SEEING SOCIAL PROBLEMS

READINGS ON CONTEMPORARY
ISSUES IN THE UNITED STATES

First Edition

Edited by
Brandon Lang and Molly Monahan Lang

cognella® | ACADEMIC PUBLISHING

Bassim Hamadeh, CEO and Publisher
Kassie Graves, Director of Acquisitions and Sales
Jamie Giganti, Senior Managing Editor
Miguel Macias, Senior Graphic Designer
John Remington, Acquisitions Editor
Monika Dziamka, Project Editor
Brain Fahey, Licensing Coordinator
Abbey Hastings, Associate Production Editor
Sue Murray, Interior Designer

Printed in the United States of America

ISBN: 978-1-5165-0474-9 (pbk) / 978-1-5165-0475-6 (br)

Contents

Dedication

For our children, Adam, Sarah, and Nathan:
May you help to make our social world a better place.

Acknowledgments

First, we would like to thank each other for this opportunity to work together. We are a married couple who have not collaborated much before. Although we are both sociologists, we study very different sociological issues. This book has given us the chance to work together and produce a document of which we are both proud.

We would also like to thank our families. Our three young children, Adam, Sarah, and Nathan, are loving, supportive, and fun. Thank you for tolerating our many hours spent completing this project. Our main Toronto relative is Ariel Lang (Brandon's mother). Thanks so much, Ariel/Mom, for always being there for us. Our main Erie relatives are Connie Monahan (Molly's mother) and Megan Monahan (Molly's sister). Thanks, you two, for everything that you have done for all of us.

We are very appreciative of all of the support given to us by those at Cognella, especially John Remington and Monika Dziamka. John is calm and personable, and he helped us navigate this project from the beginning. Similarly, Monika has been encouraging and supportive. She inspired us to work hard, take chances, and make this book as good as it could be.

We would also like to extend our appreciation to all of the contributing authors. Your chapters are insightful, timely, and perfect for this book. You all braved deadlines, the editing process, and turnarounds in a very professional manner. Thank you for helping us in this process.

Finally, we would like to thank the people with whom we work. Brandon teaches at Bloomsburg University in central Pennsylvania. He would like to thank all of his colleagues for supporting his work over the years. Molly teaches at Mercyhurst University and Penn State Erie, The Behrend College, and would like to thank her colleagues for the support and caring that they have shown her.

Preface

Sociology gives people the tools to observe, analyze, and make sense of the way that different groups of people think and act. Studying social problems is an integral part of sociology. Whether you have taken many sociology classes or none at all, learning more about social problems will give you a sense for what this vibrant and diverse discipline is all about. Our hope is that this book gives you insights to help you think critically about the many social problems in society and challenge ways that people's everyday behavior perpetuates such problems.

We are living in a very interesting time period. Immigration, global warming, the decriminalization of marijuana, and legalization of same-sex marriage are some of the many controversial issues that are affecting the country. As of the writing of this book, Hillary Clinton and Donald Trump are vying for the presidency. To think that the presidential election could be between such dissimilar candidates shows how politically divided the country is. Trump wants to build a wall along the Mexican border to keep immigrants from illegally entering the United States and opposes free trade agreements, while Clinton wants to create a pathway to citizenship and has largely supported free trade throughout her political career. Trump mainly appeals to white men, while Clinton's supporters are disproportionately minorities and women. As usual, America is not immune to controversy.

There is no shortage of social problems. Although we cannot address all of them, we aim to provide an overview of some of the main ones, and to give you the tools to critically assess all of the social problems that impact your daily lives. We have enjoyed putting this book together and working with the various authors who have contributed chapters, and we hope that you will benefit from learning more about these issues.

Brandon Lang
Molly Monahan Lang
Fall 2016

Introduction

Sociologists have been studying social problems, such as racism, sexism, and crime, for decades. In addition to wanting to understand these issues, sociologists generally have sought to lessen their negative effects. As discussed below, sociology is a progressive discipline whose practitioners are oriented toward egalitarianism and social change. An important first step in this process is to learn about the many social problems that impact our lives. This Introduction serves several purposes. First, the concept of a social problem is defined. Next, the differences between objective and subjective social problems are established. From there, the temporal and spatial variation of social problems is explained. Following this, the history of sociology, its main theories, levels of analysis, and two main types of research are examined. The Introduction concludes with a brief overview of the eight main sections of this book.

● WHAT IS A SOCIAL PROBLEM?

A social problem can be defined as an illegal act or a condition that negatively impacts a significant number of people in a physical, mental, or emotional manner. Alternatively, a social issue becomes a social problem when it meets one of several criteria. The first relates to criminal activity. When people engage in illegal behavior, that is a social problem. The next set of criteria relates to people's well-being. When lawful behavior inflicts physical harm, mental distress, or emotional suffering on others, that is also a social problem. Physical harm can occur in a variety of ways. For example, immediate physical harm could result from drinking water with lead in it or being beaten up on the playground. More long-term physical harm may arise from living near a pollution-emitting factory, or not being able to afford going to the doctor due to a lack of health insurance. It is important to consider that not all physical harm constitutes a social problem. Every day, numerous people get hurt playing sports, falling, or getting into car accidents. Car accidents do not constitute a social problem if drivers are obeying speed limits and are not intoxicated while driving. Car accidents do become a social problem if people are driving aggressively or are under the influence of illegal drugs and/or alcohol.

Social problems can also result in mental distress. When people experience mental distress, including fear and intimidation, from discrimination or oppression based on such factors as race, ethnicity, gender, sexuality, religion, physical abilities, or age, that constitutes a social problem. Similarly, emotional suffering is also associated with social problems. When people are belittled, humiliated, or shamed because of their position in society, that constitutes a social problem. All told, most forms of mental and emotional anguish that people experience at the hands of other people represent social problems.

● OBJECTIVE VERSUS SUBJECTIVE SOCIAL PROBLEMS

Sociologists differentiate between objective and subjective social problems. An objective social problem is one that is incontrovertible; most people are in agreement that a particular social condition represents a social problem. Crime is an example of this. Most agree that crime, especially serious crime, is problematic. People may have different thoughts concerning misdemeanors such as marijuana possession, but are probably going to agree that rape, murder, and kidnapping are deleterious to society. On the other hand, sociologists have established that there are subjective social problems. A subjective social problem can be defined as a social issue that lacks consensus concerning its significance. Pornography, abortion, pollution, divorce, and inadequate medical coverage are all examples of this. Many people, for instance, have grave concerns about divorce, while others see it as a necessary option. Climate change is another good example. While some believe that people should lessen their carbon footprint in order to reduce global warming, others do not see this as a pressing issue. People can disagree on whether or not certain issues are social problems, and can also disagree on the level of severity associated with them. Ultimately, most social problems are subjective in nature, meaning that they are, by definition, controversial.

The Temporal and Spatial Variation of Social Problems

Social problems are also socially constructed in that they exhibit temporal and spatial variation. In other words, they change over time and space. Just because a social condition was considered a social problem at one point in time does not mean that it will always be a social problem. In addition, new social problems emerge all the time. Social problems in one place are not always the same as social problems elsewhere. Many people, for example, consider pollution to be a social problem today, but that was not the case seventy years ago when less was known about the harmful effects of chemicals in the air. Similarly, cigarette smoking was not considered a social problem until the negative effects of smoking on the body were well-established. Another example pertains to family violence. In the past in America, men could physically harm their wives with impunity. This kind of violence was considered a private occurrence. More recently, domestic violence has become illegal; it is now widely viewed as a problem in society. Transgender discrimination is a new social problem in America, as the treatment of transgender people in society is being discussed more publicly, including in the legal realm.

Social problems also manifest themselves differently in different places. At the same point in time, a behavior can be considered a social problem in one location and not in another. It is currently a social problem when eighteen-year-olds drink beer in America or when a group of adults smokes marijuana in Turkey. But it is not considered a social problem when eighteen-year-olds drink beer in Germany, where the legal drinking age is sixteen, or when a group of adults smokes marijuana in Uruguay, where the use of marijuana is legal. Another example relates to college tuition. In America, student loan debt has become a social problem, as numerous people are graduating with unsustainable amounts of debt. In countries like Canada, where college is more affordable and more heavily subsidized, student loan debt is not considered a social problem.

● THE HISTORY OF SOCIOLOGY

In order to better understand social problems, it is important to have familiarity with the academic discipline that established the concept. Sociology is the study of people. Using sociological perspectives, sociologists seek to understand why people believe and behave the ways they do. Sociology as a discipline emerged in Europe in the mid-1800s. Auguste Comte and Emile Durkheim were two pioneers of sociology who saw the need for a discipline that explains social behavior. Both Comte and Durkheim engaged in extensive social research that increased people's awareness and understanding of social integration, religion, suicide, and criminal behavior. In the late 1800s, the first sociology program in the United States was created at the University of Chicago. In the early 1900s, several other sociology programs were developed at a number of prestigious American colleges, including the University of Wisconsin and the University of California, Berkeley.

There were still only a small number of American universities that offered sociology degrees prior to World War II. It was not until the 1950s and 1960s that sociology became a typical discipline offered in schools. Throughout the period following World War II, more and more schools began to offer sociology classes. Now, sociology classes are offered at most American universities, and tens of thousands of college students graduate with sociology degrees every year.

Sociology is known as a discipline that tends to challenge the status quo. American college campuses were hotbeds of social activism in the late 1960s and early 1970s. College students, including many sociology majors, were active in the antiwar, civil rights, and women's rights movements of that era. Many sociology students were studying racial and gender inequality in their classes and were inspired by them to protest the war in Vietnam, segregation in the American South, and opposition to the Equal Rights Amendment. As a discipline, sociology tends to attract people who not only wish to learn more about social injustice, but also want to be agents of social change.

● THINKING SOCIOLOGICALLY

There are many types of explanations that help us understand people, such as neurological, psychological, and biological. Sociological explanations are unique in that they put people's lives in a broader context. Sociologists believe that people are better understood by considering their social worlds: their place in history and their demographic and cultural surroundings. These factors guide the questions sociologists ask, and the answers they find.

Sociology is a multi-paradigmatic academic discipline. This means that, instead of being guided by one distinct paradigm or theoretical framework like the natural sciences, it is guided by multiple competing paradigms. In sociology, there are four distinct paradigms: functionalist, conflict, symbolic interactionist, and feminist. Each of these has its own guiding assumptions, affecting what is observed and what is considered important in social life.

Functionalism was developed by Emile Durkheim in the late nineteenth century, and posits that society is a social system consisting of an interdependent set of parts. Heavily influenced by the work of Herbert Spencer, functionalism borrows from the evolutionary sciences and sees social systems, large and small, consisting of a range of people whose skill sets and responsibilities complement each other. Functionalists use the metaphor of the human body to explain social life. The human body has different organs that serve disparate functions yet are essential to the overall functioning of the body. Similarly, in social systems, different parts (people) perform distinct, necessary functions for society. Some of the roles have high status while some have low, but they complement each other. Janitors, teachers, librarians, and students are interdependent in a school, just as administrative assistants, clients, and business executives are interdependent in a corporation.

Another functionalist theorist named Robert Merton developed the important concepts of manifest and latent functions. Some of the words he uses to help explain manifest functions are "intended," "conscious," and "anticipated" (Merton 1949/1968). These are the outcomes or reasons that people have in mind when they behave. Latent functions, on the other hand, are described as "not intended," "below the surface," or "not foreseen." These are neither obvious nor anticipated. Laws and other rules have both manifest and latent functions. For example, increased sentences for drug offenses in the United States had the manifest function of deterring people from committing drug crimes. The latent functions have included prison overpopulation as well as increased numbers of children growing up with parents who have spent time in prison.

The father of conflict theory is Karl Marx. His critique of capitalism has been used by many sociologists to further understand the human condition. Marx theorized that within a capitalist framework people are pitted against each other and are therefore forced to prioritize their own interests. The essence of conflict theory is that, within a capitalist setting, wealth equals power. Building on this, there are people with wealth and power who control society's resources, and people without money or power who are subject to the rules imposed on them by the ruling elite. Thus, great tensions emerge between the capitalists (the Haves) and the workers (the Have-nots) because the Have-nots want more power and the Haves want to do everything they can to preserve their power and privilege.

Symbolic interactionism is the most philosophical of the four schools of thought. Developed by the Chicago School after World War II and serving as the basis for microsociology (discussed below), this perspective establishes that ongoing interaction between people explains behavior. People use symbolic communication and interpretation, and these processes are central to our social selves and our behaviors. A central component of symbolic interactionism is what is referred to as the "definition of the situation." People do not sense their environment directly; instead, we continuously define the situation we are in, based on our interactions and internal dialogue. We may have physical responses to other people, but immediately we socially define that reality. Any situation we are in, we have to define it and continue to define it. Another important concept that exists with symbolic interactionism is social constructionism. Symbolic interactionists believe that race and gender, for example, are social constructs. They do not believe that there are essential differences between black and white people or between men and women. Rather, they believe that people perceive there to be differences between these groups, and that these perceptions have influenced people's senses of reality.

The final school of sociological thought addressed here is feminist theory. The main assumption of feminist theory is that men and women are not treated equally in American society. Feminist theory borrows heavily from conflict theory, but instead of the tension between groups being rooted in wealth, it is rooted in gender. According to this perspective, men are society's Haves and women are society's Have-nots. Men, in turn, do whatever they can to preserve their power and privilege, which ends up limiting opportunities for women. Feminist theorists contend that the underrepresentation of women in business and politics and the unequal pay for men and women for equal work are examples of gender inequality that should be addressed.

● LEVELS OF ANALYSIS

Sociologists can study social behavior using different levels of analysis, typically referred to as macro-level, micro-level, and meso-level. While using any one level of analysis it is important to keep the others in mind, as they are all significant in understanding social life. Macro-level analyses focus on the large-scale, looking at entire social systems at once. Using a macro perspective, sociologists can study democratic nation-states compared to socialist ones, or contrast countries where same-sex marriage is legal with countries where it is not. Macrosociologists could study the effects of technology on life expectancy or how civil wars affect migration.

At the micro-level, sociologists study interactions between people. Whereas macrosociologists may study technology and life expectancy at the national level, comparing countries as a whole to each other and attempting to explain the differences, microsociologists could talk with healthcare practitioners about the technology they use, or observe interactions between patients and their providers. While macrosociologists may be interested in the effects of civil wars on migratory patterns in general, microsociologists could interview refugees as they travel or observe the interactions between migrants and border guards. Sociologists using different levels of analysis may be interested in similar phenomena but look at them in different ways.

We can also discuss a third level of analysis referred to as meso-level. This sits between the interactional level and the national level. Meso-level analyses may focus on social institutions, such as the family, the economy, or the military. They may also look at organizations, such as hospitals or school boards. A meso-level focus allows us to see the influence of the large-scale on people's behaviors, while recognizing the actual people involved in the day-to-day operations of society. For example, a meso-level analysis may help us to better understand institutionalized behaviors. These are the accepted, expected, even required behaviors that have been in place for a long time in a society. Within the social institution of the family in the United States, for example, marriage is an institutionalized behavior. Within the social institutions of the economy and healthcare in the United States, the practice of connecting health insurance to employment is institutionalized. Thinking sociologically uncovers the human origins of such practices, since people tend to forget those, and to behave as if it has "always" been that way.

Quantitative and Qualitative Sociological Research

Sociologists tend to conduct either quantitative or qualitative research. Quantitative research primarily uses surveys and survey data. Respondents are asked mainly closed-ended questions about aspects of themselves, such as their political ideology, belief about abortion, amount of education, or age. These observations are turned into numbers. Quantitative researchers conduct mathematical, statistical analyses of data. This research is mainly deductive, starting with a theory and hypotheses, and testing their accuracy. As implied above, quantitative analyses use a variable language, where people are described in terms of levels of various attributes. For example, amount of education can be said to be correlated with level of prejudice, in that as education increases, levels of prejudice go down. We have to remember that there are people associated with these variables.

Quantitative research in sociology is more common than qualitative research. This may be due in part to the larger sample sizes used in such research. Large-scale surveys can be conducted on thousands of people. There is also a widespread preference for generalizability, and this can be achieved if the sample is representative of the population. However, survey data are limited due to the relatively short length of surveys that respondents are likely to tolerate. Surveys are also better measures of values and beliefs than behaviors, due to validity concerns, but they are used for all of these. We can never be completely sure of the honesty or accuracy of responses, but efforts can help encourage more of both.

Qualitative research assumes that people can be understood only by studying their everyday lives in depth. Qualitative researchers tend to use very little, if any, statistical information. They mainly conduct observational studies and/ or open-ended interviews. Due to the time-consuming nature of this research, a smaller number of people are studied. Qualitative researchers typically study dozens of people, up to perhaps a hundred at a time. However, they collect and analyze richer data, due to the length of time spent with each participant. Qualitative researchers often spend months or years with the people they study. Generalizability is not likely, but the development of concepts and/or theories can be useful elsewhere. As with quantitative research, the ultimate goal is to understand more than just the people being studied. Though qualitative researchers cannot treat their samples as representative, they can use the rich data to develop important concepts, or enhance or clarify a theory to help us better understand human beings in their social environments. It may be helpful to note that qualitative research goes along with a microsociological approach, and is used by those with a symbolic interactionist perspective in particular.

● THE ORGANIZATION OF THIS BOOK

This book is organized into eight sections. In Section 1, Socioeconomic Inequality and Poverty, the American class system is examined. There are readings on working poverty and the day-to-day lives of poor people in the era of welfare reform. Cumulative advantage and disadvantage are also discussed, particularly as they relate to the greater losses that those in the lower classes must endure. In addition, challenges in achieving upward mobility or the "American Dream" are addressed in this section.

The second section, Racial and Ethnic Inequality, has four chapters that show the extent to which racial and ethnic inequality exist in the United States. These chapters demonstrate that nativism (an opposition to new immigration) has been a persistent issue in America. They also reveal that people of different racial and ethnic backgrounds have disparate likelihoods of being questioned or detained by police officers. This section ends with a history of racial residential segregation in America and a discussion of the production and maintenance of racially integrated communities.

The third section, Gender Inequality and Homophobia, includes four chapters that document the many ways that women and people who do not exemplify the traditional and binary notion of gender experience discrimination and prejudice. This section makes clear that, in spite of many gains made in terms of gender over time, sexism and homophobia continue. In addition to chronicling the history of the feminist movement, the articles in this section explore different aspects of discrimination that many women, gay people, and transgender people experience. There is also a chapter that shows the intersections of race, gender, and social class in the use of homophobic slurs by adolescent boys.

Section 4, Crime, examines the social problems associated with a wide range of criminal activities. Though violent and property crime rates are down, drug-related crimes are increasing. The main way that the American system has responded to crime is with restitution, particularly imprisonment. This section consists of four chapters that examine mass incarceration and its consequences, the overrepresentation of minority youth in the criminal justice system, the use of capital punishment, and the prevalence and correlates of sexual assault.

The fifth section, Social Problems in Medicine and Health, considers a range of social problems that exist within the context of health and healthcare. As an affluent and advanced society, America is lauded for having one of the best healthcare systems in the world. However, not everyone is equally healthy or shares the same high-quality care. In this section, the first chapter examines why the Affordable Care Act (or "Obamacare") is so controversial. The second examines the problem of depression among college students. The third examines the problem of unhealthy eating, its consequences, and ways it is being addressed.

Social Problems in Families is the sixth section of this book. This section provides a sense of how controversial some family issues are. Although a growing percentage of people are supportive of cohabitation, same-sex marriage, and divorce, these are divisive issues. This section consists of three chapters. The first examines how family structure differs according to social class. The second explores the gender gap in pay, and gives particular attention to a phenomenon known as the motherhood wage penalty. The last chapter examines the problem of domestic violence in this country and its consequences for mothers.

The book's seventh section is entitled Social Problems in Education. There is no question that there are a number of high-quality schools at all levels in the United States. Like healthcare, however, not all groups have equal access to the same school experiences. This section includes three important chapters. The first relates to the problems associated with No Child Left Behind. The second examines bullying among adolescents and ways it can be addressed. The final chapter in this section examines challenges faced by African American college students who attend predominantly white schools.

The eighth and last section of the book is called Environmental Social Problems. In this section, three chapters consider aspects of environmental degradation and consumerism. Global warming is a controversial issue that has divided the country. The first chapter in this section examines global climate change through a sociological lens, showing its effects on rural Americans in particular. The second chapter examines how Native Americans have disproportionately high rates of exposure to water and air pollution and other environmental hazards. The third chapter charts the growing rates of consumerism and debt in the United States over time, and their consequences.

References

Merton, Robert K. 1949/1968. *Social Theory and Social Structure*. New York: Free Press.

SECTION ONE

SOCIOECONOMIC INEQUALITY AND POVERTY

I n the United States, there is substantial income and wealth inequality. On one hand, there are Americans who hold billions of dollars in assets. This includes people such as Donald Trump and Bill Gates, who can afford to lead opulent lifestyles. On the other hand, there are millions of Americans who struggle financially and do not have the money to cover even their basic needs. As of this writing, 14.5 percent of Americans are officially poor, according to the US Census Bureau (2015). In addition, there are plenty of people in between these extremes who make up the middle classes, some of whom lead lives of privilege while others live precariously close to poverty themselves. The main purpose of this section is to examine the American class system and explain how socioeconomic inequality and poverty represent significant social problems in the United States.

● WHAT IS SOCIAL CLASS?

Social class is a fairly broad concept that relates to a person's status, social standing, and economic resources. Social class can be thought of as a combination of education, occupation, income, and wealth. Sociologists conceive of gradients that use these characteristics in combination. Education can range from less than high school to postgraduate degrees. Occupations can be blue collar, where people work with their hands or bodies and are likely to be paid in wages, or white collar, where they do more mental than physical work and are likely to be paid by salary. Occupations also vary in terms of prestige, or how impressive they are perceived to be. Shoe shining is seen to be much less prestigious than being a physician, for example. Some people are impoverished in terms of income, while some earn salaries in the six figures, and a small percentage earn millions of dollars a year. Similarly, some are in great debt and others have billions in financial assets, while most are in between, with maybe a house and two cars representing their wealth.

Social class is inextricably intertwined with lifestyle. People of different social class groupings have been found to have, in aggregate, different favorite foods, décor, and hobbies. Social class can be thought of as a combination of factors that informs everything from the kinds of foods that people eat and the times that they eat meals to how they spend their free time, how they raise their kids, and the brand of car that they drive.

It is important to recognize that social class is not just about money. There are tens of thousands of people who are employed as mechanics, construction workers, and truck drivers who make more money than teachers, clergy, and even airplane pilots. Even though many blue collar people make more money than some white collar people, the two groups are likely going to have a distinct set of skills, credentials, and interests. Each group spends its money and time differently in spite of their financial standing. Bowling, for example, is generally a blue collar activity, while reading is seen as more of a white collar activity. Similarly, going to the theater or symphony is more of a white collar activity, while attending a NASCAR race is generally a blue collar activity.

● THE AMERICAN CLASS SYSTEM

Sociologists have established that people's characteristics can be combined to place everyone in a social class hierarchy. Known as social stratification, these qualities serve to order people according to their social class. The American class system can be seen as a ranking of five groups with a range of different attributes. The list of social class groupings include upper class, upper middle class, lower middle (or middle) class, working class, and poor. Each of these social class groupings is different based on the educational, social, and economic attributes of their members. Upper-class people, for example, have billions of dollars in wealth and can afford to live on the income generated from that wealth. Upper-middle-class people are distinguished by their high levels of education and professional occupations. Lower-middle-class people typically have some education beyond high school, whether an associate's or bachelor's degree, and earn around the median household income. Working-class and poor people typically work in blue collar jobs and have a high school degree or less. Working-class people make more money than poor people, however, and tend to have more financial stability. Poor people range from those working full time to those with sporadic, often part-time work histories, to those who live on public assistance.

Poverty is a significant social problem in the United States. It includes the millions of Americans who struggle to meet their food, housing, healthcare, and clothing needs on a yearly basis. Contrary to what many people think, poverty includes people who are employed but still do not make enough money to cover their basic needs. Known as working poverty, people who work low-paying service jobs generally do not receive any benefits and have their hours capped so as not to be eligible for overtime. Although the national minimum wage has been increased and many cities have even higher minimum wages to help offset high costs of living, poverty still persists across the country.

In their piece, "Organizational Behavior and the Working Poor," Leana, Mittal, and Stiehl establish that the working poor—defined here as poor people working full time—experience three types of barriers that impact such things as their job attachment, work performance, and future career attainment. Categorical barriers, for example, relate to the unskilled and often physical characteristics of low-wage work that are stigmatizing for people in those jobs. Compositional barriers, meanwhile, result in low-wage employees not having much contact with those who earn higher wages, which impacts their capacity to be noticed and rewarded for doing good work. Lastly, relational barriers limit the capacity for blue collar workers to get to know and feel supported by the white collar workers that they work with or for. All told, these barriers can impact workers' self-efficacy, which in turn can affect job performance, attitude, stress levels, outlook on life, and social capital.

● CUMULATIVE ADVANTAGE AND DISADVANTAGE

Cumulative advantage and disadvantage are important sociological concepts that can serve to reinforce social class boundaries in the United States. Cumulative advantage relates to the manner in which many opportunities seem to build on themselves over time. A person whose parents attended an Ivy League college, for example, is likely going to have an advantage getting into that school over other similarly qualified applicants who are not legacies. From there, the person may have an edge getting into graduate school or finding a well-paying job upon graduation over someone who has graduated with the same degree from a less prestigious school. That job experience may then open up even more doors over time, resulting in such possibilities as promotions at work, sound financial planning and advice, and excellent retirement benefits.

Conversely, cumulative disadvantage describes how setbacks seem to also build on themselves over time. There are thousands of people all over the country who work as roofers, cooks, or delivery people who do not have adequate health insurance. If people get hurt on the job, this may result in them not only incurring debt from lacking health insurance but also forsaking the wages that they would have earned during the recovery period. Perhaps this forces them to sell their car, which will impact their ability to return to work. All told, many people who struggle financially are one step away from a veritable downward spiral of problems that have the potential to greatly impact their day-to-day lives.

In her chapter, "'Death Always Seems to Be Around Me': Loss Privilege and Loss in Abundance in Contemporary America," Monahan Lang builds on the idea of cumulative advantage and disadvantage by explaining how people in the higher social classes tend to not only reap the financial benefits of their class privilege but also to experience fewer losses in their lives than those in the lower classes. This applies to a range of premature deaths, including infant mortality, child and youth mortality, and maternal mortality. Monahan Lang also establishes the connection between race/ethnicity, social class, and disease, and other losses such as imprisonment. She finishes the chapter by citing numerous examples of both loss privilege and loss in abundance.

● SOCIAL MOBILITY AND THE AMERICAN DREAM

The United States is considered to be an open society, which means that there is a probability of social class mobility. There are numerous examples of people who grew up in poverty or in the working class and experience upward mobility over the course of their lives. This characterizes the situations of celebrities like Oprah Winfrey, athletes like LeBron James, and numerous other businesspeople, political figures, doctors, and lawyers. Education, for example, is linked to upward mobility. Going to college and obtaining a degree creates opportunities for people to obtain different jobs than their parents and grandparents had.

When most people think about the American Dream, they associate it with a rags-to-riches story line: no matter your social class at birth, if you work hard, are goal oriented, and determined to succeed, you can achieve anything that you set your mind to. This perspective represents the optimistic view of the American Dream. The idea is that people who are hardworking and ambitious will experience success over the course of their lives. Clearly, there are numerous examples of this phenomenon. Even today, tens of thousands of people leave their families behind and enter the United States, legally and illegally, for the chance to get a foothold on the American Dream.

Not everyone is convinced, however, that hard work and ambition necessarily result in success. This perspective represents the pessimistic view of the American Dream and is summed up by the statement that "it is not what you know, it is who you know." In the United States, there are also numerous examples of people getting jobs and promotions, acceptances to prestigious schools and out of legal trouble because of their family name or social connections. Think of people such as Paris Hilton or Chelsea Clinton being given opportunities based on their family wealth and parents' social connections. But it is not just upper-class people who benefit from their social networks. Upper-middle-class people are likely to receive help from others as well. The higher your social class at birth, the greater the likelihood of having friends or family contacts that can provide information or vouch for you.

As mentioned above, higher education is often described as an important pathway to upward mobility for those born poor or working class. In their article

"Why Do First-Generation Students Fail?" Mehta, Newbold, and O'Rourke focus on college students whose parents did not graduate from college, whom they refer to as first-generation students. They discuss the challenges that first-generation students face in college, including working more hours and lacking social connections with other students. They also provide suggestions for ways that colleges and universities can help more first-generation students stay in school and succeed academically.

● PUBLIC ASSISTANCE AND WELFARE REFORM

As part of President Roosevelt's New Deal, created during the Great Depression, a social safety net was created to assist people who had fallen on hard times. Programs such as Aid to Families with Dependent Children (AFDC), Social Security, and Unemployment Insurance were created and implemented in this era. AFDC was intended to help children in low-income families who lacked one or both parents. In order to qualify to receive AFDC benefits, people had to meet indigence criteria. AFDC recipients would receive monthly checks to help them cover their rent, childcare, food, and other expenses over the course of the month. Although it was meant to be a short-term program, it became apparent in the 1970s and 1980s that many people who went on welfare ended up collecting benefits for long periods. Sociologists attribute this to the social stigma associated with being on welfare. Welfare recipients were labeled as lazy and unambitious, which made it more difficult to find gainful employment. Sociologists also identify the existence of the "welfare trap," where people can make more money on welfare than working a minimum wage job, since earnings are offset by having to pay for childcare and transportation.

In 1996, the American welfare system was overhauled under President Clinton, who signed the Personal Responsibility and Work Opportunity Reconciliation Act. This conservative welfare reform was popular because many people thought that public assistance was being overused. With this new law, AFDC was eliminated and replaced by Temporary Aid for Needy Families (TANF). Among other things, TANF limited the amount of time that someone could be on welfare, and replaced monthly checks with a voucher system mandating that people either work, go to school, or get job training. Supporters of this new legislation cite the declining number of people on welfare as evidence for success. Critics, on the other hand, are concerned that it perpetuates poverty and reinforces the growing class divide that has emerged in the United States.

In "The New Regime Through the Lens of the Old," Halpern-Meekin, Edin, Tach, and Sykes discuss the working poor within the context of the American economic safety net. They describe how welfare reform occurred and discuss other programs for those with low incomes, such as the Earned Income Tax Credit, the Supplemental Nutritional Assistance Program (formerly called food stamps), and Medicaid. They discuss the ongoing stigma associated with receiving welfare and the interactional work that low-income people do to manage that stigma. Their research shows a general agreement within American society that employment should be encouraged and rewarded, and that handouts to those deemed undeserving should be avoided.

References

United States Census Bureau. 2015. *Poverty: 2014 Highlights.* https://www.census.gov/topics/income-poverty/poverty/news-updates/updates/2014-highlights.html

CHAPTER 1

Organizational Behavior and the Working Poor

By Carrie R. Leana, Vikas Mittal, and Emily Stiehl

● INTRODUCTION

There is a great deal of evidence that shows that poverty can have a profound influence on individual perceptions, behaviors, and relationships. Yet in organizational studies, there is little attention focused on poverty, particularly the working poor. In developing theory and drawing conclusions about how people behave at work, organizational researchers have tended to study samples of industrial workers, knowledge workers, managers, and high-status professionals. Over the past 10 years (from 2000 to 2010), only about a dozen empirical studies published in *Organization Science* have included samples of workers in what could be considered low-wage jobs. Research from other fields, however, shows that the effects of poverty are present in many core aspects of a person's life, including health, family patterns, and cognitive development (e.g., Adler and Ostrove 1993, Devine et al. 2006, Durden et al. 2007). Here, we argue that low-wage work and a background of poverty—both of which are defining characteristics of the working poor—can powerfully affect work attitudes and behaviors, just as they affect other key aspects of life.

Our focus on the working poor is motivated by several transformative trends. First, this is a sizable and growing portion of the workforce in the United States and other developed economies, and many of the fastest-growing occupations (e.g., nursing aides, hospitality workers) are low-wage service jobs (Bartsch 2009). Second, the emergence of these jobs highlights a phenomenon that was largely unseen in developed manufacturing economies. As Craypo and Cormier (2000) observe, many service firms are structured like an hourglass, characterized by large wage disparities. At the top is a set of highly skilled professionals (e.g., doctors, chefs), and at the bottom is a far larger group of frontline support staff with fewer qualifications (e.g., nurse aides, waiters) and nowhere to move up. Ironically, the occupants of these jobs—the working poor—are often the primary point of contact with customers, even while they cope with low pay, lack of dignity, and difficult working conditions (Figueroa and Woods 2007). Third, from a societal perspective, the working poor often occupy jobs that entail caring for the property and even the family members of more affluent professional workers. Hemp (2004) documents the high levels of stress and lost productivity that result when professionals are unable to adequately meet family needs such as childcare and eldercare. Apart from directly contributing to the economy, then, the working poor provide positive spillover benefits to the larger society by doing jobs that buffer the personal and family demands of professionals. In the process, the working poor absorb some of the social, psychological, physical, and emotional strain associated with such care work.

Emerging research suggests that the working poor may have different models of action at work, leading them to behave in ways that do not comport with traditional theories of work motivation and performance (Stephens et al. 2007). For example, Hazel Markus and her colleagues show that middle-class students and adults are more likely to value independence and uniqueness in choices they make, whereas lower-income individuals are more likely to make choices based on a desire to be similar to others and "fit in" (Snibbe and Markus 2005). Managers may interpret such preferences negatively, as indicative of a lack of initiative or proactivity. Moreover, higher-paid coworkers and managers may have different normative beliefs regarding what constitutes agentic behavior at work (see Markus and Kitayama 2003 on class-based differences in agency). In an illuminating study, Stephens et al. (2010) examine outsiders' attributions about Hurricane Katrina survivors who evacuated prior to the storm (leavers) versus those who did not (stayers). Leavers were predominantly middle class and college educated and had the resources to leave; stayers tended to have lower income and educational attainment and often lacked basic resources that would permit them to leave (e.g., reliable transportation out of town). The researchers found that both rescue workers and "lay" subjects attributed positive motivations (e.g., agency, responsibility, independence) to leavers, whereas stayers were likely to be described as passive, irresponsible, and inflexible—regardless of differences in available resources. If similar distorted attributions about "choice" are played out in the workplace, they may have important implications for future research and for practice, as they question basic assumptions about work motivation, perceptions, and behavior for a significant segment of the workforce.

Against this backdrop, we examine how the combined conditions of past poverty and current low wages can affect attitudes and behaviors at work. We propose a framework that includes categorical, compositional, and relational approaches to understanding the condition of poverty as it pertains to work organizations. We also discuss potential mediators of the relationship between poverty and work outcomes. Our goals are threefold: (1) to heighten researchers' awareness of the potentially powerful influence of poverty on work attitudes and behaviors, (2) to stimulate reflection about theories in organizational behavior that are largely based on studies of managers and professionals, and (3) to call attention to management practice and potential interventions (in addition to enhancing pay) that may benefit the working poor.

● THE WORKING POOR

Several practical and conceptual considerations lead us to purposely limit our inquiry to full-time adult workers in the United States and other developed economies.[1] First, most of the samples used in organizational research comprise full-time paid employees in developed countries, so comparison is facilitated by this distinction. Second, focusing on full-time workers living in poverty—the working poor—belies the stereotype that poverty is the result of individuals' inability or unwillingness to work. Third, full-time jobs are generally more permanent and integrated into the fabric of the organization than part-time jobs, and full-time workers are thus more likely to be exposed to the same organizational stimuli as traditional employees, again facilitating comparisons between these two groups.

Low-Wage Workers: An Economic Definition

In the United States, the federal poverty threshold is the most common measure for defining and counting the poor (U.S. Census Bureau 2010). This tiered scale determines a household's poverty status using income and family size, and it is based on an estimate developed in 1963–1964[2] and updated annually to reflect cost-of-living increases. The poverty threshold for a household of four was $22,350 in 2011, which translates to an hourly wage of a little over $11 for one full-time employee—well above the current federal minimum wage (U.S. Department of Health and Human Services 2011).[3] In assessing poverty, some agencies (e.g., National Research Council) further consider household incomes as high as 200% of the poverty level to qualify as "poor" (Ackerman 2006).

The Working Poor: A Broadened Perspective

A somewhat more expansive definition of the working poor includes those who have jobs but do not earn enough to "afford the necessities of life," to "maintain a conventional standard of living in their community," or to "avoid poverty during periods of temporary unemployment" (Craypo and Cormier 2000, p. 31). Other researchers consider poverty not just in terms of the current economic earnings of workers but also their "background of poverty," which embodies the sociostructural factors from their past that may have led to their current situation (Gould 1999, Wilson 1987). Thus, the condition of poverty encompasses a set of past (and present) factors that affect the worker's experiences inside the organization and at home.

To elaborate on these distinctions, in Table 1 we show four groups of workers, differentiated by their current household income and their background of poverty. Cell IV contains what we label "textbook workers"—individuals with middle- to high-income backgrounds who currently hold middle- to high-wage jobs. These are the most frequent subjects of organizational research and are commonly the point of reference in organizational behavior (OB) and management textbooks. These workers have not experienced poverty in the past and are now earning high enough wages to continue to avoid it. Occupants of these jobs form the empirical basis for much of our organizational theorizing. This category includes professionals and managers who tend to have the autonomy and authority in their jobs to make significant changes in the organization or skilled and/or unionized industrial workers who can exercise power collectively. To be sure, most of the organizational research on this group focuses on the individual's current situation, assuming it to be reflective of a similar past and predictive of a relatively stable future.

Looking further at Table 1, individuals in Cell II ("Aspirants") grew up in poverty but have since obtained higher-wage jobs that provide them with middle to high income. Lubrano (2004) describes the experiences of people with working-class backgrounds who become white-collar workers, emphasizing the anxiety these individuals face as a result of the disparity between their blue-collar past and the white-collar environment of their present. Many of these workers are straddling two worlds, such that experiences that their peers take for granted are new to them and require increased effort on their part to learn. A key source of anxiety includes new work situations that they had never experienced growing up but that were commonplace for their peers (e.g., traveling abroad).

Table 1: Relationship Between Past and Current Income on Future Expectations

	CURRENT EXPERIENCE	
PAST EXPERIENCE	**LOW INCOME**	**MIDDLE TO HIGH INCOME**
POVERTY	**CELL I: WORKING POOR**	**CELL II: ASPIRANTS**
	• Consistency between past and present experience.	• Inconsistency between past and present experience.
	• High expectation that future stream of resources will be similar to their current income.	• Potential anxiety in the present because of fear that current situation is temporary and because they do not share the same developmental experiences as their peers.
	• Low expectation of escaping poverty in the future.	
MIDDLE TO HIGH INCOME	**CELL III: LOW-WAGE WORKERS**	**CELL IV: TEXTBOOK WORKERS**

- Inconsistency between past and present experience.
- Potential anxiety in the present because of loss of social contacts and status as a result of the downward change in income from past to present.

- Consistency between past and present experience.
- High expectation that future stream of resources will be similar to their current income.

Cell III, which contains "Low-wage workers," includes individuals who grew up in households with average or high levels of income but who now earn much less, either voluntarily or involuntarily. The former category may include artists and altruists who accept lower wages in exchange for the opportunity or freedom to do work they enjoy. The latter category may include those who have involuntarily taken low-wage jobs for reasons such as downsizing or a family relocation. The economic, social, and psychological toll accompanying involuntary job loss and underemployment is well documented (e.g., Leana and Feldman 1992, Newman 1998). Although these workers currently earn low wages, they are different from the working poor described in Cell I because the working poor have a past, as well as a present, circumstance that is marked by economic hardship.

Cell I, which contains the "Working poor," is the focus of this paper. Individuals in this group are defined by their background of poverty as well as their present low-wage jobs. The working poor tend to cluster into jobs such as cleaning, hospitality services, and direct care (U.S. Bureau of Labor and Statistics 2009) and, in the United States, are disproportionately female, racial minorities, and recent immigrants (DeNavas-Walt et al. 2007). As noted above, the working poor (Cell I) differ from low-wage workers (Cell III), with the former being a subset of the latter. The term "low-wage worker" describes those who are currently in low-paying jobs without regard to their past experiences or their future prospects (e.g., Muntaner et al. 2006). The working poor can be conceptualized as a subset of low-wage workers who are bounded by low household income in the past and present as well as low expectations of ameliorating their situation in the future. To illustrate, the daughter of an accountant who is working as a retail clerk for minimum wage while pursuing her college degree is not included among the working poor, because her background is not one of poverty. Moreover, she expects to obtain a better job (once she graduates) and to ameliorate her temporarily impoverished situation.

Future expectations for individuals in Cells II and III are more ambiguous than those of individuals in the other two cells. Aspirants have moved up in income but may be uneasy about the permanence of their ascent (Sennett 1998). Low-wage workers may change their situations (e.g., the starving artist "sells out" for a conventional job, or the laid-off investment analyst finds new work as a mortgage lender). Conversely, the consistencies among the past and present of those in Cells IV and I suggest a relatively predictable trajectory for the future. Just as the income trajectory for textbook employees is assumed to be relatively stable in the middle to high range, among the working poor, there is a strong expectation that the conditions associated with low income will persist in the future. Expectations about "permanent income"—i.e., future lifetime earnings—can, in turn, perpetuate behaviors that produce self-fulfilling prophecies. Thus, consistency between low current wages and past experience of poverty leads to low future expectations, defining the working poor in terms of their past, present, and future income.

Poverty and Low-Wage Work

Rather than being an attribute of the individual, poverty is a "strong situation" (Mischel 1977) that envelops the individual. A strong situation is a context that creates conditions that are sufficiently powerful so as to overwhelm the effect of individual factors, such as personality, on behaviors and associated outcomes. The power of "strong" situations comes from their ability to create a set of consistent normative expectations (Mischel 1977), which reinforce behaviors deemed desirable and appropriate. Poverty frames ambiguous information for the working poor in ways that may be very different from the frames available to those who are not poor. Stated differently, living in poverty—although not an individual attribute—provides a powerful context that shapes the individual's interpretation of information and appropriate response patterns. Being among the working poor, then, is manifested in ways that are multifaceted and that pervade several aspects of a person's life.

At the same time, we are *not* arguing that the poor are doomed to shortened lives of deprivation and stress. Although the "culture of poverty" literature (e.g., Lewis 1968, Miller 1958) implied such a deterministic view, later research has refuted such a notion. The early thesis about a culture of poverty (see Corcoran et al. 1985 for a cogent summary) suggested that the poor may have distinctive traits that are manifest in values and aspirations that persist across generations through socialization of the young, and they thus block the success of ameliorative policy efforts aimed at the poor. In contrast, more recent views suggest that there is no automatic transfer of either poverty or values from parents to children (Kane 1987). As Lubrano (2004) suggests, there are a number of exceptional individuals who have experienced poverty but are able to thrive through some combination of talent, motivation, and luck. However, poverty, like culture, provides a context with systematic and persistent influences that are substantial to the individuals living in it, even if they are not inevitable. As summarized by Stephens et al. (2007, p. 814, italics in original), "Although the material conditions of the socio-cultural context do not *determine* people's actions, they do *promote* certain kinds of actions and increase the likelihood that these actions will become normative and preferred."

● CATEGORICAL, COMPOSITIONAL, AND RELATIONAL INFLUENCES ON THE WORKING POOR

Existing theories explaining the causes and effects of poverty on the working poor are multifaceted. To understand them in an organizational context, we draw on organizational demography research (Tsui and Gutek 1999) and investigate categorical (individual-based), compositional (structural), and relational factors that can explain outcomes in the workplace and in other domains of life. We expect these factors to contribute to systematic differences in work outcomes and behaviors between the working poor and other workers. Categorical explanations of poverty focus on individual-level features that are associated with being poor, such as limited education and impoverished work experiences. A compositional explanation might focus instead on the distribution of attributes across structural dimensions, like workgroups, organizations, or communities. For example, the composition of neighborhoods, and of work places, can isolate the working poor from beneficial opportunities and experiences with nonpoor others, thus limiting job and career options. The focus of this approach is to examine how varying the composition of a group can affect individual and group functioning, the underlying assumption being that group social and psychological dynamics will vary based on the group's demographic composition. Finally, a relational explanation focuses on the working poor's relationships with other people and how social networks with few resources can be detrimental to the working poor as they pursue employment. As Tsui and Gutek (1999) explain, this approach can combine the emphases of both of the previous approaches, suggesting that the nature of the relationships of a person with other group members can be affected by the individuals' characteristics as well as the group's characteristics. Using these three perspectives, we will describe the interplay of work and nonwork factors that affect the working poor, incorporating different theoretical approaches to understanding poverty from other disciplines.

Workplace Factors and the Working Poor

There are categorical, compositional, and relational barriers in the workplace itself that can serve to isolate the working poor from opportunities that may enhance job attachment, work performance, and future career attainment. The categorical approach highlights individual factors within the organization associated with low wage work that will likely inhibit the success of the working poor. For example, a vocational perspective suggests that formal on-the-job training tends to be minimal for low-wage jobs, which may in turn limit the number and types of opportunities available to the working poor (Figueroa and Woods 2007). Additionally, the working poor are less likely to experience beneficial challenges early in their careers or to follow a planned development process like those for managerial workers (Craypo and Cormier 2000). More deeply, the working poor may be stigmatized because of the nature of work they do. Ashforth and Kreiner (1999) outline three types of "taint" associated with stigmatized work: physical, social, and moral. The working poor often perform tasks that can be tied to some or all of these and thus may be ostracized by other workers. For example, their work can involve direct contact with dirt, grime, and bodily waste (e.g., janitors), moral dilemmas between following organizational policies and accommodating the best interests of customers or patients (e.g., aides in understaffed nursing homes), and/or work that is associated with low social status (e.g., "flipping burgers"). Furthermore, the working poor are more likely to be employed in jobs that deplete physical and psychological strength (Gallo et al. 2005). Many such workers are employed in frontline and "care" work, which tends to require emotional labor as well as manual effort (England and Folbre 1999). Caregiving responsibilities associated with many low-wage jobs (e.g., maids, health aides, childcare workers) are psychologically stressful because of heightened role strain and conflict (Durden et al. 2007). High stress can negatively affect work performance (Mascaro et al. 2007), resulting in even higher levels of distress (Price et al. 2002), creating a potentially destructive cycle for the working poor.

A compositional, or structural, approach to understanding poverty and work suggests that those in low-paying jobs are not well integrated with others in the organization who earn higher wages, and thus they have limited opportunities to advance. The "hourglass" structure of labor markets in service industries suggests that a relatively small set of highly skilled professionals at the top of the structure (e.g., doctors, designers) are supported by, and separated from, a far larger group of support staff with fewer qualifications at the bottom (e.g., nurse aides, janitors). Such occupational segregation of the working poor is reinforced by policies and rules, such as unusual schedules that prevent interaction with core staff, and physical distance in the actual organizational spaces occupied by low-wage workers (Lambert and Waxman 2005). For example, the nature of direct-care work in health care requires someone to be available to patients at all times, even after administrators have gone home, reducing the interaction between these two groups. Lambert (2008) describes how employees in service work face uncertain hours, as managers shift the risks of fluctuating demand onto employees—sending them home early if demand is low and reducing the number of hours available to them in a given week. Similarly, although professionals typically have offices and conference rooms to meet with others at work, the working poor are, at best, typically provided with cramped common spaces to congregate and lockers in which to store a few personal belongings. Lambert and Waxman (2005) explain how even workplace benefits like health insurance can disadvantage the working poor relative to others because of differential marginal costs. For instance, a health-care plan with a $20 co-payment may seem like a bargain to a high-paid professional, but to the working poor, such costs could be prohibitive.

Relational barriers between the working poor and other workers are also commonplace. Between the top and the bottom levels of the organization, there may be very few, if any, opportunities for creating and fostering strong relationships (Figueroa and Woods 2007), and the feminization of many frontline service jobs isolates women in these jobs, which can negatively affect current wages and future opportunities (Pearce 1983). Thus, it is difficult for the working poor to establish relationships with high-status members of the organization who could help them to find better opportunities or advance in their careers. At the same time, the working poor rely on higher-status supervisors for evaluations and resources, even though these relationships are unlikely to persist outside the organization and nearly always involve power asymmetries. To the extent that social networks differentiate those who advance in their professions from those who do not (Seibert et al. 2001), the working poor are disadvantaged and unlikely to realize career benefits from the social interactions they do have at work.

Nonwork Factors and the Working Poor

Categorical, compositional, and relational barriers are not limited to the workplace but are also found in non-work (personal, family, and social) domains. In terms of categorical factors, various disciplines have addressed issues relevant to the working poor, including skill disparity and health. Economic and labor-market theories of poverty suggest that the individual's lack of marketable skills is a major factor contributing to poverty (Andersson et al. 2005). More generally, a background of poverty may limit the working poor's acquisition of a particular set of personal skills and characteristics (e.g., experience, education), inhibiting their ability to find better jobs and escape poverty (Willis 1981). The effects of poverty are also salient in many core aspects of a person's life, including his or her health and cognitive development (e.g., Durden et al. 2007, Adler and Ostrove 1993, Jackson et al. 2000), which can further limit the acquisition of human capital. People living in poverty have higher rates of morbidity and mortality and report poorer overall health than those in nonpoverty households (Adler and Ostrove 1993, Williams and Collins 1995). Children growing up in poverty, with unpredictable access to food, may learn to overeat when food becomes available, resulting in disproportionately higher rates of obesity and associated health problems later in life (Olson et al. 2007). Indeed, recent studies have found a widening gap in longevity between the highest and lowest income brackets in the United States (Singh and Siahpush 2006). Those living in poverty also report a higher incidence of mental health problems and lower levels of emotional well-being (Barrett and Turner 2005). They also report higher levels of stress, which can contribute adversely to an individual's physical and mental health, fostering disorders such as high blood pressure and depression (Kessler et al. 1994).

Structurally, or compositionally, sociologists have found that the poor are often separated from institutions, people, and opportunities that could help them escape poverty (Newman and Massengill 2006, Small and Newman 2001). Such separation—e.g., physical, geographic, and institutional—acts to isolate the working poor, limiting the number and types of opportunities available to them (Wilson 1987). Poor neighborhoods, characterized by high crime rates, substandard public services (e.g., transportation and recreation facilities), and a greater exposure to physical hazards (e.g., air and water pollutants, overcrowding, and noise), provide clear physical boundaries that separate the working poor from middle-class or higher-wage professionals in social settings (Taylor et al. 1997, Wilson 1987). Not only are there clear boundaries separating neighborhoods, but there are fewer resources within poor neighborhoods (e.g., shops, businesses, museums) that might otherwise encourage higher-wage individuals to enter them (Cohen et al. 2003). Even noise creates a distracting environment, making it more difficult for the working poor to effectively engage in seemingly simple activities such as sleeping or studying. Previous literature, then, suggests that living in poor neighborhoods presents structural barriers that are difficult for the working poor to escape.

Beyond physical boundaries, the lack of resources in the neighborhood and the scarcity of visits by individuals from other neighborhoods can also create social boundaries, influencing one's comfort with different experiences and understanding of the larger world (Wilson 1987). From a sociocognitive perspective, relationships and experiences shared by those in low-income neighborhoods may be mutually reinforcing, setting up behavioral norms (such as aggressive behaviors) that may be professionally deleterious (Willis 1981). Furthermore, the working poor tend to have fewer social resources or "safety nets" in their lives outside of work, making it challenging to cope with last-minute schedule changes or emergency situations. For instance, single mothers may not have social resources to arrange for adequate childcare to accommodate schedule changes at work, leading to higher role strain and problems with supervisors and coworkers who do not share such concerns (Swanberg 2005).

● THE WORKING POOR AND ORGANIZATIONAL BEHAVIOR
Work Outcomes

Having briefly summarized the existing literature in terms of categorical, compositional, and relational influences on poverty and its persistence, we now discuss the potential influences of poverty on three broad categories of work outcomes: career attainment, work performance, and job attachment. Although not an exhaustive list, these outcomes are important to both the individual and the organization and are the subjects of extensive prior research in organizational behavior. Moreover, inferences based on findings from other disciplines suggest that they are likely to be adversely affected by poverty and thus highly relevant to understanding the working poor.

Career Attainment. Career development is a life-long process often described in terms of predictable stages such as preparing for a profession, looking for a job, being hired, and improving skills along the way (Feldman 2002). There has been extensive research on virtually every stage of career development. For example, success at early stages of one's career has been found to predict future success (Hall 1976), and factors ranging from personality characteristics to social networks have been found to differentiate those who advance in their professions versus those who do not (Seibert et al. 2001). Career success is typically measured in terms of objective indicators of achievement such as vertical progression in the levels of status, responsibility, and extrinsic rewards earned over the course of one's working life.

The working poor are less likely to experience beneficial challenges early in their careers or to follow the traditional development process described in the careers literature (Craypo and Cormier 2000). Gould (1999) shows how the intersection of urban culture and discrimination inhibits the number of opportunities available to the working poor. Furthermore, factors such as running a household as a single parent or working in multiple low-level jobs might restrict the range of occupational options available to the working poor, reducing their ability to get or keep a job, advance in it, or even pursue a conventional career (Kossek et al. 1997). These circumstances leave the working poor with more limited options regarding which jobs they are likely to be hired into, their opportunities for advancement, and the likelihood of having intrinsically meaningful work. At the same time, Hall and Schneider (1973) suggest that individuals who lack challenging jobs or the autonomy to experience their own successes may stop trying to succeed, further diminishing career prospects over time. Thus, we propose that the working poor will have more difficulty realizing career success, at least as it is typically represented in the OB literature (e.g., objective progressions in status, responsibility, and rewards) compared with textbook workers, who are more commonly the subjects of organizational research.

Job Performance. Griffin et al. (2007) describe job performance in terms of an employee's proficiency (meeting the requirements of the job), adaptability (adapting to changing circumstances or roles), and proactivity (initiating change through self-directed action). We propose that the working poor may have difficulty with all three facets of performance, often as a result of circumstances they cannot control. Proficiency standards in low-wage jobs tend to be explicit and observable, offering less flexibility to the jobholder and little forgiveness of performance lapses because of off-the-job constraints. For example, punctuality is important in low-wage jobs such as retail sales or waiting tables because establishments have set business hours; however, those likely to fill such jobs may find it especially difficult to get to work on time because they lack off-the-job resources (e.g., reliable childcare or transportation) (Berg and Frost 2005; Kossek et al. 1997, 2010). Adaptive work behaviors go beyond responsibilities and actions specified by formal job requirements; they ask employees to adapt to changing needs and circumstances. As we will discuss later, the working poor often have a relatively narrow set of job skills and thus may be less adaptive to changes in their roles or work practices. Finally, proactive work behavior entails informed judgment and some level of risk taking (Grant and Parker 2009). Jobs occupied by the working poor typically discourage (and, in some cases, prohibit) deviations from standard work practice. Thus, the working poor may show lower levels of proactive behavior as well, at least that observable by management.

Job Attachment. An individual's decision to remain with or to leave the organization is the result of several forces—including those on the job and at home (Lee et al. 2004). Turnover rates tend to be higher in simple or easily monitored jobs that are more likely to be occupied by the working poor (Lane 2000). Turnover also tends to be higher for single parents and those with lower socioeconomic status (SES) (Kossek et al. 1997). The working poor may show higher rates of absenteeism and tardiness, too. With fewer slack resources or safety nets in their lives outside of work, being consistently available and on time may be more difficult than it is for workers with greater financial and social resources. Going to work may not even be economically rational some days (e.g., if the pay does not outweigh the costs of getting to work), making absenteeism a sensible decision in terms of economic value (Kossek et al. 1997). In these ways, poverty may further dampen work performance and career attainment through its association with higher levels of turnover, absenteeism, and other withdrawal behaviors.

Mediating Factors

We now attempt to address the issue of *why* differences between the working poor and textbook workers might be observed. We discuss three factors that may account for the effect of poverty on work outcomes: self-efficacy, negative affectivity, and social capital. Clearly, there are other potential mediators, but we focus on these three for three reasons. First, each has a strong research base linking the phenomenon to particular work behaviors (e.g., Gist 1987, Bandura and Locke 2003 for self-efficacy; Lerner and Keltner 2001 for negative emotional states; and Lin 2000 for social capital). Second, they collectively represent cognitive (self-efficacy), affective (negative affect), and social (social capital) routes to understanding the effects of poverty on work outcomes. These map onto the existing literature on poverty from other disciplines, as previously described. Third, there are theoretical linkages among these three factors. For instance, social capital losses may drive self-efficacy, just as lower self-efficacy may lead to lower social capital. Despite these rationales, however, it is important to emphasize that our primary goal here is to develop a framework for future research and theorizing rather than to offer a definitive model for empirical testing.

Self-Efficacy. Self-efficacy is a person's judgment about her own ability to orga-nize and execute the courses of action required to bring about a desired outcome (Bandura 1977). Self-efficacy may be generalized (i.e., global perceptions of one's ability to perform a variety of tasks) or task specific (Gist 1987), with the latter referring to self-efficacy perceptions of specific domains or tasks in an individual's personal or organizational life. A strong causal statement would be that poverty is detrimental to developing self-efficacy, which, in turn, leads to negative outcomes for the working poor. Even without ascribing a causal sequence, a useful question to ask is whether there are differences in self-efficacy perceptions between the working poor and other workers. Based on prior research, both questions can be answered largely in the affirmative. At a descriptive level, Hill et al. (1985) report data from the Panel Study of Income Dynamics, finding that beliefs about personal control, success, and efficacy are all positively correlated with family income and earnings, and that these relationships do not differ by race or gender. Subsequent studies have confirmed these findings using different samples and methodologies (Kane 1987, Sampson et al. 1997, Rosenbaum et al. 2002).

Researchers have drawn empirical and conceptual connections between poverty and self-efficacy based on categorical, compositional, and relational arguments. A categorical theory of poverty, as described earlier, suggests that those living in poverty typically have less education and/or formal training than their nonpoor counterparts (U.S. Bureau of Labor and Statistics 2009), leading to lower self-efficacy. Clausen's (1986) longitudinal analysis found that feelings of low self-competence in adolescence led to poor decisions and coping abilities and lower self-efficacy later in life. Research shows that, even as adults, individuals in poverty have more frequent occurrences of disruptive spells—both personal (e.g., pregnancy, illness) and work related (e.g., layoffs)—that can erode efficacy and perpetuate poverty (Bane and Ellwood 1986). Once such a spell occurs, the likelihood of it persisting is higher among the poor, because they lack the resources to break the spell. Bane and Ellwood (1986) find that among the poor, nearly 56% had been in a spell lasting for eight years or more.

Compositional factors suggest that poor neighborhoods lack the resources to enhance self-efficacy for residents. Poorer neighborhoods have fewer resources such as educational and recreation facilities, programs aimed at preventive health, and those aimed at developing life and professional skills (Gecas 1989, Hill et al.

1985). This is compounded by lower awareness of such programs among the poor (Coward et al. 1974) and an inability to access these programs because of constraints such as time and transportation (Gurin and Gurin 1970, Coward et al. 1974). Colocation in poor neighborhoods (Rosenbaum et al. 2002) creates a social context that affords few, if any, opportunities for the working poor to observe success and learn through vicarious observation. Such a context reinforces the dynamics of lower generalized self-efficacy in areas such as parenting, health, and other life skills (Lewis 1968, Gecas 1989), which may persist throughout life (Cervone and Palmer 1990). Mortimer et al. (1982) find that early self-competence perceptions in the domains of work and in family life affect self-efficacy perceptions 10 years later. Over time, such views of one's self-efficacy tend to become self-fulfilling.

Finally, the working poor tend to hold jobs whose basic characteristics—e.g., low pay, high monitoring—can lower self-efficacy (Andersson et al. 2005). From a relational perspective, it is likely that the working poor receive less positive feedback from their supervisors, because many work systems are designed to highlight negative exceptions (e.g., lapses) instead of positive behavior. A lack of respect by supervisors (Berg and Frost 2005) and the larger society (Stacey 2005), along with negative feedback, is a common occurrence in low-wage work. Finally, the relational perspective suggests that cohort membership and experiences of similar others who are poor can further erode perceptions of self-efficacy through vicarious learning (Bengtson et al. 1985). Thus, relational factors do little to counter—and may exacerbate—low self-efficacy among the working poor.

Turning to the effects of self-efficacy on work outcomes, the evidence is robust with studies showing that individuals with high self-efficacy tend to set higher goals, initially choose relatively more difficult tasks, persist longer in tasks, and generally perform at a higher level than individuals with lower self-efficacy[4] (e.g., Wood et al. 1990). This pattern of findings is supported at the individual (e.g., Judge and Bono 2001) and the group (Gibson 2001) levels. In his comprehensive review of self-efficacy, Gecas (1989, p. 311) concludes,

> High self-efficacy ... leads to favorable or beneficial consequences for the individual ... such as better physical and psychological health, creativity, cognitive flexibility, better problem-solving and coping skills, higher self esteem, greater involvement in political processes ... although

the direction of causality is not always clear and is probably reciprocal in most situations. Even the illusion of efficacy and control (and often it is only that) seems to be beneficial.

Findings show that lower generalized self-efficacy is related to poorer work performance, lower goals, and lower commitment to attaining those goals. This occurs in part because lower self-efficacy reduces motivation (i.e., the person believes that he simply lacks the capability to achieve desirable outcomes and therefore does not expend much effort to attain them; see Bandura and Locke 2003). Successful goal setting is a critical determinant of job performance, and setting a lower initial goal can lead to lower performance outcomes even if the goal is met (Gist 1987). Kohn and colleagues (Kohn 1969, Kohn and Schooler 1973) document that jobs associated with lower SES create environments where individuals not only lack the opportunity to set their own goals but also are more likely to experience a sense of routinization, which prohibits independent goal setting altogether. Moreover, because of more frequent job changes, the working poor can develop a sense of inefficacy and lack of control, reinforcing the practice of setting lower goals as a buffer from persistent uncertainty and/or failures (Gecas 1989).

In addition to its direct effects, generalized self-efficacy can affect performance by moderating the extent to which job stressors affect work outcomes (Fox et al. 1993). Research shows that higher self-efficacy mitigates the deleterious impact of job stressors on worker coping, stress, and other such outcomes (Schaubroeck and Merritt 1997). Similarly, self-efficacy moderates the relationship between feedback and performance. Those with lower self-efficacy are more likely to focus on negative cues and feedback (Silver et al. 1995) and to interpret otherwise objectively neutral or ambiguous cues as negative because of a focus on loss prevention (Hartlage et al. 1993, Evans and English 2002).

Self-efficacy also affects career attainment. Research shows that lowered self-efficacy about career attainment at an early age adversely affects career aspirations and goals later in life (Bandura and Locke 2003). Lower self-efficacy is associated with a lower degree of maturity about career management (Anderson and Brown 1997). Significant empirical research documents the barriers to training and self-management skills for the poor compared with others (Heckman and Smith 2004). These barriers exist in a variety of forms, including a lack of awareness about training resources, a lack of transportation to access such resources, and an inability to spend time using them (e.g., no childcare). Danziger et al. (1999) find that fewer than 15% of the poor in their large-scale study are able to utilize such resources as a result. Additionally, the working poor may have skill deficiencies that restrict their ability to move into different types of jobs laterally and certainly to better-paying jobs vertically (Burtless 1997). One reason is that although the working poor may develop specific expertise in a finite set of tasks, such a narrow skill set limits their job options beyond a set of organizations in the same industry, or to very similar jobs in other industries (Mittal et al. 2009). As a result, the job mobility of the working poor is limited compared with others who have specialized skills that are in higher demand and/or generalized skills that can transfer easily across different jobs (Lambert 1999).

Over time, a self-debilitating dynamic can ensue that manifests as lower, rather than higher, voluntary turnover, but in jobs that do not allow for further skill acquisition, career development, or significant wage increases (Vancouver et al. 2002). In this regard, the working poor can develop high task-specific self-efficacy in a very narrow task domain but low generalized self-efficacy overall (Betz and Hackett 1981), thus limiting their ability, actual and perceived, to leave their jobs. Olson and Schober (1993) construct a comprehensive model that suggests that after repeated failures, a person not only believes that it is hopeless to try to change his circumstances but that he changes his attitude to match his situation—thereby seeming satisfied in very dissatisfying circumstances. Mittal et al. (2009) offer this as one explanation for their finding of high job satisfaction among nursing home aides, despite the low pay, low status, and lack of respect by management.

At the same time, there is evidence pointing to successful interventions (Frayne and Geringer 2000, Eden and Aviram 1993) that can break the vicious cycle of efficacy decrement and career losses. For instance, Krieshok et al. (2000) report two studies among veterans seeking vocational assistance, where résumé assistance and training were offered to enhance self-efficacy. Both studies report ameliorative effects on career decision making, job seeking, and work. Similarly, Frayne and Geringer (2000) find that training sessions designed to teach participants how to overcome obstacles at work significantly improve self-efficacy, outcome expectancy, and performance relative to control groups. Follow-up over the next year found that the beneficial effects continued well after the program was complete. This is encouraging as a possible intervention in improving self-efficacy and career mobility among the working poor.

Negative Affectivity. Affective states are defined as transitory feeling states and include both target-specific emotions (e.g., anger) and more diffuse moods (e.g., feeling down). Sometimes they are also related to persistent clinical conditions such as depression (Diener and Emmons 1984). Affective states are broadly construed along two independent dimensions: valence and arousal (Russell 2003). Along the valence dimension (which is the dimension that has received the most research attention), affective states can be positive (e.g., happiness, joy) or negative (e.g., anger, fear, sadness). More recently, researchers have examined specific emotions using the appraisal-tendency framework (Lerner and Keltner 2001). Here, emotions can induce specific appraisals of the situation regarding the levels of personal control, certainty, anticipated effort, and responsibility. Differences in these appraisals may lead to different consequences for otherwise similar emotional valence. For example, Garg et al. (2005) show that anger, as compared to sadness, is characterized by high certainty.

Empirical research shows that the working poor are exposed to a relatively high number of stressors and negative life events (Dohrenwend 1973, McLeod and Kessler 1990), which can contribute significantly to negative appraisals and affective states (Kessler 1997, Gallo and Matthews 2003). A large body of research documents an inverse relationship between SES and depression[5] (Salokangas and Poutanen 1998), SES and anxiety (Warheit et al. 1975), and SES and stress (McLeod and Kessler 1990).[6] Individuals with lower SES are not only more likely to experience negative life events (Murphy et al. 1991) but are also likely to experience negative affective states more strongly and intensely after such events (McLeod and Kessler 1990). From a structural perspective, coping resources such as counseling services are less available to the working poor (Danziger and Gottschalk 1995, Gallo and Matthews 2003). From a relational perspective, the working poor have restricted social resources (Rankin and Quane 2002, Domínguez and Watkins 2003), limiting the amount of information or the number of available options (McLeod and Kessler 1990). Indeed, Brown and Moran

(1997) find that chronic episodes of negative affect are more common among the working poor than others, particularly when a social support system is lacking.

Negative affect focuses a person's attention on the negatively valenced information embedded in a situation (Hartlage et al. 1993). In some types of jobs (e.g., health care), a focus on negatively valenced cues may motivate a person to be more attentive to the potential downside risk of the situation and make him or her more mindful at work. At the same time, an inordinate focus on negative cues is likely to hamper performance in frontline service jobs that pose an expectation of gregariousness (e.g., a server at a restaurant). From a relational perspective, research shows that affective cues are sometimes inaccurate and cause perceptual misalignments, leading to counterproductive work behavior. For example, Fox et al. (2001) find that when faced with job stressors such as interpersonal conflict and perceived injustice, those experiencing higher negative affect are more likely to engage in counterproductive work behaviors. Similarly, negatively valenced affective states such as sadness can decrease the intensity of effort exerted toward the job as well as persistence in following a task to completion (Seo et al. 2004). Naquin and Holton (2002) find that those having higher negative affectivity also had lower job involvement, motivation to train, and performance outcomes. There is evidence that negative affect, particularly related to depression, can significantly curtail a person's ability to perform regular day-to-day tasks at work (Dooley et al. 2000). Thus, although there are exceptions based on specific task characteristics, negatively valenced affective states can be functionally debilitating and can adversely influence a person's job performance.

Evidence regarding career outcomes among the working poor has focused on persistent negative affect (Brown and Moran 1997), with longitudinal studies showing a causal relationship to downward career mobility (Dooley et al. 2000, Murphy et al. 1991). One type of negative affect, fear, has been shown to lead to risk aversion, particularly in assessing career-related decisions. Raghunathan and Pham (1999, p. 65) find that among those who experience fear, a job with "average salary with high job security" was more attractive than a job with "high salary with low job security." This may occur partly because fear, similar to general negative affect, focuses people's attention on potential negative consequences, which typically promotes risk aversion (Han et al. 2007). Thus, those experiencing fear may be more likely to take the safer route by staying in their current job or seeking only jobs similar to their current job, rather than risking new career options with potentially higher payoffs.

Negative states can focus the individual's attention to negatively valenced aspects of the stimuli, leading to lower satisfaction judgments (Oliver 1993) and behavioral intentions (Smith and Bolton 2008). In addition, negative affective states can exacerbate the negative impact of job dissatisfaction on feelings of job insecurity and associated coping behaviors (Jordan et al. 2002). Research has further shown that the link between high satisfaction and positive behavioral intentions can be attenuated by a negative emotional state (Smith and Bolton 2008), suggesting that negative emotions may erode or attenuate the link between job satisfaction and organizational attachment behaviors. For instance, those in emotionally taxing jobs (e.g., nurse aides) may be more likely to experience negative affect and thus may display weaker job attachment, even when they report high job satisfaction. Controlling for factors such as age, race, parental education, work experience, religiosity, area of residence, and job history, Ahituv and Lerman (2004) find a significant impact of family income on job change. Some of these findings are also consistent with the negative-affect escape model (Baron 1977) that suggests, more generally, that aversive situations lead to increased negative affect and a fight-or-flight response. In summary, research shows that the working poor may evince higher levels of negative affectivity, which, in turn, has largely negative effects on job performance and attachment as well as career attainment over time.

Social Capital. Social capital is defined in terms of the nature and the accessibility of resources embedded in relationships. In relations among individuals, social capital has at least two components: (1) social resources—assets such as information and referral benefits that are embedded in social relations, and (2) network structure and position—how contacts among people are arrayed (e.g., dense or sparse ties) and the position occupied by the individual in the social structure (e.g., centrality in the network). Lin (1983, 1999, 2000) and his colleagues (Ensel 1979, Lin and Dumin 1986) have most directly focused on access to, and mobilization of, social resources. Social resource theory states that assets such as information, referrals, and sponsorship are accessible through one's direct and indirect ties to others. Furthermore, it is not just the number of one's ties but also their quality and range that lead to positive outcomes for individuals (Lin

1982, 1999). The theory has three main propositions: (a) social resources—both their availability and their quality—affect valued outcomes such as status and wealth, (b) the individual's position in a hierarchy or SES can affect access to such resources, and (c) ties can affect outcomes such as work status, particularly for those individuals in disadvantaged initial positions. Empirical research has found support for all three propositions (e.g., Huang and Tausig 1990, Lai et al. 1998, Lin and Dumin 1986, Lin et al. 1981, Marsden and Hurlbert 1988, Seibert et al. 2001, Sparrowe et al. 2001).

Compositional and relational theories of poverty are most relevant to understanding social capital among the working poor. The working poor tend to have more impoverished social networks than their wealthier counterparts; such networks, in turn, are associated with negative individual outcomes. Green et al. (1995) find that job seekers who are economically disadvantaged are more likely to turn to neighborhood friends and relatives for job referrals, whereas the more advantaged seek out diverse sources to whom they are more distantly connected. More diverse and distant ties, in turn, have been associated with better outcomes for job seekers (Granovetter 1973, Lin 1983). Such impoverished social circumstances, moreover, tend to be self-perpetuating. As summarized by Lin (2000, p. 789), "People in lower socioeconomic status tend to use local ties, strong ties, and family and kin ties. Since these ties are usually homogeneous in resources, this networking tendency reinforces poor social capital."

There are several reasons why the economically disadvantaged may tend to associate with disadvantaged others, despite the relative paucity of social resources embedded in such relationships. The well-established phenomenon of homophily suggests that people are likely to interact with others who hold characteristics and status similar to their own (McPherson et al. 2001). From a compositional perspective, Wilson (1987) suggests that neighborhood poverty can promote social segregation, further diminishing the social resources available to residents. Individuals in poorer communities not only develop stronger social ties within the community, but they may also become an encapsulated network with poor connections (Granovetter 1985). At the same time, residents of wealthier communities are unlikely to interact with those from poorer neighborhoods, perhaps because of fear of taint or because they perceive that their lower-income neighbors have little to offer to them.

The nature of low-paying work may further limit social resources. Low-status work environments are often understaffed or require unusual work hours (Berg and Frost 2005), which limit the formation of diverse work networks. Low-status workers may also have less access to higher-status others in the organizational hierarchy, and their direct supervisors are likely to be lower-level managers with fewer high-status contacts of their own. The working poor may become isolated in organizations as well, as they are often physically or temporally segregated from other employees. As noted earlier, building janitors may share the same physical space as office workers, but they occupy that space at different times of day. Second, as previously described, low-income workers may be constrained in their interactions with higher-wage workers because of the physical and/or social taint sometimes associated with low-wage jobs.

In summary, the working poor may have limited access to social resources because of their limited association with more advantaged others. Homophily is one explanation for this, but it is not the only one. Some of the social segregation characterizing the working poor may be due to higher-status others' reluctance to associate with them for fear of taint or stigma (Ashforth and Kreiner 1999). Moreover, restricted resources in terms of time and flexibility may further isolate the working poor (Berg and Frost 2005, Stack 1974). Finally, the working poor may be physically or temporally segregated from other workers. Thus, although the working poor may be inclined, like everyone else, to gravitate toward the familiar in their social relationships, there are relational and structural factors that may further impede their access to and accumulation of social capital.

Researchers have demonstrated a link between social capital and several measures of career success, including job attainment (Granovetter 1974), mobility in the organization (Podolny and Baron 1997), and wage levels (Boxman et al. 1991). Both network structure (i.e., characteristics of the network itself and one's position in it) and the resources that can be mobilized through the network, such as information, referral, and sponsorship, can influence career success. The most influential work on social networks and career attainment is Granovetter's (1974) "strength of weak ties" hypothesis, which proposes that ties with acquaintances are more valuable in job search than are ties to family and friends because they are richer sources of unique information. There has been mixed support for this hypothesis (see, for example, Marsden and Hurlbert 1988), but arguably it is at least as applicable to the economically disadvantaged as to the professionals who tend to be the subjects of much of this research. For people at the bottom of the economic ladder, weak ties are likely to hold more resources than strong ones, if for no other reason than because when one is at the bottom, weak ties tend to reach up. Strong ties, conversely, tend to be with similar others—i.e., those who are also in low-status positions and therefore unlikely to hold unique information or valuable referrals (Rankin 2003). Indeed, Lin et al. (1981) report that the positive effect of weak ties is dependent on whether they reach up to those with more resources or whether they reach across to others in similarly disadvantaged positions.

With regard to the resources within social networks, Lin (1999) and his colleagues have provided substantial evidence that network resources like information and referrals are positively correlated with career outcomes such as work opportunities, wages, and job prestige (Boxman et al. 1991, Green et al. 1999, Lin et al. 1981). Seibert et al. (2001) also show that sponsorship by others who are more senior in the hierarchy can be particularly advantageous in terms of salary and career advancement. Moreover, they demonstrate the mediating role of network benefits (access to information, resources, and sponsorship) in the relationship between network structure and career outcomes, offering further support for Lin's social resource theory.

Seibert and colleagues (2001) describe other ways in which social capital can enhance job performance. When an individual has better access to information and resources, her job is likely to be enriched, and she is thus more motivated to excel. In addition, individuals with greater resources and information are perceived by others as more influential (Brass and Burkhardt 1993) and thus better able to secure the actual resources they need to get their work done efficiently and effectively. Finally, those who are better connected have access to more diverse information—another resource that can enhance job mobility and work performance.

With regard to job attachment, Krackhardt and Porter (1986) demonstrate the effects of social capital on turnover in a study of fast-food workers. Here, they found that employees who occupied similar roles tended to leave in clusters: when an individual observed that similar others were leaving the job, he was more likely to leave himself. In another study, Fernandez et al. (2000) report similar results with adult call center employees who could receive a bonus if they were the source of referral for a new employee. They found that referred employees were no less likely to quit their jobs than employees recruited through other means, but they were more likely to leave if the referring employee left. Castillo (2005) further reports that referred employees are initially more productive than those recruited through other means but that such performance effects dissipate over time. Overall, this work suggests that turnover may be contagious in a sense, at least among friends, which may be particularly detrimental to the working poor who do not have an abundance of alternatives.

● GENERATING ORGANIZATIONAL RESEARCH ON THE WORKING POOR

Our goals have been to initiate a theory-driven description of how being among the working poor—a background of poverty coupled with current low income—might logically affect attitudes and behavior at work, to consider how such employees might differ from their "textbook" counterparts, and to argue for future study. Toward those ends, we have touched on various research streams examining the working poor, spanning fields such as sociology, economics, education, and psychology. At the same time, the intellectual maturity of our field and the changing nature of the world economy suggest that the working poor need to be treated not at the margin of organizational studies but integrated in a more focused and attentive manner. There are likely many differences between the working poor and textbook employees—i.e., managers, professionals, and knowledge workers who are the subjects of much of the field research in OB. Our goal here is to spur future research to more fully examine them.

The working poor are situated in a very powerful context—the nexus of poverty and low-wage work. Rousseau and Fried (2001, p. 6) argue that "contextualization is a way of approaching research where knowledge of the settings to be studied is brought to bear in design and implementation decisions." They offer several suggestions for designing research studies with a stronger consideration of context, including more attention to construct comparability—e.g., does a construct mean the same thing for one group—the working poor—as another—textbook employees? For many core constructs in organizational behavior, the answer to this question might be "possibly not" or even an outright "no." For example, the literature on organizational citizenship behavior pays little heed to the potential differences among individuals in the costs they incur (e.g., time, effort) for being good citizens at work. To the extent these costs are taken into account, they are largely treated as universal threats to motivation (e.g., helping others may not further self-interest). This reflects the influence of economics in the study of work behavior, but it also reflects an inattention to differences in individuals' situations in and outside of work that may influence how they behave in their jobs. In the case of citizenship behavior, actions like helping out a colleague or staying later at work to finish a project are more costly to the worker who is already struggling to complete her own tasks and/or has nobody at home to tend to the children while she works extra hours.

Another example of how our theories of organizational behavior might be informed by a consideration of the effects of poverty is in the area of career management. Research suggests that resource depletion and repeated failure can lead to lower risk taking more generally (Mittal et al. 2002), which in turn can manifest in timidity in career planning and an undue attachment to the status quo at work. Such risk aversion might be attributed to the individual's disposition or a general lack of initiative, and it is thus coded as a motivation problem by management. But the true source of what may be interpreted as unwarranted timidity may be a lack of efficacy and overestimation of the risk of change, because any errors in judgment are inherently more costly to those with diminished resources.

We argue here for a consideration of the context of poverty in organizational science, but we recognize that individual actors are not passive recipients of context and that people who grow up in poverty can—and do—become high-wage earners. Even when they remain in low-wage jobs, there are many ways to modify the context—socially, symbolically, psychologically, and perhaps spiritually—to imbue it with meaning (see Kossek et al. 2010 for a recent example). At the individual level, the working poor may redraw the psychological boundaries of their work and the meaning they ascribe to it. Wrzesniewski and Dutton (2001) find a good deal of "job crafting" among hospital cleaning staff whose pay was generally low and formal job descriptions quite narrow. Many of the subjects in their study informally expanded the boundaries of their cleaning work (e.g., by welcoming families or attending to patients' emotional needs) to better match their own perceptions of the job's enhanced scope and importance. Socially, the working poor may create new relationships or redefine and renegotiate existing relationships. Mittal et al. (2009) find that many of the nursing home assistants in their study enrich the meaning of their jobs through emotional and spiritual relationships with their elderly residents. These workers also described their feelings of mastery and self-respect because of the importance of their work to society at large, regardless of the job's perceived low status and objective low pay. Beyond that, the working poor may also reshape their relationships with their coworkers, offering emotional and symbolic support to one another in work as well as nonwork spheres.

Another potentially fruitful line of inquiry concerns how conceptions of religiosity, spirituality, and group identity help the working poor navigate difficult jobs and personal lives. When instrumental resources are scarce, how do people extend existing social, spiritual, emotional, and cognitive resources? Furthermore, how do extant differences—in terms of gender, race, work status, and experience—hinder or facilitate such resource accumulation and sharing as it pertains to work? These are all questions to be investigated if we are to understand the variety of coping mechanisms that may be available and utilized by the working poor.

One way to do this may be to take top management team (TMT) research and turn it on its head. TMT research is predicated on the assumption that leaders are consequential to organizational outcomes and that characteristics of the TMT—categorical and compositional—matter. We suggest here that a similar approach to understanding the working poor, but not focused solely on instrumental resources, would be a useful catalyst in enhancing our theories in organization science to capture the perceptions and experiences of not just the few at the top but also the many at the bottom of the organization.

With regard to mediators of the effects of poverty on work outcomes, here we have focused on only three mediators, offered not as exhaustive but, rather, as illustrative of an approach that considers cognitive (e.g., self-efficacy), emotional (e.g., negative affect), and relational (e.g., social capital) pathways, and we focus on how they might combine in the strength and tenacity of their effects on work attitudes and behaviors. Thus, it is highly likely that social capital losses can drive lower self-efficacy as well as increase negative affect. Similarly, lower self-efficacy or negative affectivity may culminate in lower social capital because of a person's reluctance to network with others. Understanding how these factors evolve over time in ways that are mutually reinforcing, and sometimes cancelling, is a key research area.

The perspective we have outlined here, however, needs to be pursued heedfully. Like culture (and some of the early literature on the entry of women and minorities into jobs that were historically occupied by white males), there is a danger of reifying poverty as a concept and linking it directly to work outcomes. Thus, studies that simply document differences among the working poor and others, without investigating how and/or why poverty may be a causative factor, could lead to false causal attributions. We want to emphasize the critical need for articulating the underlying processes and mechanisms that are associated with poverty, which in turn may affect work outcomes. Similarly, our focus on the working poor should not be taken to suggest that the working poor represent a social class with innate characteristics. Being poor or having a low-wage job is no more an innate characteristic than is being a "physician" or a "CEO." Yet, as an initial step, an empirical body of research that can enable us to understand the experienced reality of the working poor is needed. Recognizing that these are not monoliths of people, a nuanced approach is warranted to understand what happens at the base of the organizational pyramid.

Researchers might also fruitfully study the role of locus of control among the working poor. Markus and colleagues (e.g., Snibbe and Markus 2005, Stephens et al. 2007) show that there are significant differences between working-class and middle-class individuals regarding norms about what constitutes "good" or appropriate action. In their research, middle-class students and adults are more likely to value independence and uniqueness in the choices they make, whereas working-class individuals are more likely to make choices based on a desire to be similar to others and interdependent with them. As noted previously, in an examination of Hurricane Katrina survivors by Stephens et al. (2010), outsiders attributed positive motivations like agency and responsibility to leavers (who tended to be college educated and middle class) and negative attributes like passivity and irresponsibility to stayers (who tended to have lower income and educational attainment), without regard to the differences in resources between the two groups. Equally interesting, interviews with actual survivors of Hurricane Katrina revealed divergent responses to the storm: leavers (higher SES) tended to emphasize their own actions—e.g., risk assessment, planning, and choice—and stayers (lower SES) tended to emphasize virtues like perseverance and hope.

If such results can be generalized to the work environment, they suggest that individuals who live in poverty are less likely to act in ways that are conventionally "agentic" at work—e.g., striving for recognition, control, and attainment—than are the managers and professionals who are far more often the subjects of research. In addition, norms of interdependence rather than independence, and security rather than risk taking, may be more powerful considerations for those with fewer financial resources (Stephens et al. 2007). This may lead to lower observed initiative and innovation (at least as they are conventionally measured by organizational researchers) and a more reactive rather than proactive approach to jobs. Such questions are speculative but deserve far more attention than they have received to date both because of the risk of potential bias due to restriction of range in current organizational research and because of the practical consequences of disproportionate attention to managers and professionals.

Research also needs to explore and articulate the relationship between poverty and low-wage work. We have argued that they jointly represent the working poor. However, how do the working poor come to be who they are? Especially important will be a historical and temporal account of categorical, compositional, and structural factors associated with a past of poverty that influence cognitive, affective, and social mediators at work. Research is also needed to better understand the temporal evolution of social, structural, and psychological aspects of low-wage work that likely propagate poverty.

In addition, future work should develop multilevel models (e.g., theoretical and empirical) for understanding the interplay of categorical, compositional, and relational factors. The first step would be to more precisely theorize how specific constructs need to be measured and the level at which they should be conceptualized. Although it is easier to specify categorical factors (e.g., SES, education, work experience) at an individual level, this may be more difficult for the other factors. Descriptive case studies over time as well as longitudinal studies will be useful in this regard.

Finally, there is no shortage of research on leadership in the organizations literature, but power dynamics between the working poor and their supervisors may be a particularly rich and yet underresearched area of inquiry. Kossek et al.

(2010) show the potential power of small changes in supervisor behavior on the poor workers who report to them. With this exception, much of the past research on worker–supervisor relationships has been job focused (e.g., job evaluations, job design). However, social relationships inside and outside of work are important as well. Of particular importance are the exaggerated power dynamics of these relationships. The disparity in resources may, in some ways, magnify the perceived power of the supervisor. There may also be structural aspects of low-wage work—e.g., job designs that allow supervisors to immediately document negative deviations from tight performance norms while discouraging adaptive and proactive behavior—that magnify such power disparities. To the extent that they exist, they need to be more systematically studied in terms of their influence on self-efficacy, negative affect, social resources, and other potential mediators.

● CONCLUDING COMMENTS

Bertrand et al. (2004) observe that the fundamental effect of poverty on individuals is that it leaves little room for error: missing a day at work may be inconsequential to a college professor, but the same behavior can result in a janitor's termination. Similarly, if a manager's car fails to start in the morning, she might borrow her partner's car or take a taxi into work. When a health aide faces the same problem, the result may be a reprimand and docked pay for her "unexcused tardiness" (because using public transportation may take more time) or missing work altogether.

We have argued that the nexus of past poverty and low current wages represents a strong situation that influences an individual's attitudes and behavior at work, just as it does other aspects of life, such as health and family patterns, education, social interactions, and area of residence, to mention a few. The working poor are similar in some ways to the textbook workers in organizational research in that both groups experience a consistency between their past and current economic status, which makes their futures more predictable. These groups are vastly different, however, regarding the munificence of their current and past economic lives, and it is this difference that is our focus here. We have argued that the persistence of economic deprivation that marks the lives of the working poor may present a context so powerful as to call into question the generalizability of organizational research, the focus of which has been largely on more affluent others.

As a final point, it is interesting to speculate why organizational research has been so silent with regard to the working poor. The ascension of the service sector has made such workers seemingly indispensable to the value creation model for firms in developed economies. Yet organizational researchers seem to have been slow to recognize this. One explanation is that the managers and professionals who are more often the subjects of our research are seen as contributing greater value to organizations and the economy as a whole, and they are thus more important subjects for research attention. Another explanation may rest with our own fear of "taint through association": if our research is centered on lower-status workers, maybe it too will be seen as having lower status. These two explanations are perhaps intertwined. Regardless of intention, however, both serve to maintain the status quo regarding the value we place on different kinds of jobs and the circumstances of the people who occupy them.

Acknowledgments

Authors are listed alphabetically. The authors thank Denise Rousseau and Scott Sonnenshein for helpful comments on earlier drafts of this manuscript.

Endnotes

1. At the same time, we do realize that large swaths of the world's poor live in developing and underdeveloped countries, where they face extreme living and working conditions with few government protections (e.g., labor laws) and little social assistance (e.g., income supports). We also acknowledge that many part-time workers in developed countries do not earn enough to escape poverty.

2. Originally determined by estimating the cost of food for families of different sizes and then multiplying this amount by 3 (assuming that food costs are one-third of household expenditures).

3. An individual working full time at the current federal minimum wage ($7.25 per hour) would fall below this poverty threshold. Even two adults working full time, year-round at the 2011 federal minimum wage would have a combined income that falls within 130% of the poverty threshold.

4. A related concept is learned helplessness, when people experiencing repeated failures (either through lack of control over processes or outcomes) begin to feel hopeless through reinforcement processes (Olson and Schober 1993). Learned helplessness can give way to

passivity and resignation as well as the expectation of failure as the default option. Over time, this erodes self-efficacy, perpetuating a vicious downward spiral.

5. We do not imply a dispositional or trait-based causal mechanism between poverty and negative affectivity like anger or persistent sadness. Numerous higher-paying jobs may also be associated with negative affect (Teuchmann et al. 1999, van Eck et al. 1998) and plenty of other off-work factors that may lead to persistent negative emotional states.

6. Gallo and Matthews (2003) define depression as an emotion low in pleasantness and activation, which they distinguish from clinically diagnosable depressive syndromes that reflect a clustering of negative emotions and other symptoms. They also distinguish between anxiety, an emotion low in pleasantness but high in activation, and an anxiety disorder, discriminated by its duration, intensity, or situational appropriateness.

References

Ackerman, D. J. 2006. The costs of being a child care teacher. *Ed. Policy* **20**(1) 85–112.

Adler, N. E., J. M. Ostrove. 1993. Socioeconomic status and health: What we know and what we don't. *Ann. New York Acad. Sci.* **896** 3–15.

Ahituv, A., R. Lerman. 2004. Job turnover, wage rates, and marital stability: How are they related? *Demography* **44**(3) 623–647.

Anderson, S., C. Brown. 1997. Self-efficacy as a determinant of career maturity in urban and rural high school seniors. *J. Career Assessment* **5**(3) 305–315.

Andersson, F., H. J. Holzer, J. I. Lane. 2005. *Moving Up or Moving On: Who Advances in the Low-Wage Labor Market?* Russell Sage Foundation, New York.

Ashforth, B. E., G. E. Kreiner. 1999. "How can you do it?": Dirty work and the challenge of constructing a positive identity. *Acad. Management Rev.* **24**(3) 413–434.

Bandura, A. 1977. Self-efficacy: Toward a unifying theory of behavioral change. *Psych. Rev.* **84**(2) 191–215.

Bandura, A., E. A. Locke. 2003. Negative self-efficacy and goal effects revisited. *J. Appl. Psych.* **88**(1) 87–99.

Bane, M. J., D. T. Ellwood. 1986. Slipping into and out of poverty: The dynamics of spells. *J. Human Resources* **21**(1) 1–23.

Baron, R. A. 1977. *Human Aggression*. Plenum Press, New York.

Barrett, A. E., R. J. Turner. 2005. Family structure and mental health: The mediating effects of socioeconomic status, family process, and social stress. *J. Health Soc. Behav.* **46**(2) 156–169.

Bartsch, K. J. 2009. The employment projections for 2008–18. *Monthly Labor Rev.* **132**(11) 3–10.

Bengtson, V. L., M. N. Reedy, C. Gordon. 1985. Aging and self-conceptions: Personality processes and social contexts. J. E. Birren, K. W. Schaie, eds. *Handbook of the Psychology of Aging*, 2nd ed. Van Nostrand Reinhold, New York, 544–593.

Berg, P., A. C. Frost. 2005. Dignity at work for low wage, low skill service workers. *Indust. Relations* **60**(4) 657–682.

Bertrand, M., S. Mullainathan, E. Shafir. 2004. A behavioral-economics view of poverty. *Amer. Econom. Rev.* **94**(2) 419–423.

Betz, N. E., G. Hackett. 1981. The relationship of career-related self-efficacy expectations to perceived career options in college women and men. *J. Counseling Psych.* **28**(5) 399–410.

Boxman, E. A. W., P. M. De Graaf, H. D. Flap. 1991. The impact of social and human capital on the income attainment of Dutch managers. *Soc. Networks* **13**(1) 51–73.

Brass, D. J., M. E. Burkhardt. 1993. Potential power and power use: An investigation of structure and behavior. *Acad. Management J.* **36**(3) 441–470.

Brown, G. W., P. M. Moran. 1997. Single mothers, poverty and depression. *Psych. Medicine* **27**(1) 21–33.

Burtless, G. T. 1997. Welfare recipients' job skills and employment prospects. *Future Children* **7**(1) 39–51.

Castillo, E. J. 2005. Social networks and employee performance in a call center. *Amer. J. Sociol.* **110**(5) 1243–1283.

Cervone, D., B. W. Palmer. 1990. Anchoring biases and the perseverance of self-efficacy beliefs. *Cognitive Therapy Res.* **14**(4) 401–416.

Clausen, J. A. 1986. Early adult choices and the life course. Paper presented at the American Sociological Association Annual Meeting, September, American Sociological Association, Washington, DC.

Cohen, D. A., T. A. Farley, K. Mason. 2003. Why is poverty unhealthy? Social and physical mediators. *Soc. Sci. Medicine* **57**(9) 1631–1641.

Corcoran, M., G. J. Duncan, G. Gurin, P. Gurin. 1985. Myth and reality: The causes and persistence of poverty. *J. Policy Anal. Management* **4**(4) 516–536.

Coward, B. E., J. R. Feagin, J. A. Williams Jr. 1974. The culture of poverty debate: Some additional data. *Soc. Problems* **21**(5) 621–634.

Craypo, C., D. Cormier. 2000. Job restructuring as a determinant of wage inequality and working-poor households. *J. Econom. Issues* **34**(1) 21–42.

Danziger, S., P. Gottschalk. 1995. *America Unequal*. Russell Sage Foundation, New York.

Danziger, S., M. Corcoran, S. Danziger, C. Heflin, A. Kalil, J. Levine, D. Rosen, K. Seefeldt, K. Siefert, R. Tolman. 1999. Barriers to the employment of welfare recipients. Report, Poverty Research and Training Center, University of Michigan, Ann Arbor.

DeNavas-Walt, C., B. D. Proctor, J. Smith. 2007. U.S. Census Bureau Current Population Report P60–233—Income, poverty, and health insurance coverage in the United States: 2006. U.S. Government Printing Office, Washington, DC.

Devine, C. M., M. Jastran, J. A. Jabs, E. Wethington, T. J. Farell, C. A. Bisogni. 2006. "A lot of sacrifices": Work-family spillover and the food choice coping strategies of low-wage employed parents. *Soc. Sci. Medicine* **63**(10) 2591–2603.

Diener, E., R. A. Emmons. 1984. The independence of positive and negative affect. *J. Personality Soc. Psych.* **47**(5) 1105–1117.

Dohrenwend, B. S. 1973. Life events as stressors: A methodological inquiry. *J. Health Soc. Behav.* **14**(2) 167–175.

Domínguez, S., C. Watkins. 2003. Creating networks for survival and mobility: Social capital among African-American and Latin-American low-income mothers. *Soc. Problems* **50**(1) 111–135.

Dooley, D., J. Prause, K. A. Ham-Rowbottom. 2000. Underemployment and depression: Longitudinal relationships. *J. Health Soc. Behav.* **41**(4) 421–436.

Durden, E. D., T. D. Hill, R. J. Angel. 2007. Social demands, social supports, and psychological distress among low-income women. *J. Soc. Personal Relationships* **24**(3) 343–361.

Eden, D., A. Aviram. 1993. Self-efficacy training to speed reemployment: Helping people to help themselves. *J. Appl. Psych.* **78**(3) 352–360.

England, P., N. Folbre. 1999. The cost of caring. *Ann. Amer. Acad. Political Soc. Sci.* **561**(1) 39–51.

Ensel, W. M. 1979. *Sex, Social Ties, and Status Attainment.* State University of New York at Albany Press, Albany.

Evans, G. W., K. English. 2002. The environment of poverty: Multiple stressor exposure, psycho-, physiological stress, and socio-emotional adjustment. *Child Dev.* **73**(4) 1238–1248.

Feldman, D. C. 2002. Stability in the midst of change: A developmental perspective on the study of careers. D. C. Feldman, ed. *Work Careers: A Developmental Perspective.* Jossey-Bass, San Francisco, 3–26.

Fernandez, R. M., E. J. Castilla, P. Moore. 2000. Social capital at work: Networks and employment at a phone center. *Amer. J. Sociol.* **105**(5) 1288–1356.

Figueroa, E. G., R. A. Woods. 2007. Industry output and employment projections to 2016. *Monthly Labor Rev.* **130**(11) 53–85.

Fox, M. L., D. J. Dwyer, D. C. Ganster. 1993. Effects of stressful job demands and control on physiological and attitudinal outcomes in a hospital setting. *Acad. Management J.* **36**(2) 289–318.

Fox, S., P. E. Spector, D. Miles. 2001. Counterproductive work behavior (CWB) in response to job stressors and organizational justice: Some mediator and moderator tests for autonomy and emotions. *J. Vocational Behav.* **59**(3) 291–309.

Frayne, C. A., J. M. Geringer. 2000. Self-management training for improving job performance: A field experiment involving sales-people. *J. Appl. Psych.* **85**(3) 361–372.

Gallo, L. C., K. A. Matthews. 2003. Understanding the association between socioeconomic status and physical health: Do negative emotions play a role? *Psych. Bull.* **129**(1) 10–51.

Gallo, L. C., L. M. Bogart, A. M. Vranceanu, K. A. Matthews. 2005. Socioeconomic status, resources, psychological experiences, and emotional responses: A test of the reserve capacity model. *J. Personality Soc. Psych.* **88**(2) 386–399.

Garg, N., J. J. Inman, V. Mittal. 2005. Incidental and task-related affect: A re-inquiry and extension of the influence of affect on choice. *J. Consumer Res.* **32**(1) 154–159.

Gecas, V. 1989. The social psychology of self-efficacy. *Annual Rev. Sociol.* **15** 291–316.

Gibson, C. B. 2001. Me and us: Differential relationships among goal-setting training, efficacy, and effectiveness at the individual and team level. *J. Organ. Behav.* **22**(7) 789–808.

Gist, M. E. 1987. Self-efficacy: Implications for organizational behavior and human resources management. *Acad. Management Rev.* **12**(3) 472–485.

Gould, M. 1999. Race and theory: Culture, poverty, and adaptation to discrimination in Wilson and Ogbu. *Sociol. Theory* **17**(2) 171–200.

Granovetter, M. S. 1973. The strength of weak ties. *Amer. J. Sociol.* **78**(6) 1360–1380.

Granovetter, M. S. 1974. *Getting a Job: A Study of Contacts and Careers.* Harvard University Press, Cambridge, MA.

Granovetter, M. S. 1985. Economic action and social structure: The problem of embeddedness. *Amer. J. Sociol.* **91**(3) 481–510.

Grant, A., S. Parker. 2009. Redesigning work design theories: The rise of relational and proactive perspectives. *Acad. Management Ann.* **3** 317–375.

Green, G. P., L. M. Tigges, I. Browne. 1995. Social resources, job search and poverty in Atlanta. D. A. Chekki, ed. *Research in Community Sociology*, Vol. 5. JAI Press, Greenwich, CT, 161–182.

Green, G. P., L. M. Tigges, D. Diaz. 1999. Racial and ethnic differences in job strategies in Atlanta, Boston, and Los Angeles. *Soc. Sci. Quart.* **80**(2) 263–278.

Griffin, M. A., A. Neal, S. K. Parker. 2007. A new model of work role performance: Positive behavior in uncertain and interdependent contexts. *Acad. Management J.* **50**(2) 327–347.

Gurin, G., P. Gurin. 1970. Expectancy theory in the study of poverty. *J. Soc. Issues* **26**(2) 83–104.

Hall, D. T. 1976. *Careers in Organizations*. Goodyear Publishing, Pacific Palisades, CA.

Hall, D. T., B. Schneider. 1973. *Organizational Climates and Careers: The Work Lives of Priests*. Academic, New York.

Han, S., J. S. Lerner, D. Keltner. 2007. Feelings and consumer decision making: The appraisal-tendency framework. *J. Consumer Psych.* **17**(3) 158–168.

Hartlage, S., L. B. Alloy, C. Vázquez, B. Dykman. 1993. Automatic and effortful processing in depression. *Psych. Bull.* **113**(2) 247–278.

Heckman, J. J., J. A. Smith. 2004. The determinants of participation in a social program: Evidence from a prototypical job training program. *J. Labor Econom.* **22**(2) 243–298.

Hemp, P. 2004. Presenteeism: At work—But out of it. *Harvard Bus. Rev.* **82**(10) 49–58.

Hill, M., S. Augustyniak, G. Duncan, G. Gurin, P. Gurin, J. Liker, J. Morgan, M. Ponza. 1985. *Motivation and Economic Mobility*. Institute for Social Research, University of Michigan, Ann Arbor.

Huang, G., M. Tausig. 1990. Network range in personal networks. *Soc. Networks* **12**(3) 261–268.

Jackson, A. P., J. Brooks-Gunn, C.-C. Huang, M. Glassman. 2000. Single mothers in low-wage jobs: Financial strain, parenting, and preschoolers' outcomes. *Child Dev.* **71**(5) 1409–1423.

Jordan, P. J., N. M. Ashkanasy, C. E. J. Hartel. 2002. Emotional intelligence as a moderator of emotional and behavioral reactions to job insecurity. *Acad. Management Rev.* **27**(3) 361–372.

Judge, T. A., J. E. Bono. 2001. Relationship of core self-evaluations traits—Self-esteem, generative self-efficacy, locus of control, and emotional stability—With job satisfaction and job performance: A meta-analysis. *J. Appl. Psych.* **86**(1) 80–92.

Kane, T. J. 1987. Giving back control: Long-term poverty and motivation. *Soc. Service Rev.* **61**(3) 405–419.

Kessler, R. C. 1997. The effects of stressful life events on depression. *Annual Rev. Psych.* **48** 191–214.

Kessler, R. C., K. A. McGonagle, S. Zhao, C. B. Nelson, M. Hughes, S. Eshleman, H.-U. Wittchen, K. S. Kendler. 1994. Lifetime and 12-month prevalence of DSM-III-R psychiatric disorders in the United States: Results from the National Comorbidity Survey. *Arch. General Psych.* **51**(1) 8–19.

Kohn, M. L. 1969. *Class and Conformity: A Study in Values*. Dorsey, Homewood, IL.

Kohn, M. L., C. Schooler. 1973. Occupational experience and psychological functioning: An assessment of reciprocal effects. *Amer. Sociol. Rev.* **38**(1) 97–118.

Kossek, E. E., S. Lewis, L. B. Hammer. 2010. Work–life initiatives and organizational change: Overcoming mixed messages to move from the margin to the mainstream. *Human Relations* **63**(1) 3–19.

Kossek, E. E., M. Huber-Yoder, D. Castellino, J. Lerner. 1997. The working poor: Locked out of careers and the organizational mainstream? *Acad. Management Executive* **11**(1) 76–92.

Krackhardt, D., L. W. Porter. 1986. The snowball effect: Turnover embedded in communication networks. *J. Appl. Psych.* **71**(1) 50–55.

Krieshok, T. S., J. C. Ulven, J. L. Hecox, K. Wettersten. 2000. Résumé therapy and vocational test feedback: Tailoring interventions to self-efficacy outcomes. *J. Career Assessment* **8**(3) 267–281.

Lai, G. W., N. Lin, S.-Y. Leung. 1998. Network resources, contact resources, and status attainment. *Soc. Networks* **20**(2) 159–178.

Lambert, S. J. 1999. Lower-wage workers and the new realities of work and family. *Ann. Amer. Acad. Political Soc. Sci.* **562**(1) 174–190.

Lambert, S. J. 2008. Passing the buck: Labor flexibility practices that transfer risk onto hourly workers. *Human Relations* **61**(9) 1203–1227.

Lambert, S. J., E. Waxman. 2005. Organizational stratification: Distributing opportunities for balancing work and personal life. E. E. Kossek, S. J. Lambert, eds. *Work and Life Integration: Organizational, Cultural, and Individual Perspectives.* Lawrence Erlbaum Associates, Mahwah, NJ, 99–122.

Lane, J. 2000. The role of job turnover in the low-wage labor market. K. Kaye, D. S. Nightingale, eds. *The Low-Wage Labor Market: Challenges and Opportunities for Economic Self-Sufficiency.* Urban Institute, Washington, DC. http://aspe.hhs.gov/hsp/lwlm99/lane.htm.

Leana, C. R., D. C. Feldman. 1992. *Coping with Job Loss: How Individuals, Organizations, and Communities Respond to Layoffs.* Lexington Books, New York.

Lee, T. W., T. R. Mitchell, C. J. Sablynski, J. P. Burton, B. C. Holtom. 2004. The effects of job embeddedness on organizational citizenship, job performance, volitional absences, and voluntary turnover. *Acad. Management J.* **47**(5) 711–722.

Lerner, J. S., D. Keltner. 2001. Beyond valence: Toward a model of emotion-specific influences on judgment and choice. *Cognition Emotion* **14**(4) 473–493.

Lewis, O. 1968. *A Study of Slum Culture: Backgrounds for LA Vida.* Random House, New York.

Lin, N. 1982. Social resources and instrumental action. P. V. Marsden, N. Lin, eds. *Social Structure and Network Analysis.* Sage, Beverly Hills, CA, 131–45.

Lin, N. 1983. Social resources and social actions: A progress report. *Connections* **6**(2) 10–16.

Lin, N. 1999. Social networks and status attainment. *Annual Rev. Sociol.* **25** 467–487.

Lin, N. 2000. Inequality in social capital. *Amer. Sociol. Assoc.* **29**(6) 785–795.

Lin, N., M. Dumin. 1986. Access to occupations through social tie. *Soc. Networks* **8**(4) 365–385.

Lin, N., W. M. Ensel, J. C. Vaughn. 1981. Social resources and strength of ties. *Amer. Sociol. Rev.* **46**(4) 393–405.

Lubrano, A. 2004. *Limbo: Blue-Collar Roots, White-Collar Dreams.* John Wiley and Sons, Hoboken, NJ.

Markus, H. R., S. Kitayama. 2003. Models of agency: Socio-cultural diversity in the construction of action. V. Murphy-Berman, J. J. Berman, eds. *Cross-Cultural Differences in Perspectives on Self.* Nebraska Symposium on Motivation, Vol. 49. University of Nebraska Press, Lincoln, 1–57.

Marsden, P. V., J. S. Hurlbert. 1988. Social resources and mobility outcomes: A replication and extension. *Soc. Forces* **66**(4) 1038–1059.

Mascaro, N., N. C. Arnette, M. C. Santana, N. J. Kaslow. 2007. Longitudinal relationships between employment and depressive symptoms in low-income, suicidal African-American women. *J. Clinical Psych.* **63**(6) 541–553.

McLeod, J. D., R. C. Kessler. 1990. Socioeconomic status differences in vulnerability to undesirable life events. *J. Health Soc. Behav.* **31**(2) 162–172.

McPherson, M., L. Smith-Lovin, J. M. Cook. 2001. Birds of a feather: Homophily in social networks. *Annual Rev. Sociol.* **27** 415–444.

Miller, W. B. 1958. Lower class culture as a generating milieu of gang delinquency. *J. Soc. Issues* **14**(3) 5–19.

Mischel, W. 1977. The interaction of personality and situation. D. Magnusson, N. S. Endler, eds. *Personality at the Crossroads: Current Issues in Interactional Psychology.* Lawrence Erlbaum Associates, Hillsdale, NJ, 333–352.

Mittal, V., W. T. Ross Jr. 1998. The impact of positive and negative affect and issue framing on issue interpretation and risk taking. *Organ. Behav. Human Decision Processes* **76**(3) 298–324.

Mittal, V., J. R. Rosen, C. Leana. 2009. A dual-driver model of retention and turnover in the direct care workforce. *Gerontologist* **49**(5) 623–634.

Mittal, V., W. T. Ross Jr., M. Tsiros. 2002. The role of issue valence and issue capability in determining effort investment. *J. Marketing Res.* **39**(4) 455–468.

Mortimer, J. T., M. D. Finch, D. Kumka. 1982. Persistence and change in human development: The multidimensional self-concept. P. B. Baltes, O. G. Brim Jr., eds. *Life-Span Development and Behavior.* Academic Press, New York, 263–312.

Muntaner, C., Y. Li, X. Xue, T. Thompson, H. Chung, P. O'Campo. 2006. County and organizational predictors of depression symptoms among low-income nursing assistants in the USA. *Soc. Sci. Medicine* **63**(6) 1454–1465.

Murphy, J. M., D. C. Olivier, R. R. Monson, A. M. Sobol, E. B. Federman, A. H. Leighton. 1991. Depression and anxiety in relation to social status: A prospective epidemiologic study. *Arch. General Psych.* **48**(3) 223–229.

Naquin, S. S., E. F. Holton III. 2002. The effects of personality, affectivity, and work commitment on motivation to improve work through learning. *Human Resource Dev. Quart.* **13**(4) 357–376.

Newman, K. S. 1998. *Falling from Grace: The Experience of Downward Mobility in the American Middle Class*. University of California Press, Berkeley.

Newman, K. S., R. P. Massengill. 2006. The texture of hardship: Qualitative sociology of poverty, 1995–2005. *Annual Rev. Sociol.* **32** 423–446.

Oliver, R. L. 1993. Cognitive, affective, and attribute bases of the satisfaction response. *J. Consumer Res.* **20**(3) 418–430.

Olson, G. I., B. I. Schober. 1993. The satisfied poor: Development of an intervention-oriented theoretical framework to explain satisfaction with a life in poverty. *Soc. Indicators Res.* **28**(2) 173–193.

Olson, C. M., C. F. Bove, E. O. Miller. 2007. Growing up poor: Long-term implications for eating patterns and body weight. *Appetite* **49**(1) 198–207.

Pearce, D. M. 1983. The feminization of ghetto poverty. *Society* **21**(1) 70–74.

Podolny, J. M., J. N. Baron. 1997. Resources and relationships: Social networks and mobility in the workplace. *Amer. Sociol. Rev.* **62**(5) 673–693.

Price, R. H., J. N. Choi, A. Vinokur. 2002. Links in the chain of adversity following job loss: How economic hardship and loss of personal control lead to depression, impaired functioning and poor health. *J. Occupational Health Psych.* **7**(4) 302–312.

Raghunathan, R., M. T. Pham. 1999. All negative moods are not equal: Motivational influences of anxiety and sadness on decision making. *Organ. Behav. Human Decision Processes* **79**(1) 56–77.

Rankin, B. 2003. How low-income women find jobs and its effects on earnings. *Work Occupation* **30**(3) 281–301.

Rankin, B. H., J. M. Quane. 2002. Social contexts and urban adolescent outcomes: The interrelated effects of neighborhoods, families, and peers on African-American youth. *Soc. Problems* **49**(1) 79–100.

Rosenbaum, J. E., L. Reynolds, S. Deluca. 2002. How do places matter? The geography of opportunity, self-efficacy, and a look inside the black box of residential mobility. *Housing Stud.* **17**(1) 71–82.

Rousseau, D. M., Y. Fried. 2001. Location, location, location: Contextualizing organizational research. *J. Organ. Behav.* **22**(1) 1–13.

Russell, J. A. 2003. Core affect and the psychological construction of emotion. *Psych. Rev.* **110**(1) 145–172.

Salokangas, R. K. R., O. Poutanen. 1998. Risk factors for depression in primary care findings of the TADEP project. *J. Affective Disorders* **48**(2–3) 171–180.

Sampson, R. J., S. W. Raudenbush, F. Earls. 1997. Neighborhoods and violent crime: A multilevel study of collective efficacy. *Science* **277**(5328) 918–924.

Schaubroeck, J., D. E. Merritt. 1997. Divergent effects of job control on coping with work stressors: The key role of self-efficacy. *Acad. Management J.* **40**(3) 738–754.

Seibert, S. E., M. L. Kraimer, R. C. Liden. 2001. A social capital theory of career success. *Acad. Management J.* **44**(2) 219–237.

Sennett, R. 1998. *The Corrosion of Character: The Personal Consequences of Work in the New Capitalism.* W. W. Norton, London.

Seo, M. G., L. F. Barrett, J. M. Bartunek. 2004. The role of affective experience in work motivation. *Acad. Management Rev.* **29**(3) 423–439.

Silver, W. S., T. R. Mitchell, M. E. Gist. 1995. Responses to successful and unsuccessful performance: The moderating effect of self-efficacy on the relationship between performance and attributions. *Organ. Behav. Human Decision Processes* **62**(3) 286–299.

Singh, G. K., M. Siahpush. 2006. Widening socioeconomic inequalities in US life expectancy, 1980–2000. *Internat. J. Epidemiol.* **35**(4) 969–979.

Small, M. L., K. Newman. 2001. Urban poverty after the truly disadvantaged: The rediscovery of the family, the neighborhood, and culture. *Annual Rev. Sociol.* **27** 23–45.

Smith, A. K., R. N. Bolton. 2008. The effect of customers' emotional responses to service failures on their recovery effort evaluations and satisfaction judgments. *J. Acad. Marketing Sci.* **30**(1) 5–23.

Snibbe, A. C., H. R. Markus. 2005. You can't always get what you want: Educational attainment, agency and choice. *J. Personality Soc. Psych.* **88**(4) 703–720.

Sparrowe, R. T., R. C. Liden, S. J. Wayne, M. L. Kraimer. 2001. Social networks and the performance of individuals and groups. *Acad. Management J.* **44**(2) 316–325.

Stacey, C. L. 2005. Finding dignity in dirty work: The constraints and rewards of low-wage home care labour. *Sociol. Health Illness* **27**(6) 831–854.

Stack, C. B. 1974. *All Our Kin: Strategies for Survival in a Black Community*. Harper and Row, New York.

Stephens, N. M., H. R. Markus, S. S. Townsend. 2007. Choice as an act of meaning: The case of social class. *J. Personality Soc. Psych.* **93**(5) 814–830.

Stephens, N., M. G. Hamedani, H. R. Markus, H. B. Bergsieker, L. Eloul. 2010. Why did they "choose" to stay? Perspectives of Hurricane Katrina observers and survivors. *Psych. Sci.* **20**(7) 878–886.

Swanberg, J. E. 2005. Job–family role strain among low-wage workers. *J. Family Econom. Issues* **26**(1) 143–158.

Taylor, S. E., R. L. Repetti, T. E. Seeman. 1997. Health psychology: What is an unhealthy environment and how does it get under the skin? *Annual Rev. Psych.* **48** 411–447.

Teuchmann, K., P. Totterdell, S. K. Parker. 1999. Rushed, unhappy, and drained: An experience sampling study of relations between time pressure, perceived control, mood, and emotional exhaustion in a group of accountants. *J. Occupational Health Psych.* **4**(1) 37–54.

Tsui, A. S., B. A. Gutek. 1999. *Demographic Differences in Organizations: Current Research and Future Directions*. Lexington Books, Lanham, MD.

U.S. Bureau of Labor and Statistics. 2009. A profile of the working poor, 2007. Report 1012, Washington, DC. Retrieved March 29, 2009, http://www.bls.gov/cps/cpswp2007.pdf.

U.S. Census Bureau. 2010. Poverty thresholds by size of family and number of children. Housing and Household Economic Statistics Division, Washington, DC. Retrieved January 3, 2011, http://www.census.gov/hhes/www/poverty/data/threshld/index.html.

U.S. Department of Heatlh and Human Services. 2011. The 2011 HHS poverty guidelines. Retrieved June 23, 2011, http://aspe.hhs.gov/poverty/11poverty.shtml.

Vancouver, J. B., C. M. Thompson, E. C. Tischner, D. J. Putka. 2002. Two studies examining the negative effect of self-efficacy on performance. *J. Appl. Psych.* **87**(3) 506–516.

van Eck, M., N. A. Nicolson, J. Berkhof. 1998. Effects of stressful daily events on mood states: Relationship to global perceived stress. *J. Personality Soc. Psych.* **75**(6) 1572–1585.

Warheit, G. J., C. E. Holzer III, S. A. Arey. 1975. Race and mental illness: An epidemiologic update. *J. Health Soc. Behav.* **16**(3) 243–256.

Williams, D. R., C. Collins. 1995. US socioeconomic and racial differences in health: Patterns and explanations. *Annual Rev. Sociol.* **21** 349–386.

Willis, P. 1981. *Learning to Labor: How Working Class Kids Get Working Class Jobs*. Gower, Aldershot, UK.

Wilson, W. J. 1987. *The Truly Disadvantaged: The Inner City, the Underclass, and Public Policy*. University Chicago Press, Chicago.

Wood, R., A. Bandura, T. Bailey. 1990. Mechanisms governing organizational performance in complex decision-making environments. *Organ. Behav. Human Decision Processes* **46**(2) 181–201.

Wrzesniewski, A., J. E. Dutton. 2001. Crafting a job: Revisioning employees as active crafters of their work. *Acad. Management Rev.* **26**(2) 179–201.

CHAPTER 2

"Death Always Seems to Be Around Me": Loss Privilege and Loss in Abundance in Contemporary America

By Molly Monahan Lang

Throughout history, people have had to endure the losses, by death, of those closest to them. In this chapter, I argue that in contemporary affluent nations like America, social changes have led to loss privilege for some, and loss in abundance for others. As the gap between the wealthy and the poor grows, so does the dissimilarity in their life experiences. While life expectancies are growing for those with higher incomes, they are stagnating or declining for those with lower incomes. Infant mortality rates for well-educated mothers are lower than for mothers with less education. People with lower incomes experience diseases that will eventually cause death at higher rates and at younger ages than those with higher incomes. In addition to class inequality, certain racial-ethnic groups—in particular black and Native American people—are at higher risk than other groups for premature death. Therefore, in addition to class privilege and race privilege, both of which yield numerous unearned societal benefits, we can discuss *loss privilege*: the advantage of having family members and friends who live long lives, feeling well. Those with loss privilege do not have to endure the premature deaths of loved ones on a regular basis. They are relieved of that burden, and as with other kinds of privilege, they tend to not recognize it as such.

In contrast to loss privilege is what I call *loss in abundance* (LIA). Throughout history, loss has been a common phenomenon, for all ages and racial-ethnic groups. Of course some groups experienced greater losses and likelihood of loss than others, and the circumstances surrounding the losses varied greatly, but deaths and fatal diseases were widespread until fairly recently (and still are in the least-developed nations). Over time, in more affluent nations like America, with increased understanding of germ theory and the importance of sanitation as well as vaccinations and antibiotics, deaths from infectious diseases declined and early deaths became less common. At the same time, income and wealth inequality have grown in America, with more people experiencing socioeconomic privilege in contrast to those with less. This increasing inequality is also correlated with race-ethnicity in that white people are disproportionately well-off. Loss in abundance—more than one significantly early death or other loss of a loved one—was the norm before; it was expected. But in contemporary affluent nations, there is a divide, a growing divide, between those with loss privilege and those with LIA. We are living amongst each other but understanding each other less. As income inequality grows, so does this gap.

In this chapter, I provide evidence that some groups experience loss by death at higher rates than others. I discuss life expectancy, infant mortality, child mortality, youth mortality, and maternal mortality in America, showing change over time, disparities by race-ethnicity, and disparities by social class for each. I then briefly show links between both race-ethnicity and social class and disease. Next, I discuss imprisonment as a type of loss and its effects. Lastly, I give examples of loss privilege and loss in abundance from a variety of reading materials, to show the scope of these concepts in America today.

● LIFE EXPECTANCY

Life expectancy was low throughout America's early decades, which means that loss in abundance was rampant and normalized. In fact, life expectancy did not reach forty years until 1880 (U.S. Census Bureau 1949). This was largely due to high infant and child mortality, as I discuss further below. People's chances of living a long life increased if they survived past the age of fifteen. Deaths from infectious diseases, such as tuberculosis, malaria, and cholera, were common. Unsanitary conditions, the lack of clean water or proper refrigeration, and a dearth of knowledge about the spread of disease contributed to widespread deaths. In the mid-to-late 1800s, germ theory began to replace miasma theory as the prevailing explanation for disease. Miasma theory held that diseases were caused by foul (polluted or odorous) air and that diseases did not spread between people. Eventually germ theory took hold, with the understanding that microorganisms such as bacteria caused many diseases, and that sterile conditions in medical centers and sanitary environments, in general, helped to contain the spread of disease. In the meantime, scientists discovered viruses and developed vaccines to prevent many previously fatal diseases. With vaccines to prevent, and antibiotics and other medications to treat, infectious diseases, their impact on Americans' health decreased substantially between the mid-1800s and mid-1900s (Preston and Haines 2014).

By 1960, life expectancy had reached nearly seventy years (Grove and Hetzel 1968) and a connection between social class and mortality can be established. Therefore, this is where I would place the beginnings of loss privilege in America. Kitagawa and Hauser (1973) conducted research on 1960 data that showed a correlation between education and mortality as well as one between income and mortality. As years of schooling increased, mortality decreased; as income increased, mortality decreased. This is striking: that how much education one has and how much money one makes can affect how many years one can expect to live. Additional research has corroborated this finding. In fact, Pappas, Queen, Hadden, and Fisher (1993), using data from 1986 as well as 1960, found that not only did the relationships between both income and education and death rates continue, the disparities between those with more and those with less actually increased between the two time periods.

Even more recent research shows that the gap continues to grow. Meara, Richards, and Cutler (2008), using data from the 1980s and 1990s, categorized people as low-education (12 years or fewer) or high-education (13 years or more), and found that the gap in life expectancy between the former and the latter grew during the time period. More specifically, the life expectancy for the

highly educated grew while it stayed virtually the same for those with less education. Singh and Siahpush (2006) used county-level data from 1980–82, 1989–91,
and 1998–2000, dividing counties into deciles by socioeconomic status. They
found that the life expectancy of the lower decile counties grew less than that of
the higher deciles over the time periods. Finally, Bosworth, Burtless, and Zhang
(2015) used data from 1992 to 2010 and found that, using either career earnings
or education as a measure of socioeconomic status, there have been increases
in relative mortality differences over time. The gap widens, continuing the gap
between those enjoying loss privilege and those enduring loss in abundance.

There has also been a correlation between race-ethnicity and life expectancy
throughout America's history, in that white people, on average, have had a longer
life expectancy than non-whites. For example, in 1900, life expectancy for whites
was approximately forty-eight years, versus thirty-three years for non-whites
(Arias 2015). For reasons further articulated below, I characterize that time period
as loss in abundance for virtually all Americans at the time. However, since loss
was so rampant, it was normalized and unremarkable. Giving such loss a name
was unnecessary. Over time, whites have become less likely to experience loss
in abundance. In 1960, a headline in the *Chicago Tribune* read that America's life
expectancy was "just short of 70," a real milestone (Gibbons 1960). However, the
article goes on to say that *whites*' life expectancy was indeed seventy, while non-
whites had reached just sixty-three years (emphasis mine). We now have more
specific data on race-ethnicity, and the major relevant findings show a stubborn
persistence in the gap between African Americans' and Native Americans' life
expectancies in contrast to other groups. While Americans' life expectancy has
increased to almost seventy-nine years, black Americans can expect to live just
seventy-five years, and Native Americans can expect to live seventy-seven years.

● INFANT MORTALITY

Life expectancy is just one measure of possible differences in loss. We can look
specifically at infant mortality as a way to see which people in America are more
likely to experience the tragic loss of infants in their first year of life. We can
look at the infant mortality rate (the number of deaths among infants less than

one year old per 1,000 live births) in America beginning as early as 1850, when there were 217 deaths of white infants per 1,000 live births, and 340 deaths of black infants (Haines 2008). Those numbers are staggering, and represent loss in abundance. By 1900, the numbers had decreased to 111 and 170, respectively, but were still enormously high from today's perspective. Losing an infant in his or her first year of life was still strikingly common. By 1960, the infant mortality rate in America was closer to 26, meaning that we had clearly turned a corner in terms of infant deaths (MacDorman and Rosenberg 1993).

However, as with life expectancy, there are disparities. For example, there is a continued racial-ethnic gap in the deaths of infants. As of 2013, infant mortality among whites was down to 5, whereas blacks' rate was 11 and Native Americans' was 8 (Mathews, MacDorman, and Thoma 2015). Low-birthweight babies and premature babies are at higher risk for dying in their first year of life. Within America, black babies are more likely to be born early or with a low-birthweight than whites. Native American babies are also more likely than whites to be born pre-term. Stress may be one factor that explains this differential in the incidence of prematurity. In a recent *NBC News* article, Dr. Edward McCabe, chief medical officer of the March of Dimes Foundation, is quoted as saying, "Women, especially women in underserved communities, are subjected to stress in their communities on a daily basis. There is a growing body of evidence that stress is associated with preterm birth" (Fox 2015). Regardless of the cause, mothers and other loved ones of black and Native American babies are more likely to lose those infants in their first year of life, and therefore to experience loss in abundance in America today, than whites.

There are also socioeconomic differences. A study conducted by the Center on Social Disparities in Health at the University of California (2008a) used government data from 2000 to 2002 to analyze differences in infant mortality by the educational level of the mother. Whereas the average infant mortality at that time was 6.5, the number of infant deaths per 1,000 live births of those mothers with just zero to eleven years of education was higher than average, at 7.8. The number for those mothers with twelve years of education was 7.4, again higher than average. The number for those mothers with more than twelve years of education was lower than average, however, with thirteen to fifteen years coming in at 6, and sixteen or more years at 4.2 deaths. The more education the mother has, the lower her chances of losing a baby in his or her first year of life. Higher education appears to grant some allowance of loss privilege.

● CHILD MORTALITY

Another indicator of the contrast between those with loss in abundance and those with loss privilege is child mortality. America's child mortality was troublingly high in its early years; as late as 1900, close to 15 percent of Americans did not survive childhood (Preston and Haines 2014). Preston and Haines used Census data to study child mortality in the late 1800s and found that children of all socioeconomic statuses died at high rates—again showing a shared loss in abundance. It was later in the twentieth century that social class became a crucial determinant of child mortality, expanding the gap between the life experiences of those in different social classes. Race, measured as black and white, *was* a significant factor explaining different child mortality rates throughout the centuries, similar to infant mortality. Preston and Haines emphasize the relatively hazardous conditions found in early cities, as well as a lack of understanding among parents about the importance of clean milk and water, and containing the spread of disease among persons. Indeed, they refer to deaths as "only the tip of the iceberg, a signal of the enormous morbidity that lay below" (2014, 7). The majority of children at the time contracted at least one significant illness or health concern.

A report by Singh (2010a) shows data on mortality for children aged one to four years and five to fourteen years throughout the 1900s until 2007. He shows that such mortality has declined precipitously over time. For example, in 1907, the mortality rate (deaths per 100,000) for children aged one to four years was over 1,400, but by 2007, the rate was less than 30. For children aged five to fourteen years, the rate declined from just over 300 in 1907 to 15 a century later. By 2007, less than 1 percent of Americans who survived their first year would not survive childhood. This is a major reduction, and shows a pulling away from a shared experience of loss in abundance.

As with the other measures of loss shown above, however, disparities exist. First, racial differences in child mortality in both age ranges continue. In 2007, black children aged one to four years had the highest death rate of all racial-ethnic groups, at 45 deaths per 100,000. The next highest was Native Americans at 39, and the remainder, including whites, were 26 or below. For children aged five to fourteen, blacks also had the highest death rate, at 21 per 100,000, with Native Americans at 17. All other groups had rates of 14 or below. Singh (2010a) also looked at socioeconomic differences. He analyzed child mortality rates against county-level family poverty data from the 1990 and 2000 censuses, dividing counties into low, middle, and high poverty groups. From 1969 to 2007, the mortality rate for children in the low poverty group declined faster than that of the high poverty group. This has resulted in a widening of the gap between poorer counties and those with less poverty. By 2007, children in poorer counties experienced an even higher risk of death as compared to children in more af-fluent counties than in earlier decades (Singh 2010a). In contemporary America, black families, Native American families, and those living in poorer counties are more likely than other groups to endure the deaths of their children and therefore are more likely to experience loss in abundance.

● YOUTH MORTALITY

When it comes to mortality among adolescents and young adults (those aged fif-teen to twenty-four), the most recent elaborate data comes from Singh (2010b). Using government data collected from 1935 to 2007, Singh shows that mortality for those aged fifteen to twenty-four is greater for black youths than white, and that though the gap has declined, it has persisted over time. In 2007, the youth mortality rate per 100,000 population was highest for blacks (113), followed by American Indians/Alaska Natives (103). Other groups, including non-Hispanic whites, all had rates of 77 or below. He shows the variation in causes of death for the years 1970 and 2007. In 2007, unintentional injuries (typically motor vehicle crashes) were the most common cause of death in general. However, both suicide and homicide increased in likelihood as causes of youth death during that time.

Looking more closely at racial-ethnic differences, blacks of this age group were *much* more likely than other races to die from homicide. The documentary film *Hoop Dreams* shows an illustration of this (Allen, Gilbert, James, Marx, and Quinn 1994). The film follows two black high schoolers in Chicago who dream of making it to the NBA. In one scene, one of the boys' mothers is shown making him a cake for his eighteenth birthday. She speaks to the camera, saying, "He's a bright kid. And that's another thing to be proud of. A lot of black kids don't live to his age, you know. This is his eighteenth birthday. He lived and he got to see eighteen. That's good." Her joy and relief that her son lived until age eighteen, in an affluent and advanced nation such as the United States, are a palpable reflection of those who experience loss in abundance.

Singh's (2010b) report also shows Native American youths as more likely than other races to die from suicide. Reflecting this finding, psychiatrist R. Dale Walker, who has worked on a Northern Plains reservation with particularly high young adult suicide rates, expresses the potential for these populations to be "grieved out" as a result (Almendrala 2015). This certainly shows loss in abundance, and its unequal reach in America.

In reference to social class, Starfield, Riley, Witt, and Robertson (2002, 354) studied self-reported health data from youths aged eleven to seventeen years and found that "the likelihood of being satisfied with one's health … and of being in the best health profiles were significantly and progressively greater as social class rose. Moreover, the probability of being in the poorest health profile type group was progressively higher as social class declined." Adolescents from higher social class backgrounds are more likely to report feeling well and being satisfied with their health than those from lower social class backgrounds. In addition, Fuller-Rowell, Evans, and Ong (2012, 734) studied 252 rural adolescents and found a relationship between poverty and allostatic load, which they define as "the cumulative wear and tear on the body caused by overactivation of physiological systems that respond to stress," with poor adolescents carrying a heavier burden. Interestingly, they also theorize that perceived discrimination is a mediator between poverty and allostatic load, and find support for their theory. A study analyzing The National Survey of Children's Health shows parental assessment data concerning their children aged seventeen years or less and how it relates to their household income (Center on Social Disparities in Health at the University of California 2008b). Those with incomes below the federal poverty level were significantly less likely to rate their children as being in "optimal health" than the near-poor, middle-income, or higher-income parents. In fact, as has been shown above, there is a graded increase at each level of the percentage of children in optimal health. This results in a greater potential for loss privilege for each subsequent category of income. In general, the evidence suggests that higher-income parents can expect their offspring to live long, healthy lives, and are more likely than others to see that expectation come to fruition.

When thinking about how loss in abundance manifests itself in people's lives, one study conducted by the Pew Research Center (2015) shows some possible effects. In it, data from a nationally representative sample of parents with children under the age of eighteen were analyzed. Those parents with family incomes of less than $30,000 a year were more than twice as likely as those with incomes of more than $75,000 a year to worry that their child(ren) might get shot at some point in their lives (47% to 22%, respectively). It is striking to consider that nearly half of lower-income parents in America are worried about their children possibly getting shot. Looking at race, black parents are also much more likely than white parents to share this concern (39% to 22%). This is just one type of early death that people may experience, and it is clear that black parents, and parents with lower incomes, carry this possibility around with them more than white parents or affluent ones. Loss in abundance becomes part of people's worldviews, affecting what they see as likely or possible, thereby contributing to a burden of which others are relieved.

● MATERNAL MORTALITY

Maternal mortality shows similar trends as those above. The World Health Organization (n.d.) refers to maternal mortality as "the death of a woman while pregnant or within 42 days of termination of pregnancy, irrespective of the duration and site of the pregnancy, from any cause related to or aggravated by the pregnancy or its management." Loudon (2000) shows that maternal mortality in the United States was high from the time records were first kept in the mid-1800s. In fact, a precipitous drop in maternal mortality did not really occur until the 1930s, later than would be expected given changes in understanding of disease and public health measures. Interestingly, there is evidence to suggest that in the early decades of the 1900s, upper class women were *more* likely than poor women to die this way. Loudon's explanation for this is that poor women were more likely to be treated by well-trained midwives whereas upper class women were seen by doctors who used riskier tools and procedures. Whatever the case, maternal mortality was high for all, and therefore loss in abundance was rampant in this respect. Over time, the relationship between social class and maternal mortality flipped, and now, those women living in the poorest counties in America are more likely to die this way than women in low- or medium-poverty counties, although the ratios have fluctuated over time (Singh 2010c).

There is some evidence that the maternal mortality rate may have increased more recently in the United States. Better reporting may be part of the increase, however, and more investigation is needed. Regardless, Singh's (2010c) report shows that black women have always been at higher risk than whites of dying under these circumstances. And though the black–white ratio has fluctuated over time, it still remains high. Using 2005 to 2007 data, the maternal mortality rate for black women was 34 deaths per 100,000 live births, followed by American Indians/Alaska Natives at 17 deaths. Other groups were 11 or below. In contemporary America, black and Native American women are more likely than other groups to die from pregnancy-related causes, and therefore their loved ones are more likely to experience loss in abundance.

● RACE-ETHNICITY, SOCIAL CLASS, AND DISEASE

Over time, as deaths from infectious diseases have become less common, deaths from cardiovascular disease, cancer, and diabetes have increased. There is evidence that black Americans suffer from heart disease at higher rates and younger ages than other groups (see Bibbins-Domingo et al. 2009). Blacks and Native Americans are also at greater risk for diabetes. National statistics show that 13 percent of African Americans and 16 percent of Native Americans have been diagnosed with diabetes, whereas fewer than 8 percent of whites have been (Centers for Disease Control and Prevention 2014). Kochanek, Arias, and Anderson (2013) attempt to explain the lower life expectancy of blacks than whites and find that blacks have higher death rates from heart disease, cancer, and diabetes than whites. Therefore, blacks are sicker than whites and die younger from the same diseases.

There is also a correlation between social class and disease rates. In the United States, heart disease occurs three times as often among low-income persons as among more affluent persons (Weitz 2013). Cancer rates are also gradually higher for each income level below wealthy Americans (Wilkinson 2005). In regards to diabetes, Smith (2007), uses data on adult men from the National Health and Nutrition Examination Survey for various years from 1976 through 2002. He looks at correlates with education level as a way to measure socioeconomic disparities in both diagnosed and actual rates of diabetes. He concludes,

> Those in lower education groups face a triple threat with diabetes. First, at least in more recent years, they are of slightly higher risk in contracting the disease. Second, they remain at considerably greater risk of having their diabetes undiagnosed and presumably untreated. Third, even after diagnosis, they have considerably more difficulty in successful self-management of the disease using the complex but effective treatments necessary to diminish the negative health consequences associated with diabetes. (18)

With higher disease rates come potential loss in abundance for those with lower socioeconomic statuses and their loved ones.

● OTHER LOSS: IMPRISONMENT

In my definition of loss in abundance at the beginning of this article, I included "or other loss." By this I meant imprisonment (although other areas could certainly apply, such as military deployment or drug addiction). Poor people and racial-ethnic minorities are disproportionately represented in jails and prisons throughout America (Stevenson 2014). For example, the Pew Research Center (2013) reports that in 2010, black men were more than six times as likely as white men to be incarcerated. More specifically, the incarceration rate for white men was 678 inmates per 100,000 white US residents; for black men, it was 4,347 inmates per 100,000 US black residents. The gap has increased over time. In 1960, the incarceration rate for white men was 262, and for black men it was

1,313, which means that black men were five times as likely as white men to be incarcerated in 1960.

In reference to social class, Rabuy and Kopf (2015) use data from the Survey of Inmates in State Correctional Facilities and look at pre-incarceration incomes of inmates. They find that for twenty-seven- to forty-two-year-olds, the median income of incarcerated people is 41 percent less than the median income of non-incarcerated people. They also find that a much greater percentage of incarcerated people have pre-incarceration incomes of $22,000 or less—57 percent of men and 72 percent of women (as opposed to 23% and 48% of non-incarcerated men and women, respectively). These data show that black and poor people are disproportionately incarcerated, resulting in their loved ones' greater propensity for loss.

Inmates' sentences include life without parole and death row, where prisoners are unlikely to be released into mainstream society, meaning that they are forever "lost" to their loved ones for all intents and purposes. A 2014 Bureau of Justice Statistics report shows that 42 percent of those on death row are black, despite the fact that blacks represent just 13 percent of the American population. The loved ones of these prisoners are disproportionately hit with the pain associated with loss in abundance.

In *Just Mercy* (2014), Bryan Stevenson writes about his decades of experience as an attorney representing the disenfranchised, and some of the clients with whom he has worked. A major theme of the book is the inadequate representation given to poor, rural minorities. Looking more deeply, though, the book is also about loss in abundance. At one point, Stevenson discusses an encounter with a woman in New Orleans who was present at the resentencing of some prisoners unrelated to her. Stevenson is perplexed and intrigued by her. She approaches Stevenson and tells him that she comes to support people in pain. She explains,

> My sixteen-year-old grandson was murdered fifteen years ago, and I loved that boy more than life itself.… He was killed by some other boys. I came to this courtroom for the first time for their trials and sat in there and cried every day for nearly two weeks. None of it made any sense. Those boys were found guilty for killing my grandson, and the

judge sent them away to prison forever. I thought it would make me feel better but it actually made me feel worse. (307)

Over time she decided that she was meant to help those who have lost someone. She says,

When I first came, I'd look for people who had lost someone to murder or some violent crime. Then it got to the point where some of the ones grieving the most were the ones whose children or parents were on trial, so I just started letting anybody lean on me who needed it. All these young children being sent to prison forever, all this grief and violence.... I don't know, it's a lot of pain. (308)

Here, she expresses an understanding that loss in abundance occurs not only through death but also imprisonment. Poor and black people have to endure both of these losses more than others. In fact, in the Epilogue, Stevenson writes of the death of the man whose case is the centerpiece of the book: Walter McMillian. He discusses McMillian's funeral at an African Methodist Episcopal church near Monroeville, Louisiana: "Scores of people packed the church, and dozens more stood outside. I looked at the mostly poor, rural black people huddled together with their ungrieved suffering filling the sad space of yet another funeral" (311). "Yet another funeral": a poignant way of describing the loss in abundance these people must endure.

● LOSS PRIVILEGE AND LOSS IN ABUNDANCE: EXAMPLES ABOUND

Over the last several months, as I have read various articles, news reports, blogs, and books in my day-to-day life, I have kept track of apparent examples and implications of loss privilege and loss in abundance. The variety of pieces within which I noticed these phenomena is striking. I discuss just some of them here, in no particular order, to give an idea of the scope of these concepts.

Perri Klass is a physician and author. Her 1987 memoir *A Not Entirely Benign Procedure* details her experiences training to be a physician at Harvard Medical School. As part of her training she traveled to India, to work in the pediatric department at a hospital in New Delhi. She treated a seven-month-old girl who had severe diarrhea. The child's grandmother told her that one of her other grandchildren died from diarrhea, and another died of a chest infection. As Klass looked at this grandmother and the girl's parents, she came to a realization: "All these people believe in the possibility of death, the chance that the child will not live to grow up. They've all seen many children die" (197). In an effort to better describe these people and in reiteration of her main point, she goes on to say, "They're tough and they're hopeful, but **they believe in the possibility of death**" (197, emphases mine). I have emboldened that phrase because it encapsulates loss in abundance. To these people from a poor rural village in India, loss is rampant; the death of children is common; they have all seen it and endured it. There is no need for them to name it. But Klass recognized their experiences as being different in some fundamental way from her own. She did not have a conceptual apparatus for it, but I offer one here.

As Klass continues to contrast these people's experiences and expectations with her own, she writes that in Boston where she lived, she had heard "bewildered, grieving parents say, essentially, 'Who would have believed that in the 1980s a child could just die like that?'" (Klass 1987, 197). Here, she contrasts people in a developing nation with people in an affluent nation like the United States. But she does not see that even within the United States there are people who must endure loss in abundance. She describes parents "back home, in Boston" this way: "They expect every child to live to grow up" (197). I would add that there may be social class and race differences in such expectations, that she may be inadvertently biased here. To the extent that those with socioeconomic and race privilege *expect every child to live to grow up*, they are experiencing loss privilege. While I agree with her subsequent statement that her training has taken place in a country "where all children are supposed to grow up" (198), I have shown that children in some groups are more likely to do so than others. Many people in America also "believe in the possibility of death," and this needs to be acknowledged.

As an example, I offer excerpts from *The Absolutely True Story of a Part-Time Indian*, a slightly fictionalized autobiographical account of a Native American boy's high school years (Alexie 2007). Alexie writes from the perspective of a teenager who lives on a Spokane Indian reservation but attends an all-white high school just outside of it. During the short period that the book addresses, the protagonist describes his grandmother getting fatally struck by an impaired driver, his father's best friend dying in a gun accident, and his older sister dying in a house fire. He writes, "I'm fourteen years old and I've been to forty-two funerals" (199). This is the essence of loss in abundance. Just one of these losses would be significant, but having so many in such a short time shows the amount of pain from loss that he must endure in his life. He goes on to compare his experiences with those of his classmates:

> That's really the biggest difference between Indians and white people. A few of my white classmates have been to a grandparent's funeral. And a few have lost an uncle or aunt. And one guy's brother died of leukemia when he was in third grade.... All my white friends can count their deaths on one hand. I can count my fingers, toes, arms, legs, eyes, ears, nose, ... and still not get close to my deaths. (199–200)

In describing his classmates, he poignantly articulates what I call loss privilege: the few losses by death in their lives and therefore their protection from the pain associated with abundant loss.

Another example, this one from a different racial-ethnic group and region of the United States, is Lamar Odom, an African American former professional basketball player who experienced a near-fatal drug overdose in October 2015 (Lah, McLaughlin, and Almasy 2015). In discussing his downfall, many news articles addressed the significant losses he has experienced in his life. His mother died of colon cancer when he was twelve. His grandmother, who raised him, died in 2004. Just a few years later, his seven-month-old son died of sudden infant death syndrome in his crib. Then, in 2011, his twenty-four-year-old cousin was killed. As if those were not enough, earlier in 2015 his best friend had died of complications from intravenous drug abuse. In an interview with the *Los Angeles Times*, he referenced other relatives and friends who had died early deaths. He said, "Death always seems to be around me. I've been burying people for a long time" (Turner 2011, and the source of the title for this piece). Odom is a contemporary example of someone who has not had the protections of loss privilege. He has not had the advantage of being able to expect that his loved ones would live long lives without the gnawing of impending tragedy.

To show the contrast between those with loss privilege and those with loss in abundance, I offer the book *The Same Kind of Different as Me*, in which Ron Hall and Denver Moore discuss their unlikely friendship (2006). When they meet, Hall is a wealthy, white art dealer and Moore is a black, homeless former sharecropper. In the book, each discusses his background, and Hall in particular problematizes the inequalities in their requisite upbringings and resulting fortunes. The two meet as a result of Hall's wife Deborah's philanthropic urging. Perhaps partly as a result, the book is heavily focused on her subsequent cancer diagnosis, painful and difficult treatments, and tragic death at fifty-five years of age. While the early deaths of three of Moore's beloved family members are mentioned, they are not given nearly the attention that Hall's wife's illness and death are given. It is as if Hall's loss and Moore's losses are equivalent, or even that Hall's loss is more significant. While I by no means wish to rank the importance of each death of a loved one in a person's life, I do want to point out that the tragedy and grief associated with each individual death of a person in communities with loss privilege appear to get more attention than in those with loss in abundance. I believe this is an additional advantage granted to those in privileged groups in society—more collective, public, visible sympathy concerning their losses. Just because something happens more frequently does not mean it deserves less attention. On the contrary, I would argue that in the case of abundant loss, we should be paying much more attention than we are. But without the conceptual apparatus to do so, publicly acknowledging this inequality has been difficult.[1]

To conclude this section, I provide excerpts of a short speech given by Geneva Reed-Veal at the Library of Congress in April 2016. Her speech was part of the first symposium of the Congressional Caucus on Black Women and Girls (Meyerson 2016). Reed-Veal is the mother of Sandra Bland, a 28-year-old black woman who died in a Texas jail cell in the summer of 2015. Part of her speech follows:

What I'm going to say to you is that I'm here representing the mothers who are not heard, I am here representing the mothers who have lost children as we go on about our daily lives. When the cameras and lights are gone, our babies are dead…. I will continue to speak for every mother paralyzed because of the loss of their child…. The tears are real, the pain is real, the problem is real…. I don't come to sit and be a part of a caucus where we talk and do nothing. You, you, you, you don't know my pain…. Unless you have lost a child…. We have got to stop talking and move. So I leave you with this: it is time to wake up, get up, step up, or shut up.

I interpret this speech in part as a call to action for those experiencing loss in abundance, in particular to mothers who must endure the cumulative pain that such loss engenders. With this speech, Reed-Veal tries to bring attention to loss in abundance as a social problem, and to bring people together to do something about it.

Conclusion

In this chapter, I have outlined loss in abundance as a social problem in America that largely afflicts poor and working class people, African Americans and Native Americans. People in these groups are more likely to have to endure significant losses by death or imprisonment of loved ones. Whereas loss in abundance was widespread until the mid-twentieth century in America, and therefore normalized, it has largely become the provenance of those with lower socioeconomic status and particular minority groups. Therefore, during the last fifty years we can also identify the counterpart to loss in abundance, which I call loss privilege. In addition to class privilege and racial-ethnic privilege, some people have the unearned benefit of having their loved ones live long, healthy lives. There is a growing gap in the amount of loss that people are having to endure in different social groups. As we recognize the scores of Americans who, though living in a nation of affluence, are not reaping those rewards, we need to also recognize those (often the very same people) who are not enjoying the long, healthy lives of their loved ones that such affluence seems to portend.

Notes

1. Perhaps this is part of the controversy of the Black Lives Matter movement, a social movement attempting to bring attention to the mistreatment of blacks in the criminal justice system. As has been shown here, black people are more likely than other groups to experience loss in abundance. Many are tired of it and fighting against it, partly through the activities of this movement. White people who are privileged in other ways are not likely to share this set of experiences or this perspective as a result (and even if they do, they have protections in place to buffer their suffering). More particularly, white working class or poor people may resent the Black Lives Matter movement perhaps because they *do* experience LIA but do not have a social movement to represent their anger. This may also explain in part their greater support of Donald Trump as a candidate for the United States presidency.

References

Alexie, S. 2007. *The Absolutely True Story of a Part-Time Indian*. New York: Little, Brown, and Company.

Allen, C., P. Gilbert, S. James, F. Marx, and G. Quinn. (Producers). 1994. *Hoop dreams*, DVD. Directed by S. James. Chicago, IL: Kartemquin Films.

Almendrala, A. 2015. "Native American Youth Suicide Rates Are at Crisis Levels." *The Huffington Post*, October 2. http://www.huffingtonpost.com/entry/native-american-youth-suicide-rates-are-at-crisis-levels_us_560c3084e4b0768127005591.

Arias, E. 2015. *United States Life Tables, 2011*. Hyattsville, MD: National Center for Health Statistics.

Bibbins-Domingo, K., M. J. Pletcher, F. Lin, E. Vittinghoff, J. M. Gardin, A. Arynchyn, C. E. Lewis, O. D. Williams, and S. B. Hulley. 2009. "Racial Differences in Incident Heart Failure Among Young Adults." *New England Journal of Medicine* 360: 1179–90.

Bosworth, B., G. Burtless, and K. Zhang. 2015. *Sources of Increasing Differential Mortality Among the Aged by Socioeconomic Status*. Working Paper of the Center for Retirement Research at Boston College. http://crr.bc.edu/wp-content/uploads/2015/06/wp_2015-10.pdf.

Bureau of Justice Statistics. 2014. *Capital Punishment, 2011—Statistical Tables*. Washington, DC: Author. http://www.bjs.gov/content/pub/pdf/cp11st.pdf.

Center on Social Disparities in Health at the University of California, San Francisco. (2008a). *Gaps in Infant Mortality Rates by Mother's Education: How Do States Compare?* A study conducted for the Commission to Build a Healthier America. Princeton, NJ: The Robert Wood Johnson Foundation.

Center on Social Disparities in Health at the University of California, San Francisco. (2008b). *Gaps in Children's General Health Status by Family Income: How Do States Compare?* A study conducted for the Commission to Build a Healthier America. Princeton, NJ: The Robert Wood Johnson Foundation.

Centers for Disease Control and Prevention. (2014). *National Diabetes Statistics Report: Estimates of Diabetes and Its Burden in the United States.* Atlanta, GA: U.S. Department of Health and Human Services.

Fox, M. 2015. "U.S. Infant Mortality Rate Stays High, Report Finds." *NBC News*, August 6. http://www.nbcnews.com/health/health-news/us-infant-mortality-rate-still-one-highest-developed-world-n404871.

Fuller-Rowell, T. E., G. W. Evans, and A. D. Ong. 2012. "Poverty and Health: The Mediating Role of Perceived Discrimination." *Psychological Science* 23 (7): 734–39.

Gibbons, R. 1960. "Life Span in America Now Just Short of 70." *Chicago Tribune*, December 18. http://archives.chicagotribune.com/1960/12/18/page/21/article/life-span-in-america-now-just-short-of-70.

Grove, R. D., and A. M. Hetzel. 1968. *Vital Statistics Rates in the United States, 1940–1960.* Washington, DC: U.S. Government Printing Office. http://www.cdc.gov/nchs/data/hus/hus2009tables/Table024.pdf.

Haines, M. 2008. "Fertility and Mortality in the United States." In *EH.Net Encyclopedia.* Edited by R. Whaples. http://eh.net/encyclopedia/fertility-and-mortality-in-the-united-states/.

Hall, R., and D. Moore, with L. Vincent. 2006. *Same Kind of Different as Me: A Modern-Day Slave, an International Art Dealer, and the Unlikely Woman Who Bound Them Together.* Nashville, TN: Thomas Nelson.

Kitagawa, E. M., and P. M. Hauser. 1973. *Differential Mortality in the United States: A Study in Socioeconomic Epidemiology.* Cambridge, MA: Harvard University Press.

Klass, P. 1987. *A Not Entirely Benign Procedure: Four Years as a Medical Student.* New York: Penguin Books.

Kochanek, K. D., E. Arias, and R. N. Anderson. 2013. *How Did Cause of Death Contribute to Racial Differences in Life Expectancy in the United States in 2010?* Hyattsville, MD: National Center for Health Statistics.

Lah, K., E. C. McLaughlin, and S. Almasy. 2015. "Lamar Odom Had Been Using Cocaine, Brothel Employees Say." *CNN*, October 15. http://www.cnn.com/2015/10/14/us/lamar-odom-condition/.

Loudon, I. 2000. "Maternal Mortality in the Past and Its Relevance to Developing Countries Today." *The American Journal of Clinical Nutrition* 72 (1): 241–46.

MacDorman, M. F., and H. M. Rosenberg. 1993. *Trends in Infant Mortality by Cause of Death and Other Characteristics, 1960–1988*. Hyattsville, MD: National Center for Health Statistics.

Mathews, T. J., M. F. MacDorman, and M. E. Thoma. 2015. *Infant Mortality Statistics from the 2013 Period Linked Birth/Infant Death Data Set*. Hyattsville, MD: National Center for Health Statistics.

Meara, E. R., S. Richards, and D. M. Cutler. 2008. "The Gap Gets Bigger: Changes in Mortality and Life Expectancy by Education, 1981–2000." *Health Affairs* 27 (2): 350–60.

Meyerson, C. 2016. "Read the Short, Devastating Speech Sandra Bland's Mother Just Made to Congressional Leaders." *Fusion*, April 28. http://fusion.net/story/296456/sandra-bland-mother-powerful-speech/.

Pappas, G., S. Queen, W. Hadden, and G. Fisher. 1993. "The Increasing Disparity in Mortality Between Socioeconomic Groups in the United States, 1960 and 1986." *The New England Journal of Medicine* 329 (2): 103–09.

Pew Research Center. 2013. *Incarceration Gap Widens Between Whites and Blacks*. http://www.pewresearch.org/fact-tank/2013/09/06/incarceration-gap-between-whites-and-blacks-widens/.

Pew Research Center. 2015. *Parenting in America: Outlook, Worries, Aspirations Are Strongly Linked to Financial Situation*. http://www.pewsocialtrends.org/2015/12/17/parenting-in-america/.

Preston, S. H., and M. R. Haines. 2014. *Fatal Years: Child Mortality in Late Nineteenth-Century America*. Princeton, NJ: Princeton University Press.

Rabuy, B., and D. Kopf. 2015. "Prisons of Poverty: Uncovering the Pre-Incarceration Incomes of the Imprisoned." Press Release for the Prison Policy Initiative. https://www.prisonpolicy.org/reports/income.html.

Singh, G. K. 2010a. *Child Mortality in the United States, 1935–2007: Large Racial and Socioeconomic Disparities Have Persisted over Time*. Rockville, MD: Health Resources and Services Administration, Maternal and Child Health Bureau, U.S. Department of Health and Human Services.

Singh, G. K. 2010b. *Youth Mortality in the United States, 1935–2007: Large and Persistent Disparities in Injury and Violent Deaths*. Rockville, MD: Health Resources and Services Administration, Maternal and Child Health Bureau, U.S. Department of Health and Human Services.

Singh, G. K. 2010c. *Maternal Mortality in the United States, 1935–2007: Substantial Racial/Ethnic, Socioeconomic, and Geographic Disparities Persist*. Rockville, MD: Health Resources and Services Administration, Maternal and Child Health Bureau, U.S. Department of Health and Human Services.

Singh, G. K., and M. Siahpush. 2006. "Widening Socioeconomic Inequalities in U.S. Life Expectancy, 1980–2000." *International Journal of Epidemiology* 35 (4): 969–79.

Smith, J. 2007. *Diabetes and the Rise of the SES Health Gradient.* Working Paper 12905. Cambridge, MA: National Bureau of Economic Research. http://www.nber.org/papers/w12905.pdf.

Starfield, B., A. W. Riley, W. P. Witt, and J. Robertson. 2002. "Social Class Gradients in Health During Adolescence." *Journal of Epidemiology and Community Health* 56: 354–61.

Stevenson, B. 2014. *Just Mercy: A Story of Justice and Redemption.* New York: Spiegel and Grau.

Turner, B. 2011. "Lamar Odom After Tragedies: 'Death Always Seems to Be Around Me.'" *Los Angeles Times*, August 2. http://www.latimes.com/sports/la-sp-lamar-odom-accident-20110802-story.html.

U.S. Census Bureau. 1949. *Historical Statistics of the United States, 1789–1945.* Washington, DC: Author. https://www2.census.gov/prod2/statcomp/documents/HistoricalStatisticsoftheUnitedStates1789-1945.pdf.

Weitz, R. 2013. *The Sociology of Health, Illness, and Health Care.* Boston, MA: Wadsworth.

Wilkinson, R. 2005. *The Impact of Inequality: How to Make Sick Societies Healthier.* New York: The New Press.

World Health Organization. n.d. *Maternal Mortality Ratio (per 100 000 live births).* Geneva, Switzerland: Author. http://www.who.int/healthinfo/statistics/indmaternalmortality/en/.

CHAPTER 3

Why Do First-Generation Students Fail?

By Sanjay S. Mehta, John J. Newbold, and Matthew A. O'Rourke

M ost universities today have embraced the marketing concept. Therefore, both professors and administrators at institutions of higher education need to know their customers (students). Knowing the background of these students can be beneficial in designing programs that will best serve the students they are responsible for educating. While demographic and socioeconomic information on students is collected regularly, many universities rarely use this information to design programs that provide greater value.

First-generation students (heretofore referred to as "FGS") account for nearly 50% of today's student population (Choy 2001). A FGS is defined as a student that comes from a family where neither parent/guardian graduated from college. In contrast, continuing-generation students (heretofore referred to as "CGS") are those students currently in college who have at least one parent/guardian that completed college. This study will explore the differences between FGS and CGS in today's university population. More specifically, it will identify the needs, attitudes, behaviors, and perceptions of these two disparate groups of students.

The graduation rate (persistence) among FGS is much lower than CGS (Ishitani 2006; Chen and Carroll 2005; Ishitani 2003; Warburton, Bugarin and Nunez 2001). Past research has determined that FGS work more hours and have more financial dependents (Inman and Mayes 1999; Nunez and Cuccaro-Alamin 1998) and generally feel unprepared to attend college (Rodriguez 2003. Being ill-equipped to succeed in college has tremendous consequences. It is believed that FGS enter the university with greater stress and equipped with lesser means to cope with this stress. It is expected that first-generation status impacts students' ability to be involved socially on-campus and that a combination of these factors result in lower academic performance and college dissatisfaction.

● LITERATURE REVIEW

What differentiates FGS from their peers is the fact that they did not grow up around adults that completed college. As a result, FGS are less exposed to the support and other contributing factors that provide preparation and support to CGS as they navigate through college. Rodriguez (2003) reported that FGS enter college with less knowledge of the "college-going" process, less academic preparedness, and an inability to acquire necessary funds to pay for college. FGS also reported feeling a certainty to be "discovered" as people that did not belong in college but were pretending that they did (Rodriguez 2003). In addition, FGS perceive their parents to be less supportive and less encouraging than CGS (Billson and Terry 1982; Choy 2001; Rodriguez 2003; Terenzini, Springer, Yeager, Pascarella, and Nora 1996; York-Anderson and Bowman 1991).

FGS enter college working more hours, with lower family incomes, and more financial dependents than CGS (Bui 2002; Inman and Mayes 1999, Nunez and Cuccaro-Alamin 1998). Parents and family members of FGS may not understand the time and energy that must be invested in college to be successful. As a result, these parents may expect their children to contribute to the family or move out and start their own family upon completing high school just as the parents had to do when they completed their secondary education.

Further, FGS are often reluctant to take out student loans to pay for college and also suffer from the fact that federal financial aid is not keeping up with rising tuition (Levine and Nidiffer 1996; Paulsen and St. John 2002). FGS may even lack the proper knowledge and information to access financial aid (Levine and Nidiffer 1996; Rodriguez 2003). Lundberg, Schreiner, Hovaguimian, and Slavin Miller (2007) attributed these financial struggles to a lack of "cultural capital" among FGS. *Cultural capital* refers to a general familiarity with the traditions and norms necessary to be successful at an institution of higher education (Lundberg, et al 2007). This familiarity is developed and passed on from interactions with others. In most instances, cultural capital would be learned from parents and/or peers who are attending or have successfully completed college. FGS, by definition, do not have parents/guardians with knowledge about navigating through college that they can pass on, and thus likely have less cultural capital than CGS.

Students today have a variety of demands on their time and energy—attending class, out of class academic work, jobs, family, friends, hobbies, etc. Their level of involvement in each of these activities can be measured by the amount of time that the student spends on each activity. Astin (1984; 1993) found that those activities that draw students away from campus have a negative effect on learning because the students have less time and energy for on-campus involvement. Astin (1993) also reported that success in college was related to the quality and frequency of student involvement in the "college experience."

While at college, FGS are less involved in on-campus activities (Dennis, Phinney, and Cuateco 2005; Lohfink and Paulsen 2005; Lundberg, et al 2007; Pascarella, Pierson, Wolnaik, and Terenzini 2004; Pike and Kuh 2005). Financial struggles may force FGS to work more hours, resulting in lower levels of on-campus involvement (Lundberg, et al 2007). Additionally, FGS were also found to be more likely to live off campus, resulting in lower levels of on-campus participation (Terenzini, et al, 1996).

FGS also report less involvement with student acquaintances (Lundberg, et al 2007). Again, financial need and commuter status may help explain these findings. FGS face the same academic workload as CGS but may also be required to work more hours and commute to school. It should be no surprise that students in this type of situation will be less likely to be involved with other students. Lundberg, Schreiner, Hovaguimian, and Slavin Miller (2007) also found that less student involvement among FGS had a negative effect on their learning. Peer interaction engages students more deeply in the "college experience" and consequently enhances their learning (Astin 1993).

Another area where FGS may lack the necessary "cultural-capital" is in the ways they choose to deal with stress while at college. Responses to stress can be separated into "active" and "reactive" behaviors. *Active responses* refer to actions that individuals participate in to actually deal directly with the stressful situation. Active responses are behaviors that treat stress as a problem to be solved. Active response behavior is those things that people do to 'confront' the stress head on (Shields 2001). Conversely, *reactive responses* are behaviors that attempt to address the feelings associated with stress. Instead of trying to address the 'problem' creating (causing) the stress, reactive behaviors are things that attempt to 'make you feel better' but do not directly address the stressor. Examples of active responses are behaviors like studying harder or seeking social support. Reactive responses are things such as attempting to 'escape' the stressors by focusing on a completely separate activity—such as taking a vacation.

Behavioral reaction has been identified by other researchers as a person's ability to respond to and cope with stress. In fact, one's ability to actively cope with stress has been shown to be a significant predictor of academic success (Leong, Bonz, and Zachar 1997. The extent to which one can actively cope with stress plays a critical role in the effects/outcome of stress. If students are able to actively cope, stress can be beneficial to their performance (some people perform better under pressure). In contrast, if students are not able to actively cope, stress can be detrimental to performance (some people may have a nervous breakdown), ultimately leading to poor performance and intimate withdrawal from college. Active coping leads to better adjustment to stressful events/situations and better adjustment to college. Social support was found to be an active form of coping among successful college students (Shields 2001).

Adequate finances, supportive parents, sufficient academic preparedness, on-campus/student acquaintance involvement, and ability to actively cope with stress have all been proven to be and are widely accepted academic-success promoting factors (Lundberg, et al 2007; Leong, et al 1997; Shields 2001; Astin 1984; 1993). Therefore, FGS are less prepared to succeed at college and are forced to deal with other factors to a greater degree (e.g., working and managing the financial well-being of dependents). FGS have more external demands on their time (Rendon and Hope 1996). As a result, FGS become less involved on campus and socially. Having less social involvement leaves FGS with fewer abilities to actively cope with stress. When these factors are all considered, it should be no surprise that FGS have a lower graduation rate than CGS.

● HYPOTHESES

Previous research has studied the demographic make-up of FGS (Rodriguez 2003; Paulsen and St. John 2002; Inman and Mayes 1999; Nunez and Cuccaro-Alamin 1998; Levine and Nidiffer 1996; Terenzini, et al 1996). In this study, we want to specifically determine if FGS today are significantly different from CGS.

Hypothesis 1: FGS will have different financial and time demands

Hypothesis la: FGS will report lower family incomes than CGS

Hypothesis lb: FGS will work more hours per week than CGS

Hypothesis lc: FGS will receive less financial support from their parents than CGS

Hypothesis Id: FGS will be more likely to use grants to pay for tuition than CGS

Hypothesis le: FGS will be more likely to use student loans to pay tuition than CGS

Hypothesis If: FGS will be more likely to live off campuslcommute than CGS

Greater financial and time demands will have an impact on FGS involvement. Having to spend more time working and commuting to campus will leave FGS less time to spend in social activities and on-campus activities.

Hypothesis 2: FGS will report less social involvement than CGS

Hypothesis 3: FGS will report less involvement in on-campus activities than CGS

Additionally, the result of different financial and time demands should produce higher levels of stress among FGS in those areas. It is hypothesized that the combination of lower family incomes, higher need for grants and loans, and more hours working per week will create higher levels of finance-related stress. Further, more hours commuting and working per week should leave FGS feeling like they have less time to complete their daily tasks.

Hypothesis 4: FGS will report more stress related to financial matters than CGS

Hypothesis 5: FGS will be less likely to report that they feel they have enough time in their typical day to complete all of their necessary tasks than CGS

It is also hypothesized that FGS will show different preferences for coping with stress than CGS. The ability to actively cope has been shown to be a significant predictor of academic success and social support was found to be a significant form of active coping among successful college students (Shields 2001; Leong, Bonz, and Zachar 1997). Additionally, FGS enter college with less "cultural capital" than CGS (Levine and Nidiffer 1996; Rodriguez 2003; Lundberg, et al 2007). Since active coping has been shown to be a significant predictor of college success, active coping strategies become part of the "cultural capital" that college graduates obtain. FGS have less exposure to this "cultural capital" due to the fact that they are not raised by college-educated adults. Therefore, FGS may not enter college with an understanding or an ability to engage in the active coping strategies necessary to succeed in college, which may help to explain lower graduate rates among FGS (Chen and Carroll 2005; Warburton, Bugarin and Nunez 2001). Further, we expect to find a difference in FGS active coping preferences due to the fact that we also expect to find that FGS are less socially involved (Hypothesis 2). By being less socially involved, FGS have less access to the active coping that social support can provide. In this study, we attempt to investigate if such a difference exists. Drawing from Hypotheses 2 and 3, it is hypothesize that FGS will report less social satisfaction than CGS.

Hypothesis 6: FGS will be less likely to use active coping strategies than CGS

Hypothesis 7: FGS will report less social satisfaction than CGS

FGS should report higher levels of financial and time-related stress (Hypotheses 4 and 5). However, FGS are also subjected to the same academic and personal stressors as CGS. Additionally, it is believed they will be less likely to use active (problem-solving) coping strategies (Hypothesis 6) and more reactive coping strategies.

Hypothesis 8: FGS will have higher levels of overall stress than CGS

Several factors have been proven to be predictors of academic success in college: adequate finances, social/parental support, academic preparedness, on-campus involvement, involvement with student acquaintances, and a preference to actively cope with stress. By building from Hypotheses 1–8, as well as previous studies, it can be predicted that FGS should perform lower than CGS and will be less satisfied with their college performance.

Hypothesis 9: FGS will have less academic satisfaction than CGS

Hypothesis 10: FGS will report lower GPAs than CGS

● METHOD

Questionnaire

The instrument was a self-administered, structured, undisguised questionnaire. Besides the fact that this type of instrument is the fastest, cheapest, least expensive, and most popular (Alreck and Settle 2004), our primary motivation for selecting this form of instrument was that it was the most appropriate methodology (given our sample frame, sample size, time frame, budget, etc). Recognizing the fact that the instrument is meant to measure ideas and concepts that are abstract and non-observable, extra care was taken in designing the questionnaire in terms of proper phrasing of the questions, and a neat layout of the various sections. Face validity was conducted with three researchers. A pilot study was conducted with a sample of the population to determine accuracy of instructions, wording of the questions, appropriateness of scale, etc. Since the topic under investigation was somewhat sensitive, extra care was taken to eliminate any ambiguity in the questionnaire.

Seven-point Likert scales were used extensively to assess the following:

1. Student attitudes, opinions, and reasons for being in a university,
2. Their level of involvement and participation in various university activities,
3. Their attitudes towards their work (if they did not work, they could skip this section),
4. Their social life and relationships with various reference group members,
5. Their general opinions about attending and selecting their university,
6. Their time management strategies,
7. Their attitude towards stress, and
8. Their stress coping strategies.

Approximately 3–4 items were developed to represent each construct under investigation. Nominal to ratio scales were used to obtain classification information. The survey took between 10 and 12 minutes to complete. To encourage participation from respondents, all completed responses were eligible to participate in a random drawing.

Sampling and Data Collection

The study was conducted among a projectable sample of the student population at a mid-sized southwestern state university. The overall ending sample was 452 respondents. The general demographic of the students attending this university include:

Males = 41% and Females = 59%

Whites = 71%, African Americans = 14%,

Hispanics = 12% and Others = 3%

Freshmen = 23%, Sophomores = 19%, Juniors = 20%, Seniors = 23%, and Others = 15%.

For generablizablity and the elimination of any type of bias in the responses, students of an undergraduate marketing research course were trained to obtain 5 respondents each. To ensure accuracy of data collection and completion, 5% of the student's course grade was tied into this process. A stratified sampling plan was deployed, with stratas controlling for both year in school (i.e., Freshman, Sophomore, etc.) and college attending (College of Business Administration, College of Education, etc.). The ending sample was found to represent the student population as a whole with a margin of error of ±4.5%. The validity of the sample was examined by a Chi-square goodness-of-fit test where the sample was compared to the population of the institution on key demographic variables. All Chi-squares were determined to be significant at the 0.05 level.

Data Quality

The items in the survey were developed based upon the literature review and the special circumstances of the institution where the research was conducted (Churchill and Brown 2007). For each construct, correlations between the items were examined to determine if further inclusion of each item was warranted. Following the deletion of spurious items, exploratory factor analyses were conducted for each construct utilizing principal components with varimax rotation. Factors with eigenvalues greater than 1 were retained. Since this was primarily an exploratory study, a minimum factor loading of 0.30 (Nunnally 1978) was used as a guideline for including items in a factor. The reliability of each factor was evaluated utilizing an internal consistency measure. Factors with Cronbach alpha less than 0.70 were not used for the analysis. Rather, the analysis was performed utilizing individual items.

● RESULTS

The data supported parts of Hypothesis 1. FGS were found to have significantly lower family incomes and different sources of college funding than CGS families.

Over 71% of FGS reported family incomes of less than $60,000 compared to only 42% of CGS (p = 0.00). FGS reported a greater likelihood to work more hours per week but not significant different than CGS. However, a larger percentage of FGS (42%) reported working more than 20 hours per week, compared to only 36% for CGS (p = 0.45). Further, FGS were not found to be significantly more likely to commute to campus.

The way that students paid for their tuition was significantly different between the two groups. Forty two percent of FGS reported that their parents pay for less than 5% of their annual tuition. In contrast, over 70% of CGS reported that their parents paid for more than 5% of their tuition (p = 0.008). FGS were also more likely to rely on grants and loans to pay for tuition. Over 60% of CGS reported paying none of their tuition with grants whereas over 60% of FGS reported using grants for tuition expenses (p = 0.000). Finally, only 36% of FGS said they have not taken out student loans to pay for tuition. Over 50% of CGS reported zero student loans (p = 0.025).

Finally, there was no significant difference found between FGS and CGS regarding commuter status. This may be due to the fact that the university at which this study was conducted is widely known for being a large commuter campus. The percentage of first-generation commuters was almost identical to that of continuing- generation commuters.

FGS reported lower levels of social and on-campus involvement (Hypothesis 2 was confirmed). FGS reported less social involvement but the results were not found to be significant. This may be explained in part by our similar findings that there was no significant difference between FGS and CGS in terms of number of hours worked or commuter status. It is possible that at the university where the study was conducted, FGS and CGS are both experiencing the effects that hours working and commuting has on their social involvement.

FGS were found to have significantly higher levels of stress in regards to finances. FGS also reported significant differences in their feelings about whether or not they had enough time in the day to complete all their necessary tasks.

Significant differences were found for how FGS choose to deal with stress. FGS were more likely to ask for time off of work and to deal with stress mentally by putting things in a broader mental perspective. FGS were also less likely to go to bars and attend social events.

Table 3.1: Involvement and Stress (Hypotheses 2–5)

HYPOTHESIS	FACTOR OR ITEM	FGS MEAN	CGS MEAN	SIGNIFICANCE
2	On-campus Involvement Factor	**3.92**	4.19	**0.034**
3	I am very involved with social activities in college	**3.86**	4.03	0.42
4	I am stressed because of money issues	**4.89**	4.47	**0.024**
5	I feel I have enough time in a say to complete all the necessary tasks	3.68	**3.97**	**0.087**

Table 3.2: Coping Strategies

COPING STRATEGY	FGS MEAN	CGS MEAN	SIGNIFICANCE
Ask for time off of work	**3.21**	2.62	**0.002**
Put things in a broader mental perspective	**4.83**	4.57	**0.087**
Go to a bar (social)	2.67	**3.12**	**0.028**
Attend social gatherings	3.32	**3.83**	**0.016**

To better understand how students cope with stress, our survey consisted of 19 coping strategies that were based on the results of focus groups done with undergraduate students. It is important to point out that only 4 of the 19 strategies produced significant results. Of these four, two dealt specifically with social coping mechanisms (e.g., going to bars, attending social gatherings). In both cases, FGS were less likely to engage in these activities. We consider attending bars a social coping strategy because bars are a social venue. This question did not ask if students "get drunk" as a means of coping, but only if they enter social situations (bars) where alcohol is consumed. Additionally, many of the students in the focus group reported going to bars with their friends or to meet friends which points to the social aspect of this coping mechanism. Therefore, we conclude that

FGS are less likely to use social coping strategies, which have been considered an active form of coping (Shields 2001). Additionally, active coping was defined as a "problem-solving" based form of coping. Therefore, we consider "putting things in a broader mental perspective" to be a reactive form of coping. FGS were significantly more likely to engage in this form of reactive coping. Therefore, we conclude that Hypothesis 6 was confirmed but caution drawing any conclusions from these results beyond FGS' lower social coping preference.

FGS reported significantly lower levels of social and academic satisfaction as well as lower GPAs. FGS reported higher levels of overall stress, but not at a significant level.

Table 3.3: Outcomes of First-generation Status (Hypotheses 7–9)

HYPOTHESIS	OUTCOME MEASURE	FIRST-GENERATION MEAN	CONTINUING-GENERATION MEAN	SIGNIFICANCE
7	Social Satisfaction	**5.48**	5.83	**0.010**
8	Overall Stress	4.55	4.44	0.737
9	Academic Satisfaction	**4.75**	5.0	**0.090**

Table 3.4: G.P.A.

GPA	FGS (%)	CGS (%)
Less than 2.50	**26.2**	**15.2**
2.51–3.00	32.7	34.6
3.01–3.50	**23.8**	**32.3**
3.51–4.00	17.3	17.9

(p=0.019)

● DISCUSSION

The results from this study paint a very precarious picture for FGS in that they enter college less prepared to succeed but also have greater time demands and financial commitments. The findings of this study were consistent with previous studies in that FGS were found to come from families with lower incomes, work more hours, and rely on grants and student loans to fund their education. Further, FGS were found to be less involved on-campus and socially, confirming previous studies.

This study adds to the growing knowledge about FGS in finding that FGS have different stress make-ups, feel less satisfied with their college experience (academically and socially), and earn lower grades. The study brings up the question as to what can be done to solve this situation. We propose four initiatives aimed at FGS that may make their transition to college more successful: Participation in Living-learning programs, FGS programs, transfer student programs, and increased academic peer interactions.

Participation in *living-learning programs* has been found to increase the success of academic and social transitions into college among FGS (Kurotsuchi, Daver, Vogt, and Brown 2007). Living-learning programs refer to residential programs where students live together, take courses together, and have access to planned programming, faculty, and student interaction. FGS that lived in living-learning programs reported a greater likelihood to perceive an easier academic and social transition to college (Kurotsuchi, et al 2007). Participation in structured activities, such as residence hall programming and planned faculty interaction were beneficial to FGS adjustment to college. These findings suggest that living-learning programs can help to fill the "cultural capital" gap that FGS must address in adjusting to university life.

Although involvement in living-learning programs may help FGS succeed, FGS often do not have the ability to participate in such programs. Most universities do not currently operate living-learning programs and implementing such a program will take years of planning and funding. Further, many FGS likely would not be able to participate in a living-learning program even if it was available. This study showed that FGS already feel like they do not have enough time in one day. The addition of organized living-learning program activities would only add more things for FGS to fit into their already crammed lives. Additionally, FGS have been shown to work more hours and have more financial dependents (Inman and Mayes 1999; Nunez and Cuccaro-Alamin 1998). Higher levels of commuter status are likely directly related to these characteristics. For those FGS that do not work more or have dependents, lower family incomes may make them more averse to pay for expensive, on-campus, living-learning programs. The simple fact is that, although living-learning programs can be successful, many FGS simply cannot participate in them.

However, the findings of the Kurotsuchi, Daver, Vogt, and Brown (2007) study can be combined with similar studies and frameworks that conclude that increased involvement in the "college experience" will lead to greater academic and social transitions and consequently, academic success and persistence (Kurotsuchi, et al 2007; Astin 1984; Pascarella and Terenzini 2005; Tinto 1993). Since FGS are likely to live off-campus and have higher demands on their time, creative solutions for increasing involvement are necessary.

The process of increasing involvement among FGS must start by designing *FGS programs.* FGS must be identified upon their entry to school and programs must be made available for them. Because FGS enter college with less 'cultural capital' and may be unaware of the benefits that involvement in on-campus activities brings, they must be targeted specifically with this information. This could take the form of specialized, mandatory orientation programs (Folger, Carter and Chase 2004), mailings, emails, and encouragement from professors, residence hall advisors, and on-campus employment agencies.

These programs can also take the form of less formal activities aimed at teaching FGS active coping mechanisms and the cultural capital that they lack. Mentoring programs (Ishyama 2007) with college-educated mentors or tutoring programs are two possible ways to address this problem. Mandatory counseling with academic advisors aware of FGS' particular situation may also help (Heisserer and Parette 2002).

Our study found that FGS were significantly more likely to be transfer students, therefore requiring *transfer student programs.* These students likely complete their first couple of years at community colleges and transfer to a university to complete their degree. This also explains why FGS were more likely to be at the junior and senior level of their studies. If these students attend community college and enter the university at the junior level, it should be no surprise that they struggle to adapt to college. One would imagine that the first couple of years in the college experience are very important in determining how a student is going to adapt.

At the very least, FGS that enter the university as transfer students are not exposed to first year experience programs such as freshman orientation. A transfer student orientation program could be implemented that addresses topics covered in typical freshman orientation programs. Such a program will help to increase the cultural capital for students that transfer from community colleges.

Finally, professors must be aware of students in their courses who are FGS. These professors must work to establish relationships with these students, encourage them to get involved on campus, and ensure that the students are at the very least involved with other students in the class and interactions outside of the class with the professor. This can take the form of group projects, before or after class interactions, office hour visits, and in-class discussions that require students to interact with each other. Conversely, CGS in their class is more likely to come equipped to succeed. They are more likely to have had parents explain to them the importance of attending class, asking questions, visiting the professor at their office to address concerns, and being involved on campus in organizations and with student peers.

FGS do not have this 'cultural capital,' do not understand the importance of involvement, and struggle adjusting to college. The end result of this is that FGS earn lower grades and are less socially satisfied. Other studies have shown that they have lower graduation rates.

Finally, Lundberg (2003) found that educationally related peer discussions were significant predictors of learning (in time-limited adult students). Her study concluded that adult time-limited students were able to overcome the learning void that their time-limited status could have created by participating in academic discussions with their peers. FGS report a similar time-limited status and our study found them more likely to be older. Therefore, this study could provide some insight for FGS. This information further supports the need for professors that teach FGS to encourage, perhaps require, student peer interactions that focus on academic subjects. Due to their time-limited status, it may be best to have these interactions during class in the form of small group discussions or class discussions that are facilitated by students.

● LIMITATIONS AND FUTURE RESEARCH

The results of this study are limited because this study was not a longitudinal but a cross sectional study and only involved data at one mid-sized university. To further validate these results, a longitudinal study at several universities with large FGS populations would need to be conducted.

The university that was used is well known to have high numbers of commuter students (approximately 60%) which may explain why no significant results were found for FGS being commuters. Although several previous studies showed that FGS work more hours, our study did not find this relationship to be significant. Our study found that a larger percentage of FGS (42% versus 36% for CGS) work more than 20 hours in a week, but the difference was not significant ($p = 0.45$). This may be due to the way that the question on our survey was asked. Perhaps if the ranges for hours worked were more specific, significant results may have been found. Additionally, an abnormally large percentage of the student population at this university works.

The Appendices shows that our study found that although FGS did not work significantly more hours, they had a significantly higher level of personal income. Future research may want to consider investigating the work life of FGS more fully. Perhaps they have jobs that require more responsibility because they have been working for a longer period of their life, which adds to their stress.

In general, more information about the background of FGS can be obtained. Future studies may want to focus on the geographical locations that FGS come from. It is possible that a higher percentage of students in certain school districts are more likely to be first-generation college students and that these school districts are doing an inadequate job of preparing students for college. Results from studies like this can be used to develop programs that increase the 'cultural capital' that FGS have when they enter college. Overall academic preparedness of FGS may also want to be measured.

Rode, Arthaud-Day, Mooney, Near, Bommer, and Rubin (2005) found that overall life satisfaction, as measured by the extensively validated Life Scale, had a positive correlation with college GPA. They suggested that future research focus on the factors that constitute overall life satisfaction in students to develop academic improvement policies and strategies. Our study revealed that FGS are less satisfied academically and socially. Our study did not measure overall life satisfaction, but it is likely that academic and social factors impact the overall life satisfaction of college students. Future research investigating what makes students satisfied with their lives should also focus on the special case of FGS. Since FGS have significantly different backgrounds than CGS, FGS life satisfaction may consist of other factors than CGS. An understanding of what makes FGS satisfied with their lives may shed light on ways that universities can design policies to increase FGS chances of success.

We also caution drawing any conclusions about the coping preferences of FGS from this study with the exception of their lower preference for social coping strategies. FGS were found to be more likely to "ask for time off of work" to cope with stress. It is unclear whether this is an active form of coping or a reactive form of coping. Taking time off of work could be considered an active form of coping if the extra time was used by the students to deal with stressful situations in a problem-solving manner. Conversely, if taking time off of work is simply used as an escape mechanism, it could be considered a reactive form of coping. Since our study did not measure what students used the extra time for, we cannot classify this coping strategy as either active or reactive.

Finally, the results from this study and several others could be combined to develop a model of first-generation student development at college. It is obvious that FGS face specific challenges. By developing and testing a model that explains their success at college, ways in which higher education can cater to FGS will become more evident. A greater understanding of FGS will be developed and ways to improve their academic success and satisfaction with college will be generated.

This study, along with several others, has focused on why FGS fail at college. We have identified several key differences between first-generation and continuing-generation student backgrounds and behaviors during college. We have inferred that these differences are what lead many FGS to fail to complete college. However, there are FGS that enter college from similar backgrounds and engage in similar behaviors during college that succeed (Giancola, Munz and Trares 2008). To develop a model of first-generation success, future studies would need to focus on the differences between first-generation graduates and first-generation dropouts. Do successful FGS have significantly different backgrounds? Are they more academically prepared? Do they have college educated mentors that pass on the "cultural capital?" Do successful FGS engage in different activities while in college? Do certain universities have greater success rates among FGS than others? If so, what differences can be found in the curriculum and structure of those successful universities? Again, a more comprehensive study consisting of several universities that have large first-generation populations will be needed.

References

Aldreck, P. and Settle r. (2004). *The Survey Research Handbook*. 3rd edition. McGraw-Hill.

Astin, A. W. (1984). Student involvement: A developmental theory for higher education. *Journal of College Student Personnel, 25,* 2977–308.

Astin, A. W. (1993). *What matters in college?* Four critical years revisited. San Francisco: Jossey-Bass.

Billson, J.M., and Terry, M.B. (1982). In search of the silken purse: Factors in attrition among FGS. *College and University, 58,* 57–75.

Bui, Khan Van T. (2002) First Generation College Students at a Four-Year University: Background Characteristics, Reasons For Pursuing Higher Education, and First-Year Experiences, *College Student Journal,* March 2002, Vol. 36, Issue 1 pp. 3–12.

Chen, X., and Carroll, C.D. (2005). *FGS in postsecondary education: A look at their college transcripts* (NCES 2005–171). U.S. Department of Education, National Center for Education Statistics. Washington, D.C.: U.S. Government Printing Office.

Churchill, G.J. and T.J. Brown (2007). *Basic Marketing Research*. Thomson Southwest.

Choy, S. (2001). Students whose parents did not go to college: Postsecondary access, persistence, and attainment *(NCES Statistical Report 2001–126)*. Washington, DC: U.S. Department of Education, National Center for Educational Statistics.

Dennis, J.M., Phinney, J.S., and Cuateco, L. I., (2005). The role of motivation, parental support, and peer support in the academic success of ethnic minority FGS. *Journal of College Student Development, 46,* 223–236.

Folger, Wendy, Carter, Joyce and Chase, Patricia (2004). Supporting First-Generation College Freshmen With Small Group Intervention, *College Student Journal,* September, 2004, Vol. 38, Issue 3, pp. 472–475.

Giancola, Jennifer, Munz, David, and Trares, Shawn (2008). First-Versus Continuing-Gen-eration Adult Students on College Perceptions: Are Differences Actually Because of Demographic Variance? *Adult Education Quarterly,* May 2008, Vol. 58, No. 3, pp. 214–228.

Heisserer, Dana and Parette, Phil (2002). Advising At-Risk Students in College and University Settings, *College Student Journal,* March, 2002, Vol. 36, Issue 1, pp. 69–84.

Inman, W.E., and Mayes, L. (1999). The importance of being first: Unique characteristics of first-generation community college students. *Community College Review, 26,* 3–23.

Ishitani, T.T. (2006). Studying attrition and degree completion behavior among first-generation college students in the United States. *The Journal of Higher Education, 77,* 5, pp. 861–865.

Ishitani, T.T. (2003). A longitudinal approach to assessing attrition behaviors among FGS: Time-varying effects of pre-college characteristics. *Research in Higher Education, 44,* 4, pp. 443–449.

Ishiyama, John (2007). Expectations and Perceptions of Undergraduate Research Mentoring: Comparing First-Generation, Low Income White/Caucasian and African American Students, *College Student Journal,* September 2007, Vol. 41, Issue 3, pp. 540–549.

Kurotsuchi Inkelas, K., Daver, Z., Vogt, K., and Brown Leonard, J. (2007). Living-learning programs and first-generation college students' academic and social transition to college. *Research in Higher Education, 48, 4,* 403–434.

Leong, F., Bonz, M., and Zachar, P. (1997). Coping styles as predictors of college adjustment among freshmen. *Counseling Psychology Quarterly,* 10(2), 211–220.

Levine, A., and Nidiffer, J. (1996). *Beating the odds: How the poor get to college.* San Francisco: Jossey-Bass.

Lohfink, M. M., and Paulsen, M. B. (2005). Comparing the determinants of persistence for first-generation and CGS. *Journal of College Student Development, 46,* 409–428.

Lundberg, C. (2003). The influence of time-limitations, faculty, and peer relationships on adult student learning: A causal model. *The Journal of Higher Education, 74,* 6, 665–688.

Lundberg, C., *Schreiner, L.,* Hovaguimian, K., and Slavin Miller, S. (2007). First-generation status and student race/ethnicity as distinct predictors of student involvement and learning. *NASPA Journal, 44,* 1, pp. 57–83.

Nunez, A.M., and Cuccaro-Alamin, S. (1998). First-generation students: Undergraduates whose parents never enrolled in postsecondary education *(Report No. NCES 98–082).* Washington D.C.: National Center for Educational Statistics.

Nunnally, J.C. (1978). *Psychometric Theory* 2nd edition. McGraw-Hill.

Pascarella, E.T., Pierson, C.T., Wolniak, G. C., and Terenzini, P.T. (2004). First-generation college students: Additional evidence on college experiences and outcomes. *The Journal of Higher Education, 75,* 249–284.

Pascarella, E. T. and Terenzini, P.T. (2005). *How college affects students: A third decade of research,* (2nd Ed.), San Francisco: Jossey- Bass.

Paulsen, M.B., and St. John, E.P. (2002). Social class and college costs: Examining the financial nexus between college choice and persistence. *Journal of Higher Education, 73,* 189–236.

Pike, G. R., and Kuh, G. D. (2005). First and second-generation college students: A comparison of their engagement and intellectual development. *Journal of Higher Education, 76,* 276–300.

Rendon, L., and Hope, R. (1996), *Educating a new majority: Transforming America's education system for diversity.* San Francisco: Jossey-Bass.

Rode, J., Arthaud-Day, M., Mooney, C., Near, J., Bommer, W., and Rubin R. (2005). Life satisfaction and student performance. *Academy of Management Learning and Education, 4,* 4, pp. 421–433.

Rodriguez, S. (2003). What helps some FGS succeed? *About Campus, Sept.-Oct. 2003,* pp. 17–22.

Shields, N. (2001). Stress, active coping, and academic preparedness among persisting and nonpersisting college students. *Journal of Applied Biobehavioral Research, 6,* 2, pp. 65–81.

Terenzini, P.T., Springer, L., Yeager, P.M., Pascarella, E.T., and Nora, A. (1996) First-generation college students: Characteristics, experiences, and cognitive development. *Research in Higher Education, 37,* 1–22.

Tinto, V. (1993). *Leaving college: Rethinking the causes and cures of student attrition,* (2nd Ed.), Chicago: The University of Chicago Press.

Warburton, E.C., Bugarin, R., and Nunez, A. (2001). *Bridging the gap: Academic preparation and postsecondary success of FGS.* (NCES Statisticial Analysis Report 2001–153). Washington, D.C.: U.S. Department of Education.

York-Anderson, D.C., and Bowman, S.L. *(1991).* Assessing the college knowledge of FGS. *Journal of College Student Development, 32,* 116–122

FIRST-GENERATION STUDENT PERSONAL INCOME

Income Level	FGS	CGS
Less than $15,000	79%	88%
More than $15,000	21%	12%

DESCRIPTION OF "INVOLVEMENT" FACTOR

HYPOTHESIS	ITEM(S)	CRONBACH ALPHA
2	I participate regularly in athletic activities (e.g. intramurals)	0.72
	I participate regularly in physical activities (e.g. workout)	
	I participate regularly in social activities	
	I participate regularly in leisure activities	
	I regularly attend [name of school] athletic events	

COPING STRATEGIES

STRATEGY	FGS MEAN	CGS MEAN	SIGNIFICANCE
Consider dropping out of school	2.04	2.11	0.70
Engage in mental activities	3.59	3.73	0.50
Engage in physical activities	4.58	4.81	0.21
Tell myself class is not that important	2.76	2.95	0.25
Put things in a broader mental perspective	4.83	4.57	0.08
"Zone out" in class	3.29	3.38	0.60
Skip class	3.03	3.16	0.47
Skip group or organizational meetings	2.51	2.48	0.85
Withdraw membership in clubs	2.05	2.04	0.97
Drop a course	2.32	2.41	0.63
Ask for time off of work	3.22	2.62	0.00
Quit job	1.68	1.75	0.63
Move back home	2.01	1.91	0.31
Go to a bar	2.67	3.12	0.03
Talk to instructors	2.57	2.74	0.34
Talk to a counselor	1.82	1.95	0.40
Talk to a friend	5.48	5.30	0.27
Talk to a parent	5.03	5.01	0.94
Attend social events	3.32	3.83	0.02

CHAPTER 4

The New Regime through the Lens of the Old

By Sarah Halpern-Meekin, Kathryn Edin, Laura Tach, and Jennifer Sykes

The story of the modern EITC, created in 1993 and fully implemented by 1996, must be understood in the context of the larger story of the landmark 1996 welfare reform. It was no accident that the two were forged during the same presidential administration. But converting a tiny tax credit into the program we have today—a pay raise for the working poor—was the brainchild of Harvard economist David Ellwood and a team of dedicated public servants who had worked on antipoverty legislation in Washington for decades.

Ellwood began his career as a defender of welfare after finding that its dynamics were far more complex than had been previously known. Most people claimed welfare for only short spells, suggesting that, for the typical recipient, it was a hand up and not a handout.[1] But, in 1984, Charles Murray's influential thesis—advanced in his book *Losing Ground*—gained strong currency: according to Murray, an increasingly generous welfare system caused poverty rather than alleviated it by creating perverse incentives to eschew work and marriage.

Suddenly, Ellwood found himself in the position of defending welfare against the likes of Murray. Though scholars roundly criticized Murray's statistical methods, and subsequent analysis revealed only a small negative effect on either work or marriage, the argument had broad public appeal. Because it fit so neatly into popular views of welfare recipients as behaving in reprehensible ways, it was a claim that was repeated at dinner tables across America as an incontrovertible truth.

Ellwood quickly found that there were few things less pleasant than defending welfare. Letters and phone calls came pouring in, decrying his views. Even welfare recipients were contacting Ellwood and calling him crazy for defending welfare. During those years, Ellwood recalls precious few friendly phone calls. Finally, he decided to change his strategy. As he puts it, "When everyone tells you you're drunk, lie down."

Given the ferocious reaction that Ellwood's defense of welfare had provoked, he came to the conclusion that America had to do something fundamentally different to support the poor; we couldn't merely reform welfare, we had to replace it. He took a step back and, along with Harvard colleague Mary Jo Bane, asked the following: What was it about welfare that ran so fundamentally against the American grain?[2] In his book *Poor Support,* published in 1988, Ellwood concluded that policy makers needed to devise a set of social policies to help the poor that would be consistent with American values—welfare clearly wasn't. Finally, the epiphany came—instead of asking how many poor people there were and what the government could do to help them, one should ask why people are poor and what it would take so that they wouldn't be poor, given what the government could actually control.

A key insight soon followed. The working poor were an obvious group of needy Americans that were being almost completely ignored. Cash welfare wasn't really helping them at all—AFDC punished those who worked, imposing an effective marginal tax rate on wages of nearly 100 percent. And most noncash benefits for the poor, like food stamps and Medicaid, were tied to cash welfare at the time. If you were working but poor, you couldn't win. Isn't it proposition one, Ellwood asked, that, if you work, you shouldn't be poor? More fundamentally, he wondered, how can the country justify helping some poor people when others who are undeniably playing by the rules and working—actions fully in line with America's bootstraps credo—aren't getting any meaningful assistance?

This small change in Ellwood's thinking made things fall into place in a different way. Working poverty is the one form of poverty that clearly went against Americans' beliefs; if you work, you shouldn't be poor. One would be hard pressed to find many American citizens who disagreed with that proposition; it was a simple idea that everyone could get behind. When Ellwood shared this basic notion with audiences around the country, heads would nod. After struggles with the value conundrums posed by welfare—that welfare did nothing to promote work, family, or independence, three ideals that Americans held dear—the idea of helping the working poor was immensely appealing. Work was central to the American ethos. Indeed, in America it was the equivalent of a badge of citizenship. A pay raise for the working poor was a policy that got the values straight for once. No conundrums. No more hate mail.

The trick was to identify the mechanism that could be used to fix the problem. Most economists had concluded that the strategy of raising the minimum wage wouldn't be targeted enough. Senator Russell Long had advanced this argument in the early 1970s, when alternatives to Nixon's guaranteed income scheme were being proposed. Besides, one would have to raise the minimum wage so high to fix the problem that the costs would be prohibitive—and, at that level at least, many economists believed that the consequences to the economy would have been too great.

A wage subsidy would have been ideal, Ellwood and others thought, but it was too complicated—too much information and oversight would have been required. Meanwhile, the government already had a program—a tiny tax credit that had been invented in 1975 in the wake of Nixon's failed guaranteed minimum-income proposal to offset high payroll and regressive sales taxes. The program (1) gave no money to people who were not employed and (2) was prowork: up to a certain point, the more you worked, the more you received. Why not transform this early incarnation of the EITC from a tax-relief policy into a pay raise for working-poor families?

In 1988, Democrats convened advisory panels that considered what to do about welfare, which they felt was in need of reform. Ellwood was on several of these panels. Then, at a meeting of the National Commission for Children (which Jay Rockefeller led, with Arkansas governor Bill Clinton as a member of the group), Ellwood presented a paper titled "Reducing Poverty by Replacing

Welfare." His argument centered on three key ideas: (1) if you work, you should not be poor; (2) one parent shouldn't have to do the job of two; and (3) social policy ought to give a hand up and not a handout to the able-bodied poor. In his paper, Ellwood advocated for replacing welfare with "transitional," time-limited assistance, plus assured child support (ensuring that both parents did their share). Most of the paper, though, was devoted to championing the expansion of the EITC, a position that was growing in popularity. Then Ellwood presented the paper at the National Governors Association, with Clinton again in attendance. Clinton virtually rushed the stage, exclaiming how enthusiastic he was about the paper.

During the presidential campaign that followed, Ellwood didn't meet with Clinton directly, but he worked on the candidate's platform, talking repeatedly with deputy campaign manager Bruce Reed, so much so that many in the media began calling Ellwood Clinton's welfare czar. Ellwood kept a phone line open during the presidential debates—for the back-scene moment when either candidate made a gaffe and staff had to furiously construct talking points to fix mishaps or to sharpen attacks. But welfare was not discussed once during the 1992 presidential debates. Still, welfare reform was clearly on Clinton's radar; he wanted to sound like a different kind of Democrat—one that was not as out of touch with the American people as his "tax and spend" predecessors, who lost elections. The pledge to "end welfare as we know it" became part of his standard stump speech—a signature promise of his campaign.

After Clinton won the presidency, Ellwood waited for the invitation to join the administration—he had been called the welfare czar after all—but weeks went by without a call. Finally, on the Friday before winter break, just as he was leaving his office at Harvard's Kennedy School of Government on his way home for the holidays, the phone rang. He told his assistant, "Unless it's really, really important, I'm not here." It was the newly appointed secretary of Health and Human Services, Donna Shalala, offering him a job.

All along, Clinton had hinted he was paying attention to Ellwood's mantra about the working poor: "People who play by the rules shouldn't lose the game." In his speech accepting the nomination at the Democratic convention, Clinton had offered a friendly amendment to Ellwood's oft-repeated phrase: he said, "For too long, those who play by the rules and keep the faith have gotten the shaft."[3]

Then Ellwood learned that Clinton's chief domestic policy adviser had been told to keep his paper "Reducing Poverty by Replacing Welfare" with her at all times. She had apparently done so, displaying to Ellwood a copy that had been photocopied so many times that it was barely legible. Ellwood offered to get her a clean copy.

Even before Ellwood was confirmed as the Department of Health and Human Services' assistant secretary of planning and evaluation, Clinton gave his first address—it was a budget address, because the State of the Union address doesn't occur until the president is in office for at least a year. In that 1993 speech, Clinton announced that he was going to dramatically expand the EITC, saying, "We will reward the work of millions of working poor Americans by realizing the principle that if you work 40 hours a week and you've got a child in the house, you will no longer be in poverty." Ellwood and Robert Shapiro (who invented the phrase "Make work pay") were given the job of determining just how exactly to tweak the EITC to fulfill Clinton's promise. They reworked the credit precisely so that a full-year, full-time, minimum-wage job would get a family of three out of poverty—almost to the dollar.[4]

Within days, Ellwood found himself making his first visit to the Oval Office, with the secretary of the Treasury, the undersecretary, and others in attendance, to present his plan. Clinton queried the group on the fine details of how the credit had been structured. The group turned to Ellwood to explain, and Clinton quickly saw the sense in what Ellwood had done. Ellwood walked out of that meeting thinking that he had accomplished a third of his work as undersecretary of Health and Human Services in the first week. What he didn't know was that this moment would be a high point; though a great deal would be accomplished, he would later oppose the president's decision to sign the Republican version of welfare reform, which Ellwood believed provided too few protections for families who hit the new time limits without finding a job.[5]

Any student of welfare knows that the years following 1996's landmark welfare reform coincided with the largest increase in work among single mothers in history, as well as the largest decrease in the welfare rolls the country had ever seen. Most have thus concluded that welfare reform "worked." Now, in hindsight, we have learned that the new EITC—the pay raise for the working poor—was probably a major reason why welfare reform succeeded.[6] A modest program with an innocuous name, originally crafted as tax relief for the working poor, had been called into service for a radically redefined purpose. Robert Greenstein, who was appointed to serve on the Bipartisan Commission on Entitlement and Tax Reform, worked behind the scenes, along with Wendell Primus, deputy assistant secretary of human services policy at the Department of Health and Human Services, and Bruce Reed, chief domestic policy adviser and director of the Domestic Policy Council, to get the new EITC through Congress in 1993. When they succeeded, everyone in this group knew it was a big win.[7] However, it was the 1996 welfare reform legislation—the Personal Responsibility and Work Opportunity Reconciliation Act, or PRWORA—that garnered all of the media attention, and this is the policy change that has been celebrated by politicians and the public. In contrast, the transformation of the EITC into the nation's largest antipoverty program for working families with children occurred with virtually no fanfare.[8]

Johanna and Mack Clark were just teenagers when the welfare system changed so dramatically and the modern EITC was born. For a time, Johanna was among the dwindling share of single mothers who went on welfare in the aftermath of that reform. The way Johanna, twenty-six, and Mack, twenty-nine, characterize that time offers a rich illustration of how profoundly the safety net has changed.

This white couple is raising Duncan, age seven, and Carrie, age four, in a well-maintained, four-bedroom apartment on the second floor of a triple-decker in the "Southie" neighborhood of Boston. The unit is just down the street from a bakery, an art gallery, and a health clinic, in a neighborhood of multifamily dwellings. In many respects, theirs looks like the typical American family home. Both children have their own bedrooms, with Carrie's decorated in Mattel pink, strewn with stuffed animals, and offering a TV and DVD player; they've made the fourth bedroom into a computer room for the family. The small kitchen has a sturdy table tucked against one wall, and the living room is dominated by a large TV and overstuffed furniture. The kitchen table and living room couch, side tables, and chairs have been purchased an item or two at a time each year when February rolls around and Johanna and Mack get their tax refund.

Duncan plays in his room and Carrie watches TV while Johanna and Mack sit down together at the kitchen table to tell us about their lives.

After dating for five years or so (it took a while for Mack's "cold feet" to warm up to the idea of marriage), Johanna and Mack were finally wed four years ago, after they had already had two children. Mack grew up as the baby of a family of seven children in Southie, and the Clarks still see a lot of Mack's family. Johanna had a completely different experience growing up. Because of neglect, she was removed from her mother's care when she was eleven and was shuttled between nine foster homes and a brief stay with her father after those placements failed. She met Mack when she was eighteen.

Johanna combines full-time work as a medical assistant and schooling—she is completing her prerequisites for a nursing degree—while Mack describes himself as a stay-at-home dad. Mack had been working, but he injured his foot on the job; while he was out on workers' compensation, Johanna found employment. Since they don't feel that they can afford day care and don't like strangers taking care of their children anyway, the two decided that Mack would stay home with the kids while Johanna took on the breadwinner role.

Johanna and Mack have tried hard to do the long-range thinking that they hope will ensure a more prosperous future. Soon after Duncan was born they came to the conclusion that they were never going to get ahead unless at least one of them furthered their education (both had dropped out of high school, and only Johanna had her GED). So they moved in with Mack's mother to save on rent, and Johanna enrolled in a training program that would certify her as a medical assistant. While in school, she spent six months on the welfare rolls. Once she earned her certification, she found a job and left welfare behind. Now she is taking the next step toward financial security, earning credits for a nursing degree a little at a time. But she's doing so while working full time.

With only one wage earner, the Clarks' budget demands belt tightening. Their monthly income from Johanna's regular pay plus overtime totals $2,463, which falls short of their $2,784 in monthly expenses. When Carrie begins kindergarten next year and Mack can go back to work, things will improve. This year, they had to use much of their $5,400 tax refund to pay bills they'd fallen behind on. Right now, it seems, there is not a lot of money left at the end of the month, but the Clarks are pretty happy in their current straits—anything is better than being on welfare, they say.

Like many others who have dealt with the cash welfare system—now officially known as Temporary Assistance to Needy Families (TANF)—Johanna and Mack feel they must "explain away" Johanna's days on welfare. Their strong need to justify her reliance on government benefits reflects their palpable desire to distance themselves from the unpopular image of welfare recipients. As Johanna and Mack think back on this time in their lives, we hear familiar themes: it was only for a short time; it was only because Johanna was going to school in order to better herself and to increase her ability to be self-reliant through work; it was for the good of their child; and it was a terrible experience that she would do anything to avoid again. Johanna exclaims, "I never want to be on welfare ever." Mack interrupts, "It's just no money." Johanna continues, "There really is no money, they basically give you nothing to live off of, which, I guess, is a good thing, because then it would make more people want to fend for themselves…. It definitely wasn't enough and I just didn't like the whole idea of being on welfare, like I didn't want to do it kind of thing, but you do what you have to." "She was on for such, maybe like six months, it was such a short time," Mack adds. "It was only while I was finishing up school," says Johanna. Mack interjects, "I think she might have been out of work." Johanna begins to sum up by saying, "I just didn't like the whole," and Mack completes her thought, "It's depending on other people, that's what it is." Johanna ends the discussion by asserting, "And I like to depend on myself."

In his book *Poor Support,* David Ellwood pointed to four value tenets that have shaped Americans' attitudes toward welfare for generations: self-reliance, the value of work, the primacy of family, and the importance of community. The Clarks justify Johanna's welfare receipt in astonishing correspondence to these values. Both Johanna and Mack assert the value of self-reliance through work; the implied contrast is with those who do not share the Clarks' dedication to American ideals but who are willing instead to sponge off the state. Both husband and wife work hard in this narrative to dodge the stigma that observers might attach to Johanna's spell on welfare. Such justifications, and the implied condemnation of less virtuous others, are nearly ubiquitous among those who have had any experience with government aid. This is an indication of the disreputable position of cash welfare in the moral hierarchy of government benefits—and starkly contrasts with the pride respondents take in claiming that tax refund check each year.

In this chapter, we focus specifically on families' experiences with and perceptions of what remains of the old need-based welfare system, TANF. It will quickly become clear that, at least among the families in our study, TANF is vilified. Their discussions of TANF, or "welfare," as it's usually called, sharply contrast with the tone and texture of what they say about the refundable tax credits—the EITC and the child tax credit—that they receive at tax time. Importantly, as discussed in chapter 2, they do not see these as "welfare."

In Massachusetts, TANF goes by the name Transitional Aid to Families with Dependent Children (TAFDC). As of 2005, a single parent with two children could receive some cash benefits if her monthly income fell below the equivalent of $708 per month, her car wasn't worth over $10,000, and her other assets (excluding a home) didn't exceed $2,500. If the family had no earnings, TAFDC would cut them a monthly check for $618, for a limited time. The state, which collects child support on TANF recipients' behalf, would also retain all but $50 of any child support paid in a given month as partial compensation for the cash welfare benefits. If they had earnings, the first $120 plus 50 percent of their remaining wages would be "disregarded" (not counted) in the determination of their benefit level; for any additional income, they would forfeit about fifty cents in benefits for each dollar earned. Other government programs, such as SNAP and housing subsidies, would also reduce their benefits against these earnings.

The evolution of the social safety net can be seen in the falloff in the Massachusetts welfare rolls—in contrast to the rise in the number of EITC recipients, detailed in figure 4.1. Massachusetts's trends reflect the dramatic declines in welfare rolls that have occurred across the country. These changes are nothing short of astonishing when we consider that welfare reform was tried before 1996—repeatedly—but these attempts failed, moving hardly any families off of the rolls. In 1988, for example, with 10.9 million individuals on the rolls nationwide, President Reagan and Congress passed the Family Support Act, which made work requirements a core component of welfare.[9] Nonetheless, when then-presidential candidate Bill Clinton first promised to "end welfare as we know it" in 1991, there were even more welfare recipients than there had been three years before—12.9 million. During the next five years, when states were given freedom to experiment with their own versions of welfare reform, most focused on getting recipients into jobs, but again there were no dramatic

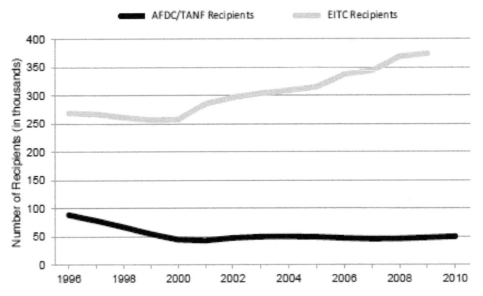

Figure 4.1. Number of AFDC/TANF and EITC recipients in Massachusetts, 1996–2010. Source: AFDC/TANF numbers from Office of Family Assistance (1996–2010). EITC numbers were obtained from Brookings Institution (2010).

declines. Though the number of welfare recipients had started to fall in 1994, it still stood at 12.3 million two years later, on the eve of the 1996 welfare reform. But by the time President Clinton left office in 2000 only 5.8 million people remained on welfare—a decline of 47 percent in only four years (see figure 4.2. which shows the changes in the total number of families receiving welfare), helped along by the booming economy of the late 1990s.

The financial crisis of the late 2000s had not yet hit when we interviewed families in 2007. Since then, many more families fell on hard times, and we revisit some of these families in the final chapter of this book to see how they have fared. But what was remarkable about the Great Recession from our point of view was that there was only a small uptick in the welfare rolls (see figure 4.3). This is a profound testament to welfare's declining role in the array of social programs aiding the poor and near poor. And this is in contrast to a marked increase in use of the Supplemental Nutritional Assistance Program—SNAP—(formerly called

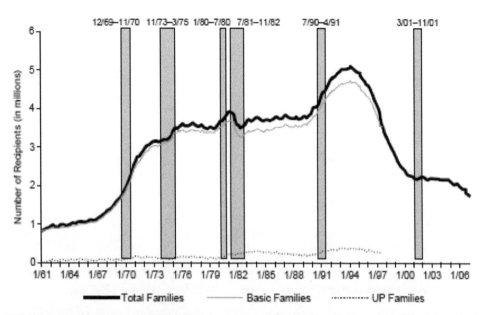

Figure 4.2. Number of families receiving AFDC/TANF in the United States, 1961–2007. "Basic Families" are single-parent families, and "UP Families" are two-parent cases receiving benefits under AFDC Unemployed Parent programs that operated in certain states before FY 1991 and in all states after October 1, 1990. The AFDC Basic and UP programs were replaced by TANF as of July 1, 1997, under the Personal Responsibility and Work Opportunity Reconciliation Act of 1996. Shaded areas indicate periods of recession as designated by the National Bureau of Economic Research. The decrease in number of families receiving assistance during the 1981–82 recession stems from changes in eligibility requirements and other policy changes mandated by the Omnibus Budget Reconciliation Act of 1981. Beginning in 2000, "Total Families" includes TANF and SSP families. Last data point plotted is March 2007. Source: Crouse, Huaun, and Rogers (2008, Appendix A).

food stamps), which started to rise when President Bush championed changes that made the program more accessible, particularly for working families, and then swelled further during the years of the Great Recession.

After the spectacular declines in the welfare rolls that followed welfare reform in 1996, some commentators cautioned that the real test of the new system would

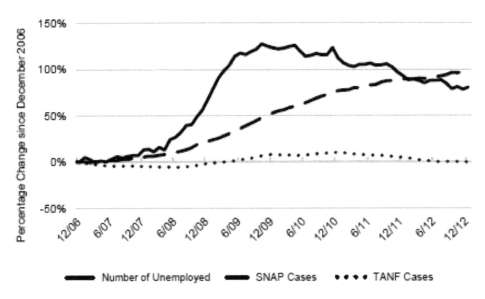

Figure 4.3. Changes in TANF, SNAP, and unemployment in the United States, 2006–12. Source: Center on Budget and Policy Priorities (2013a).

come with the first major economic downturn. That time has come, and, clearly, TANF is no longer functioning as much of a safety net, even in very difficult times—as of 2011, only 1.1 million adults and 3.3 million children remained on the rolls.[10] The very modest rise in welfare evident at the height of the recession pales in comparison to the huge cuts in the number of recipients that occurred in the preceding decade—it is clearly no longer the "Plan B" for the poor that it was before 1996. A web of in-kind support—SNAP, along with WIC, government-sponsored health insurance, and, as mentioned earlier, for the 25 percent of eligible households lucky enough to get them, housing subsidies—now serves as the safety net to catch families when they fall. The EITC, in contrast, is designed to give them a boost once they already have some traction in the labor market.

Many families we spoke with have been struggling economically for years, if not decades. This is why a relatively high proportion—44 percent—say that they have used welfare sometime in the past. Only 8 percent, though, have claimed any cash benefits in the past year. Like Johanna Clark, most say they were on the rolls for only a short time, and under conditions of acute need. This is not surprising: it is rare, at least in most states, to stay on welfare for very long.

Although nearly half of parents say they've received benefits from welfare at some point, either TANF or its predecessor, AFDC, strong negative views of the program are rampant. Perspectives on TANF, in particular, and on means-tested assistance more generally, are embedded in larger American views of which behaviors are right and wrong, and who is deserving and undeserving. We will argue that the line that these households draw between the deserving and undeserving reflects what they believe it means to be American. In this chapter, we show that one kind of government assistance ("welfare" and its in-kind ancillary, SNAP) forces claimants to "cross the road that separated the community of citizens from the outcast company of the destitute," in the words of T. H. Marshall.[11] But another radically different kind of government aid, the EITC, can actually confer benefits and privileges.

In contrast, over the past eighty years the traditional cash welfare programs, like the Elizabethan Poor Laws that Marshall was writing about, have formed the great exception to the expanding sense of the social rights of citizenship, welfare rights that are not granted solely on the basis of need but based on one's status as a citizen. As David Ellwood so painfully learned when he tried to defend it—and what many of our families would have told him—is that welfare is perceived not as an integral part of the social rights of citizenship but as an alternative to them. To claim welfare, poor households must cease to be citizens in the social sense.

This is nowhere more forcefully communicated than at the welfare office itself. In the introduction to this book, we describe the gritty exterior of the old welfare office in East Boston, with the words "OVERSEERS OF THE PUBLIC WELFARE" emblazoned above the door, marking those who passed through its doors as dependents, in need of public supervision. Take that edifice as a metaphor for how it feels to be on welfare: for generations, researchers who asked recipients to relate their experiences at the welfare office collected stories rife with complaints about rude caseworkers who "treat the money as if it's their own," long lines, and impersonal treatment, insensitive to the tragedies that often drove parents to welfare's door.

By 1975, all recipients were required to comply with child support enforcement efforts as a condition of their benefits—thus caseworkers sometimes callously pried into the sex lives of the poor, often in cubicles that provided very little privacy. Since welfare reform, privacy has been further compromised by new requirements such as the drug tests that some states and jurisdictions have tried to implement. Even the Great Recession did not lead to a reconsideration of the idea that some form of need-based cash assistance that was not predicated on behavior (work) should be an entitlement during especially bad economic times, as it had been before the 1996 welfare reform.

Historian Michael Katz writes that in the 1700s American politicians of the time sought to draw a line between the "able-bodied" and the "impotent"—those physically disabled or otherwise incapacitated through no fault of their own—in determining who should receive limited public resources.[12] He chronicles how this division morphed into a focus on rooting out the truly needy from the merely lazy in the 1800s and beyond; moral judgments of deservingness accompanied these distinctions. As Katz explains, those who are not seen as responsible for their own neediness, because of disability, old age, or uncontrollable circumstances (like being widowed or laid off), make much more sympathetic figures and are judged to be more worthy of government help. On the other hand, those who are seen as engaging in immoral behaviors (for example, having children outside marriage or eschewing work) are considered undeserving of such assistance.[13]

This dynamic plays out in public opinion surveys. Political scientist Martin Gilens finds that the belief that welfare recipients are undeserving is the largest direct predictor of public opposition to welfare spending—more than other factors such as family income, political ideology or party, or beliefs in racial stereotypes.[14] Other survey research confirms this, showing that Americans are more likely to support progressive policies when the target group is seen as deserving (e.g., physically disabled) rather than undeserving (e.g., able-bodied); in addition, progressive policies are more likely to be endorsed when the responsibility for the group's poverty is seen to lie not with the individual but with society, or when the group's poverty is seen as being due to circumstances beyond individual control.[15] Public support, therefore, rests with programs that make assistance contingent on work effort.

Johanna and Mack's story, like the stories of many others in our study, reveals that this preference is not limited to the political realm and that these labels are not just applied by the middle class and wealthy to the poor. They are also ways in which those who believe that they are among the worthy poor try to distinguish themselves from the other poor Americans who are often deemed unworthy. Interestingly, work behavior, and not whether one must approach the government for assistance, is the basis for drawing the line. Indeed, some of our households claim more from the government each year than they could have if they had quit their jobs and applied for TANF. But among the array of government programs the EITC has a very special status. For while welfare and other means-tested programs available to the poor impose the mark of being undeserving—and connote visions of lobster-eating, Cadillac-driving social parasites—the EITC is a veritable certificate of deservedness. This sense of deservedness may be felt especially keenly if you claim it at the venerable H&R Block, which publicly confers the label "taxpayer." Alone among those programs targeted at poor families with children, refundable tax credits like the EITC are citizenship affirming.

● WELFARE: "THAT'S NOT THE LIFESTYLE I CHOOSE TO LIVE"

As we saw in Johanna and Mack's story, lower-wage workers draw strong divisions between themselves and those whom they perceive to be living the "welfare lifestyle," which they characterize as choosing not to work, being on welfare for a long time, and, in general, getting benefits without being truly needy. They distance themselves from this definition as they describe their own experiences with welfare: parents routinely emphasize that they had no other choice but to go on welfare; it was only for a limited period of time; and they really needed it.

Though welfare benefits are calculated according to a stringent means test, welfare is most often discussed in moral terms, with judgments made about the values and character of those who claim it. These judgments are also made by parents who themselves have claimed benefits in the past. These parents pass judgment on others while insisting that they personally were not typical recipients; their use of the program was due to exceptional circumstances. Given their efforts to get and keep jobs, being on welfare does not give a suddenly needy mom or dad the feeling of being buoyed by the safety net; instead, it feels like a slap in the face. Unlike the EITC, which rewards work, welfare is perceived as rewarding the opposite: indolence and sloth.

Most charge that abuse of the system—claiming benefits that are not truly needed, or in lieu of efforts to provide for oneself—is the rule, rather than the exception, though none say they have been guilty of this charge. Marissa Lopez, a single Hispanic mother of three—ages five, eleven, and thirteen—in her early thirties who works as a medical assistant, describes her time on welfare as follows:

> I received it when Adriana was little, and, when I had had Jimena, that's when Governor Weld changed the law … [and] my two years was up when I had had Jimena. So that's when I went back to school and I got off of welfare completely, worked full time and went to school full time in the evening.… I was glad [I was working and going to school]. I didn't want to end up like everybody else, just sitting on welfare, getting welfare.… I could have sat on my behind and got the food stamps and the MassHealth, but my mother was like, "No, you're not going to. You're going to get up and get a job and support your kids." So I just didn't have the luxury of being able to sit on my ass.

Like many of the others we spoke with, Marissa takes pains to emphasize that she refused to "sit on welfare," opting to work and provide for her children herself. She portrays this choice as the more difficult option and details how hard she worked to get ahead. This is behavior that she says sets her apart from others who are content to depend on the government for a handout. It's interesting to note that Marissa draws this contrast even though she is aware that, since welfare reform, rules prohibit long-term benefit receipt and that in fact she herself left welfare only because she had "timed out" rather than of her own volition.

Penny McPherson, a white administrative assistant who lives with her fiancé and four-year-old son, is careful to offer a caveat to her critical evaluation of welfare recipients. Nonetheless, her views are similar to Marissa's. Penny gestures to the first-floor apartment across the street, saying,

> Like the family over there, they're on welfare, that's fine. Whatever. Everyone got to do what everyone got to do. But they take their check and spend it on drugs and addiction.… So it's kinda like,

it's going to the wrong hands. You know? Like last year, they had a birthday party, and they took their kids' birthday presents with the receipts.… They went and they returned the kids' presents [for the money]. I'm not saying that all parents on welfare do that.… But the ones who do…

Penny expresses the fairly common belief that those who receive government assistance are not using the money wisely and are engaged in an array of immoral behaviors that speak to their lack of deservedness. As a counterpoint, she offers a description of her own spending habits: "Give *me* $100 and it's not going to me!" she exclaims, noting that she prioritizes her four-year-old son over her own wants and needs. The implication is that, while the government wastes its money on her undeserving neighbors, she would have put it to good (and morally appropriate) use: her son.

A short walk from the Fields Corner subway stop in Dorchester, we find Alicia Robinson's apartment in a residential part of the neighborhood, a good distance from the hustle and bustle of the shops along Dot Ave. Alicia is a twenty-six-year-old black single mother and a current welfare recipient; until recently she worked as a personal care attendant but lost that job. Alicia says she does the best she can for her daughter, three-year-old Malia, whose photos are prominently displayed throughout their home. The apartment's interior is in much better condition than one would guess from looking at the building's shabby exterior. To enhance the homey feel, she's outfitted each of the apartment's two bedrooms with colorful bedspreads and sheets. But evidence of her limited resources appears elsewhere in the house. The living room is all but devoid of furniture—a lone table sits in the corner. The kitchen is also sparsely furnished, with just a small table and a couple of chairs.

Alicia uses the opportunity to discuss her views of the welfare system to condemn women who have more children just to get more money from welfare, which she believes is a common occurrence. She then seeks to distance herself from other recipients by emphasizing her willingness to work: "I just be like looking at these girls like, wow, you know, all these kids.… They are going to cut welfare so what are all of you going to do…? I'm not lazy like that; I will get a job." Alicia names no one in particular in telling her story but rather points to "these girls"—people she doesn't know but sees on the street when she's out and about. She makes these claims even though more than a decade has passed since Massachusetts put a "family cap" in place, which bars welfare recipients from receiving additional money if they have more children.[16] Alicia's views of the system, like those of many, are based more on supposition than on fact; she draws no obvious lessons from her own experience.

These perceptions sound remarkably similar to the stereotypes of shiftless, baby-making welfare moms that dominated the political debate prior to the transformation of the welfare system in 1996. In the pre–welfare reform days, one newspaper editorial declared, "Having babies while on welfare is wrong and we won't pay for it."[17] During the welfare reform debate in Massachusetts, Democratic state senator Michael C. Creedon claimed that "General Relief goes to people who are urinating on the floor in the bus station in Brockton and throwing up. They take that $338 and go to the nearest bar and spend it."[18] Bill Clinton, in his 1992 run for the presidency, called for an end to "permanent dependence on welfare as a way of life," despite evidence from David Ellwood and Mary Jo Bane that most welfare receipt was short term.[19] In the course of the national debates over welfare reform, some conservative congressmen compared welfare-reliant mothers to "alligators" and "wolves" in their speeches before Congress.[20]

As the proposed welfare reform legislation worked its way through the Senate in the 1990s, Republican senator Spencer Abraham of Michigan called welfare "the number one social problem in America today," and Robert Rector, of the conservative Heritage Foundation, referred to the program as "a system that promotes illegitimacy and destroys marriage."[21] It is notable that politicians have ascribed such wide-ranging powers to the welfare system, likening it to the use of a powerful narcotic.

For both Clinton and his conservative counterparts, taking a stance that was critical not only of the welfare *system* but also of the *people* who received assistance from it was a politically savvy move. In 1995, a nationwide poll revealed that 79 percent of Americans believed that those who were on welfare would never get off of it.[22] With the wide-ranging and fundamental overhaul of the welfare system in 1996, these stereotypes largely ceased to be the focus of political calls to action.[23] Nonetheless, they remain alive and well, at least among the families that we interviewed.

Massachusetts's TANF program, TAFDC, limits parents to twenty-four months of benefits in any given five-year period. Benefits are contingent on performing some sort of job search, work, or structured volunteer activity.[24] Despite the many dramatic changes in the system, meant to ensure that welfare aid is not a handout but a hand up, the program remains deeply stigmatized, and all of the old stereotypes seem to still stubbornly cling to the program.[25]

● "THEY LOOK AT YOU LIKE YOU'RE NO GOOD"

Ironically, the families in this study have often been victims of the very stereotypes they impose. Angelica Rivera, a thirty-one-year-old Hispanic project manager at a health center and a married mother of three—two in elementary school and one in high school—describes her time on welfare as follows: "It was horrible.... They give you miserable money, and then you have [them] get on your case all the time.... 'Come in the office, come in the office, come in the office.' I think [the caseworkers] look at you like you're no good because you're on assistance.... I don't think she respected me.... They were making me look like a liar.... I think they [only] gave you enough [money] for like a bar of soap."

Bryn Gamble, twenty-eight and black, lives with her boyfriend and her five-year-old daughter and is now a buyer for a health insurance company. She is still outraged over the poor treatment that she received when she went to apply for welfare after her daughter was born. Her reaction is grounded in the fact that she identifies herself as someone who plays by the rules by working and supporting herself but just happened to hit a tough time and was therefore deserving of government aid. She says,

> That's why I think a lot of them treat people the way they do, because some people just abuse and use the system, so it looks, you know, it makes it worse for the people who really do need the help. And I was one of those, you know. Are you kidding me? I paid my taxes! Do you want to see my résumé? Do you want to see my paycheck stubs? I was so mad. It was disgusting.... I'm not lazy. I like [doing it on] my own.

I really don't like for people to help me unless I really need it.... It was just so degrading and it was just so disrespectful.[26]

Tessa Morales, a thirty-year-old married white mother of three, ranging in age from five to fourteen, who works occasionally as a caterer, also felt judged by the welfare system. She describes her experience this way:

Terrible. I'll never do it again. It was the worst experience.... I was sixteen, they told me [I had] to go back to school and put Philip into a day care [to get benefits]. [But then] I'm like "Oh, fuck this." I went and got a job and got off of it. Got off and worked ever since.... It was terrible. I'll never go back to them places again. Never. It's not for me.... They took me in a little office, in the welfare office, and they had me swear in front of a judge I was gonna pay [the] $42 [they overpaid me]. I was so embarrassed. I'm like, "You are wasting the taxpayers' money to throw me into this room with a *judge* and a swearing cop?" ... I would never go back.... I swore I would work the rest of my life. I didn't care how I worked or where I worked, I would never go back there again. Never. And I didn't.

● "I WAS TOO PROUD TO TAKE WELFARE, BUT THAT WAS THE ONLY CHOICE I HAD"

Chantelle Woodward, a thirty-four-year-old black medical assistant and mother of two, ages nine and fourteen, who is separated from her husband, really "needed" welfare; that's how she justifies her time on the rolls. She explains how her daughter had severely injured her hand, requiring trips for surgery and doctors' appointments. She had to take care of her child, which precluded her from working. "I had to take care of [my daughter]. I had to physically like bathe her and it was uncomfortable for her, but she couldn't use her hand, so I had to take a couple of months off [of work] for her ... so at that point I did go on welfare.... I got all the documentation, everything that I needed so I was able to get welfare for my daughter." Chantelle's account is illustrative of a recurrent theme in people's stories about their time on welfare—they had no other choice. Furthermore, they say that they were doing it only for their children's sake, not for their own.

Chantelle continues on with her story: "I'm still gonna work. I just can't find myself sitting home all the time and not doing nothing and watching the same [TV] shows; that's not the lifestyle that I chose to live." She then draws on another recurrent theme—that leaving welfare and wanting to work are core credentials of a good parent. She says, "And not only that, but we have to survive, and I'm a role model for my daughter. I don't want them to get into that, to where it's okay to just stay home and don't work and don't think about responsibilities. I don't want that. I'm a role model for them, and I want them to know in order to get things in life and to get what you want you have to earn it, you have to go out there and get it, it's not gonna just come to you."

Fifteen years ago, researchers Kathryn Edin and Laura Lein found that, among those claiming welfare on the eve of welfare reform, there was a sharp tension between working and being a good parent; the two were often seen as being at odds with one another.[27] Although we do still hear about the difficulties of balancing work and parenthood, now many tell us that part of being a good parent is serving as a positive role model by working hard and staying employed. This sharp change in the view of work in relation to parenthood could, in part, be responsible for the strong distaste these lower-income parents have for welfare these days.

Lashara Redmond, twenty-six and black, describes her time on welfare as unavoidable and short-lived. This nutrition assistant and single mother to five-year-old Shadiah says, "I was only on welfare for a month, that's after I had my daughter, and I only did that so I could get a [child care] voucher. Because I could have [lived off of savings], but I just [went on welfare for a month] so I could get a voucher so I could get my daughter in day care because I wouldn't be able to afford that alone on my salary." For Lashara, it was okay to collect welfare because doing so is what allowed her to claim the child care subsidy that would allow her to work. Otherwise, she wouldn't be able to afford to take a job.

Maria Velasquez, a nurse's aide with a seven-year-old daughter, emigrated to the United States from Honduras as a child. She offers another Horatio Alger–type testimonial: "I try to live my life [with] whatever I have.... [In my country] they teach me, you have to work for whatever you want.... I don't like easy way. Sometime … I pray to God, 'Never [let me] go to welfare.' I know it [pays] nothing, but I know some people go over there and they don't need it." Maria believes that it is those who provide for themselves through work who deserve rewards. She knows that welfare pays little but suspects, nonetheless, that many people who receive it "don't need it."

In short, one's own past welfare receipt is seen as a regrettable necessity—only claimed in extreme situations—a source of intense shame, and woefully insufficient at the same time. These seemingly contradictory assessments of their time on the program aren't held by different groups but by the same people all at the same time. Take Tracy Sherman, a twenty-eight-year-old white single mother of two girls, ages six and eight, who works as a medical coder. She relates this story of how she ended up on welfare: "In the beginning I did it with my youngest when their dad [an alcoholic] had relapsed and I didn't want to put any of the burden on my parents. I felt like maybe I should go on it for a little while." Despite substantial misgivings, Tracy went ahead and applied for benefits. "I didn't feel good as a person, you know what I mean, like I come from a pretty good family, it's not like I'm struggling. I see people like in the lower end of Southie that really need it, and, you know, I was getting it and I could be working." Although Tracy believed that she could and should be employed, she had to sacrifice her self-worth for a while to attend to her parental duties. "[My daughter] was too young for me to go back to work … so I did it for probably like eight months, and then I got a job and my friend's mother did child day care inside her house, so she gave me a really good rate."

Even though Tracy believes that she did what she had to do in order to be a good mother, she claims she hated every minute of it.

They gave me [cash] plus they gave me food stamps for formula and everything like that. And every time I used it, though, I felt like crap.... And constant appointments that you have to go to and you've got to bring in proof and you have to have people write you letters.... It was like they were constantly in your business.... And it's like, "Is it really worth it to just be getting, you know, $50 extra a week for formula and then like maybe $200 a week for assistance?" And I'm like, "I don't think so. I'd rather go to work and do it the regular way."

For Tracy, side glances at the grocery store when she pulled the electronic benefit card out—the form that food stamps, now called SNAP, come in—gave her sharp internal feelings of shame, as did having to prove repeatedly that she needed the money. And all for so little payoff. As Woody Allen once said, "The food here is terrible, and the portions are too small."

● LEAVING THE OLD WELFARE REGIME BEHIND

Prior to welfare reform, Edin and Lein's research showed that recipients frequently worked without the knowledge of their caseworkers—often under the table for cash—in order to supplement their meager welfare benefits.[28] The new welfare rules have by and large eliminated this strategy. Because welfare recipients must be working, be involved in training, or serve as a volunteer to get benefits, they no longer have time to work covertly. In some ways, then, the package of benefits that welfare beneficiaries have to live on now is even lower than it was under the previous regime.[29] But as a result of the EITC that calculus changes dramatically when recipients leave welfare for employment. Full-time, full-year, low-wage workers with children are undoubtedly financially better off now than they have ever been before in terms of the assistance the government offers them.

The families whose stories we feature here come from widely varying backgrounds. Yet there is a consistent value system—a clear moral hierarchy—underlying their views of the acceptability of various government assistance programs. Collecting cash welfare and living in "the projects" are those forms of assistance that are most derided. The families disparage SNAP somewhat less (despite a relatively high earned-income threshold, receipt of this program is still quite "visible" because of the Electronic Benefit Transfer [EBT] card). The other main form of housing assistance, the housing choice voucher program known as "Section 8," which offers subsidies on market-rate apartments, is generally viewed as more acceptable than any of the programs above. This is probably because subsidized renters mix in with the general rental population. Unlike an address in a housing project (or even the use of an EBT card to pay for groceries), a Section 8 subsidy is largely invisible to outside observers, who have no way of distinguishing who among their neighbors has a subsidy and who does not. Government-sponsored health insurance programs (MassHealth, Medicaid, and the Children's Health Insurance Program, CHIP) hold virtually no stigma among the families we spoke with—perhaps because the programs are not restricted to the officially poor; children up to 300 percent of poverty are eligible for CHIP, for example.

The Special Supplemental Nutrition Program for Women, Infants, and Children (WIC) carries a status similar to health care, perhaps because it is limited to "nutritious foods" for pregnant women and very young children. Interestingly, at the WIC office mothers are encouraged to breastfeed, are weighed and measured to determine whether they are obese, and are given nutritional information. One might assume that potential claimants would find these intrusions offensive. Instead, many recipients welcome them. The practices even seem to add to their respect for the program, since they are "educational."

Child care subsidies and especially Head Start seem to carry no stigma either. Child care is enormously expensive in Boston, as in many other places. Nearly everyone we spoke with realizes the impossibility of paying for child care while working at a low-wage job. Besides, they say, a child care subsidy is what allows one to stay employed. In addition, Head Start (like WIC) is viewed as an educational program and draws some status from that designation. However, other than Head Start, all of these programs are to some degree seen as "welfare," while the EITC is not. As we've said, the EITC, by these households' lights, is the opposite of welfare.

Pundits and policy makers usually, though not always, agree on this view of the EITC. For example, while politicians on the right have made repeated claims that welfare perpetuates an underclass by discouraging marriage, few have made similar claims about the EITC or have even publicly worried about it. Nonetheless, as we have shown, the EITC does actually incur large marriage penalties in some cases. Americans have long been torn between judging the morality of our adult citizens (especially as evidenced by their work behavior) and wanting to provide assistance to the children in their care. The persistent critique of welfare we heard from the families in our study is based on the notion that welfare breeds immoral behavior (nonwork), which in turn breeds more poverty. To be a good role model to your kids, they say, you've got to be employed. Americans have long believed that providing support to able-bodied adults outside the paid labor force—even when they are raising children—risks the creation of a permanent dependent class. Recall that Ellwood and Bane's research had shown that this "way of life" was quite rare in reality, even back in the 1980s and '90s before welfare reform. Clinton and those who came after him castigated the system on this basis nonetheless.

The financial insecurity that lower-income families face creates a complicated relationship with government assistance programs. As we have shown, like their wealthier counterparts, the working poor hold sharply negative views of most government assistance programs. Nonetheless, many of these household heads claim SNAP or WIC, use housing subsidies, and enroll their children in Head Start or get a child care subsidy to bridge the gap between their wages and financial needs. As we showed in chapter 1, they believe that as working parents they deserve the hand up that these programs provide. The problem for the working poor is that many of these programs also serve those who don't have a job—people that they view as "undeserving." And this puts them on a moral tightrope when claiming these benefits. How do they distinguish themselves from those they deem the unworthy poor? The EITC's distinctiveness is that it offers low-wage workers an opportunity to secure government support without the baggage of the welfare label—no nonworker need apply.

Although a substantial portion of these families are not officially poor, it still rankles that their income from work isn't enough to cover their monthly expenses much of the time. The omnipresence of government assistance programs in so many of these families' lives vividly illustrates two key realities of the current labor market. First, jobs that many less educated American workers hold neither pay very much nor offer many avenues for meaningful advancement. Some Americans will spend years earning so little that supporting a family will require some form of government assistance—a housing subsidy or Medicaid, for example—much of the time. Others will come closer to the ideal of self-reliance most of the time, but an unexpected plunge in income—due to lost hours or layoffs, for example—or a sharp rise in expenses (a new baby arrives, the car breaks down, or a home repair just can't wait any longer) will prompt periodic need for government support.[30]

Turning our attention, as a society, to the working poor puts our cash assistance commitments more firmly in line with our other social support programs. Now cash benefits are seen as a right—a social right in a citizenship sense—only for those who are working and raising future citizens. Views of the EITC are most like those that Americans hold about Social Security's retirement benefits, which are also seen as a right because they are predicated on the past work behavior of the claimant or the claimant's spouse (those without a work history or without a spouse who worked can claim only a small benefit). Unemployment insurance is built on a similar premise, and importantly it requires that the job loss be involuntary. Social Security Disability Insurance, the federal disability program that serves those with a substantial work history, pays far more than its sister program, SSI, which is reserved for those without a sufficient work record. This latter program, like welfare, carries significant stigma and is viewed as problematic by our respondents, as well as society at large; the former has received much less public attention, even though the ranks of both programs are growing rapidly. Some have even charged that SSI is "the new welfare."[31]

Other forms of government assistance that are not viewed as welfare at all benefit legions of Americans; many of these are so beloved they are programmatic third rails—ones politicians would interfere with only at their own risk. The mortgage interest deduction for home owners is among the largest, along with other tax loopholes and shelters that often provide larger benefits to those higher up on the income ladder. The federal government and states also offer tax relief to those who engage in other forms of socially desirable behavior: the adoption tax credit, educational tax credits, home buyer tax credits, and credits to those who buy fuel-efficient hybrid cars are all recent examples. Like these benefits, the EITC largely escapes scrutiny, hidden among the complexities of the tax code and administered not by social service providers but by the IRS.

Economist Kenneth Boulding wrote that "social policy is that which is centered in those institutions that create integration and discourage alienation."[32] In other words, as they participate in social programs, recipients are endowed with personality traits that are the filter through which others come to see and treat them, and through which they may even come to see themselves. The EITC turns supplicants into taxpayers, even though they pay no federal and—in some states—no state taxes (except sales tax).[33] While "welfare" tries to divert potential claimants from its rolls, the EITC—often via the friendly faces at H&R Block—attempts to get the "customer" the largest possible benefit available by law.

Endnotes

1. These studies are summarized in Bane and Ellwood (1994).

2. Bane and Ellwood (1994).

3. Clinton (1992).

4. In 1996, the minimum wage was raised from $4.25 per hour to $4.75. At $4.75, a full-time, full-year worker would gross $9,500; together with an EITC of $3,556 for a working parent of two, this would be a total annual income of $13,056 against a poverty threshold of $12,641 (for a family of three that includes two children). Of course, most household heads earn a bit more than the minimum wage. Ellwood recalls that they purposely made the per-child adjustment small to get a little more cash into families' pockets. Today, the minimum wage is no longer high enough that full-time, full-year earnings combined with the EITC would boost a family above the poverty line.

5. Green (2000).

6. However, some researchers have maintained that the causal arrow was reversed—the success of welfare reform, which led women to leave welfare for work, drove up EITC receipt by expanding the pool of low-wage workers (Mead 1999).

7. And they had learned a big lesson about politics. Observers now wonder whether anyone could have predicted how large the EITC would grow; but the new version of the credit started out large—at a whopping $30 billion, an unbelievable amount for a new antipoverty program. AFDC cost only about $12 billion at the time. Ellwood claims that if he had tried to get even half that amount—another $15 billion—for welfare, the response would have been, "Do you want to give up WIC and Head Start?" But in budget discussions, especially when big tax reform is on the table and huge amounts of money are at stake, $30 billion is not a large number. Working through the tax system involves a different set of committees and people with different priorities in mind—and a much better sense of what the scope of the federal budget actually is.

8. The credit underwent significant expansions in 1986, 1990, and 1993, and temporary expansions were made in 2009 as part of the federal economic stimulus package.

9. Ultimately, this regulation lacked the teeth to revolutionize the system, and its work requirements were rarely enforced. However, this marked an important step along the path toward the overhaul of AFDC.

10. Shaefer and Edin (2012).

11. Marshall (1950, 24). *Social inclusion* is a term more often used in Europe and the rest of the English-speaking world than it is in the United States. In this view, full inclusion in society

is possible only for those who are not economically marginalized and are therefore able to conduct their lives in keeping with the community's standard of living. For example, while telegrams or letters were once the standard communication modes of the day for those who did not live in close proximity, today someone would be excluded if deprived of a telephone or access to the Internet.

12. Katz (1993).

13. Gans (1995); Jencks (1992).

14. Gilens (1999).

15. Appelbaum (2001).

16. Many with whom we spoke used the term *cap baby* to describe a child for whom you cannot receive government benefits. For example, current welfare rules stipulate that if you have an additional child while already on welfare you do not receive an accompanying increase in your benefits. Prior to the 1995 welfare reform in Massachusetts, a family on welfare would receive approximately $90 more per month for each additional child they had.

17. Richard Cohen (1995).

18. Sack (1992).

19. Clinton (1991).

20. Toner (2002).

21. Toner (1995).

22. Gilens (1999).

23. Toner (2002). However, during the 2012 presidential campaign, this issue resurfaced when Republicans sought to portray President Obama as weak on welfare for allowing states to apply for waivers from current federal welfare rules; their charge was that Obama was removing the work requirements from welfare, an argument not well supported by any available evidence.

24. The welfare reforms instituted in Massachusetts, which occurred in the year prior to the federal overhaul of the system, were known to be particularly strict and were deemed among the toughest in the nation by the National Governors Association (Wetzstein 1995). If Governor Bill Weld had had his way, the reforms would have been even more stringent; he proposed ending welfare benefits to unmarried teenage mothers, saying, "Well, we think a hundred-plus dollars a week for that stuff still makes teenage motherhood look like too much fun" (Hennrikus 2006).

25. As Robert Asen notes, "PRWORA did not end welfare as we knew it because the legislation did not—indeed, could not—repeal the contrary beliefs, competing values, and malevolent images that historically have plagued deliberations of welfare policy. Public suspicion toward persons as cheats and shirkers and public anger with governments unable to correct their pathological behavior did not end with the repeal of AFDC" (2002, 225).

26. The sense was not uncommon among families that, because they were paying taxes, they had, essentially, paid for their own benefits. In fact, taxes paid by families in the lowest income quintile (less than $3,000, on average) are far outstripped by the transfers they receive from programs like TANF, WIC, SNAP, housing subsidies, Medicaid, and the EITC; even families in the second income quintile receive as much in government assistance as they pay in taxes. Despite their strong identities as working taxpayers, most families in this study were benefiting more from government assistance than they were paying for (M. Dahl and Perese 2013).

27. See also Michalopoulos et al. (2003); London et al. (2004); Scott et al. (2001); Scott et al. (2004).

28. Edin and Lein (1997).

29. Although some states have raised their "pass through" rates, or the rates at which welfare recipients can retain their earnings from reported jobs while still receiving benefits, these rates are obviously much lower than the 100 percent of earnings respondents were able to keep from jobs performed under the table.

30. These realities are reflected in the balance of taxes families pay versus the government benefits they receive. Among nonelderly households in 2006, the bottom income quintile received far more (approximately $13,000) in cash, near-cash, and health transfers than they paid in taxes. However, reflective of the reach of work-supporting benefits and need among those higher up the income spectrum, even those in the second income quintile saw the taxes they paid basically balanced out by the government assistance they received (M. Dahl and Perese 2013).

31. Office of the Inspector General (2013); Raab (2013).

32. Boulding (1967, 7).

33. In addition to sales tax, families may pay property tax (either directly or as part of the cost of rent) and payroll taxes, even when they pay nothing in income tax. For further explanation of the taxes paid by lower-income families across states, see Newman and O'Brien (2011).

SECTION **TWO**

RACIAL AND ETHNIC INEQUALITY

Racial and ethnic inequality represent significant social problems in the United States. Although there has been substantial progress, the country is still divided along racial and ethnic lines. In this section, several important concepts that relate to race and ethnicity, such as racism, prejudice, and discrimination, are introduced. This section also consists of four chapters that examine issues relating to driving while black, prejudice, immigration, and residential segregation.

● THE DIFFERENCES BETWEEN RACE AND ETHNICITY

Many people use the terms race and ethnicity interchangeably, but they represent different concepts. Racial categories are based on observable characteristics such as skin color, eye shape, and hair texture. In the United States, people are referred to as being white, black, Asian, Native American, or Hispanic. The language of mixed-race is also used to describe people who have parents of different races. Ethnicity, on the other hand, is a cultural construct that reflects the part of the world from which people's ancestors hail. Ethnic groups are typically distinguished by shared history, religion, language, and traditions. In the United States, the general rule of thumb is that ethnic groups are followed by the term American. So, we have people who are Irish American, Chinese American, Mexican American and so forth.

When sociologists consider ethnicity, the language of thick and thin is used to describe the impact that a person's cultural background has on their daily lives. Someone with thick ethnicity is likely going to speak the language, eat the foods, and engage in the hobbies of the people in his or her home country. Consider people who live in Koreatown in Los Angeles or Little Havana in Miami. Ethnicity is a very big part of many of these people's identity. Someone with thin ethnicity is going to be more assimilated into the mainstream American culture. Many people in this group come from a mixed ethnic background and may identify with aspects of that background at some times more than others. Maybe this takes the form of an Irish American accentuating his or her ethnic heritage on St. Patrick's Day, or a German American playing up his or her heritage during Oktoberfest.

One concern that many people have with the classification of race in the United States is that the number of racial categories is limited. There is no racial category on the US Census for Hispanic or Middle Eastern, for example. This means that people who are of Hispanic or Middle Eastern descent have to decide upon a racial category that best suits them. On many job applications and government surveys, respondents can choose between the categories white of non-Hispanic origin and white of Hispanic origin. All of this points to the fact that people can share the same ethnic but not racial categorization. There are many white people, including Dave Matthews, who are African American in that they were born in Africa. Similarly, people can be the same race and have different ethnic backgrounds. For example, two people can both be Asian but one has a Chinese ethnic background and the other has a Vietnamese ethnic background.

● THE SOCIAL CONSTRUCTION OF RACE

The nature versus nurture debate represents an ongoing dialogue between sociobiologists and social scientists regarding the role that people's genetic makeup plays in their development of skills and talents. Both sides agree that heredity plays an important role in determining physical characteristics like height, hair color, eye color, and having twins. We know, for example, that people with blue eyes have to have a family member with blue eyes. Sociobiologists take this idea of genetic predisposition and apply it to other characteristics like intelligence, work ethic, and athletic ability. The idea is that people of different races have innate skills and talents that differentiate them from other people. This perspective is rejected by sociologists and other supporters of the nurture argument. Sociologists believe that people are molded by parents, siblings, coaches, and other agents of socialization to be a certain way. While people may have predispositions, their environment makes a difference in who they are. After all, we will never know how many potential Mozarts were never placed in front of a piano. Kids who are exposed to instruments and music are more likely to play and understand music than those who are not. Similarly, kids who grow up around books are more likely than other kids to read books themselves. Genetics may make a difference in how they read or what learning challenges they face, but people such as family members and teachers can help to maximize (or minimize) potential.

Many social issues can be considered through the nature and the nurture lens. Take people's SAT scores, for example. On a national level, black students score, on average, 100 to 200 points lower on the math and verbal parts of the tests compared to white students. A sociobiologist, someone who believes in nature, would see this as evidence that blacks are inherently less intelligent than whites. A sociologist, however, would explain this trend in terms of a variety of different social factors that impact a child's learning. Sociologists argue that the quality of school, commitment of teachers, after-school responsibilities, financial status, and encouragement of people to do well is often different for people with different racial backgrounds. From this perspective, it makes perfect sense that test scores are dissimilar.

When sociologists make reference to the social construction of race, we are making clear that there are not innate physiological or mental differences between people of different races. Instead, many of us have come to believe that there are essential differences between people in different racial groups that do not exist. Some of us may believe that one race is better at this activity or one race is better at that social activity. That is precisely because race is socially constructed and we have attached social meanings to unrelated biological qualities.

● RACE RELATIONS AND ETHNIC TENSIONS IN THE UNITED STATES

There have been racial tensions in the United States since its founding. The colonists questioned the Native peoples' looks and their lifestyles upon their first encounter. They thought of the Native peoples as a different race who were lower in caliber than themselves. This same set of beliefs justified the enslavement of people with African heritage for centuries. In subsequent decades, early European Americans perceived Mexicans and other Hispanics as essentially unlike themselves, in both their physical characteristics and their cultural attributes. These beliefs allowed for differential treatment with various and often severe consequences. Even many groups that are now defined as "white," such as Irish and Italian people, experienced profound racial discrimination historically in the United States, particularly in the 1800s.

More recently, the policies known as Jim Crow began in the early twentieth century, where many segments of daily life for blacks and whites were segregated. Schools, bus stations, highway rest areas, sports leagues, water fountains, restaurants, and hotels were segregated. During World War II, over a hundred thousand Japanese people were placed in internment camps with Executive Order 9066, signed by Roosevelt. Over forty-five years later, the one hundredth Congress determined that this order was based on "race prejudice, war hysteria, and a failure of political leadership" (US Congress 1987). As a response to Jim Crow and other forms of racial inequality, the civil rights movement emerged in the 1960s and laid the groundwork for a more equal and just society. The Civil Rights Acts of 1964 and 1968 outlawed discrimination in employment and housing. These were significant achievements.

Racial and ethnic inequalities continue, however. African Americans, for instance, are underrepresented in college and in white collar jobs while being overrepresented in prison and in poverty. African Americans, Hispanic Americans, and Native Americans are less likely to have health insurance, less likely to own homes and other sources of wealth, and more likely to be victims of violent crime than whites. Racial and ethnic tensions mediate the ways in which groups perceive and interact with each other.

Racism, Prejudice, and Discrimination

Several concepts that are frequently used when discussing race and ethnic relations need to be articulated before we continue. Racism is defined as beliefs and practices that promote superior treatment of the dominant racial group over another. As mentioned above, racism was much more overt prior to the civil rights movement. Generally speaking, contemporary racism is more subtle and often takes the form of what sociologists call racial microaggressions. A racial microaggression involves the telling of an inappropriate joke, the making of an assumption about a person's criminal past or level of education based on their race, or the use of an outdated and offensive word. In short, many minorities are still treated in a denigrating manner by others, whether it is intentional or not.

Two concepts related to racism are prejudice and discrimination. Prejudice is a general, negative attitude about a group, involving feelings of dislike or contempt. People can be prejudiced, for example, against short people, old people, those with mental illness, men, disabled people, and so forth. Although people can be prejudiced against any group, racist prejudice is restricted to that against a racial minority group. Discrimination involves *behavior* that results in discriminatory outcomes for people with particular characteristics. Discrimination can occur against people in minority groups or people in dominant groups, but it occurs more commonly, and more consequentially, against those in minority groups. Examples of individual discrimination against racial minorities include white landlords refusing to rent apartments to Hispanic tenants, white police officers being more likely to stop black motorists than white motorists, and white employers being reluctant to hire minority candidates. Institutional discrimination is when the policies of an organization are being followed and there are discriminatory outcomes. Institutional discrimination occurs, for example, when a bank gives people who live in minority neighborhoods higher interest rates on their mortgages or when a restaurant has a policy of not seating large groups of minorities.

White Privilege

The term white privilege was coined by Peggy McIntosh in the late 1980s to establish that many whites take racial problems for granted and largely remain oblivious to the challenges that minorities face (McIntosh 1988). McIntosh sees white privilege as "an invisible knapsack" of opportunities that many whites have access to but many minorities do not. In her article, McIntosh listed several dozen white privileges, which included being able to shop without being followed by store detectives and being able to use a credit card without having to prove that it is yours. In short, white privilege represents a way that minorities experience discrimination and are treated differently than others based on the color of their skin.

One form of white privilege is being able to drive in any type of car without regularly worrying about being pulled over by police officers. Driving while black is a social problem that has been studied extensively and documents that black motorists are not any more likely than whites to have drugs in the car or speed but are, nevertheless, more likely to be pulled over by police officers (Meeks 2010). In the chapter entitled "Exploring Black and White Accounts of Twenty-First-Century Racial Profiling: Riding and Driving While Black," Castle Bell, Hopson, Craig, and Robinson explain this phenomenon more fully. Using qualitative data from sixty interviews, the authors establish that black motorists are often fearful of being pulled over and have established techniques to get through any encounters with law enforcement without incident.

Stereotypes

One reason that white privilege is so prevalent in the United States is that many people cling to stereotypes of racial and ethnic minorities. Stereotypes pinpoint particular attributes that people in a group supposedly share, and exaggerate and overgeneralize them. Stereotypes can be positive or negative, but either way they do not allow for people in a group to be seen as individuals. Stereotypical images or discussions of minorities on the news and in other media have impacted how people perceive them. This can be particularly consequential when negative stereotypical views are held by those in positions of power. When politicians, judges, police officers, or school teachers engage in stereotyping, their decisions about the treatment of people in that group will likely be affected. An interesting consequence of this relates to the sociological theory of labeling. Labeling theory suggests that if people are continually viewed in a certain light by others, it may over time influence how they act. Thus, labeling can serve as a self-fulfilling prophesy where people begin to act in ways that are expected of them by others.

One group of people subject to stereotypes are Arab Americans. Many people are leery of those of Middle Eastern descent and make assumptions about them. Just as "driving while black" has become a social problem in the United States, so have "crossing the border while Middle Eastern" and "getting on a plane while Muslim." Awadi and Sharma identify many of these issues in their chapter entitled "The Sociological and Psychological Effects of Public Policies on Specific Communities in the United States: A Case Study on the US PATRIOT Act and Arizona SB 1070." Specific attention is focused on the psychological and social effects of religious and racial discrimination for many Arab Americans in Michigan following the September 11, 2001, attacks in New York City and Washington DC. This is also connected to anti-immigration sentiment in Arizona.

● THE CONTROVERSY SURROUNDING IMMIGRATION

Immigration is a controversial issue in the United States. On one hand, many people recognize that we are a nation of immigrants and that ethnic and racial diversity is an integral and positive aspect of America. People in this group recognize that our ancestors likely emigrated here from other countries and that the United States is really a mix of different cultures. On the other hand, many people have a negative view of immigrants, especially illegal ones, and feel that they are negatively impacting our collective quality of life. Many people think that new immigrants abuse social service programs like welfare, commit a high number of crimes, and take jobs from hard-working people. Moreover, many Americans are xenophobic and nativist in that they are fearful and judgmental of outsiders, disdainful of people whose first language is not English, and concerned that continued immigration will erode their way of life.

In his chapter entitled "Nativism as a Recurring Reaction to Immigration in US Democracy," Stodden defines nativism and explains that it has been a part of American life for hundreds of years. He establishes that nativism goes back to the mid-eighteenth century when many Americans, including Benjamin Franklin, expressed negative views concerning German and other European immigrants to the United States. From there, Stodden explains that many American politicians were openly nativist and worked to craft legislation that limited immigration and opportunities extended to immigrants. This anti-immigration sentiment has carried forward to contemporary politicians such as Donald Trump and Ted Cruz, whose nativist messages have struck a chord with many Americans who, themselves, feel that the country's immigration policies are too lenient.

● RACIAL AND ETHNIC SEGREGATION

Even though racial and ethnic segregation is no longer legislated, it is still very pronounced around the country. Whites tend to live in majority white neighborhoods, and go to schools and attend churches with other white people, while blacks and other minorities tend to live in neighborhoods, go to schools, and attend churches with minorities. This relates to the broader sociological concept of homophily. Homophily identifies that people's friends and family members tend to be similar to themselves in terms of education, race, social class, and age. As it turns out, American life is pretty divided along racial lines. Black and white youth, for example, tend to dress differently, listen to different music, and have different hobbies. People also tend to marry and have children with people who are socially similar to themselves.

In his chapter, "Racial and Ethnic Segregation and Integration in Urban America," Maly discusses racial and ethnic residential segregation. He argues that though segregated neighborhoods are common, there are notable exceptions. He gives a history of racial segregation, showing how its levels have changed over time. He contends that though this segregation has not abated over time, it is not natural nor inevitable. Levels of segregation are affected by employment trends, government policies at different levels, discrimination in banking, real estate and other organizations, and racial attitudes. He then gives an overview of community efforts to integrate and stabilize neighborhoods across the country.

● AFFIRMATIVE ACTION

As far back as John F. Kennedy's presidency, the federal government has been working to create more opportunities for historically marginalized groups, including racial minorities. Affirmative action refers to a broad array of policies put in place to rectify the effects of past and current discrimination. Places such as public institutions of higher education, companies with government contracts, and the military have all implemented race-based affirmative action initiatives in an effort to level the playing field. It was not intended to encourage the hiring of less-qualified minorities over more-qualified whites. In contrast, if generally equally qualified minorities and whites apply for a job or for admission into a university, or seek promotion at work, the minorities should be strongly considered for the position. This is meant to counteract the longstanding effects of white privilege and lessen the negative effects of racism. Also, there is evidence that diversity benefits outcomes in workplaces, and decision-making and learning experiences in schools.

Affirmative action was not meant to be a permanent program. Advocates have long agreed that it should be discontinued once workplaces and schools mirror diversity patterns around the country. Of course, this is a very controversial program. Many people see it as an important policy that promotes racial equality. On the other hand, many people feel that it contributes to discrimination, only this time against whites.

References

McIntosh, P. 1988. *White Privilege and Male Privilege: A Personal Account of Coming to See Correspondences Through Work in Women's Studies.* Wellesley, MA: Wellesley College, Center for Research on Women.

Meeks, K. 2010. *Driving While Black: Highways, Shopping Malls, Taxi Cabs, Sidewalks: How to Fight Back if You Are a Victim of Racial Profiling.* New York Coty, NY: Broadway Books.

United States Congress. 1987. *To Accept the Findings and to Implement the Recommendations of the Commission on Wartime Relocation and Internment of Civilians.* S. 1009, April 10. internment-archives.com.

CHAPTER 5

Exploring Black and White Accounts of Twenty-First-Century Racial Profiling: Riding and Driving While Black

By Gina Castle Bell, Mark C. Hopson, Richard Craig, and Nicholas W. Robinson

R acial profiling happens in numerous ways and impacts people of color in the 21st century (Schreer, Smith, and Thomas 2009; Warren and Farrell 2009). Race as a highly visible feature has been the focal point of numerous profiling arguments. Defined as "equating race with crime and using it in lieu of probable cause" (Schreer et al. 2009, p. 1432), skin color represents likelihood of committing a crime (Harris 2002, 2006).

The prevalence of profiling automobile operators (Satzewich and Shaffir 2009; Tator and Henry 2006) illustrates that the United States has not evolved into a "post–racial" society (Allen 2011). Indeed, minority drivers are regularly pulled over because of their skin color (Satzewich and Shaffir 2009). Arizona permits racial profiling through house bill SB 1070, where skin color is used to determine citizenship and officers can ask for identification (Associated Press, 2012, para. 7). Despite the Fourth Amendment prohibition of unwarranted stop and detainment by authorities, legal loopholes permit police to utilize traffic stops for investigation (Harris 1999, 2002; Harris, Henderson, and Williams 2005).

This discussion creates space for dialogue regarding racial profiling experienced by many people of color (Gabbidon 2003; Hopson 2011; Sierra, Heiser, Williams, and Taute 2010; Williams, Henderson, and Harris 2001). We position this analysis historically and are interested "discourses-in-practice," or the ways in which power is performed in "social life, in real times and places," such as while operating a motor vehicle (Holstein and Gubrium 2011, p. 344). Lived experiences with riding and/or driving while Black illustrate "discourses-in-practice" and highlight the "lived patterns of action, which historically, (presently), and institutionally 'discipline' and 'govern'" their everyday life on the road (p. 344). In this respect, prejudice is ongoing and (re)emerges in the present (Holstein and Gubrium 2011; Hopson 2011).

This article examines the following, stopping, detaining, and even harassment of Blacks or African Americans based on their racial identity (Allen 2011; Harris et al. 2005; Satzewich and Shaffir 2009), otherwise known as driving while Black (DWB). While past research depicts only Black participants' views about DWB, this study presents Black and White voices on the topic. White participants identified instances of DWB as 21st-century forms of prejudice affecting Black "community members" (Heuman 2004). Black people are not fabricating stories—in many circumstances, profiling experiences with DWB are factual, "routine, and regular" (Satzewich and Shaffir 2009, p. 200). DWB occurs when law enforcement officers shadow and stop Blacks and/or African Americans while operating a motor vehicle (Hopson 2001, 2011; Lundman 2010; Withrow 2006). DWB targets individuals because they have Black skin not because they violated traffic laws (Dixon 2006; Dixon and Linz 2000; Tanovich 2006). DWB reflects a 21st-century abuse of power by those possessing a legitimate form of authority. Such abuse violates trust in law enforcement officials who promise to protect and to serve. Instead of protecting, DWB racially "discriminates, subjugates, and oppresses" (Hylton 2010, p. 338).

We position DWB as an abusive, 21st-century form of prejudice and/or racial profiling. Prejudice is defined as a personal thought process (Ting-Toomey and Chung 2012) and involves having a preference for or against specific individuals or particular cultural group members (Allen 2011; Orbe and Harris 2008). Embedded within prejudice is the tendency to accept or reject cultural values, ideas, and groups because of one's individual, personal thoughts. Here, racial profiling indicates a preference for or against individuals belonging to specific racial groups. The following phrases exemplify prejudice: I do not like (or I only like) *tall people, short people, democrats, republicans, people who do not use proper English, Latino(a) people, Black people, White people, rednecks, rich people, gay people, fat people, Asian people, old people, poor people, Hispanics, Mexicans, immigrants, slow people, or people who suck at driving*. These examples of prejudice illustrate the "lingering effects of [mental and physical] enslavement" today (Allen 2011; Asante 2003, p. 8).

Media serves as part of a hegemonic institution perpetuating a polarizing presentation of perpetrators. Dixon and Linz (2000) noted that Blacks are overwhelmingly represented as perpetrators of crimes in television news, whereas Whites are typically underrepresented as perpetrators (Dixon 2006; Entman and Rojecki 2000). Fictional and non-fictional media production content establishes what Hebl, Tickle, and Heatherton (2000) described as stigmatized and non-stigmatized individuals. *Stigmatized individuals* (traditionally marginalized and/or co-cultural group members) have negative connotative ideologies ascribed to their existence and social position, while *non-stigmatized individuals* (dominant group members) are less likely to embody such pejorative associations. Unfortunately, all too often, the media portray Black individuals as dangerous, violent, aggressive, and likely to steal from you, sexually assault you, or sell you drugs; Blacks, as depicted on the media, are unable to be trusted (Boylorn 2008; Brown 2008, 2011; Collins 2000, 2004; Dixon 2006; Entman and Rojecki 2000). Essentially, Blacks' bodies are criminalized through television representations and then penalized personally in daily life through encounters with DWB and other forms of societal, institutional, or social prejudice.

The communication of distrust and suspicion through skin-color-based traffic stops informs Black community members that, regardless of their character, their skin continues to stigmatize. For some Black individuals, this may involve DWB. With this in mind, the following research questions are proposed:

RQ1: How do Black or African American automobile operators experience racial tensions in 21st-century United States?

RQ2: How does DWB influence drivers' and passengers' experiences when encountering law enforcement?

● METHODOLOGICAL FRAMEWORK

Sixty communicators who self-identified as either (a) Black or African American (N = 31) or (b) White or Caucasian (N = 29) and (c) who were 18 years or older were interviewed about 21st-century Black and White communication in the United States. Participants ranged from 18 to 75 years of age and were from 20 different states. Participants were recruited through snowball sampling to identify and include participants in a comfortable manner (Keyton 2014; Lindlof and Taylor 2002). Qualitative interviews were employed to gather data in person or through Skype or Facetime. The semi-structured interview schedule was pilot-tested, and changes to question wording were made (Maxwell 2005; Silverman 1993). Interviews lasted approximately 25 to 75 min and were audio-recorded for accuracy. Data were fully transcribed and re-examined to maintain accuracy (Maxwell 2005).

Owen's (1984) and Braun and Clarke's (2006) thematic analysis procedures were employed for data analysis. First, data were examined for recurrence, repetition, and forcefulness (similar meanings, repeated key words, and emphasis; Owen, 1984). Braun and Clarke's (2006) guidelines were utilized while coding: "(1) familiarize yourself with the data; (2) generate initial codes; (3) search for themes; (4) define and name themes; and (5) produce the report" (p. 87). Member checks and respondent validation served as qualitative forms of proof to clarify information and to ensure that data reflected participants' perspectives (Golafshani 2003; Lindlof and Taylor 2002; Maxwell 2005).

● DATA AND ANALYSIS

The prevalence of DWB narratives illustrates the existence of racial prejudice in 21st-century United States. Both Black and White participants explained the existence of racial tensions by discussing their experiences while operating or riding in a motor vehicle. Experiences with DWB emerged naturally during two interview moments. The first author asked participants if they ever witnessed or experienced something they felt was race related. In response, from 60 total participants, nearly 20 of the 31 Black participants and 9 of the 29 White participants shared about having experiences with DWB. Participants' easy recall of such moments demonstrates a considerable impact on their perceptions of racial tensions and prejudice. Black and White participants shared several DWB experiences representing three major themes. For Black participants, two major themes emerged: (a) Getting pulled over: Making sure I can drive away; and (b) Fear of being pulled over: The ghost of slavery. For White participants, (a) Driving while Black when White was a major theme. Each of these three themes are presented, defined, and analyzed as follows.

Getting Pulled Over: "Making Sure I Can Drive Away"

Black participants' concerns while operating automobiles centered around preparing for being pulled over, what to do when one is pulled over, and the fear of being pulled over. This theme emerged naturally when participants were asked to share experiences with 21st-century racism. *Getting pulled over* provides the context for racial tensions when stopped by law enforcement officials, while *making sure I can drive away* highlights a desire to survive the experience successfully. Out of the Black participants who explained that they feared police officers, eight identified with the need to survive the experience or drive away from it. They equally worried about the consequences of being stopped by White police officers for a traffic violation. As follows, we reflect on Black participants' thoughts about getting pulled over and surviving the experience. The best quotations and descriptions of this particular theme are provided here.

Ronald, a Black male in his 40s, explained that 21st-century racism is present while driving. To illustrate this, he discussed his experiences of being pulled over for traffic violations:

> I have been pulled over more than I care to imagine by police officers. I've had my car searched for drugs countless times and I have never once tried or experimented with illegal substances. It has happened everywhere I've ever lived: Delaware, Northern Virginia, North Carolina. I've had my car searched for drugs. I've never owned a car that I would identify as a drug dealer's car. Yet, I have had dogs go through my car a couple of times. Depending on where they catch me, I carry

myself differently. I ask questions which let the officers know that I'm not going to be the easy victim. Or so they know that I'm not going to give them a reason to overreact. I'm becoming more studious with age. Police officers scare me in a really big way … they walk around with guns and sticks. So they are already in a position of power because I don't carry a gun or a stick. Police officers are in a position to exert their power with very little repercussions or restraint in the moment. Afterwards, you know, there is a law that can review cases. But if I'm dead, that law doesn't matter. I have to make sure that I survive every police encounter. It really is about making sure that when I get pulled over by a police officer, I can drive away.

Ronald uses his personal experience with law enforcement to illustrate the power dynamic that exists between some White police officers and some Black males in different locations. He identified their carrying a gun as a powerful part of the law enforcement official-civilian relationship. Thus, not only does carrying a firearm add to the power dynamic, the location of the stop matters, too.

Finally, Ronald discussed being searched without cause. He felt that his car was not a typical prototype of a drug dealer's vehicle, yet he recounted having it searched several times. Ronald asserted that these searches occurred because he is a Black male. For Ronald, the circumstances surrounding being pulled over heighten 21st-century racial tensions and magnify the ways in which he worried about, and hoped to survive, being pulled over. In addition to hoping to survive the encounter with law enforcement officials, some Black participants also described their fears of being pulled over.

Fear of Being Pulled Over: "The Ghost of Slavery"

Almost all Black participants, 28 out of 31, described their fears of White police officers and explained dreading being pulled over. Kayla, a 21 year-old Black female, described her fear of police and DWB encounters, "Every Black person I've talked to is afraid of police officers. I'm afraid of the cops. I've never been pulled over by the cops, but I understand the fear …" For

Kayla, police officers and the possibility of a DWB encounter evoked fear and anxiety; she was not alone. Like Kayla, Vanessa, a 21 year-old some Black female from Virginia, said:

I've never been pulled over. If I ever got pulled over by any police officer, but especially a White officer, I would keep driving with my turn signal on until I got somewhere really safe. The thought of it (DWB) scares the hell out of me. I have negative thoughts about police. I've seen lots of movies and lots of news and that's scary. Hearing about those experiences, and seeing it in the media. It's not limited to the media. There are so many stories about how there was a Black person who got pulled over who reached into their pocket and got shot to death, for reaching for something that was not a weapon … It's hard to hear those stories and then get pulled over by a police officer or have interaction with a police officer and not think about it.

Vanessa feared a racially tense communication encounter would ensue if pulled over by a White police officer. Below, Rabbijn, a 40 year-old Black male, expressed how he feared driving "in his Black skin" during his 2002 drive through southern Indiana:

When I was driving through Indiana, it was late at night, I kept saying, 'Please God don't let anything happen to me or my car, because if something happens and I get pulled over, I'm going to be missing or hanging from a tree.' These are the kinds of things implanted in my head. I still think like that because of the past. It's a part of history. They [Whites] didn't like us. Even when we had Martin Luther King in the 60s, they were like, the n-word won't go away. We're going to block you from going to class. We're going to block you from going into restaurants, you can't sit on the bus, and violence happened. And we still see it on television. We have TV film footage. And so, I've got to be cautious. It was 2002 and what goes through my mind? I'm going to be missing if I get pulled over. It is terrible. It's the ghost of slavery.

Rabbijn described fearing DWB encounters, specifically the possibility of being brutally beaten and disappearing thereafter. For these specific Black participants, fear of police officers and DWB encounters transforms driving into a racially tense communicative experience. Black participants were not alone in noticing or experiencing DWB. Several White participants also shared experiences of DWB as a form of racism or racial profiling that occurred while driving as passengers with Black friends.

Driving While Black, When White

This theme illustrates White participants' perceptions that Black drivers are pulled over, not for breaking traffic laws but because they are targeted by police through racial profiling. Below, participants share experiences of being in the car with a Black friend while DWB occurred. Whites described these occasions as evidence of 21st-century racial prejudice. Matt, a 20 year-old White male from West Virginia, commented on his DWB experience:

> I think there is definitely a few things that make life a little bit more difficult if you're not White. Like, driving, this actually happened in my hometown. I've seen Black people get pulled over for absolutely nothing. I've been sitting in the car with them, driving, when it's like my friend gets pulled over. I asked him, 'Man, what were you doing?' And he was like, 'I have no idea, man, just don't talk.' I didn't see anything that he did wrong. I mean, if I would have been doing the same thing, I don't think that I would have gotten pulled over.

Matt explained how DWB is an example of racial tension that he witnessed personally. Matt's response highlighted the dividing line between different sides of town, making the divisions between Blacks and Whites visible to White participants. Next, Monica, a 23 year-old White female from Maryland, shares an experience similar to Matt's, being pulled over while in the car with a Black driver:

I've had this with my boyfriend [he is Black]. It was in Baltimore. Like we've been pulled over when I'm going the speed limit like just so the officer can come and get into his face because he's Black. And like making sure that, I was pulled out of the car, to make sure that I was okay. Like all kinds of shit, just because you know. Because like I said, we were going the speed limit. We looked a little bit lost because we were like driving into Baltimore and I don't know where I'm going. And uh, he pulled us over and didn't even acknowledge me for the first five minutes … He didn't even acknowledge me for the first five minutes that we were interacting. He pulled me over. He came over to my, the passenger side of the car, not the driver's side. And proceeded to get into the car—like get his face into the car window and be like nose to nose with my boyfriend. And like, where are the drugs? I know that they're here. And like there were drugs in the car. It was never, it was not a situation like that at all. And he just automatically assumed that we were trafficking drugs across state lines because I had an out-of-state license plate, and an out-of-state driver's license, and because it was me and my Black boyfriend driving in the car.

Monica, a White female, witnessed and personally experienced DWB, as a police officer questioned her and her Black boyfriend, who was driving the car. In addition to DWB reflecting racial profiling, Monica explained that the situation became increasingly racially tense as the police officer, asked "… Where are the drugs…?," assuming they were trafficking drugs across state borders. Monica noticed the police officer assumed the worst about her Black boyfriend. DWB led Monica and Matt to consider the persistence of covert racial tensions.

Discussion

Research Question 1 inquired how Black or African American automobile operators experience racial tensions in 21st-century United States. Data indicate that some Black individuals experience racial tensions while operating a motor vehicle. Not only did Black participants overwhelmingly respond by sharing experiences of DWB, they also revealed their primary objective: surviving the traffic violation. Black participants also noted changing their communicative behavior when they were pulled over in different regions. In many respects, the first research question illustrates the ways in which Black community members utilize varying strategies to mitigate racial tensions during traffic violations, whether the violation was real or fabricated. Although co-cultural theory was not involved in this analysis, participants' actions reveal the utilization of various communicative strategies to help them achieve their overall goal: survival.

Research Question 2 explored how DWB influences drivers' and passengers' experiences when encountering law enforcement. Results indicate that DWB affects Black drivers and White passengers alike. Black participants explained that their fear of police officers rises during traffic stops. Black community members also indicated a general fear of being pulled over while operating a motor vehicle. The power that law enforcement officials hold during traffic stops, and the historical representations of power throughout slavery, reconstruction, Jim Crow, the U.S. civil rights movement, and beyond, all affected the mindset of Black drivers. Further, Black participants were also influenced by stories about DWB from friends and through the media. Narratives recounted by friends, loved ones, or television also created fear for Black drivers and White passengers. Fear makes DWB a racially tense communicative interaction for drivers and passengers alike.

Finally, White passengers also noticed DWB and were influenced by Black drivers' fears. Therefore, for the White passengers, there was no doubt about it: There was no traffic violation, yet their Black friend's car was pulled over. In many respects, although unfortunately so, White participants' voices add legitimacy to an argument some people attribute to "hyper-tense," oversensitive Black perspectives. DWB is real in different ways because Whites experienced it; however, perhaps it is only more present. Arguably, the White recognition of DWB adds credibility from the non-stigmatized community to the voices of the stigmatized Black community. From the results of this research, further study of White perceptions of DWB could address political and social implications relating to racial profiling and seek to bring about change.

Conclusion

For some time now, it has been understood that members of the Black community have expressed experiencing racial prejudice and tension as a result of racial profiling while operating automobiles. Surprisingly, exposure for the White community has come not only through the retelling of these experiences by Blacks and media reports, but also through personal experience. White participants report instances of profiling—where they witnessed Black drivers being pulled over by police officers, although no traffic violation occurred. Participants' experiences insinuate a continued racial tension between Black individuals and White law enforcement officers. While the United States has made valuable strides, we still have prejudices to overcome.

References

Allen, B. J. (2011). *Difference matters: Communicating social identity*. Long Grove, IL: Waveland Press.

Asante, M. K. (2003). *Erasing racism: Survival of the American nation*. NY: Prometheus Books.

Associated Press. (2012, September 5). Judge Oks "show me your papers" provision of Arizona law SB 1070. Retrieved from http://www.npr.org/blogs/thetwo-way/2012/09/05/160635960/judge-oks-part-of-arizonas-immigration-law

Boylorn, R. M. (2008). As seen on TV: An autoethnographic reflection on race and reality television. *Critical Studies in Media Communication, 25*(4), 413–433.

Braun, V., and Clarke, V. (2006). Using thematic analysis in psychology. *Qualitative Research in Psychology, 3*, 77–101.

Brown, T. (2011). Scripting the Black male athlete: Donovan McNabb. In R. L. Jackson and M. Hopson's (Eds.), *Masculinity in the black imagination: Politics of communicating race and manhood* (pp. 147–168). New York: Peter Lang.

Brown, T. J. (2008). "I am who I am": Black masculinity and the interpretation of individualism in the film *Barbershop. Qualitative Research Reports in Communication, 9*, 46–61.

Collins, P. H. (2000). *Black feminist thought*. New York: Routledge.

Collins, P. H. (2004). *Black sexual politics: African Americans, gender, and the new racism*. New York: Routledge.

Dixon, T. L. (2006). Psychological reactions to crime news portrayals of Black criminals: Understanding the moderating roles of prior news viewing and stereotype endorsement. *Communications Monographs, 73*, 162–187.

Dixon, T. L., and Linz, D. (2000). Overrepresentation and underrepresentation of African Americans and Latinos as lawbreakers on television news. *Journal of Communication, 50*, 131–154.

Entman, R. M., and Rojecki, A. (2000). *The Black image in the White mind: Media and race in America*. Chicago, IL: The University of Chicago Press.

Gabbidon, S. L. (2003). Racial profiling by store clerks and security personnel in retail establishments: An exploration of "shopping while Black." *Journal of Contemporary Criminal Justice, 19*, 345–364.

Golafshani, N. (2003). Understanding reliability and validity in qualitative research. *The Qualitative Report, 8*, 597–607.

Harris, D. A. (1999). Driving while Black: Racial profiling on our nation's highways. *American Civil Liberties Union special report*. Retrieved from http://www.aclu.org/racial-justice/driving-while-black-racial-profiling-our-nations-highways

Harris, D. A. (2002). *Profiles in injustice: Why racial profiling cannot work*. New York: The New Press.

Harris, D. A. (2006). The war on terror, local police, and immigration enforcement: A curious tale of police power in post-9/11 America. *Rutgers Law Journal, 38*, 1–60.

Harris, D. A., Henderson, G. R., and Williams, J. D. (2005). Courting customers: Assessing consumer racial profiling and other marketplace discrimination. *Journal of Public Policy and Marketing, 24*, 163–171.

Hebl, M. R., Tickle, J., and Heatherton, T. F. (2000). Awkward moments in interactions between non-stigmatized and stigmatized individuals. In T. F. Heartherton, R. E. Kleck, M. Hebl, and J. Hull (Eds.), *The social psychology of stigma* (pp. 276–306). New York: Guilford Press.

Heuman, A. N. (2004). *Toward an ethic of speaking with: Articulating a politics of location in cultural communication research* (Unpublished Doctoral Dissertation). Bowling Green State University, Bowling Green, Ohio.

Holstein, J. A., and Gubrium, J. F. (2011). The constructionist analytics of interpretive practice. In N. K. Denzin and Y. S. Lincoln (Eds.), *The SAGE Handbook of Qualitative Research* (pp. 341–357). Thousand Oaks, CA: Sage.

Hopson, M. C. (2001). Observations of DWB: A very real issue. *The Journal of Intergroup Relations*, 77–79.

Hopson, M. C. (2011). *Notes from the talking drum: Exploring Black communication and critical memory in intercultural communication contexts*. Cresskill, NJ: Hampton Press.

Hylton, K. (2010). How a turn to critical race theory can contribute to our understanding of "race," racism and anti-racism in sport. *International Review for the Sociology of Sport, 45*, 335–354.

Keyton, J. (2014). *Communication research: Asking questions, finding answers*. New York: McGraw-Hill.

Lindlof, T. R., and Taylor, B. C. (2002). *Qualitative communication research methods*. Thousand Oaks, CA: Sage.

Lundman, R. J. (2010). Are police-reported driving while Black data a valid indicator of the race and ethnicity of the traffic law violators police stop? A negative answer with minor qualifications. *Journal of Criminal Justice, 38*, 77–87.

Maxwell, J. A. (2005). *Qualitative research design: An interactive approach*. Thousand Oaks, CA: Sage.

Orbe, M. P., and Harris, T. M. (2008). *Interracial communication: Theory into practice* (2nd ed.). Thousand Oaks, CA: SAGE Publications, Inc.

Owen, F. (1984). Interpretive themes in relational communication. *Quarterly Journal of Speech, 70*, 274–287.

Satzewich, V., and Shaffir, W. (2009). Racism versus professionalism: Claims and counter-claims about racial profiling. *Canadian Journal of Criminology and Criminal Justice, 51*, 199–226.

Schreer, G. E., Smith, S., and Thomas, K. (2009). Shopping while Black: Examining racial discrimination in a retail setting. *Journal of Applied Psychology, 39*, 1432–1444.

Sierra, J. J., Heiser, R. S., Williams, J. D., and Taute, H. A. (2010). Consumer racial profiling in retail environments: A longitudinal analysis of the impact on brand image. *Brand Management, 18*, 79–96.

Silverman, D. (1993). *Interpreting qualitative data*. Thousand Oaks, CA: Sage.

Tanovich, D. M. (2006). *The colour of justice: Policing in Canada*. Toronto: Irwin Law.

Tator, C., and Henry, F. (2006). *Racial profiling in Canada: Challenging the myth of "a few bad apples."* Toronto: University of Toronto Press.

Ting-Toomey, S., and Chung, L. C. (2012). *Understanding intercultural communication*. New York, NY: Oxford University Press.

Warren, P. Y., and Farrell, A. (2009). The environmental context of racial profiling. *The Annals of the American Academy of Political and Social Science, 623*, 52–53.

Williams, J. D., Henderson, G. R., and Harris, A. M. G. (2001). Consumer racial profiling: Bigotry goes to market. *Issues and Views, 17*, 22–24.

Withrow, B. L. (2006). *Racial profiling: From rhetoric to reality*. Upper Saddle River, NJ: Pearson/Prentice Hall.

CHAPTER 6

The Sociological and Psychological Effects of Public Policies on Specific Communities in the United States: A Case Study on the US PATRIOT Act and Arizona SB 1070

By Ali Awadi and Meena Sharma

● INTRODUCTION

The devastating attacks on September 11, 2001 affected how Arab American Muslims are perceived by many in America (American–Arab Anti-Discrimination Committee 2011). The negative perceptions surrounding them increased the challenges for members of this religious and cultural group to fully integrate and assimilate into American society (Syed 2006). Historically, many Muslim immigrants found that they could best assimilate by attempting to conceal their

Ali Awadi and Meena Sharma, "The Sociological and Psychological Effects of Public Policies on Specific Communities in the United States: A Case Study on the US PATRIOT Act and Arizona SB 1070," *Middle East Review of Public Administration*, vol. 1, no. 1, pp. 2-7. Copyright © 2015 by Association for Middle Eastern religious and ethnic identities. After 9/11, Arabs and Muslims in the United States found it increasingly difficult to change the negative perceptions about their communities (Alsultany 2012). Regardless of these obstacles, many in this community kept their focus on retaining their religious and cultural identities while still working towards assimilation and integration. Arab American Muslims continue to develop productive ways to confront these issues while more actively participating in the social and political arenas of American society (Smith 2011).

The vast amount of diversity in the Arab American Muslim communities has challenged researchers. In order to report how the population is affected by internal and external forces, qualitative researchers have studied a multitude of experiences that are as complex as assimilation and integration, particularly in the milieu of increased anti-Islam and anti-Arab sentiment since 9/11 (Ali, et al. 2011; Pew Research Center 2011). The feeling of being a target in society has resulted in both subtle and apparent lifestyle changes that impact on their freedom to practice the Islamic faith without fear. Arab Muslims in the United States today continue to face challenges of identity, educational and occupational choices and opportunities, dress, religious expression, and acculturation with various racial and ethnic Muslim groups (Haddad 2007).

In recent times, many nations have enacted laws or policies that unequivo-cally target Muslim residents (Kuru 2009). These decisions were solely or partially related to a violent incident caused by the actions of extremists' who claim to be Muslim. Consequently, policies that affect an ethnic or religious group create a recipe for disorder and betrayal. For this reason, it has become increasingly important for public policy professionals to understand the impact of policy in relation to actual assimilation and integration experiences of the current minor-ity groups in America (Pew Research Center 2011). Current research indicates that these policies can serve as a deterrent for Arab Muslims in America to fully assimilate into mainstream American culture (Awadi 2014). Therefore, the abil-ity to have policies and decisions implemented effectively has been a concern for public policy makers in the aftermath of 9/11. In actuality, the creation, implementation, and delivery of particular policies that were intended to make life easier for Arab Americans have caused them more discomfort.

● IMPACT OF THE USA PATRIOT ACT

It is without a doubt that the attacks of 9/11 uncovered the United States' vulnerability to violence. As a result, the US enhanced their anti-terrorist strategies in hopes of preventing future attacks by directing their attention to both foreign and domestic terrorists. For example, one month after the dreadful attacks on the World Trade Centers, Congress passed the USA PATRIOT Act of 2001. The title of this Act is constructed of a ten-letter backronym (USA PATRIOT), which stands for Uniting and Strengthening America by Providing Appropriate Tools Required to Intercept and Obstruct Terrorism. This Act provided unlimited strength and resources to law enforcement agencies at all levels in the United States. Many agencies used this boost of power to keep a watchful eye on anyone who appeared to be tied to the Muslim faith not limited to Arab, African, Hispanic, and Asian Americans. However, what the government did not foresee is the discrimination factor in this policy, or they were ignorant of the psychological and sociological effects of this maltreatment. Muslims who practice their faith have described feelings of intimidation, shame, and discouragement from openly engaging in activities such as attending prayer services at a local mosque (Shamas and Arastu 2012).

● THE IMPLICATIONS OF THE USA PATRIOT ACT: IMPACT ON PHYSICAL AND MENTAL HEALTH

From a social science perspective, there exists both psychological and sociological adverse effects of public policies. An example, the USA PATRIOT Act inadvertently targeted Arab and Muslim Americans or anyone who resembled that group by allowing law enforcement agencies to investigate without rights or constitutional limitations. Although, this Act is just one legal element affecting human rights in the United States, it appears to be the one that has had the largest impact on this population.

For instance, a study of Arab American Muslims in Michigan (Awadi 2014), revealed how this policy has led participants to experience racial and religious discrimination that affected their family situations, education, career advancement opportunities, or even continue to work without incident at their job. Awadi (2014) explained that participants in the study either decided to continue to practice their Islamic faith or distance themselves from their religion altogether. Some of the themes derived from the study presented how the effects of 9/11 impacted their assimilation efforts along with cultural and religious identity. Additionally, the study revealed that discrimination against Arabs and Muslims caused them to experience various psychological issues. As a result of these unfortunate circumstances, participants began to employ their coping methods, which varied between these two generations.

● COPING WITH POLICY: FIRST AND SECOND GENERATION DIFFERENCES

Differences in assimilation efforts for first generation and second generation Arab American Muslims were personally expressed during interviews. The way in which these two generations reacted to, and were affected by, the public policy counter-terrorism initiatives, such as the USA PATRIOT Act, was especially interesting. First-generation participants, who experienced government-sanctioned religious and political repression and witnessed racial discrimination against others in their homelands, were much more tolerant of the ramifications of the post 9/11 US public policy initiatives. This group was also overwhelmingly grateful and relieved to be able to live in relative freedom. On the other hand, second-generation participants were more likely to feel that the United States was their country and therefore felt that their rights as American citizens were being attacked and invalidated. They expressed disappointment with American government policies that they felt were threatening their rights as native-born American citizens (Awadi 2014). This generation recognized that to assimilate into American society, they must understand that elected officials of federal, state, and local governments will continue to perpetuate the notion that Arabs, Muslims, Islam, and Shari 'a are threats to the security of the United States and disrupt the American way of life (Pew Research Center 2007).

ARIZONA SB 1070: SUPPORT OUR LAW ENFORCEMENT AND SAFE NEIGHBORHOODS ACT

Lopez (2011) conducted a qualitative study that focused on the impact of the Arizona's immigration law on its youth. This legislative act was signed into law in 2010 is known as the "Support Our Law Enforcement and Safe Neighborhoods Act" and is the harshest anti–illegal immigration law in the United States to date. Similar to the USA PATRIOT Act, Lopez (2011) describes an abundance of evidence that reveals the negative implications of SB 1070 on both individuals and their families. The complexities of immigration status has not only been on undocumented immigrants but also for many young citizens and legal residents facing problems such as instability in families, limited educational opportunities and a constant fear of institutions and law enforcement. The USA PATRIOT Act and the Arizona immigration law (SB 1070) both focus on the sociological and psychological ramifications of public policy.

THE IMPLICATIONS OF SB 1070: IMPACT ON PHYSICAL AND MENTAL HEALTH

While SB 1070 was not the first Arizona state law that addressed the illegal immigration issue, it was the most powerful one because it required many youth and their families to undergo a wide range of emotions and lifestyle changes. Interestingly, many (Mexican) families only heard about the law from television and radio media and it soon became the most talked about at home (Lopez 2011). Participants in this study used keywords such as "panic" and "fear" when describing their reaction after the law was passed. The 9/11 Commission encouraged Americans to establish a border and immigration system, including law enforcement, that sends a message of welcome and tolerance (Ong Hing 2006). Clearly that was not the case with this law and many Mexican families felt they were the intended target of SB 1070, which affected their emotions on a more personal level. As a result, this exposure to stressful family circumstances could inevitably leave a damaging impact on physical and mental health.

Likewise, Thoits (2010) describes "stress proliferation" as a process in which an initial stressor gives rise to additional stressors. This idea is parallel to a rippling effect where one problem leads to another in ones' life and can multiply immediately or over time. Her research highlights a critical finding that occurs in childhood. In this early stage of life, events and strains that generate stressful experiences, led to further stressors in later life. Thus, childhood stressors harm adult mental health both directly and indirectly through a process of stress accumulation. Furthermore, stress proliferates across the generations. For example, this proliferation spans to close social relationships, adversely affecting the members (Thoits 2010).

Accordingly, stress proliferation processes play a part in the reproduction of social disadvantage from one generation to the next. The SB 1070 passage created a path for destruction for Mexican families in Arizona. Lopez (2011) discusses how one family's tension over the potential departure from Arizona caused the parents to separate. As a result, an older daughter dropped out of college and returned home to assist her family financially while the parents were separated. The "fear" factor within the affected families caused vast amounts of confusion and anger. Lopez (2011) also described how some youth had conflicts with their parents about leaving Arizona. Additionally, distress manifested itself on school grounds when a school volunteer witnessed seeing Mexican children "giving little pieces of paper to the other kids" and telling them "have these papers so that they don't stop and take you" (Lopez 2011). It was also reported that schools had an increased level of stress-related health problems as a result of increased anger and aggression by many youth and their family members.

● THE COMPLEXITY OF POLICY: THE USA PATRIOT ACT AND SB 1070

The mixture of xenophobia and racism is fueled by lawmakers who enact policies without merit or research. A possible result of this could be a negative perception from the greater American society towards the targeted ethnic or religious community. Hence, the reaction to these policies may cause fear, hatred, and discrimination. Research conducted on two distinct populations in the United States show similar issues as a result of unfounded and improper policies. Research carried out by Awadi (2014) demonstrated how Arab and Muslim Americans are forced to change their ethnic and religious identity out of fear and anxiety while Lopez (2011) explained how policies put the safety of Arizona's youth in jeopardy, has undermined education, and has destroyed Mexican families. Both papers established a common outcome, which is the feeling of betrayal by the American people resulting from the public policies enacted.

Conclusion: Policy Recommendation and Future Research

Part I of this research will provide public policy professionals with additional scholastic knowledge that will aid in the design and implementation of policies. It is of the utmost importance to have appropriate policies in place since it is not only crucial to the well-being of individual groups in society but to also establish a rule of law within a nation. However, prior to policies being imposed, they must be supported by factual and intensive research in order to prevent the segregation of ethnic, racial, and religious communities that are directly affected. Furthermore, public policy officials will gain a better understanding of the vast array of diversity that is considered the fabric of the United States.

What is needed now is for researchers and policymakers to pay more attention to the unique issues that these populations must confront. Often times, what is hidden from public view are the daily stressors endured. The evidence clearly documents an abundance of daily stress, mental health needs and inadequate coping resources. The various stressors encountered will further substantiate both physical and mental health over time for these individuals. Further research on the daily stressors endured due to government policies that ultimately effect mental health and well-being will be conducted in Part II of this study.

References

Ali, W., Clifton, E., Duss, M., Fang, L., Keyes, S., and Shakir, F. (2011). *Fear, Inc.: The roots of the Islamophobia Network in America*. Center for American Progress. Washington: Center for American Progress.

Alsultany, E. (2012). *Arabs and Muslims in the Media: Race and Representation after 9/11*. New York: New York University Press.

American-Arab Anti-Discrimination Committee. (2011, June 15). *Action Alerts*. Retrieved June 15, 2011, from American-Arab Anti-Discrimination Committee: http://adc.org

Awadi, A. (2014). *How the Events of 9/11 Shaped the Lives of Arab American Muslims in American*. Walden University. Dearborn: Dissertation.

COJEP International. (2010, October 8). *A proposed definition of Islamophobia*. Retrieved May 14, 2012, from COJEP International: http://www.cojep.com/en/islamofobia_varsova.html

Haddad, Y. (2007). The Post-9/11 Hijab as Icon. *Sociology of Religion, 68*(3), 253–267.

Kuru, A. T. (2009). *Secularism and State Polices Toward Religion: The United States, France, and Turkey*. New York: Cambridge University Press.

Lopez, T. (2011). *LEFT BACK: The Impact of SB 1070 on Arizona's Youth*. Tucson: The University of Arizona.

Ong Hing, B. (2006). Misusing Immigration Policies in the Name of Homeland Security. In B. Ong Hing, *Deporting Our Souls; Values, Morality, and Immigration Policy* (pp. 140–163). New York: Cambridge University Press.

Pew Research Center. (2007). *Muslim American, Middle Class and Mostly Mainstream*. New York: Pew Research Center.

Pew Research Center. (2011). *Muslim Americans: No signs of growth in alienation or support for extremism*. Washington: Pew Research Center for the People and the Press.

Shamas, D., and Arastu, N. (2012). *Mapping Muslims: NYPD Spying and its Impact on American Muslims*. City University New York. New York: CUNY School of Law.

Smith, J. (2011, April 3). *Patterns of Muslim Immigration*. Retrieved January 30, 2013, from Muslim Life in America: http://infousa.state.gov/education/overview/muslimlife/immigrat.htm

Syed, F. (2006). *A comparative study of immigrant Muslims in the United States and the United Kingdom*. The University of Pennsylvania, The Lauder Institute. Philadephia: The University of Pennsylvania.

Thoits, P. (2010). Stress and Health: Major Findings and Policy Implications. *Journal of Health and Social Behavior*, pp. 41–53.

U.S. Department of Justice. (2006, March). *Patriot Act Report by the DOJ Inspector General*. Retrieved July 2012, from United States Department of Justice: http://www.usdoj.gov/oig/special/03-06/chapter1.htm

Xie, Y., and Greenman, E. (2005). *Segmented assimilation theory: A reformulation and empirical test.* University of Michigan Institute for Social Research, Population Studies Center. Ann Arbor: University of Michigan Population Studies Center.

CHAPTER 7

Nativism as a Recurring Reaction to Immigration in US Democracy

By William P. Stodden

W hy did nativism and distrust of immigrants suddenly gain traction in the 2016 election? What does the adoption of this ideology among populist politicians and their supporters in the electorate mean for the future of the Republican Party, and the United States as a whole? To find answers to these questions, one need only briefly review the history of nativism in the United States. Doing so reveals that the turn against immigrants and toward nativism is a regularly recurring theme in the history of US democracy. We can also notice from a historical perspective that the groups that adopt nativism soon disappear from the political scene in the United States. But socially speaking, nativism is a tool of opportunistic political leaders who seek to stoke the fear and apprehension of people who suffer from unmet expectations. Nativism is a social problem that is a product of the democratic process itself.

In this chapter, I first discuss what nativism is, specifically in the context of the United States of America. Then I recount the history of nativism among American voters throughout our 225-year history. Finally, I draw parallels between historical nativist movements and the most recent example in 2016, and suggest some possible vectors for future development of the movement. In all, this chapter demonstrates that the 2016 episode of nativism is more or less a response to unmet expectations following the financial crisis of 2008 and the election of the nation's first black president. But if history is any indication, it will ultimately backfire on its practitioners and adherents in a way that will ensure more, not less, openness to immigration and socially progressive policy in the United States.

● THEORIES OF NATIVISM: DISTRUST AND UNMET EXPECTATIONS

Nativism, for the purposes of this discussion, is defined as "the active opposition to new immigrants and the changes they bring to the larger society" (Burghart and Zeskind 2012). Within this definition, there are several key points that conceptually separate nativism from racism and xenophobia, though these two concepts are often undercurrents in nativism. In nativism, the focus is on *new* immigrants: the new immigrants could hypothetically come from the same country of origin as the nativist's own ancestors, and would therefore be of the same "race" and maybe even the same ethnicity or nationality, but the opposition to late arrivals is what defines nativism. It is therefore not correct to say that nativists are opposed to immigration, nor do they have any problem with the fact that their own ancestors were immigrants. They are actually opposed to *new arrivals*.

Additionally, the opposition is not necessarily based on a fear of foreigners who remain "at home" or the cultural and ethnic characteristics of foreigners, but on their arrival here and the changes that will result in the inevitable mixing of the cultures of the recently arrived and the native population. Because of these important distinctions, it is not appropriate to confuse nativists with racists and xenophobes: a nativist may very well be a racial supremacist and/or have an enduring hatred or fear of those things that are foreign, but it is also possible that a nativist merely seeks to protect what she or he has from change which she or he believes will adversely affect his or her life.

We must also be very careful when using the term "nativism" itself, because this term is loaded with meaning and connotation. When we talk about nativism, we implicitly raise matching questions about "Who is the native?" and "Who is the outsider?" More importantly, we must also ask, what is the native culture, how did it get that way, and who decides this? To answer these questions, it is important to remember that culture itself is constructed by those who live it. What is "American" in 2016 has a completely different set of cultural characteristics than those belonging to people living in the nineteenth century. Whether nativists wish to acknowledge it or not, our "culture" is the product of a nearly constant aggrandizement by people arriving from different places. Nonetheless, nativists across the history of our country have asserted that there is not only a specific "culture" in the United States at any given time, but that recent arrivals would somehow diminish that "cultural experience" for those already living here. So while it may be very difficult for an outsider to nail down specifically what it is that nativists are attempting to defend, for the nativist, the thing they are attempting to protect is quite clear, and very real for them.

Nativism arises from a lack of trust of people or groups that are perceived to be "outside" of the mainstream, as it is currently construed. Mutual identification and recognition of similar cultural traits aids in the building of trust between communities—the farther apart these traits between two groups are, the less likely the two groups are to trust one another (Crepaz, Polk, Bakker, and Singh 2014). This trust is important because it lessens people's anxieties and allows us to be at ease around those who we do not know personally. But this trust is an individual feature: an individual who tends to trust those like him or her more than those who are not part of his or her own group tends to be more inclined to adopt nativism. Conversely, those who tend to trust outsiders as much or more than members of their own group tend to be less inclined toward nativism. Another way to see this concept is a strong *particularized trust* in those who share many of the same cultural traits, or a more *generalized* type of trust in people who may or may not share the same cultural indicators: the particularized form of trust is indicative of high *in-group trust*, while the more generalized trust demonstrates high *out-group trust* (Lei and Vesely 2010).

This definition has important implications for nativism in an age of high uncertainty, both about domestic economic and social conditions and international insecurity being driven by militant religious groups with radical political motivations. We see that people who do not already possess strong out-group trust tend to experience anxiety about people who are not "like them." This anxiety stems from uncertainty: the social and cultural norms of the United States are rapidly changing around us, the economic outlook is no longer certain for large segments of America's working populace, and terrorism and fanaticism is seemingly everywhere abroad. For those people who do not embrace the rapidity of the changes occurring, the turbulence can be disconcerting, and this can lead to great resentment and decreasing levels of trust among individuals toward people who do not look, act, or think like them.

When looking for the source of nativist appeals in society, it may be tempting to place the onus on economic hardship and dislocation associated with the regular boom-bust cycle of capitalism alone. Conventional wisdom and classic liberal economic theory holds that economic crises feeds nativism. According to the argument, during a contraction of the economy, a nativist appeal can be very attractive for the segment of the population that will be hurt most by increasing direct competition for fewer and fewer jobs (see, e.g., Goldstein and Peters 2014; Rogowski 1987).

A competing argument, however, which is borne out with empirical data consisting of actual voter behavior, suggests that nationalist political appeals based on the fear of economic competition by themselves often fail to persuade native workers who see immigrant competition as suffering from the same set of circumstances that they are. When people believe that pain is being *shared* across society, rather than being borne disproportionately by themselves, the appeal of demagogues promoting a populist and nativist message tends to evaporate, because workers begin to see themselves as being "all in the same boat" (Bloom 2012). But seeing this shared pain requires a sense of commonality, as well as the perception that the pain is indeed shared equally across all groups in society: if those two criteria are missing, the nativist appeal becomes more attractive.

Bearing this in mind, other data demonstrate that perception of cultural assimilation or simply a prejudicial attitude toward immigrants has some bearing on an individual's susceptibility to nativist appeals (Goldstein and Peters 2014). The argument states that a perceived rapid and massive influx of new arrivals with a culture that is seen to be either foreign or incompatible with the receiving society, and who have not yet begun to assimilate into the larger society, will be a source of insecurity for the native population. This effect, which some argue overrides even economic competition, tends to be compounded further if the native population contains a strongly negative prejudice against the arriving population. If one is already prejudiced against other groups who are culturally distant from one's own group, their feelings of distrust and fear will likely be transferred onto all immigrant populations who are viewed as being culturally distant as well. This effect would go to explain why, for example, some minority groups who have lived in the United States for generations may nonetheless support nativism, even though they themselves might experience prejudice from the cultural majority (Dugan 2015).[1]

One other interesting feature of strong in-group trust is willingness to participate in elections and expressed preference for adherence to laws. Those who are prone to nativism also tend to be more civically minded (Crepaz et al. 2014). Briefly, the 2016 GOP contest, which was marked by high nativism, also had record turnout among Republican primary voters. Donald Trump's candidacy was given most of the credit for the high turnout, but it is also possible that those who express nativist sympathies also have an affinity for using the existing process and institutions to protect the society that they view as being under threat (Dinan 2016). In the 2016 primary contest, civic-mindedness among nativist voters was expressed often as strangers being a threat to their way of life. Among groups targeted by nativists were refugees of the Syrian civil war, whom nativists opposed because Syrians held a culture believed to be completely incompatible with the American experience.

One final explanation for the appeal of nativism has to do with a famous theory about unmet expectations and relative deprivation. In his classic work on revolutions, James Davies described a scenario where individuals have constantly rising expectations (Davies 1962). They match these expectations with their actual experience. Overall, there is likely to be a gap between the improvement in their life that they expect and the improvement that they experience, but most of the time, this gap is tolerable. Revolution, according to Davies, occurs when there is a brief setback in the meeting of these expectations, though expectations continue to increase, and the gap between expectation and reality becomes intolerable. Combined with Vanneman and Pettigrew's (1972) theory of relative deprivation, where a person perceives that his or her own group is unfairly doing worse than some other out group, nativist appeals suddenly become very salient.

There were plenty of examples of this explosive combination in the 2016 primary contest: many voters, especially among Republicans, saw society as both stacked against white, lower-educated, working-class people (which it possibly is) and as favoring social advancement of people who do not fit into the white working class, who do not share the values of the white working class, and who in many ways do not look like the white working class. This combination of unmet expectations on the part of undereducated white workers and a sense of relative deprivation made support for Trump look, in many ways, like a revolutionary movement, seemingly single-mindedly focused on ending immigration from Mexico and the Middle East as the solution to all of America's economic woes.

● HISTORICAL NATIVISM IN THE UNITED STATES

As long as the United States has existed, there has been a segment of the population, itself inevitably the descendants of previous waves of immigrants, that resented new arrivals and sought to develop policy designed to limit or eliminate further immigration. Nativist appeals are older than the United States itself. Benjamin Franklin, the early US statesman, complained that Pennsylvania was being overrun by Germans, who could "never adopt our language and customs, any more than they could adopt our complexion" (Franklin 1751). Later, Thomas Jefferson complained about the arrival of foreign "monarchists" who would influence American legislation in the direction of absolutism and "render [legislation] into a heterogeneous, incoherent, distracted mess" (Jefferson 1977a, 125). Both statements by such crucial members of the founding generation, and people who were thought to be both liberal and enlightened, demonstrate the deep roots of nativism in the experience of the country. Both statements were made concerning recent arrivals to the country, and demonstrated a sort of fear of the anticipated change that new arrivals would bring to the character of the fledgling country.

The earliest anti-immigration measures, signed into law in 1798 by President John Adams, were the Naturalization Act, the Alien Friends Act, and the Alien Enemies Act. These were more famously known as the Alien and Sedition Acts.

These laws aimed to make it more difficult for a foreigner to become a citizen of the United States, and gave the president the power to exclude, imprison, and deport foreigners who were deemed to be "dangerous" to the government (National Immigration Forum 2001). Ostensibly passed to enhance US national security during the early Undeclared War with France, some (then–Vice President Thomas Jefferson among them) also saw them as an effort to limit political opposition to the Federalist Party, and argued that the government of the United States had no power to limit the migration of individuals nor to deport them under the Constitution (Jefferson 1977b). When Jefferson became President in 1801, he allowed the Naturalization Act and Alien Friends Act to expire, though the law for deportation of "enemies" of the country, known as the "Alien Enemies Act" remained on the books with some slight modification, and was used in later episodes of deportation of foreigners.

During the 1830s, the United States experienced a massive influx of desperately impoverished immigrants from Catholic areas in Europe, specifically Ireland and Germany. Beginning in 1845, the Great Famine in Ireland, combined with various restrictive British land laws, drove nearly an eighth of the population out of Ireland, many of whom came to the United States: by the early 1850s, a quarter of the population of Boston was Irish. Land hunger was the main driving factor in German immigration during this period, though most Germans quickly moved off the east coast onto the newly opened lands of the Louisiana Territory and the old Northwest.

Nativism was the response to the large influx of Catholics from northern and central Europe. Nativist and anti-Papist political organizations soon formed, arguing that American culture was essentially Protestant and the new arrivals owed their allegiance to the monarchical Pope in Rome rather than to the republican institution in Washington, a claim that echoed the sentiments of Thomas Jefferson. These nativist organizations merged Protestantism with politics, and sought to generate exclusionary laws designed to protect an insecure population against forces over which they had no other form of control. The irony of this nativist movement was that it occurred against a backdrop of Jacksonian populism: during Andrew Jackson's administration, "the common man" was generally promoted, and the perceived leveling of American society masked a turbulent shift in the American economy from a largely land-based, rural agricultural economy to a factory-based, urban society in much of the North, while the South was being transformed from a largely small-farm subsistence agriculture economy to one dominated by cotton and heavily reliant on slavery.

One of the most significant critiques of immigration, therefore, was that foreign influences were coming to the United States and served to undermine this rise of populism and shared identity among the white Protestant population. Forgotten were the warnings about Germanization of the state of Pennsylvania and the "heterogeneous, incoherent, distracted mess" in Virginia caused by earlier waves of immigrants. The grandchildren of those immigrants now sought to use the democratic institutions and traditions of the nation to exclude others who were coming for many of the same reasons that their grandparents had come. The wave of anti-Catholic nativism, which began in the 1830s as a result of Jacksonian populism, resulted in the rise, by the 1840s, of the Native American Party, known to history as the Know-Nothings.

The Know-Nothings took their name from a nativist secret society: if asked about the society, members were instructed to answer that they "know nothing" (Levine 2001). The Know-Nothings entered politics as the Native American Party and later shortened it to the American Party, and were one of the beneficiaries of the disintegration of the old Whig Party over the issue of slavery in territories recently acquired from Mexico. The Know-Nothing Party was composed primarily of conservative, anti-Catholic, anti-immigrant former Whigs, who nominated former President Millard Fillmore, himself not a member of the American Party, *in absentia* in 1856 to run for president. Fillmore finished third in the election, behind the Democratic Party and the newly formed anti-slavery Republican Party. The Know-Nothings, however, did manage to elect governors in six states, as well as majorities in the state legislatures of nine states (National Immigration Forum 2001). This tactic of winning at the state level what they could not win at the national level has become one of the keys to nativist success ever since.

The defeat in the 1856 general election did not at the time appear to be a fatal blow to the Know-Nothings, but very soon, all concerns about Catholics and immigrants were pushed aside while the country descended into the bloody fraternal apocalypse of the Civil War, and the issue of slavery exploded as the primary cultural cleavage in American society. Following the 1857 *Dred Scott* decision, the anti-slavery Know Nothings, who opposed slavery because slaves, like immigrants, competed with free white labor for jobs, joined the Republican Party, while the pro-slavery nativists first backed John Bell's Constitutional Union bid for president in the 1860 election, and then disappeared as an organized political force, fading into the opposition, pro-slavery Democratic Party.

Nativism, however, did not disappear from the United States; it was merely forced underground for a while. Anti-immigrant sentiments reappeared just five years after the Civil War, as slavery receded from the national discussion following its abolition by the Thirteenth Amendment. Anti-Catholic nativist sentiment, mixed with white supremacism inherent in neo-Confederate sympathy, took hold of the Democratic Party in the South, and formed the nucleus of the Ku Klux Klan. Meanwhile, in California, nativists in the newly formed and tremendously popular Workingman's Party led the populist movement, which successfully promoted a new constitution for the state and various acts designed to exclude recent Chinese immigrants from legal protection and opportunities to work.

Chinese immigrants had begun arriving in California in 1850, to participate in the gold rush, and soon began finding other types of work. Generally, they prospered, and this prosperity led to resentment by Americans who arrived from the eastern states (Kanazawa 2005). White laborers, and the politicians who represented them, argued that Chinese immigrants depressed wages, practiced strange, un-American customs in their closed communities, and debased white manhood through opium addiction. By the late 1870s, the California legislature passed laws designed to exclude Chinese labor from most workplaces in California, and the US Congress passed the first Chinese Exclusion Act in 1882. The act was designed specifically to prevent any additional Chinese immigration, and remained in force in one form or another for sixty-one years.

Cultural nativism experienced another major moment in the first decades of the twentieth century. In 1906, Congress required new immigrants to possess the ability to speak and understand English as a condition of naturalization. A federal study conducted in 1911 found that immigrants who had been arriving since the 1870s from eastern and southern Europe—as opposed to those who had arrived from northern and central Europe earlier in the decade—possessed a substantially different "character." The new immigrants "were less skilled and educated, more clannish, slower to learn English, and generally less desirable than the 'old immigrants'" (Schmid 2002). The report echoed the distrust of people who were culturally further from the predominant western and central European stock, which now composed much of the American population. Other concerns once more repeated Jefferson's fear: many of the new immigrants came from despotic monarchies, and their arrival in the United States raised not only a fear that the republicanism of American society would be undermined, but also that radical ideas would spread and socialism and anarchism would take root. In 1917, Congress required a strict literacy test for all immigrants and specifically barred immigrants from Asia, which was seen as the most different from US culture of all the places in the world currently sending immigrants to the United States.

National quotas were established in the 1920s, which served to greatly limit immigration from eastern and southern Europe. Nativists in the United States saw people from these areas as genetically inferior to the Anglo-Saxon race—by which they meant western and northern Europeans, and felt that these inferior people would never assimilate into a more dominant US culture. As World War II loomed for the United States, all alien residents were required to register with the government, and many US citizens whose ancestors had come from Japan, Germany, or Italy were forced into internment camps for the duration of the war. Meanwhile, their property was infamously expropriated by their white neighbors, who offered the owners no compensation for the acquisition.

Those who sought exclusion based on cultural characteristics were not the only people who supported restrictive new laws. Organized labor was a major force in pushing for restriction at the end of the nineteenth and most of the twentieth century. The American Federation of Labor (AFL), led by immigrant Samuel Gompers, championed Chinese exclusion on the grounds that non-unionized Chinese laborers competed with higher-paid American laborers who had the right to organize in unions (Briggs 2001). In the 1920s, the AFL advocated for a zero-immigration policy from Asia and eastern and southern Europe, for many of the racialized reasons that other non-union nativists did. The AFL joined nativists in the legislature and in states in the west in seeking to end competition with Mexican labor during the 1940s, and opposed any guest worker provisions. The AFL supported strong anti-hiring laws in the 1980s, but by the 1990s had switched to supporting immigration for the opportunity to unionize immigrant labor, because the white working class was being affected by

Reagan-era policies. The switch for the AFL was a matter of survival, rather than a strong desire for inclusion.

Following World War II, nativist sentiment sunk once more below the surface, as the threat of atomic annihilation loomed over the world. Beginning in 1943, the first guest worker programs that applied to immigrants from Latin America were passed. This led to the third major wave of immigration into the United States, as low-skilled workers from Central America joined the Latinos who had lived in the United States for generations, since before Mexican losses in 1848. It is the height of irony that Latinos in the United States had always experienced discrimination from white North Americans who had first entered their territory, and then seized it by force, meanwhile promoting laws that denied legal protection to Latinos who had lived in the new territories, using nativist appeals to do all of this. Those laws were based, as we expect, on the notion that Latinos would never assimilate into mainstream American culture: they spoke a different language, were devoutly Catholic, and were not white. Also, because they were systematically denied any sort of legal protection against discrimination, they were treated as competition for jobs, and therefore, were resented by white workers. The new arrivals from the south had these same characteristics, and often experienced discrimination from the older, long-settled Latino population as well as the white population when they arrived.

The elimination of "nation of origin" quotas in 1964 was accompanied by a return of nativism, this time in the form of the English-Only Movement. The movement gained steam throughout the 1960s, and focused primarily on Latin American immigration. In 1979, the anti-immigrant cause organized into the Federation of American Immigration Reform (FAIR). FAIR had seven main principles: they sought to strictly limit the number of legal immigrants coming into the United States, oppose all amnesty and guest worker measures, tie any immigration to high wages for native labor, enforce anti-hiring restrictions and harsh penalties on American employers who hired illegal immigrants, cut down on refugee and asylum-seeking immigration, limit immigration to merely "stabilize" the American population, and eliminate special preferences for immigrants from certain countries (Federation for American Immigration Reform n.d.).

While, on the surface, this seven-point program might have seemed moderate compared to past restrictions, FAIR represented a new organized movement designed to promote "enforcement-only" immigration policies. In other words, FAIR promoted, and won, legislative battles designed to specifically limit immigration, and strengthen and enforce existing immigration policy, without any path for those who were in the United States illegally to remain here under any circumstances. In addition to their strict anti-immigration position, FAIR and other nativist organizations often expressed strongly racist and white supremacist overtones in the way they discussed immigration. The organization's founder was reportedly animated by racist concerns (Burghart and Zeskind 2012). FAIR worked closely with the Minuteman movement, which patrolled the border with Mexico, and were implicated in a number of fatal shootings of individuals attempting to enter the United States from Mexico. But this nativist impulse, like others in the past, was overshadowed by crisis: the terrorist attacks of 9/11 overshadowed other concerns, and as the focus of the nation shifted from the border with Mexico to the Middle East, border control shifted to an emphasis on national security, rather than culture.

FAIR, for its part, simply adapted. During the George W. Bush administration, this anti-immigration "establishment" exercised an effective veto on immigration reform. By 2008, the anti-immigrant establishment counted more than 1.2 million Americans as members (Burghart and Zeskind 2012). The election of Barack Obama, son of a Kenyan immigrant and an American woman, gave new impetus to the nativist movement. The president was a constant reminder that someone whose name did not sound like, and who did not look like the majority of the population of the United States, had still acquired tremendous power and influence over the direction of American life. Before Obama was elected, efforts were launched to delegitimize his candidacy for the office of president, to paint him as some sort of "other," and to represent him as a threat to the American way of life. A liberal president with an immigrant father also posed an existential threat to the anti-immigrant establishment. But the nativists remained undaunted: following Obama's election, the Tea Party appeared, seemingly out of nowhere, and its rise corresponded to the decline and replacement of FAIR and organizations of the anti-immigrant establishment.

Ostensibly, the Tea Party was opposed to being taxed to pay for the housing bailout following the financial crisis of 2008, but the nativists in the Tea Party quickly took over the faltering anti-immigrant, anti-foreigner movement. It did not start out as a nativist organization, but it soon began attracting nativist Americans, away from the "establishment" organizations. In 2010, the Tea Party ran a string of populist candidates on the national, but more importantly, on the state and local level, dedicated to, among other things, "enforcement-only" immigration policy, and experienced large victories all across the United States. Arizona's nativist governor, Jan Brewer, in league with nativist Maricopa County Sherriff Joe Arpaio, passed incredibly restrictive laws that gave state and local police the power to detain people who could not prove that they were American citizens, and seek their deportation (Burghart and Zeskind 2012). These state laws were seen as more stringent than the federal law and were challenged in federal court.

Other states also passed very strict anti-immigrant laws, and nearly a dozen states went so far as to explicitly ban Shari'a law, which serves as the basis for law in much of the Muslim world (Schachtel 2016). Immigration reform stalled out in Congress in the face of this strong anti-immigrant impulse, and Obama's executive actions taken on behalf of illegal immigrants were roundly criticized and challenged by the Republican Party, who had fully absorbed, and were largely under the dominance of, the Tea Party following the 2014 midterm elections.

● NATIVISM IN THE 2016 PRIMARY CONTEST

Both Donald Trump and his main rival during the final months of the 2016 nomination contest, Texas Senator Raphael "Ted" Cruz, used nativist sentiment to garner support during the 2016 primary contest. Both candidates called for efforts to secure both the US–Mexico border as well as a more virtual border that may potentially be crossed by political refugees from the Middle East. Trump's rhetoric, specifically, took on overtones of nativism and xenophobia very early in his campaign. In June 2015, he announced his candidacy with a speech that included the following words:

> When Mexico sends its people, they're not sending their best.... They're sending people that have lots of problems, and they're bringing those problems with us. They're bringing drugs. They're bringing crime. They're rapists. And some, I assume, are good people.... It's coming

from more than Mexico. It's coming from all over South and Latin America, and it's coming probably—probably—from the Middle East. But we don't know. Because we have no protection and we have no competence, we don't know what's happening. And it's got to stop and it's got to stop fast. (Trump 2015b)

From there, Trump went on to promise to build a wall between the United States and Mexico, and make Mexico pay for it (Trump 2015c); to force China to quit devaluing its currency and deploy the US Navy to the South China Sea to signal to China that "the US is back in the global leadership business" (Trump 2015d); and to deport eleven million undocumented immigrants from the United States, and to ban Muslims from entering the United States, "until our country's representatives can figure out what is going on" (Trump 2015a). Cruz—himself the son of a US citizen and a Cuban immigrant—essentially agreed with many of these proposals (see, e.g., Bendary 2016), and therefore offered no significant alternative to the nativist message coming from the front of the GOP pack. The nativist rhetoric used by both the Republican frontrunners virtually ensured that nativism would be a major campaign theme in the 2016 general election, and will therefore be a major force in Republican Party politics for years to come.

One indication of nativism is the preference for stronger immigration restrictions. In late March 2016, candidate Ted Cruz's proposal to give law enforcement the power to patrol Muslim neighborhoods had the support of an astonishing 70 percent of Republicans, and 45 percent overall, according to a YouGov.com and *Huffington Post* survey of a thousand voters conducted following his statements to that effect (Moore 2016). A Pew Research Center poll of 2,254 voters taken a few days later showed that 84 percent of those who backed Trump and 64 percent of those voting for Cruz supported the building of a massive wall on the US–Mexico border to prevent overland immigration. One-third of Republicans overall supported the wholesale and unmitigated deportation of immigrants who are in the United States illegally. Meanwhile, the vast majority, though certainly not all, of Democratic voters opposed these proposals (Pew Research Center 2016).

A corollary to nativism, especially in US border states, has to do with resentment at having to offer people who are in the country illegally a path to acquisition of legal protections and benefits. For example, Texas and twenty-five other Republican-dominated states filed suit in federal court against President Barack Obama's executive orders that would provide some four million immigrants a temporary legal status. The plaintiffs in this case argued that temporary legal status would make undocumented immigrants eligible for federal and state benefits. Texas claimed that legal status would make immigrants eligible for driver's licenses, which Texas claims would cost them millions of dollars (Totenburg 2016). Driver's licenses being the least of the benefits legalized undocumented workers would hypothetically acquire, opponents of reform also worry that legalized immigrants with the vote might use it to expand access to programs like Social Security, Medicaid, public schooling, and unemployment protection in states that have been trying for a long time to roll those programs back (Nowrasteh 2015).

For the anti-immigrant rhetoric of the GOP campaign, there were no corresponding calls to secure the US "border" from western European immigration or other nations that are sending the United States highly skilled immigrants. In fact, the Republican Party struggled to find a policy that simultaneously expanded the use of H–1B visas, which encourage immigration from wealthy and highly skilled populations, while ending immigration from lower-skilled and poorer places in Latin America (Trujillo 2015). Both Trump and Cruz at one time advocated for the expansion of H–1B visas (Zillman 2016), which are also favored by tech companies and other companies short on native, high-skilled labor. But as soon as the campaign began, both frontrunners changed their position on H–1B visas to fit the nativist narrative that they had adopted, calling for reform in the system to protect American workers from foreign competition. Cruz even went so far as to require an advanced degree for visa consideration and a statement from the hiring companies that detailed the efforts to hire American workers first (Cruz 2015).

Clearly, nativism was in full swing during the 2016 primary election contests. A combination of economic and cultural insecurity drove the largest number of Republican primary voters to the polls since 1980. Much of that turnout was due to Donald Trump's candidacy: his populist message was one of restoration of American "greatness" and anti-immigrant nativism. This message resonated with millions of American voters, who sought some explanation for the large-scale marginalization and alienation that they felt when economic gains of the widely touted "economic recovery" went to people who did not live like them, and social gains were made among groups who had previously been largely excluded from mainstream American society. Interestingly, the nativism expressed by Trump deflected any criticism of the socioeconomic system, which largely benefitted Trump himself, as one of the wealthiest men in the United States, and many individuals like him.

● CONCLUSION: NATIVISM IN 2016

The above exploration of nativism and its history in the United States demonstrates that there really is nothing new about the Republican Party's nativist appeal. Nativism in the 2016 primary contest is just the latest episode of a long debate between those who oppose the arrival of new immigrants and those who embrace it. One interesting trend that history shows is that nativism is always pushed aside during a war or a major national crisis. The rise of Jefferson, the Civil War, the World Wars, and the Cold War are all examples of events that occurred in the middle of a nativist wave and pushed anti-immigration sentiment beneath the surface. It always rose again, however, at a later date, when the emergency was over. And even if this wave is, like the others, subsumed below some great national crisis, it is always likely that it will be resurrected a few years later. I argue that nativism is, itself, a response to the style of democracy in this country, where people are asked what they want to do with people who themselves have no say in their fate. Of course people will fight to defend what they have, especially when they can be convinced that others are attempting to take it away from them.

More interestingly, the adoption of a hard line toward immigration by a political party appears to lead to that party fracturing and collapsing. The result has been either party disintegration, as in the case of the Federalist Party following the Alien and Sedition Acts, or the Whig Party following the Compromise of 1850 and the rise of Free Soil, or party impotence, as was the case of the Democratic Party in the second half of the nineteenth century, or the Republican Party after the anti-immigration measures of the 1920s. This is not to say that there is hard empirical evidence that demonstrates a causal relationship between nativism and party irrelevance, but the historical trend seems to suggest that there may be at least a non-random relationship between the two phenomena.

What is less clear is whether nativism hastens party demise, or the adoption of nativism is the result of party decay and collapse that is already occurring. Given the susceptibility of at least a significant portion of the electorate at any given moment to the appeals of nativism and immigrant scapegoating, politicians may adopt this platform plank as a measure of securing otherwise uncertain political support. But if this is the case, it is possible that nativism does not make for a sustainable platform, and its adoption for short term gains undermines a party's long-term base, many of whom must not be susceptible to nativist appeals, and many of whom may decide to actively oppose it. Such a split along ideological lines is fatal to a party, and at best will doom it to the political wilderness for a generation or more.

What is clear is that, by spring 2016, nativism and anti-immigrant sentiment was alive and well in the United States, specifically in the Tea Party–era Republican Party. The Republican Party leadership appeared to have largely lost all control over their party, as populist forces stormed the gates and threatened to upend the fiscal and social conservative coalition that the Republican Party built in the 1970s. Whether the Republican Party will survive this populist revolution being led, ironically, by the party's nominee for president is entirely uncertain. But what is clear is that Trump's success was due to this fear and uncertainty, much of it nativist opposition to new arrivals. This is nothing new, nor is it the last time it will likely happen. This is just another episode of voters expressing their desire to keep the blessings of American democracy and the goods provided by American economic predominance for themselves, to ensure that they get what they believe they are entitled to, and that people they believe are undeserving do not come and attempt to take a share of it away.

● NOTES

1. For example: The poll asks Latino respondents, half of whom said they were immigrants themselves, whether immigration has been good for the country, and four out of five said yes, but one in five said no. Support for *increased* immigration among Latinos is only at 36

percent, while 21 percent of Latinos born in the United States and 31 percent born outside the United States reported said they wanted decreased levels of immigration.

● REFERENCES

Bendary, J. (2016). "Obama: Ted Cruz is 'Just as Draconian' on Immigration as Donald Trump. Huffington Post, April 5. http://www.huffingtonpost.com/entry/obama-ted-cruz-immigration_us_5703eb8ce4b0a06d580705c6.

Bloom, S. 2012. "Does a Nationalist Card Make for a Weak Hand? Economic Decline and SharedPain." *Political Research Quarterly* 65 (1): 166–78.

Briggs Jr., V. M. 2001. "American Unionism and US Immigration Policy." *Faculty Publications-Human Resource Studies*. Ithaca, NY: Cornell University Center for Immigration Studies

Burghart, D., and L. Zeskind. 2012. *Beyond FAIR: The Decline of the Anti-Immigrant Organizations and the Rise of TEA Party Nativism*. Kansas City, MO: Institute for Research and Education on Human Rights.

Crepaz, M. L., J. T. Polk, R. S. Bakker, and S. P. Singh. 2014. "Trust Matters: The Impact of Ingroup and Outgroup Trust on Nativism and Civicness." *Social Science Quarterly* 94 (4): 938–59.

Cruz, T. 2015. *Cruz Immigration Plan*. https://www.tedcruz.org/cruz-immigration-plan/.

Davies, J. C. 1962. Toward a Theory of Revolution. *American Sociological Review* 27 (1): 5–19.

Dinan, S. 2016. "Donald Trump Drives GOP's Record Turnout; Democrats Lack Enthusiasm." *Washington Times*, March 1. http://www.washingtontimes.com/news/2016/mar/1/donald-trump-drives-republican-turnout-to-record-d/.

Dugan, A. 2015. "US Support for Increased Immigration up to 25%." *Gallup*, August 15. http://www.gallup.com/poll/184529/support-increased-immigration.aspx.

Federation for American Immigration Reform. n.d. "7 Principles for Truly Comprehensive Immigration Reform." http://www.fairus.org/about/7-principles-of-true-comprehensive-immigration-reform.

Franklin, B. 1751. "Observations Concerning the Increase of Mankind."http://www.archive.org/stream/increasemankind00franrich/increasemankind00franrich_djvu.txt.

Goldstein, J. L., and M. E. Peters. 2014. "Nativism or Economic Threat: Attitudes Toward Immigrants During the Great Recession." *International Interactions* 40 (3): 376–401.

Jefferson, T. 1977a. "Notes on the State of Virginia." In *The Portable Thomas Jefferson*. Edited by Merrill D. Peterson. London, UK: Penguin Press. 23–232

Jefferson, T. 1977b. "The Kentucky Resolutions." In *The Portable Thomas Jefferson*. Edited by Merrill D. Peterson. London, UK: Penguin Press. 281–289.

Kanazawa, M. 2005. "Immigration, Exclusion, and Taxation: Anti-Chinese Legislation in Gold Rush California." *The Journal of Economic History* 65 (3): 779–805.

Lei, V., and F. Vesely. 2010. "In-Group Versus Out-Group Trusta: The Impact of Income Inequality. *Southern Economic Journal* 76 (4): 1049–63.

Levine, B. 2001. "Conservatism, Nativism, and Slavery: Thomas R. Whitney and the Origins of the Know-Nothing Party." *The Journal of American History* 88 (2): 455–88.

National Immigration Forum. 2001. "Cycles of Nativism in US history." http://www.immigrationforum.org/Facts/cyclesofnativism2001.html. http://www.colorado.edu/AmStudies/lewis/1025/cyclesnativism.pdf

Pew Research Center. 2016. "Campaign Exposes Fissures over Issues, Values and How Life Has Changed in America," March 31. http://www.people-press.org/2016/03/31/campaign-exposes-fissures-over-issues-values-and-how-life-has-changed-in-the-u-s/.

Moore, P. 2016. "Divide on Muslim Neighborhood Patrols, but Majority Now Back Muslim Travel Ban." *YouGov.com*, March 28. https://today.yougov.com/news/2016/03/28/divide-muslim-neighborhood-patrols/.

Nowrasteh, A. 2015. "The Best Argument Against Immigration." *The Cato Institute*. http://www.cato.org/publications/commentary/best-argument-against-immigration.

Rogowski, R. 1987. "Political Cleavages and Changing Exposure to Trade." *American Political Science Review* 81 (4): 1121–37.

Schachtel, J. 2016. "South Carolina House Passes Bill Excluding Sharia Law from State Courts." *Breitbart News Network*, January 28. http://www.breitbart.com/big-government/2016/01/28/exclusive-south-carolina-house-passes-bill-banning-sharia-law/.

Schmid, Carol. 2002. "The Politics of English-Only in the United States: Historical, Social and Legal Aspects." In *Language Ideologies: Critical Perspectives on the Official English Movement Vol. 1*. Edited by Gonzalez, D. Rosann, and Ildiko Melis. National Council of Teachers of English. 62–86.

Totenburg, N. 2016. "Supreme Court to Review if Obama Immigration Actions Were 'Faithfully Executed.'" *National Public Radio*, January 19. http://www.npr.org/2016/01/19/463622789/supreme-court-agrees-to-review-obama-executive-actions-on-immigration.

Trujillo, M. 2015. "GOP Divided on Immigration Changes." *The Hill*, March 17. http://thehill.com/policy/technology/235948-gop-divided-on-high-skilled-immigration-changes.

Trump, D. 2015. "Donald J. Trump Statement on Preventing Muslim Immigration." https://www.donaldjtrump.com/press-releases/donald-j.-trump-statement-on-preventing-muslim-immigration.

Trump, D. 2015. "Here's Donald Trump's Presidential Announcement Speech" [Transcript]. *Time*, June 16. http://time.com/3923128/donald-trump-announcement-speech/.

Trump, D. 2015. "Immigration Reform That Will Make America Great Again." https://www.donaldjtrump.com/positions/immigration-reform. https://www.donaldjtrump.com/images/uploads/Immigration-Reform-Trump.pdf

Trump, D. 2015. "Reforming the US-China Trade Relationship to Make America Great Again." https://www.donaldjtrump.com/positions/us-china-trade-reform. https://www.donaldjtrump.com/press-releases/reforming-the-u.s.-china-trade-relationship-to-make-america-great-again

Vanneman, R. D., and T. F. Pettigrew. 1972. "Race and Relative Deprivation in the Urban United States." *Race* 14 (4): 461–86.

Zillman, C. 2016. "The Race Is on for Tech Companies to Snag Foreign Workers." *Fortune*, April 1. http://fortune.com/2016/04/01/h-1b-visa/.

CHAPTER 8

Racial and Ethnic Segregation and Integration in Urban America

By Michael Maly

    " Segregation then, segregation tomorrow, and segregation forever," shouted George Wallace on a chilly Inauguration Day in 1963 in Montgomery, Alabama. While Wallace's insistent cry was a broad rejection of integration in general, he may as well have been talking about how Americans organize residential space. Even after the Fair Housing Act of 1968, U.S. urban areas remain tremendously segregated. This should come as no surprise; a look around any metropolitan area in the United States reveals the familiar pattern—a sizable number of blacks concentrated in central cities (usually impoverished) and whites living in the suburbs or, as George Clinton of Parliament Funkadelic put it, "chocolate cities and vanilla suburbs." Most of us seem to accept this pattern as inevitable, even natural. For many Americans, residential diversity and integration may sound appealing but seem unworkable in practice, as scholars and the media highlight segregated and homogenous environments and ignore integrated ones. In our current urban landscapes, the presence of gated communities, fortresslike building developments, private security forces, racial ghettos, and a patchwork of isolated, racially homogeneous sprawling suburbs suggests that Wallace was right.

While the weight of evidence indicates that residential segregation has been a predominant feature of modern urban life, it is neither inevitable nor even universal. Racially integrated neighborhoods do exist and can remain stable. Places like Chicago's Uptown, Queens's Jackson Heights, and Oakland's San Antonio–Fruitvale exemplify this reality. And while the focus of this book is not to revisit the existence, causes, and consequences of residential segregation by race highlighted in many scholarly accounts (see Massey and Denton 1993), a brief recounting of the historical and cultural context that supports segregation as a normative, if not valued, feature of modern urban growth and development will set the stage for the story of these three racially integrated communities.

This historical and cultural context is part of what makes it difficult for us to consider integrated neighborhoods as viable and sustainable. Organizer Saul Alinsky echoed a common misperception when he characterized racial integration as merely the time between "the entrance of the first black family and the exit of the last white family" (Sanders 1970: 86). Yet there have been numerous efforts to create and promote racially and ethnically integrated communities in the United States during the last half century. Hundreds of interracial organizations in both urban and suburban communities have actively pursued and achieved stable racially integrated residential environments. The focus of this chapter is the "open housing" movement, which has largely been ignored, given the severity of segregation and its accompanying virulent effects. Communities involved in this movement have proven that despite formidable institutional and individual forces, segregation does not have to be inevitable or "forever"—integration is possible.

● THE LEGACY OF RACIAL RESIDENTIAL SEGREGATION

Segregation in U.S. urban areas did not just happen; there was nothing "natural" about the way urban residential settlement became racially homogenous. Persistent patterns of segregation and the always tenuous possibility of integration evolved over the last century. Before World War I, urban neighborhoods were not as segregated as they are today. Blacks were only slightly residentially segregated from whites and European immigrant groups of similar economic circumstances, as there were few institutional structures to concentrate residents and workers in densely populated areas (Spear 1967; Yancey, Ericksen, and Juliani 1976; Hershberg 1981; Binder and Reimers 1995). Industrialization altered this arrangement, creating densely clustered worker housing and a segregated workforce (Drake and Cayton 1945; Greenberg 1981).[1] The availability of jobs drew both European immigrants and southern black migrants to northern cities. European immigrants initially lived in isolated neighborhoods, but this isolation was short-lived and enclaves were rarely homogenous (Lieberson 1963, 1980; Binder and Reimers 1995). The story was quite different for the large number of southern black migrants recruited to resolve worker shortages and serve as naïve strikebreakers (Grossman 1989; Trotter 1985).[2] Most whites in this period viewed the increasing numbers of blacks with fear, animosity, and hostility. Whites maintained the residential color line through a variety of violent acts, ranging from personal harassment to mob attacks to bombing (Rudwick 1964; Osofsky 1968; Kusmer 1976; Philpott 1978; Hirsch 1983). After the 1920s, more subtle methods such as neighborhood "improvement associations" sprang up to maintain racial boundaries by implementing restrictive covenants and restrictions on interracial sales (Helper 1969; Connolly 1977; Bauman 1987).[3] By 1940, all the major industrial centers in the North had substantially segregated zones and maintained significant levels of segregation between whites and blacks (Cutler, Glaeser, and Vigdor 1999).

These strict racial lines in residential patterns would solidify between 1940 and 1970, as the percentage of blacks in northern cities grew dramatically after World War II.[4] Newly arriving blacks found their housing choices circumscribed to select and narrowly bounded neighborhoods. White attitudes continued to support racial discrimination in housing and the systematic exclusion of blacks from white neighborhoods (Helper 1969).[5] These attitudes translated into action; if blacks did move into the neighborhood, incumbent whites moved out and most white home seekers simply avoided the neighborhood, guaranteeing resegregation (Molotch 1972). Even before restrictive covenants were declared unenforceable in 1948, some real estate agents "eagerly exploited whites' fears by blockbusting likely areas—selling to a black family, spreading fear among whites that the neighborhood was about to change; buying property from the panicked whites at bargain basement prices; then selling it to middle-class blacks looking for a nice neighborhood at higher prices" (Judd and Swanstrom 1998: 194).[6] In addition, until the 1970s realtors were obligated to steer potential home seekers to neighborhoods whose residents shared their race or nationality (Helper 1969). These private efforts made it less necessary for prejudiced whites to use personal or communal violence to defend their neighborhoods from integration or racial change.

Federal policies institutionalized many of these discriminatory acts and exacerbated racial tensions and color lines in cities. From the 1930s through much of the 1960s, the federal government provided financial support for a housing boom that was effectively put off-limits for blacks. For example, between 1930 and 1960, the Federal Housing Administration (FHA) and Veteran's Administration (VA) provided loan guarantees that accelerated suburban development by insuring loans and easing the task of purchasing a home (Jackson 1985).[7] And while FHA and VA programs provided tremendous housing and social opportunities to households in the postwar period, they were open only to white home seekers desiring suburban locales.[8] Federal administrators of insured financing programs promoted segregated housing and neighborhoods by favoring segregation over integration, suburbs over cities, and redlining of racially mixed or minority areas (Bradburn, Sudman, and Gockel 1971).[9]

In addition, government-backed urban renewal and public housing policies sharply limited the housing supply for black home buyers and renters, contributing to racial tensions and sharp lines of racial segregation (Judd and Swanstrom 1998). The housing acts of 1949 and 1954 gave local authorities federal funds to check blight and ghetto expansion by clearing "slum" properties for redevelopment, while turning to the construction of public housing to guarantee replacement housing (Bauman 1987). During the 1950s and 1960s, local public officials with tremendous private sector pressure used urban renewal and public housing, largely in black neighborhoods, to clear and rebuild on land in growing black areas that threatened white business districts and elite institutions (Rainwater 1970; Hirsch 1983). Thus, whites had more opportunities and great incentives to leave their communities, while blacks had fewer options as urban renewal, public housing, and discrimination narrowly defined the communities open to them. Combined with discriminatory institutional practices, racial transition became a striking urban process. The ghetto expanded as a "rolling tide" or "wave" over neighborhoods as a cumulative pattern of invasion and succession took place in U.S. cities (Goodwin 1979). In a relatively short time, the population of various northern cities became virtually all black.[10] Data indicated that in the thirty largest metropolitan areas from 1940 through 1970, segregation levels peaked in northern cities in 1950, edging downward slightly by 1970. In sum, by the end of the 1960s, the average black and white lived in a residential area where the vast majority of his or her neighbors were of the same race, making meaningful contact between whites and blacks outside the workforce extremely unlikely. As a result, integrated neighborhoods were deemed temporary and unstable, bound to resegregate regardless of local efforts to alter the outcome.

Since 1970, there has been some progress toward more integrated cities and regions. For example, from 1970 to 2000, the number of metropolitan areas with exceedingly high segregation indices decreased significantly, and the number of moderately segregated metropolitan areas increased (Glaeser and Vigdor 2001; Farley and Frey 1994). Also, the percentage of whites living in homogeneous white neighborhoods decreased dramatically in both cities and suburbs over this same period (Ellen 1998; Alba et al. 1995). However, racial segregation, particularly for blacks, remains a continuing and significant factor for understanding the spatial patterns of metropolitan areas and cities. For example, the greatest declines in segregation have come in places where fewer blacks reside and where a long history of segregation does not exist (e.g., fast-growing cities in the South and West), while segregation remains high in metropolitan areas with the largest black populations (Denton 1999; Glaeser and Vigdor 2001). Also, black suburbanization did little to desegregate metropolitan areas or eliminate black-white differences in residential quality.[11] While the movement of blacks to the suburbs did signal the lifting of the suburban–urban barrier for blacks, any optimism about greater residential integration between whites and blacks was short-lived.

Finally, there remains alarming evidence that minorities (particularly African Americans) experience continued and systematic discrimination in the real estate, lending, and insurance industries. Over the last three decades, real estate markets have continued to discriminate (e.g., steering minorities away from particular areas) by excluding minorities from certain neighborhoods, particularly in racially mixed (or potentially mixed) neighborhoods (Galster 1990; Turner, Struyk, and Yinger 1991; Urban Institute 1991; Yinger 1996). Financial institutions have extended far less private credit, fewer federally insured loans, and less total mortgage money to blacks and racially mixed areas than to socioeconomically advantaged white areas (Bradbury, Case, and Dunham 1989; Shlay 1989; Squires 1994). The practice of redlining certain neighborhoods continued between the 1970s and 1990s.[12] More than thirty years after the passage of Title VIII of the 1968 Civil Rights Act, which made it illegal to discriminate based on race, racial and ethnic discrimination in the real estate and lending industries has not abated. Discriminatory practices maintain significant levels of isolation and segregation, stack the deck against racially mixed communities, and perpetuate the assumption that mixed communities are not viable.

What accounts for these variable trends? We can look to two post–civil rights changes: shifts in individual attitudes regarding integrated neighborhoods and the enactment of legal barriers to discrimination. First, as noted, attitude surveys indicated that whites largely endorsed racial segregation in the 1950s and 1960s. However, by 1990, only 20 percent of white respondents agreed with the statement that "white people have a right to keep blacks out of their neighborhoods if they want to, and blacks should respect that right," down from 60 percent in 1964 (Schuman, Steeh, and Bobo 1985). Also, several studies indicate that whites' tolerance of black neighbors has increased over time and they have expressed less desire to move as the percentage of black in-migrants increased (Farley, Schuman et al. 1978; Farley, Steeh et al. 1994). White tolerance for black neighbors, however, drops substantially when blacks represent a sizable proportion of the population (Clark 1986; Schuman, Steeh, and Bobo 1985). Whites appear to accept racially mixed neighborhoods as long as whites are the clear majority, while blacks are more likely to accept an equal proportion of blacks and whites. This gap between white and black attitudes toward integration is central to understanding the persistence of segregation.

Second, since the 1960s, the federal government has passed legislation that was meant, at least in spirit, to "dismantle systems of discrimination" that maintain racial segregation (Squires 1996: 224). The Federal Fair Housing Act of 1968 and the Equal Credit Opportunity Act of 1974 prohibited discrimination in housing and housing finance markets. The passage of the Home Mortgage Disclosure Act in 1975 and the Community Reinvestment Act in 1977 provided communities greater access to information on the location of mortgages and required depository institutions to affirmatively ascertain and be responsive to the credit needs of their entire service areas. These statutes have not eliminated discrimination in mortgage lending and real estate practices, largely because the acts put the onus on individuals and communities to recognize and fight discriminatory behavior. However, at a minimum, these acts have provided community groups tools to successfully fight discrimination and disinvestment. Though it is impossible to measure, the law and the publicity surrounding successful lawsuits arguably have served to liberalize attitudes (Farley and Frey 1994) and to deter some lenders and realtors from discriminatory practices. However, such legislation seems unlikely to unravel decades of federal and local policies that mandated segregation.

● DIRECTING DIVERSITY: THE PRO-INTEGRATION MOVEMENT

It should be obvious that the racial environment in which residential areas have existed over the last century has been one of tremendous segregation. Scholars and researchers have suggested that integrated neighborhoods are the exception, temporary, fragile, and doomed to eventual resegregation. Harvey Molotch, in his study of Chicago's South Shore neighborhood, went so far as to say that no amount of intervention is likely to reverse the process of racial transition (1972). This view, however, neglects the complexity of an important part of U.S. urban history. Urban and suburban communities over the last half century have organized and struggled to maintain a stable integrated racial composition.

Although these communities have been largely ignored or discounted by scholars as anomalies, no discussion of residential segregation and integration is complete without examining their experience. The efforts to promote stable integration, like the reality of pervasive racial segregation, are part of the sociopolitical context in which neighborhoods and residents existed during the second half of the twentieth century. These communities emerged out of the distinctive social conditions of the 1950s and 1960s, particularly the last wave of southern black migrants to northern cities, neighborhood racial transition, and the civil rights movement. Taken collectively, their efforts formed a social movement that has been referred to as the "open housing," "neighborhood stabilization," or "pro-integrative" movement. Regardless of the label, the movement centers on local reaction to racial change, reaction that includes organized and active intervention to prevent racial transition and to preserve racial integration.

These communities emerged from the civil rights movement and involved interracial coalitions working to promote the benefits of integration by developing an array of organizations, social networks, and institutions that focused directly on fostering stable integration (Nyden et al. 1998). Although these communities differ from the diverse communities that have emerged in the last two to three decades (outlined in Chapters Three, Four, and Five), there is much to be learned from them, as they provide a counterpoint to studies of racial segregation. The movement to maintain racially integrated communities provides invaluable lessons for those wishing to break down the barriers of segregation and its harsh effects. These communities show that segregation was not as universal as many scholars or common perceptions might suggest. However, their experience also reveals the depth and strength of the forces that encourage segregation.

Neighborhood Stabilization/Pro-integration

In the early 1950s and 1960s, the last wave of the Great Migration and overcrowded conditions in the established ghettos increased the number of black home seekers in northern cities. Urban renewal, public housing policies, and discriminatory practices reduced the available supply of quality housing open to blacks and as a result forced (or lured) many blacks to look for housing in older white neighborhoods. As blacks entered previously all-white neighborhoods, a variety of factors encouraged racial transition and what scholars have referred to as "invasion and succession."[13] The pattern typically went like this: a few middle-class black families, seeking to escape overcrowded conditions in the segregated zones and to gain better housing, would move into a predominantly white neighborhood. As blacks moved in, many whites took their presence as a harbinger of "change" and "decline." White fear of blacks, unscrupulous acts by the real estate community (e.g., blockbusting, racial steering), discriminatory bank policies in newly integrated areas, and other local factors (e.g., media coverage) quickened the pace of racial transition.[14] A common understanding of racial transition that emerged from this period suggests that when the size or composition of a relatively homogenous area is altered, racial transition occurs. For example, Carole Goodwin, in her book *The Oak Park Strategy*, demonstrates the link between increased black in-migration and racial change in Chicago's Austin neighborhood. As Austin's black population increased from less than 1 percent in 1960 to 32.5 percent in 1970, so did racial transition. Goodwin reports that between 1966 and 1973, 148 blocks changed from white to black, with most of this transition occurring between 1970 and 1973 as 113 blocks changed racial occupancy (1979: 48). This process occurred in city after city across the country and contributed to the notion that racially integrated neighborhoods were temporary and unstable.

In the light of rapid transitions of formerly all-white neighborhoods, a "tipping point" hypothesis emerged. This hypothesis assumes that racial transition moves gradually until the proportion of blacks reaches a threshold, the point (obviously variable) when whites no longer feel comfortable with integration or the presence of blacks in the neighborhood. Once this threshold is crossed, whites move out (often rapidly) and fewer whites are interested in moving in; the result is resegregation. A cycle is created that predictably leads to conditions that accelerate racial turnover, assures resegregation, and maintains a perception that segregation is the "natural" and inevitable outcome of city life (Keating and Smith 1996; Ottensmann 1995). The expectation is that as "other" groups "invade," the neighborhood is deemed vulnerable, making resegregation seem inevitable and integration temporary.

The tipping point, however, was not the result simply of individual preferences or comfort levels. A variety of mediating institutions and groups were influential in hastening the process of racial transition. Consider the following four: real estate brokers, lending agents, schools, and the media. The real estate community has a long history of blockbusting newly integrated areas and reaping hefty profits from the workings of the dual housing market while steering white home seekers away from black or integrated areas. Banks and other lending institutions continue to withdraw credit from commercial and residential areas experiencing racial change. Schools, a major factor in housing choices, can also work against integration. The reality is, regardless of objective standards, that predominantly white schools are perceived as superior and predominantly black schools as inferior. School officials who ignore racial imbalance in schools can prompt resegregation by fueling negative perceptions of the quality of the schools. The media has a substantial influence on individual opinion and perception, and, by and large, mass media accounts of integrated neighborhoods have been unfavorable. Terms like "open housing" or "equal-opportunity housing" are code words for housing for minorities. In sum, since larger social forces always influence individual housing and investment choices, to understand the nature of neighborhood racial change we must consider how these and other mediating institutions can (though they do not always) accelerate the process and pace of racial change. By devaluing integrated neighborhoods as attractive and inviting places to reside, these institutions have contributed to neighborhood racial change and segregated residential spaces.

Fortunately, these mediating institutions do not have complete control over the fate of a neighborhood. Residents in neighborhoods experiencing racial change do not live and move at the whim of discriminatory market forces; not all neighborhoods "tip." External factors favoring segregation cannot be downplayed, but a neighborhood's internal reactions to change also require careful consideration. In any area experiencing racial change there is always some "combination of interests, motives, and concrete acts by individuals and groups" that shapes the fate of the community (Goodwin 1979: 4). Existing residents and incoming residents react to change and thus set in motion processes that alter how communities perceive, define, and experience themselves. These processes, along with external factors, have significant impacts on the likelihood of resegregation.

A good example of this syndrome began to occur in communities experiencing racial change between 1950 and the mid-1970s. Neighborhood groups committed to integration maintenance emerged in almost every U.S. city where black in-migration and neighborhood racial change and transition occurred. For example, during the 1950s, neighborhood groups surfaced in the Boston-Edison section of Detroit, Park Hill in Denver, Shaker Heights in Ohio, Shepard Park in Washington, D.C., West Mount Airy in Philadelphia, South Shore in Chicago, and Teaneck, New Jersey.[15] Scores of other groups came to life in the 1960s and 1970s as "the knowledge and experience of earlier groups spread, as civil rights gained increasing national sympathy, and as the dynamic of racial transition reached into a greater number of neighborhoods and suburbs" (Wiese 1995: 114).[16] Although groups formed independently, in most cases the patterns of resisting resegregation were strikingly similar. Organizations began interracially and demonstrated a mixture of postwar liberalism, sympathy to civil rights, and enlightened self-interest (Wiese 1995). Group members attempted to prevent racial transition in the hope of stabilizing their community, maintaining racial integration, and avoiding resegregation (Saltman 1990). While many community members held liberal attitudes toward racial integration and civil rights, they also valued their homes, wanting neither to move nor to have their housing values plummet. As these groups became aware of each other, a national movement or umbrella organization called National Neighbors was formed in 1969. By the mid-1970s, National Neighbors represented more than two hundred such groups (Saltman 1990).

In many communities, initial organizing efforts did not center solely on racial integration, but on broad concerns of neighborhood stabilization. For example, the Sherman Park Community Association, representing a west-side Milwaukee neighborhood, was initially formed "not in response to an outside threat, but to improve the quality of life" in the area (Valent and Squires 1998). Also, it has been suggested that religious leaders in the West Mount Airy section of north Philadelphia became actively involved in efforts to prevent resegregation so members of their congregations and synagogues would not move to the suburbs (Ferman, Singleton, and DeMarco 1998). These early efforts to "defend" the community from destabilizing forces (Suttles 1972) quickly led to more "conscious communities" (Hunter 1978) and a stronger promotion of racial integration. These conscious communities reacted to racial change by adopting an interventionist approach.

The interventionist approach suggests that residents can achieve neighborhood stabilization and racial integration if they mobilize sufficient resources and institutional networks for collective action early on in the process of change (Galster 1987; Helper 1986; Saltman 1990; Taub, Taylor, and Dunham 1984). This approach puts a premium on organized community efforts to effect change. Richard Taub and colleagues expressed this view after reviewing racial change in various Chicago neighborhoods in the 1970s: "Ecological facts do not, in fact, unidirectionally determine neighborhood outcomes. Corporate and individual decisions always intervene and sometimes modify the connection between eco-logical circumstances and neighborhood outcomes.… What is clear is that inter-ventions can and do work, and that they sometimes do in situations that might be considered unpromising on the basis of historical understandings" (Taub, Taylor, and Dunham 1984: 187).

While it is often assumed that individual or community-level group action gives way in the face of brute economic forces or embedded racist institutional practices, the effect of local interventions on neighborhood outcomes requires us to factor in grassroots involvement in neighborhood development. Decades of community studies have shown that local organized efforts can intervene to shape the outcome of a neighborhood (R. Fisher 1994). And researchers have shown that community groups faced with racial change and the institutional factors that promote racial transition can intervene through an array of local (and regional) organizations, social networks, and institutions. I refer to these communities as "diverse by direction" because local groups intentionally focused on integration. Groups attempt to direct the future of their neighborhood toward stable integration by ensuring that existing white households do not panic and that the overall stability and racial balance of the neighborhood is maintained.

Pro-integration Strategies

Over the last four decades, as part of the neighborhood stabilization movement or pro-integrative efforts, numerous communities have employed intervention strategies to promote neighborhood stability and racial integration. Diverse-by-direction communities face common struggles, including proposed zoning changes that threaten existing land use (e.g., urban renewal or highway construction), the workings of mediating institutions (noted earlier), and commercial and residential deterioration—all of which encourage racial transition and segregation. In all cases, local groups shape or direct their community toward stable racial integra-tion by managing perceptions through a specific set of responses or interventions.

General Aim of Pro-integrative Efforts

In urban America, the identities of residential areas result from comparisons to other neighborhoods (Suttles 1972). This means that residential areas are sym-bolic as well as physical entities that maintain a general identity and are shaped by perceptions, real or imagined. Any neighborhood's "desirability" and the related demand for housing are strongly linked to the image of the community (Goetze 1979). Communities undergoing racial transition establish new identities, particularly in contrast to nearby or similar communities. Given the normative nature of segregation in the United States, it is no surprise that integrated neighborhoods are usually perceived as changing and unstable. Change is perceived negatively and assumed to bring lower property values, increased criminal activity, fewer municipal services, and deteriorating schools, businesses, and housing.

To promote positive views of a neighborhood's "type" and "future," communities attempting to sustain racial integration must challenge and change perceptions. Although image is not everything in a community, in the context of white racism, pervasive discrimination, and segregation, it is a key element in maintaining integrated communities. Communities experiencing racial change have taken notice of the importance of image, working to challenge the perception of instability as well as to promote positive images of racial integration. Indeed, communities experiencing success in maintaining racial integration make conscious efforts to change the social and cultural character of the community and to redefine its values and norms through private and public support for integration (Goodwin 1979; Saltman 1990; Nyden, Maly, and Lukehart 1997). This has meant making integration a stated goal, promoting it as a community strength and a part of all organizing efforts.

Communities challenging perceptions have employed a variety and combination of intervention strategies or models. One model relies on "pro-integrative" policies in area housing. Pro-integrative housing efforts involve everything from the promotion of fair and open housing to rehabilitation of existing housing stock to "affirmative marketing" strategies. These intervention strategies take aim at the dual housing market. Another general model has been referred to as community development or community building. Efforts conforming to this model deal primarily with quality-of-life and neighborhood-quality issues (e.g., crime, schools, economic development) as well as strengthening neighborhood networks and organizations to encourage greater interaction across racial lines. Underlying both intervention models is an awareness that challenging negative perceptions of racially integrated neighborhoods is a necessary step to maintain the racial balance.

Pro-integration Housing Interventions

Communities working toward maintaining racial integration must attend to the fear that racial integration will bring neighborhood decline, particularly through a lowering of housing quality and property values. Real estate agents who practice blockbusting and racial steering, owners who do not maintain their properties, lending institutions that redline the neighborhood, and interest groups who seek to alter the zoning of the neighborhood from residential to other uses—all are common enemies of integrated neighborhoods (Saltman 1990: 373). In diverse-by-direction communities, local organizations intervene in the local housing market to challenge the forces promoting segregation and pushing neighborhoods toward resegregation. Their interventions can be divided into those that seek to manage or maintain the racial integration and those that aim to encourage racial diversity (commonly referred to as "affirmative marketing") (Chandler 1992).

Interventions aimed at managing or maintaining racial integration work to replace the dual housing market with a unitary market in which all can participate (Lauber 1991). Initially, pro-integration groups focus on improving the quality of the housing stock by seeking rehabilitation funds for deteriorating properties. For example, in the late 1970s, the Sherman Park Community Association (SPCA) employed yearly windshield surveys to identify building-code violations and building deterioration. SPCA then worked with other agencies to secure block-grant funds to help low-income homeowners make home repairs (Valent and Squires 1998). Other communities have set up similar housing committees to preserve their housing stock. Given that integrated neighborhoods are typically older neighborhoods, housing maintenance and repair are vital to maintain the quality of life in a community.

However, while rehabilitating housing is initially important, the larger challenge for racially changing or integrated neighborhoods lies with the workings of the discriminatory housing market. Diverse-by-direction communities must commit significant time and energy to fair and open housing efforts if they wish to combat the forces supporting segregation. Direct pro-integration efforts use a variety of strategies to take aim at local real estate and lending institutions to maintain integration. For the most part, such groups implement anti-solicitation regulations to discourage panic peddling and blockbusting, ban For Sale signs to avoid perceptions of racial transition, lobby to prevent an overconcentration of public housing in the community, and offer equity insurance programs to protect property values of incumbent residents (Keating 1994; Lauber 1991; Saltman 1990; R. Smith 1993). For example, in the early 1970s, leaders in suburban Park Forest, Illinois, adopted several integration-maintenance ordinances. The ordinances prohibited racial steering of prospective home buyers and redlining by lenders, established a fair-housing review board to regulate real estate brokers, and empowered the village manager and the human relations committee to review complaints of racially discriminatory housing practices (Helper 1986; Berry et al. 1976).

Another strategy involves monitoring and testing for housing discrimination. Integrated communities across the United States have combated illegally discriminatory housing practices by documenting them through fair-housing audits.[17] In the 1970s, community groups worked with National Neighbors to conduct local and regional tests for real estate discrimination (Saltman 1990). Communities often team up with city- and regionwide fair-housing centers to conduct testing. In many cases, such efforts uncover discriminatory action, and these centers assist communities and individuals in obtaining legal recourse. These efforts allow pro-integration communities to face head-on actions detrimental to the maintenance of diversity.

A final and most controversial strategy employed by pro-integration groups is affirmative marketing. Pro-integration groups quickly realized that if there was demand for housing from just one racial group in a racially changing area, resegregation would quickly result. Thus, communities, particularly suburban ones, saw that the only way to maintain long-term racial integration was to attract white buyers to the market through affirmative marketing strategies. These strategies are designed to initiate and maintain racial integration, while expanding freedom of choice in housing (DeMarco and Galster 1993). Affirmative marketing strategies are considered choice expanding because they encourage "people of the race least likely to consider moving to an area to do so" (i.e., blacks to white areas, whites to integrated ones) (Saltman 1990: 402). The techniques communities use to encourage racial groups to make nontraditional and choice-expanding moves include the use of financial incentives for prodiversity moves, promotion of mixed-race rental or owner properties, and use of Federal Section 8 rental assistance to promote prodiversity moves (Chandler 1992).[18]

Affirmative marketing strategies are race-conscious attempts to counteract hundreds of years of racial steering and denial of housing opportunity. Usually this means trying to "fix" the problem of diminishing white demand for housing in racially changing neighborhoods (Richie 1990; Wiese 1995). For communities working toward stable integration, the reality is that, without whites moving into an integrated area, resegregation is a likely result. This has been true for the groups founded in the 1950s as well as for current efforts. For example, in 1995, local officials in Matteson, Illinois (a southern suburb of Chicago), employed affirmative marketing practices in an attempt to attract more white residents to protect the community's racial balance. Officials suggested that while the effort to maintain racial diversity might be painful, it was a necessary remedy for many residents who did not want to appear racist but were also concerned about property values (Lifson 1995).

Affirmative marketing strategies to attract whites have met with substantial criticism that emanates from different interpretations of the goal of the Fair Housing Act of 1968. One position holds that the act was meant to eliminate discrimination, not necessarily to ensure stably integrated neighborhoods. Thus, affirmative marketing limits freedom of choice, stigmatizes blacks, denies the viability of an all-black neighborhood, limits the ability of blacks to improve their own housing conditions, and ignores the reality that obtaining good housing is a higher priority than integration (Woodson 1988; Kearney-King and Marquis 1989; Leigh and McGhee 1986). The other position, shared by those implementing affirmative marketing strategies, argues that the ultimate purpose of the Fair Housing Act is to promote stable integration. It is argued that even without overt housing discrimination, housing markets would continue to behave in ways that produce and maintain racially separate communities, because institutionally embedded practices ensure that individuals do not have full knowledge of available housing options (DeMarco and Galster 1993; Galster 1992; Polikoff 1985, 1986). Affirmative marketing strategies differ fundamentally from the discriminatory practice of racial steering in that they are intended to expand housing choices, not limit them. A legal note titled "Benign Steering and Benign Quotas" (1980: 938) in the *Harvard Law Review* suggests that pro-diversity incentives are critical because "every time a community resegregates, the pattern of racial separation and hostility is reinforced ... [and thus] the movement toward racial equality will continue to languish until some communities break out of the cycle of resegregation by creating a stable interracial environment that demonstrates racial harmony that is not only desirable but attainable."

These efforts to initiate and maintain racial integration over the long term through intervention in the housing market are critical to the success of stable integration. Such race-conscious policies would be unnecessary if U.S. culture did not discriminate. Since this is not the case, the interventions by local organizations to eliminate housing discrimination and lending continue to challenge images of racially integrated neighborhoods as unstable. They demonstrate that residents in racially changing areas are not helpless to prevent racial transition. Affirmative marketing efforts, however, cannot stand alone; interventions in the housing market are not sufficient to challenge the common perception of racially integrated communities as unstable. This is not lost on community leaders who are intervening in community processes to promote and maintain integration, as they have focused enormous time and energy on what I refer to as community-building efforts, mostly to improve neighborhood quality.

Community Building

To improve neighborhood quality, intervening communities require a well-organized community-based group. This is one factor that all diverse-by-direction communities share—community organizations actively involved in motivating grassroots awareness and involvement in neighborhood concerns (Saltman 1990). Key leaders have emerged to form these organizations and provide the impetus to maintain them. Usually all it took was a handful of people to start the process. For example, in the Sherman Park neighborhood, organizing efforts to promote diversity can be traced back to 1970, when seven families established a local organization to address neighborhood concerns (Valent and Squires 1998). In Indianapolis, four families (two white, two black) are considered the founders of the Butler-Tarkington Neighborhood Association, formed to "achieve an ideal racially integrated, beautiful neighborhood" (Saltman 1990: 38). A similar pattern emerged in other communities. Often religious congregations and ecumenical groups played a lead role in directing and sustaining efforts to maintain integration. These groups, drawing on decades of race dialogue, were situated in prominent positions of leadership (Nyden et al. 1998). As the fight for integration continued, successful communities had organizations that presented "unified, strong, stubborn images and succeeded in influencing key decision makers on local and state levels" (Saltman 1990: 374).

The primary concern of community-building activities is improving or maintaining the quality of life of the community. However, quality of life means different things to different people. In diverse-by-direction communities it means improving the overall image of the area by strengthening social networks, promoting the community, and balancing schools. Community-building efforts usually strike a balance between strengthening social ties and upgrading the neighborhood's physical quality. Indeed, all communities face this task. Where racially heterogeneous neighborhoods differ from racially homogeneous ones is in the priority given to maintaining racial integration. In the former, community building is that much more important. Leadership is required to direct local groups to improve neighborhood quality and to do so with the intent of stable integration.

Community leaders attend to neighborhood quality by working to sustain positive intergroup relations and networks through the formation of parent-teacher associations, religious groups, interfaith groups, Chambers of Commerce, youth recreational leagues, political parties, and block clubs. These groups create an environment that promotes more positive associations among individuals and communal groups, especially across racial lines (Saltman 1990; Nyden et al. 1998). When these efforts were labeled multicultural, the emphasis in the community shifted from black and white to the idea of a mingling of all races and ethnic backgrounds (Goodwin 1979). These social networks strengthen the sense of community in an area, and when their emphasis shifts toward interracial alliances, it creates a positive perception of racial integration and the changes taking place. In integrated areas, such efforts go a long way toward strengthening a community's social and cultural character.

Strong community associations, however, are just part of the picture. In racially integrated neighborhoods, residents often fear that economic development will flounder and crime will increase. Community organizations, realizing that these issues must be dealt with to reverse the perceived link between racial change and neighborhood decline, have begun to work with other organizations to pump life into sagging commercial strips. Although commercial marketing and maintenance largely has been left to the private sector, community organizations realize the importance of economic development in fostering a positive community image. Local organizations may leverage funds for façade and landscaping improvement, for example, to ensure the physical quality of the community.

More importantly, however, it is the efforts by groups to improve the social quality of the community, particularly in the areas of safety and crime, which are most important to changing perceptions. Studies indicate that racially integrated neighborhoods are perceived to have higher crime rates than racially homogeneous ones (Taub, Taylor, and Dunham 1984; Bratt 1983). Local groups, taking concerns over safety into account, have developed specific safety or crime-prevention programs. In Denver's Greater Park Hill neighborhood, for example, concerns over increased violence and gang activity spurred local volunteers to begin a block- and sector-organizing program that encouraged residents to meet one another, confer about crime problems, and be trained to respond to the needs of their neighbors in terms of safety and crime (K. Woods 1998: 98). Similarly, Milwaukee's Sherman Park neighborhood established a "watch" program that includes block-club organizing, graffiti cleanup, and crime-watch patrols (Valent and Squires 1998). These physical and social maintenance programs are necessary for racially integrated neigh-borhoods to alter perceptions that such areas are unstable and undesirable.

The racial mix of a neighborhood and its public school population are also intertwined. Schools tend to resegregate before housing markets do. If there are no efforts to ensure integration in the schools, white households will likely perceive the neighborhood as undesirable and resegregation can quickly follow (Saltman 1990). Various communities have recognized this by working with local school districts to get involved with citywide desegregation efforts. This was the case in Sherman Park, where citywide desegregation reduced fears that neighborhood children would be denied educational resources if minorities moved into the neighborhood (Valent and Squires 1998). In some communities, efforts were made to establish in the neighborhood a citywide magnet school with a special curriculum. In other cases, especially in suburbs, communities and school boards worked together to ensure desegregation. For example, in 1967 and 1968, the Shaker Heights (a suburb of Cleveland) Board of Education addressed racial imbalance in the school system by voluntarily instituting busing and magnet schools

(Keating 1994: 102). In fact, school administrators in Shaker Heights helped fund pro-integrative efforts. These desegregation strategies are crucial for improving the perception of the neighborhood and maintaining integration.

A final element in maintaining the quality of life in a racially integrated neighborhood involves direct promotion of the community. Diverse-by-direction communities have realized the necessity of creating a positive identity, both internally and externally, through the telling of positive stories of the community (from crime reduction to festivals to the diversity itself). Using various media outlets, local groups have promoted their community through shaping how the community is represented. Communities have intervened through "direct marketing and promotional efforts touting the positive aspects of the community, pressuring local media to report positively on the community, and monitoring media and public officials' statements or comments about the neighborhood and responding to such statements when they appear damaging to the community" (Nyden, Maly, and Lukehart 1997: 516). Many communities publish local newspapers to create an internal sense of neighborhood identification. Memphis's Vollintine-Evergreen neighborhood, for example, established the *VE News*, which announces meeting dates, publishes articles about neighborhood residents and businesses, and features stories that celebrate the success of the neighborhood and its diversity. In terms of fostering a positive image of the neighborhood, some claim that the *VE News* is the "single most important institution in Vollintine-Evergreen" (Kirby 1998: 70).

In sum, community-building efforts are aimed at improving or maintaining the quality of life of the community. While some of these efforts are no different from those in racially homogeneous neighborhoods, they are even more vital in integrated ones. These efforts help deflect negative perceptions and promote integration as a positive community quality. Key to understanding the importance of such efforts is the realization that organizations in integrated communities undertook these efforts to improve neighborhood conditions *in order to* maintain stable racial integration.

Diverse-by-direction communities are unique. In them, leaders and organizations direct their efforts toward maintaining stable racial integration. Whether through intervening in the housing market or improving the quality of life in the neighborhood, these efforts intentionally seek to break the cycle of segregation-change-resegregation. These laudable efforts have proven successful in many communities. It is important to keep in mind, however, that neither affirmative marketing strategies nor other interventions guarantee stable integration. Affirmative marketing has generated controversy and has had difficulty attracting support from blacks, many of whom view such efforts as placing a negative value on black residents. Moreover, not all diverse-by-direction communities are successful. Juliet Saltman chronicles the failure of some communities to maintain their mobilizing organization and leadership, and ultimately their racial balance. In other communities, intervention efforts have served only to hold resegregation at bay, slowing down the process of racial transition by a decade or so. Some leaders, like Bobbie Raymond, former director of the Oak Park Housing Center, claim that pro-integration efforts are costly, impeding long-term success. The facts back Raymond's experience—it is estimated that Oak Park spends over $300,000 annually on integration efforts (Wiese 1995).

There is little doubt that the movement to maintain stable integration has been fragile. However, it is important to remember that one of the reasons these interventions and the communities they are trying to maintain are fragile is the sociohistorical legacy of racism. I agree with Saltman's suggestion that when neighborhoods become racially integrated in this country, they initially assume the "same status that the incoming minority group has in the society at large. As such they … are subject to the same levels of domination, discrimination, and segregation in the local community as the minority group experiences in the larger society" (1990: 394). This is what produces resegregation. Local interventions are vital, though sometimes insufficient, in breaking the cycle that produces resegregation. Despite the fragility and costs, such efforts are instrumental in maintaining racial integration and proving that segregation is not inevitable.

The Pro-integration Movement: Then and Now

The neighborhood stabilization movement has waxed and waned since the 1950s. Some observers have rung the death knell for the pro-integration movement, claiming that with the end of the Great Migration, fewer whites vigorously support open housing or racial integration, and the mainstream of middle-class African America has become increasingly weary of integration as an overt social goal. It has been suggested that pro-integrative groups have had a hard time attracting a new base of support, particularly among whites, who have always been its base constituency. This is visible in the support for pro-integration within the fair-housing coalition during the 1980s. Among the 460 fair-housing agencies and organizations surveyed by National Neighbors in 1994, just 68 (15 percent) included any kind of pro-integrative program (Wiese 1995: 117). Of these sixty-eight, half represented communities or neighborhoods working toward stable racial integration. Andrew Wiese sums up one perspective on the pro-integrative movement: "As the neighborhood diversity movement entered its fifth decade, changing social and demographic forces had conspired to produce a movement with proven tools but dwindling resources and an ever narrowing constituency" (1995: 17).

While there is evidence to support this rather dour outlook, there are signs of hope. In the 1990s, the movement received attention as several communities new to the pro-integration movement began employing its "proven tools" to promote neighborhood stability and racial integration. The cases presented in this book—while not necessarily part of the pro-integration movement—are examples of such communities. Also, Matteson, Illinois, for example, a middle-class-to-affluent community in south suburban Chicago, took on an ambitious affirmative marketing campaign in an effort to improve perceptions and maintain integration. Matteson achieved a good deal of media coverage, including an hour-long *Dateline* special, "Why Can't We Live Together?" broadcast by NBC on June 27, 1997, and hosted by Tom Brokaw. Finally, the Fund for an Open Society, founded in 1973 to promote integration in the Philadelphia area, emerged in the 1990s as "America's only national nonprofit working to promote thriving racially and ethnically inclusive communities" (Fund for an Open Society 2003). This organization moved to the forefront of the movement, attracting a national audience to its annual conferences. These conferences are the organization's most obvious attempts to fulfill its mission by equipping communities that seek to become racially inclusive with the skills and resources necessary, and by promoting the benefits of living in integrated communities to a wide range of audiences. While the overall movement may have declined, these examples suggest that reports of the movement's death are exaggerated.

Was George Wallace correct in his implication that racial segregation will (and should) persist in U.S. urban neighborhoods? Indeed, the evidence confirms that segregation has become a prominent feature of urban America. Any discussion of residential settlement patterns by race in the United States must acknowledge that segregation is the norm and that it is maintained through a series of institutionally embedded practices that continue regardless of federal legislation declaring them illegal. However, this same discussion must also consider that local communities can act to promote and maintain racially integrated communities. While such efforts may not be widespread enough to effect immediate meaningful change in the pattern of racial separation that occurs at the neighborhood level, they do call into question the assumption that segregation must or will remain forever. Indeed, the color line can never be discounted as a meaningful force in shaping where people live, what type of services they receive, and what the quality of their lives is. Nevertheless, it can be and has been challenged. Although segregation is perceived as normal in the United States, it is not normal in any inevitable sense. Such a mindset takes residents, activists, policy analysts, and scholars away from examining ways in which to support communities working to maintain their racial and ethnic mix.

Endnotes

1. David Gordon suggests that manufacturers initially located their factories in cities to capitalize on an urban environment that gave them the upper hand in labor disputes. Because both heavy manufacturing and residential areas for its employees were located away from the central core, and individuals in nonindustrial or light industrial work were packed in or near the central business district, there was little opportunity for the two groups of workers to see themselves as potential allies (1984: 32–40). Industrialization segmented social and urban space in this way to prevent interaction among various groups.

2. Between 1910 and 1930, approximately 1.4 million African Americans left southern farms and cities to move north (Farley and Allen 1987).

3. Before 1900, the main way to restrict blacks from buying property was through deed restrictions on single land parcels. Restrictive covenants were devised to allow local real estate boards or neighborhood organizations to establish rules forbidding real estate agents from selling to blacks or anyone else whose presence was deemed "detrimental to property values in that neighborhood" (Massey and Denton 1993; Helper 1969; Trotter 1985).

4. The second wave of southern migrants, greater than the post–World War I wave, brought a net flow north of approximately three million blacks between 1950 and 1960 (Farley and Allen 1987; Massey and Denton 1993).

5. For example, in 1942, 84 percent of white Americans polled answered affirmatively to the question "Do you think there should be separate sections in towns and cities for Negroes to live in?" and in 1962, 61 percent of whites surveyed agreed that "white people have the

right to keep blacks out of their neighborhood if they want to, and blacks should respect that right" (Allport 1958; Schuman, Steeh, and Bobo 1985).

6. Blockbusting has been described as a practice of real estate agents to exploit the color line for profit (Massey and Denton 1993: 37–38). Blockbusting agents would select a promising area for racial turnover, one that often bordered the black ghetto and contained older housing, poorer families, aging households, and some apartment buildings. Agents would quietly purchase a small number of homes and apartments in the area, renting or selling them to carefully chosen black families. Whites inevitably reacted with violence and resistance. Agents countered this with deliberate attempts to increase white fears and spur black demand, often going door-to-door warning white residents of the impending "invasion" and offering to purchase or rent homes on generous terms. As the number of panicking whites increased, realtors would advertise widely within the black community, quickly expanding black demand. Realtors would then inflate the price when selling to blacks. Given that most blacks were more than eager to escape the overcrowding and deplorable conditions of the ghetto, they succumbed to inflated prices, ensuring tremendous profits for real estate agents.

7. Both FHA and VA programs, by insuring up to 80 percent of the value of a property, lowered a lending institution's risk and allowed the borrower to pay a low down payment, with the remaining principal and interest spread out over a twenty-five- or thirty-year period, making it possible for millions of white families to realize the "suburban dream."

8. Between 1935 and 1975, the FHA insured about 9.5 million housing units representing a face value of more than $109 billion (Bureau of National Affairs 1976).

9. Between 1946 and 1959, blacks purchased less than 2 percent of all housing financed with the assistance of federal mortgage insurance (Gelfand 1975).

10. Taeuber and Taeuber report examples such as Chicago's south and west sides, Cleveland's east side, Philadelphia's north and west sides, and most of central city Newark, Detroit, Baltimore, and Washington, D.C. (1965).

11. Segregation levels among whites and blacks in the suburbs (an index of dissimilarity score of 70) were not dramatically lower than in central cities (77) (Massey and Denton 1993). In addition, suburbs accepting black residents were older, lower in socioeconomic status, and densely populated (Clay 1979; Lake 1981; Logan and Schneider 1984).

12. For example, studies indicate that areas with small or declining black populations receive a greater share of mortgage money and that mortgage credit is reduced in areas where black population growth is occurring (Dane 1991; Hula 1981; Squires, Velez, and Taeuber 1991; Yinger 1999).

13. Ernest Burgess, a prominent scholar at the University of Chicago, used this phrase to refer to the cycle through which the character and composition of urban land areas changed as cities grew. Burgess noted that invasion-succession occurred through four stages, not clearly distinguished, but overlapping and blending into one another. The stages included: (a) first entry of newcomers or new land uses (i.e., invasion); (b) reaction to the entry by existing inhabitants; (c) continued entry by newcomers and abandonment of the area by

original inhabitants; and (d) complete displacement of the original inhabitants or land uses by the new ones (i.e., succession) (1928). Racial change, however, was just one example of the invasion-succession model. The model has been used broadly to explain how cities grow and develop (see Keating and Smith 1996).

14. Real estate brokers, standing to reap tremendous profits, unscrupulously promoted rapid racial transition. Brokers would attempt to exploit white fears of living in a black area and losing the value of their housing investment by spreading rumors that the neighborhood was declining and changing. A vicious cycle would be created—as more white homeowners put their houses up for sale, others were frightened and encouraged to sell. White fear and desire to leave the neighborhood rapidly allowed brokers and speculators to purchase these homes cheaply. Brokers and speculators would then sell these houses at inflated prices to middle-income blacks (most of whom were eager to escape the current conditions of the ghetto), creating a dual housing market, one for whites and one for blacks.

15. Chicago's Hyde Park–Kenwood Community Conference, organized in 1949, was the first (Saltman 1990).

16. For instance, in the 1960s and early 1970s, community groups emerged in the following areas: Oak Park and Park Forest, Illinois; Shaker Heights, Ohio; Butler-Tarkington in Indianapolis; Sherman Park in Milwaukee; Crenshaw in Los Angeles; Volluntine-Evergreen in Memphis; Rochester New York's Nineteenth Ward; Blue Hills in Hartford; the west side of Akron; and Belmont-Hillsboro in Nashville.

17. A fair-housing audit is a survey technique designed to isolate the impact of a person's minority status on the way he or she is treated when inquiring of either a landlord or real estate agent about available housing. Audits consist of "successive visits to the same housing agent by two audit teammates who are equally qualified for housing but who differ in minority status" (Yinger 1996: 22). Each teammate then independently fills out a detailed audit survey form, describing what he or she has been told and how he or she was treated (see Yinger 1996).

18. Incentives may include "deal sweeteners" such as low-cost appraisals and closing fees, or even low-interest mortgage loans for those making pro-integrative moves (Keating 1994; DeMarco and Galster 1993).

● REFERENCES

Alba, Richard, Nancy Denton, Shu-yin Leung, and John Logan. 1995. "Neighborhood Change under Conditions of Mass Immigration: The New York City Region, 1970–1990." *International Migration Review*. 24(3): 625–656.

Bauman, John. 1987. *Public Housing, Race, and Renewal*. Philadelphia: Temple University Press

Berry, Brian, Carol Goodwin, R. Lake, and K. Smith. 1976. "Attitudes toward Integration: The Role of Status in Community Response to Racial Change," in Barry Schwartz (ed.), *The Changing Face of the Suburbs*. Chicago: University of Chicago Press.

Binder, Frederick, and David Reimers. 1995. All the Nations under Heaven. New York: Columbia University Press. Blakely, Edward. 1988.

Bradburn, Norman, Seymour Sudman, and Galen Gockel. 1971. *Side by Side: Integrated Neighborhoods in America*. Chicago: Quadrangle Books.

Bradbury, Katherine, Karl Case, and Constance Dunham. 1989. "Geographic Patterns of Mortgage Lending in Boston: 1982–1987." *New England Economic Review*. September/October: 3–30.

Bratt, Rachel. 1983. "People and Their Neighborhoods: Attitudes and Policy Implications," in Phillip Clay and Robert Hollister (eds.), *Neighborhood Policy and Planning*. Lexington, Mass.: Lexington Books.

Chandler, Mittie Olion. 1992. "Obstacles to Housing Integration Program Efforts," in George Galster and Edward Hill (eds.), *The Metropolis in Black and White: Place, Power, and Polarization*. New Brunswick, N.J.: Rutgers University Press.

Clark, William A.V. 1986. "Residential Segregation in American Cities." *Population Research and Policy Review*. 5:95–127.

Connolly, Harold X. 1977. *A Ghetto Grows in Brooklyn*. New York: New York University Press

Cutler, David, Edward Glaeser, and Jacob Vigdor. 1999. "The Rise and Decline of the American Ghetto." *Journal of Political Economy*. 107(3): 455–490.

Denton, Nancy. 1999. "Half Empty or Half Full: Segregation and Segregated Neighborhoods 30 Years after the Fair Housing Act." *Cityscape: A Journal of Policy Development and Research*. 4(3): 107–122.

Drake, St. Clair, and Horace Cayton. 1945. Black Metropolis. New York: Harcourt, Brace.

Ellen, Ingrid. 1998. "Stable Racial Integration in the Contemporary United States: An Empirical Overview." *Journal of Urban Affairs*. 20(1): 27–42.

Farley, Reynolds, and William Frey. 1994. "Changes in Segregation of Whites from Blacks during the 1980s." *American Sociological Review*. 59(1): 23–45.

Farley, Reynolds, Howard Schuman, Suzanne Bianchi, Diane Colasanto, and Shirley Hatchett. 1978. "Chocolate City, Vanilla Suburbs: Will the Trend toward Racially Separate Communities Continue?" *Social Science Research*. 7: 319–44.

Farley, Reynolds, Charlotte Steeh, Tara Jackson, Maria Krysan, and Keith Reeves. 1994. "Stereotypes and Segregation: Neighborhoods in the Detroit Area." *American Journal of Sociology*. 100(3): 750–780.

Ferman, Barbara, Theresa Singleton, and Don DeMarco. 1998. "West Mount Airy, Philadelphia." *Cityscape: A Journal of Policy Development and Research.* 4(2): 29–59.

Fisher, Robert. 1994. *Let the People Decide: Neighborhood Organizing in America.* New York: Twayne.

Fund for an Open Society. 2003. *About Us.* [www.opensoc.org/] Accessed January 8, 2004.

Galster, George. 1987. "Federal Fair Housing Policy in the 1980s." Working Paper No. 5. Cambridge: MIT Center for Real Estate Development.

———. 1992. "The Case for Residential Integration," in George Galster and Edward Hill (eds.), The Metropolis in Black and White. New Brunswick, N.J.: Rutgers University Press.

Galster, George, and Mark Keeney. 1988. "Race, Residence, Discrimination, and Economic Opportunity." *Urban Affairs Quarterly.* 24:87–117.

Glaeser, Edward, and Jacob Vigdor. 2001. *Racial Segregation in the 2000 Census: Promising News.* Brookings Institution. April. [www.brook.edu/dybdocroot/es/urban/census/glaeser.pdf] Accessed June 23, 2002.

Goetze, Rolf. 1979. *Understanding Neighborhood Change: The Role of Expectations in Urban Revitalization.* Cambridge, Mass.: Ballinger

Goodwin, Carole. 1979. *The Oak Park Strategy.* Chicago: University of Chicago Press.

Greenberg, Stephanie. 1981. "Industrial Location and Ethnic Residential Patterns in an Industrializing City," in T. Hershberg (ed.), Philadelphia: Work, Space, Family, and Group Experience in the Nineteenth Century. New York: Oxford University Press.

Grossman, James. 1989. Land of Hope: Chicago, Black Southerners, and the Great Migration. Chicago: University of Chicago Press.

Helper, Rose. 1969. *Racial Policies and Practices of Real Estate Brokers.* Minneapolis: University of Minnesota Press.

———. 1986. "Success and Resistance Factors in the Maintenance of Racially Mixed Neighborhoods," in John Goering (ed.), *Housing Desegregation and Federal Policy.* Chapel Hill: University of North Carolina Press.

Hershberg, Theodore. 1981. "Free Blacks in Antebellum Philadelphia: A Study of Ex-Slaves, Freeborn, and Socioeconomic Decline," in Hershberg (ed.), Philadelphia: Work, Space, Family, and Group Experience in the Nineteenth Century. New York: Oxford University Press.

Hirsch, Arnold. 1983. *Making the Second Ghetto.* Chicago: University of Chicago Press.

Hunter, Albert. 1978. "Symbols of Incivility: Social Disorder and Fear of Crime in Urban Neighborhoods." Paper presented at the annual meeting of the American Society of Criminology, Dallas, Texas. November.

Jackson, Kenneth. 1985. *Crabgrass Frontier*. New York: Oxford University Press.

Judd, Dennis, and Todd Swanstrom. 1998. *City Politics: Private Power and Public Policy*. 2d edition. New York: Longman.

Kearney-King, J., and H. Marquis. 1989. "Freedom of Choice versus Integration Maintenance." *Trends in Housing*. 28:16–17.

Keating, Dennis. 1994. *The Suburban Racial Dilemma*. Philadelphia: Temple University Press.

Keating, Dennis, and Janet Smith. 1996. "Neighborhoods in Transition," in Dennis Keating, Norman Krumholtz, and Philip Star (eds.), *Revitalizing Urban Neighborhoods*. Lawrence: University of Kansas Press.

Kirby, Michael. 1998. "Vollintine-Evergreen, Memphis." *Cityscape: A Journal of Policy Development and Research*. 4(2): 61–87.

Kusmer, Kenneth. 1976. *A Ghetto Takes Shape: Black Cleveland, 1870–1930*. Urbana: University of Illinois Press.

Lauber, Daniel. 1991. "Racially Diverse Communities: A National Necessity," in Philip Nyden and Wim Wiewel (eds.), *Challenging Uneven Development: An Urban Agenda for the 1990s*. New Brunswick, N.J.: Rutgers University Press.

Leigh, Wilhelmina, and James McGhee. 1986. "A Minority Perspective on Residential Racial Integration," in John Goering (ed.), *Housing Desegregation and Federal Policy*. Chapel Hill: University of North Carolina Press.

Lieberson, Stanley. 1963. Ethnic Patterns in American Cities. New York: Free Press. ———. 1980. A Piece of the Pie. Berkeley: University of California Press.

Lifson, Edward. 1995. "Middle-Class Recruiting." *All Things Considered*. National Public Radio. May 13.

Massey, Douglas, and Nancy Denton. 1993. American Apartheid. Cambridge: Harvard University Press. McKinney, Scott, and Ann Schnare. 1989. "Trends in Residential Segregation by Race: 1960–1980." Journal of Urban Economics. 26(3): 269–280.

Molotch, Harvey. 1972. *Managed Integration*. Berkeley: University of California Press.

Nyden, Philip, John Lukehart, Michael Maly, and William Peterman. 1998. "Neighborhood Racial and Ethnic Diversity in U.S. Cities." *Cityscape: A Journal of Policy Development and Research*. 4(2): 1–17.

Osofsky, Gilbert. 1968. *Harlem: The Making of a Ghetto*. New York: Harper Torchbooks.

Ottensmann, John. 1995. "Requiem for the Tipping-Point Hypothesis." *Journal of Planning Literature*. 10(2): 131–141.

Philpott, Thomas. 1978. *The Slum and the Ghetto: Neighborhood Deterioration and Middle-Class Reform, Chicago, 1880–1930*. New York: Oxford University Press

Polikoff, Alexander. 1985. "What's in a Name?—The Diversity of Racial Diversity Programs.". Consultation/Hearing of the U.S. Commission on Civil Rights. Washington, D.C. November 12–13.

Rainwater, Lee. 1970. *Behind Ghetto Walls: Black Life in a Federal Slum*. Chicago: Aldine.

Richie, Winston. 1990. "Pro-Integrative Policy and Incentives." Paper presented at the National Conference of the National Federation for Neighborhood Diversity. Cleveland. June 15.

Rudwick, Elliot. 1964. Race Riot in East St. Louis: July 2, 1917. Urbana: University of Illinois Press.

Saltman, Juliet. 1990. *A Fragile Movement: The Struggle for Neighborhood Stabilization*. New York: Greenwood Press.

Sanders, Marion. 1970. *The Professional Radical: Conversations with Saul Alinsky*. New York: Harper and Row.

Schuman, Howard, Charlotte Steeh, and Lawrence Bobo. 1985. *Racial Attitudes in America*. Cambridge: Harvard University Press.

Shlay, Ann. 1989. "Financing Community: Methods for Assessing Residential Credit Disparities, Market Barriers, and Institutional Reinvestment." *Journal of Urban Affairs*. 11(3): 201–223.

Squires, Greg. 1994. *Capital and Communities in Black and White*. New York: SUNY Press.

———. 1996. "Friend or Foe? The Federal Government and Community Reinvestment," in Dennis Keating, Norman Krumholz, and Philip Star (eds.), *Revitalizing Urban Neighborhoods*. Lawrence: University Press of Kansas.

Smith, Richard. 1993. "Creating Stable Racially Integrated Communities." *Journal of Urban Affairs*. 15(2): 115–140.

Spear, Allan. 1967. *Black Chicago: The Making of the Negro Ghetto, 1890–1920*. Chicago: University of Chicago Press.

Suttles, Gerald. 1972. *The Social Construction of Communities*. Chicago: University of Chicago Press.

Taub, Richard, Garth Taylor, and Jan Dunham. 1984. *Paths of Neighborhood Change*. Chicago: University of Chicago Press.

Trotter, Joe William. 1985. *Black Milwaukee*. Urbana: University of Illinois Press.

Turner, Margery Austin, Raymond Struyk, and John Yinger. 1991. *Housing Discrimination Study*. Washington, D.C.: Department of Housing and Urban Development.

Urban Institute. 1991. *Housing Discrimination Study: Methodology and Data Documentation.* Washington, D.C.: Department of Housing and Urban Development, Office of Policy Development and Research.

Valent, Edward, and Gregory Squires. 1998. "Sherman Park, Milwaukee." *Cityscape: A Journal of Policy Development and Research.* 4(2): 105–130.

Wiese, Andrew. 1995. "Neighborhood Diversity: Social Change, Ambiguity, and Fair Housing." *Journal of Urban Affairs* 17(2): 107–129.

Woods, Katherine. 1998. "Park Hill, Denver." *Cityscape: A Journal of Policy Development and Research.* 4(2): 89–103.

Woodson, R. L. 1988. "Integration Maintenance: Noble Intentions, Ignoble Results." Hearings before the Subcommittee on Civil and Constitutional Rights of the Committee on the Judiciary, U.S. House of Representatives, December 12, 151–154. Washington, D.C.: U.S. Government Printing Office.

Yancey, William, Eugene Ericksen, and Richard Juliani. 1976. "Emergent Ethnicity: A Review and Reformulation." American Sociological Review. 41:461–491.

Yinger, John. 1996. *Closed Doors, Opportunities Lost.* New York: Russell Sage

SECTION **THREE**

GENDER INEQUALITY AND HOMOPHOBIA

Like poverty and racism, gender inequality and homophobia represent significant social problems in the United States. Many women and gay people experience subjugation in a variety of ways that impact their pursuit of education, employment, housing, and even their safety. This section consists of four informative chapters that chronicle the history of the feminist movement, the meaning of sexual harassment, challenges experienced by trans people, and the intersection of gender, sexuality, and race in adolescence.

● THE DIFFERENCES BETWEEN SEX AND GENDER

As with race and ethnicity, many people use the terms sex and gender interchangeably. However, sociologists distinguish between these important concepts. The term sex refers to a person's biological makeup and is typically categorized as male or female. Gender, conversely, is more of a social construct. Accepted gender categories include girl and boy for youths, and woman and man for adults. Typically, people see sex and gender in binary terms where people fit into one category or another. Sociologists recognize that people can be more complicated than that.

● THE SOCIAL CONSTRUCTION OF SEX AND GENDER

The nature versus nurture debate can be applied to sex and gender, just as it is applied to race. On one hand, there are people who think that there are innate differences between males and females based on differing body chemistry. This view represents the nature view and is held by sociobiologists who contend that people's skills and abilities are dictated by genetics. This lends itself to a common view that males and females are each best suited for a different set of roles and responsibilities, ranging from work to household responsibilities and parenting. The competing view, nurture, is maintained by sociologists who contend that gender is social, and that there are not essential differences between the skills or abilities of those people categorized as male and those categorized as female. According to this perspective, people are heavily influenced by agents of socialization. Boys and men "do" masculinity, and girls and women "do" femininity because they have learned how to do so from significant people in their culture. They are held morally accountable to do so and are likely to feel badly about themselves if they do not. So while there are differences between the groups, the differences have social more than biological roots.

Gender is an integral part of the everyday lives of people in society. People categorize each other based on the appearance of physical characteristics such as body hair, breasts, and shoulder size; and self-presentation, including clothing and accessories. We do not see people's genitalia or hormones or chromosomes, so we look for other cues that suggest sex. We then expect people to perform the gender expectations that align with their sex category. Femininity and masculinity denote gender expectations—how a person is supposed to appear, feel, think, and behave, in order to be seen as an appropriate man or woman. These expectations depend upon the particular cultural and historical context, meaning that gender is a social construction. Think of how women and men are supposed to behave in contemporary American homes, workplaces, and public areas. While there are uniquenesses in each place, women are generally expected to smile and be pleasant, while men are expected to be decisive. Women are expected to care about their appearance and try to look attractive, while men should be brave and productive. We learn these expectations and become used to them, so that we are likely to be uncomfortable with situations that defy our overall view of gender, such as when we see female police officers, female construction workers, or male receptionists.

Sociologists have challenged conventional notions of gender for decades. Gender limits each of our human potential, and makes us live according to a set of rules that are arbitrary and contrived. In the United States, people are often sanctioned when they act in ways that violate gender norms. Think of the language that exists to emasculate men when they display emotion and concern for others. Similarly, think of the language that exists to insult women when they exhibit assertiveness and dominance. Despite all of the changes in gender over time, we continue to expect men to be breadwinners and decision makers and women to be caretakers for others. This is socially problematic, not only because it views men and women differently, but also because it diminishes, undervalues, and takes for granted the roles that many women undertake. In a truly egalitarian society, men and women would be able to act in similar ways without being sanctioned.

● SEXISM AND THE DOUBLE STANDARD IN SOCIETY

Sexism is to women what racism is to racial minorities. Sexist behavior and beliefs rank people by sex category, rewarding and valuing males and masculinity over females and femininity. Sexism takes a variety of forms, from telling an inappropriate joke to not hiring or promoting a qualified woman. Like racism, sexism is not generally as obvious and blatant as it was in times past. One hundred years ago, American women could not vote and were severely limited in their educational and career advancement. There was substantial prejudice in that women were generally thought to be less competent and more capricious than men. While there has been progress, the opportunity and reward structure in America still favors men and masculinity. Moreover, many women are treated in a condescending and belittling manner by men because of their sex. Two terms that are closely related to sexism are patriarchy and misogyny. To say that we live in a patriarchal society means that men have more power, and control more of society's resources than women. Meanwhile, misogyny is a stronger term that describes the contempt and disdain that some people have towards women.

Many sociologists have noted that there is a double standard when it comes to gender in the United States. Women are judged more harshly for certain things than men. The sexual double standard, where men are allowed to have multiple sexual partners but women are negatively sanctioned for doing so, is a long-standing and definitive example. Having a messy home is also frowned upon for women but acceptable and perhaps expected for men, and contributes to women spending more time doing housework than men, a seemingly ubiquitous form of gender inequality. In addition, choosing not to have children is an example of the double standard of gender. Women are expected to want children as part of a complete and satisfactory life, whereas men are allowed to see children as one of many possible options. When women do not want children, as is true of many millennial women, they may be viewed as lacking the nurturance and selflessness required as part of appropriate femininity. Parenting is also judged differently in that men need to perform very little childcare in order to be applauded. The substantial unpaid work that women do is often invisible labor in society, and this represents a form of male privilege.

● THE FEMINIST MOVEMENT

Feminism is the belief that men and women are equal and should be treated as such. Many people assume that feminism is a radical ideology. There are plenty of stereotypes of feminists as angry and aggressive, summed up by the use of the term "feminazi" by Rush Limbaugh to disparage Gloria Steinem, Susan Sarandon, and other women who are working to promote equal rights for men and women. This is likely why many women and most men are reluctant to identify with the term feminist. It is politically charged and connected to a host of controversial issues, such as women's reproductive rights; it is generally not seen as a positive term. However, at its core, feminism is about egalitarianism. And though many people are uncomfortable with the term, even people who do not identify as feminist often support what it represents.

In her chapter, "Riding the Waves of US Feminism over the Centuries," Allen chronicles the history of the feminist movement in the United States. The first wave of feminism occurred in the early twentieth century and achieved its goal of giving American women the right to vote. The second wave of feminism emerged in the middle part of the century and established that women should have the same opportunities to attend college, work outside of the home, and engage in family breadwinning as men. Furthermore, this era is marked by women campaigning to raise awareness about such issues as domestic violence and marital rape. The third wave recognizes the importance of seeing gender inequality as part of a broader social phenomenon that is also connected with the marginalization of racial, sexual, and other minorities. Third-wave feminism also allows for more individual empowerment of girls and women, rather than solely collective empowerment.

● WOMEN'S EMPLOYMENT AND SEXUAL HARASSMENT

In the United States, women have historically been less likely to participate in the paid labor force than men. Beginning in the 1960s, in conjunction with the second wave of feminism, increasing numbers of women—including wives and mothers—sought employment. This meant that women were often entering bastions of masculinity. Numerous women have received unwelcome sexual propositioning or have been treated as sex objects in the workplace. In the 1970s, American feminists coined the term sexual harassment, and pushed for laws against such treatment. Although sexual harassment is now illegal, it is an ambiguous and controversial phenomenon.

In the chapter "Introduction: The Making of a Concept," Saguy discusses the background of sexual harassment in the United States and in France. She describes how sexual harassment is conceptualized differently in the two countries, with America viewing it as a form of discrimination and France seeing it as interpersonal violence. In America, sexual harassment is when unwelcome sexual behavior is either a condition for entrance or advancement (quid pro quo) or interferes with working or learning (hostile environment). The latter occurs much more frequently, but as Saguy discusses, in order for it to qualify it must not only be unwelcome, but also severe or pervasive. These are relative terms. Clearly, if women and men are going to work in the same places, both groups need to feel safe. Sexual harassment laws are in place to encourage such safety, but preventing and rectifying harassment requires efforts at all levels, making the goal quite challenging.

● THE TRANSGENDER COMMUNITY

Gender minority is a broad term used to describe a wide range of people who do not fit into the conventional binary categories of sex and gender used by most Americans. Transgender is a term used to describe people whose gender identity is different from their assigned sex. In addition to prejudice and misunderstanding, one of the biggest challenges impacting trans people is the use of bathrooms. As an illustration, consider the House Bill 2 controversy in North Carolina after Governor Pat McCrory signed an executive order mandating that people use the public bathrooms that match their biological sex.

In her chapter, "Understanding the Transgender Community: Support and Resiliency in the Face of Discrimination," Rosalind Kichler uses Meyer's minority stress model to explain the discrimination, both distal and proximal, that sexual and gender minorities often experience. Trans people, as a gender minority group, have experienced profound effects of discrimination, such as a high rate of mental health problems, along with physical health issues and psychological distress. Kichler's chapter identifies how people have responded to this discrimination and its effects, endeavoring to achieve support and resiliency. Kichler pushes the conceptualization of community in her piece, using the actions of both sexual minorities and trans people as her guides.

● HOMOPHOBIA AND INTERSECTIONALITY

Homophobia describes an aversion to gayness and gay people, often resulting in negative treatment of sexual minorities. Like racism and sexism, American society is not as blatantly homophobic as it was fifty or a hundred years ago. Same-sex marriage is legal in every state, many American cities have pride weeks, and many workplaces offer benefits for same-sex partners. All of these would have been unheard of even twenty years ago. However, gay people are still discriminated against, quietly judged, and openly mocked because of their sexuality.

Intersectionality

Though we have examined concepts such as race, social class, and gender in relative isolation, in real life people experience all of these components together. The term "intersectionality" was established to show that these different concepts should be analyzed in combination with each other. People can simultaneously experience different kinds of oppression or privilege based upon their combined race, class, gender, and sexuality. A poor, black, lesbian woman not only experiences inequality differently than a wealthy, white, heterosexual man, or even a poor, white, lesbian woman, but also experiences it to a more elevated degree than members of those two other groups. As such, discrimination experienced by people who experience race, class, gender, and sexual inequality is compounded compared to a person who experiences fewer dimensions of oppression. Many sociologists believe that whenever one of these concepts is focused on in analyses of social life, the others should be considered as well.

In her chapter, "'Dude, You're a Fag': Adolescent Male Homophobia," C. J. Pascoe uses an intersectional approach to show how teenage boys use homophobic slurs to police each other's masculinity. Based on her qualitative research, she emphasizes the term "fag" as a negative sanction used particularly by and against purportedly heterosexual boys. She shows how the patrolling of gendered norms can differ between boys and girls, and between whites and African Americans in a high school setting, including how terms such as "ghetto" introduce social class into the mix.

CHAPTER 9

Riding the Waves of US Feminism over the Centuries

By Mallary Allen

F eminism is a major ideological force in US society today, and represents an important identity for about one-fifth of American adults (YouGov 2013). The concept of feminism, which many define quite simply as a belief in the social equality of women and men and/or an activist movement working to bring about this equality, has, however, a long and complex history. In this reading, we will ride the exciting and sometimes bumpy waves of feminism over more than a century of history, uncovering trends, values, and related movements of the past, and look ahead to feminism's implications for our present lives and beyond.

● FEMINISM'S FIRST WAVE: ABOLITION, THE RIGHTS OF WIVES, AND WOMEN'S SUFFRAGE

The history of feminism in the United States is often divided into three distinct waves, which are, upon closer inspection, not always perfectly distinct. Feminism's first wave is most closely associated with women's suffrage, or the social movement for women's voting rights. This was rooted in the sentiment that women should have status equal to men, a timeless belief attributed to cultures all over the world. Although this wave represented the first public demonstrations for gender equality, it is important to note that this is not where the movement for women's equality in the United States actually began.

Many early movers and shakers for women's equality in the United States first became involved in the cause through the abolition movement, which sought to end slavery in the seventeenth, eighteenth, and nineteenth centuries and, ultimately, became a formidable force for change in the decades preceding the Civil War. Realizing that the cause of liberation for slaves and liberation for women were fundamentally similar, many American women lent their voices to both causes.

When their fellow abolitionists failed to see the relatedness of the two causes, or even prohibited them from speaking publicly at abolition events, many women diverted their activist energy to women's rights in particular. At the famed women's rights conference known as the Seneca Falls Convention in 1848, feminists unfurled their *Declaration of Rights and Sentiments*, authored chiefly by abolitionist and women's rights activist Elizabeth Cady Stanton. Modeled after the US Declaration of Independence, this document highlighted the sexism of the day and made appeals for, among other things, property ownership, public speaking, and voting rights for women.

While many abolitionists supported the Seneca Falls Convention and others like it all over the country in the years that followed, tension between the causes remained. Former slave and abolitionist Sojourner Truth highlighted this tension with her 1851 speech addressed to the Ohio Women's Rights Convention, "Ain't I a Woman?" In it, Truth recounted her life under slavery, which she argued was every bit as challenging as a man's, and called for *human* rights for women and men of every race.

Many feminists influential to the success of the voting rights campaign for decades afterwards, like Alice Paul, a Quaker who saw universal human rights as a Christian imperative, would continue to see the causes of racial justice and women's rights as linked. Not all would, however. As women's suffrage became the basis of a distinct movement following the Emancipation Proclamation of 1863 and the 1865 ratification of the Thirteenth Amendment, which effectively gave black men the right to vote, activists not sympathetic to the cause of abolition and racial justice also joined feminism's ranks.

Some of these feminists drew upon turn-of-the-century racial anxieties and, in turn, racist ideologies to promote the cause of women's suffrage in the early 1900s. Carrie Chapman Catt, suffragist and founder in 1920 of the League of Women Voters, emphasized women's suffrage as a way to temper the political influence of "undesirable" voting populations. Decades removed from the abolitionist feminists who worked to articulate the goals and grievances that would come to define the early first wave, women like Catt warned that voting among immigrants, Native Americans, and African Americans threatened US civil society, and offered the "civilized" votes of white women as an urgent and effective solution.

Apart from this racist ideology, Catt's beliefs were also representative of *maternal feminism*, or feminism which situates the struggle for women's rights within claims of their moral superiority and importance as wives and mothers. While feminists were divided on the rhetorical tactic of emphasizing gender role differences, maternal feminism spawned prolific suffrage propaganda featuring images of mothers with children accompanied by slogans like "Women bring all voters into the world." Other feminists, many of them graduates of new, elite women's colleges, would become the nation's first social workers—or, in the words of Jane Addams (1914), "civic housekeepers"—volunteering their time and energy to promote shorter workdays for female industrial workers and poor relief for widows based on the idea that working mothers were needed at home.

With few exceptions, feminists were also the United States' first prohibitionists, leading a temperance movement that condemned alcohol as a threat to family life. Women's rights and banning alcohol may not seem like complementary causes, but rallying against alcohol allowed women to combat lesser-acknowledged issues many saw as related to excessive drinking. In the nineteenth century, wives were the legal property of their husbands, and few had effective means of resisting the physical and sexual abuse of oftentimes drunken husbands that we today call domestic violence and marital rape. Such issues were nearly unspeakable at the time, but speaking out against the sins of alcohol was consistent with women's assumed roles as moral compasses of the home and family.

Other early feminists, some radical and gender-expectation defying, and others more traditional, hoped to improve the status of wives and eliminate sexual abuse in marriage by promoting a cause they termed "voluntary motherhood" (Gordon 1973). Given that the turn of the twentieth century was marked by the formal illegalization of abortion and by anti-obscenity laws that prohibited the mailing of contraceptive devices and information, we might assume that feminist proponents of voluntary motherhood demanded access to these banned practices and materials. This was not the case, however. By and large, women's rights advocates publicly opposed birth control and abortion because they saw these as further facilitating women's mistreatment, enabling husbands to rape their wives without consequence of unwanted pregnancy (Gordon 1973).

The voluntary motherhood movement of the nineteenth century, like the women's temperance movement, was a way for feminists to advocate the basic rights of women. As women were primarily understood as wives and mothers, much of the rhetoric of improving women's lives at this time was centered on transforming the institution of marriage in a way that sentimentalized romance and motherhood, and in turn institutionalized what we today think of as the traditional family. But by emphasizing the benefits of smaller family size and spacing of children through the female-directed practices of periodic celibacy, early feminists were also, in fact, advocating women's rights to consensual sex.

By the 1920s, first-wave feminists' successes were widespread and visible, beginning with the ratification of the Nineteenth Amendment in 1920, which gave women the right to vote. Women soon also won the rights to own property independent of their husbands and to keep their own wages. Age at marriage increased throughout the 1920s and 1930s, while divorce laws were liberalized, meaning that women had greater freedom to avoid and to leave abusive marriages. Women's workforce participation inclined steadily, and more women went to college. Though alcohol use continued to thrive under Prohibition (effective from 1907 to 1930), underground bars or "speakeasies" widely incorporated women into drinking establishments for the first time, and the public norms and culture surrounding alcohol that took root following Prohibition was in many ways transformed from the rowdy male saloons of the past.

The social transformations brought about in large part by first-wave feminists would soon be eclipsed by the hard times of the Great Depression, however, and eventually give way to complacency in the prosperous economy of the post–World War II era. During this period, feminist activism continued, but in ways less visible to the mainstream culture. Like many social movements, feminism went into abeyance, or a period of low visibility and activity, until being reinvigorated by new activists and causes decades later (Taylor 1989).

● THE SECOND WAVE: PUBLIC SPHERE OPPORTUNITIES AND A POLITICS OF THE PERSONAL

Just as was the case one hundred years prior, the 1950s and 1960s were a time of immense social movement activity and incredible change. The visibility and successes of the civil rights movement spurred a lively activist environment on college campuses, and many students protested against a variety of issues, including the Vietnam War. Bringing with them competencies learned from their involvement in the civil rights and anti-war movements, and also feeling excluded from leadership in other campus-based causes, numerous women on these campuses began to forge a distinct movement for women's rights in the mid-to-late 1960s.

As wives and mothers working in the home, many first-wave feminists couched their calls for social reform within the assumptions of women's ideal roles in the private sphere. The women's liberation movement of the 1960s and 1970s, however, made women's rights to access opportunities and equality in the public sphere of US society its primary goal. Thus, women were encouraged to pursue higher education, work in fulfilling paid careers, and defy any private-sphere gender expectations by advocating women's rights to birth control and abortion.

Like their first wave predecessors, however, the activists and causes associated with second-wave feminism were diverse and can be organized somewhat generationally. Older second-wave feminists frequently worked in professional capacities to bring about formal legal and political changes associated with liberal feminism. This brand of feminism is consistent with economic liberalism, which strives to make changes to the existing society without rejecting capitalism and its related institutions. Younger, college-going women were often associated with the more radical women's liberation movement.

These younger feminists promoted the idea that "the personal is political" and, through discussing their personal experiences with sexism in consciousness-raising circles, grassroots publications, and various protests and demonstrations, sought to challenge existing social institutions. These women promoted frank discussions of domestic violence, illegal abortions, sexual assault, and objectification in media. Some rejected the institutions of marriage and motherhood as bastions of female oppression, and others organized collectives so that women could rely on one another for health care and nutritional needs, publish feminist literature together, and/or live and work together separate from mainstream society to varying degrees.

Born to the World War II generation during the baby boom, which began in the late 1940s and peaked in the mid-1950s, many of these younger second wavers grew up in middle-class, racially segregated suburban communities. In addition to being raised in an era of remarkable prosperity and traditionalism, their mothers were likely to get married at younger ages and have more children than their grandmothers (Fischer and Hout 2005). As Betty Friedan famously described in her 1963 book *The Feminine Mystique*, many boomer women felt stifled by this anomalous traditionalism. This served as something of a rallying cry for middle-class women who were dissatisfied with compulsory homemaking.

With college-age women leading a movement to change the way we think about women's roles, and older professional women leading political campaigns, winning anti-discrimination lawsuits, and organizing professional networks like the National Organization for Women, feminism was once again an American institution by the mid-1970s. Throughout the 1970s, boomer women and their professional counterparts increasingly joined ranks: In 1971, for example, 1930s-born journalists Gloria Steinem and Dorothy Pitman Hughes founded the feminist magazine *Ms.* with editors and contributors many years younger than they. In 1972, senator Patsy Mink, born in 1927, co-sponsored Title IX, the educational equality bill which promotes, among other things, women's and girls' access to school sports, while younger athletes like Billie Jean King and Kathrine Switzer popularized the notion of women's athletic equality. In 1973, twenty-eight-year-old attorney Sarah Weddington argued before the Supreme Court and won the case that would legalize abortion in the United States, *Roe v. Wade*. Throughout the ensuing years, women born in the 1920s, 1930s, 1940s, and 1950s contributed to a rich and diverse corpus of feminist academic and mainstream literature and worked together in many other fields to bring about legal and social victories, like the founding of women's shelters and legal recognition of victims of spousal and acquaintance rape.

In spite of its victories, the mainstream second-wave feminist movement was not without internal divides and tensions. To women marginalized within society not only by their gender but also by their racial, socioeconomic, sexual, parental, or ability statuses, the women's movement appeared primarily concerned with the empowerment of privileged, heterosexual, white, college-going and professional women. Women of color, for example, were essential to the founding of feminist organizations like NOW and the establishment of collectives and publications, but they were not recognized as activists to nearly the same degree as their white counterparts. As such, many of the movement's most visible causes did not seem to represent their concerns.

As second-wave feminism so often equated women's empowerment with public sphere success in highly paid careers and framed other issues, like abortion rights, as supporting these pursuits, women facing the compounded issues of racism, economic inequality, and homophobia articulated new feminisms with attention to multiple sources of social privilege and oppression. Angela Davis and Florynce Kennedy are good examples of high-profile figures in the second-wave feminist movement who fought to bring attention to multiple oppressions simultaneously. Davis, for example, worked in conjunction with the black liberation movement, while Kennedy focused her attention on race, sexuality, socioeconomic status, and issues such as abortion.

This time, feminism would not retreat into the prolonged abeyance of the 1930s through the early 1960s. Instead, a new wave of feminism would emerge from diverse feminists' critiques of the second wave's shortcomings, and from their efforts to discern new feminisms against mainstream exclusions. Even as its visibility in mainstream society began to diminish by the 1980s, it had proliferated into many discernable types: black feminism, Chicana feminism, lesbian feminism, socialist feminism, and more. In the third wave, these diverse and sometimes less visible new conceptions would attempt to change US society once again.

● THIRD-WAVE FEMINISM: INTERSECTIONALITY, NEW CRITIQUES, AND NEW FORUMS

It is difficult to pinpoint a timeline for the third wave of feminism. It is hard to say when it began, what its unifying messages have been, and when it ended (or if it indeed has). There are good reasons for the confusion. To begin with, important critiques of mainstream feminism, particularly its lack of racial, sexual, and socioeconomic diversity, were articulated during the second wave movement itself by peers of mainstream activists. These critiques represented diverse causes and identities, meaning that, once these marginalized voices began to gain recognition, they offered a wider array of issues to pay attention to. These issues extended beyond the relatively straightforward goals of public sphere inclusion and the freedom to make choices about private sphere roles. At the same time, by the late 1970s, mainstream society was no longer the primary audience paying attention to feminist voices. Instead, feminist identities and theories proliferated and continued to take root in academic circles, while the popular social movement went into abeyance throughout the 1980s.

In some ways, then, third-wave feminism began when feminism came back into mainstream culture in the 1990s. After a period of marked conservatism and widespread public condemnation of feminism and of feminists, magazines, music, and new Internet forums helped to raise awareness about gender inequality and bring people together. In academic circles, the continued and diversifying role of feminism was further enriched by the eventual articulation of *intersectionality theory* by Kimberlé Crenshaw in 1989. Intersectionality refers to the unique experiences of privilege and oppression that correspond to the multiple social statuses that individuals embody simultaneously, like race and class, in addition to gender. Academic feminisms especially became more accountable to issues of intersectionality. This trend is exemplified by the enduring political critiques of Angela Davis, the cultural and literary criticism of bell hooks and Adrienne Rich, the linguistic and colonial histories recounted by Gloria Anzaldúa and Paula Gunn Allen, the psychological and developmental theories of Sandra Bem, and the social and sexual analyses of Patricia Hill Collins.

In the mainstream culture, efforts among young women to bring feminist goals again to the forefront of popular attention were more visible—and more varied. For many, third-wave feminism brings to mind the emergence of female musicians, like the rap group Salt-N-Pepa, whose lyrics promoted and boasted of women's independence and sexual autonomy. It is also associated with the birth of the Riot Grrrl movement, a musical culture centered on female grunge and punk bands and their informal feminist publications known as zines. It also brings to mind young women who combined their support for abortion rights with their support for mainstream Democratic politicians like Bill Clinton, who popularized the mantra that abortion should be "safe, legal, and rare" and made reproductive rights a campaign issue. At the same time, scholars observe that the institutionalization of the pro-choice movement within mainstream society ushered in a new era of more conservative, moralizing, and qualified support for abortion rights among young feminists especially (Tonn 1996; Rohlinger 2002).

Third-wave feminism is also associated with the rise of new forums for feminist voices. While notable rhetorical landmarks of third-wave feminism, like Rebecca Walker's *Ms.* magazine article "Becoming the Third Wave," which formally heralded the movement in 1992, or Naomi Wolf's bestselling book *The Beauty Myth* (Wolf 1991), demonstrate the enduring power of traditional media forms to revitalize a cause or social movement, young feminists were also beginning to take activism online. By the mid-1990s, activists promoted established ideas regarding women's empowerment through educational and career fulfillment and reproductive rights on Internet message boards. They also took issue with earlier standbys.

Many second-wave feminists, like authors Catherine McKinnon and Andrea Dworkin, were staunchly opposed to pornography, for instance, and saw it as degrading and dehumanizing as well as promoting a culture of violence against women. Some second-wave feminists also argued that these patterns of exploitation and objectification existed within the private sexual lives of ordinary women and men, whom they argued could not share a completely consensual sexual relationship within the context of an unequal society. Third wavers initially coined the term *sex positive*, then, to refer to a rejection of earlier feminists' critical orientation to pornography and heterosexuality.

Third-wave feminism is far from unified on this topic or nearly any other, however, leading some to believe that the less-pronounced nature of third-wave feminism may have to do not just with the proliferation of issues activists promote, but a lack of unifying message. Sociologist J. Jack Halberstam (2012) has coined the term "gaga feminism" to refer to the contemporary character of feminism in the United States. Gaga, which means crazy, refers to the movement's seeming lack of continuity as much as it reflects the importance of one of its icons—Lady Gaga. Due to its varied character and affinity for such an ironic ambassador—a pop star who wears stiletto heels and conforms to feminine beauty standards earlier feminists might find oppressive, Halberstam summarizes today's feminism as, to some degree, reactionary. Halberstam says that feminism is thriving but transformed and eager to eke out an identity that is queerer, more sexually expressive, and more accommodating of popular culture.

Others worry that a lukewarm commitment to serious goals and a declining willingness, especially among young women, to identify as feminists signal not a transformation but a post-feminist orientation (McRobbie 2009). This is the belief that the work of feminism is done and that a social movement dedicated to gender equality is no longer needed. Some worry, too, that the popularity of feminism among a visible faction of celebrity women has diluted earlier, radical messages and lacks intersectional awareness—thus rendering "feminist" a meaningless identity label accommodating of nearly any personal choice or action by a woman (Zeisler 2016).

Still, many look with assurance to the proliferation of feminism worldwide, to the growing commitment of some "ecofeminists" to bringing about economic and social equality through socially and environmentally sustainable practices, and the growing leadership of young women in new social movements like Black Lives Matter. Others point to the growth of feminist blogs and the use of social media to raise awareness and mobilize for action, as pro-choice activists did with the 2015 anti-abortion stigma Twitter movement #ShoutYourAbortion, as well as young feminists' continued use of traditional legal and political avenues. In recent years, for instance, college students Andrea Pino and Annie Clark filed a Title IX lawsuit against their school for failing to adequately address their sexual assaults perpetrated by fellow classmates, experiences they later chronicled in a book (Clark and Pino 2016).

Conclusion

Whether feminism is currently in abeyance is open to debate. On one hand, lower levels of feminist identification among young people along with the institutionalization of intersectionality have impacted the movement. Many people seem to take for granted what first- and second-wave feminists fought so hard for. On the other hand, feminism continues to represent a thriving and instrumental social movement. Continued activism throughout institutions ranging from legal and academic to religious and environmental have demonstrated its vitality, relevance, and social significance. Just as hindsight allows us to look back upon more than a hundred years of feminism and identify distinct causes, strategies, and trends, history may allow us to one day look back upon the past couple of decades with certainty as to the distinctive features and boundaries of feminism's third wave. Alternately, we may look back upon the feminist ideologies and activities of today's society as mere features of an enduring system of beliefs and goals.

References

Addams, J. 1914. *Twenty Years at Hull-House*. New York: McMillan.

Clark, A. E., and A. L. Pino. 2016. *We Believe You: Survivors of Campus Sexual Assault Speak Out*. New York: Holt.

Fischer, C. S., and M. Hout. 2005. "The Family in Trouble? Since When? For Whom?" In *Family Transformed: Religion, Values, and Society in American Life*, 120–40. Edited by S. M. Tipton and J. Witte, Jr. Washington DC: Georgetown University Press.

Friedan, B. 1963. *The Feminine Mystique*. New York: Dell.

Gordon, L. 1973. "Voluntary Motherhood: The Beginnings of Feminist Birth Control Ideas in the United States." *Feminist Studies* 1 (3/4): 5–22.

Halberstam, J. J. 2012. *Gaga Feminism: Sex, Gender, and the End of Normal*. Boston: Beacon.

Crenshaw, K. 1989. "Demarginalizing the Intersection of Race and Sex: A Black Feminist Critique of Antidiscrimination Doctrine, Feminist Theory, and Antiracist Politics." *University of Chicago Legal Forum* 1989 (1): 139–67.

McRobbie, A. 2009. *The Aftermath of Feminism: Gender, Culture and Social Change*. New York: Sage.

Rohlinger, D. A. 2002. "Framing the Abortion Debate: Organizational Resources, Media Strategies, and Movement-Countermovement Dynamics." *The Sociological Quarterly* 43 (4): 479–507.

Taylor, V. 1989. "Social Movement Continuity: The Women's Movement in Abeyance." *American Sociological Review* 54 (5): 761–75.

Tonn, M. B. 1996. "Donning Sackcloth and Ashes: Webster v. Reproductive Health Services and Moral Agony in Abortion Rights Rhetoric." *Communication Quarterly* 44 (3): 265–79.

Walker, R. 1992. "Becoming the Third Wave." *Ms.* 12 (2): 86–88.

Wolf, N. (1991). *The Beauty Myth: How Images of Beauty are Used Against Women*. London, UK: Vintage.

YouGov. 2013. Omnibus Poll, April 11–12. http://big.assets.huffingtonpost.com/toplines_gender_0411122013.pdf.

Zeisler, A. 2016. *We Were Feminists Once: From Riot Grrrl to CoverGirl, the Buying and Selling of a Political Movement*. New York: PublicAffairs.

CHAPTER 10

The Making of a Concept

By Abigail C. Saguy

During the two years that Teresa Harris worked as a manager at Forklift Systems, an equipment rental company, Charles Hardy, the company's president, often insulted her and made her the target of unwanted sexual innuendos. Charles asked Teresa on several occasions, in the presence of other employees, "You're a woman, what do you know?" or said things such as "We need a man as the rental manager"; at least once, he told her she was "a dumb-ass woman." Again in front of others, he suggested that the two of them "go to the Holiday Inn to negotiate Teresa's raise." Charles occasionally asked Teresa and other female employees to get coins from his front pants pocket. He threw objects on the ground in front of Teresa and other women, and asked them to pick the objects up. He made sexual innuendos about Teresa's and other women's clothing.

When Teresa complained to Charles about his conduct, the latter expressed surprise that Teresa was offended, claimed he was only joking, and apologized. Based on his promises that he would stop his behavior, Teresa stayed on the job. But then the behavior began anew: While Teresa was arranging a deal with one of the company's customers, Charles asked her, again in front of other employees, "What did you do, promise the guy some sex Saturday night?" Shortly after this incident, Teresa collected her paycheck and quit.[1]

Is this sexual harassment? Actually, it depends on when and where the behavior took place. Before 1993, when the U.S. Supreme Court ruled in favor of Teresa Harris in *Harris v. Forklift Systems*[2] reversing the Court of Appeals for the Sixth Circuit, Charles Hardy's behavior was arguably not severe or pervasive enough to constitute sexual harassment under American law. Less than twenty years before that, the term "sexual harassment" did not exist in the United States or in American law. Today, the meaning of sexual harassment in the United States is still in a state of flux. However, the behavior that Teresa Harris suffered at the hands of Charles Hardy falls squarely within one of two legally recognized forms of sexual harassment: hostile environment, in which a boss or colleague creates an abusive or hostile environment by making unwanted sexual comments, demands for sex, sexual jokes, or sexist insults that are "sufficiently severe or pervasive as to alter the conditions of a victim's employment and to create an abusive working environment."[3] If Charles Hardy had told Teresa Harris that unless she gave in to his sexual advances he would fire or demote her or take away some of her job benefits, she would have been subject to the second kind of sexual harassment: quid pro quo sexual harassment.[4]

Though the concept of sexual harassment has spread across the globe, it still means different things in different places.[5] For instance, during the time the research for this book was conducted, French law only recognized the quid pro quo version of sexual harassment, so that the kind of behavior suffered by Teresa Harris would not be sexual harassment under French law.[6] Unlike American law, which defined sexual harassment as a form of group-based discrimination, French law framed it as a form of interpersonal violence. This legal framing was preserved in subsequent legal reform, suggesting that predictions about cultural and political convergence across the globe[7] are incomplete.

These national legal differences stem from the fact that although feminists demanded sexual harassment laws in both countries, they encountered distinct political, legal, and cultural constraints and resources. Particularly important were understandings of group-based discrimination and discrimination law in the United States and the salience of hierarchical boundaries, interpersonal violence, and anti-American sentiment in France. As is shown in subsequent chapters, these legal differences have had a far-reaching impact on wider social understandings of sexual harassment in the two countries. Rather than simply reproducing national legal definitions of sexual harassment, however, American and French corporations and the press responded to national sexual harassment law based on their own institutional practices and traditions, as well as external constraints and resources. Likewise, national legal definitions of sexual harassment greatly informed the way in which individuals conceptualized sexual harassment. However, individuals also innovated upon legal definitions to varying degrees, based on the extent of their training in the law combined with the degree to which legal definitions coincided with broader, taken-for-granted social assumptions about right and wrong.

● THE IMPORTANCE OF NAMING SEXUAL HARASSMENT

The past three decades have seen an influx of women into the paid labor market[8] and growing legitimacy of the *idea* that women are equal, rather than subservient, to men. The greater acceptance of the concept that women are men's equals has made sexual harassment laws possible, and the existence of such laws has, in turn, further legitimized and enforced gender equality. Coined in 1975 by American feminists,[9] the concept of "sexual harassment" assumed a worldview in which women were not always flattered by sexual attention but could instead be extremely aggravated by it. By labeling as "sexual harassment" the way many men treat their female coworkers as sex objects, feminist activists and, later, the courts suggested that sexual or sexist aggression should not be an unavoidable part of women's employment. In so doing, they challenged cultural assumptions about gender (the social implications of being a man or a woman), sexuality, and the workplace.[10] Moreover, this new label potentially transformed the way women who are ogled, propositioned, or groped at work experience and respond to such behavior, as well as their level of outrage or self-blame. Likewise, naming sexual harassment transformed how the men who ogle, proposition, or grope them regard their own behavior and the sense of entitlement or guilt they feel. The belief that such behavior is wrong arguably serves to prevent some men from committing such acts at all.

The formulation of sexual harassment as a concept and a body of law *at all,* as well as the particular way it is conceptualized, thus has important implications for gender equality, for expectations and behaviors linked to sexuality, and for what sorts of social interactions are considered appropriate or desirable in the workplace in particular and in other public and private spheres more generally. Yet, we know very little about how and why this term has been transformed so quickly from an esoteric phrase to a taken-for-granted concept. The bulk of American research on sexual harassment assumes a priori that there exists a particular definition of sexual harassment, one usually based on current legal doctrine. In so doing, these studies take current legal definitions for granted rather than examining how they are historically and nationally contextual. They lose sight of the fact that earlier in United States history "sexual harassment" meant something different or nothing at all. They do not examine the meaning sexual harassment has outside of the courtroom or for different individuals. Moreover, they do not capture how, given different institutional or ideological conditions such as those found abroad, we may have ended up with a very different understanding of what "sexual harassment" entails and why it is wrong.

● THE INADEQUACY OF ESSENTIALIST NATIONAL CHARACTER EXPLANATIONS

That sexual harassment is conceptualized differently in the United States and France makes intuitive sense to many people. Americans having lived in France share anecdotes about France's more "laissez-faire" sexual environment, where physical touching and sexual banter is still a common and even valued feature of French workplaces. Others talk more critically about how in France the climate is more sexist and oppressive for women, and sexual coercion and humiliation remain commonplace, to the detriment of female workers. Few French are surprised to hear that sexual harassment is taken more seriously in the United States. For many, this information coincides with their impressions of American workplaces as repressive and intolerant of sexual innuendo. For others, the United

States is "ahead of" France in matters of gender equity. For many, the United States is a country of contradictions, a place where workplaces are both more women-friendly and also dangerously invasive of people's personal lives.

However, when people venture to explain such national differences, they usually appeal to essentialist accounts of national character, which explain national variation as the product of exaggerated and ahistorical "cultural" differences. The mass media in both countries affirm that Americans are uptight and puritanical compared to the French, who are more at ease with matters sexual. For instance, a *New York Times* article on sexual harassment policy in France[11] reports:

> When one thinks of France, certain images spring to mind. The accordion. Foie gras. Ah, yes, the French lover, whose seductive skills have long seemed as much a birthright as a good Bordeaux. Eroticism has helped define the country. The disclosure by the former president, François Mitterrand, of a decades-long relationship with a mistress created barely a ripple—and when it did, it was an approving one.

This article and others like it gloss over the fact that surveys show that most French *dis*approve of marital infidelity.[12] Indeed, they say nothing about how this disapproval kept Mitterrand's extramarital affair a dirty secret during his lifetime. More importantly, however, reports such as this one treat cultural differences as widely agreed upon and unchanging.

In fact, culture, whether this term is used to denote norms, values, beliefs, expressive symbols, or any number of the "totality of man's products,"[13] is multivalent and highly contested.[14]

The issue of sexual harassment is fascinating from a sociological point of view precisely because it represents a crack in previous configurations of gender and sexuality, a place where cultural change is taking place. The popular French view that Americans are obsessed with sexual harassment because they are "puritans" fails to account for how ideas about what are appropriate and inappropriate ways for men to treat their female coworkers or subordinates have changed tremendously in the past several decades. As an American woman in her seventies told me recently: "When I was working, my boss used to chase me around his desk. It happened when we were alone in the office and I hated to go into his office to ask him something because of that, but other than that, he wasn't a bad guy." This woman's comments reveal the extent to which cultural expectations about work, gender, sexuality, and hierarchical authority have changed in the United States during her lifetime. The formulation of sexual harassment as a social problem is part of this process. As such, it needs explaining, and the ahistorical supposition that Americans are puritanical and the French are sexually permissive will not do.

Indeed, the "permissive" French have had laws against sexual harassment since the early 1990s and the "puritanical" Americans have prohibited sexual harassment not because it is a form of deviant sexuality but because it compromises women's employment opportunities. According to American jurisprudence, employers can be held liable for sexual harassment occurring among employees and be made to pay compensatory and punitive damages under Title VII of the Civil Rights Act of 1964, which makes it illegal to discriminate on the basis of race, color, religion, sex, or national origin.

In contrast, under French law, a male supervisor who fires a female subordinate because she refuses to have an affair with him has committed a penal misdemeanor, for which he alone (and not his employer) is held responsible. His action is not condemned as an instance of sex discrimination.[15] Rather, this man has committed a misdemeanor akin to the crime of rape by using his authority as supervisor to try to coerce a woman into having sexual relations with him, much as a rapist uses physical force to compel his victim into having sexual relations. Indeed the connection between sexual harassment and rape is made in the French penal code, which classifies sexual harassment with rape, sexual battery, and exhibitionism in the section on sexual violence, rather than with group-based discrimination. While rape is a *crime,* however, the other three, including sexual harassment, are *délits* (misdemeanors), which are tried in a different court and carry much lighter penalties. Although the sexual harassment penal statute allows for a maximum penalty of one year behind bars or a fine roughly equivalent to $14,000, actual sentences typically involve only suspended jail sentences of two months, a couple of thousand dollars in fines, and small compensatory damages paid to the plaintiff (usually less than the equivalent of $3,000).

These distinct legal approaches have important material consequences, including the kind of relief a victim of sexual harassment can receive, the likelihood that employers will take preventive or remedial measures against sexual harassment, as well as the kinds of punishment sexual harassers can expect. Moreover, these legal distinctions affect the ways in which people understand the harm done when they or others sexually harass or are harassed and how seriously they take such behavior. More generally, these legal approaches shape a variety of taken-for-granted understandings of political rights, acceptable and unacceptable behavior, and social responsibility, to list a few prominent examples.

While legal institutions have shaped both American and French conceptions of sexual harassment, sexual harassment is not solely a legal issue in either country. American employers have created their own rules and regulations that define sexual harassment differently from American law. Within such companies, some behavior, like sexist jokes or comments that fall short of the legal test of severity or pervasiveness, is considered sexual harassment in the company. Moreover, rather than condemn the behavior as sex discrimination, many American human resource departments condemn sexual innuendo of any kind because it is considered to detract from the bottom line and standards of professionalism. Likewise, the American mass media, which also play a role in defining sexual harassment, often lose sight of the discrimination component when they report on high-profile sexual harassment cases as sexual and often political scandals.

That sexual harassment is a form of interpersonal violence, rather than a form of sex discrimination, is the dominant view in French law and corporations. Some French feminist activists, however, have promoted an analysis of sexual harassment as a form of sex discrimination. These activists have also argued that the French Parliament should prohibit the kind of behavior that American courts classify as hostile environment sexual harassment, an argument with which many French people agree.[16] Finally, the French media reports focus on *American* sexual harassment scandals as revealing American excesses of litigiousness, feminism, and puritanism.

The view that current American conceptions of sexual harassment are the product of a natural evolution toward a more gender-equal society overlooks how these particular understandings of sexual harassment are situational. Indeed, the contrast with France shows how a different institutional, political, historical, and cultural context can foster an extremely different conception of sexual harassment. The way sexual harassment is understood and addressed has important consequences for gender equality, sexuality, and the workplace, yet we know very little about why and how this problem has been conceptualized differently in different countries. This book seeks to answer this question, using as case studies the United States and France, major industrialized democracies with strong commitments to civil rights but which have adopted different definitions of sexual harassment. Not only important in its own right, this question is also useful for shedding light on the more general question of how social meaning is created, reproduced, and challenged.

● GENERAL ARGUMENT OF THE BOOK

I argue that, in both the United States and France, the career of "sexual harassment," as social concept, body of law, and object of company rules, has been shaped by concerted efforts on the part of local social actors, like feminists, to change taken-for-granted assumptions about gender, sexuality, and the workplace. I thus embrace the concept of "social agency," or the idea that social actors have "free will" or autonomy to change their social environment. However, I further argue that the key social actors involved in struggles over legal and nonlegal definitions of sexual harassment were constrained and enabled by *social structure, relations among institutions and countries,* and *cultural and political traditions* specific to their national and institutional context.

"Social structure" is a sociological concept that refers to stable patterns of social behavior or rules that limit what sorts of conduct are possible or likely in a given social context. Social structures are often conceptualized as contained within particular institutions, such as the courts or the legislature. However, interconnections among different institutions, which vary cross-nationally, have had important implications for the conceptualization of sexual harassment and other social problems, as have interactions between the United States and France, an aspect too often neglected by cross-national research. By "cultural and political traditions," I am referring to collective customs, beliefs, and reasoning that govern everyday interactions or, more specifically, political behavior. My distinction between social structure, relations among institutions and countries, and cultural and political traditions is a heuristic device, a useful starting point for unpacking complex social behavior. In reality, as the empirical data will show, the lines among these concepts are often blurred. For instance, institutions are often considered the building blocks of social structure. However, they can also be analyzed as practical norms in routine activity.

Legal systems function as social structure by dictating who can make or change laws (such as lawmakers, judges, lobbyists, dictators, and so on) and through which processes (such as legislative debates, court precedent, decree, and so on). A common-law system, like that of the United States, for instance, allows courts discretion in building case law through jurisprudence to an extent that is unparalleled in a civil law system, like that of France. In the case of sexual harassment, the common-law system provided American feminists a valuable entryway into the lawmaking process that their French counterparts did not enjoy. This structural opportunity also entailed inherent constraints. For instance, to win their case, American feminists and lawyers have had to make a *legal* case in U.S. courtrooms that sexual harassment violates an existing statute. For strategic and intellectual reasons, they chose to build sexual harassment jurisprudence on Title VII. This, in turn, has compelled them to stress certain aspects of the harm of sexual harassment, such as group-based discrimination and employment consequences, and downplay others, such as sexual violence and behavior outside of the workplace. Preexisting laws, such as Title VII in the United States, were thus also part of the social structure that influenced the ways in which sexual harassment could or could not be legally defined.

French feminists faced different structural opportunities and constraints. Because of French legal structure, the avenue for legal reform lay not in the courts but in Parliament, especially in 1991 when a *window of opportunity* emerged in the form of penal code reform. Here state feminists (feminists employed by the state, in roles such as minister or secretary of women's rights, or as independent lawmakers) were obliged to engage in political compromise to get sufficient support for their bill, a standard practice of the parliamentary process. In French parliamentary debates, state feminists thus narrowed the scope of the sexual harassment bill to target only quid pro quo forms of sexual harassment and framed[17] the problem as an abuse of hierarchical power rather than gender discrimination in order to convince their (male) socialist colleagues to vote for their bill. French feminists were less able to build on discrimination law, as it was narrowly defined, poorly enforced, and lacked legitimacy in France. Rather, the French sexual harassment penal statute was ultimately inscribed in the preexisting section on sexual violence, a placement that had consequences for how the wrong of sexual harassment would be conceptualized and addressed.

Other institutions are governed by their own sets of rules and routines. The American mass media, often controlled by business and dependent on advertisement revenues, are under great pressure to produce news that sells, making sexual harassment scandals particularly compelling. Due largely to the more narrow scope and recent passage of sexual harassment law in France as well as greater legal constraints on the media, there were no home-grown French sexual harassment scandals before 2002.[18] However, the French press, which also faces intense competition, has found that American scandals make for titillating stories with a moral: beware of "American excesses." Corporations tend to be driven by profit-maximization, assuming that the government does not heavily subsidize them. In the case of the United States, this has led corporations to address sexual harassment largely as a practice that can hurt the bottom line, not only through costly lawsuits but also by affecting reputation and employee productivity.

The courts, corporations, and mass media have further interacted in ways that have increased attention to sexual harassment in the United States. By holding employers liable for sexual harassment occurring in their workplace, American sexual harassment law has accorded employers with "ownership"[19] of this social problem to a far greater extent than has French law, which holds only individual harassers, and not employers, legally responsible for their behavior. In the United States, corporate responses to the law can have a feedback effect on the courts.[20] For instance, American corporations initially enacted sexual harassment policies and training programs in the hopes that they could be used to shield themselves from liability. Over the years, the U.S. courts have officially recognized these policies as important elements of an affirmative defense against employer liability.[21]

By reporting on the most expensive sexual harassment lawsuits, the mass media inflate the perceived risks of legal action for employers, thereby increasing the odds that companies will take preventive action.[22] According to several commentators, media reporting on Anita Hill's accusations against Clarence Thomas and her treatment during the Senate hearings facilitated President Bush's signing of the Civil Rights Act of 1991, which greatly strengthened sexual harassment law, in particular by allowing plaintiffs to sue for punitive damages.[23]

In addition to their structural aspects, laws also function as *cultural symbols* that legitimize *cultural and political traditions.*[24] For instance, the existence of affirmative action and Title VII makes Americans likely to think that group-based discrimination, such as racism or sexism, is an important source of inequality, or at least to see race and gender as salient social categories.[25] Even if they believe group-based discrimination is exaggerated or that antidiscrimination law goes too far, Americans will, on the whole, be more familiar with the concept than their French counterparts, who have neither a political history of civil rights equivalent to the American movement nor strong employment discrimination laws.[26] This means that Americans are more likely to conceptualize a range of behavior, including sexual harassment, as forms of gender discrimination. The French, on the other hand, are more likely to conceptualize inequality in terms of class divisions and hierarchy, since ideas about class struggle and abuse of power are embedded in French social history and are perpetuated by state institutions like the French Communist and Socialist parties. Similarly, America's developed antidiscrimination jurisprudence institutionalizes and legitimizes expectations that (labor) markets should be fair, a more important and central belief in the United States, where there is a low degree of "decommodification" and a high degree of liberalism, than in France, where there is greater suspicion of the market.[27]

Based on peoples' perceptions of dominant cultural and political traditions, individuals also have different expectations about what their peers are willing to believe or do. For instance, even though the French state-feminist supporters of the 1991 sexual harassment bills were personally sympathetic to the argument that sexual harassment is a form of gender discrimination and violence against women, they framed the behavior as a form of hierarchical abuse because they thought this argument would resonate more with their male Socialist colleagues. Sometimes there is a considerable gap between what members of a community personally believe and what beliefs they ascribe to their peers, so that groups of people may act contrary to their own wishes because they falsely believe they are conforming to the larger group.[28]

These cultural differences have been accentuated by "boundary work"[29] on the part of French individuals. For instance, French lawmakers engaged in "boundary work" against the United States by drawing on the French media's representations of the "excesses" of American sexual harassment law to argue that French law should be more cautious in its approach to sexual harassment. According to the official French Senate report: "Recent press articles report that in [the United States] 'simply holding the door open for a woman can incite a severe reprimand,' and that most men admit to being very wary in interacting with women in the workplace."[30] The desire to avoid alleged American excesses was one of the reasons given by this senator, in his report, for limiting the scope of French sexual harassment laws. In his words: "It is certain that the excesses that are a product of exaggerated protective concern against sexual harassment in North America motivates the preference for a more restrictive but more realistic definition." Such negative perceptions of American responses to sexual harassment have also raised concern among French judges and the public at large about the danger of falling into "American excesses," a fear that has increased the stigma attached to sexual harassment victims and their advocates.[31]

This study follows in a tradition of work in cultural sociology, in which cultural attitudes and cultural content cannot be understood divorced from the organizational contexts in which they are produced.[32] While most studies focus on one institutional setting, this research triangulates among several, concentrating especially on the law, mass media, and corporations. It seeks to make sense of larger national patterns by examining how key national institutions have addressed sexual harassment, as well as the ways in which their respective approaches interact with each other.

I focus on four key groups of actors, including (1) feminist scholars, activists, and associations; (2) lawmakers, judges, and lawyers; (3) journalists and public figures; and (4) human resource managers and union activists. I examine how the actions of these social actors have been enabled and constrained by the three main institutional settings that have been primary sites for the conceptualization of sexual harassment: (1) the law; (2) the mass media; and (3) corporations.

● METHODS AND DATA

This study draws on several sources of data, which were collected using multiple methods. First, I examined the major French and American sexual harassment legal texts, including statutes and jurisprudence. Second, using a detailed coding scheme and statistical analysis, I analyzed over six hundred randomly sampled articles about sexual harassment from the French and American press, published in 1975–2000. Third, I conducted almost sixty in-depth interviews with feminist activists, public figures (including Catharine MacKinnon, Phyllis Schlafly, Camille Paglia, Marie-Victoire Louis, Françoise Giroud, and Elisabeth Badinter), lawyers, human resource personnel, and union activists. Rather than a representative sample of French and Americans, the respondents are cultural entrepreneurs, who, through their jobs or volunteer activity, are likely to have a particular impact on the conceptualization of this social problem. I use the interviews with the activists to help reconstitute the legal and social movement history of sexual harassment. I also draw on the interviews with the activists, public figures, lawyers, human resource managers, and union representatives in my analysis of the actual meaning laws and press reports have for victims of sexual harassment and their advocates.

I further draw on the interviews with human resource personnel and union activists to examine the meaning of sexual harassment in the workplace of large multinational corporations. These respondents were employed in one of four work sites, including an American or French branch of an American multinational that I call "AmeriCorp," or an American or French branch of a French multinational that I call "Frenchco." In the case of the United States, I draw on secondary literature to put my findings from the American branches in a larger perspective. Because there is no comparable literature on French corporations, I conducted a series of short telephone interviews with representatives of twenty-three French branches of large multinational corporations. I draw on these to evaluate how French corporations respond to sexual harassment laws.[33]

● BOOK OUTLINE

The next chapter, "Sexual Harassment Law on the Books: Opportunity Loss v. Violence," examines how and why American and French sexual harassment laws differ by body of law and definition of harm, scope, and remedy. In both countries, key social actors (feminists in both countries, lawyers and judges in the United States, lawmakers in France) mobilized for sexual harassment laws, but they encountered very different structural constraints and resources, institutions and institutional networks, and cultural and political traditions. These different national contexts, as well as global politics (namely negative French sentiment towards the United States) shaped the goals and strategies of social actors and, ultimately, the sexual harassment laws that ensued. In the United States, political traditions of antidiscrimination, a product of the 1960s civil rights movement, as well as antidiscrimination statutes and jurisprudence, made it particularly likely that American feminists would successfully conceptualize sexual harassment as a form of sex discrimination. In France, the legal system did not offer a ready-made mechanism like civil rights laws. On the other hand, two other kinds of resources were decisive: (1) the importance given to hierarchical boundaries, which are also institutionalized in French law; and (2) anti-American rhetoric, developed by the French media, on which certain influential lawmakers drew to argue that American sexual harassment law should not be taken as the model for France.

Chapter 2, "Sexual Harassment Law in Action: Legitimacy and Liability," examines the legal and corporate environment of sexual harassment.[34] This chapter shows how the differences that exist in sexual harassment laws have been compounded by the very different status sexual harassment has as a body of law and a social problem in each country. Briefly, the interviews demonstrate that the issue is taken much more seriously in the United States than in France. This chapter attributes this finding to national differences in cultural attitudes towards sexism and money, corporate cultures, legal differences (not limited to sexual harassment law), and the way in which national institutions, like courts, corporations, and mass media, interact or overlap. I further show how French social actors have reinforced these national differences by drawing symbolic boundaries against the United States.

Chapter 3, "Sexual Harassment in the Press: National Scandal, Pride, or Superiority?" examines how six of the main American and French presses have reported on sexual harassment. The American press has focused primarily on stories of sexual harassment as political scandal by covering accusations against high-profile political figures, like Supreme Court Justice Clarence Thomas or President Bill Clinton. Despite this focus, a substantial proportion of the American press has framed sexual harassment as an important social problem and a women's issue. The French press has reported less on sexual harassment than the American press, and when it has, it has focused on *American* rather than homegrown scandals. Analyses further show that when reporting on sexual harassment in the United States, as compared to reporting on France, French journalists are more likely to discredit plaintiffs and trivialize sexual harassment as a social problem, focusing instead on "American excesses" of feminism, puritanism, and litigiousness. As will become clear in the following chapters, the way the French media has presented sexual harassment as an "American problem" effectively discredits feminist activists, plaintiff lawyers, victims of sexual harassment, and others who are exposed to this problem in France. These patterns of reporting reflect both different "realities" in each country, such as the different scope of national sexual harassment laws and litigation, and media routines that favor simplification, individualism, symbolism, and "gotcha journalism."[35]

Chapter 4, "Discrimination, Violence, Professionalism, and the Bottom Line: How Interview Respondents Frame Sexual Harassment," analyzes how the interview respondents conceptualize sexual harassment. Three principal frames emerge: (1) a "discrimination frame," in which sexual harassment is condemned as a form of sex discrimination in employment, which was most common among the American respondents, especially the activists; (2) the "violence frame," in which sexual harassment is wrong because it is a form of interpersonal violence, which was more common among the French respondents; and (3) a "business frame," also common among the American respondents, especially human resource personnel, according to which sexual harassment is wrong because it is not "professional" and does not "add [economic] value" to companies. Chapter 4 thus complements Chapters 1 and 3 by demonstrating the extent to which individuals draw on public representations of sexual harassment produced by the legislature, courts, or mass media to make sense of this issue and the ways in which they innovate upon public definitions. This chapter reveals that strong national patterns exist but that individuals also demonstrate creativity as they improvise upon official definitions of sexual harassment.

The Conclusion, "Institutions, Framing, and Political Power," summarizes how the institutional patterns explored in Chapters 1–4 play out in the United States and France. I discuss the ways in which the law, corporations, and media interact, as well as how the interview respondents draw from different "cultural toolkits,"[36] depending on their national and institutional context. I conclude this chapter by discussing some of the lessons this study holds for sociology and by considering the political implications of debates regarding how sexual harassment should be defined.

As this book was going to press, French lawmakers revised French law to address sexual harassment among coworkers, and a scandal erupted around alleged incidents of sexual harassment in higher education. I address these events in the Epilogue, "Plus ça change, plus c'est la même chose." I argue that although these incidents seem to suggest that France is finally coming to resemble the United States in matters of sexual harassment, closer analysis reveals that important cross-national differences persist. For instance, although legal reform extended French sexual harassment laws to coworker harassment, it reinforced the French framing of sexual harassment as a form of interpersonal violence, rather than as an instance of group-based discrimination, and did little to reinforce employer liability. Media reporting on charges of sexual harassment in higher education revealed that for many French social commentators "universal" or gender-neutral questions of professors' power over students and class inequalities, and not sexism or sexual violence, remain the fundamental problems at stake. The events of 2002 also reveal that anti-American rhetoric remains an important political strategy for discrediting those who try to address the problem of sexual harassment in France.

Endnotes

1. These events are recounted in *Harris v Forklift Systems,* 510 US 17 (1993).

2. *Harris v Forklift Systems,* 510 US 17 (1993).

3. *Harris v Forklift Systems,* 510 US 17, 17 (1993). See also Catharine Mac-Kinnon, *Sexual Harassment of Working Women* (New Haven, Conn.: Yale University Press, 1979).

4. *Barnes v Costle,* 561 F2d 983 (DC Cir 1977).

5. For a discussion of how sexual harassment has been defined in Austria, see Mia Cahill, *The Social Construction of Sexual Harassment Law* (Aldershot: Ashgate, 2001). For a discussion of sexual harassment in Sweden, see R. Amy Elman, *Sexual Subordination and State Intervention: Comparing Sweden and the United States* (Providence, R. I.: Berghahn Books, 1996). On Spain, see Celia Valiente, "Sexual Harassment in the Workplace: Equality Policies in Post-Authoritarian Spain," in *Politics of Sexuality: Identity, Gender, Citizenship,* ed. Terrell Carver and Veronique Mottier (London: Routledge, 1998), 169–79. On Germany, see Kathrina Zippel, "Comparative Perspectives of Sex Equality Policies in Germany, the European Union, and the United States: The Example of Sexual Harassment," Ph.D. diss., Department of Sociology,

University of Wisconsin, Madison, 2000. On India, see Martha Nussbaum, "The Modesty of Mrs. Bajaj: India's Problematic Route to Sexual Harassment Law," *New Directions in Sexual Harassment Law,* ed. Reva Siegel and Catharine MacKinnon (New Haven: Yale University Press, in press).

6. Code pénal [C. Pén.] art. 222–33 (Fr.). As this book was going to press, the French Parliament extended the French legal definition of sexual harassment to coworkers, suggesting that a threat of economic retaliation is no longer necessary for there to be sexual harassment. However, the sexual harassment labor statute *only* prohibits retaliation and not the sexual harassing behavior itself, and both the labor and penal statutes still define sexual harassment as "the act of harassing another for the purpose of obtaining sexual favors." It is unclear whether a judge would see Charles Hardy's behavior, as offensive as it was, as a plot to obtain "sexual favors" from Teresa Harris. As the French legal reform is not retroactive, it will be some time before we see the concrete impact of this reform. For a discussion of these legislative changes, see the Epilogue.

7. John Boli and George M. Thomas, "World Culture in the World Polity: A Century of International Non-Governmental Organization," *American Sociological Review* 62, no. 2 (1997): 171–90; See also John W. Meyer, John Boli, and George M. Thomas, "Ontology and Rationalization in the Western Cultural Account," in *Institutional Environments and Organizations: Structural Complexity and Individualism,* ed. Richard Scott and John Meyer (Thousand Oaks, Calif.: Sage, 1994); John W. Meyer, David Kamens, Aaron Benavot, Yun Kyoung Cha, and Suk-Ying Wong, "Knowledge for the Masses: World Models and National Curricula, 1920–1986," *American Sociological Review* 56, no. 1 (1991): 85–100; David Strang and John Meyer, "Institutional Conditions for Diffusion," *Theory and Society* 22 (1993): 487–511.

8. See Christine Cousins, "Women and Employment," in *Society, Work and Welfare in Europe* (London: Macmillan Press, 1999), pp. 72–96.

9. According to MacKinnon, *Sexual Harassment of Working Women,* p. 250, "Working Women United Institute … seems to have been the first to use these words as anything approaching a term of art … [in] 1975."

10. Both American and French sexual harassment law is gender neutral, meaning that men and women can harass someone of either sex. However, it is widely recognized that most of the time it is men who harass women. For the sake of simplicity, I often refer to the sexual harasser as "he" or "him" and the victim as "she" or "her."

11. Vivienne Walt, "Regarding Sexism on the Job: Plus Ça Change …," *New York Times,* 24 May 2000, sec. G, col. 1–3, p. 1.

12. See Abigail C. Saguy, "Puritanism and Promiscuity? Sexual Attitudes in France and the United States," *Comparative Social Research* 18 (1999): 227–47.

13. Peter L. Berger, *The Sacred Canopy: Elements of a Sociological Theory of Religion* (New York: Anchor Books, 1969), p. 6; cited in Wendy Griswold, *Cultures and Societies in a Changing World* (Thousand Oaks, Calif.: Pine Forge Press, 1994), p. 8.

14. There are more than 160 meanings of culture in the social scientific literature. See Alfred L. Kroeber and Clyde Kluckhohn, *Culture: A Critical Review of Concepts and Definitions* (Cambridge, Mass.: Harvard University Peabody Museum of American Archaeology and Ethnology, 1952); cited in Griswold, *Cultures and Societies in a Changing World,* p. 8. This study focuses on cultural or social assumptions about how the world works, which I regard as historically embedded, socially changing, and contested. I employ the concept of cultural repertoire to capture how individuals choose from among a varied but limited set of cultural "tools," based on their social situation, especially their national and institutional context.

15. See Françoise Dekeuwer-Defossez, "Le harcèlement sexuel en droit français: Discrimination ou atteinte à la liberté?" *La Semaine juridique* 3662, no. 13 (1993): 137–41.

16. See Chapter 4; Jacqueline Remy, "Les françaises accusent," *L'Express,* 13 March 1999. In 2002, the French Parliament expanded sexual harassment laws to cover coworker harassment, but the violence frame was preserved. See the Epilogue.

17. I borrow the concept of frame from social movement research (William Gamson, *Talking Politics* [Cambridge: Cambridge University Press, 1992]; David Snow and Robert D. Benford, "Ideology, Frame Resonance and Participant Mobilization," *International Social Movement Research* 1 [1988]: 197–217; Sidney Tarrow, "Mentalities, Political Cultures, and Collective Action Frames: Constructing Meanings Through Action," in *Frontiers in Social Movement Theory,* Aldon D. Morris and Carol McClurg Mueller, eds. [New Haven, Conn.: Yale University Press, 1992], pp. 174–202.). According to Snow and Benford ("Ideology, Frame Resonance and Participant Mobilization," p. 198), social movements "frame, or assign meaning to and interpret, relevant events and conditions in ways that are intended to mobilize potential adherents and constituents, to garner bystander support, and demobilize antagonists." The way social movement theorists use the term is quite different from Goffman's original concept of "frame" (Erving Goffman, *Frame Analysis: An Essay on the Organization of Experience* [New York: Harper Colophon, 1974]; see Nathalie Heinich, "Pour introduire la cadre-analyse," *Critique* 535 [1991]: 936–53.).

18. In February 2002, a small (by American standards) media scandal erupted in France over a sexual harassment charge by a doctoral candidate against her dissertation advisor, a well-known Parisian intellectual. See the Epilogue for a discussion of what facilitated the media's treatment of this event and how the press represented these charges.

19. See Joseph R. Gusfield, *The Culture of Public Problems: Drinking-Driving and the Symbolic Order* (Chicago: University of Chicago Press, 1981).

20. See Lauren B. Edelman, Christopher Uggen, and Howard S. Erlanger, "The Endogeneity of Legal Regulation: Grievance Procedures as Rational Myth," *American Journal of Sociology* 105, no. 2 (1999): 406–54.

21. *Burlington Industries v Ellerth,* 524 US 742 (1998); *Faragher v City of Boca Raton,* 524 US 775 (1998).

22. Lauren Edelman, Steven E. Abraham, and Howard S. Erlanger, "Professional Construction of Law: The Inflated Threat of Wrongful Discharge," *Law and Society Review* 26, no. 1 (1992):

47–83; Erin Kelly and Frank Dobbin, "Civil Rights Law at Work: Sex Discrimination and the Rise of Maternity Leave Policies," *American Journal of Sociology* 105, no. 2 (1999): 455–92.

23. Terry Morehead Dworkin, "Harassment in the 1990s: Sexual Harassment in the Workplace: Women in Business," *Business Horizons* 36, no. 2 (1993): 52; "Thank You, Anita Hill, for the Civil Rights Act of 1991," *Christian Science Monitor,* 29 October 1991, sec. Editorial; for a discussion of the merits of these claims, see Roger Clegg, "A Brief Legislative History of the Civil Rights Act of 1991," *La. L. Rev.* 54 (1994): 1459–71.

24. See Robin Stryker, "Rules, Resources, and Legitimacy Processes: Some Implications for Social Conflict, Order and Change," *American Journal of Sociology* 99, no. 4 (January 1994): 847–911.

25. For an excellent history of affirmative action, see John David Skrentny, *The Ironies of Affirmative Action: Politics, Culture and Justice in America* (Chicago: University of Chicago Press, 1996).

26. See Erik Bleich, *Race Politics in Britain and France: Ideas and Policy-Making since the 1960s* (New York: Cambridge University Press, in press).

27. See Gosta Esping-Andersen, *The Three Worlds of Welfare Capitalism* (Princeton, N.J.: Princeton University Press, 1990); Michèle Lamont and Lau-rent Thévenot, eds., *Rethinking Comparative Cultural Sociology: Polities and Repertoires of Evaluation in France and the U.S.* (Cambridge/Paris: Cambridge University Press and the Presses de la Maison des Sciences de l'Homme, 2000); Erik Olin Wright, Janeen Baxter, and Gunn Elizabeth Birkelund, "The Gender Gap in Workplace Authority: A Cross-National Study," *American Sociological Review* 60, no. 3 (1995): 407–35.

28. See Deborah A. Prentice and Dale T. Miller, "Pluralistic Ignorance and the Perpetuation of Social Norms by Unwitting Actors," *Advances in Experimental Social Psychology* 28 (1996): 161–209.

29. I borrow the concept of boundary work from sociologist Michèle Lamont (*Money, Morals and Manners: The Culture of the French and American Upper-Middle Class* [Chicago: University of Chicago Press, 1992]) who, in her cross-national work on the culture of upper-middle-class men in France and the United States, points to the way in which people often emphasize, through boundary work, their identity in relation to others. By drawing inclusive boundaries, individuals affirm similarities between themselves and specific others, thereby affirming some group identity. In contrast, by drawing exclusive boundaries, individuals define their own identity in opposition to others. Though Lamont uses the concept of symbolic boundaries to explain interpersonal behavior, I show that it is also useful for understanding more macro political and cultural processes. From this perspective, the kind of macro cultural convergence noted by students of globalization can occur when political elites affirm international similarities, often as a way of gaining political legitimacy. However, political elites can alternatively reject international cultural models by drawing exclusive boundaries.

30. Frank M. Serusclat, "Rapport du sénat," *Seconde session ordinaire de 1991–1992* 350 (1992), pp. 16–17.

31. For an excellent overview of elite French writings about America, both negative and positive, see Jean-Philippe Mathy, *Extrême-Occident: French Intellectuals and America* (Chicago: University of Chicago Press, 1993). See also Stanley Hoffmann, "Deux universalismes en conflit," *Tocqueville Review* 21, no. 1 (2000): 65–71, which attributes such conflict to centuries-old competition over visions of universalism.

32. See Diana Crane, ed., *The Sociology of Culture: Emerging Theoretical Perspectives* (Oxford: Basil Blackwell, 1994); Joshua Gamson, *Freaks Talk Back: Tabloid Talk Shows and Sexual Nonconformity* (Chicago: University of Chicago Press, 1998).

33. For further details about the methodology, see the Appendix.

34. This chapter thus follows in a tradition of work that examines the meaning of law in people's everyday lives, e.g., Patricia Ewick and Susan S. Silbey, *The Common Place of Law: Stories From Everyday Life* (Chicago: University of Chicago Press, 1998). However, it also pays particular attention to the effect of national and institutional context on personal perceptions of the law.

35. See W. Lance Bennett, *News: The Politics of Illusion* (New York: Longman, 2001); Steven Brill, "War Gets the Monica Treatment," *Brill's Content,* 99–137 (July/August 1999); Robert Entman, *Democracy Without Citizens: Media and the Decay of American Politics* (Oxford: Oxford University Press, 1989); Herbert Gans, *Deciding What's News* (New York: Pantheon, 1979), 78–80; Todd Gitlin, *The Whole World Is Watching: Mass Media in the Making and Unmaking of the New Left* (Berkeley: University of California Press, 1980).

36. Ann Swidler, "Culture in Action: Symbols and Strategies," *American Sociological Review* 51, no. 2 (1986): 273–86.

CHAPTER 11

Understanding the Transgender Community: Support and Resiliency in the Face of Discrimination

By Rosalind Kichler

In June 2014, *Time* magazine's cover featured now well-known transgender actress and activist Laverne Cox standing tall next to the headline "The Transgender Tipping Point: America's Next Civil Rights Frontier." Yet as of early 2016, only thirteen states have laws in place to facilitate gender marker change on both birth certificates and driver's licenses, only twenty states prohibit housing and employment discrimination based on gender identity, and, despite the promises of the Affordable Care Act (2011), insurance coverage for medical transition services, such as sex hormones and gender reassignment surgery, is still not guaranteed (Human Rights Campaign 2016a). In 2015, twenty-one anti-trans state laws were proposed; this number more than doubled in 2016 to forty-four as of this writing (Human Rights Campaign 2016b). In 2015, more than twenty trans persons, primarily trans women of color, were murdered simply for being transgender (National LGBTQ Task Force 2016). Moreover, the National Transgender Discrimination Survey (NTDS) found almost two-thirds (63%) of respondents had experienced a serious act of discrimination; twenty-three percent of respondents had experienced at least *three* such serious acts of discrimination (Grant et al. 2011). Although there may be increased visibility for trans identities and trans issues, trans persons still experience overwhelming discrimination.

Yet to speak only of discrimination ignores the incredible efforts of trans persons to survive and even thrive in these adverse conditions. The minority stress model (Meyer 2003) provides one framework for understanding how *resiliency*, defined as "anything that can lead to more positive adaptations to minority stress," can be developed despite increased exposure to discrimination (Meyer 2015, 210). Specifically, the minority stress model predicts that stigmatized minorities such as transgender persons suffer from worse mental health due to exposure to discrimination (minority stress), but identification with and support from communities of similarly stigmatized others can ameliorate the deleterious effects of this discrimination (Meyer 2003). While stigmatized individuals can and do develop resilience, Meyer (2015) argues resiliency is best understood as a *community-level* resource. Although trans persons are often assumed to have access to and support from "the" LGBTQ community or "the" trans community, many may not understand themselves as members of this community nor feel supported by it.

In this chapter, I bring together scholarship on the minority stress model and on lesbian, gay, bisexual, and transgender (LGBT) community and communities. Despite the importance of community to the minority stress model, community remains an underdeveloped concept (Frost and Meyer 2012). Moreover, within both bodies of scholarship, research on gender minorities has lagged behind research on sexual minorities. In particular, research on the transgender community has been almost entirely limited to health needs assessments. Through an examination of transgender community and communities, researchers can contribute to the sparse but growing sociological literature on transgender lives. Further, a focus on transgender community enables social scientists to suggest interventions capable of addressing the mental health inequalities currently experienced by transgender persons.

● DEFINING TRANSGENDER IDENTITIES: A BRIEF OVERVIEW OF RELEVANT TERMINOLOGY

Just as there are no universally agreed-upon definitions of lesbian, gay, bisexual, and queer identity, there is no agreed-upon definition of transgender. Transgender is commonly used as "an umbrella term to include everyone who challenges the boundaries of sex and gender" (Feinberg 1996, x). Thus transgender includes any persons whose gender identity, defined as "one's subjective sense of being a boy, girl, man, woman, or some combination thereof," and/or gender expression, defined as the "social presentation of gender in everyday life (through dress, bodily comportment, vocal expressions, etc.)" does not match the sex and/or gender they were assigned at birth (Pfeffer 2010, 167). Gender is assigned at birth based on doctors' categorization of babies' sex as either male or female. Although as many as one in a thousand babies are likely born intersex, meaning their genitals, hormones, and chromosomes do not exactly align with the supposedly discrete categories of "male" or "female,"[1] gender is assumed to follow from sex: male babies are boys who will grow up to be men, and female babies are girls who will grow up to be women.

Because of the distinction drawn between sex and gender, some distinguish trans*gender* persons from trans*sexual* persons. In this classificatory scheme, transsexual individuals are those who seek to change their *sex* by pursuing medical transition, whereas transgender individuals only seek to change their *gender* and thus do not pursue medical intervention. However, given queer theoretical critiques that sex is "always already" gender (see Butler 2008 for more) and the complexities of self-definitions,[2] transgender or simply "trans" is increasingly used to refer to all persons who *transverse* the sex and/or gender they were assigned at birth. Trans people may be trans women, trans men, or nonbinary (i.e., genderqueer). Trans persons falling in this latter category hold a gender that falls either outside or between the binary categorizations of male/man and female/woman. "Gender minority" is also an increasingly popular term used to describe trans persons, however it is also used as an umbrella term for *any* person who describes themselves as gender nonconforming, even if they do not identify as trans (Reisner, Greytak, Parsons, and Ybarra 2015).

Although many scholars refer to trans women as "female-to-male" (FTM) and trans men as "male-to-female" (MTF), there is a desire to move away from these labels because they serve to both reify binary and (Western) constructions of sex/gender and overemphasize the importance of sex in determining gender (Feinberg 1996, xi). In agreement with this logic, I do not use the terms FTM or MTF in this chapter and instead employ only the terms trans woman and trans man. Additionally, many trans persons have pushed to introduce the term "cisgender" (cis) to mark persons whose gender identity and expression does match the sex/

gender they were assigned at birth. Cis should be used instead of "non-transgender," as the latter terminology normalizes cisgender identity, further contributing to the stigmatization and marginalization of transgender identities. Consequently, cissexism refers to the system of oppression that normalizes and privileges cisgender over transgender, creating prejudice, stigmatization, discrimination, and marginalization against all trans people (Hibbs 2014; for more on the operations of cissexism, see Schilt and Westbrook 2009; Westbrook and Schilt 2014).

● THE MINORITY STRESS MODEL AND TRANS PERSONS

The minority stress model (Meyer 2003, 1995) was developed to explain mental health disparities between sexual minority persons (primarily lesbian, gay, and bisexual, but also other sexual identities associated with same-sex/gender attraction, such as queer) and their heterosexual counterparts. According to this model, these inequalities can be explained by sexual minority persons' exposure to unique discrimination stressors related to their stigmatized sexual minority status. Minority stress ranges from distal to proximal. Distal stressors are objective experiences of discrimination, whereas proximal stressors are more subjective and thus more closely related to individuals' self-identifications. Meyers (2003) identifies three types of proximal stressors: expectations of discriminatory events and the constant vigilance such expectations require, concealment of sexuality, and internalized homophobia. However, according to the minority stress model, sexual minority status conveys unique *group-level* resources, too (Meyer 2003). These resources, specifically identification with and support from other sexual minority persons, are conceptualized under the framework of "minority coping" and can attenuate the deleterious effects of minority stress by providing support and enabling the development of resiliency.

Trans people, even straight trans persons, have often been included as members of the sexual minority community for a variety of reasons,[3] as indicated by the commonly used acronym LGBT. Considering that trans persons are in many ways already members of the community, the minority stress model seems particularly applicable to them. In fact, Meyer (2015, 209) notes, "Although I originally developed minority stress in the context of sexual orientation, gender identity is similarly implicated." Thus a small but growing body of research has begun empirically testing the minority stress model as an explanation for the worse mental health of transgender persons (Bockting, Miner, Swinburne, Hamilton, and Coleman 2013; Budge, Rossman, and Howard 2014; Goldblum et al. 2012; Miller and Grollman 2015; Reisner et al. 2015; Su et al. 2016; Testa, Jimenez, and Rankin 2014; Testa et al. 2012).

Just as sexual minority persons are exposed to unique heterosexist discrimination stressors due to their sexual orientation, trans persons face unique cissexist discrimination stressors due to their transgender status. The National Transgender Discrimination Survey (NTDS), the most extensive survey of trans persons to date, found almost two-thirds (63%) of respondents had experienced a serious act of discrimination, defined as events that would have a major impact on a person's quality of life and ability to sustain themselves financially or emotionally; twenty-three percent of respondents had experienced at least *three* such serious acts of discrimination (Grant et al. 2011). Trans persons suffer from worse mental and physical health than their cis peers. According to NTDS (Grant et al. 2011), an astronomical 41 percent of respondents reported having attempted suicide, compared to 1.6 percent of the general population. Trans persons were also found to have higher rates of lifetime cigarette, alcohol, and drug use (Grant et al. 2011). One of the benefits of using the minority stress model is that it establishes that the poorer mental health of trans persons is not a result of being transgender, but of exposure to gender minority stress. Application of the minority stress model thus helps counter the pathologization of trans identities (Hendricks and Testa 2012).

The minority stress model has been found to be highly applicable to trans persons. The poor mental health of trans persons, as indicated by high suicidality (Clements-Noelle, Marx, and Katz 2006; Goldblum et al. 2012; Miller and Grollman 2015; Su et al. 2016; Testa et al. 2012, 2014), depression (Budge et al. 2014; Gonzalez, Bockting, Beckman, and Duran 2012; Nuttbrock et al. 2010; Su et al. 2016), substance use (Reisner et al. 2015; Wolf and Dew 2010), and general psychological distress (Bockting et al. 2013; Sanchez and Vilain 2009), can be explained by their exposure to gender minority stress. As with sexual minority stress, this stress ranges from distal to proximal, including objective experiences of discrimination such as physical and sexual assault (Testa et al. 2012) or gender-based victimization (Goldblum et al. 2012); expectations of discrimination and the constant vigilance these require, as exemplified by feelings of fear when first understanding oneself as trans (Testa et al. 2014); attempts to conceal one's stigmatized identity, such as being able to live only "part time" in one's gender (Gonzalez et al. 2012); and internalized transphobia. As a form of stigma visibility, gender nonconformity may moderate the relationship between transgender status and experiences of discrimination; if others can read one as trans, then discrimination becomes more likely (Miller and Grollman 2015).

Identification with and support from other gender minority persons attenuates the deleterious effects of minority stress through the development of resiliency (Bocking et al. 2013; Follins, Walker, and Lewis 2014; Sanchez and Vilain 2009; Su et al. 2016; Testa et al. 2014). At high levels, peer support has been shown to fully moderate the relationship between enacted stigma (objective experiences of discrimination) and psychological distress for trans persons (Bockting et al. 2013). More proximally, higher levels of self-acceptance of trans identity have been found to greatly reduce trans respondents' likelihood of experiencing depressive symptoms (Su et al. 2016). Among genderqueer trans persons, social support is significantly and negatively associated with both depression and anxiety (Budge et al. 2014).

Many of the above studies examine resilience as an *individual-level* construct. Although personal resiliency is important, a focus on individual resilience is potentially hazardous because "it can remove or reduce social responsibility to protect disadvantaged populations" (Meyer 2015, 211). Instead, Meyer (2015) urges greater attention to *community-level* resilience in order to maintain the minority stress model's emphasis on the social conditions related to stigma, discrimination, and prejudice, which are responsible for producing negative mental health outcomes for disadvantaged populations. Further, much of individual resilience is developed through contact with sexual and gender minority communities that provide alternative norms, values, role models, and opportunities for social support to the similarly stigmatized (Meyer 2003, 2015). For example, among trans women, the more positively respondents felt about being a part of a "transsexual" community, the less psychological distress they experienced (Sanchez and Vilain 2009). Similarly, both trans men and women who had prior awareness of other trans persons at the time when they first felt they were transgender were significantly less likely to report feeling fearful; trans men and women were also significantly less likely to report feeling suicidal when they first began identifying as transgender if they had prior awareness of other trans people or had met another trans person (Testa et al. 2014). However, the relationship between having prior awareness of other trans people or having met another trans person and decreased fearfulness and suicidality when first experiencing feelings of being transgender did not hold for nonbinary trans persons (Testa et al. 2014). This is likely a consequence of the relative invisibility and lack of resources for nonbinary trans people in many trans communities.

Just as there is no monolithic sexual minority community that supports all its members (Frost and Meyer 2012), there is no monolithic supportive gender minority community. Yet minority stress model research often measures connectedness to "the" gender minority (or sexual and gender minority) community as a proxy for resilience (Frost and Meyer 2012). Unfortunately, "the" LGBT community is frequently understood as white, middle class, male, and biphobic. Consequently, sexual and gender minority persons of color, poor and working-class LGBT persons, women, and bisexual persons may feel less connected to "the" LGBT community. Although Frost and Meyer (2012) do not theorize how "the" trans community may privilege other intersecting identities, it is likely similarly white and middle class. Further, there may be an emphasis on trans persons who undergo (or at least desire to undergo) medical transition (Siebler 2012). Such an emphasis likely excludes trans persons who do not desire medical transition (especially nonbinary trans persons), or cannot afford it. Without an empirically grounded understanding of community, minority stress model research is likely to miss much of the support that comes from trans persons' communities, but not "the" trans community. Because research on trans community is extremely limited, in the following section, I primarily explore studies on sexual minority persons' understandings and experiences of community but provide parallels to trans understandings and experiences wherever possible.

● COMMUNITY AND COMMUNITIES

Within the social sciences, there is little agreement on the definition of community. Over fifty years ago, Hillery (1955) identified ninety-four distinct definitions of community; however, he notes that approximately two-thirds of those definitions agreed upon social interaction, shared ties, and an area context (shared geographic location) as fundamental to community. In a more updated examination of community, MacQueen et al. (2001, 1929 found community is best defined as "a group of people with diverse characteristics who are linked by social ties, share common perspectives, and engage in joint action in geographical locations or settings." Shared geographic locations may be especially important to the development of sexual minority communities, as these communities have frequently been "imagined" (see Anderson 2006) to be located exclusively in urban, coastal cities like San Francisco (Weston 1995). Yet in a "post-gay" era where gay identity is increasingly assimilationist (Ghaziani 2011), sexuality has been gradually unbound from geography. For example, a study of urban gay men found that social connection with other gay men, but not residence in a gay enclave neighborhood, drove respondents' feelings of attachment to gay community (Kelly, Carpiano, Easterbrook, and Parsons 2014).

Much of the research on sexual minority communities has worked to complicate the imagined "gay" community (Easterbrook, Carpiano, Kelly, and Parsons 2013; Fraser 2008; Heath and Mulligan 2008; Holt 2011; LeBeau and Jellison 2009; Lehavot, Balsam, and Ibrahim-Wells 2009; Peacock, Eyre, Quinn, and Kegeles 2001; Woolwine 2000). Among a relatively homogenous sample of twenty-six gay men belonging to the San Francisco gay community, *thirty-two* different sub-communities were identified (Peacock et al. 2001). LaBeau and Jellison (2009) found little agreement in gay and bisexual men's conception of the gay community, with some believing it was locally bounded while others viewed it as a global community encompassing all sexual (and even gender) minority persons; further, participants differed on whether they conceived of the gay community as an informal friendship network or as a collection of formal institutions such as community centers and gay bars and clubs. Trans persons, who may participate in LGBT communities, likely also hold multiple, competing conceptualizations of both LGBT community and transgender community.

In a mixed sample of sexual minority men and women, divides were found based on sexual identity such that gay men were more likely to socialize with other gay men, lesbian women were more likely to socialize with lesbian women, and so on (Easterbrook et al. 2013). Similarly, lesbian and bisexual women participate in distinct communities based on their different sexualities (Heath and

Mulligan 2008; Lehavot et al. 2009). Sexual minority women's communities are further strained not only by biphobia, which ostracizes bisexual women from lesbian communities, but also by racism and classism (Lehavot et al. 2009). Trans communities may similarly segregate by gender and by specific trans identity, such as binary and nonbinary identities. Race and class differences may place additional strains on trans communities.

Despite these challenges to community, many sexual minority persons still imagine a gay community united by sameness (Easterbrook et al. 2013; Fraser 2008; Holt 2011; Woolwine 2000). Unfortunately, this imagined sameness has real, negative consequences. Amongst a sample of young, Australian gay men, Fraser (2008) found many participants felt excluded from the gay community due to their perceived differences from it. Researchers have thus begun to advocate for understanding gay community and communities as *personal* communities (Holt 2011; Morris, McLaren, McLachlan, and Jenkins 2015; Wilkinson et al. 2012; Woolwine 2000). Woolwine (2000) argues that gay men experience community in three ways: as an imagined community (albeit one that participants recognized as divided), as centered around specific gay or AIDS-related organizations and institutions, and as personal communities. Personal communities created through friends and friendship networks provided "the most pure primary experience of community" (Woolwine 2000, 31). Similarly, Holt (2011) found that gay male participants expressed ambivalence about the gay community and instead found a sense of belonging in personal communities. Path analysis shows a sense of belonging to a general gay community was determined by a gay man's sense of belonging to gay groups and with gay friends; in turn, a sense of belonging to the general community significantly reduced depressive symptoms (Morris et al. 2015).

Families of choice (Weston 1991) are similar to personal communities, although the latter is perhaps more inclusive, as it does not necessarily reify the distinction between family and friendship (Pahl and Spencer 2004). Families of choice are familial-like relationships of intimacy that are chosen, instead of defined by legal or blood ties (Weston 1991). Families of choice emerge from specific historical relations. With regards to the LGB community, it was the emergence of a coherent "homosexual" identity (see Foucault 1990 for a detailed theoretical discussion of the emergence and crystallization of homosexual identity) that necessitated the creation of communities specifically for "homosexuals," especially as heightened gay visibility also brought heightened discrimination against sexual minorities. Yet, "gay" identity was not enough to unite all sexual minority persons, who varied by sexuality, gender, race/ethnicity, class, age, geography, and so on; nor could the gay community provide support to all its members as families are expected to. Thus it was necessary for LGB persons to form specific, intentional ties with other sexual minority persons in order to build their own close, familial relationships, based on mutual love and capable of providing support to all members (Weston 1991).

Currently, there is no research explicitly utilizing a families of choice perspective in order to understand the lives of trans persons. One study of black, gay families in the South (Levitt, Horne, Puckett, Sweeney, and Hampton 2015) interviewed ten self-identified gay men, of which half identified with female roles, used she/her pronouns and had feminine presentations. However, none of these participants identified as transgender and thus conclusions about trans families of choice are difficult to draw. It seems likely that when trans identity emerged as a divisive category of difference serving to marginalize trans persons in the mainstream gay community, trans persons responded by forming their own families of choice with other trans persons. Further, as trans persons become more visible and more individuals are able to claim a trans identity, it is likely that variation in other identities may preclude the formation of a functioning, singular trans community. Thus, given the historical moment in which we find ourselves, when trans visibility is greater than ever, yet legal and social discrimination against trans persons remains high, families of choice may provide a valuable framework for understanding trans communities.

Research on transgender communities has been almost exclusively limited to health needs assessments, although there are exceptions. Hines (2007) and Schrock, Holden, and Reid (2004) have conducted research with trans support groups, which may very well be considered communities. Yet both studies utilize a social movements perspective and are thus interested in how these groups facilitate mobilization and activism, not community. Siebler (2012) focuses specifically on online trans community; however, her examination is more theoretical than empirical. She suggests that, while online trans communities may offer needed information and counter trans individuals' feelings of isolation, ultimately these communities present "a singular and unified pedagogy of transgender identity: be who you are, but you need to spend money to align your body with who you really are; your natural state *is* one that is unnatural and needs remediation" (Siebler 2012, 95). Thus, her study fits better within the more extensive, albeit still limited, literature on trans identity. Factor and Rothblum (2008) provide perhaps the only studies to ask trans participants about their feelings of connection to both the LGB community and the trans community. The authors find no differences in feelings of connection to the trans community when comparing trans men, trans women, and genderqueer trans people; however, genderqueer participants did feel significantly more connection to the LGB community than both trans men and trans women (Factor and Rothblum 2008).

● CONCLUSION

Support is an important component of the minority stress model (Meyer 2003) because it enables stigmatized minorities, like trans persons, to cope with persistent experiences of discrimination and develop resiliency. However, within this model, support is unique in that it springs from communities of similarly stigmatized others. Hence, without an understanding of community, minority stress scholars cannot accurately capture support or resiliency. While the concept of community has been interrogated for sexual minorities (Easterbrook et al. 2013; Fraser 2008; Heath and Mulligan 2008; Holt 2011; LeBeau and Jellison 2009; Lehavot et al. 2009; Morris et al. 2015; Peacock et al. 2001; Wilkinson et al. 2012; Woolwine 2000), the same cannot be said for gender minorities. Future research must begin to untangle the imagined trans community from trans persons' actual experiences of community. Much support provided by trans communities may be missed when participants are asked only about support in reference to "the" LGBTQ and/or "the" trans community.

An advantage of using the minority stress model is that it clearly establishes that the poorer mental health of trans persons is not a result of being transgender, but of exposure to gender minority stress, and thus helps counter the continued pathologization of trans identities and lives (Hendricks and Testa 2012). It therefore identifies societal interventions aimed at reducing cissexism, such as allowing trans persons to use facilities (restrooms, changing rooms, dormitories, et cetera) consistent with their gender, facilitating the process of changing gender markers on identity documents, mandating coverage of medical transition services, and enacting antidiscrimination laws, as solutions for reducing transgender mental health inequalities. Encouraging the development of resiliency, particularly by supporting trans persons to construct and maintain strong communities, is another solution for addressing these mental health inequalities. Focusing on community, support, and resiliency enables researchers to bring in the lived experiences of trans persons in a way that positions them as agentic actors who, despite facing cissexist discrimination, stigmatization, and marginalization on a daily basis, are able to survive and even thrive by creating unique communities for themselves.

● NOTES

1. See the Intersex Society of North America (2008) for more information.

2. According to Feinburg (1996, x), "not all transsexuals choose surgery or hormones; some transgender people do."

3. An exploration of these reasons is beyond the scope of this literature review; for an excellent ethnographic account of the emergence of transgender as an identity category distinct from sexual identity, see Valentine (2007).

● REFERENCES

Anderson, B. 2006. *Imagined Communities: Reflections on the Origin and Spread of Nationalism*. New York: Verso. (Original work published 1983 by Verso Books, London, UK.)

Bockting, W. O., M. H. Miner, R. E. Swinburne, A. Hamilton, and E. Coleman. 2013. "Stigma, Mental Health, and Resilience in an Online Sample of the US Transgender Population." *American Journal of Public Health* 103 (5): 943–51.

Budge, S. L., H. K. Rossman, and K. A. S. Howard. 2014. "Coping and Psychological Distress Among Genderqueer Individuals: The Moderating Effect of Social Support." *Journal of LGBT Issues in Counseling* 8 (1): 95–117.

Butler, J. 2008. *Gender Trouble: Feminism and the Subversion of Identity*. New York: Routledge. (Original work published 1990 by Routledge, Abingdon-on-Thames, UK).)

Clements-Noelle, K., R. Marx, and M. Katz. 2006. "Attempted Suicide Among Transgender Persons: The Influence of Gender-Based Discrimination and Victimization." *Journal of Homosexuality* 51 (3): 53–69.

Easterbrook, A., R. M. Carpiano, B. C. Kelly, and J. T. Parsons. 2013. "The Personal Experiences of Community Among Urban Gay Men, Lesbians, and Bisexuals: Melting Pot or Mosaic?" *Social Science Quarterly* 95 (3): 682–700.

Factor, R., and E. Rothblum. 2008. "Exploring Gender Identity and Community Among Three Groups of Transgender Individuals in the United States: MTFs, FTMs, and Genderqueers." *Health Sociology Review* 17 (3): 235–53.

Feinberg, L. 1996. *Transgender Warriors: Making History from Joan of Arc to RuPaul.* Boston: Beacon Press.

Follins, L. D., J. J. Walker, and M. K. Lewis. 2014. "Resilience in Black Lesbian, Gay, Bisexual, and Transgender Individuals: A Critical Review of the Literature." *Journal of Gay & Lesbian Mental Health* 18 (2): 190–212.

Foucault, M. 1990. *The History of Sexuality Volume 1: An Introduction,* translated by R. Hurley. New York: Vintage Books. (Original work published 1976 by Gallimard, Paris, Fr.)

Fraser, S. 2008. "Getting out in the 'Real World': Young, Men, Queer and Theories of Gay Community." *Journal of Homosexuality* 55 (2): 245–64.

Frost, D. M. and I. H. Meyer. 2012. "Measuring Community Connectedness Among Diverse Sexual Minority Populations." *The Journal of Sex Research* 49 (1): 36–49.

Ghaziani, A. 2011. "Post-Gay Collective Identity Construction." *Social Problems* 58 (1): 99–125.

Goldblum, P., R. J. Testa, S. Pflum, M. L. Hendricks, J. Bradford, and B. Bongar. 2012. "The Relationship Between Gender-Based Victimization and Suicide Attempts in Transgender People." *Professional Psychology: Research and Practice* 43 (5): 468–75.

Gonzalez, C. A., W. O. Bockting, L. J. Beckman, and R. E. Duran. 2012. "Agentic and Communal Personality Traits: Their Association with Depression and Resilience Among Transgender Women." *Sex Roles* 67 (9): 528–43.

Heath, M., and E. Mulligan. 2008. "Shiny Happy Same-Sex Attracted Woman Seeking Same": How Communities Contribute to Bisexual and Lesbian Women's Well-Being." *Health Sociology Review* 17 (3): 290–302.

Hendricks, M. L., and R. J. Testa. 2012. "A Conceptual Framework for Clinical Work with Transgender and Gender Nonconforming Clients: An Adaptation of the Minority Stress Model." *Professional Psychology: Research and Practice* 43 (5): 460–67.

Hibbs, C. 2014. "Cissexism." In *Encyclopedia of critical psychology*, 235–37. Edited by T. Thomas. New York: Springer.

Hillery, G. A., Jr. 1955. "Definitions of Community: Areas of Agreement." *Rural Sociology* 20: 111–23.

Hines, S. 2007. "Transgendering Care: Practices of Care Within Transgender Communities." *Critical Social Policy* 27 (4): 462–86.

Holt, M. 2011. "Gay Men and Ambivalence About "Gay Community": From Gay Community Attachment to Personal Communities." *Culture, Health & Sexuality* 13 (8): 857–71.

Human Rights Campaign. 2016a. *Anti-Transgender Legislation Spreads Nationwide, Bills targeting Transgender Children Surge.* http://hrc-assets.s3-website-us-east-1.amazonaws.com//files/assets/resources/HRC-Anti-Trans-Issue-Brief-FINAL-REV2.pdf. Human Rights Campaign. 2016b. Maps of State Laws and Policies. http://www.hrc.org/state_maps.

Intersex Society of North America. 2008. Frequently asked questions. http://www.isna.org/faq.

Kelly, B. C., R. M. Carpiano, A. Easterbrook, and J. T. Parsons. 2014. "Exploring the Gay Community Question: Neighborhood and Network Influences on the Experience of Community Among Urban Gay Men." *The Sociological Quarterly* 55 (1): 23–48.

LeBeau, R. T., and W. A. Jellison. 2009. "Why Get Involved? Exploring Gay and Bisexual Men's Experiences of the Gay Community." *Journal of Homosexuality* 56 (1): 56–76.

Lehavot, K., K. F. Balsam, and G. D. Ibrahim-Wells. 2009. "Redefining the American Quilt: Definitions and Experiences of Community Among Ethnically Diverse Lesbian and Bisexual Women." *Journal of Community Psychology* 37 (4): 439–58.

Levitt, H. M., S. G. Horne, J. Puckett, K. K. Sweeney, and M. L. Hampton. 2015. "Gay Families: Challenging Racial and Sexual/Gender Minority Stressors Through Social Support." *Journal of GLBT Family Studies* 11 (2): 173–202.

MacQueen, K., E. McLellan, D. S. Metzger, S. Kegeles, R. P. Strauss, R. Scotti, … R. T. Trotter, II. 2001. "What Is Community? An Evidence-Based Definition for Participatory Public Health." *American Journal of Public Health* 91 (12): 1929–38.

Meyer, I. H. 2015. "Resilience in the Study of Minority Stress and Health of Sexual and Gender Minorities." *Psychology of Sexual Orientation and Gender Diversity* 2 (3): 209–13.

Meyer, I. H. 2003. "Prejudice, Social Stress, and Mental Health in Lesbian, Gay, and Bisexual Populations: Conceptual Issues and Research Evidence." *Psychological Bulletin* 129 (5): 674–97.

Meyer, I. H. 1995. "Minority Stress and Mental Health in Gay Men." *Journal of Health and Social Behavior* 36 (1): 38–56.

Miller, L. R., and E. A. Grollman. 2015. "The Social Costs of Gender Nonconformity for Transgender Adults: Implications for Discrimination and Health. *Sociological Forum* 30 (3): 809–31.

Morris, S., S. McLaren, A. J. McLachlan, and M. Jenkins, M. 2015. "Sense of Belonging to Specific Communities and Depressive Symptoms Among Australian Gay Men." *Journal of Homosexuality* 62 (6): 804–20.

Grant, J. M., L. A. Mottet, J. Tanis, J. Harrison, J. L. Herman, and M. Keisling. 2011. *Injustice at Every Turn: A Report of the National Transgender Discrimination Survey.* Washington, DC: National Center for Transgender Equality and National Gay and Lesbian Task Force.

National LGBTQ Task Force. 2016. *Stop Trans Murders.* http://www.thetaskforce.org/stop-trans-murders/.

Nuttbrock, L., S. Hwahng, W. Bockting, A. Rosenblum, M. Mason, M. Marci, and J. Becker. 2010. "Psychiatric Impact of Gender-Related Abuse Across the Life Course of Male-to-Female Transgender Persons." *Journal of Sex Research* 47 (1): 12–23.

Pahl, R., and L. Spencer. 2004. "Personal Communities: Not Simply Families of "Fate" or "Choice." *Current Sociology* 52 (2): 199–221.

Peacock, B., S. L. Eyre, S. C. Quinn, and S. Kegeles. 2001. "Delineating Differences: Sub-Communities in the San Francisco Gay Community." *Culture, Health & Sexuality* 3 (2): 183–201.

Pfeffer, C. A. 2010. "'Women's Work?' Women Partners of Transgender Men Doing Housework and Emotion Work." *Journal of Marriage and Family* 72 (1): 165–83.

Reisner, S. L., E. A. Greytak, J. T. Parsons, and M. L. Ybarra. 2015. "Gender Minority Social Stress in Adolescence: Disparities in Adolescent Bullying and Substance Use by Gender Identity." *The Journal of Sex Research* 52 (3), 243–56.

Sanchez, F. J., and E. Vilain. 2009. "Collective Self-Esteem as a Coping Resource for Male-to-Female Transsexuals." *Journal of Counseling Psychology* 56 (1): 202–09.

Schilt, K., and L. Westbrook. 2009. "Doing Gender, Doing Heteronormativity: 'Gender Normals,' Transgender People, and the Social Maintenance of Heterosexuality." *Gender & Society* 23 (4): 440–64.

Schrock, D., D. Holden, and L. Reid. 2004. "Creating Emotional Resonance: Interpersonal Emotion Work and Motivational Framing in a Transgender Community." *Social Problems* 51 (1): 61–81.

Siebler, K. 2012. "Transgender Transitions: Sex/Gender Binaries in the Digital Age." *Journal of Gay & Lesbian Mental Health* 16 (1): 74–99.

Su, D., J. A. Irwin, C. Fisher, A. Ramos, M. Kelley, D. A. R. Mendoza, and J. D. Coleman. 2016. "Mental Health Disparities Within the LGBT Population: Comparison Between Transgender and Nontransgender Individuals." *Transgender Health* 1 (1): 12–20.

Testa, R. J., C. L. Jimenez, and S. Rankin. 2014. "Risk and Resilience During Transgender Identity Development: The Effects of Awareness and Engagement with Other Transgender People on Affect." *Journal of Gay & Lesbian Mental Health* 18 (1): 31–46.

Testa, R. J., L. M. Sciacca, M. L. Hendricks, P. Goldblum, J. Bradford, and B. Bongar. 2012. "Effects of Violence on Transgender People." *Professional Psychology: Research and Practice* 43 (5): 452–59.

Valentine, D. 2007. *Imagining Transgender: An Ethnography of a Category.* Durham, NC: Duke University Press.

Weston, K. 1995. "Get Thee to a Big City: Sexual Imagery and the Great Gay Migration." *GLQ: A Journal of Lesbian & Gay Studies* 2 (3): 253–77.

Weston, K. 1991. *Families We Choose: Lesbians, Gays, Kinship.* New York: Columbia University Press.

Westbrook, L., and K. Schilt. 2014. "Doing Gender, Determining Gender: Transgender People, Gender Panics, and the Maintenance of the Sex/Gender/Sexuality System." *Gender & Society* 28 (1): 32–57.

Wilkinson, J., M. Bittman, M. Holt, P. Rawstorn, S. Kippax, and H. Worth. 2012. "Solidarity Beyond Sexuality: The Personal Communities of Gay Men." *Sociology* 46 (6): 1161–77. Wolf, E. C. M., and B. J. Dew. 2010. "Understanding Risk Factors Contributing to Substance Use Among MTF Transgender Persons." *Journal of LGBT Issues in Counseling* 6 (4): 237–56.

Woolwine, D. 2000. "Community in Gay Male Experience and Moral Discourse." *Journal of Homosexuality* 38 (4): 5–37.

CHAPTER 12

"Dude, You're a Fag": Adolescent Male Homophobia

By C. J. Pascoe

The sun shone bright and clear over River High's annual Creative and Performing Arts Happening, or CAPA. During CAPA the school's various art programs displayed students' work in a fairlike atmosphere. The front quad sported student-generated computer programs. Colorful and ornate chalk art covered the cement sidewalks. Tables lined with student-crafted pottery were set up on the grass. Tall displays of students' paintings divided the rear quad. To the left of the paintings a television blared student-directed music videos. At the rear of the back quad, a square, roped-off area of cement served as a makeshift stage for drama, choir, and dance performances. Teachers released students from class to wander around the quads, watch performances, and look at the art. This freedom from class time lent the day an air of excitement because students were rarely allowed to roam the campus without a hall pass, an office summons, or a parent/faculty escort. In honor of CAPA, the school district bussed in elementary school students from the surrounding grammar schools to participate in the day's festivities.

Running through the rear quad, Brian, a senior, yelled to a group of boys visiting from the elementary schools, "There's a faggot over there! There's a faggot over there! Come look!" Following Brian, the ten-year-olds dashed down a hallway. At the end of the hallway Brian's friend Dan pursed his lips and began sashaying toward the little boys. As he minced, he swung his hips exaggeratedly and wildly waved his arms. To the boys Brian yelled, "Look at the faggot! Watch out! He'll get you!" In response, the ten-year-olds raced back down the hallway screaming in terror. Brian and Dan repeated this drama throughout the following half hour, each time with a new group of young boys.

Making jokes like these about faggots was central to social life at River High. Indeed, boys learned long before adolescence that faggots were simultaneously predatory and passive and that they were, at all costs, to be avoided. Older boys repeatedly impressed upon younger ones through these types of homophobic rituals that whatever they did, whatever they became, however they talked, they had to avoid becoming a faggot.

Feminist scholars of masculinity have documented the centrality of homophobic insults and attitudes to masculinity (Kimmel 2001; Lehne 1998), especially in school settings (Burn 2000; Kimmel 2003; Messner 2005; Plummer 2001; G. Smith 1998; Wood 1984). They argue that homophobic teasing often characterizes masculinity in adolescence and early adulthood and that antigay slurs tend to be directed primarily at gay boys. This chapter both expands on and challenges these accounts of relationships between homophobia and masculinity. Homophobia is indeed a central mechanism in the making of contemporary American adolescent masculinity. A close analysis of the way boys at River High invoke the faggot as a disciplinary mechanism makes clear that something more than simple homophobia is at play in adolescent masculinity. The use of the word *fag* by boys at River High points to the limits of an argument that focuses centrally on homophobia. Fag is not only an identity linked to homosexual boys but an identity that can temporarily adhere to heterosexual boys as well. The fag trope is also a racialized disciplinary mechanism.

Homophobia is too facile a term with which to describe the deployment of *fag* as an epithet. By calling the use of the word *fag* homophobia—and letting the argument stop there—previous research has obscured the gendered nature of sexualized insults (Plummer 2001). Invoking homophobia to describe the ways boys aggressively tease each other overlooks the powerful relationship between masculinity and this sort of insult. Instead, it seems incidental, in this conventional line of argument, that girls do not harass each other and are not harassed in this same manner. This framing naturalizes the relationship between masculinity and homophobia, thus obscuring that such harassment is central to the formation of a gendered identity for boys in a way that it is not for girls.

Fag is not necessarily a static identity attached to a particular (homosexual) boy. Fag talk and fag imitations serve as a discourse with which boys discipline themselves and each other through joking relationships. Any boy can temporarily become a fag in a given social space or interaction. This does not mean that boys who identify as or are perceived to be homosexual aren't subject to intense harassment. Many are. But becoming a fag has as much to do with failing at the masculine tasks of competence, heterosexual prowess, and strength or in any way revealing weakness or femininity as it does with a sexual identity. This fluidity of the fag identity is what makes the specter of the fag such a powerful disciplinary mechanism. It is fluid enough that boys police their behaviors out of fear of having the fag identity permanently adhere and definitive enough so that boys recognize a fag behavior and strive to avoid it.

An analysis of the fag discourse also indicates ways in which gendered power works through racialized selves. The fag discourse is invoked differently by and in relation to white boys' bodies than it is by and in relation to African American boys' bodies. While certain behaviors put all boys at risk for becoming temporarily a fag, some behaviors can be enacted by African American boys without putting them at risk of receiving the label. The racialized meanings of the fag discourse suggest that something more than simple homophobia is involved in these sorts of interactions. It is not that gendered homophobia does not exist in African American communities. Indeed, making fun of "negro faggotry seems to be a rite of passage among contemporary black male rappers and filmmakers" (Riggs 1991, 253). However, the fact that "white women and men, gay and straight, have more or less colonized cultural debates about sexual representation" (Julien and Mercer 1991, 167) obscures varied systems of sexualized meanings among different racialized ethnic groups (Almaguer 1991). Thus far male homophobia has primarily been written about as a racially neutral phenomenon. However, as D. L. King's (2004) recent work on African American men and same-sex desire pointed out, homophobia is characterized by racial identities as well as sexual and gendered ones.

● WHAT IS A FAG? GENDERED MEANINGS

"Since you were little boys you've been told, 'Hey, don't be a little faggot,'" explained Darnell, a football player of mixed African American and white heritage, as we sat on a bench next to the athletic field. Indeed, both the boys and girls I interviewed told me that *fag* was the worst epithet one guy could direct at another. Jeff, a slight white sophomore, explained to me that boys call each other fag because "gay people aren't really liked over here and stuff." Jeremy, a Latino junior, told me that this insult literally reduced a boy to nothing, "To call someone *gay* or *fag* is like the lowest thing you can call someone. Because that's like saying that you're nothing."

Most guys explained their or others' dislike of fags by claiming that homophobia was synonymous with being a guy. For instance, Keith, a white soccer-playing senior, explained, "I think guys are just homophobic." However, boys were not equal-opportunity homophobes. Several students told me that these homophobic insults applied only to boys and not to girls. For example, while Jake, a handsome white senior, told me that he didn't like gay people, he quickly added, "Lesbians, okay, that's *good*." Similarly Cathy, a popular white cheerleader, told me, "Being a lesbian is accepted because guys think, 'Oh that's cool.'" Darnell, after telling me that boys were warned about becoming faggots, said, "They [guys] are fine with girls. I think it's the guy part that they're like ewwww." In this sense it was not strictly homophobia but a gendered homophobia that constituted adolescent masculinity in the culture of River High. It is clear, according to these comments, that lesbians were "good" because of their place in heterosexual male fantasy, not necessarily because of some enlightened approach to same-sex relationships. A popular trope in heterosexual pornography depicts two women engaging in sexual acts for the purpose of male titillation. The boys at River High are not unique in making this distinction; adolescent boys in general dislike gay men more than they dislike lesbians (Baker and Fishbein 1998). The fetishizing of sex acts between women indicates that using only the term *homophobia* to describe boys' repeated use of the word *fag* might be a bit simplistic and misleading.

Girls at River High rarely deployed the word *fag* and were never called fags. I recorded girls uttering *fag* only three times during my research. In one instance, Angela, a Latina cheerleader, teased Jeremy, a well-liked white senior involved in student government, for not ditching school with her: "You wouldn't 'cause you're a faggot." However, girls did not use this word as part of their regular lexicon. The sort of gendered homophobia that constituted adolescent masculinity did not constitute adolescent femininity. Girls were not called dykes or lesbians in any sort of regular or systematic way. Students did tell me that *slut* was the worst thing a girl could be called. However, my field notes indicate that the word *slut* (or its synonym *ho*) appeared one time for every eight times the word *fag* appeared.

Highlighting the difference between the deployment of *gay* and *fag* as insults brings the gendered nature of this homophobia into focus. For boys and girls at River High *gay* was a fairly common synonym for "stupid." While this word shared the sexual origins of *fag,* it didn't *consistently* have the skew of gender-loaded meaning. Girls and boys often used *gay* as an adjective referring to inanimate objects and male or female people, whereas they used *fag* as a noun that denoted only unmasculine males. Students used *gay* to describe anything from someone's clothes to a new school rule that they didn't like. For instance, one day in auto shop, Arnie pulled out a large older version of a black laptop computer and placed it on his desk. Behind him Nick cried, "That's a gay laptop! It's five inches thick!" The rest of the boys in the class laughed at Arnie's outdated laptop. A laptop can be gay, a movie can be gay, or a group of people can be gay. Boys used *gay* and *fag* interchangeably when they referred to other boys, but *fag* didn't have the gender-neutral attributes that *gay* frequently invoked.

Surprisingly, some boys took pains to say that the term *fag* did not imply sexuality. Darnell told me, "It doesn't even have anything to do with being gay." Similarly, J. L., a white sophomore at Hillside High (River High's cross-town rival), asserted, "*Fag,* seriously, it has nothing to do with sexual preference at all. You could just be calling somebody an idiot, you know?" I asked Ben, a quiet, white sophomore who wore heavy-metal T-shirts to auto shop each day, "What kind of things do guys get called a fag for?" Ben answered, "Anything ... literally, anything. Like you were trying to turn a wrench the wrong way, 'Dude, you're a fag.' Even if a piece of meat drops out of your sandwich, 'You fag!'" Each time Ben said, "You fag," his voice deepened as if he were imitating a more masculine boy. While Ben might rightly *feel* that a guy could be called a fag for "anything … literally, anything," there were actually specific behaviors that, when enacted by most boys, could render them more vulnerable to a *fag* epithet. In this instance Ben's comment highlights the use of *fag* as a generic insult for incompetence, which in the world of River High, was central to a masculine identity. A boy could get called a fag for exhibiting any sort of behavior defined as unmasculine (although not necessarily behaviors aligned with femininity): being stupid or incompetent, dancing, caring too much about clothing, being too emotional, or expressing interest (sexual or platonic) in other guys. However, given the extent of its deployment and the laundry list of behaviors that could get a boy in trouble, it is no wonder that Ben felt a boy could be called fag for "anything." These non-sexual meanings didn't replace sexual meanings but rather existed alongside them.

One-third (thirteen) of the boys I interviewed told me that, while they might liberally insult each other with the term, they would not direct it at a homosexual peer. Jabes, a Filipino senior, told me, "I actually say it *[fag]* quite a lot, except for when I'm in the company of an actual homosexual person. Then I try not to say it at all. But when I'm just hanging out with my friends I'll be like, 'Shut up, I don't want you hear you any more, you stupid fag.'" Similarly J. L. compared homosexuality to a disability, saying there was "no way" he'd call an actually gay guy a fag because "there's people who are the retarded people who nobody wants to associate with. I'll be so nice to those guys, and I hate it when people make fun of them. It's like, 'Bro do you realize that they can't help that?' And then there's gay people. They were born that way." According to this group of boys, gay was a legitimate, or at least biological, identity.

There was a possibility, however slight, that a boy could be gay and masculine (Connell 1995). David, a handsome white senior dressed smartly in khaki pants and a white button-down shirt, told me, "Being gay is just a lifestyle. It's someone you choose to sleep with. You can still throw around a football and be gay." It was as if David was justifying the use of the word *fag* by arguing that gay men could be men if they tried but that if they failed at it (i.e., if they couldn't throw a football) then they deserved to be called a fag. In other words, to be a fag was, by definition, the opposite of masculine, whether the word was deployed with sexualized or nonsexualized meanings. In explaining this to me, Jamaal, an African American junior, cited the explanation of the popular rap artist Eminem: "Although I don't like Eminem, he had a good definition of it. It's like taking away your title. In an interview they were like, 'You're always capping on gays, but then you sing with Elton John.' He was like 'I don't mean gay as in gay.'" This is what Riki Wilchins (2003) calls the "Eminem Exception. Eminem explains that he doesn't call people 'faggot' because of their sexual orientation but because they're weak and unmanly" (72). This is precisely the way boys at River High used the term *faggot*. While it was not necessarily acceptable to be gay, at least a man who was gay could do other things that would render him acceptably masculine. A fag, by the very definition of the word, could not be masculine.

This distinction between fag as an unmasculine and problematic identity and gay as a possibly masculine, although marginalized, sexual identity is not limited to a teenage lexicon; it is reflected in both psychological discourses and gay and lesbian activism. Eve Sedgwick (1995) argues that in contemporary psychological literature homosexuality is no longer a problem for men so long as the homosexual man is of the right age and gender orientation. In this literature a homosexual male must be an adult and must be masculine. Male homosexuality is not pathologized, but gay male *effeminacy* is. The lack of masculinity is the problem, not the sexual practice or orientation. Indeed, the edition of the *Diagnostic and Statistical Manual of Mental Disorders* (a key document in the mental health field) that erased homosexuality as a diagnosis in the 1970s added a new diagnosis in its wake: Gender Identity Disorder. According to Sedgwick, the criteria for diagnosis are different for girls and boys. A girl has to actually assert that she is a boy, indicating a psychotic disconnection with reality, whereas a boy need only display a preoccupation with female activities. The policing of boys' gender orientation and of a strict masculine identity for gay men is also reflected in gay culture itself. The war against fags as the specter of unmasculine manhood appears in gay male personal ads in which men look for "straight-appearing, straight-acting men." This concern with both straight and gay men's masculinity not only reflects teenage boys' obsession with hypermasculinity but also points to the conflict at the heart of the contemporary "crisis of masculinity" being played out in popular, scientific, and educational arenas.

● BECOMING A FAG: FAG FLUIDITY

"The ubiquity of the word *faggot* speaks to the reach of its discrediting capacity" (Corbett 2001, 4). It's almost as if boys cannot help shouting it out on a regular basis—in the hallway, in class, or across campus as a greeting. In my fieldwork I was amazed by the way the word seemed to pop uncontrollably out of boys' mouths in all kinds of situations.[1] To quote just one of many instances from my field notes: two boys walked out of the PE locker room, and one yelled, "Fucking faggot!" at no one in particular. None of the other students paid them any mind, since this sort of thing happened so frequently. Similar spontaneous yelling of some variation of the word *fag,* seemingly apropos of nothing, happened repeatedly among boys throughout the school. This and repeated imitations of fags constitute what I refer to as a "fag discourse."

Fag discourse is central to boys' joking relationships. Joking cements relationships among boys (Kehily and Nayak 1997; Lyman 1998) and helps to manage anxiety and discomfort (Freud 1905). Boys both connect with one another and manage the anxiety around this sort of relationship through joking about fags. Boys invoked the specter of the fag in two ways: through humorous imitation and through lobbing the epithet at one another. Boys at River High imitated the fag by acting out an exaggerated "femininity" and/or by pretending to sexually desire other boys. As indicated by the introductory vignette in which an older boy imitated a predatory fag to threaten little boys, male students at River High linked these performative scenarios with a fag identity. They also lobbed the *fag* epithet at each other in a verbal game of hot potato, each careful to deflect the insult quickly by hurling it toward someone else. These games and imitations made up a fag discourse that highlighted the fag not as a static but rather as a fluid identity that boys constantly struggled to avoid.

In imitative performances the fag discourse functioned as a constant reiteration of the fag's existence, affirming that the fag was out there; boys reminded themselves and each other that at any moment they could become fags if they were not sufficiently masculine. At the same time these performances demonstrated that the boy who was invoking the fag was *not* a fag. Emir, a tall, thin African American boy, frequently imitated fags to draw laughs from other students in his introductory drama class. One day Mr. McNally, the drama teacher, disturbed by the noise outside the classroom, turned to the open door, saying, "We'll shut this unless anyone really wants to watch sweaty boys playing basketball." Emir lisped, "I wanna watch the boys play!" The rest of the class cracked up at his imitation. No one in the class actually thought Emir was gay, as he purposefully mocked both same-sex sexual desire (through pretending to admire the boys playing basketball) and an effeminate gender identity (through speaking with a lisp and in a high-pitched voice). Had he said this in all seriousness, the class most likely would have responded in stunned silence. Instead, Emir reminded them he was masculine by immediately dropping the fag act. After imitating a fag, boys assure others that they are not a fag by instantly becoming masculine again after the performance. They mock their own performed femininity and/ or same-sex desire, assuring themselves and others that such an identity deserves derisive laughter.

Boys consistently tried to force others into the fag position by lobbing the *fag* epithet at each other. One day in auto shop, Jay was rummaging through a junk-filled car in the parking lot. He poked his head out of the trunk and asked, "Where are Craig and Brian?" Neil responded with "I think they're over there," pointing, then thrusting his hips and pulling his arms back and forth to indicate that Craig and Brian might be having sex. The boys in auto shop laughed. This sort of joke temporarily labeled both Craig and Brian as faggots. Because the fag discourse was so familiar, the other boys immediately understood that Neil was indicating that Craig and Brian were having sex. However, these were not necessarily identities that stuck. Nobody actually thought Craig and Brian were homosexuals. Rather, the fag identity was fluid—certainly an identity that no boy wanted but that most boys could escape, usually by engaging in some sort of discursive contest to turn another boy into a fag.

In this way the fag became a hot potato that no boy wanted to be left holding. One of the best ways to move out of the fag position was to thrust another boy into that position. For instance, soon after Neil made the joke about Brian having sex with Craig, Brian lobbed the *fag* epithet at someone else, deflecting it from himself, by initiating a round of a favorite game in auto shop, the "cock game." Brain said quietly, looking at Josh, "Josh loves the cock," then slightly louder, "Josh loves the cock." He continued saying this until he was yelling, "JOSH LOVES THE COCK!" The rest of the boys laughed hysterically as Josh slunk away, saying, "I have a bigger dick than all you motherfuckers!" These two instances show how the fag could be mapped, for a moment, onto one boy's body and how he, in turn, could attach it to another boy, thus deflecting it from himself. In the first instance Neil made fun of Craig and Brian for simply hanging out together. In the second instance Brian went from being a fag to making Josh into a fag through the "cock game." Through joking interactions boys moved in and out of the fag identity by discursively creating another as a fag.

Given the pervasiveness of fag jokes and the fluidity of the fag identity, it is difficult for boys to consistently avoid the brand. As Ben stated, it almost seemed that a boy could get called a fag for "anything." But most readily acknowledged that there were spaces, behaviors, and bodily comportments that made one more likely to be subject to the fag discourse, such as bodily practices involving clothing and dancing.

According to boys at River, fags cared about the style of their clothes, wore tighter clothes, and cared about cleanliness. Nils explained to me that he could tell that a guy was a fag by the way he dressed: "Most guys wear loose-fitting clothing, just kind of baggy. They [fags] wear more tight clothes. More fashionable, I guess." Similarly, nonfags were not supposed to care about dirtying their clothes. Auto shop was a telling example of this. Given that the boys spent two hours working with greasy car parts, they frequently ended up smudged and rumpled by the end of class. While in the front of the classroom there was a room boys could change in, most of them opted not to change out of their school clothes, with a few modifying their outfits by taking their shirts off and walking around in their "beaters." These tank tops were banned at River High because of their association with gang membership. Auto shop was the one place on campus where boys could wear them with impunity. Like most of the boys in auto shop, Ben never changed out of his jeans or heavy-metal T-shirts. After working on a particularly oily engine he walked in to the classroom with grease stains covering his pants. He looked down at them, made a face, and walked toward me laughing, waving his hands around with limp wrists, and lisping in a high-pitched singsong voice, "I got my good panths all dirty!" Ben's imitation indicated that only a fag would actually care about getting his clothes dirty. "Real" guys didn't care about their appearance; thus it didn't matter if they were covered in grease stains. Of course, to not care about one's clothes, or to make fun of those who care about their clothes, ironically, is to also care about one's appearance. In this sense, masculinity became the carefully crafted appearance of not caring about appearance.

Indeed, the boys' approach to clothing and cleanliness mirrored trends in larger society and the ascendance of the "metrosexual." *Metrosexual* is the recently coined label for straight men who care about their appearance, meticulously piecing together outfits, using product in their hair, and even making manicure appointments (for clear polish, of course). Because these sorts of grooming practices are associated with gay men, straight men developed a new moniker to differentiate themselves from other straight men and from gay men.

Dancing was another practice that put a boy at risk of being labeled a fag. Often boys would jokingly dance together to diffuse the sexualized and feminized meanings embedded in dancing. At dances white boys frequently held their female dates tightly, locking their hips together. The boys never danced with one another unless they were joking or trying to embarrass one another. The examples of boys jokingly dancing together are too numerous to discuss, but the following example was particularly memorable. Lindy danced behind her date, Chris. Chris's friend Matt walked up and nudged Lindy aside, imitating her dance moves behind Chris. As Matt rubbed his hands up and down Chris's back, Chris turned around and jumped back, startled to see Matt there instead of Lindy. Matt cracked up as Chris turned red and swore at his friend.

A similar thing happened at CAPA as two of the boys from the band listened to another band play swing music. These two boys walked toward each other and began to ballroom-dance. Within a second or two they keeled over in laughter, hitting each other and moving away. This ritualized dance, moving closer and then apart, happened again and again when music played at River High. Boys participated in this ritualized exchange to emphasize that indeed they weren't fags.

When boys were forced to dance with one another, as in classroom activities, this sort of joking escalated. In the drama class Mr. McNally walked the students through an exercise that required them to stand so close to each other that most parts of their bodies touched. He instructed the students to stand in two circles on the stage, with each person on the outer circle directly behind someone in the inner circle. He began to play a haunting instrumental song with no vocals. As the song continued Mr. McNally told the students in the inner circle to close their eyes and let their bodies go limp, while still standing. He instructed the students in the outer circle to move the person in front through an interpretive dance, following his lead as he moved the student in front of him. As the music continued, most of the students in the outer circle watched Mr. McNally's movements intently, trying their best to mirror his actions. The result was an intimate and beautiful puppet-and-puppeteer–like dance with the student in back moving the student in front through slow, fluid poses. Instead of following Mr. McNally's movements like the rest of the class, one pair of white sophomores, Liam and Jacob, barely touched. Jacob stood in back of Liam and, instead of gently holding Liam's wrist with their full arms touching as the other students did, picked up Liam's wrist with two fingers as if picking up something repulsive and flung Liam's hand to its destination. He made jokes with Liam's arm, repeatedly flinging it up against Liam's chest in a movement that indicated Liam was "retarded." The jokes continued as the students switched places, so that the inner circle became the outer circle, with Liam now "in control" of Jacob. Liam placed Jacob's hand against his forehead as if saluting, made his arms flap like birds, and used Jacob's finger to poke at his eyes, all the while, unlike the other students, never letting the majority of his body touch Jacob's. At the end of the exercise Mr. McNally asked for the students' feedback. One of the girls said, a little embarrassed, "I hate to say it, but it was almost sexual." To which Mr. McNally responded, "Yeah, it's full physical contact," at which point Liam and Jacob took two steps apart from one another. Even though the entire class was assigned to touch one another simultaneously, Jacob and Liam had a hard time following the instructions because it was so dangerous to actually "dance" together like this. Even in a class situation, in the most nonsuspect of interactions, the fag discourse ran deep, forbidding boys to touch one another.

The constant threat of the fag regulated boys' attitudes toward their bodies in terms of clothing, dancing, and touching. Boys constantly engaged in repudiatory rituals to avoid permanently inhabiting the fag position. Boys' interactions were composed of competitive joking through which they interactionally created the constitutive outside and affirmed their positions as subjects.

● EMBODYING THE FAG: RICKY'S STORY

Through verbal jockeying, most boys at River continually moved in and out of the fag position. For the one boy who permanently inhabited the fag position, life at River High was not easy. I heard about Ricky long before I met him. As soon as I talked to any student involved with drama, the choir, or the Gay/Straight Alliance, they told me I had to meet Ricky. Ricky, a lithe, white junior with a shy smile and downcast eyes, frequently sported multicolored hair extensions, mascara, and sometimes a skirt. An extremely talented dancer, he often starred in the school's dance shows and choreographed assemblies. In fact, he was the male lead in "I've Had the Time of My Life," the final number in the dance show. Given how important other students thought it was that I speak to him, I was surprised that I had to wait for nearly a year before he granted me an interview. His friends had warned me that he was "heterophobic" and as a result was reluctant to talk to authority figures he perceived were heterosexual. After I heard his stories of past and present abuse at the hands of negligent adults, cruel teenagers, and indifferent school administrators, I understood why he would be leery of folks asking questions about his feelings, experiences, and opinions. While other boys at River High engaged in continual repudiatory rituals around the fag identity, Ricky embodied the fag because of his homosexuality and his less normative gender identification and self-presentation.

Ricky assumed (rightly so in this context) that other people immediately identified him with his sexuality. He told me that when he first met people, "they'll be like, 'Can I ask you a personal question?' And I'm like, 'Sure.' And they say, 'Are you gay?' And I'm like, 'Yeeeaahh.' 'Okay, can I ask you another question?' And I'm like, 'Sure.' And they'll go, 'Does it hurt?' It always goes …'" He rolled his eyes dismissively, telling me, "They go straight up to the most personal question! They skip everything else. They go straight to that. Sometimes I'll get the occasional 'Well, how did you know that you were [gay]?'" He answered with "For me it's just always been there. I knew from the time I could think for myself on. It was pretty obvious," he concluded gesturing to his thin frame and tight-fitting tank top with a flourish.

Ricky lived at the margins of school, student social life, and society in general. His mother died when he was young. After her death, he moved around California and Nevada, alternately living with his drug-addicted father, a boyfriend's family, his aunt, his sister, and his homophobic grandmother (who forbade him to wear nail polish or makeup). The resulting discontinuities in his education proved difficult in terms of both academics and socialization:

> It's really hard to go to a school for a period of time and get used to their system and everything's okay. Then when all of a sudden you have to pick up and move the next week, get into a new environment you have no idea about, you don't know how the kids are gonna react to you. You don't know what the teachers are like and you don't know what their system is. So this entire time I have not been able to get used to their system and get used to the environment at all. That's why I had to say, "Fuck it," cause for so long I've been going back and going back and reviewing things I did in like fifth grade. I'm at a fourth-grade math level. I am math illiterate, let me tell you.

In addition to the continual educational disruptions, Ricky had to contend with intense harassment. Figuring out the social map of the school was central to Ricky's survival. Homophobic harassment at the hands of teachers and students characterized his educational experience. When he was beat up in a middle school PE class, the teacher didn't help but rather fostered this sort of treatment:

> They gave them a two-day suspension and they kind of kept an eye on me. That's all they could do. The PE coach was very racist and very homophobic. He was just like "faggot this" and "faggot that." I did not feel comfortable in the locker room and I asked him if I could go somewhere else to change, and he said, "No, you can change here."

Sadly, by the time Ricky had reached River High he had become accustomed to the violence.

> In a weird sense, in a weird way, I'm comfortable with it because it's just what I've known for as long as I can remember. I mean, in elementary

school, I'm talking like sixth grade, I started being called a fag. Fifth grade I was called a fag. Third grade I was called a fag. I have the paperwork, 'cause my mom kept everything, I still have them, of kids harassing me, saying "Gaylord," at that time it was "Gaylord."

Contrary to the protestations of boys earlier in the chapter that they would never call someone who was gay a fag, Ricky experienced this harassment on a regular basis, probably because he couldn't draw on identifiably masculine markers such as athletic ability or other forms of dominance to bolster some sort of claim on masculinity.

Hypermasculine environments such as sporting events continued to be venues of intense harassment at River High. "I've had water balloons thrown at me at a football game. Like, we [his friends Genevieve and Lacy] couldn't have stayed at the homecoming game. We had to go." The persecution began immediately at the biggest football game of the year. When he entered with his friend Lacy, "Two guys that started walking up to get tickets said, 'There's the fucking fag.'" When Ricky responded with "Excuse me?" the boy shot back, "Don't talk to me like you know me." The boy and his friends started to threaten Ricky. Ricky said, "He started getting into my face, and his friends started saying, 'Come on, man, come on, man'" as if they were about to hit Ricky. Ricky felt frustrated that "the ticket people are sitting there not doing a damn thing. This is right in front of them!" He found Ms. Chesney, the vice principal, after the boys finally left. While Ms. Chesney told him, "We'll take care of it," Ricky said he never heard about the incident again. Later at the game he and Lacy had water bottles thrown at them by young boys yelling, "Oh look, it's a fag!" He said that this sentiment echoed as they tried to sit in the bleachers to watch the half-time show, which he had choreographed: "Left and right, 'What the fuck is that fag doing here?' 'That fag has no right to be here.' Blah blah blah. That's all I heard. I tried to ignore it. And after a while I couldn't take it and then we just went home." While many of the boys I interviewed said they would not actually harass a gay boy, that was not Ricky's experience. He was driven out of the event he had choreographed because of the intense homophobic harassment.

Ricky endured similar torment at CAPA, the event at which Brian and Dan socialized the young boys to fear faggots by chasing them. Boys reacted with revulsion to Ricky's dance performances while simultaneously objectifying the girls dancing on the stage. The rear quad served as the stage for CAPA's dancers. The student body clustered around the stage to watch the all-female beginning jazz dance class perform. Mitch, a white senior, whose shirt read, "One of us is thinking about sex. It must be me," muttered, "This is so gay" and began to walk away. Jackson yelled after him, "Where are you going, *fag?*" As Mitch walked away, Jackson turned back to the dancing girls, who now had their backs to the boys, gyrating their behinds in time to the music, and shouted, "Shake that ass!" Jackson reached in his pocket to grab his glasses. Pablo commented, "He's putting on his glasses so he can see her shake her ass better." Watching the girls' behinds, Jackson replied, as he pointed to one of them, "She's got a *huge* ass." Mitch turned to Pablo and asked, seriously, "Why are there no guys?" Pablo responded, "You're such a fag."

The advanced dance troupe took the stage with Ricky in the center. Again, all the dancers sported black outfits, but this time the pants were baggy and the shirts fitted. Ricky wore the same outfit as the girls. He danced in the "lead" position, in the front and the center of the dance formation. He executed the same dance moves as the girls, which is uncommon in mixed-gender dance troupes. Usually the boys in a mixed-gender dance troupe perform the more "physical" moves such as flips, holding up the girls, and spinning them around. Ricky, instead, performed all the sexually suggestive hip swivels, leg lifts, arm flares, and spins that the girls did.

Nils and his group of white male friends made faces and giggled as they stared at Ricky. Soon Nils turned to Malcolm and said, "It's like a car wreck, you just can't look away." Both shook their heads in dismay as they continued to watch the "car wreck" with what can only be described as morbid absorption. Other boys around the stage reacted visibly, recoiling at Ricky's performance. One of them, J. R., a hulking junior and captain of the football team, shook his head and muttered under his breath, "That's disgusting." I asked him, "What?" J. R. turned to me with his nose wrinkled in revulsion and responded, "That guy dancing, it's just disgusting! Disgusting!" He again shook his head as he walked off. Soon afterward an African American boy turned to his friend and admiringly said of Ricky, "He's a better dancer than all the girls! That takes talent!" He turned to me and said, "Can I wiggle my hips that fast?" and laughed as he tried.

The white boys' revulsion bordering on violence was common for boys when talking about Ricky and his dancing. More surprising was the African American boys' admiration, if tinged with humor, of these skills. In these moments boys faced a terrifying, embodied abject, not just some specter of a fag.

Even though dancing was the most important thing in his life, Ricky told me he didn't attend school dances because he didn't like to "watch my back" the whole time. Meanings of sexuality and masculinity were deeply embedded in dancing and high school dances. Several boys at the school told me that they wouldn't even attend a dance if they knew Ricky was going to be there. In auto shop, Brad, a white sophomore, said, "I heard Ricky is going in a skirt. It's a hella short one!" Chad responded, "I wouldn't even go if he's there." Topping Chad's response, Brad claimed, "I'd probably beat him up outside." K. J. agreed: "He'd probably get jumped by a bunch of kids who don't like him." Chad said, "If I were a gay guy I wouldn't go around telling everyone." All of them agreed on this. Surprised and somewhat disturbed by this discussion, I asked incredulously, "Would you really not go to prom because a gay guy would be in the same room as you all?" They looked at me like I had two heads and said again that of course they wouldn't. Ricky's presentation of both sexual preference and gender identity was so profoundly threatening that boys claimed they would be driven to violence.

Ricky developed different strategies to deal with the fag discourse, given that he was not just *a* fag but *the* fag. While other boys lobbed the epithet at one another with implied threats of violence (you are not a man and I am, so watch out), for Ricky that violence was more a reality than a threat. As a result, learning the unwritten rules of a particular school and mapping out its social and physical landscape was literally a matter of survival. He found River High to be one of the most homophobic schools he had attended: "It's the most violent school I think that I've seen so far. With all the schools the verbal part about, you know the slang, 'the fag,' the 'fuckin' freak,' 'fucking fag,' all that stuff is all the same. But this is the only school that throws water bottles, throws rocks, and throws food, ketchup, sandwiches, anything of that nature."[2]

While there is a law in California protecting students from discrimination based on sexual identity, when Ricky requested help from school authorities he was ignored, much as in his interaction with the vice principal at the homecoming game. Ricky responded to this sort of treatment with several evasion strategies. He walked with his eyes downcast to avoid meeting other guys' eyes, fearing that they would regard eye contact as a challenge or an invitation to a fight. Similarly he varied his route to and from school:

> I had to change paths about three different times walking to school. The same people who drive the same route know, 'cause I guess they leave at the same time, so they're always checking something out. But I'm always prepared with a rock just in case. I have a rock in my hand so if anything happens I just chuck one back. I always walk with something like that.

Indeed, when I was driving him home from the interview that day, boys on the sidewalk glared at him and made comments I couldn't hear. He also, with the exception of the homecoming football game, avoided highly sexualized or masculinized school events where he might be subject to violence.

Soon after my research ended, Ricky dropped out of River High and moved to a nearby city to perform in local drag shows. While other boys moved in and out of the fag position, Ricky's gendered practices and sexual orientation forced him to bear all that the other boys cast out of masculinity. His double transgression of sexual and gender identity made his position at River High simply unlivable. The lack of protection from the administration meant facing torture on a daily basis. The abuse that was heaped on him was more than one person, certainly more than one parentless, undereducated, sweet, artistic adolescent, could bear.[3]

● RACIALIZING THE FAG

While all groups of boys, with the exception of the Mormon boys, used the word *fag* or fag imagery in their interactions, the fag discourse was not deployed consistently or identically across social groups at River High. Differences between white boys' and African American boys' meaning making, particularly around appearance and dancing, reveal ways the specter of the fag was racialized. The specter of the fag, these invocations reveal, was consistently white. Additionally,

African American boys simply did not deploy it with the same frequency as white boys. For both groups of boys, the *fag* insult entailed meanings of emasculation, as evidenced by Darnell's earlier comment. However, African American boys were much more likely to tease one another for being white than for being a fag. Precisely because African American men are so hypersexualized in the United States, white men are, by default, feminized, so *white* was a stand-in for *fag* among many of the African American boys at River High. Two of the behaviors that put a white boy at risk for being labeled a fag didn't function in the same way for African American boys.

Perhaps because they are, by necessity, more invested in symbolic forms of power related to appearance (much like adolescent girls), a given African American boy's status is not lowered but enhanced by paying attention to clothing or dancing. Clean, oversized, carefully put together clothing is central to a hip-hop identity for African American boys who identify with hip-hop culture. Richard Majors (2001) calls this presentation of self a "cool pose" consisting of "unique, expressive and conspicuous styles of demeanor, speech, gesture, clothing, hairstyle, walk, stance and handshake," developed by African American men as a symbolic response to institutionalized racism (211). Pants are usually several sizes too big, hanging low on the hips, often revealing a pair of boxers beneath. Shirts and sweaters are similarly oversized, sometimes hanging down to a boy's knees. Tags are frequently left on baseball hats worn slightly askew and perched high on the head. Meticulously clean, unlaced athletic shoes with rolled-up socks under the tongue complete a typical hip-hop outfit. In fact, African American men can, without risking a fag identity, sport styles of self and interaction frequently associated with femininity for whites, such as wearing curlers (Kelley 2004). These symbols, at River High, constituted a "cool pose."

The amount of attention and care given to clothing for white boys not identified with hip-hop culture (that is, most of the white boys at River High) would certainly cast them into an abject, fag position, as Ben indicated when he cried, jokingly, "I got my good panths all dirty!" White boys were not supposed to appear to care about their clothes or appearance because only fags cared about how they looked. However African American boys involved in hip-hop culture talked frequently about whether their clothes, specifically their shoes, were dirty. In drama class both Darnell and Marc compared their white Adidas basketball shoes. Darnell mocked Marc because black scuff marks covered his shoes, asking incredulously, "Yours are a week old and they're dirty, I've had mine for a month and they're not dirty!" Both laughed. Monte, River High's star football player, echoed this concern about dirty shoes. Looking at the fancy red shoes he had lent to his cousin the week before, he told me he was frustrated because after his cousin used them the "shoes are hella scuffed up." Clothing, for these boys, did not indicate a fag position but rather defined membership in a certain cultural and racial group (Perry 2002). Especially for poor African American boys (as most were at River High), clean clothing was an indicator of class status. If one had enough money to have clean shoes one was not "ghetto," in the parlance of the students at River.

As in many places in the United States, racial divisions in Riverton line up relatively easily with class divisions. Darnell grabbed me at lunch one day to point this out to me, using school geography as an example. He sauntered up and whispered in my ear, "Notice the separation? There's the people who hang out in there (pointing toward the cafeteria), the people who hang out in the quad. And then the people who leave." He smashed one hand against the other in frustration: "I talk to these people in class. Outside we all separate into our groups. We don't talk to each other. Rich people are not here. They got cars and they go out." He told me that the "ball players" sat in the cafeteria. And he was right: there were two tables at the rear of the cafeteria populated by African American boys on the basketball and football teams, the guys whom Darnell described to me as his "friends." He said there were "people who leave, people who stay and the people over there [in the quad]. The people who stay are ghetto." He added, "*Ghetto* come to mean 'niggerish.' That reflects people who are poor or urban."

Carl and his friend James, both African American basketball players, were also clear about the ways race lined up with class at River: "White people always take us to lunch cause black people don't have cars." Because African American boys lacked other indicators of class such as cars and the ability to leave campus during lunch, clean expensive basketball shoes took on added symbolic status.

Dancing was another arena that carried distinctly fag-associated meanings for white boys but masculine meanings for African American boys who participated in hip-hop culture. White boys often associated dancing with fags. However, dancing did not carry this sort of sexualized gender meaning for all boys at

River High. For African American boys dancing demonstrates membership in a cultural community (Best 2000). At River, African American boys frequently danced together in single-sex groups, teaching each other the latest dance moves, showing off a particularly difficult move, or making each other laugh with humorous dance moves. In fact, while in drama class Liam and Jacob hit each other and joked through the entire dancing exercise, Darnell and Marc seemed very comfortable touching one another. They stood close to one another, heel to toe, as they were supposed to. Their bodies touched, and they gently and gracefully moved the other's arms and head in a way that was tender, not at all like the flailing of the two white boys.

Dancing ability actually increased an African American boy's social status. Students recognized K. J., along with Ricky, as the most talented dancer at the school. K. J. was a sophomore of mixed racial descent, originally from the Philippines, who participated in the hip-hop culture of River High. He continually wore the latest hip-hop fashions. His dark complexion and identification with hip-hop culture aligned him with many of the African American boys at River High. Girls hollered his name as they walked down the hall and thrust love notes folded in complicated designs into his hands as he sauntered to class. For the past two years K. J. had won first place in the talent show for dancing. When he danced at assemblies the auditorium reverberated with screamed chants of "Go K. J.! Go K. J! Go K. J.!" Because dancing for boys of color, especially African American boys, placed them within a tradition of masculinity, they were not at risk of being labeled a fag for engaging in this particular gendered practice. Nobody called K. J. a fag. In fact, in several of my interviews boys of multiple racial/ethnic backgrounds spoke admiringly of K. J.'s dancing abilities. Marco, a troublemaking white senior, said of K. J., "Did you know he invented the Harlem Shake?" referring to a popular and difficult dance move. Like Ricky, K. J. often choreographed assembly dance routines. But unlike Ricky, he frequently starred in them at the homecoming and Mr. Cougar rallies.

None of this is to say that participation in dancing made boys less homophobic. K. J. himself was deeply homophobic. But like the other boys, it was a gendered homophobia that had to do with masculine gender transgressions as much as sexuality. His sister, for instance, identified as a lesbian, and he looked up to and liked her. But he loathed Ricky. Because of their involvement with dance, the two came into contact relatively frequently. Stylistically, they mirrored one another. Both sported long hair: K. J.'s in cornrows and Ricky's lengthened with highlighted extensions. Both wore elaborate outfits: K. J. favored oversized matching red and white checked shorts and a button-down shirt over a white tank top, while Ricky sported baggy black pants, combat boots, and a white tank top. Both were thin with delicate facial features and little facial hair. But the meanings associated with what might seem like gender transgressions by both of them were mediated by their racial and sexual identities, leading to K. J.'s popularity and Ricky's debasement. K. J.'s appearance identified his style as hip-hop, a black, masculine cultural style, whereas Ricky's style identified him as gender transgressive and feminine.

Not surprisingly, K. J. and Ricky were the stars of the dance show at River High. As the day of the show arrived, K. J. asked me for what must have been the hundredth time if I was planning to attend. He said, "Everyone is sayin' that Ricky is my competition, but I don't think so. He's not my competition." K. J. continued to tell me that he was very upset with Ricky because the night before at the dress rehearsal Ricky had walked up to him, saying, "Hey, K. J., awesome dance." Ricky had put his hand on K. J.'s back when he said this. Angry and red, K. J. said to me, "I wanted to hit him hella bad! Then he came up *again*. I was like 'Oh My God!' Ugh!" Trying to identify exactly who Ricky was, another boy said, "I think that's the same guy who is in our history class. The guy who looks like a girl?" K. J., wanting to make sure the other boys knew how repulsive Ricky was, said, "You know how you look at girls like they are hella fine? That's how he looks at guys, dude! He could be looking at you!" All the boys groaned. K. J. expressed relief that he was "safe," saying Ricky "only checks out white guys." K. J. took pains to differentiate himself from Ricky by saying that Ricky wasn't his competition and that Ricky didn't even look at him as a sexual object because of his race. The respect K. J. commanded at River was certainly different from the treatment Ricky received because the meanings associated with African American boys and dancing were not the same as the ones associated with white boys and dancing. K. J.'s dancing ability and carefully crafted outfits bolstered his popularity with both boys and girls, while Ricky's similar ability and just as carefully chosen outfits placed him, permanently, in a fag position.

None of this is to say that the sexuality of boys of color wasn't policed. In fact, because African American boys were regarded as so hypersexual, in the few instances I documented in which boys were punished for engaging in the fag discourse, African American boys were policed more stringently than white boys. It was as if when they engaged in the fag discourse the gendered insult took on actual combative overtones, unlike the harmless sparring associated with white boys' deployments. The intentionality attributed to African American boys in their sexual interactions with girls seemed to occur as well in their deployment of the fag discourse. One morning as I waited with the boys on the asphalt outside the weight room for Coach Ramirez to arrive, I chatted with Kevin and Darrell. The all-male, all-white wrestling team walked by, wearing gold and black singlets. Kevin, an African American sophomore, yelled out, "Why are you wearing those faggot outfits? Do you wear those tights with your balls hanging out?" The weight-lifting students stopped their fidgeting and turned to watch the scene unfold. The eight or so members of the wrestling team stopped at their SUV and turned to Kevin. A small redhead whipped around and yelled aggressively, "Who said that?!" Fingers from wrestling team members quickly pointed toward Kevin. Kevin, angrily jumping around, yelled back as he thrust his chest out, "Talk about jumping me, nigger?" He strutted over, advancing toward the small redhead. A large wrestler sporting a cowboy hat tried to block Kevin's approach. The redhead meanwhile began to jump up and down, as if warming up for a fight. Finally the boy in the cowboy hat pushed Kevin away from the team and they climbed in the truck, while Kevin strutted back to his classmates, muttering, "All they know how to do is pick somebody up. Talk about jumping me … weak-ass wrestling team. My little bro could wrestle better than any of those motherfuckers."

It would seem, based on the fag discourse scenarios I've described thus far, that this was, in a sense, a fairly routine deployment of the sexualized and gendered epithet. However, at no other time did I see this insult almost cause a fight. Members of the white wrestling team presumably took it so seriously that they reported the incident to school authorities. This in itself is stunning. Boys called each other fag so frequently in everyday discussion that if it were always reported most boys in the school would be suspended or at least in detention on a regular basis. This was the only time I saw school authorities take action based on what they saw as a sexualized insult. As a result Mr. J. explained that somebody from the wrestling team told him that Kevin was "harassing" them. Mr. J. pulled Kevin out of weight-lifting class to discuss the incident. According to him, Kevin "kept mouthing off" and it wasn't the first time he had been in trouble, so they decided to expel him and send him to Hillside.

While Kevin apparently had multiple disciplinary problems and this interaction was part of a larger picture, it is important that this was the only time that I heard any boy (apart from Ricky) tattle on another boy for calling him gay or fag. Similarly it was the only time I saw punishment meted out by the administration. So it seems that, much as in the instance of the Bomb Squad at the Dance Show, intentionality was more frequently attributed to African American boys. They weren't just engaging in the homophobic bantering to which teachers like Mr. Kellogg turned a blind eye or in which Mr. McNally participated. Rather, they were seen as engaging in actual struggles for dominance by attacking others. Because they were in a precarious economic and social position, the ramifications for African American boys for engaging in the fag discourse were more serious. Precisely because some of them were supposed to be attending, not River High, but the "bad" school, Chicago, in the neighboring school district, when they did encounter trouble their punishment was more severe.

● WHERE THE FAG DISAPPEARS: DRAMA PERFORMANCES

While, for the most part, a boy's day at River entailed running a gauntlet of competitive and ritualized sexual insults, there were two spaces of escape—the Gay/ Straight Alliance and drama performances. Theater productions were not the same as the drama classroom, where I have already indicated that Mr. McNally sometimes drew upon the fag discourse for laughs and to forge rapport with male students. Drama performances typically didn't involve all of the students in drama classes. Rather, students who were involved were ones who identified as drama students and cared about the theater; some of them envisioned trying to make a career out of it. Drama is notoriously a fag space in high schools. The ironic result of this connection is that the insult disappears. Not only does the insult disappear, but drama becomes a space where male students can enact a variety of gender practices.

The opening night of the yearly spring musical illustrates how the *fag* insult disappeared and male students enacted a variety of gender practices without negative ramifications. Drama students ran around in various stages of costuming and undress in the backstage area of the River High auditorium as they prepared for the opening night of the spring musical, *Carousel*. As the balmy spring air blew through the stage door, I smiled as I thought back to my high school days and felt that same nervous energy as we prepped for choir concerts and musicals like *Fiddler on the Roof*. Squealing, giggling, and singing, students frantically searched for spare props, costume parts, and makeup. Students flew past me in clouds of hairspray, carrying parasols or sailor paraphernalia as they readied themselves to perform this relatively dark musical about romantic betrayal, domestic violence, and murder.

I leaned against the wall outside the dressing rooms as students costumed themselves and each other. Girls quickly and carefully applied makeup under the bright yellow bulbs. Boys lined up waiting for an available girl to apply makeup. I waited for the inevitable fag comment as the girls plastered rouge, lip gloss, and eye shadow on the boys' faces. Surprisingly, even though all but one of the boys (Brady) participating in this musical were straight, I heard not a one. Instead Trevor, the handsome blond lead, and the other boys checked out the girls' handiwork in the surrounding mirrors, suggesting slight changes or thanking them for their help. Squealing with delight at their new look, the boys ran back into the beehive of noise and activity that constituted the backstage area outside the dressing rooms. That reaction and their impromptu singing surprised me as much their pride in sporting makeup. The normally tough and competitive exterior that they displayed in the rest of the school disappeared, and the boys showed as much excitement as the girls did, smiling and giggling as they anticipated their performance.

Soon the backstage area quieted down as students took their marks and the orchestra, really a group of four musicians, played the opening bars. Students danced around the stage, depicting a picnic, a fair, and other tableaus of small-town American life in the 1900s. Remarkably, all the students watched or sang a musical number entitled "You're a Queer One, Julie Jordan" without cracking a single joke about fags or homosexuality. This refusal to engage in insults, homophobic comments, or sexist joking continued throughout the evening. Conditioned as I was at this point to hearing the fag discourse, I was stunned at the myriad opportunities to levy the epithet and the seeming refusal by all of these boys, gay and straight, to invoke it.

The most striking example of this refusal occurred midway through the play as eight boys dressed as sailors tumbled over each other as they prepared to go on stage. They joked about their lack of "sailorness" as they waited excitedly in the wings. Brady, surveying his fellow soldiers, admonished the boys laughingly to "act like sailors, men!" Jake laughed back in a loud whisper, "Oh yeah, right!" Randy sarcastically said, "We look sooo much like sailors," puffing out his chest and mock-strutting across the stage. The boys all giggled at this performance. They soon gathered around Brady, who, as part of his effort to appear like a tough sailor, had had his friend draw a temporary tattoo on his hairy bicep. It was a truly sailorlike tattoo, a mermaid. But this mermaid was more a visual pun than anything else because she was not a sultry, buxom siren but Ariel from the Disney movie *The Little Mermaid*. Brady beamed as he showed it off to everyone. The other boys admired the artwork and remarked, with a tinge of jealousy, that it was a great tat-too. They heard their cue and strutted on stage, eventually forming a semicircle and singing: "Blow high, blow low / Away then we will go / We'll go away in the sailin' away / Away we'll go / Blow me high an' low." During the song, boys took their turns performing a short solo dance. Some performed typically masculine moves such as flips or swaggers, while others performed pirouettes or delicate twirls.

Sailors, in the contemporary United States, are already laden with all sorts of gay innuendo. From the sailor member of the famous gay disco group the Village People to actual sailors stuck on ships with all-male crews, to jokes about "sea men," sailors represent a subtext of same-sex desire. So a bunch of sailors jumping around singing a song that relies upon the repeated lyrics "blow me" is pretty funny. However, the boys took an approach to this that was, more than anything, simply playful.

Watching this scene unfold, I was surprised that given all of the fag iconography in this moment—sailors, dancing, Disney cartoons, and the repeated singing of the word *blow* (which by itself can get boys joking for hours)—I didn't hear a single invocation of the fag discourse. At the end of the night I turned to David and asked why no one uttered the word *fag* the entire night. He explained, "That's cause we're drama freaks." In a sense, because these boys were near the bottom of the social hierarchy at River High, they were, by default, fags. But I think the lack of the fag discourse during that evening was a more complicated story.

The boys had fun with the double entendres and played with masculinity. Brady's tattoo functioned as a sort of queering of masculinity in which he visually punned by drawing a mermaid who was not so much sexy as a singing heroine for little girls. The theater is a place for all sorts of experimentation, so why not a metaphorical and physical space for gender and sexual experimentation? After watching what boys endured daily at River High, I found this dramatic performance a space of liberation and relaxation. The boys were able to try on gender identities, integrating masculine and feminine gender practices, without fear of being teased. Instead of constantly policing their own and others' gender displays, they were able to be playful, emotional, and creative. It was as if, because they were in a space where they were all coded as fags anyway and couldn't be any lower socially, it didn't matter what they did. Such is the liberatory potential of the theater. These boys had nothing left to lose socially, which meant that, ironically, they were free from the pressures of adolescent masculinity, at least temporarily (though it should be noted here that the boys involved in drama productions weren't among the most ardent users of the fag discourse, even outside dramatic performances). What they weren't able to do, however, was to engage in these sorts of playful practices around gender outside the drama performance space.

● REFRAMING HOMOPHOBIA

Homophobia is central to contemporary definitions of adolescent masculinity. Unpacking multilayered meanings that boys deploy through their uses of homophobic language and joking rituals makes clear that it is not just homophobia but a gendered and racialized homophobia. By attending to these meanings, I reframe the discussion as a fag discourse rather than simply labeling it as homophobia. The fag is an "abject" (Butler 1993) position, a position outside masculinity that actually constitutes masculinity. Thus masculinity, in part, becomes the daily interactional work of repudiating the threatening specter of the fag.

The fag extends beyond a static sexual identity attached to a gay boy. Few boys are permanently identified as fags; most move in and out of fag positions. Looking at fag as a discourse in addition to a static identity reveals that the term can be invested with different meanings in different social spaces. *Fag* may be used as a weapon with which to temporarily assert one's masculinity by denying it to others. Thus the fag becomes a symbol around which contests of masculinity take place.

Researchers who look at the intersection of sexuality and masculinity need to attend to how racialized identities may affect how *fag* is deployed and what it means in various social situations. While researchers have addressed the ways in which masculine identities are racialized (Bucholtz 1999; Connell 1995; J. Davis 1999; Ferguson 2000; Majors 2001; Price 1999; Ross 1998), they have not paid equal attention to the ways *fag* might be a racialized epithet. Looking at when, where, and with what meaning *fag* is deployed provides insight into the processes through which masculinity is defined, contested, and invested in among adolescent boys.

Ricky demonstrates that the fag identity can, but doesn't have to, inhere in a single body. But it seems that he needed to meet two criteria—breaking both gendered and sexual norms—to be constituted as a fag. He was simultaneously the penetrated fag who threatened psychic chaos (Bersani 1987) and the man who couldn't "throw a football around." Not only could he not "throw a football," but he actively flaunted his unmasculine gender identification by dancing provocatively at school events and wearing cross-gendered clothing. Through his gender practices Ricky embodied the threatening specter of the fag. He bore the weight of the fears and anxieties of the boys in the school who frantically lobbed the *fag* epithet at one another.

The *fag* epithet, when hurled at other boys, may or may not have explicit sexual meanings, but it always has gendered meanings. When a boy calls another boy a fag, it means he is not a man but not necessarily that he is a homosexual. The boys at River High knew that they were not supposed to call homosexual boys fags because that was mean. This, then, has been the limited success of the mainstream gay rights movement. The message absorbed by some of these teenage boys was that "gay men can be masculine, just like you." Instead of challenging gender inequality, this particular discourse of gay rights has reinscribed it. Thus we need to begin to think about how gay men may be in a unique position to challenge gendered as well as sexual norms. The boys in the drama performances show an alternative way to be teenage boys, which is about playing with gender, not just enforcing gender duality based on sexual meanings.

● ENDNOTES

1. In fact, two of my colleagues, both psychotherapists, suggested that the boys exhibited what we could think of as a sort of "Fag Tourette's Syndrome."

2. Though River was not a particularly violent school, it may have seemed like that to Ricky because sexuality-based harassment increases with grade level as gender differentiation becomes more intense. As youth move from childhood into adolescence there is less flexibility in terms of gender identity and self-presentation (Shakib 2003).

3. There were two other gay boys at the school. One, Corey, I learned about after a year of fieldwork. While he wasn't "closeted," he was not well known at the school and kept a low profile. The other out gay boy at the school was Brady. While he didn't engage in the masculinity rituals of the other boys at River High, he didn't cross-dress or engage in feminine-coded activities as did Ricky. As such, when boys talked about fags, they referenced Ricky, not Brady or Corey.

● REFERENCES

Almaguer, Tomas. 1991. "Chicano Men: A Cartography of Homosexual Identity and Behavior." *Differences* 3, no. 2:75–100.

Baker, Janet G., and Harold D. Fishbein. 1998. "The Development of Prejudice towards Gays and Lesbians by Adolescents." *Journal of Homosexuality* 36, no. 1:89–100.

Bersani, Leo. 1987. "Is the Rectum a Grave?" *AIDS: Cultural Analysis/Cultural Activism*, no. 43:197–222.

Best, Amy. 2000. *Prom Night: Youth, Schools, and Popular Culture*. New York: Routledge.

Bucholtz, Mary. 1999. "You Da Man: Narrarating the Racial Other in the Production of White Masculinity." *Journal of Sociolinguistics* 3, no. 4:443–60.

Burn, Shawn Meghan. 2000. "Heterosexuals' Use of 'Fag' and 'Queer' to Deride One Another: A Contributor to Heterosexism and Stigma." *Journal of Homosexuality* 40, no. 2:1–11.

Butler, Judith. 1993. *Bodies That Matter: On the Discursive Limits of "Sex."* New York: Routledge.

Connell, R. W. 1995. *Masculinities*. Berkeley: University of California Press.

Corbett, Ken. 2001. "Faggot = Loser." *Studies in Gender and Sexuality* 2, no. 1:3–28.

Davis, James Earl. 1999. "Forbidden Fruit: Black Males' Constructions of Transgressive Sexualities in Middle School." In *Queering Elementary Education: Advancing the Dialogue about Sexualities and Schooling*, edited by William J. Letts IV and James T. Sears, 49–59. Lanham, MD: Rowan and Littlefield.

Ferguson, Ann. 2000. *Bad Boys: Public Schools in the Making of Black Masculinity*. Ann Arbor: University of Michigan Press.

Freud, Sigmund. 1905. *The Basic Writings of Sigmund Freud*. Translated by A. A. Brill. New York: Modern Library

Julien, Isaac, and Kobena Mercer. 1991. "True Confessions: A Discourse on Im-206/References ages of Black Male Sexuality." In *Brother to Brother: New Writings by Black Gay Men*, edited by Essex Hemphill, 167–73. Boston: Alyson Publications.

Kehily, Mary Jane, and Anoop Nayak. 1997. "'Lads and Laughter': Humour and the Production of Heterosexual Masculinities." *Gender and Education* 9, no. 1:69–87.

Kelley, Robin D. G. 2004. "Confessions of a Nice Negro, or Why I Shaved My Head." In *Men's Lives*, edited by Michael Kimmel and Michael Messner, 335–41. Boston: Allyn and Bacon.

King, J. L. 2004. *On the Down Low: A Journey into the Lives of Straight Black Men Who Sleep with Men*. New York: Broadway Books.

Kimmel, Michael S. 2001. "Masculinity as Homophobia: Fear, Shame, and Silence in the Construction of Gender Identity." In *The Masculinities Reader*, edited by Stephen Whitehead and Frank Barrett, 266–87. Cambridge: Polity Press.

———. 2003. "Adolescent Masculinity, Homophobia, and Violence: Random School Shootings, 1982–2001." *American Behavioral Scientist* 46, no. 10:1439–58.

Lehne, Gregory. 1998. "Homophobia among Men: Supporting and Defining the Male Role." In *Men's Lives*, edited by Michael Kimmel and Michael Messner, 237–49. Boston: Allyn and Bacon.

Majors, Richard. 2001. "Cool Pose: Black Masculinity and Sports." In *The Masculinities Reader*, edited by Stephen Whitehead and Frank Barrett, 208–17. Cambridge: Polity Press.

Messner, Michael. 2005. "Becoming 100% Straight." In *Gender through the Prism of Difference*, edited by Maxine Baca Zinn, Pierrette Hondagneu-Sotelo, and Michael Messner, 227–32. New York: Oxford University Press.

Perry, Pamela. 2002. *Shades of White: White Kids and Racial Identities in High School*. Durham: Duke University Press.

Plummer, David C. 2001. "The Quest for Modern Manhood: Masculine Stereotypes, Peer Culture and the Social Significance of Homophobia." *Journal of Adolescence* 24, no. 1:15–23.

Price, Jeremy. 1999. "Schooling and Racialized Masculinities: The Diploma, Teachers and Peers in the Lives of Young, African American Men." *Youth and Society* 31, no. 2:224–63.

Ross, Marlon B. 1998. "In Search of Black Men's Masculinities." *Feminist Studies* 24, no. 3:599–626.

Riggs, Marlon. 1991. "Black Macho Revisited: Reflections of a Snap! Queen." In *Brother to Brother: New Writings by Black Gay Men*, edited by Essex Hemphill, 253–60. Boston: Alyson Publications.

Sedgwick, Eve Kosofsky. 1995. " 'Gosh, Boy George, You Must Be Awfully Secure in Your Masculinity!' " In *Constructing Masculinity*, edited by Maurice Berger, Brian Wallis, and Simon Watson, 11–20. New York: Routledge

Smith, George W. 1998. "The Ideology of 'Fag': The School Experience of Gay Students." *Sociological Quarterly* 39, no. 2:309–35.

Wilchins, Riki. 2003. "Do You Believe in Fairies?" *Advocate*, February 4, 72.

Wood, Julian. 1984. "Groping Towards Sexism: Boy's Sex Talk." In *Gender and Generation*, edited by Angela McRobbie and Mica Nava, 54–84. London: Macmillan.

SECTION **FOUR**

CRIME

Crime is a significant social problem in the United States that impacts the lives of millions of Americans every year. Although violent and property crime rates have been declining for years, rates of drug-related crime have been increasing during that same period. Overall, tougher sentences are being imposed and American prisons are expanding well beyond their intended capacities. In this section, crime is defined and several important issues are examined, which include crime trends over time, mass incarceration, capital punishment, and sexual assault on American college campuses.

● WHAT IS CRIME?

Crime is defined as an act that violates a local, state, or federal law. Crime is a wide-ranging and broad concept that can be broken down by types of crimes that people commit or the severity of those crimes. For example, criminologists, politicians, and lawyers make clear distinctions between property, drug, violent, and white collar types of crime. Similarly, the language of misdemeanor and felony is used to distinguish between less severe and more severe criminal acts, respectively. Jaywalking and coasting through a stop sign are examples of illegal acts that many of us commit on a routine basis. They are considered to be misdemeanors and people do not go to prison for engaging in such activities.

The punishment for these offenses generally involves paying a fine. Felonies, on the other hand, are more serious crimes that generally involve people being arrested, going to jail, and getting charged with an offense punishable by prison.

● THE TEMPORAL AND SPATIAL VARIATION OF CRIME

As with social problems, crimes vary across time and space. What may have been a crime at one point in time in a certain location may no longer be against the law. And new laws against behaviors can be passed at any time. Similarly, what may be considered a criminal act in one part of the world or country may not be in another. "Sexting" is a good example here, as laws against this practice are recent and in flux. Some countries and states have laws against sexting, which includes sending nude or sexual photos over a computer or mobile device, and some do not. We expect more countries and states to develop laws regulating this activity and other activities conducted through technology in the future.

In the United States, seatbelt and car seat laws represent another good example of the temporal and spatial variation of crime. Before 1984, seat belt use was not mandatory. Then the state of New York passed a law and was subsequently followed by the other states, although details of each state's law vary. Similarly, car seats began to be mandatory in 1977, and within eight years all fifty states had some sort of law requiring particular car restraints for children. The relative recency of these laws may lead to interesting conversations with your parents or grandparents about their typical practices in automobiles when they were young.

Gambling is another good example. Sports betting is legal in a few states, such as Nevada and Delaware, but illegal in every other state. However, innumerable people violate the law by betting on sports through bookies or offshore websites, which are out of US jurisdiction. Betting on horse races is legal in some parts of the United States and some parts of the world, and each country or state has particular limitations or rules in place, many of which have changed over time. Nevada and Louisiana are the only two states where casino gambling is legal statewide. In other states it is completely illegal, whereas others have local allowances and restrictions.

● CRIME TRENDS

Upon examining American crime trends over time, it becomes clear that there have been several substantial changes over the course of the past three decades. One clear trend is that rates of both violent crime and property crime have been steadily declining for years. As encouraging as this is, however, some more alarming trends have emerged. One is that drug-related crime is higher than it has ever been. People can make lots of quick money making and selling drugs. More people also seem to be using drugs to help them cope with stress, depression, chronic pain, and a plethora of other issues. It is not just that people are using and selling drugs at a higher rate than before, but that penalties have gotten tougher. The "War on Drugs" has created many mandatory minimum sentences and resulted in increasing numbers of people going to prison. Another trend is that rates of recidivism, or re-offending upon being released from prison, are very high.

Youth and Crime

There are tens of thousands of American youth who are involved with the criminal justice system. As with adult facilities, more youth facilities are being filled beyond capacity to accommodate all of the youth offenders. There are many reasons why young people commit crime. As outlined by social learning theory, youth are highly impressionable and may imitate friends or family members who, themselves, have broken the law. Youths may also see theft or selling drugs as a way to escape poverty. Youth disillusionment may also be a factor. Finally, they may lack meaningful social connections with others and join a gang or other criminal group to gain a sense of family with others.

Shoenberger's chapter, "Disproportionate Minority Contact in the Criminal Justice System," examines reasons why young minorities in particular have higher rates of contact with the police and courts than whites. For example, economically disadvantaged neighborhoods often have a greater police presence than wealthier ones, and police officers and others in the criminal justice system may hold racial biases. She also addresses the data showing higher rates of offending by young minorities. Shoenberger identifies several strategies that have been used to reduce rates of disproportionate minority contact with law enforcement. Much

of this revolves around awareness raising and diversity training for people working in the criminal justice field. Shoenberger concludes her piece by discussing
the goals and strategies of the Black Lives Matter movement.

● REHABILITATION VERSUS RESTITUTION

There are two basic philosophies that people have regarding the punishment
of criminals. The first of these has a clear orientation towards helping and
rehabilitating people who have been found guilty of crimes. The idea is that
social programming strategies, including counseling, anger management, skill
building, and education, are valuable tools in helping convicted offenders learn
from their mistakes and successfully reintegrate into society upon their release
from prison. Other programs, like parole, conjugal visits, and halfway houses, are
used to incentivize good behavior and help people's transition to life outside of
prison. Halfway houses embody the spirit of rehabilitation in that inmates find
jobs, open bank accounts, and have a built-in support system that is designed to
reduce the likelihood of people reoffending upon being released from prison.
Rehabilitation used to be the main penal philosophy in the United States. It has
been long criticized by people, however, for being too lenient on people who
break the law.

The second penal philosophy, restitution, is rooted in the tough-on-crime
mindset that has been espoused by many conservative political candidates over
recent years. People who are restitution oriented feel that inmates should be
punished to the fullest extent of the law. Therefore, this perspective supports
the discontinuation of programs like parole and conjugal visits. This has also
led to the creation of new super-max style facilities, where inmates have longer
lockdown times, more restricted recreation, and fewer contact visits. Using this
model, mandatory minimum sentences were created to dissuade people from
using and selling drugs, three strikes laws were passed to thwart the revolving
door of crime, and the death penalty has been used in capital cases. In Chapter
14, "The Collateral Consequences of Mass Incarceration in the Twenty-First
Century," Lesneskie discusses the exponential increase in the imprisoned population in the United States that began in the 1970s. He goes over some reasons

for the increase, including the War on Drugs and "tough-on-crime" laws such as mandatory minimum sentencing. The bulk of his piece concerns the unintended consequences of mass incarceration for individuals, families, and communities in the United States. For individuals, he discusses the continued effects on people after completing their prison terms, such as restrictions on voting, housing, and employment. For families, he discusses how imprisonment influences marriage and divorce as well as parent and child relationships. For the community, he shows how imprisonment is concentrated in certain neighborhoods, resulting in constant disruption for the people who live there. He completes his chapter with ideas about ways to rectify these latent but significant effects on people's lives.

● CAPITAL PUNISHMENT

Historically, dozens of countries used the death penalty as a way to both punish offenders and deter people from committing violent crimes. Rooted in the belief of "an eye for an eye," supporters of capital punishment have felt that people should have things taken away from them that they have taken from other people. The death penalty was used extensively in the United States through the first half of the twentieth century to punish aggravated murderers, rapists, and other violent offenders. The four main methods of execution during this time were firing squad, electric chair, gas chamber, and hanging. Some states allowed the death-row inmates to choose their method of death, while other states only had one option available to them.

By the mid-twentieth century, a growing number of Americans voiced moral concerns with the death penalty. Many people felt that the methods of execution were cruel and that they should be discontinued. During this time, many legal petitions were established challenging the constitutionality of capital punishment, and the number of executions decreased. In fact, between 1967 and 1977, there were no executions. As a result of a Supreme Court decision in 1972, inmates who were sentenced to death had their sentences changed to life without parole. In 1977, Utah became the first state to reinstate the death penalty under state law. Since then, thirty-one other states have followed suit. Several new policies, however, were implemented. One is that only aggravated murderers could be sentenced to death. Another is that lethal injection was established as the only acceptable method of execution.

The death penalty is clearly very controversial. On one hand, many people support it because it is punitive. Many victims and victims' advocates, for example, have been so devastated by the death of a loved one that they wish ill will on the perpetrator of that crime. Many feel that execution will bring them a sense of closure. On the other hand, many people still have grave concerns with the death penalty. One is that the appeals process is very time-consuming and expensive. The second is that it is seen as being inhumane. A third is that African Americans and poor people are overrepresented on death row. The concern here is that many people have been wrongfully convicted or inordinately harshly sentenced due to their race and/or inability to hire a legal team capable of providing them with an adequate defense.

In her piece, "Capital Punishment, the Court, and Racial Discrepancy Research," Flexon shows that capital punishment is not racially neutral. In other words, there is racial discrepancy in its application. For instance, black murderers who kill white victims are seven times more likely to receive the death penalty than white murderers who kill black victims. Flexon also contends that since capital jury members must be death-qualified—or willing to invoke the death penalty—this introduces bias into the deliberation process.

● SEXUAL ASSAULT

Sexual assault is an important social problem that impacts us all. In general, men are the perpetrators of sexual assault, a criminal act that affects a high rate of women. One explanation for this is that rape is less about sex than it is power. The disempowerment of men may lead to sexual assault in an effort to exercise power and control. Another important factor involves consent. By definition, sexual assault means that sexual acts are done without mutual consent. But as with sexual harassment, men and women—in fact each individual—may define consent differently. Americans are not accustomed to discussing these issues with each other, often resulting in confusion and sometimes in criminality. The incredible access to pornography that the Internet affords does not help clarify boundaries between healthy and unhealthy sex. Rape can be eroticized, actors can play parts that should not be imitated in real life, and consumers of pornography may be left with a misguided understanding of how sex can be accomplished both pleasurably and lawfully.

In her chapter, "Measuring Sexual Assault," James establishes that ascertaining actual sexual assault rates is a very difficult proposition. Also, it is estimated that only a quarter of actual sexual assaults are reported to police, due to victims being fearful of reprisal from perpetrators, being blamed for what happened, and/or not being taken seriously by authorities. One group of people who experience particularly high rates of sexual assault are college-age women. College-age women are four times more likely to be sexually assaulted than women in other age groups. In addition to age, James considers several characteristics of victimization and documents that rates of sexual assault vary according to women's race and ethnicity, place of residence, time of day, and lifestyle.

CHAPTER 13

Disproportionate Minority Contact in the Criminal Justice System

By Nicole A. Shoenberger

E ric Garner, John Crawford, Michael Brown, Dante Parker, Tamir Rice, and Freddie Gray are some of the young black men who have been killed by police since Trayvon Martin died at the hands of George Zimmerman, a neighborhood watch volunteer in 2012. This select group of men has helped to publicly raise the important issue of disproportionate minority youth contact within the criminal justice system. Disproportionate minority contact (DMC) has come to be understood as the overrepresentation of young minorities in the criminal justice system (CJS). This not only means overrepresentation for imprisonment, but also an overrepresentation at all contact points in the CJS, including arrest, referral to court, diversion, case petitions, secure detention, delinquency finding, probation, confinement in a secure correctional facility, confinement in out-of-home residential placement, and case transfer to adult criminal court. This purpose of this chapter is to examine the causes of DMC and to consider various strategies that have been implemented to reduce DMC over the last twenty-five years.

● BACKGROUND

Although minority youth comprise only one-third of youth in America, they represent over two-thirds of all youth currently held in juvenile institutions (Armour and Hammond 2009). American criminal justice agencies have known about this for two or more decades and have created a diverse range of initiatives to try and reduce this problem. Unfortunately, these efforts have not been very successful and national trends illustrate an increase in the rate of disproportionate minority contact. In 1990, for example, the Relative Rate Index (RRI), a measure developed to examine the issue that divides the rate of activity in a contact point for minority youth by that of white youth contact, illustrated that arrests for blacks was 2.0 whereas the rates for whites (the comparison group) was 1.0. Although this rate decreased through the 1990s, the rate began to increase in 2005 and rose to 2.2 by 2011 (Puzzanchera and Hockenberry 2014). Though blacks account for only 15 percent of the United States population, black youth account for 26 percent of juvenile arrests, 21 percent of adjudications, 20 percent of out-of-home placements, and 46 percent of cases that are waived to adult court (Dillard 2013).

DMC is not a new issue and has a long history in the United States. After the de-institutionalization era of the 1970s, conservative politics in the early 1980s influenced a more punitive era that corresponded with an increase in rates of incarceration. This increase was led by minority youth, who consisted of 93 percent of the incarceration increase (Davis and Sorensen 2013). In 1986, in front of the House Subcommittee on Human Resources, Ira Schwartz provided testimony that, despite the number of minority youth in prison, data did not illustrate that minority youth committed a disproportionate amount of crime. In doing so, Schwartz used the phrase disproportionate minority contact (DMC) and provided the first legislative account of DMC on record (Davis and Sorensen 2013). Since then, coalitions, mandates, legislation, and programs have been created and implemented to address the issue of DMC in the United States.

● CAUSES OF DISPROPORTIONATE MINORITY CONTACT

Evidence of racial disparity within the juvenile justice system has been apparent for decades, yet there is little agreement concerning the causes of DMC. Even though numerous studies have sought to explain DMC, the results are mixed (Feyerherm 1995). Detailed examinations of each stage of the CJS, for example, have revealed both racial disparities and no evidence of disparity (DeJong and Jackson 1998). Though there is mixed evidence of disparities at all stages, one assumption has been maintained through the research: later disparities typically result from disparities that occur in the early processing stages (Davis and Sorensen 2013). Therefore, it follows that if racial disparity occurs during an arrest or through the intake process, minority youth will experience a cumulative barrage of disparity throughout punishment, detention, and institutionalization as they move through the system.

One cause of DMC relates to differential involvement and offending, or the idea that there are differences in offending for whites and minorities (Piquero 2008; Bridges and Steen 1998; Bridges, Conley, Beretta, and Engen 1993). For example, official data illustrate that black males are more likely to commit serious violent offenses compared to white males (Kakar 2006). These offenses include armed robbery, homicide, and aggravated assault—all of which are violent and typically have a victim who has a higher likelihood of knowing his or her perpetrator. These offenses are more likely to catch the attention of police, as they are more likely to be reported by the victim or a bystander. This, in turn, increases contact in the criminal justice system for minority youth. Depending on the severity of the offense, the youth may be detained at various stages of the process. Ultimately, this perspective asserts that standard police tactics can lead to the overrepresentation of minorities in the criminal justice system, as they are perceived, through *official*[1] data, to be committing higher reported criminal activity.

Within this differential offending framework, scholars have examined other contextual issues that might increase the likelihood that minority youth would have more contact with the CJS. For example, scholars point to multidimensional factors that increase the risk of contact. Sampson, Morenoff, and Raudenbush (2005) have long pointed out that economically disadvantaged neighborhoods have decreased levels of collective efficacy, which creates unstable and danger-ous neighborhoods. Within these neighborhoods, supporting institutions such as schools perform at substandard rates, which limits children's investment in education and causes many of them to eventually drop out of school (Sharkey and Sampson 2010). Many of these youth then rely upon or make friends with delinquent peers (Anderson 1999). Further, many of these youth come from unstable family units, and have incarcerated parents or erratic parental supervi-sion and discipline; all of which are correlated with higher rates of delinquency (Sampson, Morenoff, and Raudenbush 2005). The accumulation of these risk factors increases the likelihood of many youth having contact with police, there-fore increasing their contact with the CJS.

Others argue that DMC extends beyond the standard criminal justice prac-tice of processing crimes that are most likely to be reported to the police. As such, some argue that the *differential selection/ treatment and processing* of youth within the criminal justice system is the root cause of DMC. The argument here is that the system may actually treat minorities and whites differently at various stages of the process (Piquero 2008; Snyder and Sickmund 1999; Bridges, Conley, Engen and Price-Spratlen, 1995; Dunn, Perry, Cernkovich, and Wicks 1993). This perspective highlights that minority youth are more likely to receive harsher punishments, more likely to be detained more often, and less likely to benefit from diversion programs because of police or judicial discretion and bias. Here, police officers might be more likely to arrest minority youth simply through racial profiling or bias. Further, judges may give preferential treatment to white youth compared to minority youth. Some probation officers may provide a second chance to white youth compared to minority youth. Differential selection also explains the greater police presence in lower-class and minority neighborhoods, which creates more chances for police to see and apprehend minority youth offenders (Kempf-Leonard 2007).

One critique of the criminal justice system is that police officers and judges have too much discretionary power. Given the increase of punitive justice, some police may be more inclined to "provide a lesson" to certain youth in certain situations (Kempf-Leonard 2007). This may further extend to the courts, where judges may feel more inclined to process minority youth due to their presumed family and community situations, in hopes to help these youth overcome situational deficits (Kempf-Leonard 2007). In this regard, both police and courts may unfairly process minority youth to either teach them a lesson, help them receive treatment, or remove them from a bad environment.

Differential processing tends to be a favored argument concerning DMC, though some scholars argue that it is a combination of differential processing and the offenses committed (Piquero 2008). Through this combination, a cumulative effect may increase the disparity as youth move through the system (Davis and Sorensen 2013). Kempf-Leonard (2007) states that minority youth in urban areas may be more likely to have the police called against them for an infraction that police believe these youth commit more than whites. This means police patrol these areas more and arrest these youth more. Other members of the CJS come to see these youth as the perpetrators of these crimes because of these arrests, and feel the need to punish them more harshly for these crimes. In this scenario, both the crime committed and police's differential patrolling and decision making initially play a role in the arrest of the youth, which then has an influence on the differential processing of the youth in future events in the system.

Other explanations focus on geographical differences, regardless of police contact. Research illustrates that living in certain regions of the country may affect police contact. Similarly, living in certain states or cities may affect DMC, and living in rural or suburban areas plays a part in police contact. Geographical differences are also associated with the severity of punishment that a youth receives (Armour and Hammond 2009). The Office of Juvenile Justice and Delinquency Prevention (OJJDP) provides data indicating that youth who commit crime in urban areas are more likely to receive a harsher punishment than similar cases in other jurisdictions (i.e., suburban or rural). This might be influenced by visibility factors, in which minority youth may be more likely to participate in crime in public, visible areas. Not only do these crimes, such as drug exchanges, draw the attention of police, but also many of them, by the statutes of the law, carry stiffer punishments. Even though whites also commit these acts, they are likely to live in different jurisdictions and are more likely to commit these acts inside their homes (Armour and Hammond 2009). Therefore, criminal activities among whites that tend to carry severe punishments are out the eye of police because crime in rural and suburban areas plays out differently than crime in urban areas.

Many scholars argue that the explanation for DMC is extremely complex and includes multiple factors, such as system bias, differential involvement, policies, and macro-level structural conditions such as family situations, poverty, and social inequalities (Kakar 2006; Pope, Lovell and Hsia 2002). Furthermore, as recent cases have come to light since the Trayvon Martin case, many argue that an overarching cause of DMC is racial bias both within and outside of the system. If this is the case, simply addressing policies for fair treatment may not be enough, as the systemic issues are rooted in cultural beliefs, which means to address DMC, society needs to address its issues regarding race.

● ATTEMPTS TO REDUCE DMC

Feyerherm (1995) posited that DMC is so complex that changes need to go beyond simply removing a type of treatment or providing the same successful program to all. As such, multiple studies done over the years have produced mixed results in terms of pinpointing root causes and solutions to the problem. These ambiguous results may be attributable to how researchers have attempted to study DMC. Kempf-Leonard (2007) argues that examining DMC and its reduction is not as simple as comparing youth just by race. Instead, comparisons need to be drawn from "similar situated" youth who happen to differ by race. To do so would require multiple pieces of the puzzle—information on families, communities, the actual persons, and the criminal justice system processing the individuals. Moreover, one would need to study equality in opportunities within the communities and within the criminal justice systems. Clearly, all of these are very difficult to achieve.

Though results are mixed, states have received federal funding to focus on examining the causes of DMC in order to make it less prevalent. These initiatives have led to increased data collection, minority trainings for judges, and pilot projects (Armour and Hammond 2009). Though there have been considerable attempts at reducing DMC, it is clear that more programs and policies are needed (Kempf-Leonard 2007).

The most common intervention strategies are direct services, training and education, and system change (Leiber and Rodriguez 2011). Direct services are programs that are geared towards addressing factors that directly impact youth. Needs such as education, positive relationship development, and parent training are addressed while the youth are in the system. Direct services may include specific diversion programs and alternatives to secure detention (Leiber and Rodriguez 2011). When diverting youth from institutionalization, youth may be directed to social service agencies or community service. These programs still hold the youth responsible for their actions; however, they are not formally processed by the court (Leiber and Rodriguez 2011). Though the above programs are popular, most attention is focused on alternative means of punishing youth without placing them in secure detention. These programs attempt to reduce confinement of youth while still increasing public safety, reducing minority confinement, and reducing the cost of juvenile justice (Mendel 2009; see also Leiber and Rodriguez 2011).

Training and educational programs represent another popular strategy that has increased over the last twenty-five years. Specifically, these programs include cultural diversity training that educates local law enforcement and juvenile justice personal on stereotypes and racial biases (Leiber and Rodriguez 2011). Increasing awareness of cultural differences may help police and judges understand the decisions some of these youth have to make in their day-to-day lives. Some training, such as the Pennsylvania DMC forums, include education on brain development of youth, which is an important factor in understanding why youth may not think of the consequences of their actions. Further, conferences and forums that law enforcement may attend provide extensive training to officers in how to handle youth differently than adults (Leiber and Rodriguez 2011).

Lastly, Leiber and Rodriguez (2011) state that the third type of intervention, though slow to occur, is system change. This type of intervention relies heavily on legislation, administrative changes, and structural changes concerning the entire criminal justice process. Some reform has seen legislation passed that makes states accountable for collecting data on DMC and has states justify current and new policies that affect it. Leiber and Rodriguez (2011) note that one of the best examples of legislation having an effect is the focus on reducing and changing secure detention procedures.

Armour and Hammond (2009) argue that one way to address DMC is to increase people's awareness of institutional biases. This takes the form of increasing awareness of the issue among community leaders, parents, the police, and other stakeholders. Further, this might extend to trainings, seminars, and forums that contain cultural diversity information. To be effective in reducing DMC, the Office of Juvenile Justice and Delinquency Prevention (OJJDP) has offered guidelines for intervention programs that establish the importance of developing a comprehensive, multisystemic approach; prioritizing strategies based on critical decision points within a jurisdiction; implementing strategies that have community support; relying on evidence-based strategies; and drawing on and evaluating successful DMC initiatives and strategies (Leiber and Rodriguez 2011). A few programs have followed the outline provided by the OJJDP and have identified and focused on major contact points to create initiatives to reduce DMC, with moderate success. Among these are the Models for Change, the Juvenile Detention Alternatives Initiative, and the Pennsylvania DMC Forums. Each is discussed further below.

Models for Change

Funded through the MacArthur Foundation in 2004, the Models for Change Initiative attempts to achieve a bias-free juvenile justice system. To do so, the states participating in the program are to complete routine compliance monitoring and are supplied with resources that help specify possible disparities in the system, with plans on how to address these issues. Some of the programs include diversity within the agencies involved in handling youth, the use of standardized criteria for processing, and the creation of newer alternatives to detention (Armour and Hammond 2009; Nellis and Richardson 2010).

Juvenile Detention Alternatives Initiative

The Juvenile Detention Alternatives Initiative (JDAI), funded by the Annie E. Casey Foundation, was founded in 1992 to address one particular area of DMC—pretrial detention. By focusing on pretrial detention, the JDAI created a risk assessment for detention screenings. They also introduced alternative detention programs that are operated by the community, such as Evening Reporting Centers. The JDAI supports faster processing of youth to reduce the time spent in secure facilities while also proposing new policies that address probation violations (Armour and Hammond 2009; Nellis and Richardson 2010).

A subcommittee of the Pennsylvania Commission on Crime and Delinquency was formed to address the unequal treatment of racial minorities in the state. From this, a curriculum for law enforcement was created to help law enforcement work with and understand youth. This project has brought together local stakeholders including police, judges, public defenders, and probation officers with minority youth in a series of forums where youth and officers get to candidly discuss police tactics, arrests, and how youth perceive law enforcement. Further, youth and officers spend the day together discussing and role-playing realistic situations that may involve minority youth (DMC Youth/Law Enforcement Corporation 2015; Armour and Hammond 2009).

● A CALL TO ACTION: #BLACK LIVES MATTER

In 2015, the Black Lives Matter movement placed fourth on *Time* magazine's Person of the Year list. As *Time* notes, the movement is a force to be reckoned with, as it has badgered police chiefs, helped in prosecutions, and very publicly came to the forefront of the hunger strike that led to the resignation of the University Missouri's president (Altman 2015). The movement has helped groups form national conferences, provided an outlet to strategize, and launched a medium for many to voice their concerns about systemic injustice. It might be argued that the Black Lives Matter movement has done more for DMC in the public sphere than many of the policies implemented by the system that caused the problem in the first place. In this movement, many have witnessed the words of Margaret Mead ring true: "Never doubt that a small group of thoughtful, committed citizens can change the world; indeed, it's the only thing that ever has."

The #BlackLivesMatter handle was formulated by Alicia Garza, Opal Tometi, and Patrisse Cullors in response to both the acquittal of George Zimmerman, who is famously known for the killing of Trayvon Martin in 2012, and the current anti-black racism that is still apparent in American society (Edwards and Harris, 2016). Unlike many movements, Black Lives Matter gained widespread recognition in both the media (Twitter, Facebook, general Internet searches, and TV shows) and on the streets, where protests and marches have sprung up on college campuses, in inner cities, and at the sites of the killings of unarmed black men by police officers. Many initiatives to combat the unfair treatment of minorities have been formal and made possible through foundations and state policies. The Black Lives Matter movement is a movement by the people for the people. Grassroots in nature, it is an on-the-ground initiative to which everyday individuals can contribute and feel as though they are doing something to reduce the disproportionate treatment of racial minorities in multiple arenas of everyday life.

The women who started the movement argue that Black Lives Matter is not a narrow-minded movement to call on black people to love their fellow black peers. They argue that "it is a tactic to (re)build the Black liberation movement" (Garza 2014, 2). This restructuring is meant to address the multilayered deprivation that many black men and women still face at the hands of America's institutions—not just the prison state. In doing so, the creators of the movement attempt to create conversation around the ways in which "Black people are left powerless at the hands of the state" and to provide an avenue for people to fight against this powerlessness for all realms of inequality (Black Lives Matter 2016).

Though the movement has gained popularity and has been applauded for its work, the movement is not without scrutiny. Handles such as "All Lives Matter," "White Lives Matter," and "Blue Lives Matter" have sprung up to argue that people should not place focus on one group over the other. Some argue that if those of the Black Lives Matter movement are looking for equality then why focus their efforts only on blacks. Further, the biggest counter to the countless lives of young black men and women are the lives of many police officers who have died in the line of duty, and that these are the lives that should matter as these men and women put their lives on the line for the protection of society. The founders of the Black Lives Matter movement argue that the movement does not mean that other lives do not matter or that black lives are more important. It is recognition that not all lives are *free*. Not all lives are *liberated*. In understanding this, if society moves towards the end of what Garza (2014, 3) refers to as the "hyper-criminalization and sexualization of Black people and end the poverty, control, and surveillance of Black people, every single person in this world has a better shot at getting and staying free." If society truly liberates black lives, then in turn, it has helped everyone—making it a handle for everyone to get behind.

● SUMMARY AND CONCLUSION

Though the system has attempted to address DMC, it is a very difficult and complex issue to face, as the causes of DMC are not as clear-cut as society would like them to be. There are issues of differential offending where some youth, by artifacts of where they live, their family life, and peer influence, are more likely to commit certain crimes that are on the police radar, which places them in the line of sight of police for arrests and eventually secure detention. There are arguments of differential selection/treatment that places the burden on CJS personnel and their own personal biases, and may affect how police, judges, and intake officers use their own discretion when making arrests, filing petitions, and placing youth in secure detention. Some argue that it is a combination of differential offending and treatment of minority youth. One supported argument does remain: racial disparity that occurs during the arrest or through the intake process will affect minority youth throughout the system, which creates a cumulative barrage of punishment, detention, and institutionalization.

In recent years, Americans have learned about the disproportionate minority youth contact in the criminal justice system, an issue that has been on the radar of the criminal justice system for twenty-five years. Though the public's attention has been focused on the deaths of many minority men and women, this over-representation of minority youth in the system affects youth at *all* contact points in the system—arrest, intake, referrals to court, diversion, case petitions, secure detention, delinquency findings, probation, confinement in a secure correctional facility, out-of-home placement, and cases waived to adult court. In response, the government and the CJS have attempted to address the issue through mandates and initiatives that focus on direct services, training and education, and system change.

Many of these projects attempt to educate police, judges, probation officers, and other CJS personnel on DMC and perceived biases while providing diversity training. Further, programs attempt to address issues in the community such as violence, education, and family influences. As noted earlier, system change is the slowest of them all, but some states have passed mandates while also introducing legislation to change how the system deals with secure detention. Among these initiatives are some promising programs, such as Models for Change, the Juvenile Detention Alternatives Initiative, and the Pennsylvania DMC Forums. Beyond the responses of the CJS and the government, a grassroots movement, Black Lives Matter, has provided an outlet for those who are most affected by DMC. This movement has been vocal in attempting to hold the system accountable for the perceived injustice that has been occurring for decades.

Believed to be historically rooted in institutional racism, DMC has allowed for the continuance of the unfair treatment of racial minorities at all contact points in the system. Though the CJS has recognized this to be the case, and has ultimately placed efforts and funding to eradicate the issue, it still exists. It is the hope of those supportive of the Black Lives Matter movement that the CJS can make better efforts to reduce the disparity before there are more Eric Garners, John Crawfords, Michael Browns, Dante Parkers, Tamir Rices, or Freddie Grays.

● NOTES

1. Official is italicized as there is evidence that there are differences in crime rates when using official data compared to self-reported and victimization data. Official data are used here as they are the data used for calculations for RRIs and for official reports of crime by the FBI.

● REFERENCES

Altman, A. 2015. "Person of the Year: The Short Lists No. 4: Black Lives Matter: A New Civil Rights Movement Is Turning a Protest Cry into a Political Force." *Time*, 186 (25/26). http://time.com/time-person-of-the-year-2015-runner-up-black-lives-matter/.

Anderson, E. 1999. *The Code of the Streets: Decency, Violence, and the Moral Life of the Inner City*. New York: Norton.

Armour, J., and S. Hammond. 2009. "Minority Youth in the Juvenile Justice System: Disproportionate Minority Contact." National Conference of State Legislatures Report, Denver, CO.

Bridges, G. S., D. J. Conley, R. L. Engen and T. Price-Spratlen. 1995. "Racial Disparities in the Confinement of Juveniles: Effects of Crime and Community Social Structure on the Punishment." In *Minorities in Juvenile Justice*. Edited by K. K. Leonard, C. E. Pope, and W. Feyerherm. Thousand Oaks, CA: Sage. 128–152.

Black Lives Matter. 2016. About the Black Lives Matter Network. http://blacklivesmatter.com/about/.

Bridges, G., D. Conley, G. Beretta, and R. Engen. 1993. *Racial Disproportionality in the Juvenile Justice System* (Final Rep. to the Commission on African American Affairs). Olympia, WA: Department of Social and Health Services.

Bridges, G. S., and S. Steen. 1998. "Racial Disparities in Official Assessments of Juvenile Offenders: Attributional Stereotypes as Mediating Mechanisms." *American Sociological Review* 63 (4): 554–70.

Davis, J., and J. Sorensen. 2013. "Disproportionate Minority Confinement of Juveniles: A National Examination of Black-White Disparity in Placements, 1997–2006." *Crime & Delinquency*, 59 (1): 115–39.

DeJong, C., and K. Jackson. 1998. "Putting Race into Context: Race, Juvenile Justice Processing and Urbanization." *Justice Quarterly* 15 (3): 487–504.

Dillard, D. 2013. "Limited Disproportionate Minority Contact Discourse May Explain Limited Progress in Reducing Minority Over-Representation in the US Juvenile Justice System." *Youth Justice* 13 (3): 207–17.

DMC Youth/Law Enforcement Corporation. 2015. "The Pennsylvania DMC Reduction Story." https://padmc.org/the-pennsylvania-story/.

Dunn, C., R. L. Perry, S. R. Cernkovich, and J. Wicks. 1993. *Race and Juvenile Justice in Ohio: The Overrepresentation and Disproportionate Confinement of African American and Hispanic Youth.* Bowling Green, OH: Bowling Green State University.

Edwards, S.B., and D. Harris. 2016. *Black Lives Matter*. North Mankato, MN: Abdo Publishing

Feyerherm, W. 1995. "The DMC Initiative: The Convergence of Policy and Research Themes." In *Minorities in Juvenile Justice,* 1–15. Edited by K. K. Leonart, C. E. Pope, and W. H. Feyerherm. Thousand Oaks, CA: Sage.

Garza, A. 2014. "A Herstory of the #BlackLivesMatter Movement." *The Feminist Wire*, October 7. http://www.thefeministwire.com/2014/10/blacklivesmatter-2/.

Kakar, S. 2006. "Understanding the Causes of Disproportionate Minority Contact: Results of Focus Group Discussions." *Journal of Criminal Justice* 34 (4): 369–81.

Kempf-Leonard, K. 2007. "Minority Youths and Juvenile Justice: Disproportionate Minority Contact Nearly 20 Years of Reform Efforts." *Youth Violence and Juvenile Justice* 5 (1): 71–87.

Leiber, M., and N. Rodriguez. 2011. "The Implementation of the Disproportionate Minority Confinement/Contact (DMC) Mandate: A Failure or Success?" *Race and Justice* 1 (1): 103–24.

Mendel, R. 2009. *Two Decades of JDAI: A Progress Report.* Baltimore, MD: Annie E. Casey Foundation.

Nellis, A., and B. Richardson. 2010. "Getting Beyond Failure: Promising Approaches for Reducing DMC." *Youth Violence and Juvenile Justice* 8 (3): 266–76.

Piquero, A. 2008. "Disproportionate Minority Contact." *The Future of Children* 18 (2): 59–79.

Pope C. E., Lovell R., Hsia H. M. (2002). Disproportionate Minority Confinement: A Review of the Research Literature from 1989 through 2001. Washington, DC: Office of Juvenile Justice and Delinquency Prevention.

Puzzanchera, C., and S. Hockenberry. 2014. *National Disproportionate Minority Contact Databook.* Developed by the National Center for Juvenile Justice for the Office of Juvenile Justice and Delinquency Prevention. http://www.ojjdp.gov/ojstatbb/dmcdb/.

Sampson, R., J. Morenoff, and S. Raudenbush. 2005. "Social Anatomy of Racial and Ethnic Disparities in Violence." *American Journal of Public Health* 95 (2): 224–32.

Sharkey, P., and R. Sampson. 2010. "Destination Effects: Residential Mobility and Trajectories of Adolescent Violence in a Stratified Metropolis." *Criminology* 48 (3): 639–81.

Snyder, H. N., and M. Sickmund. 1999. *Minorities in the Juvenile Justice System.* Washington, DC: U.S. Department of Justice, Office of Justice Programs, Office of Juvenile Justice and Delinquency Prevention.

CHAPTER 14

The Collateral Consequences of Mass Incarceration in the Twenty-First Century

By Eric G. Lesneskie

C rime is arguably one of the most agreed–upon social problems occurring in any society. The monetary costs of crime alone in the United States are staggering. It is estimated that yearly criminal offenses cost approximately 15 billion dollars in economic losses to the victims, and the price tag for law enforcement, courts, and corrections to deal with these crimes is estimated to be close to 179 billion dollars annually (Department of Justice 2005). These financial expenses associated with the criminal justice system are straightforwardly quantified, but other costs are more latent, and the effects of these cannot not be easily determined. Less measurable, but equally important costs include psychological harm to victims and families, fear of crime, and diminished quality of life. With all of these tolls and effects, rightly, the prevention of crime should be of upmost importance. However, the question of how to best reduce crime remains unanswered. The United States' chosen approach has been to punish offenders through imprisonment. The main purpose of this chapter is to illustrate the collateral consequences resulting from the changes that have occurred in imprisonment laws and policies in the United States since the 1970s.

● MASS INCARCERATION: HOW DID WE GET HERE?

For the last four decades, the United States has attempted to reduce crime and to punish offenders, in part, through mass incarceration. The prison population began to surge in 1972 and this unrelenting growth was maintained across the country until 2010 (Clear and Frost 2014). Specifically, from 1980 to 2010 the prison population increased by 373 percent, and the jail population increased by 324 percent (Guerino, Harrison, and Sabol 2011).[1] This growth has resulted in the United States having the highest incarceration rates of all Western countries (Clear and Frost 2014; Nagin 2014; Tonry 2014).

Criminologists, for the last few decades, have attempted to distinguish what prompted this era of mass imprisonment. Increasing crime, the War on Drugs, and/or simply changes in laws and policies have all been examined as possible rationales for the imprisonment binge. But, still to this day, there is not one explanation for the more than forty years of prison growth. For example, at face value, increasing crime is hypothesized to correlate with increased prison growth. Pragmatically, this makes sense; as crime rates increase, arrests rates rise correspondingly, and finally prison populations begin to grow. But, in the case of the United States, this causal relationship is not consistently seen. Yearly crime and imprisonment trends since the 1970s indicate that crime rates fluctuated but imprisonment rates consistently increased. Accordingly, the relationship between crime rates and imprisonment rates is uncertain and varying. Crime cannot be entirely unrelated from or entirely determinate of imprisonment, thus crime as the sole indicator and explanation for increased prison growth is problematic (see Clear and Frost 2014).

There is more evidence to suggest that policy and legal changes, both correctional and social, had greater influence on the rise of the prison populations in the United States than crime. First, in part, a change in correctional philosophy from a rehabilitative-based to a deterrence-based system occurred (Zimring 2001). The belief, at the time, was that rehabilitation practices were ineffective in preventing crime (Clear and Frost 2014; Martinson 1974; Zimring 2001). This shift to more of a deterrence-based system increased the likelihood of someone being imprisoned. If an individual was convicted of a crime, the odds or risk of imprisonment increased drastically starting in the early 1970s. This increased risk of imprisonment was not just for serious violent offenders; the odds also increased substantially for low-level offenders.

Second, in the 1980s, the War on Drugs further contributed to the rise of prison populations across the United States (Zimring 2001). Fueled by the crack epidemic, concerns about drug distribution and usage reached all-time highs. This time period is criticized on many fronts for the failure to focus on the problem of drug addiction, which fuels markets and provides an endless supply of users (Clear and Frost 2014). Instead of addressing addiction and other demand-side issues, efforts fixated on the arrest of sellers and deterring individuals from becoming involved in the drug trade through long and harsh sentences. The Sentencing Reform Act of 1984 produced punitive sanctions with mandatory minimum prison sentences for selling illegal substances (Zimring 2001). Now drug offenders, in addition to other low-level offenders, experienced greater risk of imprisonment (Clear and Frost 2014; Zimring 2001). By 2010, individuals imprisoned for drug crimes represented 20 percent of the prison population, while in the 1970s, just 5 percent of the prison population was imprisoned for drug offenses (Clear and Frost 2014).

Next, starting in the mid-1990s, the focus was turned to reducing violent crime. In order to reduce crime, laws and policies were implemented to impose more lengthy sentences (Zimring 2001). Truth-in-sentencing laws, which require offenders to complete 85 percent of their sentence, were the cornerstones of this time period (Clear and Frost 2014). The idea was to punish individuals longer, which will then prevent crime and recidivism through incapacitation. However, legislation during this time period increased sentence length for not just violent and repeat offenders, but for all offending types, including nonviolent, first-time offenders (Clear and Frost 2014).

Three-strike laws, mandatory minimum sentences, truth-in-sentencing, and determinate sentencing are a few of the better known "tough-on-crime" laws and policies that were implemented during the aforementioned mass imprisonment binge.[2] These were enacted and large numbers of people were incarcerated.

Crime is costly, both economically and socially, and violent offenders should be punished and incarcerated. However, large numbers of nonviolent offenders were also sentenced to confinement in this era of mass imprisonment due to the implementation of these "tough-on-crime" laws and policies. About two-thirds of people entering prison each year are incarcerated for nonviolent crimes, such as property, drug, and public order offenses (Clear and Frost 2014). In many instances, punishment is continued after being released due to restrictions placed on this large number of ex-offenders returning to society. These restrictions produce collateral consequences, such as the inability to find housing and employment, the disruption of the family unit, and reduction in the social organization of neighborhoods.

Prison, in and of itself, places hardships on those incarcerated and in most respects, rightly, it should. However, keep in mind the terms "*ex*-felon" or "*ex*-offender." I italicize "*ex*" throughout this chapter to reinforce the notion that individuals have already concluded their prison sentence and paid their prescribed debt to society. I use these terms, not to categorize, but to further illustrate the issues facing individuals returning to society from prison. The effects of serving time go beyond the prison walls and extend through the re-entry process and in some instances even longer. Almost 95 percent of individuals incarcerated will eventually be released (Prager 2007) and an average of ten thousand individuals are released from state and federal prisons each week (see Clear 2007). Additionally, race and socioeconomic status are obstinately linked to imprisonment and re-entry. It is estimated that one in nine black males between twenty and thirty-four years of age are imprisoned on a given day (PEW 2008). Since the prison population is disproportionately poor, young, minority, and male, imprisonment and re-entry, as well as the collateral consequences, are thus concentrated amongst poor minority males (Clear 2007).

The United States continually punishes large numbers of individuals long after they are released from prison. Voting disenfranchisement, housing restrictions, and being banned from certain employment settings are a few of the restrictions that continue to punish individuals after they are released from custody. Many of these restrictions placed on *ex*-offenders maintain the stigmatization of being a criminal and prohibit the integration and the building of bonds with society. On simply the basis alone of such criminological theories as labeling (Lemert 1967) and social bond (Hirschi 1969), this cannot be good practice. The ultimate outcome of this continued stigmatization and maintenance of broken bonds and low levels of social control is recidivism. Empirical evidence indicates this, with two-thirds of all *ex*-offenders recidivating within three years of release (see Cnaan, Draine, Frazier, and Sinha 2008).

Prison and these restrictions have obvious collateral consequences on the individual. However, research has also consistently shown how imprisonment produces collateral and negative consequences for the families of those incarcerated and the neighborhoods for which large segments of the population are imprisoned and released (see Clear 2007). I contend that the era of mass imprisonment did more harm than good by producing continued collateral consequences for society. The rest of this chapter will detail some of the collateral consequences of imprisonment on individuals, families, and neighborhoods, and the subsequent effects that it has on crime.

● UNINTENDED CONSEQUENCES AT THE INDIVIDUAL LEVEL

There are many unintended consequences of mass incarceration that exist at the individual level. The first is voting disenfranchisement. The second relates to housing. The last one is employment. Each of these compound each other and impact the abilities of *ex*-offenders to fully integrate into mainstream society.

1. Voting Disenfranchisement

Serving time in prison produces educational, economic, and social inequalities for the individual upon release (Wakefield and Uggen 2010). Often driving these inequalities have been laws and policies that prevent *ex*-offenders from fully removing the stigma of being a criminal and developing strong bonds with society. One such restriction that fails to remove the criminal stigma and prohibits building of bonds is voting disenfranchisement. Each state has its own rules and restrictions for felon and *ex*-felon voting rights. Across the United States, it is estimated that five million citizens are restricted from voting due to felon disenfranchisement (Uggen and Inderbitzin 2010).[3] Of this estimated five million felony disenfranchised individuals, 74 percent are individuals who are not incarcerated (Uggen and Inderbitzin 2010). These individuals are either under supervised release or are no longer under supervision. Disproportionately, the number of felony disenfranchisement individuals are racial minorities, with one in twelve African Americans restricted from voting due to felony convictions (King 2006).

Reasonably, forty-eight states prohibit felons who are currently serving prison sentences from voting within prison (Sentencing Project 2015). However, twelve states have post-release voting disenfranchisement for *ex*-offenders (Sentencing Project 2015). These states either totally deny voting rights for certain types of crimes or have a post-release waiting period before re-enfranchisement. The trend across the country is slowly moving towards the easing of restrictions and the restoration of voting rights for *ex*-offenders; however, the process of re-enfranchisement is often burdensome and few individuals take advantage of it (Sentencing Project 2015).

Even if they are still under supervised release, such as probation or parole, *ex*-offenders are citizens who pay taxes, have children who go to school, and are residents of a neighborhood. Re-enfranchising voting rights may help with the re-entry process for these *ex*-offenders. By re-enfranchising, the categorization of "felon" or "offender" can start to be diminished. Further, by enabling political action, *ex*-felons have the opportunity to participate in community activities, thereby promoting a sense of being a stakeholder in the community (Uggen and Inderbitzin 2010). Being a community stakeholder can increase social capital and strengthen bonds that may have a protective effect by integrating the individual into the community and thus reducing the odds of recidivism. There is some empirical evidence to suggest that voting participation may reduce re-offending. Uggen, Inderbitzin, and Vuolo (2007) found that probationers and parolees who voted had lower recidivism rates than those who did not. Although it may appear to be a trivial consequence for having committed a crime, by disenfranchising *ex*-offenders we are continually punishing and prohibiting these individuals from being fully re-integrated as members of society.

2. Housing Policy

Finding housing is also a barrier to successful re-entry for many *ex*-offenders. In the mid-to-late 1990s, during the height of the imprisonment boom, on any given day in California about 10 percent of state parolees were homeless (CA-DOC 1997). When disaggregated by city, this percentage was even higher for San Francisco (50%) and Los Angeles (30%; CA-DOC 1997). Unfortunately, even today, finding a place to live is still an issue facing many *ex*-offenders. Often with little money and bleak opportunities for employment, the only option other than homelessness is to attempt to reside in public or HUD-subsidized housing. Yet this can prove difficult. Local Public Housing Authorities (PHAs) have the power to reject and deny the housing applications of potential residents with a criminal record or a history of drug or alcohol abuse (Popkin, Gwiasda, Olson, Rosenbaum, and Buron 2000; Popkin, Cunningham, and Woodley 2003; Roman and Travis 2004).

Restrictive policies also have an influence on the family residing in subsidized housing. Residing with family is often the most stable environment for the *ex*-offender. However, if the family resides in public or HUD-assisted housing, residential security for the *ex*-offender is frequently unable to be achieved. According to Roman and Travis (2004), a large number of public housing residents have relatives or significant others with criminal histories. Therefore, often, the leaseholder is forced to make a decision on whether to allow the relative or significant other with a criminal record to live with them illegally or to turn their back on them (Roman and Travis 2004). Venkatesh (2002) indicates that almost half of the households surveyed in Chicago's Robert Taylor Homes expected a family member to be released from prison within nine months, and the returning offenders' only option might be to reside in public housing developments "off-the-lease" with their family (Popkin et al. 2003; Venkatesh 2002). Thus, the burden of housing is not just for the *ex*-offender; often the burden is shared with family and loved ones.

Similar to states and voting rights, the implementation of housing restrictions is left up to the local PHAs (see Moreno et al. n.d.). As such, there is tremendous variability on how these restrictions are implemented. Some PHAs allow *ex*-offenders to be residents on a case-by-case basis, or have separate housing for individuals with a felony record. Other PHAs allow residence for all *ex*-offenders, with the exception of those who are convicted of producing methamphetamine on public housing premises and those convicted of crimes that lead to lifetime registration under a state sex offender program.

Changes are occurring, yet the barriers to establishing housing for individuals with a criminal record are still present. Failing to establish housing often hinders reintegration and being productive members of society. The stigma of having to live in separate housing and/or being denied housing continually punishes the individual. Similar to what was discovered for *ex*-offenders who voted (Uggen et al. 2007), Roman and Travis (2004) indicate that *ex*-offenders who do not have housing experience higher rates of parole violations, thus leading to arrest. Similarly, Metraux and Culhane (2004) find that stable and supportive housing reduces crime rates and improves outcomes for *ex*-offenders. By reducing the barriers for housing, positive bonds may be strengthened and the stigma of a criminal record may be diminished, thereby potentially reducing recidivism.

3. Employment

Research has continually indicated that a felony conviction makes individuals significantly less employable (see Prager 2007). Roughly 60 to 75 percent of released offenders remain unemployed up to a year after release (Travis 2005; Petersilia 2003). The felony conviction works independently of other factors to lessen the opportunity for the gainful employment of *ex*-offenders (see Prager 2007). Even for employed *ex*-offenders, job stability is sporadic and earnings typically average $9,000 a year with little growth potential (Western 2006).

There are numerous ways that a felony conviction can reduce the odds of employment. First, being incarcerated can lead to a reduction in employable human capital skills, such as formal education, applied experience and skills, and "soft skills" such as human relations (Duran, Plotkin, Potter, and Rosen 2013). Second, imprisonment can contribute to a reduction in social networks (Duran et al. 2013). These social networks can often lead to job opportunities, which increase the odds of employment. However, when incarcerated, the networks are fragmented. Third, in some states, a felony conviction places limitations on government employment and professional licensing (Duran et al. 2013).

Being incarcerated or being a convicted felon can reduce the aforementioned skills and opportunities, but it also invokes a stigma that further makes employment less likely. This stigma is compounded even further when race is introduced into the context. As Prager (2007) illustrates with her research, the stigma of being a felon interacting with race further hinders large numbers of individuals from gainful employment. Thus, Prager (2007) contends that a black male with a criminal record is less likely to be hired by an employer than a white male with a criminal record. It appears, from this important research, that a criminal record, as well as race, are stigmatizing characteristics that produce and maintain social and economic inequality.

Surprisingly, most research indicates that a weak statistical relationship exists between employment and recidivism, and only a few studies show a direct relationship (see Wilson, Gallagher, and MacKenzie 2000; Visher, Debus, and Yahner 2008). However, pragmatically, employment should be an important tool in reducing recidivism, even if the relationship is indirect. Sampson and Laub (1993) suggest that stable employment can be a turning point that leads to desistence from offending. Employment with job stability, job commitment, and interpersonal relationships at the place of work can be a stabilizing influence on a person's trajectory (Sampson and Laub 1993). Basically, the social capital produced in the work environment produces bonds and social control over the individual and thus can lead to a reduction in criminal behavior. Employment may be an important first step in re-entering society for *ex*-offenders; however, if never given the opportunity for employment, individuals are never fully integrated into the community.

● UNINTENDED CONSEQUENCES FOR FAMILIES

As was indicated in the previous sections, *ex*-offenders often face continued punishments and collateral consequences upon release. These continued punishments and consequences do not just apply to the *ex*-offender, but extend to the family by influencing marital and parenting relationships, and also child functioning.

Marriage

Similar to employment, marriage can be a positive turning point for an individual. Attachment to a spouse can hinder involvement in crime due to the marital bonds producing social control (Sampson and Laub 1993). These bonds and informal social control can start the desistence process to stop engaging in crime and/or prevent criminal behavior altogether. However, going to prison substantially reduces the likelihood of marriage (Thomas 2005). This holds true across all racial groups, though the effect is most substantial for African American males over the age of twenty-four. For this group of males, the likelihood of marriage is reduced by 50 percent by being incarcerated (Thomas 2005). There are even consequences for those who are married prior to incarceration, due to imprisonment increasing the odds of separation and divorce (Western 2006). Thus, males who are not married may find it more difficult to develop prosocial relationships than males who are married, thereby reducing informal social bonds and control and increasing the potential for recidivism.

Parenting and Child Functioning

More than half of those incarcerated in state and federal prisons are parents of children under the age of eighteen (Harrison and Beck 2002). Long distances often separate those incarcerated and their children, reducing the opportunities for contact between parent and child. Average distances between incarcerated mothers and their children is 160 miles, while for incarcerated fathers the average distance between them and their children is 100 miles (see Travis, McBride, and Solomon 2005). Sheer distance separation is an issue, but incarceration also affects the lives of children psychologically, socially, and financially. Shame, the social stigma of having a parent incarcerated, increased delinquency, and poor school performance are some of the psychological and social outcomes of parental incarceration (Travis et al. 2005). Further, most parents (71%) were employed either full or part time a month prior to imprisonment, and once imprisoned that income was lost (Travis et al. 2005). Keep in mind, many of these families are already living in poverty and the loss of wages from being imprisoned further burdens the children and the family.

The negative effects do not just stop once the parent is released and reunited with their child. Barriers can prevent the returning parent from re-establishing parental roles, with such barriers including new spousal relationships, home re-location, and feelings of resentment (Travis et al. 2005). *Ex*-offenders are not the only ones influenced by imprisonment; families are also affected when a member, especially a parent, is incarcerated.

UNINTENDED CONSEQUENCES FOR THE COMMUNITY

Neighborhoods in the United States are often segregated by race and socio-economic status, and incarceration is demographically concentrated by race and socioeconomic status (Clear 2007). Subsequently, the collateral consequences of incarceration are concentrated in poor minority neighborhoods across the United States. For instance, Clear and Rose (2003) indicate that for predominately African American neighborhoods in Brooklyn, the incarceration rate is 12.4 per 1,000 residents. However, for white neighborhoods in Brooklyn, the rate is significantly lower at 2.7 per 1,000 residents.

As indicated in the first couple of paragraphs of this chapter, 95 percent of offenders are eventually released (Prager 2007). Due to this concentration of incarceration geographically in poor minority neighborhoods, naturally re-entry is often concentrated geographically within the same neighborhoods due to *ex*-offenders returning to the areas in which they resided prior to being imprisoned (Clear 2007). Even further, large numbers of *ex*-offenders typically return to just a small number of cities, counties, and neighborhoods (Morenoff and Harding 2011; Sampson and Loeffler 2010). Specifically, Morenoff and Harding (2014) found that half of all of Michigan's parolees were living in just 12 percent of census tracts in 2004.

Large proportions of individuals being imprisoned, released, experiencing continued stigmatization, and then imprisoned again from a small number of locations has adverse effects on the overall functioning of the community. First, the local economy is affected by the reduction in the supply of potential employees, which then limits outside investors and employers from establishing commerce in the community (Clear 2007; Morenoff and Harding 2014). Further, this reduction in potential workers and investors reduces earnings and tax bases for the community (Clear 2007; Morenoff and Harding 2014).

The removal of criminally prone individuals from a neighborhood should theoretically have an incapacitation effect and provide positive outcomes for the community. However, as outlined by Clear (2007), incarceration and re-entry can have negative effects on a community, and can actually increase crime within a neighborhood through a mechanism called coercive mobility. Coercive mobility is essentially the disruptive effects of population turnover by the continued cycling of offenders between the community and prison, which then reduces the aforementioned protective effects of incarceration (Clear 2007; Rose and Clear 1998). When coercive mobility reaches a high level, it is believed to reduce the neighborhood's ability to exert informal social control (Bursik and Grasmick 1993; Clear 2007; Rose and Clear 1998).

Empirically, as indicated by the coercive mobility thesis, moderate and high rates of imprisonment and re-entry in neighborhoods were linked with higher rates of crime (Clear 2007; Dhondt 2012). Further, research conducted by Hipp and Yates (2009) in Sacramento also finds that neighborhoods with higher rates of re-entry experience lower levels of social organization and higher levels of crime. These findings lend support to the negative effects and collateral consequences of incarceration on individuals, families, and institutions of a neighborhood by reducing the overall organization and climate of the community.

● DISCUSSION

The tremendous increase in prison growth since the 1970s has affected large segments of US citizenry. Many of the individuals incarcerated during this era of prison growth were first-time, nonviolent offenders (Clear 2007; Clear and Frost 2014; Prager 2007) and the restrictions placed on these *ex*-offenders have continued impact on not just these individuals, but also on their families and their community. In many ways, an *ex*-offender has never truly paid their full debt to society with these continued restrictions and limitations. These restrictions and limitations, in many ways, have adverse effects, such as continued stigmatization and ultimately recidivism. Incarceration has a detrimental influence on families, but when family bonds are re-broken due to recidivism, the effects are that much more drastic. Similar issues take place at the aggregate level in the community.

These issues are well documented and changes are starting to occur. On November 2, 2015, President Barack Obama attended a roundtable discussion on mass imprisonment and re-entry at the Center for Law and Justice at Rutgers University in Newark, New Jersey (Fox Nixon 2015). This discussion centered on how to inform policies that ease the process for *ex*-offenders, families of *ex*-offenders, and communities fin which *ex*-offenders reside. A program discussed during this roundtable was the New Jersey Scholarship and Transformative Education in Prisons (NJ-STEP) program (see njstep.newark.rutgers.edu). This initiative across New Jersey partners together the Department of Corrections, the Parole Board, and institutions of higher education. College courses are provided to eligible offenders who are incarcerated in state correctional facilities.

The program also helps to ease the re-entry process for those released by assisting with the changes to life in college and the community. Interestingly, NJ-STEP is not government funded; all funding comes from private supporters and donors. Other initiatives to reform the criminal justice process in the United States were discussed, and President Obama encouraged changes to the system by promoting initiatives designed to inspire reintegration and rehabilitation. Providing adult re-entry education grants, guidelines on screening *ex*-offenders in public and HUD-assisted housing, and "banning the box" for federal employment were all initiatives discussed at this roundtable (Fox Nixon 2015). The latter initiative allows for *ex*-offenders to receive equal and fair opportunities to achieve federal employment. Essentially, "banning the box" initiatives promote delaying the disclosure of a criminal record on initial job applications. Delaying this disclosure during the job hiring process provides better odds of employment for *ex*-offenders. *Ex*-offenders will then have opportunities to present themselves and explain their criminal histories to potential employers, rather than simply being rejected at the initial phases due to "checking a box" that indicates they have a criminal record (see Prager 2007). Delaying the disclosure of a criminal record to the secondary stages will help to reduce continued stigmatization and increase the odds of employment for *ex*-offenders.

The prison population began to decline in 2010 (Clear and Frost 2014). States are moving towards voting re-enfranchisement, local PHAs are starting to reduce restrictions for housing, and methods for promoting employment for *ex*-offenders are starting to come to fruition. These efforts, put into action, will have positive influences for society. Recidivism will be reduced, families bonds will be strengthened, and communities will become more socially organized. By addressing the continued punishment of *ex*-offenders by easing restrictions and limitations, the stigmatization of being a criminal will be reduced. Then, maybe, *ex*-offenders will have finally paid their debt to society.

● NOTES

1. This growth of the prison population naturally produced an increase in the number of individuals on parole and probation (Guerino et al. 2011).

2. Detailed explanations of these laws and policies are beyond the scope of this chapter.

3. Prior to the mass incarceration binge, the estimated total felony disenfranchised population was about 1.2 million individuals (Uggen and Inderbitzin 2010).

● REFERENCES

Bursik, R., and H. G. Grasmick. 1993. *Neighborhoods and Crime: The Dimensions of Effective Community Control.* New York: Lexington Books.

Clear, T. R., and D. R. Rose. 2003. "Individual Sentencing Practices and Aggregate Social Problems." In *Crime Control and Criminal Justice: The Delicate Balance.* Edited by D. F. Hawkins, S. Myers, and R. Stone. Westport, CT: Greenwood. 27–52.

Clear, T. R. 2007. *Imprisoning Communities: How Mass Incarceration Makes Disadvantaged Neighborhoods Worse.* New York: Oxford University Press.

Clear, T. R., and N. A. Frost. 2014. *The Punishment Imperative: The Rise and Failure of Mass Incarceration in America.* New York: New York University Press.

Cnaan, R. A., J. Draine, B. Frazier, and J. W. Sinha. 2008. "Ex-Prisoners' Re-Entry: An Emerging Frontier and a Social Work Challenge. *Journal of Policy Practice* 7 (2–3): 178–98.

California Department of Corrections (CA-DOC). 1997. *Preventing Parolee Failure Program: An Evaluation.* Sacramento: California Department of Corrections.

Dhondt, G. 2012. "The Bluntness of Incarceration: Crime and Punishment in Tallahassee Neighborhoods, 1995 to 2002." *Crime, Law and Social Change* 57 (5): 521–38.

Department of Justice (2005). *Justice Expenditure and Employment in the United States.* Washington, DC: Bureau of Justice Statistics.

Duran, L., M. Plotkin, P. Potter, and H. Rosen. 2013. *Integrated Reentry and Employment Strategies: Reducing Recidivism and Promoting Job Readiness.* New York: Council of State Governments Justice Center.

Fox Nixon, F. 2015. "President Obama Visits RU-N and Talks Criminal Justice Reform." Rutgers University Press Release. http://www.newark.rutgers.edu/news/president-obama-visits-ru-n-and-talks-criminal-justice-reform.

Guerino, P., P. M. Harrison, W. J. Sabol. 2011. *Prisoners in 2010*. Washington, DC: Bureau of Justice Statistics.

Harrison, P., and A. Beck. 2002. *Prisoners in 2001*. Washington, DC: Bureau of Justice Statistics.

Hipp J. R., and D. K. Yates. 2009. "Do Returning Parolees Affect Neighborhood Crime? A Case Study of Sacramento." *Criminology* 47 (3): 619–56.

Hirschi, T. 1969. *Causes of Delinquency*. Berkeley: University of California Press.

King, R. 2006. *A Decade of Reform: Felony Disenfranchisement Policy in the United States*. Washington, DC: The Sentencing Project.

Lemert, E. 1967. *Human Deviance, Social Problems, and Social Control*. Englewood Cliffs, NJ: Prentice Hall.

Martinson, R. 1974. "What Works? Questions and Answers About Prison Reform." *The Public Interest* 35 (Spring): 22–54.

Metraux, S., and D. P. Culhane. 2004. "Homeless Shelter Use and Reincarceration Following Prison Release. *Criminology & Public Policy* 3 (2): 139–60.

Moreno, E., P. Patterson, K. Peirce, V. Rogers, E. Shryock, and J. Zapata, J. n.d. *Best practices for Housing Former Offenders to Promote Family Reunification*. Austin, TX: The Austin/Travis County Reentry Roundtable.

Morenoff, J. D., and D. J. Harding. 2014. "Incarceration, Prisoner Reentry, and Communities." *Annual Review of Sociology* 40 411–29.

Nagin, D. S. 2014. "Reinventing Sentencing in the United States." *Criminology & Public Policy* 13 (4): 499–502.

Petersilia, Joan. 2003. *When Prisoners Come Home: Parole and Prisoner Reentry*. New York: Oxford University Press.

PEW. 2008. *One in 100: Behind Bars in America 2008*. Washington, DC: PEW Charitable Trusts.

Popkin, S. J., V. E. Gwiasda, L. M. Olson, D. P. Rosenbaum, and L. Buron. 2000. *The Hidden War: Crime and the Tragedy of Public Housing in Chicago*. New Brunswick, NJ: Rutgers University Press.

Popkin, S., M. Cunningham, and W. T. Woodley. 2003. *Residents at Risk: A Profile of Ida B. Wells and Madden Park*. Report to the Ford Foundation. Washington, DC: The Urban Institute.

Prager, D. 2007. *Marked: Race, Crime, and Finding Work in an Era of Mass Incarceration*. Chicago: University of Chicago Press.

Rose, D. R., and T. R. Clear. 1998. "Incarceration, Social Capital, and Crime: Implications for Social Disorganization Theory." *Criminology* 36 (3): 441–79.

Roman, C., and J. Travis. 2004. *Taking Stock: Housing, Homelessness, and Prisoner Reentry.* Washington, DC: The Urban Institute.

Sampson, R. J., and J. H. Laub. 1993. *Crime in the Making: Pathways and Turning Points Through Life.* Cambridge, MA: Harvard University Press.

Sampson, R. J., and C. Loeffler. 2010. "Punishment's Place: The Local Concentration of Mass Incarceration." *Daedalus* 139 (3): 20–31.

The Sentencing Project. 2015. *Felony Disenfranchisement: A Primer.* Washington, DC: The Sentencing Project.

Travis, J. 2005. *But They All Come Back: Facing the Challenges of Prisoner Reentry.* Washington, DC: Urban Institute.

Travis, J., E. C. McBride, and A. L. Solomon. 2005. *Families Left Behind: The Hidden Costs of Incarceration and Reentry.* Washington, DC: Urban Institute.

Thomas, A. 2005. The Old Ball and Chain: Unlocking the Correlation Between Incarceration and Marriage. Unpublished manuscript.

Tonry, M. 2014. "Remodeling American Sentencing: A Ten-Step Blueprint for Moving Past Mass Incarceration. *Criminology & Public Policy* 13 (4): 503–33.

Uggen, C., M. Inderbitzin, and M. Vuolo. 2007. *What Happens When Probationers and Parolees Vote? Community Supervision and Civic Reintegration.* Atlanta, GA: American Society of Criminology.

Uggen, C., and C. Inderbitzin. 2010. "The Price and the Promise of Citizenship: Extending the Vote to Non-Incarcerated Felons." In *Contemporary Issues in Criminal Justice Policy.* Edited by N. A. Frost, J. D. Freilich, and T. R. Clear. Belmont, CA: Wadsworth. 61–68.

Wakefield, S., and C. Uggen. 2010. "Incarceration and Stratification." *The Annual Review of Sociology* 36: 387–406.

Western, B. 2006. *Punishment and Inequality in America.* New York: Russel Sage.

Wilson, D. B., C. A. Gallagher, and D. L. MacKenzie. 2000. "A Meta-Analysis of Corrections-Based Education, Vocation, and Work Programs for Adult Offenders." *Journal of Research in Criminal and Delinquency* 37 (4): 347–68.

Venkatesh, S. 2002. *The Robert Taylor Homes Relocation Study: A Research Report from the Center for Urban Research and Policy.* New York: Columbia University.

Visher, C., S. Debus, and J. Yahner. 2008. *Employment After Prison: A Longitudinal Study of Releases in Three States.* Washington, DC: Urban Institute.

Zimring, F. E. 2001. "Imprisonment Rates and the New Politics of Criminal Punishment." *Punishment & Society* 3 (1): 425–36.

CHAPTER 15

Capital Punishment, the Court, and Racial Discrepancy Research

By Jamie L. Flexon

● INTRODUCTION

As previously discussed, the system governing the disposition of the death penalty has always been fraught with problems, and racial disparity in capital case outcomes persists as one of those problems. The issues of racial stereotype and associated biases has found its way into the discourse in the social sciences and legal arenas. In addition, the Supreme Court ruled in a number of cases presenting 14th Amendment challenges concerning discriminatory application of the law based on race, e.g., housing, employment practices, and public facilities. However, the standards the Court used in those cases is not consistent with the showing necessary to prove that equal protection violations are occurring in capital cases (see Ellsworth, 1988 –for discussion; Baldus, Woodworth, and Grosso, 2007).[1]

In *McCleskey v. Kemp*, 481 U.S. 279 (1987), the Supreme Court dealt with the issue of racial discrimination in capital sentencing by answering the following question: Whether a complex statistical study that indicates a risk that racial considerations enter into capital sentencing determinations proves that petitioner McCleskey's capital sentence is unconstitutional under the 8th and 14th Amendments? The defendant, McCleskey, was a black man convicted and sentenced to death for killing a white police officer during the course of a robbery. McCleskey offered no mitigating evidence at sentencing. On appeal, McCleskey argued that his 8th and 14th Amendment rights were violated through the Georgia death penalty statute. The defendant argued that statistical evidence demonstrated discriminatory intent by the Georgia statute in violation of the Equal Protection Clause of the 14th Amendment. McCleskey further argued that his sentence of death was in violation of the 8th Amendment, because it was disproportionate compared to offenders with white victims, and the level of juror discretion allowed for racial prejudices to enter into decisions (see also Patterson, 1995, p. 83).

McCleskey introduced a study that was performed by David Baldus, Charles Pulaski, and George Woodworth (hereafter, the Baldus study) in support of his claims of discrimination (*McCleskey v. Kemp*, 1987, pp. 287–288). The Baldus study examined over 2000 murder cases in Georgia during the 1970s and controlled for over 230 variables. The study showed that black defendants who kill white victims were more likely to be put to death than any other interracial defendant and victim combination. "Thus, the Baldus study indicates that black defendants, such as McCleskey, who kill white victims have the greatest likelihood of receiving the death penalty." (*McCleskey v. Kemp*, 1987, p. 288).

The breakdown of those receiving the death penalty by interracial combination of defendant and victim was reported to the Court as follows (*McCleskey v. Kemp*, 1987, p. 287):

DEFENDANT/VICTIM	PERCENT OF DEFENDANTS RECEIVING THE DEATH PENALTY
Black/White	22%
White/White	8
Black/Black	1
White/Black	3

Nevertheless, while acknowledging racial *disparities* in capital sentencing, the Court reasoned that the Baldus study was "insufficient to support an inference that any of the decision makers in the case acted with discriminatory purpose" (*McCleskey v. Kemp*, 1987, p. 296). To support the equal protection challenge, McCleskey would have to prove that the *purpose* of the Georgia death penalty statute was to create and maintain an anticipated discriminatory effect (*McCleskey v. Kemp*, 1987, p. 299). According to the *McCleskey* Court (1987, p. 299):

> There was no evidence then [Gregg], and there is no evidence now, that the Georgia Legislature enacted the capital punishment statute to further racially discriminatory purpose. Nor has McCleskey demonstrated that the Legislature maintains the capital punishment statute because of the racially disproportionate impact suggested by the Baldus study.

In other equal protection cases, the defendant has the burden of establishing a *prima facie* case showing that a law created a disparate impact which gives rise to an inference of discriminatory purpose. The use of statistical evidence to show discrepancies in application of the law had been enough to support such a showing. Once a *prima facie* case is established, the burden of proof shifts to the State to explain reported discrepancies. The *McCleskey* Court offered that other cases allowing for similar statistical evidence, such as the Baldus study, dealt with too few entities to disturb the system (*McCleskey v. Kemp*, 1987, p. 296). The Court also asserted that, unlike other Equal Protection case contexts, "the State has no practical opportunity to rebut the Baldus study" (*McCleskey v. Kemp*, 1987, p. 297; see also Patterson, 1995, p. 83).

In *McCleskey*, the burden of proof could not shift to the State to explain the discriminatory impact from the statute on death penalty sentencing (see Patterson, 1995, pp. 81–82, 85). The Court's decision and rationale created the following situation; In denying McCleskey's use of statistical evidence concerning the death penalty for establishing a *prima facie* case, the Court created a new standard of proof for the defense. Aggregate statistical evidence was not enough to support McCleskey's equal protection claim. The Court's remedy was to maintain that the defendant has the burden of showing that deliberate and invidious discrimination was occurring among the decision makers in each case.

The race of the victim was at the heart of McCleskey's 8th Amendment claim. The Baldus study showed that defendants with Black victims received the death penalty in only 1% of death penalty cases, and defendants who killed White victims received the death penalty in 11% of cases (*McCleskey v. Kemp*, 1987, p. 287). The logic for McCleskey's 8th Amendment claim followed that his death sentence for killing a White victim was disproportionate to *similarly situated* defendants who killed Black victims, and this form of discrimination also was the result of unfettered juror discretion which created a *risk* of discrimination (see also Patterson, 1995).

The Court noted that after controlling for 39 nonracial variables, defendants charged with killing White victims were 4.3% times more likely to receive the death sentence than similar cases with Black victims (*McCleskey v. Kemp*, 1987, pp. 287–288). However, McCleskey's 8th Amendment claim failed because the Court relied on its holding in *Gregg*, which stated that safeguards had been established that addressed defendant McCleskey's concerns (see *Gregg v. Georgia*, 1976). Georgia's death penalty sentencing guidelines contained *focused* discretion. The Court reasoned:

> Despite the imperfections [in the system], our consistent rule has been that the constitutional guarantees are met when "the mode" [for determining guilt or punishment] itself has been surrounded with safeguards to make it as fair as possible. Where the discretion that is fundamental to our criminal process is involved, we decline to assume that what is unexplained is invidious (*McCleskey v. Kemp*, 1987, p. 314).

The *McCleskey* Court rationalized that to find for the defense would create precedent too far reaching and render all cases vulnerable to arguments of discrimination based on any number of physical characteristics, e.g., facial characteristics of court actors, victims, or defendants (see also Lawrence, 1987). The Court requires a showing in each case of deliberate and *invidious* discrimination before it will sustain a challenge based on equal protection violations. The burden is on the defendant to prove that intentional discrimination was taking place by the decision makers in a case.

However, the Court's orientation to equal protection challenges to the death penalty is based on individual cases and is likely to miss much of the discrimination. Most stereotyping and prejudice takes place without cognitive awareness. The proof required of the defendant will not be soon forthcoming in the sense necessary to overcome the Court's jurisprudential hurdle given what is known about stereotyping. It appears that in the context of the death penalty, racial challenges are "different" than in any other type of case.[2]

● DEATH QUALIFICATION: REQUIREMENTS FOR A CAPITAL JURY

Another legal difficulty surrounds selecting a jury for a capital case. The process used to choose a capital jury has the potential to create discriminatory outcomes that would likely be dismissed using the Court's standards for reviewing constitutional claims regarding the death penalty. The process of death qualification for capital juries and the impact this has on the system of justice has been implicated as contributing to the race-based disparities. As discussed in the previous chapter, death qualification refers to the process at *voir dire* examination which excludes jurors from a capital case who cannot or will not, due to their beliefs, impose a death sentence (*Wainwright v. Witt,* 1985; see also *Witherspoon v. Illinois,* 1968; *Lockhart v. McCree,* 1986).

The *Witt* Court set the standard as to when a prospective capital juror may and may not be excused for cause. The Court ruled that "a juror may not be challenged for cause based on his views about capital punishment unless those views would prevent or substantially impair the performance of his duties as a juror in accordance with his instructions and his oath" (*Wainwright v. Witt,* 1985, p. 424). Those who are capable of rendering a verdict of death are referred to as "death qualified" and able to sit on a capital jury. Concomitantly, a capital juror must also be "life qualified," that is, capable of giving a life sentence. Individuals who would always vote for a death sentence upon a conviction for murder are referred to as automatic death penalty individuals and are not life qualified (see Blume et al., 2001).

The Court has found that death qualification of capital jurors is constitutionally permissible and consistent with previous rulings concerning the 6th and

14th Amendments, while excusing claims that the removal of jurors through death qualification creates a conviction-prone jury. In *Lockhart v. McCree*, 476 U.S. 163 (1986), the Court dealt with the question: Does the Constitution prohibit the removal for cause, prior to the guilt phase of a bifurcated capital trial, of prospective jurors whose opposition to the death penalty is so strong that it would prevent or substantially impair the performance of their duties as jurors at the sentencing phase of the trial?

In *McCree*, the defendant raised 6th and 14th Amendment claims.[3] The defendant argued that death qualification removed from the capital jury an important representation of attitudes and thereby violated his rights to an impartial jury selected from a representative cross-section of the community. To support McCree's claim, studies were introduced to the court showing that death qualified juries were more likely to convict (conviction-prone) than juries that included individuals whose level of opposition to the death penalty prohibited them from serving on a capital case.

The Court rejected McCree's argument and reasoned that it has "never invoked the fair cross-section principle to invalidate the use of either for-cause or peremptory challenges to prospective jurors, or to require petit juries, as opposed to jury panels or venires, to reflect the composition of the community at large" (1986, p. 174). The *McCree* Court (1986, p. 168) relied on the premise that jurors excluded from serving on a capital case based on their beliefs do not constitute a *distinctive group* in the community:

> The essence of a fair-cross claim is the systematic exclusion of a "distinctive group" in the community—such as blacks, women, and Mexican-Americans—for reasons completely unrelated to the ability of members of the group to serve as jurors in a particular case. Groups defined solely in terms of shared attitudes that would prevent or substantially impair members of the group from performing one of their duties as jurors, such as "Witherspoon-excludables" at issue here, are not "distinct groups" for fair-cross-section purposes. "Death Qualification" is carefully designed to serve the State's legitimate interest in obtaining a single jury that can properly and impartially apply the law to the facts of the case at both the guilt and sentencing phases of a capital trial.

The Court further rationalized that jurors excluded from a capital case based on their beliefs are singled out for an attribute that is within the individual's control.

McCree argued that death qualification produced a constitutionally impermissible "slant" in the jury toward favoring convictions. The Court concluded that excluding a segment of attitudes that was determined by researchers to be important to balancing out capital juries did not violate the Constitution. The Court determined that impartial juries conscientiously apply the law and find the facts. Further, the impartial jury requirement was secured by statute that channeled discretion, particularly in the context of determining guilt and innocence in capital cases.

Irrespective of the Court's orientation to the problem, the research examining conviction-proneness on capital juries is valuable for examining sentencing disparities. The research examining the impact of death qualification on conviction-proneness suggests that capital juries are partial, and that this partiality influences jury decisions, even when the discretion is guided at the guilt phase of the bifurcated system. One would expect the same or similar dynamics to operate in both the guilt phase and sentencing phase, although more discretion is allowed at the sentencing phase. Of note, the more discretion individuals have available to them, the more reliance there is on stereotyped information (Bargh, 1999; Bodenhausen and Macrae 1998). Therefore, one would expect to see a greater influence of biases at the sentencing phase of a capital trial versus the guilt phase. Attitudes are influential in the jury deliberation process and are tied to the more global construction of attitudes toward crime control and indicated by support for the death penalty. The implications for attitude extremity, jury composition and polarization are thus highly problematic to the capital punishment context. With regard to jurors who think that their deliberation had no element of bias, it seems fundamentally that they are likely unaware participants in a symbolically formalized and social process that may promote discriminatory outcomes (Ellsworth, 1993, see also Hart, 1995; Landy and Aronson, 1969; Lerner and Goldberg, 1999; Moran and Cutler, 1991; Villemur and Shibley-Hyde, 1983).

In sum, repeated empirical evidence suggests that racial discrimination is active on capital juries. The Supreme Court and others are uninformed about the processes involved with stereotypes and more covert processes that yield discrimination. The misapprehension of stereotype processes has apparently contributed to an impasse between the Court, empirical researchers, and others.

● THE FUNDAMENTALS OF CRIME CONTROL V. DUE PROCESS

Herbert Packer (1968) articulated the *crime control* and *due process* models of the criminal justice process. The crime control orientation is frequently mentioned in connection with research concerning racial discrimination in capital sentencing.

The value system that underscores "the Crime Control Model is based on the proposition that repression of criminal conduct is by far the most important function to be performed in the criminal justice process" (1968, p. 158). The aim of law enforcement is to secure tight control of criminal conduct, which is viewed as compromising human freedom through the breakdown of public order (Packer, 1968, p. 158). There also is an emphasis on efficiency, speed, and finality with the crime control orientation, and a presumption of factual guilt as opposed to concerns over legal guilt, which begins to operate before the 'suspect' becomes a 'defendant'" (Packer, 1968, pp. 159–160). Also, informal, extrajudicial processes are preferred to formal, judicial processes (Packer, 1968, p. 159). According to Packer, there is a "heavy reliance on the ability of investigative and prosecutorial officers, acting in an informal setting in which their distinctive skills are given full sway, to elicit and reconstruct a tolerably accurate account of what actually took place in an alleged criminal event" (Packer, 1968, p. 163).

The Due Process Model emphasizes procedural safeguards to protect individuals' rights from State activity and the possibility of error when subduing criminal conduct. The due process model is concerned with a presumption of innocence that is based on normative and legal grounds over issues of factual guilt (Packer, 1968, pp. 161–162). According to Packer, "The presumption of innocence is, then, a direction to the authorities to ignore the presumption of guilt in their treatment of the suspect. It tells them, in effect, to close their eyes to what will frequently seem to be factual probabilities (1968, pp. 161–162).

The conflict between the due process model and the crime control model rests with the reliability of fact-finding practices (Packer, 1968, p. 163). Due process individuals do not embrace the idea that the police and authorities will protect and observe individual rights when conducting investigations (Packer, 1968, p. 163).

● JUROR CHARACTERISTICS

A jury's deliberation is affected by the characteristics and beliefs of the members. The demographic differences and beliefs of jurors have been found to influence sentencing decisions in previous research (Lynch and Haney, 2000; 2009). Research has shown that there are demographic differences and differences in the constellation of attitudes and beliefs between and among death qualified and non–death qualified individuals (see e.g., Fitzgerald and Ellsworth, 1984; Young, 2001; 2004). Recognizing the belief system of jurors as racially biased with a crime control perspective before being called to sit on a jury should give important insight for how such jurors might orient themselves in deliberation.

Juror characteristics that have been identified by previous research as having a correlation with capital sentencing decisions include sex, age, race, education level, region of domicile, religious beliefs, and political affiliation (e.g., Applegate, 2000; Bohm, 1998; Boots et al., 2003; Eisenberg et al., 2001; Thompson et al., 1984). Consistently, females are less likely to favor capital punishment than males (ABC/Washington Post poll, 2001; Bohm, 1998; Cochran and Sanders, 2009). Blacks are less likely to favor the death penalty than Whites (Barkan and Cohn, 1994; Bohm, 1998; Cochran and Chamlin, 2006; Flexon, 2006; Peffley and Hurwitz, 2007; Unnever, Cullen, and Jonson, 2008; Young, 2001; see also Unnever and Cullen, 2010) and more recent research to be discussed later has identified racial beliefs as an important component. Those under age 30, college graduates, as well as Easterners and Southerners also are less likely to support the death penalty than Westerners and Midwesterners (Bohm, 1998; see also Barkan and Cohn, 2010 for further delineation on the role of race and regional differences in support for the death penalty). Prior research has found limited support for the idea that religious affiliation has an impact on capital punishment attitudes. Research has found that the discerning feature of religion is not denominational variation, which was traditionally used for measuring and testing the effects of religion on criminal justice attitudes. Applegate et al., (2000) found that the discerning feature in attitudes is the degree of fundamentalism. More fundamentalist Protestant individuals are likely to be more punitive in their criminal justice attitudes than Christian non-fundamentalist Protestants (Applegate et al., 2000; but see Wozniak and Lewis, 2010). There also is an association between fundamentalism and Republican conservatism that had grown over the 1980's and 90's (Applegate et al., 2000). Republicans are twice as likely to favor the death penalty compared to Democrats and Independents (ABC/Washington Post poll, 2001; see also Jacobs and Carmichael, 2002 for a discussion of the political sociology of the death penalty).

Fitzgerald and Ellsworth (1984) examined attitudes of potential jurors for possible biases against capital defendants. The researchers examined demographic and attitudinal differences related to crime control, court actors, and punitive orientation among death qualified and non-death qualified respondents.[4] The researchers found demographic differences between the two groups that is consistent with the body of research in this area (see e.g., Bronson, 1971; Ellsworth, 1993; Jurow, 1971; Zeitsel, 1968; see also Flexon, 2006). The findings indicated that death qualified juries are more likely to agree with prosecution arguments and embrace a general crime control orientation over due process (see Ellsworth, 1993; Fitzgerald and Ellsworth, 1984; Sandys, 1998). Of note, greater proportions of Blacks and females were excluded through the process of death qualification (1984, p. 46).

Previous research has shown that individuals supporting the death penalty are likely to espouse a constellation of punitive beliefs and attitudes related to the criminal justice system, and that support for the death penalty is considered a "symbolic attitude" of such beliefs (see Ellsworth, 1993, p. 50). According to Ellsworth (1993, pp. 49–50) death penalty supporters are "…more concerned about high levels of violent crime," less sympathetic toward criminal defendants, "more suspicious of defense attorneys," and "exhibit more favorable attitudes toward prosecuting attorneys and the police" (see also Fitzgerald and Ellsworth, 1984).

Although death qualification has been tied to a jury's conviction proneness, research has been unable to explain how the sifting of the juror pool creates an atmosphere that is ripe for discrimination. The above research findings suggest that stereotyping processes are at work. During deliberations, jurors can learn new arguments from like minded individuals that reinforce preexisting views (Lynch and Haney, 2009; see also Flexon, 2006). Ideas that are not consistent with one's attitude may be dismissed. Here, one would expect that if a prospective juror holds racially negative stereotypes and is crime control oriented, that his or her beliefs will be strengthened by input during deliberations from other, like minded jurors (Lynch and Haney, 2009; see also Flexon, 2006). It is likely that the death qualification process deposits like minded individuals on capital juries. This concentration of individuals with like attitudes may operate to create an atmosphere where jurors reinforce each others' preexisting views about race and crime.

In sum, several variables are important when examining attitudes related to capital punishment. Demographic variables including sex, race, age, region, religion, education, political affiliation are correlated with death penalty attitudes. Research also has identified attitudes relating to criminal justice that are important when evaluating death penalty attitudes that have the potential to influence juror decisions (e.g., Flexon, 2006, see also Unnever and Cullen, 2010).

● CONCLUSION

In *McCleskey,* the Court considered empirical findings showing racial discrepancies in the imposition of the death penalty. The Court is fully aware of other associated research pertaining to disparities, biasing influences of death qualification (see *Lockhart v. McCree,* 1986), and, that in cases where the defendant was Black and the victim was White, the defendant was (is) more likely to be put to death. Recent research has identified particular scenarios where discriminatory outcomes are more or less likely to occur, and this pattern suggests a process yielding discrimination in capital sentencing is taking place. Bowers' et al. (2001) findings from the Capital Jury Project merit particular attention, since it appears that a complex, interactive and identifiable (group) process promotes discriminatory application of death sentences. These findings will be discussed in the next chapter.

Much also has been assumed about stereotype processes in the sociological literature, by legal scholars, and by the Court. However, it appears as though much remains misunderstood. The process by which stereotyping occurs is complex and, to a great extent, cognitively covert. Stereotypes and attitudes generally (e.g., Bargh, 1999; Bodenhausen and Macrae, 1998; Devine and Monteith, 1999), and negative stereotypes and attitudes specifically, are largely biasing (see e.g., Abelson, 1995; Fitzgerald and Ellsworth, 1984; Thompson et al., 1984), and resistant to change (e.g., Bargh, 1999; Devine and Monteith 1999). This holds true irrespective of statutory guidelines and the Court's jurisprudentially based assumptions (see Bodenhausen and Macrae, 1998; for further discussion see Baldus et al., 2007). Empirical research on racial discrimination via jury deliberation in capital cases in large part has been a response to the Court's use of social science research (and/or solid and generally accepted empirical findings)—and a reluctance to use aggregated statistical data as evidence in this area. Again, the Supreme Court acknowledges the research and the existence of racial *disparities* in capital sentencing. The majority of the Court, however, is dismissive of the notion that the disparities are based on racial stereotyping processes resulting in discrimination from jurors (see *McCleskey v. Kemp*, 1987).

Presumptively, one source of disparate outcomes in death cases is emanating from the jury. The commonly held belief is that an intentional and overt form of racial prejudice is motivating jurors' decisions. Recent research has attempted to find influences of prejudice on capital juries (e.g., Bowers et al., 2001; Lynch and Haney, 2009). Juror questionnaires often are used to examine the nature of such biases. However, the use of post-trial interviews and questionnaires to provide answers to this problem has shortcomings. Many jurors do not recognize stereotypical processes and outcomes as emanating from themselves or other jurors (Ellsworth, 1993). Juror recounts also have the same issues that are associated with use of survey instruments for data collection concerning past events, such as forgetfulness and non-deliberate observation of events leading to decisions. This leads to inaccurate accounting of events, and here, rationalizations are likely due to misunderstanding the decision making process.

McCleskey points to an important void in the research in this area. The missing link appears to be the lack of understanding for how stereotypes originate and operate rather than a general process of conscious and deliberate discrimination. This prior concern tends to be the focus for much criminal justice research. However, given the extent to which future research findings relate what is known about death qualification, criminal justice attitudes, and conviction proneness to corollary attributes explaining racial bias, an appreciable void would be filled. Just as informing would be research relating how such biases play out in the group dynamics and decision processes of juries—specifically relating jury demographic make-up to the interracial combinations of Black defendants and White victims (the main focus of discriminatory effects in death outcomes). Recent research has begun to do just that (Lynch and Haney, 2009).

It also is known that death qualified jurors share some similar attitudes and beliefs. Identifying a more complete index of influential characteristics of jurors who are more or less likely to convict is only an initial stage of inquiry into the above concern. Bridging research from different disciplines is necessary for efforts to understand juror characteristics known to influence capital sentencing, such as possible racial bias. The issues raised thus far will be examined in more detail throughout the remaining discussion in order to further explain the contours of prejudice and how capital jurors can discriminate based on race.

● ENDNOTES

1. Cases frequently identified with racial discrimination challenges in outcome are: *Furman v. Georgia* (1972); *Gregg v. Georgia* (1976); *Turner v. Murray* (1986); more recently, *McCleskey v. Kemp* (1987). The list is not exhaustive, but encompasses much of the discussion in specifically this area. For (some) other cases which are tied, but generally identified with jury composition and the impact of death qualification on conviction proneness specifically, see *Lockhart v. McCree* (1986); *Witherspoon v. Illinois* (1968).

2. The reference to "death is different" is taken from the opinion of Justices Stewart, Powell, and Stevens in *Woodson v. North Carolina*, 428 U.S. 280 (1976, p. 305), "The penalty of death is qualitatively different from a sentence of imprisonment, however long. Death, in its finality, differs more from life imprisonment than a 100-year prison term differs from one of only a year or two. Because of that qualitative difference, there is a corresponding difference in the need for reliability in the determination that death is the appropriate punishment in a specific case."

3. The 6th Amendment right to a jury selected from a representative cross-section of the community rests on the Incorporation Doctrine, where constitutional rights are applied to the States through the 14th Amendment.

4. Using the *Witherspoon* standard, 17.2% of subjects were identified as non-death qualified (Fitzgerald and Ellsworth, 1984, p. 42; see also *Witherspoon v. Illinois*, 1968). The *Witherspoon* standard removes jurors who said they could never vote to impose the death penalty.

● REFERENCES

ABC News/Washington Post Poll. (2001). *The death penalty revisited.* (May). Retrieved June 26, 2003, from International Communications Website: http://www.icrsurvey.com/Study.aspx?f=ABC_deathpen050201.html

Abelson, R.P. (1995). Attitude extremity. In R.E. Petty and J.A. Krosnick (Eds.), *Attitude strength: Antecedents and consequences* (pp. 25–42). Mahwah, NJ: Erlbaum.

Applegate, B.K., Cullen, F.T., and Vander Ven, T. (2000). Forgiveness and fundamentalism: Reconsidering the relationship between correctional attitudes and verdicts. *Criminology*, 38, 719–754.

Baldus, D.C., Woodworth, G., and Grosso, C.M. (2007). Race and proportionality since McCleskey v. Kemp (1987): Different actors with mixed strategies of denial and avoidance. *Columbia Human Rights Law Review*, 39, 143–177.

Bargh, J.A. (1999). The cognitive monster: The case against the controllability of automatic stereotype effects. In S. Chaiken and Y. Trope (Eds.), *Dual-process theories in social psychology* (pp. 361–382). New York, NY: The Guilford Press.

Barkan, S.E., and Cohn, S.F. (1994). Racial prejudice and support for the death penalty by Whites. *Journal of Research in Crime and Delinquency*, 31, 202–209.

Barkan, S.E. and Cohn, S.F. (2010). Contemporary regional differences in support by Whites for the death penalty: A research note. *Justice Quarterly, 27*, 458–471.

Blume, J.H., Johnson, S.L., and Threlkeld, A. B. (2001). Probing "life qualification" through expanded voir dire. *Hofstra Law Review*, 29, 1209–1264.

Bodenhausen, G.V., and Macrae, C.N. (1998). *Stereotype activation and inhibition. In R.S. Wyer, Jr. (Ed.), Stereotype activation and inhibition: Advances in social cognition, Volume XI* (pp. 1–52). Mahwah, NJ: Erlbaum.

Bohm, R.M. (1998). American death penalty opinion: Past, present, and future. In J. R. Acker, R.M. Bohm, and C.S. Lanier (Eds.), *America's experiment with capital punishment: Reflections on the past, present, and future of the ultimate penal sanction*, (pp. 25–76). Durham, NC: Carolina Academic Press.

Bohm, R.M. (2007). *Deathquest, III.* Newark, NJ: LexisNexis.

Boots, D.P., Cochran, J.K., and Heide, K.M. (2003). Capital punishment preferences for special offender populations. *Journal of Criminal Justice*, 31, 553–565.

Bowers, W.J., Steiner, B.D., and Sandys, M. (2001). Death sentencing in black and white: An empirical analysis of juror's race and jury racial composition. *Pennsylvania Journal of Constitutional Law*, 3, 171–275.

Bronson, E. (1970). On the conviction-proneness and representativeness of the death-qualified jury: An empirical study of Colorado veniremen. *University of Colorado Law Review*, 42, 1–32.

Cochran, J.K., and Chamlin, M.B. (2006). The enduring racial divide in death penalty support. *Journal of Criminal Justice*, 34, 85–99.

Cochran, J.K., and Sanders, B.A. (2009). The gender gap in death penalty support: An exploratory study. *Journal of Criminal Justice*, 37, 525–533.

Devine, P.G., and Monteith, M.J. (1999) Automaticity and control in stereotyping. In S. Chaiken and Y. Trope (Eds.), *Dual-process theories in social psychology* (pp. 339–360). New York, NY: The Guilford Press.

Eisenberg, T., Garvey, S., and Wells, M. (2001). Forecasting life and death: Juror race, religion, and attitude toward the death penalty. *Journal of Legal Studies, Vol. XXX*, June, 277–311.

Ellsworth, P.C. (1993). Some steps between attitudes and verdicts. In Reid Hastie (Ed.), *Inside the Juror: The psychology of juror decision making* (pp. 42–64). New York, NY: Cambridge University Press.

Ellsworth, P.C. (1988). Unpleasant facts: The Supreme Court's response to empirical research on capital punishment. In K.C. Hass and J.A. Inciardi (Eds.), *Challenging capital punishment: Legal and social science approaches* (pp. 177–212). Newbury Park, CA: Sage.

Fitzgerald, R., and Ellsworth, P.C. (1984). Due process v. crime control: Death qualification and jury attitudes. *Law and Human Behavior*, 8, 31–51.

Flexon, J.L. (2006). Cognitive predisposition to prejudice and discrimination on capital juries: Can race be ignored in the jury room? *Dissertation Abstracts International, A. The Humanities and Social Sciences, 67*, 2329 (UMI No. 3221100).

Hart, A.J. (1995). Naturally occurring expectation effects. *Journal of Personality and Social Psychology*, 68, 109–115.

Jacobs, D., and Carmichael, J.T. (2002). The political sociology of the death penalty: A pooled time-series analysis. *American Sociological Review, 67*, 109–131.

Jurow G. (1971). New data on the effects of a death-qualified jury on the guilt-determination process. *Harvard Law Review, 84*, 567–611.

Landy, D., and Aronson, E. (1969). The influence of the character and his victim on the decisions of simulated jurors. *Journal of Experimental Social Psychology*, 5, 141–152.

Lawrence, C.R. (1987). The id, the ego, and equal protection: Reckoning with unconscious racism. *Stanford Law Review*, 39, 317.

Lerner, M., and Goldberg, J.H. (1999). When do decent people blame victims?: The differing effects of the explicit/rational and implicit/experiential cognitive systems. In S. Chaiken and Y. Trope (Eds.), Dual-process theories in social psychology (pp. 627–640). New York, NY: The Guilford Press.

Lynch, M., and Haney, C. (2000). Discrimination and instructional comprehension: Guided discretion, racial bias, and the death penalty. Law and Human Behavior, 24, 337–358.

Lynch, M., and Haney, C. (2009). Capital jury deliberation: Effects on death sentencing, comprehension, and discrimination. Law and Human Behavior, 33, 481–496.

Moran, G., and Cutler, B.L. (1991). The prejudicial impact of pretrial publicity. *Journal of Applied Social Psychology*, 21, 345–367.

Packer, H.L. (1968). *The limits of the criminal sanction*. Stanford, CA: Stanford University Press.

Patterson, C.M. (1995). Race and the death penalty: The tension between individualized justice and racially neutral standards. *2 Tex. Wesleyan Law Review*, 45, 80–95.

Peffley, M., and Hurwitz, J. (2007). Persuasion and resistance: Race and the death penalty in America. *American Journal of Political Science*, 51, 996–1012.

Sandys, M. (1998). Stacking the deck for guilt and death: The failure of death qualification to ensure impartiality. In J.R. Acker, R.M. Bohm, C.S. Lanier (Eds.), *America's experiment with capital punishment: Reflections in the past, present, and future of the ultimate penal sanction* (pp. 285–308, 1st Edition; 385–411, 2nd Edition). Durham, NC: Carolina Academic Press.

Thompson, W.C., Cowan, C.L., Ellsworth, P.C., and Harrington, J. (1984). Death penalty attitudes and conviction proneness: The translation of attitudes into verdicts. *Law and Human Behavior, 8*, 95–113.

Unnever, J.D., and Cullen, F.T. (2007). The racial divide in support for the death penalty: Does white racism matter? *Social Forces, 85*, 1281–1302.

Unnever, J.D., and Cullen, F.T. (2010). Racial-ethnic intolerance and support for capital punishment: A cross-national comparison. *Criminology*, 48, 831–862.

Villemur, N. K., and Shibley-Hyde, J. (1983). Effects of sex of defense attorney, sex of juror, and age and attractiveness of the victim on mock juror decision making in a rape case. *Sex Roles*, 9, 89–889.

Wozniak, K.H., and Lewis, A.R. (2010). Reexamining the effect of Christian denominational affiliation on death penalty support. *Journal of Criminal Justice, 38*, 1082–1089.

Young, R.L. (1991). Race, conceptions of crime and justice, and support for the death penalty. *Social Psychology Quarterly*, 54, 67–75.

Young, R.L. (2004). Guilty until proven innocent: Conviction orientation, racial attitudes, and support for capital punishment. *Deviant Behavior*, 25, 151–167.

Zeitsel H. (1968). *Some data on juror attitudes toward capital punishment*. Monograph Center for Studies in Criminal Justice, University of Chicago Law School.

● CASES CITED

Gregg v. Georgia, 428 U.S. 153 (1976)

Lockhart v. McCree, 476 U.S. 162 (1986)

McCleskey v. Kemp, 481 U.S. 279 (1987)

Wainwright v. Witt, 469 U.S. 412 (1985)

Witherspoon v. Illinois, 91 U.S. 510 (1968)

CHAPTER 16

Measuring Sexual Assault

By Veronyka James

For a variety of reasons, it is difficult to determine the exact incidence and prevalence of sexual assault. According to Rozee and Koss (2001), the lifetime prevalence of rape and attempted rape ranges between 21 percent and 27 percent among college-aged women (in industrialized nations). In the United States, it has been found that, in general, the prevalence of rape is between low-end estimate of 15 percent (Rozee and Koss, 2001) and 18 percent (Breiding et al., 2014; CDC, 2012) and high-end estimate of 44 percent (Russell, 1986; O'Sullivan, 2013). Koss and Burkhart (1989) estimated that between 15 and 22 percent of women have been raped at some point in their lifetime, though few rape victims seek assistance for this victimization. It is likely that only approximately 25 percent or fewer of actual assaults are ever reported to police (Fisher et al., 2003, 2010; Gross, Winslett, Roberts, Gohm, 2006; Karjane et al., 2005; Ward et al., 1991). It may be that victims decide not to report the crime for fear of being blamed (Felson and Pare, 2005; Rennison et al., 2013; Russell, 1982), fear of reprisal from the perpetrator (who is often known to the victim)

(Fisher et al., 2003, 2010; Kilpatrick et al., 2007; Planty et al., 2013; Russell, 1982; Sampson, 2002; Ward et al., 1991), or believe that those within the justice system will not accept the report as valid and will fail to investigate or prosecute the crime (Sampson, 2002; Taylor and Norma, 2012).

● INCIDENCE AND PREVALENCE

Although it is difficult to know the exact prevalence of sexual assault because of different methodologies and research techniques employed to estimate prevalence, researchers have used both victimization surveys and official reports to determine an estimate. The prevalence of sexual assault of women in the general population varies widely depending upon variations in data collection and methodology (e.g., *Uniform Crime Reports* (UCR) versus *National Crime Victimization Survey* (NCVS) data) (S. Holmes and R. Holmes, 2009; Kilpatrick et al., 2007; O'Sullivan, 2013; Reddington and Kreisel, 2009; Russell, 1982). According to the Centers for Disease Control and Prevention [CDC], nearly 18.3% (or 1-in-5) women have reported being raped in their lifetime (see also, Breiding et al., 2014; Kilpatrick et al., 2007). In 2013, based on data from the Uniform Crime Reports (UCR), there were an estimated 79,770 forcible rapes (reported to law enforcement) and an estimated rape rate of 25.2 per 100,000 (UCR, 2013). For 2011, the rape rate was 52.7 per 100,000 (UCR, 2011); however, "reports like the UCR [Uniform Crime Reports], which rely on estimates from reported and founded cases of rape only, will grossly underestimate the total occurrence of rape" (Kilpatrick and McCauley, 2009, p. 11).

The use of victimization surveys can yield better data on the scope (though still only provide an estimate) of sexual assault victimization, though according to Kilpatrick and McCauley (2009) the sensitivity of the assessment influences the measurement of the crime (Fisher et al., 2010; Rozee and Koss, 2001; Russell, 1982). Although, the National Crime Victimization Survey (NCVS), a major victimization study administered in the United States by the Bureau of Justice Statistics, can yield more data than the UCR, this source has been criticized as well for underestimating the extent of victimization (Kilpatrick and McCauley, 2009; Fisher et al., 2010). According to Planty et al. (2013), using data from the

National Crime Victimization Survey [NCVS], found that for 2010, "females nationwide experienced about 270,000 rape or sexual assault victimizations" (p. 1) and that the rate of completed rape/sexual assault declined from 3.6 per 1,000 to 1.1 per 1,000 between 1995 and 2010. However, the rate of attempted rape or threat of rape remained relatively constant during this time (Planty et al., 2013).

Russell (1982) argued that using victimization interview methods offered a better understanding of the rates of sexual assault because victims may be more willing to report their victimization to researchers who were trained to deal with sensitive topics. Russell (1982) examined several different studies of sexual victimization and discovered that an accurate measure of the prevalence of rape did not exist. With her own study, her goal was to find a more accurate estimate of these rates by creating a detailed interview schedule and interviewing 930 randomly selected adult women in the San Francisco area. Yet, by combining both rapes and attempted rapes, the prevalence rates that she reported might be overestimates.

Russell attempted to gain more disclosure by specifically designing an interview schedule that encouraged the development of good rapport with respondents. Interviewers were given two weeks of sensitivity training, and they were selected because of their understanding of and sensitivity to the issue of rape. Interviews were held in private areas as much as possible, and sincere attempts were made to match the race and ethnicity of the respondent and the interviewer to the fullest extent possible. In her study a 36 percent refusal rate was experienced. Russell was unable to compare the social characteristics of the sample with adult women in San Francisco except on the variables of race and ethnicity. This limitation did not allow the study to determine if the sample was representative of the population of adult women in San Francisco, or adult women in the U.S. in general. This limitation also made it difficult to generalize the results due to the unknown representativeness of the sample.

Russell (1982) compared her results to the 1979 edition of the *Uniform Crime Reports* (UCR). In the 1979 UCR, there were 583 reported rapes and attempted rapes of women of all ages in San Francisco during 1978. According to Russell, these data yielded a rape rate of 1.71 per 1,000 women of all ages in 1978 in San Francisco. Russell's sample of 930 women reported 33 extramarital rapes and attempted rapes from mid-1977 to mid-1978 (12 months prior to the interview), but 8 of the rapes/attempted rapes occurred outside of San Francisco, which is a final measure of 25 rapes. Using these 25 rapes of 930 women, Russell estimated the total number of extramarital rapes and attempted rapes of women 17 years old and older in 1978 in San Francisco to be 7.625. Russell (1982) calculated that this is 13 times higher than the total incidence reported by the UCR for women of all ages. Russell's estimate of the incidence rate of rape was 3 percent. The UCR, however, does not give information on the age of victims, whereas Russell's study was limited to women 17 years old and older. Also, Russell only examined residents of the city and not others, unlike the UCR.

Russell also discussed the rate of unfounding (i.e., police finding that no forcible rape offense or attempt occurred) of rape cases, and although there are no statistics for 1978 on the unfounding rate, Russell reported the rate of unfounding for 1976 (the last year rates of unfounding were given) as 18%. Russell explained that her rates are higher than those of the UCR because of the fact that the rapes she measured were not unfounded and included unreported rapes.

Based on the interviews conducted with the 930 women, 41 percent reported at least one experience that conformed to the legal definition of rape or attempted rape (Russell, 1982). Russell suggested that this estimate does not capture the full extent of the problem since many of her study participants were still unwilling to disclose their experiences even with the training and known sensitivity of the interviewers. Based on these results the reporting of this crime might be low even when researchers take extra steps to gain the trust of respondents and increase the likelihood of victimization disclosure.

Bachman (1998) examined data about rape and sexual assaults from the redesigned National Crime Victimization Survey (NCVS) for the years 1992 to 1994. Although the NCVS measures a variety of sexual assaults, Bachman limited the examination to incidents that only involved one male offender and a female victim 18 years old and older occurring in the United States. Thus, other types of sexual assaults are excluded from Bachman's analysis (i.e., gang rapes), which may possibly lower the actual incidence of sexual assault and rape. Bachman examined the reporting of the victimizations to the police and found that only 25 percent of the victimizations experienced were reported to police. Rape victims were the ones who informed the police in 67 percent of instances of the victimization. Bachman also found that completed rapes were <u>not</u> reported more often than attempted rapes and other sexual assaults; however, Bachman did not discuss the prevalence rates of sexual assault.

Breiding et al., (2014) used the 2011 National Intimate Partner and Sexual Violence Survey (NISVS) to determine more recent national prevalence data on sexual violence, rape, stalking, and intimate partner violence victimization. This survey is administered by the Centers for Disease Control and Prevention and entails a nationally representative sample. It is administered by random–digit dialing non–institutionalized individuals within the United States who are 18 years and older. A total of 14,155 interviews were conducted in the 2011 administration of the survey. As with previous studies, this survey included behaviorally specific questions "that assessed being a victim of sexual violence, stalking, and intimate partner violence over the respondent's lifetime and during the 12 months before interview" (p. 3). Specifically, the survey asked respondents about rape, forced penetration that was completed or attempted, as well as drug-facilitated penetration, other types of sexual violence (e.g., penetrating a perpetrator, sexual coercion), unwanted sexual contact (e.g., fondling), and unwanted sexual experiences that did not include physical contact (e.g., being flashed). Respondents were also asked about being a victim of stalking and intimate partner violence, which also included sexual violence, as well as physical violence and psychological aggression.

Breiding et al. (2014) found that within the United States "an estimated 19.3% of women (or >23 million women) have been raped during their lifetimes" (p. 4). With completed forced penetration, an estimated 11.5% of women (or >13 million) experienced this victimization and an estimated 9.3% of women (or >11 million) experienced drug or alcohol-facilitated rape within their lifetimes. In the 12 months prior to the survey, an estimated 1.6% of women (or > 1 million) experienced rape and an estimated 1.0% of women (> 1 million) experienced drug or alcohol-facilitated penetration. For the other types of sexual violence examined (i.e., made to penetrate, sexual coercion, unwanted sexual contact, and unwanted, non-contact, sexual experiences), an estimated 43.9% of women (>52 million women) experienced these types of victimization within their lifetimes. In the 12 months prior to the survey, an estimated 5.5% of women (or >6 million) experienced these types of victimization. Breiding et al. (2014) also found that "among female victims of completed rape….this form of sexual violence was first experienced by an estimated 78.7% before age 25 years, [and] by an estimated 40.4% before 18 years…" (p. 11).

Although Breiding et al. (2014) were able to gather information on a variety of types of sexual violence and were able to show sexual victimization affects a significant number of women, both during their lifetimes and during the previous 12 months, within the United States, their study is not without noteworthy limitations. As indicated by the researchers themselves, the response rate of the 2011 NISVS was "relatively low (33.1%)" (p. 17). Despite efforts by the researchers to reduce nonresponse by completing a "nonresponse follow-up in which randomly selected nonresponders were contacted again and offered increased incentive for participation" (p. 17), this did not translate into an increased response rate. Additionally, although researchers did examine a wide range of different types of self-reported victimization, and used behaviorally-specific questions, there is still a likelihood that even what was reported by respondents is an underestimation of the true incidence and prevalence of sexual victimization. As with other self-report studies, the data could be subject to recall bias by respondents or respondents could have decided, for a variety of reasons, not to disclose all their victimization experiences. As a result, the estimates could be lower than actual rates of the sexual violence experienced by respondents. Another limitation would have to do with how the survey was conducted. Since the study was conducted using random-digit dialing, despite efforts by researchers to reach out to those without a landline (i.e., they included a cellular telephone sample), "…a telephone survey might be less likely to capture some populations that could be at higher risk for victimization (e.g., persons living in nursing homes, military bases, prisons, or shelters, or those who are homeless)" (p. 17). This could also result in an underestimation of actual prevalence and incidence rates, since these populations might have experienced sexual victimization (and possibly higher rates than the population surveyed) and because they were not included, these victimizations were not captured by this research.

● COLLEGE WOMEN

Although they also could be included in the overall population of women as potential victims, college women constitute a distinct subset of women highly worthy of study. Studies consistently find that those with the highest rate of victimization are women in their late teens to early 20s (Breiding et al., 2014; Fisher et al., 2000, 2003, 2010; Kilpatrick and McCauley, 2009; Planty et al.,

2013; Sinozich and Langton, 2014; Tjaden and Thoennes, 2000). Fisher et al. (2010) maintain that women within this age bracket "are almost *four times* more likely to be raped than all other female age groups" (p. 65, emphasis added). This is especially true for women within this age group who are enrolled in colleges and universities (Banyard et al., 2005, 2007; Fisher et al., 2000, 2003, 2010; Gross et al., 1991; Karjane et al., 2005; Krebs et al., 2009; Sampson, 2002; Tjaden and Thoennes, 2000). As a result of their living arrangements, lifestyle, age, and their community, the prevalence of rape among college women should be examined separately from that of women in the general population.

Although most researchers find that females aged 18 to 24 have the highest rate of victimization (Breiding et al., 2014; Fisher et al., 2000, 2003, 2010; Kilpatrick and McCauley, 2009; Planty et al., 2013; Sinozich and Langton, 2014), and most researchers have found that those within this age group enrolled in colleges/ universities are at an increased risk for victimization, the study by Sinozich and Langton (2014) contradict this. Sinozich and Langton examined data from the National Crime Victimization Study (NCVS) for the period 1995–2013 to compare the rape and sexual assault victimization of students to nonstudents. They found that "the rate of rape and sexual assault was 1.2 times *higher* for nonstudents (7.6 per 1,000) than for students (6.1 per 1,000)" (p. 1). However, this finding could be due to the different methodologies and measurement differences employed by the NCVS versus the college-specific victimization surveys (e.g., National College Women Sexual Victimization Survey, Campus Sexual Assault Study). Not only are the foci of these studies different (i.e., NCVS is a survey about crime in general while some of the others, such as the CSA, are surveys about public health), but also the definitions of rape and sexual assault vary, as do how the survey questions are worded. This set of differences likely led to the difference in prevalence and incidence reported by the NCVS versus other studies.

Ward et al. (1991) examined the issue of sexual assault within college social situations. Data were collected by distributing questionnaires in undergraduate classrooms in an attempt to get a better response rate of a cross-section of the student population and to keep information anonymous. Twenty classes were selected, and they yielded a sample of 524 women and 337 men which represented approximately 10 percent of the undergraduate population at the university in question.

The questionnaire employed in the survey asked students about the amount of unwanted sexual contact, unwanted attempted sexual intercourse, and unwanted completed sexual intercourse that the men participated in and the women had experienced during the current academic year. Incidents that reportedly occurred on campus were separated from those that had occurred elsewhere. The Ward et al. (1991) study had some limitations in that their sample was not truly representative of the undergraduate population of the university since it overrepresented female students, freshmen, and those in the college of liberal arts. By overrepresenting freshmen, this may make the estimates of the prevalence of assault inflated, because according to Ward et al. (1991), freshmen are the most likely victims of sexual assaults. Ward et al. (1991) found that 34 percent of the women sampled had experienced unwanted sexual contact, 20 percent had experienced unwanted attempted intercourse, and 10 percent had experience unwanted completed intercourse.

Fisher, Cullen and Turner (2000, 2010) examined the sexual victimization of college women using the National College Women Sexual Victimization (NCWSV) study. The NCWSV attempted to overcome some of the previous limitations of studies on sexual assault by getting a better estimate of the prevalence of sexual assault among college-aged women. The NCWSV used a telephone-based survey of a randomly selected national sample of 4,446 women attending 2- or 4-year universities with 1,000 or more students during the fall of 1996. The NCWSV used a two-stage methodology to estimate rates of victimization. First, respondents were asked a series of behaviorally-specific screening questions to see if they had experienced a range of different types of sexual victimizations. If a respondent answered yes to a screening question, it was followed by an incident report to clarify information about the victimization and collect information about different aspects of the incident (i.e., victim-offender relationship). The NCWSV collected incident-based data for the 1996–1997 academic year along with data on demographic characteristics, lifestyles, and routine activities of the respondents.

Twelve types of victimization were measured by the NCWSV, which included both completed and attempted rape, threats of rape, completed, attempted, and threatened sexual coercion, and other unwanted sexual contact. The NCWSV also examined stalking and verbal and visual forms of sexual victimization that other studies had not examined when looking at sexual victimization. Fisher et al. (2000, 2010) found that 2.8 percent of the sample had experienced either a completed or attempted rape. Some women were found to be victimized more than once, and as a result the rates of incidents were higher than the rate of victims (35.3 per 1,000 students). Of the 123 victims, 22.8 percent were victims of multiple rapes. Fisher et al. (2000) also projected the findings to get an estimate of the rate of victimization for a whole year (not only a school year, approximately 7 months). This estimate of the rate of victimization for a period of one year was about 5 percent, and when projected over a whole college career (average of 5 years) the rate of victimization rises to between one-fifth and one-quarter[1].

Fisher et al. (2000, 2010) also compared the results of the NCWSV to estimates from the National Crime Victimization Survey (NCVS) and found that the estimates generated from the NCWSV were 11 times greater than those found with the NCVS for completed rape, and for attempted rape 6 times greater. Fisher et al. (2000, 2010) suggested that these differences were due to the wording of the questions. The NCWSV used behaviorally-specific screening questions while the NCVS does not. It is possible that by using the behaviorally-specific questions respondents who may either be reluctant to report or do not classify what happened to them as a sexual assault will report the victimization (Fisher et al., 2000, 2010).

Sampson (2002) found that women, especially women in college, are at high-risk of being victims of sexual assault and that approximately 25 percent have been victims of attempted or completed sexual assaults. Sampson (2002) also found that women in college are at more risk of being sexually assaulted than women in the 16 to 24 age group who are not in college[2]. This suggests that women in college are a high risk population, quite possibly more at risk that those women not in college. Therefore, it is important to examine this population in depth.

Although researchers have not been able to specify clearly the prevalence or incidence of sexual assault, all agree that it is a serious crime and that it affects many women, particularly those in college and universities. Fisher et al. (2000, 2010) found that for a period of one year about 5 percent of college women are assaulted, and over 5 years (a typical college career) the figure rises to between one-fifth and one-quarter of college women. Researchers also agree that virtually all women are vulnerable to sexual assault, though there are some characteristics that are more common among victims than non-victims.

● CHARACTERISTICS OF VICTIMIZATION

Although college men can be assaulted too, women in college are more likely than men of their same age to become victims of sexual assault (Krebs et al., 2009; Hines et al., 2012; Russell, 1982; Sinozich and Langton, 2014).

Age

Research indicates that college women between the ages of 16 and 24 years old are victimized at a higher rate than any other age group (Fisher et al., 2003, 2010; Sampson, 2002; Ward et al., 1991). It is possible that college women in this age group engage in behaviors (e.g., drinking alcohol) that put them at a higher risk for victimization (Krebs et al., 2009; Hines et al., 2012; Lawyer et al., 2010; Ward et al., 1991). In addition, women within this age group tend to experience multiple sexual assaults (Fisher et al., 2000, 2010; Gross et al., 2006; Sampson, 2002; Ward et al., 1991). Women are most vulnerable to sexual assault during the first few weeks of their freshman and sophomore years, particularly the first few days of their freshman year; this represents the period of highest risk for victimization (Sampson, 2002; Ward et al., 1991). Gross et al. (2006) found that 84.4 percent of victims experienced victimization sometime during the first four semesters (or first two years) on campus.

Race/Ethnicity

Though some researchers have found a general relationship between ethnicity and victimization (Riedel and Welsh, 2002), much of the sexual victimization research has not found any correlation between race and ethnicity and being a victim of sexual assault. Researchers examining sexual assault often do not report information on ethnicity or any findings associated with ethnicity and victimization. Although they may have gathered relevant information about the demographics of survey respondents, Ward et al. (1991) did not report findings on race and ethnicity in their examination of sexual assault.

Sinozich and Langton (2014) found that for the period of 1995–2013, "there were no significant differences in the student and nonstudent rates of rape and sexual assault for black non-Hispanics, Hispanics, or persons of other races... among female students, the rate of rape and sexual assault was slightly higher for whites (6.7 per 1,000) than for Hispanics (4.5 per 1,000), but did not differ significantly from the rate for blacks (6.4 per 1,000)" (p. 10).

According to Belknap (2000), African-American women are more at risk for assault than other groups, though the types of assault may differ. She determined that while Caucasian women are more at risk for acquaintance rapes, African-American women were more at risk for stranger rapes. Although Belknap (2000) did not identify why African-American females may be more at risk for stranger rapes than white females, Gross et al. (2006) found that African-American female college students who are victims of assault report higher rates of physical force and emotional pressure than victims who are white. Gross et al. (2006) found that there is no clear correlation between rape and ethnicity, but found that there was greater alcohol usage with white victims relative to African-American victims. Unfortunately, other races and ethnicities were not examined by Gross et al. (2006). Additionally, Kilpatrick et al. (2007) found "that African-American women had a prevalence of [forcible rape] that was about 50% higher than Caucasian and Hispanic women" (p. 27).

According to Mustaine and Tewksbury (2002), African-American women have a victimization rate that is 14 percent higher than that of white women. Rozee and Koss (2001), in their review of sexual assault research, stated that the prevalence rate of rape for white women was found to be the same as that of African-American women in many studies, though others have found a lower rate for African-American women when compared to white women. It was also acknowledged that many of the studies that sample college women do not include a random sample of African-American women (Rozee and Koss, 2001). This bias in sampling may be why there is a dearth of research of the interaction between ethnicity and victimization.

As with Gross et al. (2006), most research ignores or has weakly examined the possible interaction between sexual victimization and ethnicity. By not examining victim race and ethnicity, researchers may be missing critical information regarding the experiences and causes of sexual victimization.

Residence

The location of the victimization is important to consider when examining sexual assault, and, in particular, assaults committed by acquaintances and against college-aged women. Existing research suggests that these events occur on campus, and most often in the victims' residences (Sampson, 2002; Ward et al., 1991). Sampson (2002) reported that 45 percent of attempted rapes of college women occur on campus and 34 percent of completed rapes occur on campus. Sampson (2002) reported that approximately 60 percent of the completed rapes that occur on campus take place at the victims' residences, about 31 percent occur at another campus-area residence, and about 10 percent at a fraternity. A sexual assault involving an acquaintance may occur either at a residence following a date or in a vehicle, but stranger rapes tend to occur on campus in isolated areas (e.g., garages) or in the victims' residences (Sampson, 2002).

Fisher et al. (2000, 2010) discovered that a majority of sexual victimizations among college women occurred in living quarters, with almost 60 percent occurring in the victim's own residence. Fisher et al. (2000, 2010) also found that among college women victimization is more common within off-campus residences.

Time

Similar to the issue of residence, temporal associations with victimization are important to consider, though not many researchers have examined the question of precisely when victimizations occur. Sampson (2002) found that sexual assaults tend to happen after 6 p.m., with the majority occurring after midnight. Fisher et al. (2000, 2010) also found that many victimizations occurred after 6 p.m., with a majority (51.8 percent) occurring after midnight. This is possibly due to the fact that within these hours there is little natural light and also these may be the hours when individuals are not most alert (either due to natural biorhythms or to imbibing alcohol/drugs). The combination of the lack of light and less alert individuals may make an environment where it is easier for offenders to commit assaults than might be the ease earlier in the day.

Lifestyles

Research has shown that the way individuals live affects not only their lifestyle, but also their risk of victimization (Armstrong and Griffin, 2007; Cohen and

Felson, 1979)–including the risk of sexual assault victimization. Routine activities theory (Cohen and Felson, 1979) and lifestyle exposure theory (Hindelang et al., 1978) may help explain why female college students tend to have higher victimization rates than other women (even among other women in the same age group). Routine activities theory states that victimization and crime can occur when there are motivated offenders who come in contact with suitable victims and there is a lack of capable guardians (Cohen and Felson, 1979). The theory proposes that crime can occur during the course of routine activities (e.g., going to school or work). Capable guardianship can include additional lighting or other physical security devices that improve ongoing surveillance (Cohen and Felson, 1979).

Lifestyle exposure theory suggests that variation in risk to victimization can be attributed to differences in an individual's lifestyle characteristics (Armstrong and Griffin, 2007; Hindelang et al., 1978). Certain individuals may be more susceptible to victimization due to their exposure to dangerous people, places, or times, which then increases the situations where victimization can occur. As a result, one woman, due to her lifestyle activities (both personal and professional) may have an increased risk of victimization versus another woman despite being similar in all other ways (e.g., age, race, and socioeconomic status) (Armstrong and Griffin, 2007; Hindelang et al., 1978).

It may be that suitable targets (i.e., women who are intoxicated) come into contact with motivated offenders (i.e., men who are intoxicated or who have experienced peer support toward victimization) more often in situations related to college and university social scenes. In addition, it is possible that this convergence of suitable targets and motivated offenders occurs in conjunction with a lack of capable guardians (i.e., in isolated dorm rooms, or at parties where others are intoxicated) (Hines et al., 2012; Ward et al., 1991).

According to Ward et al. (1991), the majority of acquaintance sexual assaults among college-aged victims and offenders involve alcohol and/or drug use by both the victim and perpetrator. Ward et al. (1991) found in their examination that in over 75 percent of the college and university victimizations, the male perpetrators had consumed alcohol, and, in over half the incidents, the female victims had consumed alcohol.

Additionally, Kilpatrick et al. (2007) found with their study that an estimated 3% of college women were raped. Of these, a little over 2% (2.1%) experienced a drug or alcohol-facilitated rape or an incapacitated rape (see also Fisher et al., 2010). Expanding on this research, Lawyer et al. (2010) also examined forcible, drug-facilitated and incapacitated rape and sexual assault among college students. Of their sample of 314 female students, 93 (29.6%) reported drug-related assaults. Of these 93 victims, 77 victims answered follow-up questions about the nature of the drug related-assault (i.e., whether they consumed the drug(s) voluntarily). "When this subsample of women was considered, 84.4% (n = 65) of the respondents reported an incapacitated assault (they reported consuming the alcohol or drugs voluntarily) and 15.6% (n = 12) described a drug-facilitated assault..." (Lawyer et al., 2010, p. 456).

Gross et al. (2006) suggest that in over half of these incidents, either the victim or perpetrator used alcohol. This may be one of the reasons why college women are more susceptible to acquaintance rape since there is often an atmosphere conducive to drinking on college and university campuses (Gross et al., 2006).

Schwartz and Pitts (1995) suggested that women are more likely targets for sexual assault and have a higher risk of victimization than others regardless of lifestyle choices. They also suggested that due to the "rape-supportive" culture of the United States, men are motivated to sexually assault women. Capable guardianship is diminished because there are men who assault women and feel no guilt or shame. Low penalties for men who assault women also contribute to this lowered guardianship. Schwartz and Pitts (1995) argued that a college campus is a hot spot for this convergence of suitable targets, motivated offenders, and lack of guardianship. Their study examined the factors that increased the pursuit of suitable targets by potential offenders. Women who had male friends who got women drunk for the purpose of sexual assault and women who drank more often were found to be more likely to be sexually assaulted than women who did not engage in these behaviors. However, they did not look into other lifestyle choices that might increase a women's chance of victimization.

Mustaine and Tewksbury (2002) examined sexual assault using routine activities theory to expand on the research of Schwartz and Pitts (1995). They expanded the range of lifestyle activities in an attempt to understand how lifestyles may predispose a woman to victimization due to making her a more suitable target. They also examined whether these factors that influence sexual assault vary with varying degrees of severity of victimization. Data from women on 12 college campuses collected from self-administered surveys were examined. Mustaine and Tewksbury (2002) found that none of the variables measuring self-protective behaviors was a significant predictor of sexual assault, suggesting that guardianship behavior did not influence whether a women was seen as a suitable target for victimization. In their final model, none of the variables associated with categories of demographics and those related to alcohol or lifestyle statuses were significant predictors of victimization. They suggest that by adding more lifestyle behaviors into the analysis and thereby controlling for more behaviors, the variables that are typically found to be significant predictors of victimization in more limited studies (i.e., alcohol use) are no longer significant. Though they did not find alcohol-related lifestyle behaviors to be significant, they imply that it may be other activities in association with drinking alcohol that influence a woman's suitability as a target (i.e., not drinking, but with whom she is drinking). However, they did find that when lifestyle behavior relating to drug usage was included in the models, the significance of the alcohol measures disappear, suggesting that drug usage may have a greater influence on a woman's risk for victimization than alcohol use. Mustaine and Tewksbury (2002) found that victimization risks were primarily influenced by proximity or exposure to rape-supportive male peer groups, with measures of victim attractiveness/suitability being less influential.

Colleges and universities may also contain environmental characteristics where the likelihood of being assaulted is greater (e.g., mixed social functions, co-ed dormitories). According to Ward et al. (1991), women may also trust those with whom they interact on a relatively regular basis (i.e., have class or study with them) and not have as much fear of being victimized if they associate with these individuals. Victimizations often do occur within social situations where women are not predisposed to be fearful (e.g., they are with their friends at a party), and therefore, women may inadvertently put themselves at risk because they do not believe they will be assaulted. The problem is compounded by the reports that college women disproportionately fear stranger-based sexual assaults and may take steps to avoid these events (e.g., not walking alone on campus at night), but exhibit less concern with becoming intoxicated with relatively unknown acquaintances (Gross et al., 2006; Mustaine and Tewksbury, 2002; Sampson, 2002; Ward et al., 1991).

College men may also not consider taking advantage of an intoxicated female student as rape and other acquaintances may facilitate the event by encouraging male perpetrators and female victims simply out of ignorance (Sampson, 2002; Mustaine and Tewksbury, 2002; Rozee and Koss, 2001; Ward et al., 1991). Since college students may not define these incidents as rape when they occur to a friend or acquaintance, they may be less likely to define them as such if these incidents happen to them (Fisher et al., 2010; Sampson, 2002; Ward et al., 1991).

The lifestyle of a college student may affect their victimization risk. Engaging in risky activities, such as drinking, may lessen their ability to protect themselves from victimization, especially sexual assault. Also, women in college may come in more proximity or spend more time with males who are part of rape-supportive peer groups increasing their risk of victimization (Mustaine and Tewksbury, 2002). With some confusion related to the definition of sexual assault, it is likely that many events that qualify as sexual assaults also go unreported.

● REPORTING OF SEXUAL ASSAULT

Research consistently finds that sexual assault is vastly underreported to authorities, and is one of the least reported of all crimes (Banyard et al., 2005, 2007; Belknap, 2010; Lizotte, 1985; Fisher et al., 2000, 2003, 2010; Gross et al., 2006; Ménard, 2005; Miller et al., 2011; Reddington and Kreisel, 2009; Rennison et al., 2013; Sable, Dabis, Mauzy, and Gallagher, 2006; Sampson, 2002; Sinozich and Langton, 2014; Tjaden and Thoennes, 2000; Weiss, 2009, 2010). Studies examining victimization of students have found that typically only 5% of assaults are reported to university authorities and/or police (Fisher et al., 2000, 2003, 2010; Karjane et al., 2005; Koss et al., 1987; Ménard, 2005; Miller et al., 2011). Other research estimates the reporting rate as approximately 25 percent (Fisher et al., 2003, 2010; Gross et al., 2006; Sampson, 2002), but this is still alarmingly low. Research suggests that victims often tell someone, most likely a friend or a roommate, and do not tell a person of authority (Ahrens et al., 2007; Banyard et al., 2005; Fisher et al., 2003, 2010; Sampson, 2002). Part of the reason reporting is low with sexual assault could be the embarrassing nature of the crime. Others posit that it is because many of the assaults involve acquaintances and alcohol, and that many victims may not realize that what happened was a sexual assault (Fisher et al., 2000, 2010; Ward et al., 1991; Sampson, 2002).

Ambiguity Concerning Assault

Many victims may not report their victimization because they may not realize that what had happened constitutes sexual assault, particularly if the assault involves someone known to the victim (Fisher et al., 2003, 2010; Gross et al., 2006; Rennison et al., 2013; Russell, 1982; Sampson, 2002; Ward et al., 1991; Weiss, 2011). Since the assault often does not take the form of the stereotypical stranger-in-the-bushes assault, victims may fail to recognize and label the experience as a sexual assault, and they will see no need to report it as a crime (Gross et al., 2006). Fisher et al. (2000, 2010) found in their examination of sexual assault that in almost half the incidents (48.8 percent) the respondents did not consider the incident rape while 4.7 percent stated that they did not know if it constituted rape.

Research indicates that this is especially true with college and university women who are assaulted. Sexual assaults committed against college and university women predominately involve a perpetrator whom the victim knows or has recently met, the use of alcohol, and occur within a social scene where the victim may not characterize what happened as sexual assault (Ward et al., 1991). Also, these assaults may not result in physical injuries and the victims may not have fought the perpetrator, despite protesting against sexual conduct or being unable (due to intoxication) to properly consent (Ward et al., 1991). As a result, victims may not characterize these assaults as true sexual assaults, and therefore do not report them (Fisher et al., 2003, 2010; Gross et al., 2006; Sampson, 2002; Ward et al., 1991).

Researchers describe the typical sexual assault as not the stereotypical event that most women fear, but rather victimization at the hands of someone known to them (Fisher et al., 2010; Lizotte, 1985; Reddington and Kreisel, 2009). Both Belknap (2000) and Russell (1982) have described the stereotypical rape as one involving a lone woman, being grabbed by someone, usually a stranger hiding in the bushes, being assaulted at night, and in an isolated area. In this view, there are injuries due to a physical confrontation. Research indicates that sexual assaults are more likely to involve a perpetrator who is known to the victim, either casually or intimately, usually involves alcohol, and results in few if any physical injuries (Fisher et al., 2000, 2010; Russell, 1982; Ward et al., 1991). As a result, many women may not define what occurred to them as sexual assault because it does not fit their conception of a sexual assault (Fisher et al., 2000; Ward et al., 1991). When researchers attempt to gather information on the rates of assaults, women who do not define what happened as sexual assault may allow their victimization experiences to go unmeasured and unreported (Fisher et al., 2000, 2003, 2010; Russell, 1982; Weiss, 2010).

Fear of Retaliation

Since a majority of the sexual assaults that occur on campuses are committed by offenders known to the victims, one possible reason for victims not reporting is fear of reprisal by the assailant(s) (Sampson, 2002; Tjaden and Thoennes, 2000). Bachman (1998) found that more than 1-in-10 university women who are victims did not report because they were afraid of reprisal from the offender. Victims may not only fear reprisal from the assailant, but also from the assailant's friends, who may also be known to the victim and the victim's own friends. Since oftentimes victims are not believed (especially if the assault does not conform to stereotypical events or if there was a prior relationship between victim and offender), sexual assault victims also may fear social stigma as a form of reprisal (Fisher et al., 2003, 2010; Sampson, 2002; Weiss, 2011).

Research indicates that those who know their attackers are even less likely to notify authorities (and/or delay telling anyone) than those who are assaulted by strangers due to possible fear of reprisal (Bachman, 1998; Fisher et al., 2003, 2010). Victims may fear that someone known to them would be more prone to retaliation than a stranger (Bachman, 1998). Bachman found in her work that this is even the case despite finding that victimizations perpetrated by known offenders may be more likely to result in an arrest compared to those committed by strangers. This proximity of victim and attacker creates an even larger problem with reporting assaults of college women since the majority of these involve offenders known to the victim.

Victim Blaming/Secondary Victimization

Many victims may choose not to report the assault because of fear of being blamed for the assault occurring (Felson and Pare, 2005; Fisher et al., 2003, 2010; Reddington and Kreisel, 2009; Weiss, 2010). Despite being a traumatic experience in and of itself for the victims, sexual assault is also the only crime where the victim can be and often is socially stigmatized and blamed for becoming a victim (Russell, 1982). Victims may also come to blame themselves for allowing the assault to occur. The victim may believe that the incentives to avoid reporting outweigh any possible benefits of reporting (Russell, 1982). Victims may also believe that nothing can or will be done about it despite being stigmatized and blamed. Therefore, they still choose not to report to authorities, though they may still disclose information to close friends (Ahrens et al., 2007; Gross et al., 2006; Ménard, 2005; Sampson, 2002; Ward et al., 1991).

Since the majority of assaults also involve drinking and/or drug use by the victim, those who are assaulted while under the influence may fear being blamed or receiving sanctions if they go to university officials to report the incident (Karjane et al., 2005; Ward et al. 1991). Women may fear that because they had been drinking at the time of the assault they may not be believed, or worse yet they will be blamed for allowing the victimization to occur. If the sexual assault victimization was committed by someone known to the victim, the victim again may fear that authorities will not believe an assault occurred or think that she is only reporting "to get back at the male" or because of a "bad date" (Belknap, 2000, 2010; Sampson, 2002). The victim may decide that it is more beneficial not to report than to be ceaselessly questioned about the assault; the victim may want to just forget it happened and go on with her life without reliving the painful victimization (Belknap, 2000; Sampson, 2002; Weiss, 2011).

Those Who Report

Some victims do choose to report their victimization to authorities. Often times those who disclose being victimized do so first to friends or other intimate acquaintances before deciding to go to authorities (often at the urging of these friends) (Ahrens et al., 2007; Fisher et al., 2003, 2010; Kilpatrick et al., 2007; Paul et al., 2013; Rennison, 2002; Sampson, 2002). Research indicates that more than three-fourths of victims tell someone about the incident, usually a friend, rather than disclose the information to police (Ahrens et al., 2007; Paul et al., 2013; Fisher et al., 2003, 2010), since only approximately 5 percent to 25 percent of assaults are reported to authorities (Fisher et al., 2003, 2010; Karjane et al., 2005). As with non-reporting, research has attempted to determine what factors influence victims to report their victimization to authorities to allow for better reporting practices overall. This section discusses those factors that have been found to be correlated with reporting sexual assaults to authorities.

According to Karjane et al. (2005), if victims are treated fairly (without blame), if there is coordination between the community and authorities, and if there are easily accessible victim services available, reporting is more likely to occur. They also discovered that policies on campuses that encourage anonymous and confidential reporting encourage both victims and others to report sexual assaults. Additionally, Greeson, Campbell and Fehler-Cabral (2014) found that "sexual assault victims have positive experiences with the police [when they] are treated with compassion and sensitivity, whereas some have negative experiences [when they] are treated in a cold, intimidating manner" (p. 646). Fisher et al. (2003, 2010) found in their research that victims were more likely to report if they hold favorable attitudes of those taking the reports (e.g., if victims felt the police will handle the case efficiently and considerately).

Research also indicates that there are characteristics specific to the actual assault that increase the likelihood of reporting. If the victim shows evidence of the assault (i.e., physical harm and injuries), it is more likely to be reported because the victim believes she is more likely to be taken seriously and viewed as a victim (Bachman, 1998; Felson and Pare, 2005; Lizotte, 1985; Ménard, 2005; Russell, 1982). If someone unknown to the victim commits the assault, she is more likely to report (Bachman, 1998; Belknap, 2000; Fisher et al., 2003; Ménard, 2005; Russell, 1982).

Victim characteristics also have been identified as increasing the likelihood to report. Older victims are more likely to report than those who are younger (Ménard, 2005), and research indicates that the more education a woman has the less likely she is to report the assault (Lizotte, 1985). This observation is possibly due to the fact that by being more educated a woman understands more fully how she may be secondarily victimized by the justice system and what she will experience if she reports the victimization and participates in the prosecution of the offender (Fisher et al., 2003; Lizotte, 1985; Weiss, 2011). Research has also shown that if the victim feels that the assault conformed to the stereotypical rape then the assault is more likely to be reported to authorities (Felson and Pare, 2005; Fisher et al., 2003; Karjane et al., 2005; Patterson and Campbell, 2010; Russell, 1982; Sampson, 2002).

● CONCLUSION

Though the true prevalence of sexual assault is exceedingly difficult to determine due to lack of reporting, many researchers agree that it is a serious problem for women, especially women aged 16 to 24 who are in college (Fisher et al., 2003, 2010; Kilpatrick and McCauley, 2009; Gross et al., 2006; Krebs et al., 2009; Miller et al., 2011; Russell, 1982; Sampson, 2002; Ward et al., 1991). Research has shown that the majority of these sexual assaults are committed by those known to the victims and occur during the course of common social interaction. These two characteristics greatly decrease the likelihood of reporting. There are many reasons why victims may not report the crime to the authorities, including fear of reprisal, fear of being blamed, and ambiguity over qualification of the assault (Fisher et al., 2003, 2010; Planty et al., 2013; Rennison, 2002; Rennison et al., 2013; Russell, 1982; Ward et al., 1991; Weiss, 2009, 2010). There are also reasons why victims may choose to report despite these fears, including the thought that they will be taken seriously and treated considerately by the authorities when reporting (Fisher et al., 2003, 2010; Greeson et al., 2014; Karjane et al., 2005). This suggests that those universities that are located in places where a good relationship exists between students and law enforcement may wish to recognize and foster such a relationship that facilitates the reporting of sexual assault.

Universities where officials understand the complex nature of the crime and comprehend the reasons behind both reporting and non-reporting may also be able to enact policies that help prevent sexual assault. The following chapter reviews the interaction between the public and police, and it identifies the importance of this relationship and suggests how it can be improved to enhance the timely reporting of crimes in general and sexual assault in particular.

● ENDNOTES

1. Karjane et al. (2005) found the same results as Fisher et al. (2000, 2010) that 5 percent of women during a year will be victims of rape, and over a five-year period this figure rises to one-fifth of college women.

2. *Sampson (2002) did not explain how she came to the conclusion that college women are more at risk for sexual assault than women 16 to 24 years old who are not in college.*

● REFERENCES

Ahrens, C. E., Campbell, R., Ternier-Thames, N. K., Wasco, S. M., and Sefl, T. (2007). Deciding whom to tell: Expectations and outcomes of rape survivors' first disclosures. *Psychology of Women Quarterly, 31*, 38–49.

Armstrong, G. and Griffin, M. (2007). The effect of local life circumstances on victimization of drug-involved women. *Justice Quarterly, 24*(1), 80–105.

Bachman, R. (1998). The factors related to rape reporting behavior and arrest: New evidence from the National Crime Victimization Survey. *Criminal Justice and Behavior*, 25(1), 8–29.

Banyard, V. L., Plante, E. G., Cohn, E. S., Moorhead, C., Ward, S. and Walsh, W. (2005). Revisiting unwanted sexual experiences on campus: A 12-year follow-up. *Violence Against Women, 11* (4), 426–446.

Belknap, J. (2010). Rape: Too hard to report and too easy to discredit victims. *Violence Against Women, 16*(12), 1335–1344.

Belknap, A. (2000). Sexual Victimization in *The Invisible Woman: Gender, Crime, and Justice*, (pp. 227–266). Belmont, CA: Wadsworth.

Breiding, M., Smith, S., Basile, K., Walters, M., Chen, J., and Merrick, M. (2014). Prevalence and characteristics of sexual violence victimization—National Intimate Partner and Sexual Violence Survey, United States, 2011. *Morbidity and Morality Weekly Report, Surveillance Summaries, 63* (8), 1–18. Retrieved from http://www.cdc.gov/mmwr/preview/mmwrhtml/ss6308a1.htm?s_ci d=ss6308a1_e#Table1.

Centers of Disease Control and Prevention. (2012). *Sexual violence: Facts at a glance*. Retrieved April 13, 2015 from http://www.cdc.gov/violenceprevention/sexualviolence/datasource s.html.

Cohen, L. and Felson, M. (1979). Social change and crime rate trends: A routine activity approach. *American Sociological Review, 44*, 588–608.

Felson, R. and Pare, P. (2005). The reporting of domestic violence and sexual assault by non-strangers to the police. *Journal of Marriage and Family*, 67, 597–610.

Fisher, B., Cullen, F., and Turner, M. (2000*). The Sexual Victimization of College Women*. Washington, D.C.: U.S. Department of Justice, National Institute of Justice and Bureau of Justice Statistics.

Fisher, B., Daigle, L., Cullen, F., and Turner, M. (2003). Reporting sexual victimization to the police and others: Results from a national-level study of college women. *Criminal Justice and Behavior*, 30(1), 6–38.

Fisher, B., Daigle, L., and Cullen, F. (2010). *Unsafe in the Ivory Tower: The Sexual Victimization of College Women*. Los Angeles: Sage Publications.

Gross, A., Winslett, A., Roberts, M., and Gohm, C. (2006). An examination of sexual violence against college women. *Violence Against Women, 12* (3), 288–300.

Hines, D. A., Armstrong, J. L., Reed, K. P., and Cameron, Amy Y. (2012). Gender differences in sexual assault victimization among college students. *Violence and Victims, 27* (6), 922–940.

Holmes, S. T and Holmes, R. M. (2009). *Sex Crimes: Patterns and Behavior* (3rd edition). Los Angeles: Sage Publications.

Karjane, H., Fisher, B., and Cullen, F. (2005). *Sexual Assault on Campus: What Colleges and Universities are Doing About It*. Washington, D.C.: U.S. Department of Justice, National Institute of Justice, (December), 1–16.

Kilpatrick, D. and McCauley, J. (2009). *Understanding National Rape Statistics*. Harrisburg, PA: VAWnet, a project of the National Resource Center on Domestic Violence. Retrieved 04/07/2013, from: http://www.vawnet.org

Kilpatrick, D. G., Resnick, H.S., Ruggiero, K.J., Conoscenti, L. M., and McCauley, J.M. (2007). *Drug-facilitated, Incapacitated, and Forcible Rape: A National Study*. (NCJ 219181-Final Report). Washington, DC: U.S. Department of Justice, National Institute of Justice.

Koss, M. and Burkhart, B. (1989). A conceptual analysis of rape victimization. *Psychology of Women Quarterly*, 13, 27–40

Krebs, C. P., Lindquist, C. H., Warner, T. D., Fisher, B. S., and Martin, S. L. (2009). College women's experiences with physically forced, alcohol- or other drug-enabled, and drug-facilitated sexual assault before and since entering college. *Journal of American College Health*, 57(6), 639–647.

Lawyer, S., Resnick, H., Bakanic, V., Burkett, T., and Kilpatrick, D. (2010). Forcible, drug-facilitated, and incapacitated rape and sexual assault among undergraduate women. *Journal of American College Health, 58*(5), 453–460.

Lizotte, A. (1985). The uniqueness of rape: Reporting assaultive violence to the police. *Crime & Delinquency, 31*(2), 169–190.

Menard, K.S. (2005). *Reporting Sexual Assault: A Social Ecology Perspective*. El Paso, TX: LFB Scholarly Publishing, LLC.

Miller, A., Canales, E., Amacker, A., Backstrom, T., Gidycz, C. (2011). Stigma-threat motivated nondisclosure of sexual assault and sexual revictimiztion: A prospective analysis. *Psychology of Women Quarterly, 35*(1), 119–128.

Mustaine, E. and Tewksbury, R. (2002). Sexual assault of college women: A feminist interpretation of a routine activities analysis. *Criminal Justice Review, 27*(1), 89–123.

O'Sullivan, C. S. (2013). Sexual violence victimization of women, men, youth, and children. In R. C. Davis, A. J. Lurigio, and S. Herman (Eds.), *Victims of Crime* (4th edition) (3–28). Los Angeles: Sage Publications.

Planty, M., Langton, L., Krebs, C., Berzofsky, M. and Smiley McDonald, H. (2013). *Female Victims of Sexual Violence, 1994–2010*. Washington, D.C.: U.S. Department of Justice, Bureau of Justice Statistics.

Paul, L.A., McCauley, J. L., Ruggiero, K. J., Resnick, H. S., and Kilpatrick, D. G. (2013). College women's experiences with rape disclosure: A national study. *Violence Against Women, 19*(4), 486–502.

Reddington, F. P. and Kreisel, B. W. (2009). *Sexual Assault: The Victims, the Perpetrators, and the Criminal Justice System* (2nd edition). Durham, N.C.: Carolina Academic Press.

Rennison, C. M., Dragiewicz, M., and DeKeseredy, W. S. (2013). Context matters: Violence against women and reporting to police in rural, suburban, and urban areas. *American Journal of Criminal Justice*, 38, 141–159.

Riedel, M. and Welsh, W. (2002). *Criminal Violence: Patterns, Causes, and Prevention*. Los Angeles: Roxbury Publishing Company.

Rozee, P. and Koss, M. (2001). Rape: A century of resistance. *Psychology of Women Quarterly, 25* (2001), 295–311.

Russell, D. (1986). *The Secret Trauma: Incest in the Lives of Girls and Women*. New York: Basic Books.

Russell, D. (1982). The prevalence and incidence of forcible rape and attempted rape of females. *Victimology: An International Journal, 7* (1–4), 81–93.

Sable, M.R., Danis, F., Mauzy, D.L., and Gallagher, S.K. (2006). Barriers to reporting sexual assault for women and men: Perspectives of college students. *Journal of American College Health, 55*(3), 157–162.

Sampson, R. (2002). *The Problem of Acquaintance Rape of College Students.* Washington D.C.: U.S. Department of Justice, Office of Community Oriented Policing Services *[Problem-Oriented Guides for Police Services #17, 1–45].*

Schwartz, M. and Pitts, V. (1995). Exploring a feminist routine activities approach to explaining sexual assault. *Justice Quarterly, 12* (1), 9–31.

Sinozich, S. and Langton, L. (2014). *Rape and Sexual Assault Victimization Among College-Age Females, 1995–2013.* Washington, D.C.: U.S. Department of Justice, Bureau of Justice Statistics. Retrieved from http://www.bjs.gov/content/pub/pdf/rsavcaf9513.pdf.

Taylor, S.C. and Norma, C. (2012). The "symbolic protest" behind women's reporting of sexual assault crime to police. *Feminist Criminology*, 7(1), 24–47.

Tjaden, P., and Thoennes, N. (2000). *Full Report of the Prevalence, Incidence, and Consequences of Violence Against Women.* Washington, D.C. United States Department of Justice, Office of Justice Programs; National Institute of Justice. Retrieved from http://ncjrs.gov/pdffiles1/nij/183781.pdf?PHPSESSID=d240499cb e6d011c51f08c6d312bef.

Ward, S., Chapman, K., Cohn, E., White, S. and Williams, K. (1991). Acquaintance rape and the college social scene. *Family Relations*, 40, 65–71.

Weiss, K. G. (2009). "Boys will be boys" and other gendered accounts: An exploration of victims' excuses and justifications for unwanted sexual contact and coercion. *Violence Against Women, 15*(7), 810–834.

Weiss, K. G. (2010). Too ashamed to report: deconstructing the shame of sexual assault. *Feminist Criminology, 5*(3), 286–310.

SECTION FIVE

SOCIAL PROBLEMS IN MEDICINE AND HEALTH

Medicine and healthcare are important sociological issues that affect everyone. The quality of health care, in general, has increased dramatically over the decades. A wide range of diseases that were once seen as life-threatening are now managed, cured, or prevented. The main social problem associated with medical care is that everybody does not have equal access to it. Health care is very expensive and represents something that reinforces inequality in society. The purposes of this section are to examine US health care reform, the medicalization of society, mental health issues, and the social problem of unhealthy eating.

● HEALTH CARE DELIVERY IN THE DEVELOPED WORLD

There are two main models of health care delivery that exist in the developed world. In the United States there is a user-pay system, where most people obtain insurance through a health maintenance organization (HMO) to pay for treatment. This is in contrast to the universal health care model that exists in Canada and other developed countries. Under this system, taxes are higher than they are in the United States but social programs like health care are heavily subsidized by the government. Each of these models has its strengths and weaknesses.

The US Health Care System

The American health care system is one of the best in the world. American doctors are trained at some of the highest-ranked medical schools and American hospitals are global leaders in terms of medical research, training, and treatment. People come to the United States from other countries for cancer treatments, bypass operations, and organ transplants. What differentiates the US health care system from the ones in other developed countries is that it is a user-pay system. This means that people are expected to pay for all medical services rendered, either on their own or through insurance coverage provided by an HMO.

Medical procedures and treatments tend to be very expensive in the United States. A typical night in the hospital costs upwards of $1,000, giving birth to a child with no complications costs around $15,000, and having open-heart surgery can easily cost $100,000. Because of these high costs, most HMOs place restrictions on the benefits that they pay in claims. HMOs, like other businesses, are in existence to generate profits. They want to make sure that the premiums that people pay exceed the costs of their claims. As such, they may, for example, only cover three sessions of physical therapy after a broken limb or two nights in the hospital after a woman gives birth.

One of the many social problems associated with American health care is that millions of people lack coverage. Because of the increasing costs of premiums and deductibles, more than 10 percent of the American population does not have any medical insurance. This means that if they require any medical attention they have to pay out-of-pocket for those services, often making payments on a long-term plan to the hospital. The probability is high, however, that the amount owed will be so large that they will default on their payments and even consider bankruptcy. Low-income people and racial minorities are disproportionately uninsured (Kaiser Family Foundation 2015), which results in compounded inequalities for these groups. Ultimately, American health care is greatest for those with the most comprehensive health coverage.

One of the reasons for the inequality in insurance is that those with pre-existing conditions have historically been denied coverage. This means that people diagnosed with such chronic conditions as HIV, epilepsy, or multiple sclerosis would not be able to access insurance after the fact. The cost of managing these conditions with drugs is expensive. Tivicay, for example, is a very effective drug in helping people to manage HIV but costs $14,000 a year. Insurance companies have been reluctant to cover people with chronic conditions because they do not want to lose money. From a business perspective, it does not make much financial sense to cover someone, for example, who pays $6,000 in yearly premiums but will need $20,000 in medical treatment. However, without coverage, most people with chronic conditions cannot afford adequate medical treatment. As such, many argue that denying coverage to people with pre-existing conditions is a social problem.

The Universal Health Care Model

The universal health care model is very different than the American one. In England, Canada, Germany, and other developed countries, health care is considered a right of citizenship. Outside of the United States, taxes are generally higher but the government uses that money to subsidize education, health care, and other social programs. Therefore, people living in these countries have access to the medical treatment that they need. In these countries, there are no co-pays or restrictions placed upon people with pre-existing conditions. This system is by no means perfect, however. Oftentimes, people outside of the United States are subject to long waits and delays compared to Americans. Moreover, the hospitals outside of the United States tend to have less recent technology and fewer amenities than their American counterparts.

Obamacare

One of the first issues that President Obama tackled after he took office was health care reform. He sought to overhaul the existing system and implement a variety of controversial changes. First, he wanted people with pre-existing conditions to be able to access health insurance. Second, he wanted everyone to be covered. In fact, people would be fined if they did not have coverage. Third, he wanted any business with more than two hundred employees to be mandated to cover their employees' health coverage costs. Fourth, he advocated for the creation of the health care marketplace and a government insurance option to compete with for-profit insurance companies and lower the costs of plans.

Written by James Petre, Chapter 17 is entitled "An Examination of Public Support for the Affordable Care Act." In this chapter, Petre offers a detailed history of this controversial legislation and establishes why health care reform has been such a contentious issue in American politics for the last seventy years. Even though many Americans are supportive of insurance companies being obligated to cover people with pre-existing conditions and of raising the age that young people can remain on their parents' coverage, the Affordable Care Act (ACA) has become politicized. Liberals have been more likely to endorse the plan while most conservatives have derided it, seeing it as an expression of socialism and even "un-American." Petre's chapter concludes by examining the implications of health care reform.

● THE MEDICALIZED SOCIETY

Many people also consider the increasing medicalization of American life to be a social problem. Medicalization can be defined as the process through which conditions or behaviors become defined as medical problems requiring medical solutions. Some examples of medicalized conditions are attention-deficit/hyperactivity disorder, anxiety, menopause, infertility, sex addiction, chronic dry eye syndrome, and obesity. They have become defined in medical terms, are now described using medical language, and are subsequently treated with medical interventions. There are degrees of medicalization in that not all conditions are universally acknowledged as medical problems. However, there are typically interested parties who gain from such acknowledgment. For example, doctors and pharmaceutical companies benefit from conditions being seen as medical, as people then have to see doctors and are frequently prescribed medications as a result of diagnosis.

The concerns that people have with the process of medicalization are threefold. First, it assumes that any problem that people experience can be diagnosed and treated medically, when many conditions may have numerous sources that are left uncovered in the medical process. Second, it overemphasizes pharmaceutical treatment and underemphasizes cognitive and social treatment of ailments. It is simpler to write a prescription for a drug than it is to fix a person's family problems or help them learn how to read. Third, it reinforces the superiority of the Western medical model over the naturopathic and holistic practices that are used in many parts of the world. Although acupuncture, nutrition, and meditation are widely accepted practices for promoting health, mainstream medical practitioners reject them as ineffective and unnecessary.

● MENTAL HEALTH

Millions of Americans suffer from mental health problems ranging from anxiety to schizophrenia. The medical model of mental illness assumes that mental illness is measurable with scientific tests and that the source of the disorder is biochemical in nature. Psychotropic medications are the most common treatment, although talk therapy is often recommended. In response, sociologists emphasize the subjectivity involved in the defining and diagnosing of mental illnesses. We point out that mental distress reflects a particular social setting as well as individual behavior or biology. Sociologists are also concerned about the social and psychological consequences of psychotropic medications.

Regardless of what causes mental distress, or how we respond to it, the suffering itself is real. And it is certainly an improvement that Americans are discussing these issues rather than hiding them, as Americans have done for generations. Mental illness is still stigmatized, however, and is physically and emotionally debilitating for numerous Americans.

One group of people who are especially susceptible to anxiety and depression are college students. In their article entitled "The Prevalence and Correlates of Depression Among College Students," Lindsey, Fabiano, and Stark establish that the amount of stress that college students experience is very high. In their study of 618 students at Western Washington University, the authors found that one in four respondents experienced depression in the past year. Students suffering from depression were more likely to also be experiencing such issues as chronic pain, learning disabilities, relationship difficulties, and stress. Rates of depression were also higher among students who rated their overall health as being fair or poor, smoked cigarettes, or identified as being LGBT. The authors provide some ways in which colleges can help prevent or respond to students' depression.

● UNHEALTHY EATING

A final social problem addressed in this section concerns Americans' eating habits. In her chapter, "From Basic 7 to MyPlate: How the USDA Attempts to Promote Healthy Eating," Elizabeth Petre establishes that Americans tend to eat unhealthily. The typical American diet is not only high in fat, sugar, and salt, but many foods, including bacon and sausage, are linked to a host of medical ailments including high blood pressure, stroke, diabetes, and cancer. As a way to promote healthy eating and educate the American public about nutrition, the United States Department of Agriculture (USDA) has produced a number of different food guides. Petre traces the history of these food guides and evaluates each of them. Her piece concludes by working through many of the challenges that exist when it comes to promoting healthy eating around the country.

References

Kaiser Family Foundation. 2015. *Key Facts About the Uninsured Population.* Menlo Park, CA: Author. http://kff.org/uninsured/fact-sheet/key-facts-about-the-uninsured-population/.

CHAPTER 17

An Examination of Public Support for the Affordable Care Act

By James T. Petre

The United States spends more money on health care than any other nation ("Why Is Obamacare So Controversial?" 2014). Paradoxically, it does not provide universal health care coverage for its citizens (Vladeck 2003). Although particular programs differ, virtually all other developed nations provide health care coverage for their citizens. The fact that many Americans either do not have, or have inadequate coverage is a social problem that continues to vex the United States. While the Patient Protection and Affordable Care Act of 2010 (ACA) does not provide universal coverage, it constitutes a significant step in this direction. However, the ACA (often referred to as "Obamacare") remains less than popular in public opinion polls.

There are both simple and complex reasons for the ACA's relative unpopularity among Americans. The simple answer to why the ACA is unpopular is that the so-called *public option* was removed during final negotiations over the bill. The more complex answer to the ACA's unpopularity lies in ideological differences among Americans regarding the proper role of government.

Put simply, conservatives are unified in their opposition to the ACA, considering it a government overreach. Meanwhile, liberals are split on the issue. Although a significant portion of liberals support the ACA, other liberals oppose it because they believe it does not go far enough to provide universal coverage. The purpose of this chapter is to trace the history of the ACA and to examine why it is so controversial. Several significant implications and strategies going forward will also be discussed.

● WHAT IS THE AFFORDABLE CARE ACT?

Passed in 2010 and phased in through a series of steps over ensuing years, the Patient Protection and Affordable Care Act of 2010 is a significant and controversial piece of legislation. While the bill fell short of offering universal health insurance coverage, several key reforms were implemented.[1] For example, insurance companies could no longer deny coverage due to a pre-existing condition;[2] Medicaid was expanded to provide coverage to citizens earning low incomes; children could stay covered on their parents' health insurance plan until the age of twenty-six; and health insurance exchanges were created to allow consumers to compare different plans and buy their own health insurance ("Summary of the Affordable Care Act" 2013).

The ACA also included an individual mandate requiring that all American citizens and legal residents have qualifying health coverage ("Summary of the Affordable Care Act" 2013, 2), and the creation of the health care exchanges was supposed to foster competition and help keep costs low. The bill required everyone to have health insurance to ensure that healthy people as well as sick people purchased insurance. If a person did not receive coverage through his or her employer, he or she would be required to purchase it. However, subsidies would be offered for those who could not afford to purchase insurance on their own ("Summary of the Affordable Care Act" 2013).

As stated above, the bill was controversial, and passed only after a long and arduous process. In the end, the bill received absolutely no Republican support in Congress (House of Representatives or Senate), and many concessions were made to keep several disaffected Democrats on board. This process will be explained in more detail below. However, before the specifics are discussed, some important concepts and contexts must be explained.

● KEY TERMS

There are several key terms to consider in relation to the issue of health care reform. Specifically, it is critical to have a clear understanding of what the concepts *universal health care*, *single-payer*, and *public option* refer to. According to the World Health Organization (WHO), "the goal of universal health coverage is to ensure that all people obtain the health services they need without suffering financial hardship when paying for them" ("What is Universal Health Coverage?" 2014, 1). The United States stands out as one of a very small number of developed nations that does not provide universal health care (Fisher 2012, 1).

The ACA created several health insurance exchanges and required that people purchase their own insurance through these exchanges if they did not already have insurance through their employer. Thus, the ACA has helped to bring the United States closer to universal coverage, as recent data indicate that the uninsured rate is the lowest on record (Broaddus and Park 2015). However, according to Census data, 10.4 percent of the population still do not have health insurance coverage (Smith and Medalia 2015). While this number is down from recent years and indicates that progress is being made, the social problem of providing universal health insurance coverage still has not been solved.

Another key term is *single-payer*. As explained on the Physicians for a National Health Program website,

> Single-payer national health insurance, also known as "Medicare for all," is a system in which a single public or quasi-public agency organizes health care financing, but the delivery of care remains largely in private hands. Under a single-payer system, all residents of the U.S. would be covered for all medically necessary services, including doctor, hospital, preventive, long-term care, mental health, reproductive health care, dental, vision, prescription drug and medical supply costs. ("What is Single Payer?" 2016, 2)

Throughout the history of health care reform efforts, the idea of a single-payer system emerged repeatedly, but never received passage in the United States. It is important to note that while single-payer health care is often inaccurately labeled as "government-run health care … it is government *financed* health care, but all of the players—doctors, nurses, hospitals, drug companies, medical device companies, and so on—remain private" (Altman and Shactman 2011, 68–69). Although many nations have universal health care, relatively few follow a pure single-payer model to achieve universal coverage.

Two examples of nations that use a single-payer model are Canada and Taiwan (Rovner 2016). This raises the question of how other nations offer universal health care to their citizens if they do not follow the single-payer model. Some countries use a mixed public–private system that guarantees basic coverage for everyone, while giving wealthy citizens the option to purchase supplemental coverage through a private insurer (Khazan 2016, 4–5). Others, like Germany, have plans that resemble the ACA but are more affordable for patients since the insurance companies are less profit oriented than American insurers (Khazan 2016, 4). In the United States, citizens must purchase their own insurance (if it is not provided through an employer). However, they are limited to choosing among different for-profit insurance companies, rather than a mix of public (or non-profit) and for-profit insurance providers.

This difference in choices available in the United States as opposed to many other nations of the world calls forth the importance of the final key term: the *public option*. According to Brasfield (2011, 456), the "public option" refers to the creation of "a publicly sponsored insurance entity" that would "compete with private plans." In other words, when choosing between health care plans on an open marketplace, a consumer could elect to purchase insurance through a public entity or a private entity. Proponents of the public option supported the idea because it was a mechanism to control costs (Holahan and Blumberg 2009). If private providers charged too much on their premiums, consumers could choose the public option if they found it to be more affordable. Alternatively, if wealthy citizens wished to purchase an insurance plan that offered more deluxe features, they could choose to purchase a more expensive private plan. The public option was one of the most popular features of the ACA while the bill was being debated. Unfortunately, as will be discussed later in this chapter, the public option was removed from the final version of the bill passed by Congress.

The concepts *universal health care*, *single-payer*, and *public option* are important to the present discussion, and will be referenced throughout this essay. Along with providing an understanding of these key concepts, it is also important to briefly explain the historical context of health care reform efforts in the United States. Although the ACA is a relatively new law, health care reform is an issue that has been debated for decades.

● HISTORICAL CONTEXT

There is a long and fascinating history when it comes to health care reform in the United States.[3] However, far more twists and turns exist regarding health care reform than can be fully recounted in these pages. Since it is not possible to provide an exhaustive explanation of every development, I will instead provide a brief overview of the major moments and efforts regarding health care reform, with a focus on those most pertinent to the present topic.

It is interesting to note that the notion of a governmental role in ensuring comprehensive health care dates back to the founding of the nation. According to Emanuel (2014, 127), "There was compulsory health coverage in Revolutionary America. In 1790 the very first US Congress enacted a law requiring owners of ships of more than 150 tons to buy medical insurance for their seamen." While few steps were taken over the next several decades (in the United States or elsewhere), several other nations instituted health care reform in the late nineteenth and early twentieth centuries, beginning with Germany in 1883 (Emanuel 2014). However, little action regarding health care reform took place in the United States until 1912, and a comprehensive health care plan eluded passage until the ACA was passed by Congress and signed into law by President Obama in 2010 (Emanuel 2014).

When Theodore Roosevelt (unsuccessfully) ran for president in 1912, he made national health insurance a part of his campaign (Emanuel 2014, 129). That same year, the American Association of Labor Legislation (AALL) formed a "committee on social welfare" and focused on health insurance (Palmer 1999).

In 1915, the AALL proposed a plan that would "insure low-income workers and their dependents" (Altman and Shactman 2011, 97). The American Medical Association (AMA) actually supported the plan initially, but it was opposed by the American Federation of Labor (AFL) because AFL president Samuel Gompers thought benefits should be provided by unions, rather than the government (Altman and Shactman 2011). To make matters more difficult for reformers, the AMA decided to reverse its position and no longer supported the AALL plan (Altman and Shactman 2011). US entry into World War I in 1917 was the final nail in the coffin for this early reform, because national health insurance was seen as a "German" idea (since, as mentioned above, Germany was the first nation to pass health care reform in 1883 [Palmer 1999]). In addition, during the "Red Scare," opponents of a national health care plan associated the idea with socialism (Palmer 1999).

Talk of health care reform did not re-emerge in a significant way until Franklin D. Roosevelt's presidency. Roosevelt's administration elected to leave health care reform out of the 1935 Social Security Act because many worried that it would compromise passage (Palmer 1999). Roosevelt would try again later, in 1938, when he made national health a priority in the 1938 midterm elections (Altman and Shactman 2011). Unfortunately for proponents of health care reform, this support was short lived because the midterm elections that year resulted in conservative gains in Congress, making further actions on social policy very difficult (Palmer 1999, 4). Thus, when Senator Robert Wagner tried to pass a bill that would create national health insurance, "FDR did not endorse the effort, and it was easily defeated by political opponents and the AMA" (Altman and Shactman 2011, 101). Later, the Wagner-Murray-Dingell Bill would be initially proposed in 1943 and reintroduced in every congressional session for fourteen years, but failed to gain passage, despite Harry Truman's support for a national health insurance plan (Palmer 1999). In fact, Truman emphasized health care reform in the 1948 election, but opponents successfully defeated efforts at reform by again linking it to socialism (Palmer 1999).

Efforts at health care reform would lay dormant until the election of John F. Kennedy, as Medicare was an important component of John F. Kennedy's domestic agenda (Altman and Shactman 2011). However, it would not be passed until 1965 (Altman and Shactman 2011), two years after Lyndon Johnson became president following Kennedy's tragic assassination. This time, more effort was directed at taking a piecemeal approach. Rather than a national health insurance program, the focus was on creating a program that would provide health insurance for the elderly and the poor. Thus, Medicare Part A, Medicare Part B, and Medicaid were born (Altman and Shactman 2011). While it was piecemeal in the sense that it did not cover everyone, many people, mostly political liberals, were hopeful that it would be represent a first step toward single-payer health care (Altman and Shactman 2011).

A few years later, Richard Nixon sought to shepherd a national health care bill through Congress in the early 1970s (Emanuel 2014). In fact, Nixon's plan was quite similar to the ACA of 2010 (Altman and Shactman 2011). However, because of Nixon's involvement in the Watergate scandal (and eventual resignation), and House Ways and Means Chairman Wilbur Mills's involvement in a sex scandal, "health care reform drowned along with Nixon's presidency and Wilbur Mills's political career" (Altman and Shactman 2011, 17). Once again, while reforms were pursued in the intervening years, comprehensive health care reform would not be addressed again in a significant way until Bill Clinton was elected president in 1992.

The issue of health care reform received a great deal of attention in the 1992 campaign, and Bill Clinton's administration focused on passing a comprehensive health care plan following his election victory. Rather than a single-payer system, Clinton supported the idea of managed competition (Emanuel 2014, 149), a system in which health insurers compete against one another in a regulated marketplace (Altman and Shactman 2011). Shortly after his inauguration, Clinton created the Task Force on National Health Care Reform, which was chaired by Hillary Clinton (Emanuel 2014, 149). The resulting bill (known as the Health Security Act) ended up being 1,342 pages long when it was submitted to Congress in November 1993 (Emanuel 2014, 149). The Clinton plan "included an employer mandate [to provide health insurance to employees], a government-defined benefit package, fifty state-based health alliances, a national health board, insurance premium caps, and a global budget" (Altman and Shactman 2011, 94). However, as seen with previous efforts, his administration met several roadblocks in Congress, and the bill failed to gain passage.

The Democrats lost their congressional majority in the 1994 midterm elections, and Bill Clinton spent the rest of his presidency with a Republican majority in Congress. Thus, efforts at a national health plan remained stalled. After Republican George W. Bush took office in 2000, discussion and debate over a national health insurance plan did not re-emerge until Barack Obama's election in 2008, which led to the eventual passage of the ACA. While far from perfect, the ACA constituted the first successful effort at passing a national health insurance plan, almost one hundred years after the efforts of Teddy Roosevelt in 1912 and the AALL in 1915.

● THE AFFORDABLE CARE ACT

The prospect of universal health care was not addressed after the failure of the Health Security Act of 1994 until it re-emerged as a campaign issue in the 2008 presidential election. Several candidates in the 2008 election focused on health care reform, and Barack Obama continued to push for a national health care plan following his victory in the 2008 election over John McCain. However, it is important to note the context of the beginning of Obama's presidency in 2009. The nation was in the depths of the Great Recession, and Obama's first major policy initiative was the passage of the American Recovery and Reinvestment Act of 2009 to try to get the economy moving again. Had the economy been in a better state, the formation and passage of the ACA may have taken a different shape.

As stated above, the ACA was passed after a long and arduous process that took a little over one year. The Obama administration held its first "health care summit" on March 5, 2009, and the final version of the ACA passed on March 21, 2010 (Smith 2012). There was initial hope for a bipartisan health care bill, as Senators Max Baucus (a Democrat) and Charles Grassley (a Republican) formed the "gang of six" (consisting of three Democrats and three Republicans) to find a bipartisan compromise (Altman and Shactman 2011). Unfortunately, "Republican senators came under intense pressure from their leadership not to reach any compromise with Democrats" (Altman and Shactman 2011, 276). Furthermore, several members of Congress were confronted in town hall meetings held in August 2009 by angry Tea Party members and conservatives opposed to health care reform (Smith 2012). However, the Democrats still had large enough majorities in the House and Senate at that time to pass the ACA (through various stages between fall 2009 and spring 2010) without any Republican support. The House bill was passed on November 7, 2009, and the Senate bill was passed on December 24, 2009 (Smith 2012). As stated above, the final version of the bill was passed on March 21, 2010. Finally, the Patient Protection and Affordable Care Act of 2010 was signed into law by President Obama on March 23, 2010 (Altman and Shactman 2011).

The ACA contained several important features. The health insurance exchanges created by the ACA were designed in a similar fashion to the Massachusetts health care plan signed into law by former Republican governor Mitt Romney (Dzieza 2012). Rather than a single-payer national health care plan, the ACA required individuals who were not already covered through an employer's health insurance plan to purchase their own insurance coverage ("Summary of the Affordable Care Act" 2013). Subsidies were to be included for individuals who could not afford the full cost of an insurance plan, and Medicaid would be expanded to those who earned low incomes but did not previously qualify. Furthermore, "individuals and small businesses with up to 100 employees" would be able to purchase insurance through health insurance exchanges ("Summary of the Affordable Care Act" 2013). A key component of the ACA that was taken out of the final bill was the public option, which would have allowed individuals to purchase a health insurance plan offered by the government. Having a public option was thought to control costs, as health insurance corporations would have to compete with a non-profit entity and could therefore not engage in price gouging. However, critics claimed that it functioned as a "Trojan horse" that would lead to a single-payer system down the road (Brasfield 2011).

Despite the fact that there were similarities with the Massachusetts plan signed into law by Romney, the ACA was vehemently opposed by Republicans in Congress. While there were several reasons for GOP opposition, some, like Republican Senate Leader Mitch McConnell, believed a bipartisan bill was more likely to be accepted by the public (Ornstein 2015, 6). This opposition also fit into a broader GOP strategy to "fight Obama on everything," which was devised in a meeting of Republican leaders on the night of Obama's inauguration in 2009 (Khan 2013). Others argued that the Massachusetts plan was acceptable because it was implemented by an individual state, but it would be inappropriate for the federal government to mandate health insurance coverage.[4]

Since the bill received no Republican support, Democratic leaders were forced to ensure that few Democrats (particularly in the Senate) opposed the bill. It was especially important to make sure that absolutely no Democratic senators would be willing to filibuster the bill. Throughout most of the process, the Democrats had a "filibuster-proof" majority in the Senate (i.e., 60 votes) that could pass health care legislation if all Democrats were on board (or at least willing to allow the legislation to come up for a vote without a filibuster).[5] However, the relatively weak position brought about by absolutely no GOP support forced the Democratic leadership to make concessions to appease unsatisfied Democratic senators. For example, Senator Joe Lieberman[6] opposed having a public option in the bill, and "said he would vote for the bill only if the public option was stripped out" (Potter 2015, 2). Furthermore, a few conservative Democrats, including Senator Ben Nelson, threatened to filibuster the bill if there was a public option included (Klein 2013, 1).

Opposition from Lieberman, Nelson, and others forced the popular public option to be removed from the final version of the ACA bill. While concessions like these allowed the ACA to eventually pass and become law, the bill was less popular than it was when it contained a public option. Understanding the implications of these concessions is critical to the investigation of why the ACA is still unpopular with the American public. As I will demonstrate below, the ACA enjoyed greater popularity prior to the removal of the public option from the bill. However, once the public option was removed, support for the ACA never fully recovered.

The various struggles and controversies surrounding the passage of the ACA called forth a significant amount of scholarly investigation. In what follows, I provide a brief overview of several scholarly contributions. Following this review, I investigate the impact jettisoning the public option had on public opinion regarding the ACA.

● STUDIES OF THE AFFORDABLE CARE ACT

Since the ACA constituted a landmark piece of legislation and was considerably controversial, a plethora of studies exist regarding its passage and implementation. For example, several scholars investigated public opinion and different interpretations related to the new law. Specifically, Corman and Levin (2016, 114) provided an exhaustive overview of public polling data in order to explore changes in Americans' views on how involved the government should be in health care. The authors compared Americans' current perceptions of government involvement in health care with perceptions that were held prior to the debate over the ACA, and examined whether passage of the ACA led to a decrease in public support of government involvement (Corman and Levin 2016, 115). While Americans' opinions seemed to fluctuate based on a current issue or concern, they found that there is a certain "equilibrium range" that Americans eventually come back to (Corman and Levin 2016, 174).

Richardson and Konisky (2013) also studied public opinion regarding health care. They used a survey to assess prospective and retrospective evaluations of Americans' attitudes toward health care reform, and how these would affect voting behaviors (Richardson and Konisky 2013). Prospective indicates "that voters seek to elect political parties that they believe will do the best job of representing their interests," while retrospective means "that vote choice is largely a referendum on the incumbent administration" (Richardson and Konisky 2013, 923). Within prospective and retrospective evaluations, Americans had differing views based on whether they focused on how health care reform would affect them personally (i.e., personal assessments) versus how it would impact society more broadly (i.e., collective assessments) (Richardson and Konisky 2013). Specifically, they found that personal and collective prospective assessments, as well as collective retrospective assessments, were important factors, but that personal retrospective evaluations were mixed (Richardson and Konisky 2013, 922). Thus, Richardson and Konisky (2013, 950) conclude the following:

> Citizens' perceptions of the reform were … partly driven by their collective (and sometimes personal) assessments of the current US health care system, as well as their expectations about how the reform would affect their future health care and that of their family and the country as a whole.

Both studies mentioned above are quite illuminating in terms of understanding how Americans view the issue of health care reform in broad terms, and what serves as a basis for shaping those viewpoints.

Other scholars investigated party identification and additional factors as predictors of agreement or disagreement with the passage and implementation of the ACA. For example, Hindman (2012) argues that political party identification, rather than education level, was a significant predictor of one's knowledge about specific aspects of the ACA. Furthermore, Hindman (2012, 598) states,

> Republicans appeared to know less about the components in the health care law in April of 2010 than they did three months earlier. In an era of political polarization in which political elites map themselves into intractable positions opposite that of their opponents, knowledge of heavily publicized and politically contested issues does not accumulate; instead, *beliefs about knowledge* accumulate in directions that serve the political objectives of the parties.

Hindman's study demonstrates that, in the current era of hyper-partisanship, one's politics (rather than education level) are more illustrative when trying to discern that person's level of knowledge about a controversial issue such as the ACA.

Additional predictors of one's perceptions regarding the ACA are one's tendencies toward nativist beliefs and stereotyping. Knoll and Shewmaker (2015, 88–89) argue that people inclined toward nativist beliefs were more likely to accept a link between "un-American foreign-ness" and the ACA. In fact, the authors found that nativism had a stronger effect than economic self-interest or racial resentment in terms of determining one's attitude toward the ACA (Knoll and Shewmaker 2015). Wetherell, Reyna, and Sadler (2013, 61) examined stereotypes about people who would potentially purchase a public option (if one existed), and found that they "were stereotyped as *low-status* value violators." Interestingly, "whether or not beneficiaries are seen as violating values of hard work was the most consistent predictor of attitudes toward reform policies" (Wetherell, Reyna, and Sadler 2013, 61). Taken as a whole, these studies demonstrate the role that partisanship, tendencies toward nativism, and stereotyping can play in predicting one's perception of the ACA and its related policies.

Additional studies examine issues and controversies specific to the ACA itself. For example, Elder (2015) provides an overview of the difficulties surrounding the problematic and widely criticized rollout of the health care exchange through the Healthcare.gov website in 2013. She claims that "state resistance to the ACA" and "the fundamental way the government does business" both contributed to the failings of the initial rollout of Healthcare.gov (Elder 2015, 3481–82). For instance, the government relied on large contractors rather than smaller IT firms, which could have allowed more productivity in the management of the website's rollout (Elder 2015). Despite the rough beginnings, Elder (2015, 3482) notes that "one could argue that Healthcare.gov was a success" because "the number of people the Obama administration had initially set as an enrollment benchmark had been met and exceeded."

Finally, Hopper (2015) explores how the use of the term "Obamacare" rather than the "Affordable Care Act" functions in the media. She argues that linking "Obamacare" to negative coverage about health care reform allowed Obama's opponents to effectively define this legislative accomplishment in a negative light (Hopper 2015). However, she also notes,

> As the effort to reframe Obamacare was followed by a modest increase in positive news content across all four media outlets and (except in the *Times*) a substantial increase in neutral content, it stands to reason that a more sustained campaign might have yielded greater success for the president. (1293).

In other words, opponents of the ACA were successful at turning "Obamacare" into a *bad word*, but the president and his administration had success when trying to recover the term and it may be strategically useful for them to continue such efforts.

Clearly, various issues and debates have been thoroughly examined by a multitude of scholars. However, there has not been an investigation into the reasons for the relative unpopularity of the ACA by dissecting the different responses of contemporary public opinion polls. As stated in the beginning of this chapter, I argue that there are both simple and complex reasons for the ACA's relative unpopularity. The simple answer deals with the jettisoning of the public option during negotiations over the ACA's final passage. The more complex answer involves ideological differences among Americans regarding the proper role of government in relation to health care policy. I will address these reasons (both simple and complex) in the remaining sections of this essay.

● PUBLIC SUPPORT FOR THE AFFORDABLE CARE ACT (OR LACK THEREOF)

In trying to understand why the ACA is not more popular with the general public, it can be illuminating to explore the nuances of public opinion poll responses. First, it is important to note that while more people tend to disapprove of it than approve, the level of disapproval is closer to a simple majority. Nevertheless, for the most part, the ACA (when named in a poll) tends to yield more negative responses than positive. For example, a Gallup poll (2015) showed 44 percent of respondents approved of the ACA, while 52 percent disapproved. Similarly, in a Quinnipiac poll (2015), 43 percent of respondents approved while 52 percent disapproved. Although the specific number may move by a few points, the overall trajectory has been one in which more people disapprove of the ACA than approve since it was passed in 2010.

If one simply views polls showing that a majority disapproves of the ACA, one may incorrectly assume that the ACA is seen as a liberal overreach. However, this may not be the case if one looks a little bit deeper into the nuances of the poll responses. For example, a recent Kaiser Family Foundation poll (2015) showed that 58 percent of respondents supported a "national health plan in which all Americans would get their insurance through an expanded, universal form of Medicare-for-all." Such a plan would actually be further to the political left than the ACA as currently conceptualized, suggesting that some may oppose the current policy because it does not go far enough toward a single-payer model. In fact, prior to the removal of the public option as part of the ACA, polls consistently demonstrated that it was one of the most popular aspects of the entire proposal. Its importance was evident in a Rasmussen Reports (2009) poll that included the headline "Without [a] public option, enthusiasm for health care reform, especially among Democrats, collapses." Prior to the passage of the bill that removed the public option, 59 percent of respondents to a CBS/*New York Times* poll (2009) favored the inclusion of that option. This viewpoint was reflected in several other polls, as a CNN/Opinion Research Corporation poll (2009b) showed that 61 percent of respondents supported a public option, and in an ABC/*Washington Post* poll (2009), 53 percent of respondents also supported a public option.[7] While polls soliciting opinions regarding the ACA as a whole fluctuated between support and disapproval prior to the removal of the public option,[8] after the public option was removed from the bill support for the ACA fell to under 50 percent, and is yet to fully resurface.[9]

These issues point to the fact that several respondents may claim they disapprove of the ACA, but it is because they feel the ACA should go further than it currently does to expand coverage and control costs. For example, in a CNN/ORC poll (2015), 43 percent of respondents said they favored the ACA, while 55 percent opposed it. However, an additional question asked respondents if they disapproved because it was "too liberal" or "not liberal enough." Taking these numbers into account, 43 percent of respondents supported the ACA, 15 percent opposed because it was not liberal enough, while 37 percent opposed because it was too liberal (the remaining 3% said that they opposed the ACA for "another reason"). Based on these findings, it appears that adding a public option to the ACA would draw a solid majority of support among Americans. This line of thinking is borne out in a CBS/*New York Times* poll (2014), in which 59 percent of respondents favored a "government-administered health insurance plan—something like the Medicare coverage that people 65 and older get—that would compete with private health insurance plans."

Furthermore, when people are asked about their opinion regarding specific aspects of the ACA (rather than the name itself or "Obamacare"), a majority of respondents tend to express positive sentiments. For example, in a Reuters poll, 56 percent opposed the ACA overall, while 44 percent supported it (Zengerle 2012). However, when asked about specific aspects of the bill, 82 percent supported the ban on denying coverage for pre-existing conditions, and 61 percent supported children being able to stay on their parents' insurance plan until age twenty-six. At the same time, only 39 percent supported the individual mandate, while 61 percent opposed it. These results underscore the complexities of the ACA. While the individual mandate tends to be unpopular, it is necessary in order to be able to ban the denial of coverage due to a pre-existing condition. In other words, the system would not work if younger and healthier people are not required to purchase insurance to be able to offset the costs of those who are more expensive to insure. These numbers demonstrate that it is a misconception to interpret the entire ACA as unpopular, and I argue that including a public option as a competitor in the marketplace would make the ACA more popular as a whole.

As stated above, removing the public option provides a simple explanation of why the ACA is not supported by a majority of Americans. However, I argue that this is only one piece of the puzzle. A related but broader issue speaks to the dynamics of differing perceptions among Americans regarding the proper role of government. By and large, as noted above, the ACA is opposed by conservatives (who tend to identify as Republicans, but some identify as right-leaning independents). In some instances, this opposition may be due to a desire to prevent President Obama and the Democrats from achieving a historic policy milestone. In other instances, it may be due to philosophical disagreement over the approach taken in the law.

Conservatives are typically opposed to government intervention in the marketplace, and tend to oppose the ACA because they do not believe that the government should play a role in mandating or providing health insurance coverage for Americans (particularly at the federal level). Most likely, someone supporting a conservative position on health care would argue that health care costs are high due to too much regulation and too many malpractice lawsuits. Thus, a way to cut costs (from a conservative point of view) would be to cut regulations and implement tort reform.[10] In addition to cutting regulations, conservatives typically support more tax cuts to allow Americans to keep more of their own money (which could presumably be used to purchase their own health insurance if it is not provided by their employer). They also (but not always) may favor state governments playing a role in promoting health insurance exchanges to foster competition in the marketplace (and may even support a mandate to purchase insurance, as Romney did in the plan he signed into law as governor of

Massachusetts), but not to mandate coverage or impose regulations at the federal level.

Meanwhile, liberals (who typically identify as Democrats, but some identify as left-leaning independents) are more divided over the ACA. Liberals are typically more supportive of the idea of the government (including the federal government) intervening in the marketplace than conservatives are. Thus, liberals tend to be more comfortable with government playing a role in health care reform than conservatives, and many liberals support the ACA. However, other liberals express disapproval with the ACA because they think it does not do enough to control costs and provide universal coverage. By and large, liberal opponents of the ACA want at least a public option, and would likely prefer a single-payer plan that guarantees coverage to all Americans.

The solid opposition to the ACA by conservatives and the divided support among liberals skews the numbers and makes it seem like the ACA is unpopular due to a government overreach. However, I argue that in fact it is unpopular to some (mostly conservatives) because they see it as a government overreach, and it is also unpopular with others (mostly liberals) because they think it does not go far enough. Meanwhile, independents may align themselves in a variety of ways along this spectrum. Thus, the popularity of the ACA (or lack thereof) cannot simply be viewed with a binary "like/don't like" lens.

● IMPLICATIONS

It is clear that most politicians have a plan to address (if not solve) the social problem of providing universal health insurance coverage. However, these plans differ greatly based on one's political and ideological affiliations. By and large, Republicans (who tend to be conservative) want to solve the problem through some combination of private competition, tort reform, and tax credits. Democrats (who tend to be liberal) are more divided. Some Democrats also support private market solutions, while others support the idea of a single-payer national insurance plan. A compromise among Democrats could exist in the form of adding a public option to the ACA. However, when Republican influence is also factored in, implementing this compromise would be difficult due to GOP unity against such a plan. Future successes and failures related to the ACA and its policies will likely determine the direction future Congresses, presidents, and citizens take regarding health care reform. If Republicans fail to repeal the ACA, and Democrats are able to successfully implement a public option, the ACA may enjoy a renaissance of support among the general public.

Oddly enough (considering the opposition of the usually pro-business Republicans), one major reason for supporting universal health care is that it could promote entrepreneurship and mobility. On the White House blog, Furman (2014, 5) points out that "before the ACA, many Americans' only source of secure health insurance coverage was through their jobs." People would be reluctant to switch jobs or start their own businesses out of fear of losing their health care. According to Furman (2014, 6), the passage of the ACA

> allows people to take risks that further their careers and benefit the economy as a whole, like going part-time in order to go back to school, leaving a job in order to start a business, or moving to a better job, perhaps at an employer that does not offer coverage.

While I would agree with Furman that the ACA addresses this issue somewhat, a major shortcoming of the ACA as it is currently constituted is that there is no mechanism in place to control costs, which can reduce one's willingness to take a risk. As noted above, due to the lack of a public option, the ACA essentially created health insurance exchanges with the hope that competition among insurance companies would keep down costs. Although the law requires certain thresholds of coverage, there is nothing in place that ensures competition, or prevents companies from charging excessive premiums. A public option would have served this exact purpose, but was removed.[11]

Nevertheless, taken as a whole, the health insurance marketplace created by the ACA does promote greater competition than existed previously. This, along with other provisions such as banning denial of coverage due to pre-existing conditions and expanding Medicaid, demonstrates that the ACA is an important first step toward universal health insurance coverage. However, US political leadership does not seem to be following through on the interests and desires of their constituencies to improve the ACA. By and large, as noted above, Americans want a public option. I argue that providing one would not hinder competition; it would actually promote it. It would also serve as a mechanism for controlling costs. Furthermore, it could benefit the economy in unanticipated ways. The existence of a public option could encourage individuals to start businesses, and not be forced to stay in jobs simply for their insurance coverage. Finally, including a public option would likely make the ACA more popular with the public and bring the United States closer to universal coverage.

While moderately unpopular, the ACA contains many elements that garner public support, so it is still too early to judge it as a success or a failure. Instead, I hope this chapter has fleshed out some of the nuances of the US health care debate and provided more complex ways of understanding public opinion regarding the ACA. While the ACA serves as an important step toward universal coverage, it is clear that the social problem of providing health insurance coverage to all Americans is far from solved. In essence, the ACA serves as a beginning, not an end, to negotiating our way toward a resolution.

● NOTES

1. For purposes of simplicity, I focus on a few of the most well-known elements of the ACA. For a helpful overview of the entire law, see the Kaiser Family Foundation's "Summary of the Affordable Care Act" (2013).

2. A pre-existing condition refers to "people who have a health condition (such as an illness or pregnancy) or who are at higher than average risk of needing health care" (Claxton, Pollitz, and Levitt 2012, 1).

3. For a comprehensive history of US health care reform movements, see Altman and Shactman (2011) and Emanuel (2014).

4. In a controversial 5–4 ruling in 2012, the Supreme Court "upheld the mandate as a tax," but "concluded it was not valid as an exercise of Congress' commerce clause power" (Sacks 2012, 1).

5. Republican Scott Brown won a special election to the Senate following Ted Kennedy's death, which ended the Democrats' filibuster-proof majority (Cooper 2010). Instead, the Democrats would pass the final version of the ACA through a process known as "reconciliation," in which they could "bypass the filibuster in the Senate" (Ornstein 2015, 7).

6. Joe Lieberman actually won re-election in 2006 as an independent, but still caucused with the Democrats (Simon 2008).

7. While there are fluctuations among the various polls, almost all of the polls showed a majority of support for a public option.

8. For example, a CNN/Opinion Research Corporation poll (2009a) taken in September 2009 showed that 51 percent of respondents favored "Barack Obama's plan to reform health care." However, a Quinnipiac University poll (2009) taken later that month showed that only 40 percent of respondents supported his plan and 47 percent opposed. This divergence is indicative of the fluctuation in different polls at this time.

9. There were a few minor exceptions. For example, in a Kaiser Family Foundation poll (2010) taken in July 2010, 50 percent of respondents expressed a favorable opinion of the ACA. However, this is the only instance of support reaching 50 percent or above in this monthly tracking poll between June 2010 and January 2016.

10. Tort reform involves the capping of medical awards and damages in lawsuits. Generally speaking, conservatives favor this more than liberals.

11. I argue elsewhere that Obama and the Democrats could have been tougher negotiators to ensure the preservation of the public option in the final bill (see Petre 2012).

● REFERENCES

ABC News/Washington Post poll [Health policy]. 2009. *Polling Report*, November 12–15. http://www.pollingreport.com/health9.htm.

Altman, S., and D. Shactman. 2011. *Power, Politics, and Universal Health Care: The Inside Story of a Century-Long Battle.* Amherst, NY: Prometheus Books.

Brasfield, J. 2011. "The Politics of Ideas: Where Did the Public Option Come from and Where Is It Going?" *Journal of Health Politics, Policy and Law* 36 (3): 455–59.

Broaddus, M., and E. Park. 2015. "Census Data Show Historic Coverage Gains in 2014." *Center on Budget and Policy Priorities*, September 18. http://www.cbpp.org/research/health/census-data-show-historic-coverage-gains-in-2014.

CBS News/New York Times poll [Health policy]. 2009. *Polling Report*, December 4–8. http://www.pollingreport.com/health9.htm

CBS News/New York Times poll [Health policy]. 2014. *Polling Report*, December 4–7. http://www.pollingreport.com/prioriti.htm.

Claxton, G., K. Pollitz, and L. Levitt. 2012. "What Do They Mean When They Talk About Pre-Existing Health Conditions?" *The Henry J. Kaiser Family Foundation*, October 19. http://kff.org/health-reform/perspective/what-do-they-mean-when-they-talk-about-pre-existing-health-conditions/.

CNN/Opinion Research Corporation poll [Health policy]. 2009a. *Polling Report*, September 11–13. http://pollingreport.com/health10.htm.

CNN/Opinion Research Corporation poll [Health policy]. 2009b. *Polling Report*, October 16–18. http://pollingreport.com/health9.htm.

CNN/ORC poll [Health policy]. 2015. *Polling Report*, May 29–31 http://pollingreport.com/health2.htm.

Cooper, M. 2010. "G.O.P. Senate Victory Stuns Democrats." *The New York Times*, January 19. http://www.nytimes.com/2010/01/20/us/politics/20election.html?_r=0.

Corman, J., and D. Levin. 2016. "The Polls—Trends: Support for Government Provision of Health Care and the Patient Protection and Affordable Care Act." *Public Opinion Quarterly* 80 (1): 114–79.

Dzieza, J. 2012. "Romneycare and Obamacare Differ Only in Inconsequential Ways." *The Daily Beast*, March 6. http://www.thedailybeast.com/articles/2012/03/06/romneycare-and-obamacare-differ-only-in-inconsequential-ways.

Elder, K. 2015. "HealthCare Dot Flub: An Examination of the Politics and Administrative Processes Contributing to the Strained Launch of the Federal Health Insurance Exchange." *International Journal of Communication* 9: 3477–84.

Emanuel, E. J. 2014. *Reinventing American Health Care: How the Affordable Care Act Will Improve Our Terribly Complex, Blatantly Unjust, Outrageously Expensive, Grossly Inefficient, Error Prone System.* Philadelphia, PA: PublicAffairs.

Fisher, M. 2012. "Here's a Map of the Countries That Provide Universal Health Care (America's still not on it)." *The Atlantic*, June 28. https://www.theatlantic.com/international/archive/2012/06/heres-a-map-of-the-countries-that-provide-universal-health-care-americas-still-not-on-it/259153/.

Furman, J. 2014. "Six Economic Benefits of the Affordable Care Act." *The White House*, February 6. https://obamawhitehouse.archives.gov/blog/2014/02/06/six-economic-benefits-affordable-care-act.

Gallup poll [Health policy]. 2015. *Polling Report*, November 4–8. http://pollingreport.com/health2.htm.

Hindman, D. B. 2012. "Knowledge Gaps, Belief Gaps, and Public Opinion About Health Care Reform." *Journalism & Mass Communication Quarterly* 89 (4): 585–605.

Holahan, J., and L. J. Blumberg. 2009. "Is the Public Plan Option a Necessary Part of Health Reform?" *The Urban Institute Health Policy Center.* http://www.urban.org/research/publication/public-plan-option-necessary-part-health-reform/view/full_report.

Hopper, J. 2015. "Obamacare, the News Media, and the Politics of 21st-Century Presidential Communication." *International Journal of Communication* 9: 1275–99.

Kaiser Family Foundation poll [Health policy]. 2010. *Polling Report*, July 8–13. http://pollingreport.com/health6.htm.

Kaiser Family Foundation poll [Health policy]. 2015. *Polling Report*, December 1–7. http://pollingreport.com/health2.htm.

Khan, A. 2013. The Republicans' Plan for a New President. *Frontline*, January 15. http://www.pbs.org/wgbh/frontline/article/the-republicans-plan-for-the-new-president/.

Khazan, O. 2016. "Americans Don't Know What "Single Payer" Means." *The Atlantic*, February 26. https://www.theatlantic.com/health/archive/2016/02/people-have-no-idea-what-single-payer-means/471045/.

Klein, E. 2013. "Whatever Happened to the Public Option?" *The Washington Post*, March 22. https://www.washingtonpost.com/news/wonk/wp/2013/03/22/whatever-happened-to-the-public-option/?utm_term=.5313b9ca854c.

Knoll, B. R., and J. Shewmaker. 2015. "'Simply un-American': Nativism and Support for Health Care Reform." *Political Behavior* 37 (1): 87–108.

Ornstein, N. 2015. "The Real Story of Obamacare's Birth." *The Atlantic*, July 6. https://www.theatlantic.com/politics/archive/2015/07/the-real-story-of-obamacares-birth/397742/.

Palmer, K. S. 1999. "A Brief History: Universal Health Care Efforts in the US." *Physicians for a National Health Program.* http://www.pnhp.org/facts/a-brief-history-universal-health-care-efforts-in-the-us.

Petre, J. T. 2012. *Realignments of Doxa in U.S. American Politics: Tracing the Rhetorical Histories of Franklin Roosevelt, Ronald Reagan, and Barack Obama* (Doctoral dissertation). http://opensiuc.lib.siu.edu/dissertations/493/.

Potter, W. 2015. "Elimination of 'Public Option' Threw Consumers to the Insurance Wolves." *Center for Public Integrity*, February 16. https://www.publicintegrity.org/2015/02/16/16766/elimination-public-option-threw-consumers-insurance-wolves.

Quinnipiac University poll [Health policy]. 2009. *Polling Report*, September 29–October 5. http://pollingreport.com/health10.htm.

Quinnipiac University poll [Health policy]. 2015. *Polling Report*, July 23–28. http://pollingreport.com/health2.htm.

Richardson, L., and D. M. Konisky. 2013. "Personal and Collective Evaluations of the 2010 Health Care Reform." *Journal of Health, Policy and Law* 38 (5): 921–56.

Rovner, J. 2016. "Debate Sharpens over Single-Payer Health Care, But What Is It Exactly?" *NPR*, January 22. http://www.npr.org/sections/health-shots/2016/01/22/463976098/debate-sharpens-over-single-payer-health-care-but-what-is-it-exactly.

Sacks, M. 2012). Supreme Court Health Decision: Individual Mandate Survives. *The Huffington Post*, June 28 http://www.huffingtonpost.com/2012/06/28/supreme-court-health-care-decision_n_1585131.html.

Simon, R. 2008. "Lieberman Frustrates Democrats." *Los Angeles Times*, June 12. http://articles.latimes.com/2008/jun/12/nation/na-lieberman12.

Smith, E. 2012. "Timeline of the Health Care Law." *CNN*, June 28. http://www.cnn.com/2012/06/28/politics/supreme-court-health-timeline/.

Smith, J. C., and C. Medalia. 2015. "Health Insurance Coverage in the United States: 2014." *United States Census Bureau*. https://www.census.gov/content/dam/Census/library/publications/2015/demo/p60-253.pdf.

Summary of the Affordable Care Act. 2013. *The Henry J. Kaiser Family Foundation*, April 25. http://files.kff.org/attachment/fact-sheet-summary-of-the-affordable-care-act.

Vladeck, B. 2003. "Universal Health Insurance in the United States: Reflections on the Past, the Present, and the Future." *American Journal of Public Health* 93 (1): 16–19. http://www.ncbi.nlm.nih.gov/pmc/articles/PMC1447684/.

Wetherell, G., C. Reyna, and M. Sadler. 2013. "Public Option Versus the Market: Perceived Value Violations Drive Opposition to Healthcare Reform." *Political Psychology* 34 (1): 43–66.

"What Is Single Payer?" n.d. *Physicians for a National Health Program*. http://www.pnhp.org/facts/what-is-single-payer.

"What Is Universal Health Coverage?" 2014. *World Health Organization*, December. http://www.who.int/health_financing/universal_coverage_definition/en/.

"Why Is Obamacare So Controversial?" 2014. *BBC News*, March 28. http://www.bbc.com/news/world-us-canada-24370967.

"Without Public Option, Enthusiasm for Health Care Reform, Especially Among Democrats, Collapses." 2009. *Rasmussen Reports*, August 19. http://www.rasmussenreports.com/public_content/politics/current_events/healthcare/august_2009/without_public_option_enthusiasm_for_health_care_reform_especially_among_democrats_collapses.

Zengerle, P. 2012. "Most Americans Oppose Health Law But Like Provisions." *Reuters* June 24. http://www.reuters.com/article/us-usa-campaign-healthcare-idUSBRE85N01M20120625.

CHAPTER 18

The Prevalence and Correlates of Depression Among College Students

By Billie J. Lindsey, Patricia Fabiano, and Chris Stark

D epression in young adults is a common health problem and growing public health concern (Voelker 2003; Lewinsohn, Rohde, and Seeley 1998).
Depression impairs psychosocial development and academic success (Birmaher
et al. 1996). It is a strong predictor of suicide, which is the third leading cause of
death in 15–24 years olds and the second leading cause of death among college
students (Hass, Hendin, and Mann 2003). Early onset of depression is also a
predictor of more serious illness in adulthood (Weissman et al. 1999). This article
describes the prevalence and correlates of depression among students, from a
mid-size Northwestern regional public university, who participated in the 2002
National College Health Assessment (NCHA), a survey used to assess students'
health status, health problems, and health behaviors.

The primary purpose of this study was to analyze the NCHA data to assess
the prevalence and correlates of depression and depressive symptoms within this
specific college population. Its secondary purpose was to explore and compare
the relationship between self-reported depressed and non-depressed students'

health-related behaviors and factors associated with academic performance. Colleges and universities that take an active role in early detection, intervention, and treatment of depression and depressive symptoms are more likely to meet the mental health objectives of *Healthy People* 2010 (U.S. Department of Health and Human Services Office of Disease Prevention and Health Promotion 2000) and *Healthy Campus* 2010 (18–9b) (American College Health Association 2002) and mitigate the progress and chronicity of depression among college students and its wasteful hindrance of their academic performance and corrosion of the collegiate social milieu.

According to the National Institute of Mental Health, major depressive disorder (MDD) affects about 5% of the adult population in a given year and 15–20% of the population during a lifetime. Another 5.4% of adults experience dysthymic disorder: chronic, mild depression lasting at least 2 years (National Institute of Mental Health 2003). An analysis of the Centers for Disease Control and Prevention's third *National Health and Nutrition Examination Survey* (NHANES) found that 7.5% of 15–19 year olds met the criteria for MDD, 35.5% reported at least two weeks of depressed mood, and 5.9% reported at least two years of depressed mood. Among 20–24 year olds, 9.7% met the criteria for MDD, 40.5% reported at least two weeks of depressed mood, and 7.95% reported at least two years of depressed mood (Riole 2002). The Centers for Disease Control and Prevention (CDC) report that in 18–24 year olds, 12.3% of women and 7.8% of men experience frequent distress, a key indicator for depression (National Mental Health Association 2004).

These data suggest that traditional aged college students, as a subset of the U.S. population group, may be at particular risk for depression or depressed mood. Gallagher found that 10–15% of college students struggle with depressive illness (Gallagher 2002). Furr, Westefeld, McDonnell, and Jenkins (2001) reported that 53% of students experienced depression at some point during their college careers. Benton, Robertson, Tseng, Newton, and Benton (2003) found an alarming increase in depression and other mental health problems during a 13 year period: the number of students seeking help for depression doubled and the number of suicidal students tripled. *Results of Your First College Year Survey* found that 10% of women and 15% of *men frequently* felt depressed and 43% of first year women and men frequently felt overwhelmed by all they had to do (Sanderson 2003).

In Spring 2002, 44 colleges and universities used random sampling to administer the American College Health Association's (ACHA) *National College Health Assessment* to 28,000 students. This assessment surveyed students' health status and behavior, including depression and depressive symptoms, for their last academic year. The top health problems experienced by students were back pain (44.8%), allergy (40.4%), sinus infection (26.8%) and depression (16.8%). Nineteen percent of women and 13% of men reported they had experienced depression at some time during the previous year. Eleven percent of women and 6% of men reported anxiety disorder and 5% of women and 3% of men reported seasonal affective disorder. Thirteen percent of women and 9% of men attributed academic impairment to "depression/anxiety/seasonal affective disorder." In addition to the numbers of students who reported experiencing depression, 14% of women and 7% men reported that they had actually been diagnosed with depression at some time in their lives. Of those diagnosed with depression, 25% of women and 21% of men were currently in therapy for depression and 38% of the women and 28% of men were taking medication for depression (ACHA 2004a).

Students also reported depressive symptoms. On five or more occasions, 27% of women and 21% of men felt things were hopeless; 69% of women and 50% of men felt overwhelmed by all they had to do; 64% of women and 49% of men felt exhausted; 41% of women and 28% of men felt very sad; and 20% of women and 13% of men felt so depressed it was difficult to function. Ten percent of women and 9% of men seriously considered suicide and 1% of women and 1% of men attempted suicide (ACHA 2004a).

Depression is complex. The factors associated with its occurrence and continuance in adolescence and young adulthood are many. Contributing familial factors are a lack of physical affection among family members and a lack of verbal intimacy with parents (Field, Diego, and Sanders, 2001); parent divorce (Short 2002); lack of positive reinforcement (Lewinsohn et al. 1998); family violence, low family cohesion, and a family history of depression and substance abuse (Reinherz, Paradis, Giaconia, Stashwick, and Fitzmaurice 2003); child abuse and neglect (Brown, Cohen, Johnson, and Smailes 1999); and trauma (Turner and Butler 2003). Intrapersonal factors include low global self-esteem (Smith and

Betz 2002); self-criticism, introversion, low assertiveness, dependency, and a need to please others (Gudleski and Shean 2002); difficulty in adjusting to new and changing circumstances (Beeber 1999); feeling hopeless and helpless (Furr et al. 2001); and harboring negative beliefs about the self, world, and future (Birmaher et al. 1996). Low socioeconomic status (Goodman and Huang 2002; Weitzman 2004); female gender (Rushton, Forcier, and Schectman 2002); gender role conflict (Zamarripa, Wampold, and Gregory 2003; Wong and Whitaker 1994); sexual orientation (West-efeld, Maples, Buford, and Taylor 2001); body weight and body satisfaction (Womble et al. 2001); eating disorders (Franko and Omori 1999); learning disabilities (Spencer, Beiderman, and Wilens 1999); and physical illness (Rawson, Bloomer, and Kendall 1994) have also been associated with depression in young adults.

Other factors associated specifically with college student depression include stressful life events and daily hassles (O'Neil and Mingie 1998; Segrin 1999; D'Angelo and Wierzbicki 2003); stress reactivity (Felsten 2002); conflict between work and family (Zamarripa et al. 2003); relationship problems, financial concerns, and poor grades (Furr, et al. 2001); lack of social support or networks (Beeber 1999; O'Neil and Mingie 1988; D'Angelo and Wierzbicki 2003); a sense of not belonging (Hagerty and Williams 1999); having fewer friends (Field, Diego, and Sanders 2001); and experiencing loneliness (D'Angelo and Wierzbicki 2003). Other research supports that depressed students more than non-depressed students, smoke cigarettes (Allgower, Wardle, and Steptoe 2001); engage in heavy alone drinking (Christiansen, Vik, and Jarchow 2002); use illicit drugs (Field et al. 2001); use the internet for activities such as shopping, playing games, and doing research [vs. email and instant messaging] (Morgan and Cotten 2003); cope with maladaptive eating behaviors (Hawkins, McDermott, Seeley, and Hawkins 1992); and have experienced unwanted sexual contact (Larimer, Lydum, Anderson, and Turner 1999).

● METHOD

Participants and Procedures

This study was conducted at mid-size public university in the Pacific Northwest in conjunction with the American College Health Association's National College Health Assessment. Based on data provided by the university registrar, a random sample of 2,500 students was drawn from a population of 11,189. After approval by the University Institutional Review Board, each student received a mailed packet, which included a cover letter, the *National College Health Assessment* (NCHA), and a stamped business envelope in which to return the surveys. Students were offered a chance to win $1000.00 as an incentive to participate in the survey. They were assured anonymity by instructing them to mail a postcard for the drawing, separately, from the survey. One month after the initial mailing, a reminder was mailed. Limited funding prevented a second mailing of the survey.

Instrument

The NCHA, developed in 1998, has demonstrated its reliability and validity and is used by the American College Health Association in random surveys of college students across the country (American College Health Association 2004b). The NCHA is a 58-item survey with multiple components to each item. The survey included questions related to demographics, work, sources of health information, sexual activity, exercise, alcohol, tobacco, and other drug use, as well as checklists about specific illnesses and conditions that students experienced during the past school year, including seven items of depressive symptoms. Students were asked to indicate whether they had experienced these symptoms from zero to 11 or more times during the past school year. Students were also asked if they had ever been diagnosed with depression, and if so, was it during the last school year; were they currently in therapy; and were they currently taking medication for depression. In separate items, students were asked to identify if they experienced depression or anxiety or seasonal affective disorder in the last school year, and whether they had ever been diagnosed with depression, the latter being a repeated question. In a final item, students were asked, among other conditions, if they had experienced "depression/anxiety disorder/seasonal affective disorder" (all one choice), and if so, if "it" had affected their academic performance.

To determine the prevalence of depression and its correlates, we used the question "Within the last school year, have you had depression?" Additional comparative analyses were conducted in which we used students who had also been diagnosed with depression.

Statistical Analysis

Frequency distributions were used to outline the characteristics of the sample on various survey items. In addition, we employed the Chi-square test of independence to infer differences between depressed and non-depressed students in regards to year in school. All other inferential statistics were independent t-tests.

● RESULTS

Participant Characteristics

Of the sample of 2500 students, 618 returned the survey, for a response rate of 25.1%. Women comprised the majority (71.5%). The largest ethnic groups were European Caucasian Americans (81.1%) followed by Asian American (6.3%) and unknown/multi-cultural (5.8%). The majority were single (53.7%), full-time (95.1%), and juniors/seniors (28.2% were 3rd year and 25.0% 4th year). Over 56% worked for pay and 40.2% worked from 10 to over 40 hours per week. Nearly one in three (28.8%) volunteered between 1–9 hours per week. See Table 18.1 for full listing of participants' characteristics.

Depression, Anxiety, and Seasonal Affective Disorder

Twenty-six percent (27% women and 25.3% of men) of all students reported experiencing depression in the last school year, making it the third highest reported health problem experienced by this group of college students [More students experienced back pain (50.3%) and allergy (42.7%).] More women (19.3%) than men (12.2%) reported they had actually been diagnosed with depression at some point in their lives, [$\chi2$ (1, N = 595) = 4.14, p = .042]; 36.3% were diagnosed in the last school year. A higher proportion of women (20%) than men (3.8%) reported being in treatment for depression [$\chi2$ (1, N = 121) = 3.86, p = .049]; and a higher proportion of women (31%) than men (8%) were currently taking medication for depression [$\chi2$ (1, N = 120) = 6.11, p = .013]. Students in their second year (19.3%), third year (21.8%), fourth year (19.1%), and fifth year (19.7%), were more likely to have been diagnosed with depression than first years (5.8%) [$\chi2$ (5, N = 61) = 12.73, p = .026]. Depressed students (11.3%) were more likely to report their health status as fair or poor than non-depressed

Table 18.1 Demographic Characteristics of Participants (N=618)

GENDER
- Female — 71.5%
- Male — 28.5%

AGE
- 18–20 — 42.1%
- 21–25 — 48.6%
- 26+ — 9.4%

YEAR IN SCHOOL
- 1st year — 18.4%
- 2nd year — 15.8%
- 3rd year — 28.2%
- 4th year — 25.0%
- 5th year — 12.6%

ETHNICITY
- White — 84.9%
- Black — 0.5%
- Hispanic or Latino — 2.7%
- Asian/Pacific Islander — 5.1%
- American Indian or Alaskan Native — 0.5%
- Other — 6.3%

RELATIONSHIP STATUS
- Single — 53.7%
- Married — 6.9%
- Engaged — 37.7%
- Separated — 0.7%
- Divorced — 0.8%
- Widowed — 0.2%

Continued

WORK FOR PAY

- 0 hours   43.8%
- 1–9 hours   16.0%
- 10–19 hours   20.9%
- 20–29 hours   14.9%
- 30–39 hours   2.7%
- 40 hours   0.8%
- more than 40 hours   0.8%

HOURS VOLUNTEERED

- 0 hours   68.2%
- 1–9 hours   28.8%
- 10–19 hours   2.0%
- 20–29 hours   0.7%
- 30–39 hours   0.3%
- 40 hours   0.0%
- more than 40 hours   0.0%

students (6.1%) [$\chi2$ (1, N = 574)= 4.20, p = .041]. In addition to depression, 14.4% of women and 7.6% of men reported anxiety disorder [$\chi2$ (1, N = 582) = 4.71, p = .030]; and 14.2% of women and 8.3% of men reported seasonal affective disorder.

Work, Volunteerism, and Credit Card Debt

To assess the effect of work and the prevalence of depression, we compared students who didn't work for pay to those who did. There were no significant differences between non-working and working students and reported depression. Likewise, a comparison of students who worked nine or fewer hours to those who worked 10 or more hours found no relationship to reported depression. There were differences, however, when the total number of hours students worked was added to the total number of hours they volunteered per week. Students who worked and volunteered 10 or more hours per week (22.4%) were more likely to be depressed than students who worked and volunteered nine or fewer hours (29.9%) [$\chi 2$ (1, N = 571) = 4.20, p = .041].

Significant differences were found in the number of volunteer hours between depressed and non-depressed students, t (570) = 2.78, p = .006. Students responded to a 7-point Likert scale with answers ranging from "1 = 0 hours" to "7 = more than 40 hours" for time spent volunteering. Students who were depressed, volunteered fewer hours per week (M = 1.25, SD = 0.48) than students who were not depressed (M = 1.42, SD = 0.66). Finally, students carrying a monthly balance of credit card debt (34.3%) reported depression more frequently than students (13.4%) carrying no credit card debt [$\chi 2$ (1, N = 586) = 12.98, p < .001].

Weight, Weight Satisfaction, and Eating Disorders

Students were asked to describe their weight on a 5-point Likert scale with answers ranging from "1 = very underweight" to "5 = very overweight" Women (42%) perceived their bodies as more overweight (M = 3.37, SD = 0.73) than men (24%) (M = 3.05, SD = 0.73) [t (580) = 4.71, p <.001] and more women (57%) than men (25%) wanted to lose weight [$^{-}2$ (1, N = 581) = 50.35, p < .001], In spite of this, there were no significant differences between students who had ever been diagnosed with depression or who reported experiencing depression during the last school year and how they described their weight. Likewise, there were no differences between depressed and non-depressed women in regards to wanting to lose weight. Five percent of students reported they had experienced either anorexia or bulimia in the past year. These students were more likely also to report depression than non-depressed students [$\chi 2$ (1, N = 578) = 14.99, p < .001; $\chi 2$(l, N = 577) = 12.58, p < .001].

Sexual Orientation

Gay/lesbian, bisexual, transgender, or unsure (GLBTU) students were more likely than heterosexual students to have been diagnosed with depression as well as experience depression during the last year. Nearly one third (31.6%) of GLBTU students compared to 16.7% of heterosexual students had ever been diagnosed with depression [$\chi 2$ (1, N = 583) = 5.41, p = .02]; and 59.5% of GLBTU students experienced depression in the past year compared to 24.4% of heterosexual students [$\chi 2$ (1, N = 570) = 21.76, p < .001].

Depressive Symptomotology

Besides experiencing depression, many students also reported depressive symptoms. On five or more occasions, 23.1% of women and 21.7% of men felt things were hopeless, 69.6% of women and 54.9% of men felt overwhelmed by all they had to do, 63.7% of women and 50.3% of men felt exhausted, 40.7% of women and 34.0% of men felt very sad, and 19.1% of women and 16.7% of men felt so depressed it was difficult to function. Nearly 8% (7.9%) of women and 13.0% of men seriously considered suicide, and 2 women and 3 men attempted suicide. Students who reported being depressed in the last school year experienced all of these depressive symptoms more frequently than did non-depressed students. See Table 18.2 for results of independent samples t-test.

Tobacco, Drugs, and Alcohol

Next we explored the relationship of depression in the past year and frequency of drug and alcohol use within the past 30 days. Students responded to the drug and alcohol items using an 8-point Likert scale with response options ranging from "1 = never used" to "8 = all 30 days." An independent t-test revealed differences between depressed students (M = 2.84, SD = 2.47) and non-depressed students (M = 2.06, SD = 1.88) and smoking frequency [$t(580) = 4.71, p < .001$]. Depressed students (M = 2.25, SD = 1.91) and non-depressed students (M = 1.87, SD = 1.44) displayed differences in marijuana use in the past thirty days [$t(577) = 2.60, p = .009$]. Moreover, depressed students (M = 1.18, SD = 0.58) reported more cocaine use than non-depressed students (M = 1.09, SD = 0.40) [$t(577) = 2.16, p = .031$], On the other hand, there were no significant differences between depressed and non-depressed students' use of alcohol, amphetamines, rohypnol, GHB, or Liquid X.

Academic Impairment

Students were asked if a variety of physical or psychological conditions impaired their academic performance within the last year. Depressed students were more likely to identify Attention Deficit Hyperactivity Disorder (ADHD), chronic pain, depression/anxiety/seasonal affective disorder, drug use, eating disorders, learning disabilities, relationship difficulties, sinus infections/bronchitis/strep

Table 18.2 Results of Independent t-test with "Had Depression in the Past Year" (yes/ no) as the Independent Variable and Depressive Symptoms as the Dependent Variable.

DEPRESSIVE SYMPTOM	MEAN SCORE FOR DEPRESSED STUDENTS	MEAN SCORE FOR NON-DEPRESSED STUDENTS	T-VALUE	DF	P-VALUE
Felt things were hopeless	4.00	2.13	11.63	572	<.001
Felt overwhelmed by all you had to do	5.36	4.37	5.67	575	<.001
Felt exhausted not from physical activity	5.46	4.04	7.71	573	<.001
Felt very sad	5.06	2.98	12.34	575	<001
Felt so depressed it was difficult to function	3.88	1.64	14.87	574	<.001
Seriously considered attempting suicide	1.53	1.06	6.54	573	<.001
Attempted suicide	1.06	1.00	2.63	573	=.009

throat, sleep difficulties, and stress as sources of academic impairment than non-depressed students (See Table 18.3). No differences were found for academic impairment attributed to alcohol use, allergies, colds/flu/sore throat, physical or sexual assault, concern for troubled friends or family members, chronic illness, death of a friend or family member, injury, internet use/computer games, mono-nucleosis, pregnancy, or STDs between depressed and non-depressed students.

Sexual Activity, Exercise, and Other Variables

There were no differences between depressed and non-depressed students' sexual activity or exercise behaviors. There were no differences in full or part-time student status, GPA, ethnicity, or relationship status between depressed and non-depressed students.

Discussion

As stated at the outset, the primary purpose of this study was to analyze the NCHA survey data of this university to determine the prevalence of depression and depressive symptoms as well as the correlates of depression, and secondarily to research the relationship between depressed and non-depressed students' health-related behaviors and factors associated with academic performance.

Table 18.3 Results of Independent t-test with "Had Depression in the Past Year" (yes/no) as the Independent Variable and Issues Affecting Academic Performance as the Dependent Variable.

ISSUES AFFECTING ACADEMIC PERFORMANCE	MEAN SCORE FOR DEPRESSED STUDENTS	MEAN SCORE FOR NON-DEPRESSED STUDENTS	T-VALUE	DF	P-VALUE
Attention Deficit Hyperactivity Disorder (ADHD)	1.32	1.12	3.18	565	=.002
Chronic pain	1.29	1.16	2.59	568	=.010
Depression/anxiety/seasonal affect disorder	2.69	1.30	16.72	566	<.001
Drug use	1.31	1.20	2.00	566	=.046
Eating disorders	1.21	1.04	4.75	567	<.001
Learning disabilities	1.24	1.12	2.09	565	=.037
Relationship difficulties	1.97	1.56	4.93	564	<.001
Sinus infection/bronchitis/strep throat	1.57	1.39	2.60	564	=.010
Sleep difficulties	2.27	1.87	4.73	566	<.001
Stress	2.69	2.14	6.45	565	<.001

Mean scores reflect responses on a 1–6 Likert scale with higher scores indicating a more severe academic impairment.

Primarily, the study found depression to be a serious health problem warranting an attention consistent with the mandate of colleges and universities to maximize educational opportunity for their students. Secondarily, the study uncovered data that supports that depressed students are at higher risk than non-depressed students for a number of health problems and academic impairment. In the service of our primary purpose, the authors articulate six distinct areas of concern: (1) the impetus of the college experience to depression and depressive symptoms; (2) the relationship between findings on depression and seasonal affective disorder; (3) a rise in male depression; (4) the impact of sexual orientation and depression; (5) the impact of financial insecurity; and (6) the long range consequences of depression upon a college population.

The overall number of students (17.5%) who had ever been diagnosed with depression was higher than the national 2002 NCHA data in which 10.5% of students reported a depression diagnosis at some time in their lives. Although the prevalence in both groups was comparable to the estimated 10–15% of college students with MDD as reported by Gallagher (2002), it is considerably greater than the analysis of the CDC NHANES in which 9.7% of 20–24 year olds across the country met the criterion for MDD (Riole 2002). The college experience could be, in and of itself, a contributing factor to depression in this age group.

The number of students who experienced depression in the past year and the relation of such experience to seasonal affective disorder (SAD) is puzzling and warrants further investigation. More students at our campus reported depression (26.2%) and SAD (22.5%) than did students nationwide (16.8% and 8%, respectively). This finding points to the need to determine what role SAD plays in student depression. It could be possible that SAD explains, at least in part, the difference between students at this Pacific Northwest campus and students nationwide.

As has been noted in previous research (Rushton et al. 2002), women more than men reported diagnosed depression (19.3% vs.12.2%); but, nearly as many men (25.9%) as women (26.8%) reported feeling depressed during the last year. While we do not presume that everyone feeling depressed will meet the criteria for major depressive disorder, the realization that one out of every four men feels depressed supports implementing an outreach program to specifically target depression in college men.

Students who identified as gay, lesbian, trans-gender, bisexual, or unsure were more than *twice* as likely to report depression than heterosexual students. Questioning one's sexual orientation, coming out, and fearing rejection weigh heavily on emotional and mental health. An environment that supports GLBT student organizations and gay-straight alliance groups, faculty members who recognize and include diversity of student lifestyles and sexual orientations in their classroom curricula, as well as faculty and staff who are "out" and can mentor students, are positive and perhaps necessary elements of any serious address to this pressing campus concern. Indeed, indications that gay and lesbian youth have a high suicide attempt rate make the cultivation of a supportive campus environment imperative (Garofalo, Wolf, Wissow, Woods, and Goodman 1999; Paul et al. 2002).

Students who worked and volunteered more hours reported feeling depressed more than students who worked and volunteered few or no hours. This finding warrants careful consideration of the impact of the current trend toward requiring more service learning in the college curricula. Also the amount of credit card debt carried by students correlated with self-reported depression. Colleges and universities and their counseling services in particular should be alert to the toll of financial burdens upon the emotional lives of students. As the cost of collegiate education escalates and financial aid diminishes, more and more students are obliged to work considerable hours to meet expenses. The correlation between work and volunteer hours and debt and depression suggests that campuses should offer financial management services and examine credit card company presence on campus. Future research should determine whether college student depression and depressive symptoms are in any way caused or exacerbated by financial strain and determine how a school's own loan-debt policy affects student mental health and academic performance.

Depressive symptoms are often an indicator of major depressive disorder or a predictor for later-life major depression. In our study, depressed students reported all depressive symptoms more frequently than non-depressed students, and women reported all symptoms more frequently than men. Serious consideration of suicide was the exception, reported more frequently by men than women. A disconcerting number of our total student sample reported that they felt overwhelmed by all they had to do, exhausted, so depressed it was difficult to function, hopeless, and very sad.

Our findings suggest that there may be factors in the campus climate that contribute to disturbing mental and physical self-report. Some factors may include curricular and pedagogical factors that undermine student effort and student health. For example, requiring students (particularly those already working to pay their way) to also engage in unpaid volunteer and service learning projects may contribute to their feelings of being overwhelmed, exhausted, and depressed. Another example might be a changing pedagogy focused more upon experience-based learning and group projects that require more student time and contribute to these reports of stress and depression. This warrants further attention and research.

The secondary purpose of this study was to assess students' health behaviors that were correlated with depression. Our findings differ in two respects from findings of other research. Unlike other research, we did not find an association between depression and alcohol use. The higher rates of alcohol consumption on the college campuses generally may be masking or diluting our ability to detect a relationship between alcohol and depression. For certainly, depressed students who reported alcohol problems did more often report academic impairment than did non-depressed students with alcohol problems. Whether or not the reported academic impairment was caused by the depression, alcohol, or a combination, is, therefore impossible to determine. Unlike other research, we did not find a correlation between depression and Internet use, sexual assault, and body weight.

On the other hand, our study, like others, did find a correlation between depression and cigarette, marijuana, and cocaine use. The fact that use of these drugs is common among depressed students should alert medical and counseling staff to explore the possibility of depression with students who smoke and use other drugs.

Since there was a correlation between the self-reports of depression and self-perceived health status, clinicians, when taking a medical history, should ask students to describe their overall health as excellent, very good, good, fair, or poor. Fair/poor choices of response should lead to further questions about depression. The U.S. Preventive Service Task Force recommends asking two questions that may be as effective as using a longer depression screening instrument. These include (1) "Over the past two weeks, have you felt down, depressed, or hopeless?" and (2) Over the past two weeks, have you felt little interest or pleasure in doing things?" (U.S. Preventative Services Task Force 2002). Based on our research findings, clinicians should also ask about a student's workload, financial circumstance, and credit card debt.

Our research did find that depressed students were more likely to encounter academic problems if they had learning disabilities, chronic pain, relationship problems, sleep difficulty, sinus/bronchitis/strep throat infections, and stress than were non-depressed students with these problems. For these reasons, campus disability services should be particularly alert to students with ADHD and learning disabilities; medical and counseling services should seek to alleviate some of the negative consequences of pain, poor sleep, and stress; and student services should enhance educational programs and services related to relationships, stress and time management, and sleep. Based on our research, campuses should offer programs and/or services for financial management, substance misuse and abuse, gay/lesbian/transgender support, seasonal affective disorder, and depression screenings.

Our survey did not include questions about friendship, loneliness, self-esteem, or family of origin issues, all which have all been implicated in young adult depression. We believe, however, that campuses should consider ways they can help students make connections and build friendships, and to make counseling services more accessible and encourage their use.

Limitations

We note several limitations to our study. This study reports the results of the NCHA at one campus in the Pacific Northwest, limiting generalizability. Women were disproportionately represented and the response rate overall was 25%. Also, NCHA is a self-report survey. It is possible that students interested in health or their own health status were more likely to respond, thereby skewing the results. Secondly, there are many factors associated with young adult depression that were described in the introduction that were not assessed in this survey. We do not assume that the correlates of depression that we found are the causes of depression. However, our findings do provide new and important insight into the problems that many college students are experiencing which are related to depression, as well as identify important areas for future research.

Conclusion

Our study highlights the seriousness of depression on the college campus and points to the desirability of campuses to participate in the American College Health Association's NCHA and tailor services and programs to the unique needs of their students. Creating a campus climate that is supportive and protective of students' mental and physical health will help ensure their academic success and would go some way toward meeting the obligation of such institutions to their own ostensible aim of education for the common good.

References

Allgower, A., Wardle, J., and Steptoe, A. (2001). Depressive symptoms, social support, and personal health behaviors in young men and women. *Health Psychology,* 20(3), 223–225.

American College Health Association. (2002). Healthy Campus 2010: *Making it happen.* Baltimore, MD: American College Health Association.

American College Health Association (2004a). *National College Health Assessment: Mental and physical health.* Retrieved October 2004, from http://www.achancha.org/data/PHYSM ENTALFA02.html.

American College Health Association. (2004b). *National College Health Assessment:* Reliability and validity analysis 2000. Baltimore, MD: American College Health Association.

Beeber, L.S. (1999). Testing an explanatory model of the development of depressive symptoms in young women during a life transition. *Journal of American College Health,* 47(3), 227–234.

Benton, S. A., Robertson, J.M., Tseng, W.C., Newton, F.B., and Benton, S.L. (2003). Changes in counseling center client problems across 13 years. *Professional Psychology Research and Practice,* 34(1), 66–72.

Birmaher, B., Ryan. N.D., Williamson, D.E., Brent, D.A., Kaufman, J., Dahl, R., et al. (1996). Childhood and adolescent depression: A review of the past 10 years. Part I. *Journal of the American Academy of Child & Adolescent Psychiatry,* 35(11), 1427–1439.

Brown, J., Cohen, P., Johnson, J.G., and Smailes, E.M. (1999). Childhood abuse and neglect: Specificity of effects on adolescent and young adult depression and suicidality. *Journal of the American Academy of Child & Adolescent Psychiatry,* 38(12), 1490–1496.

Christiansen, M., Vik, P.W., and Jarchow, A. (2002). College student heavy drinking in social contexts versus alone. *Addict Behavior,* 27(3), 393–404.

D'Angelo, B., and Wierzbicki, M. (2003). Relations of daily hassles with both anxious and depressed mood in students. *Psychological Reports, 92,* 416–418.

Felsten, G. (2002). Minor stressors and depressed mood: Reactivity is more strongly correlated than total stress. *Stress and Health,* 18(2), 75–81.

Field, T., Diego, M., and Sanders, C. (2001). Adolescent depression and risk factors. *Adolescence,* 36(143), 491–499.

Franko, D.L., and Omori, M. (1999). Subclinical eating disorders in adolescent women: A test of the continuity hypothesis and its psychological correlates. *Journal of Adolescence,* 22(3), 389–396.

Furr, S.R., Westefeld, J.S., McConnell, G.N., and Jenkins, J.M. (2001). Suicide and depression among college students: A decade later. *Professional Psychology Research and Practice,* 32(1), 97–100.

Garofalo, R., Wolf, R.C., Wissow, L.S., Woods, E.R., and Goodman, E. (1999). Sexual orientation and risk of suicide attempts among a representative sample of youth. *Archives of Pediatric and Adolescent Medicine,* 153(5), 487–493.

Gallagher, R. (2002). *National Survey of Counseling Center Directors.* Alexandria, VA: International Association of Counseling Services, Inc.

Goodman, E., and Huang, B. (2002). Socioeconomic status, depressive symptoms, and adolescent substance use. *Archives of Pediatric & Adolescent Medicine,* 156(5), 448–453.

Gudleski, G.D., and Shean, G.D. (2002). Depressed and nondepressed students: Differences in interpersonal perceptions. *Journal of Psychology,* 134(1), 56–63.

Hawkins, W.E., McDermott, R.J., Seeley, J., and Hawkins, M.J. (1992) Depression and maladaptive eating practices in college students. *Women Health,* 18(2), 55–67.

Hagerty, B.M., and Williams, R.A. (1999). The effects of sense of belonging, social support, conflict, and loneliness on depression. *Nursing Research,* 48(4), 215–219.

Hass, A.P., Hendin, H., and Mann J.J. (2003). Suicide in college students. *American Behavioral Science,* 46(9), 1223–1240.

Larimer, M.E., Lydum, A.R., Anderson, B.K, and Turner, A.P. (1999) Male and female recipients of unwanted sexual contact in a college student sample: Prevalence rates, alcohol use-and depression symptoms. *Sex Roles,* 40(4), 295–308.

Lewinsohn, P.M., Rohde, P., and Seeley, J.R. (1998). Major depressive disorder in older adolescents: Prevalence, risk factors, and clinical implications. *Clinical Psychology Review,* 18(7), 765–794.

Morgan C., and Cotton, S.R. (2003). The relationship between internet activities and depressive symptoms in a sample of college freshmen. *Cyberpsychological Behavior,* 6(2), 133–142.

National Institutes of Mental Health. (2003). *Depression in Children and Adolescents: A fact sheet for physicians.* Retrieved October 22, 2003, from http://www.nimh.nih.gov/publicaty depchildres fact.cfm.

National Mental Health Association. *Finding hope and help: College student and depression initiative.* Retrieved September, 2004. fromhttp://www.nmha.org/camh/college/index.cfm.

O'Neil, M.K., and Mingie, P. (1988). Life stress and depression in university students: Clinical illustrations of recent research. *Journal of American College Health,* 36(1), 235–240.

Paul, J.P., Catania, J., Pollack, L., Moskawitz, J., Canchola, J., Mills, T., et. al. (2002). Suicide attempts among gay and bisexual men: Lifetime prevalence and antecedents. *American Journal of Public Health,* 92(8), 1338–1346.

Rawson, H.E., Bloomer, K., and Kendall, A. (1994). Stress, anxiety, depression, and physical illness in college students. *The Journal of Genetic Psychology,* 155(3), 321.

Reinherz, H.Z., Paradis, A.D., Giaconia, R.M., Stashwick, C.K., and Fitzmaurice, G. (2003). Childhood and adolescent predictors of major depression in the transition to adulthood. *American Journal of Psychiatry,* 160(12), 2141–2147.

Riole, S.A. (2002). *Depression common in teens but few seek help.* Paper presented at the annual meeting of the American Academy of Child and Adolescent Psychiatry, San Francisco, CA. Retrieved September, 2004, from http://preventdisease.com/news/articles/depre_ssion_common_teens_few seek help.shtml

Rushton, J.L., Forcier, M., and Schectman, R.M. Epidemiology of depressive symptoms in the National Longitudinal Study of Adolescent Health. *Journal of the American Academy of Child & Adolescent Psychiatry,* 41(2), 199–205.

Sanderson, R.A. (2003) *Your first college year survey results.* Oregon State University Division of Student Affairs. Retrieved November, 2004.from http://www.gseis.ucla.edu/heri/findings.html.

Segrin, C. (1999). Social skills, stressful life events, and the development of psychosocial problems. *Journal of Social and Clinical Psychology,* 18(1), 14–34.

Short, J.L. (2002). The effects of parental divorce during childhood on college students. *Journal of Divorce & Remarriage,* 38(1), 143–155.

Smith, H.M., and Betz, N.E. (2002). An examination of efficacy and esteem pathways to depression in young adulthood. *Journal of Counseling Psychology,* 49(4), 438–448.

Spencer, T., Beiderman, J., and Wilens, T. (1999). Attention-deficit/hyperactivity disorder and comorbidity. *Pediatric Clinics of North America,* 46(5), 915–927.

Turner, H.A., and Butler, M.J. (2003). Direct and indirect effects of childhood adversity on depressive symptoms in young adults. *Journal of Youth and Adolescence,* 32(2), 89–104.

U.S. Department of Health and Human Services (DHHS) Office of Disease Prevention and Health Promotion. (2000). *Healthy People 2010: Understanding and improving health.* Washington, D.C: U.S. Government Printing Office.

U.S. Preventive Services Task Force. (2002). Screening for depression: Recommendations and rationale. *Annals of Internal Medicine,* 136(10), 760–764.

Voelker, R. (2003). Mounting student depression taxing campus mental health services. *The Journal of the American Medical Association,* 289(16), 2055–2056.

Weissman, M.M., Wolk, S., Goldstein, R.B., Moreau. D., Adams, P., Greenwald, S., et al. (1999). Depressed adolescents grown up. *Journal of the American Medical Association,* 281, 1701–1713.

Weitzman, E.R. (2004). Poor mental health, depression, and associations with alcohol consumption, harm and abuse in a national sample of young adults in college. *Journal of Nervous & Mental Disease,* 192(4), 269–277.

Westefeld, J.S., Maples, M.R., Buford, B., and Taylor, S. (2001). Gay, lesbian, and bisexual college students: The relationship between sexual orientation and depression, loneliness, and suicide. *Journal of College Student Psychotherapy,* 15(3), 71–82.

Womble, L.G., Williamson, D.A., Martin, C.K., Zucker, N.L., Thaw, J.M., Netemyer, R., et al. (2001). Psychosocial variables associated with binge eating in obese males and females. *International Journal of Eating Disorders,* 30(2), 217–221.

Wong, J.L., and Whitaker, D J. (1994) The stability and prediction of depressive mood states in college students. *Journal of Clinical Psychology,* 50(5), 715–722.

Zamarripa, M.X., Wampold, B.E., and Gregory, E. (2003). Male gender role conflict, depression- and anxiety: Clarification and generalizability to women. *Journal of Counseling Psychology,* 50(3), 333–338.

CHAPTER 19

From Basic 7 to MyPlate: How the USDA Attempts to Promote Healthy Eating

By Elizabeth A. Petre

The typical American diet—consisting of high levels of fat, sugar, and salt—is unhealthy and leads to a variety of chronic diseases, including type 2 diabetes, heart disease, stroke, cancer, and obesity. Unfortunately, chronic diseases are on the rise (Ratzan 2004), and represent the leading causes of death and disability in the United States (Centers for Disease Control and Prevention 2016). These diseases are directly linked to people's eating habits, which makes unhealthy eating a social problem that various public health measures have sought to address. While there are several campaigns dedicated to curbing Americans' unhealthy eating habits, this chapter explores how the food guides created by the United States Department of Agriculture (USDA) attempt to promote healthy eating.

Over the past century, the USDA has designed and distributed seven food guides, each responding to the needs and contexts of the time.[1] In this chapter, I analyze the development and dietary advice of the seven USDA food guides to highlight how these images have attempted to address the social problem of unhealthy eating. Some readers of this chapter might recognize these images, particularly the 1992 Food Guide Pyramid[2] and the 2011 MyPlate. However, recognition does not necessarily equate to action; unfortunately, despite the USDA's efforts, Americans by and large still do not eat healthily. I argue that this is due, in part, to the competing interests of different constituencies involved in promoting dietary advice. Investigating the history and messages of the USDA food guides helps uncover the key difficulties of trying to get Americans to adopt healthy eating practices. Before the food guides are analyzed, it is important to understand why unhealthy eating is such a problem.

● THE SOCIAL PROBLEM OF UNHEALTHY EATING

As a whole, Americans do not eat healthily. First, Americans tend to eat too much. People often overeat for emotional reasons (including comfort, stress, or boredom) and as a result of environmental triggers (such as food advertisements, social gatherings, or to mirror others' behaviors; Walton 2012). Second, Americans often do not eat healthy foods, as the typical American diet is high in fat, sugar, and salt (Kessler 2009). Americans also eat a lot of meat, carbohydrates, and "empty calories" consisting of soda, candy, and processed foods that lack nutritional value. For instance, 90 percent of Americans consume too much sodium (Sifferlin 2015). Daily consumption of fruits and vegetables is also low, with the average American adult eating fruit 1.1 times per day and vegetables 1.6 times per day (Centers for Disease Control and Prevention 2013). The *2010 Dietary Guidelines for Americans* recommends consumers eat more fruits and vegetables to meet healthy dietary needs (United States Department of Agriculture and United States Department of Health and Human Services 2010).[3] Over the last several decades, the size, portions, and constant availability of food has also increased, making it easier for Americans to snack throughout the day and consume calories in excess of their dietary needs (Suchetka 2010).

Unfortunately, as mentioned above, these unhealthy eating habits lead to a variety of chronic health problems, including type 2 diabetes, cardiovascular diseases, certain forms of cancer, and obesity. For example, a recent report published in the *Mayo Clinic Proceedings* identified added sugar as a "primary driver" of diabetes (DiNicolantonio, O'Keefe, and Lucan 2015, 372).[4] This is troubling news because Americans typically consume large amounts of sugar daily in the form of packaged foods and beverages (Kessler 2009). In addition, diets including high levels of processed meats, eggs, red meats, and high-fat dairy products have been linked to an increased risk for cardiovascular diseases (Kerver, Yang, Bianchi, and Song 2003). Furthermore, research has documented the growing connections between meat consumption and cancer, as a recent study by the World Health Organization (WHO) expressly linked consumption of bacon, sausage, and hot dogs to raising a person's risk of colon cancer (O'Connor 2015). In fact, the WHO report put processed meats in the same category of cancer risk as cigarette smoking and asbestos exposure (Aubrey 2015).

There is also evidence to suggest that diets high in red meat are linked to pancreatic and prostate cancer based on chemicals released during the cooking process (O'Connor 2015). Another possible outcome of unhealthy eating habits is obesity, which has more than doubled in the United States since 1960 (Fryar, Carroll, and Ogden 2014). In fact, data from the 2011–2012 National Health and Nutrition Examination Survey indicates that over two-thirds of all Americans are either overweight or obese (Fryar, Carroll, and Ogden 2014). Chronic diseases are also expensive, with costs to treat type 2 diabetes, cardiovascular diseases, cancers, and obesity each in the billions of dollars annually (Centers for Disease Control and Prevention 2016).

Conversely, eating healthily helps promote good health. Diets rich in vegetables, fruits, and whole grains reduce the risk of chronic diseases listed above. For example, Nestle (2006, 62) observes that people who eat more fruits and vegetables daily had "half the cancer risk of people who eat only two servings" per day. Typically, vegetarians and those who eat mostly fruits, vegetables, and whole grains have lower rates of heart disease and cancer (Nestle 2006). One study even showed that daily consumption of whole fruits and vegetables daily "was associated with a substantially longer survival and lower rate of overall mortality" (Bellavia, Larsson, Bottai, Wolk, and Orsini 2013, 457). For instance, the Mediterranean diet—consisting mostly of fruits, vegetables, fish, and non-packaged foods—has been found to keep bones strong, maintain healthy brain functioning, and lower the risk of cardiovascular diseases, among other benefits (Manella 2016). Eating fruits and vegetables also helps people feel more full, which allows them to manage their weight better (Centers for Disease Control and Prevention 2015). In sum, healthy eating habits put less stress on our bodies and can increase life expectancy and improve overall quality of life.[5]

As this overview indicates, unhealthy eating habits can have serious, potentially life-threatening health consequences, but adopting healthy eating habits can help avert chronic diseases and lead to good long-term health. Public health measures like the USDA food guides represent important ways to address the social problem of unhealthy eating by promoting healthy eating habits. In what follows, I analyze the seven USDA food guides developed over the past century to explore how they encouraged Americans to eat more healthily.

● EARLY USDA FOOD GUIDES

Created in 1862, the USDA was charged with two purposes. The first is to promote access to a safe and plentiful food supply and the second is to provide Americans information about what to eat (Nestle 2002). It is this second purpose that led to the creation of food guidance materials and dietary advice in the early part of the twentieth century, focused on preventing dietary deficiencies and malnutrition.[6] USDA nutritionist Caroline Hunt developed the "Food for Young Children" pamphlet in 1916, followed by the "How to Select Foods" guide for adults in 1917 (Davis and Saltos 1999). These initial pamphlets established the food-group format (Nestle 2002). In 1941, the US National Academy of Sciences developed the first set of Recommended Dietary Allowances (RDAs), which gave recommendations for daily consumption of calories and nine essential nutrients (Davis and Saltos 1999). The RDAs were incorporated into a stand-alone image that the USDA released to correspond with the National Wartime Nutrition Guide in 1943. This image became known as the "Basic 7" (Nestle 2002). As its name suggests, the image consisted of seven food groups that consumers were recommended to alternate in instances of limited supplies.[7]

After national surveys in the early 1950s indicated that "the diets of many Americans were below standard for several nutrients" (Nestle 2002, 36), the USDA began working on a new food guide to help simplify dietary advice. This image was called the "Basic Four" and featured four food groups based on what soldiers typically received while serving in the armed forces: meat, milk, vegetables and fruits (in one group), and bread (Kamps 2011). The Basic Four became a staple of American dinners, and was the first food guide to specify the number and size of servings of each food group (Nestle 2002). Both the Basic 7 and the Basic Four focused on making sure Americans ate enough nutrients daily to maintain good health, and eating healthily was linked to patriotism (Mudry 2010). Interestingly, the Basic Four was the primary food guide used in the United States for the following two decades (Nestle 2002).

However, US dietary guidance began to shift in the 1960s and 1970s as levels of obesity, type 2 diabetes, and heart disease started to rise (Nestle and Porter 1990). Nutritionists and physicians had been highlighting the link between chronic diseases and diet since the late 1950s, and Congress began conducting hearings on this relationship nearly two decades later (Nestle 2006). The hearings resulted in a select Senate committee (led by Senator George McGovern) that released *Dietary Goals for the United States* in 1977. This document recommended that Americans reduce their consumption of meat, eggs, dairy, and both high-fat and high-sugar foods (Nestle 2002). Consequently, *Dietary Goals* received a great deal of push-back from ranchers, egg producers, sugar producers, and the dairy industry (Nestle 2002). Members of the food industry demanded additional hearings on *Dietary Goals*, arguing that Congress was essentially telling the "public that their products were bad for health" (Nestle 2002, 40). For instance, one of the most contested recommendations stated that people should eat less meat. As a result, the report was subsequently revised and re-released later that year.

Despite the uproar from the food industry, in 1979 USDA nutritionists designed a new publication and corresponding image called "Food: The Hassle-Free Guide to a Better Diet" to help Americans follow *Dietary Goals*. This image became known as the "Hassle-Free Guide" (see Figure 19.1). The Hassle-Free Guide essentially used the Basic Four food groups and added a fifth—the fats, sweets, and alcohol group—to be consumed in moderation (Davis, Britten, and Myers 2001). Readers will notice that the food groups in Figure 1 are stacked vertically and contain photographic collections of food items along with informative text. the fats, sweets, and alcohol group included at the bottom is half the size of the others (with a yellow "Caution" sign) to indicate moderation, which "marked the first time a [USDA food] group's visual illustration mirrored its

Figure 19.1 The 1979 Hassle-Free Daily Food Guide.

recommended consumption relative to other foods" (Perelman 2011, 62). The Hassle-Free Guide was quite popular among the American public, as a former Assistant USDA Secretary for Food and Consumer Services claimed that it was the organization's most requested publication that year (Nestle 2002). Shortly after its release, the USDA joined with the Department of Health and Human Services (formerly the Department of Health, Education, and Welfare) to develop a new document called *Dietary Guidelines for Americans*. Congress created a mandate that *Dietary Guidelines* be updated every five years, and that the recommendations be incorporated into any future federal materials providing advice to the American public on what to eat (Nestle 2002).

Although the Hassle-Free Guide was popular, the release of the *1980 Dietary Guidelines* prompted the development of another food guide that was a joint effort between the USDA and the American Red Cross (Welsh, Davis, and Shaw 1992a). In 1984, "Food Wheel: A Pattern for Daily Food Choices" was released. The Food Wheel (see Figure 19.2), as it became known, was the first food guide to focus on the issue of proportionality in terms of daily food consumption (Perelman 2011). As readers can see, the pie chart–style graphic is divided into six sections of varying degrees, with silverware positioned on either side of the wheel. Although the information about recommended serving sizes corresponded to *Dietary Guidelines*, based on the sheer number of food items mentioned in each category, it seemed as though Americans were being encouraged to eat more food. The Food Wheel was widely used in federal publications throughout the mid-1980s (Davis and Saltos 1999). However, the USDA determined that the Food Wheel was visually cluttered

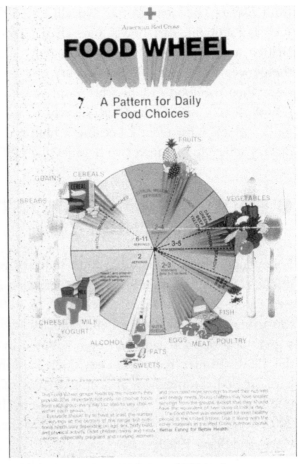

Figure 19.2 The 1984 Food Wheel.

and complicated to interpret (Nestle 2002); so once again, the USDA continued to work on developing another food guide to help Americans eat healthily.

In 1988, the USDA contracted with Porter Novelli, a Washington, DC–based public relations and consumer-research firm, to design an image that would convey the ideas of variety, proportionality, and moderation in a singular graphic (Welsh, Davis, and Shaw 1992b). *Variety* referred to selecting foods from multiple groups, *proportionality* meant selecting the appropriate number of servings within each group, and *moderation* highlighted restrictions on fat and sugar (Nestle 2002). This new image was also supposed to incorporate the nutritional recommendations from *Dietary Guidelines.* Porter Novelli tested different graphic representations, such as a shopping cart, bowls, a pie chart, a picnic design, and a pyramid (Davis, Britten, and Myers 2001). It was ultimately determined that people understood the concepts of variety, proportionality, and moderation in daily food selection best when the food groups were displayed horizontally in a triangle/pyramid (Nestle 2002). This finding led directly to the development of the new food guide, which subsequently became a highly recognized icon of governmental dietary advice for the next two decades: the USDA Food Pyramid (Nestle 2002).

● FOOD PYRAMIDS AND STEPS TO A HEALTHIER YOU

Following a flood of negative food industry response and extended time for public comment on an initial image (Perelman 2011), the Food Guide Pyramid (see Figure 19.3) was released on April 28, 1992. Many readers will recognize this iconic image for governmental dietary advice. The Food Pyramid received a great deal of praise, and was even adopted by different countries throughout the 1990s (Painter, Rah, and Lee 2002). Researchers in a variety of disciplines have studied the messages and effectiveness of the Food Pyramid extensively (see Davis, Britten, and Myers 2001; Kennedy 1998; Mudry 2010; Nestle 1993, 2002; Nestle and Porter 1990; Noland and Meirelles 2008; Perelman 2011; Welsh, Davis, and Shaw 1992b).

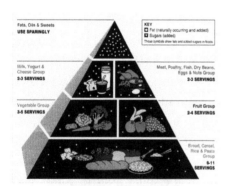

Figure 19.3 The 1992 Food Guide Pyramid.

The Food Pyramid featured five food groups, with informative text about the recommended number of servings people should consume daily. The food groups were arranged in a hierarchy, with the bread, cereal, rice, and pasta group as the base, and then decreasing quantities of the other four groups, culminating with a section of fats, oils, and sweets—to be used sparingly—at the top. The Food Pyramid was very well-known, so readers viewing Figure 19.3 may remember the colorful cartoon images of food featured in each group, along with tiny yellow circles and white triangles sprinkled throughout. While the recommended daily servings in each category mirrored the advice of the 1984 Food Wheel, seeing the pictures of food items paired with the text encouraged viewers to observe how much food this really is. Not only is this a large number of recommended daily servings, if one counts the number of individual food items pictured in the Food Pyramid, the image may seem to suggest that one would need to eat all this food in a single day—quite a hefty task.

Within three years of its release, about half of American adults surveyed said they had heard of the Food Pyramid (Nestle 2002). In 2005, 80 percent of Americans recognized this image; however, few reported following its recommendations (Severson 2005). Even though many consumers seemed to be aware of the federal image, Davis, Britten, and Myers (2001) claimed that there were inconsistencies between people's nutrition knowledge and eating behaviors. In short, most Americans recognized the Food Pyramid as an image, but did not follow its principles. Thus, many different organizations and nutritionists called for the need to change the Food Pyramid (Kennedy 1998). As the number of overweight and obese Americans steadily increased in the decade following the release of the Food Pyramid (d'Elgin 2005), many nutritionists claimed this image was at least partially responsible for misinformation about food consumption choices. For example, the base of the Food Pyramid recommended a large number of servings of the bread, cereal, rice, and pasta group, and in general the image did not distinguish between *healthy* and *unhealthy* food choices. Hellmich (2002) notes that nutrition scientists criticized the content and design of the Food Pyramid, which led them to develop numerous alternative food guides.

By 2002, Steven Christensen, acting director of the Center for Nutrition Policy and Promotion (CNPP), acknowledged that many people recognized the graphic, but failed to incorporate the information into their daily eating habits. In an interview with *USA Today*, he claimed that the Food Pyramid had become a "stand-alone image, and people don't necessarily associate it with the text that goes with it" (Hellmich 2002, 1). The Food Pyramid was also criticized for taking a "one-size-fits-all" approach that did not allow consumers to "personalize" their eating habits (Hellmich 2005, 1–2). Krisberg (2003) explained how federal agencies began to revise their official dietary advice for Americans as a response

Figure 19.4 The 2005 MyPyramid.

to increased levels of obesity. As a way to address these concerns, Porter Novelli was again hired to design a new graphic.

On April 19, 2005, the USDA released the MyPyramid image (see Figure 19.4). In addition to the three messages of *variety, proportionality*, and *moderation* that the Food Pyramid sought to emphasize, MyPyramid added the elements of *physical activity, personalization*, and *gradual improvement* (Haven and Britten 2006). In a special issue of the *Journal of Nutrition Education and Behavior*, executive director of the CNPP Eric J. Hentges (2006, S77) explained how MyPyramid "moves from the one-size-fits-all approach to more individualized guidance, with interactive tools and more personalized dietary recommendations."

As readers can see when viewing the image, MyPyramid featured an equilateral triangle divided vertically into six segments of varying width, with three-dimensional steps protruding to the left. A black cartoon stick figure is climbing the steps, with the website ("MyPyramid.gov") and the slogan ("Steps to a Healthier You") positioned below the image. Each segment's color corresponded to a food group, and viewers could learn what the colors represented by visiting the website.[8] There, consumers could observe that the titles of each food group were more simplified when compared to the Food Pyramid; for instance, the "Meat, Poultry, Fish, Dry Beans, Eggs, and Nuts Group" in the original food pyramid was reduced to just "Meat & Beans" in MyPyramid. MyPyramid was the first USDA food guide to not have instructional text providing information on which foods groups and how much within each group to consume daily. It was also the first food guide to incorporate recommendations about exercise directly into the message, and to include a government website on the actual image itself.

Some experts responded favorably to MyPyramid. Dawn Jackson Blatner, a registered dietician at Northwestern Memorial Hospital's Wellness Institute, claimed that MyPyramid was easier to understand than the 1992 Food Pyramid because MyPyramid "doesn't try to jam everything into a graphic that people don't understand" ("MyPyramid Has a Mixed Response," 2005). D'Elgin (2005, 25) praised MyPyramid for including a message about physical activity, and stated that "as an overweight, diseased population, we [Americans] need the fresh start MyPyramid provides and the better fuel it recommends." Stephanie Childs, a spokesperson for the Grocery Manufacturers of America, expressed support for the new symbol, as did General Foods Corporation and other food companies (Hellmich 2005). In general, the food industry responded positively to the image that was "frequently described as the Food Guide Pyramid flipped on its side" (Perelman 2011, 68). With MyPyramid there was no visual hierarchy to indicate that some foods were better than others. On the day it was released, the MyPyramid.gov website received 1.8 million hits in the first hour, which led many journalists to suggest that the public was very interested in viewing the new graphic (Hellmich 2005).

However, many critics emerged for a variety of reasons. Although MyPyramid retained the pyramid name, a main criticism was that the hierarchy is lost in the vertical division of the colors (Perelman 2011). This made it challenging for viewers to distinguish the proportions of each food group. In addition, many experts disliked the image because it lacked pictures of food ("MyPyramid Has a Mixed Response" 2005). Walter C. Willett (2006), nutritionist at the Harvard School of Public Health, criticized the fact that this information is only available online and not on the graphic itself. In order to comprehend the dietary messages of MyPyramid, people must have Internet access. At the time of MyPyramid's release, the CNPP used a February 2004 Nielsen/NetRatings Survey statistic to assert that 75 percent of US households (or 204.3 million Americans) had Internet access at home, and 99 percent of public schools and 95 percent of public libraries provided access to the Internet ("Public Response to MyPyramid" 2005). Based on these statistics, a majority of Americans had Internet access, which presumably gave them the ability to study the components of MyPyramid on their own. While these numbers were encouraging, they ignored the disparities that exist with regard to Internet access, income level, educational level, and dial-up versus high-speed Internet service in the United States ("Home Internet Access in U.S." 2009). Moreover, having Internet access does not guarantee a visit to MyPyramid.gov or any future online USDA food guides.

MyPyramid was also criticized for not including any visual information about *healthy* food choices. Nestle (2002) claims that it is in the interest of food companies for consumers to be unable to distinguish between *healthy* and *unhealthy* foods. Following this logic, if there is "no such thing as a 'good' food (except when it is theirs)" and no such "thing as a 'bad' food (especially not theirs)" then *all* foods that a food company produces can be incorporated into a healthy diet (Nestle 2002, 21). In addition, visual design research suggests that people have a difficult time distinguishing proportions based on solid colors positioned next to one another (Noland and Meirelles 2008), which could prevent viewers from understanding how much of each food group to consume daily. The image was also confusing because it included a yellow band in the face of the image to stand for oils, but the website indicated that oils were actually *not* considered a food group. In contrast to the 1992 Food Guide Pyramid, little information was released on the development and creation of MyPyramid. Nestle (2002, 380) opined, "It remains a mystery how the USDA came up with a food guide that illustrates physical activity but is completely devoid of food." Because MyPyramid lacked clear information about food groups on the graphic itself, many nutritionists did not believe the image effectively promoted healthy eating.

● CHOOSING MYPLATE

The USDA acknowledged that confusion began to grow with some consumers using the "old Pyramid" and others using the "new Pyramid" ("Executive Summary of Formative Research" 2011, 1). In addition, as mentioned above, few people were successfully following the dietary recommendations of either Pyramid (Haack and Byker 2014). Many nutritionists documented the rise in obesity, particularly during the 1990s and 2000s, as indicative of the American public rejecting the advice of both pyramids. Another criticism that emerged about both food pyramids was that Porter Novelli also serves corporate clients including the Campbell Soup Company, the Dole Food Company, and McDonald's, leading some critics to suggest that the company had a conflict of interest in designing governmental images on dietary advice (Severson 2005). With the release of the updated *2010 Dietary Guidelines*, the White House Childhood Obesity Task Force issued a report stating that the federal government should work with local communities to "disseminate information" about *2010 Guidelines*. The report recommended the government focus on using "simple, easily actionable messages for consumers," which included a "next generation Food Pyramid" ("Executive Summary of Formative Research" 2011, 2). This set the stage for a new food guide. On June 2, 2011, the USDA announced the creation of MyPlate (see Figure 19.5).

On the day of MyPlate's release, First Lady Michelle Obama, Agriculture Secretary Tom Vilsack, and Surgeon General Regina Benjamin unveiled this "new generation icon with the intent to prompt consumers to think about building a healthy plate at meal times and to seek more information to help them do that by going to www.ChooseMyPlate.gov" (United States Department of Agriculture 2011, 1). In doing away with the pyramid shape, MyPlate differs significantly from the previous two USDA food guides. The unifying elements of MyPlate are the fork, the plate (divided into quarters), and the cup. Readers will notice the one-word titles of (what can be presumed to be) five food groups clearly labeled on each quarter-section of the plate and the center of the cup. The proportions indicated by the size of each labeled food group (in relation to one another) corresponds to *2010 Guidelines*.

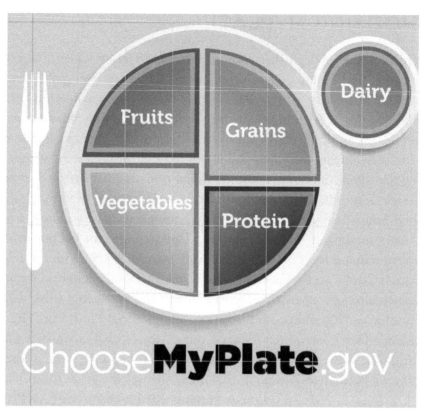

Figure 19.5 The 2011 MyPlate.

In many ways, MyPlate represents a combination of the previous six USDA food guides. It features a circular shape like the Basic 7 and the Food Wheel; utilizes concise food group titles as the key explanatory text like the Basic Four and the Hassle-Free Guide; and includes bright colors with white lines separating the food groups like the Food Guide Pyramid and MyPyramid. MyPlate extends MyPyramid by invoking the "my" prefix, implying this image is meant to be understood as advice for an individual to follow, and that *my* plate can be altered and changed based on individual dietary needs. Similar to MyPyramid, viewers can learn more about the contents of the image by visiting the featured website, ChooseMyPlate.gov. In relation to the five food groups, the website advises the following: (1) "Make half your plate fruits and vegetables;" (2) "Make half your grains whole grains;" (3) "Move to low-fat or fat-free dairy;" (4) "Vary your protein routine;" and (5) "Compare the saturated fat, sodium, and added sugars in your foods and beverages" ("Start with Small Changes" 2016). The wording of these instructions is designed to be simple and easy to follow, so as to encourage Americans to practice healthy eating habits. Unlike the previous USDA food guides that provided advice for daily food consumption, MyPlate differs by focusing on one meal at a time.

Shortly after MyPlate's release, experts including Marion Nestle and David Kessler expressed positive opinions of the new image (Park 2011). As we can infer from the labels and divisions of the plate, viewers are encouraged to fill half of their plates with fruits and vegetables at meal time—advice that clearly corresponds to healthy eating practices. Looking closely at the image, it indicates that vegetables and grains are two of the largest quarter-sections on the plate, implying that more of one's meal should consist of these food items (and, implicitly, less from the other ones). Using the word "Protein" allows for broader interpretations of foods that could be included in this category, and represents the first time a USDA food guide does not explicitly include "Meat" as part of a food group. In addition, placing a cup labeled "Dairy" off to the side of the plate is significant, as this represents the first USDA food guide to not feature "Milk" as its own food group appearing within the main graphic itself (i.e., the plate). By visually encouraging people to eat more vegetables, fruits, and grains while recommending fewer proteins and dairy food items, the image was one nutritionists praised as a helpful reminder about how to eat healthily. On the day MyPlate was released, its simplicity was applauded, as dietician Bonnie Taub-Dix stated in a *USA Today* article that "we eat on plates, not pyramids" (Hellmich 2011, 1).

While there are many aspects to praise about MyPlate, there are also some criticisms worth noting. First, as with MyPyramid, Internet access is necessary to fully understand the colors and symbols of MyPlate. Fortunately (and unlike MyPyramid), MyPlate does feature informative text on the image itself to encourage viewers to know what each color category stands for. Other criticisms based on focus-group research are that there are many meals where people do not use plates, which might make it difficult for consumers to translate MyPlate's advice into their daily eating habits ("Executive Summary of Formative Research" 2011). While this style of eating might apply to some meals, many meals involve different combinations of foods that would be hard to categorize in terms of the correct servings of each food group. In addition, the visual design critiques of MyPyramid can apply to MyPlate in that "our visual systems are not good at judging spatial relations or at measuring angles, chords, or areas of wedges precisely" (Noland and Meirelles 2008, 10). This could work to the advantage of the food industry, which tends to favor nonhierarchical shapes (like bowls or circles) for food guidance images. Finally, MyPlate does not indicate how large or small the plate should be, which could cause people to remain confused about portion size. This confusion might also lead to continued overeating as consumers might feel pressure to endlessly clean their plates. It remains to be seen how effective MyPlate will be, but for now, this image represents the US government's most recent attempt at encouraging Americans to eat healthily.

● CHALLENGES OF PROMOTING HEALTHY EATING IN THE UNITED STATES

The history of the USDA food guides illustrates several key difficulties of trying to address the social problem of unhealthy eating. First, within the development of each food guide are the competing interests of nutritionists, government officials, numerous food industry lobby groups, and the American public. These groups played a role during the development and promotion of each food guide, at some moments differently than others. For instance, nutritionists gained prominence in the late nineteenth and early twentieth centuries, and their focus on quantifying the types of nutrients that each food item contained was highly influential in how we conceptualize food as fuel for the body (Mudry 2010). Nutritionists work to provide the public with the most updated advice on how to eat healthily in ways that will meet people's dietary needs. Nutritionists at the USDA also have to contend with the competing interests of other governmental entities that are tasked with food-related concerns. In fact, Nestle (2010) identified over twelve agencies that play some role in monitoring, evaluating, and recommending food choices to Americans.

In addition, the food industry plays a large role in the development of the USDA food guides. The food industry consists of producers, distributors, marketers, and servers that combined account for 8 percent of US gross national product, and employ 12 percent of the nation's labor force (Nestle 2002). To keep profits high, the food industry does not want the government to explicitly recommend that the public avoid consuming *their* products. Since the USDA has the dual roles of both promoting access to and giving advice about food, this can be a tricky balance. For instance, as mentioned above, the now-infamous release of the 1977 *Dietary Goals* was met with wide resistance from cattle ranchers, egg producers, sugar manufacturers, and dairy farmers, which caused the congressional committee to re-release its recommendations (Nestle 2002). In fact, the original *Dietary Goals* document was one of the last USDA-related publications that explicitly advised Americans to eat less meat. In the edited version, the language changed to "choose 2 to 3 servings of … lean meats," and "limit … intake of high-fat processed meats" (Nestle 2002, 44). Today, in regard to meat, *2010 Dietary Guidelines* recommends that consumers "choose a variety of protein foods" or "replace protein foods that are higher in solid fats with choices that are lower in solid fats and calories and/or are sources of oils" (United States Department of Agriculture and United States Department of Health and Human Services 2010, xi). Advice such as this is vague and complicated at the same time. This is problematic because it does not explicitly encourage a decrease in total daily meat consumption, which as research has shown, can help reduce one's risk of chronic diseases.

Second, this history demonstrates how dietary advice has shifted over the twentieth century and how these recommendations can lead to confusion about what to eat. Of course, there is the overarching shift of the USDA's focus on preventing dietary deficiencies and malnutrition with the first two food guides to promoting healthy eating habits as a way to reduce one's risk for chronic diseases (Nestle 2002). However, these recommendations can be perceived as confusing when new studies are released that seem to contradict one another. For instance, because of the amount of cholesterol an egg has, some studies deem eggs as healthy, while others say they are not (Berardi 2013). Red wine is another example, with some evidence indicating that moderate consumption can have health benefits, while other research points to potential health risks (McCoy 2015). There are also commonly consumed foods and beverages (including water, coffee, and chocolate) that do not make it into any USDA food guide, leaving consumers confused about where these items would fit into a healthy diet. Different dietary trends, such as low-fat foods or the Atkins diet, might also be difficult to fit into the food guides. As a result, many Americans remain confused about what constitutes a healthy diet (Goldberg et al. 2004). This confusion works to the advantage of food producers, who are constantly developing "new and improved" ingredients and products to sell. In fact, Pollan (2008, 9) identifies an interesting "American paradox" related to our eating habits: "a notably unhealthy population preoccupied with nutrition and diet and the idea of eating healthily."

It is also important to consider that not all Americans have access to the same types of foods that would allow them to fulfill the recommendations of any food guide. In fact, 23.5 million Americans live in "food deserts" across the country (Corapi 2014). These are areas that do not have supermarkets or other places where people can access fresh and nutritious foods (Corapi 2014). Other challenges that can make healthy eating difficult include the large number of people living in poverty and experiencing, as the USDA calls it, food insecurity. This situation reflects Cherry-Chandler's (2009, 45) description of "America's secret": "the growing number of its citizens … stationed on the periphery of plenty." Individuals who do not have access or resources to purchase (or grow) healthy foods would experience difficulty with trying to fulfill the messages of any governmental food guide, no matter how clear it is.

Finally, I argue that the history of the USDA food guides points to the reluctance of the American public to follow governmental advice. Throughout the twentieth century, the USDA attempted to improve on each previous food guide to develop a more effective image that would encourage people to eat healthily. However, as Haack and Byker (2014) observe, Americans might be aware of federal nutrition guides, but fail to use them. In fact, their survey of thirty-one studies on how well Americans know and use the Food Pyramid, MyPyramid, and/or MyPlate revealed that there was "no conclusive evidence" that these food guides had any impact on consumers' eating habits (Haack and Byker 2014, 621).

Ironically, at the same time, Americans want advice on how to eat healthily—just in a particular way. For example, during the development of MyPlate, the USDA used focus groups to test messages about the recommendations in *2010 Dietary Guidelines for Americans*. Not surprisingly, participants chose directives that they perceived to be the easiest to incorporate into their daily routine.

These phrases included "Enjoy what you eat, just eat less of it," "Save half your plate for fruits and vegetables," and "Snack wisely" ("Executive Summary of Formative Research" 2011, 4). However, the messages that were ranked as least favorable were ones that participants believed were irrelevant or required difficult changes to adopt, such as "Switch to 1% or fat-free milk," "Break the sugary drink habit," and "Know your personal calorie limit" ("Executive Summary of Formative Research" 2011, 4). While participants wanted to learn nutritional information that would positively impact their health, an interesting trend emerged as many people did not want to feel as though they were being told what to do. The participants wanted to feel "empowered" and "in control" of their own food habits. Although there were only 112 participants in the focus groups, this idea of resisting governmental advice is very prominent today. In fact, by and large, Americans are distrustful of the government, as a recent Pew Research Center survey (2015) reveals that only 19 percent of Americans report that they trust the federal government to do what is right "just about always" (3%) or "most of the time" (16%). Public trust in government remains at historic lows, and this could have a negative impact on Americans' willingness to accept and adopt dietary advice from the USDA, or any governmental entity for that matter.

● CONCLUSION

This chapter has focused on how the USDA food guides have sought to address the social problem of unhealthy eating. Exploring the history of the USDA food guides reveals that there are competing interests of different constituencies that played a role in the development of each image, and this affects the content and the messages of the various food guides. Starting with the 1943 Basic 7 and the 1958 Basic Four, the USDA focused on getting Americans to consume more nutrients as a way to prevent malnutrition and promote a strong population. Federal dietary advice shifted as the prevalence of chronic diseases began to rise. The 1979 Hassle-Free Guide and the 1984 Food Wheel reflected a focus on the number of daily servings paired with more images of foods people could eat. Moving to more contemporary food guides, the 1992 Food Guide Pyramid, the 2005 MyPyramid, and the 2011 MyPlate encouraged consumers to think more about variety, proportionality, and moderation while also expanding the purview of daily food guides by including exercise and online guidance materials.

Unfortunately, this history also demonstrates that the USDA has struggled to get Americans to adopt healthy eating habits. While there have been various groups and individuals involved in the creation of these food guides, I argue that the difficulties in getting Americans to follow this advice stems primarily from the competing interests of nutritionists, the food industry, and the American public. First, nutritionists are focused on providing advice about the amount of nutrients the public should consume to maintain good health. This focus often leads to more specific and detailed instructions (e.g., "increase consumption of foods that contain fiber, calcium, and vitamin D") of seemingly simple ideas (e.g., "eat more vegetables").

Second, as mentioned above, the food industry does not want nutritionists or the government to issue negative news about their products. An illustrative example comes from the aforementioned studies linking processed meat consumption to cancer. In response to the WHO report, Barry Carpenter, president of the North American Meat Institute, stated, "Scientific evidence shows cancer is a complex disease not caused by single foods and that a balanced diet and healthy lifestyle choices are essential to good health" (Aubrey 2015, 3). In short, the food industry wants everyone to keep consuming their products (whatever they may be). Finally, the American public has a strong desire to get healthy. Millions of dollars are spent each year on new diets, supplements, products, and gym memberships. However, as mentioned earlier, Americans tend to not like being told what to do. Surprisingly, for nearly every news article featuring a story about the connections between certain foods leading to chronic diseases, at least one comment would be a posting criticizing the research as an attempt to boss us around. As trust in government continues to remain low, there is a continued resistance to the so-called nanny state.[9]

It is also important to note that changes in the food industry have presented additional challenges to solving the social problem of unhealthy eating. For example, portion sizes have increased greatly since the 1970s, making it difficult to calculate the number of servings being consumed in a meal (Ledikwe, Ello-Martin, and Rolls 2005). Kessler (2009) documents how processed foods containing high levels of fat, sugar, and salt actually alter brain chemistry, which then prevents people from knowing when they are full. Criticisms that function purely at the individual level draw our focus away from the means of production and the corporations involved in food production. In addition, governmental recommendations and public policies do not always align. For instance, although MyPlate recommends that half of one's plate should consist of fruits and vegetables, Haack and Byker (2014, 623) note that "production of these crops receives less than 2% of funding from the 2008 Farm Bill." As this chapter demonstrates, due to the various factors involved, our eating habits need to be addressed from multiple angles.

While the USDA food guides have not been fully successful in getting Americans to adopt healthy eating habits, at the present moment, they do represent a comprehensive way to transmit dietary advice to the American public. The USDA is one governmental agency that has over a century's worth of data and knowledge about which foods to consume and how much. A quick visit to ChooseMyPlate.gov reveals pages upon pages of sample meals, daily tracking calculators, and ways to take charge of our eating habits. And MyPlate itself provides helpful advice in terms of filling half of our plates with fruits and vegetables, and using the labels of "Protein" and "Dairy" (instead of "Meat" and "Milk") to allow for broader interpretations of foods that can fit into a healthy diet.

Some people may have good intentions about adopting healthy eating habits, but admittedly, change is hard. Until Americans become more willing to accept and enact changes in their eating habits and possibly their views on governmental advice, it may be difficult for any USDA food guide to be effective. However, solving the social problem of unhealthy eating does not rest solely on individual behaviors, as the food industry would have to be willing to accept some changes, too. These may take the form of lower profits, or less access to government subsidies—or even restrictions on portion sizes or what goes into our food (e.g., added sugar, salt, et cetera). We are all connected to this problem. It is in all of our interests to reduce the growing rates of type 2 diabetes, cardiovascular diseases, cancer, and obesity by striving to practice and maintain healthy eating habits throughout our lives.[10] Criticizing the government is the easy part. Finding solutions that both the food industry and the American public would be willing to enact—that's food for thought.

● NOTES

1. Each of the seven food guides discussed in this chapter are available to view in "A Brief History of USDA Food Guides" (2011), which was produced by the USDA's Center for Nutrition Policy and Promotion.

2. I conducted a visual rhetorical analysis of the 1992 Food Guide Pyramid and the 2005 MyPyramid in my dissertation, and portions of this essay appeared in parts of my dissertation (see Petre 2012).

3. I rely on *2010 Dietary Guidelines for Americans* in this chapter because these recommendations were used to develop the MyPlate image, and have received more recent scholarly attention. While writing this document, *2015–2020 Dietary Guidelines* were released and made available to the public at http://health.gov/dietaryguidelines/2015.

4. Researchers are also beginning to document links between added sugar consumption and depression (Gangwisch et al. 2015).

5. Some readers might be inclined to ask, what about exercising? Although exercise plays an important role in maintaining a healthy lifestyle and it is recommended that people exercise regularly, when it comes to our overall health, dietary choices matter more. For example, exercise expends fewer calories than many people think. Consuming a twelve-ounce can of Coca-Cola that contains 140 calories and ten teaspoons of sugar would take three miles of rigorous walking to burn off (O'Connor 2015); in most cases, simply choosing to drink water instead would have the same result. Exercise also can increase appetite, causing people to overeat, which undercuts any potential weight loss from exercise (Thomas et al. 2012).

6. Dr. Marion Nestle (2002, 2006, 2010), a professor of nutrition, food studies, and public health at New York University, has written extensively on food and the food industry. I rely on her descriptions of the history of how different USDA food guides were created throughout the twentieth century. Interested readers should consult pages 29 to 94 of Nestle (2002), *Food Politics: How the Food Industry Influences Nutrition and Health.*

7. The Basic 7 consisted of seven food groups: (1) green and yellow vegetables; (2) oranges, tomatoes, and grapefruit; (3) potatoes and other vegetables and fruits; (4) milk, and milk products; (5) meat, poultry, fish, or eggs; (6) bread, flour, and cereals; and (7) butter and fortified margarine (Welsh, Davis, and Shaw 1992a, 9).

8. The colors featured in MyPyramid were positioned in the six bands in the following order from left to right: orange, green, red, yellow, blue, and purple. These colors represent the food groups, and the bands vary in size to indicate the proportion of each food group a person should consume daily. The MyPyramid website showed which food groups correspond to which colors: (1) Grains are orange, (2) Vegetables are green, (3) Fruits are red, (4) Oils are yellow, (5) Milk is blue, and (6) Meat and Beans are purple.

9. Nanny state is a pejorative term used to indicate excessive government involvement in our lives. It is commonly used by conservatives to refer to the actions of government as excessive. For example, in 2010 Sarah Palin called Pennsylvania a "nanny state run amok" because of the state's proposed guidelines to limit the amount of sugary sweets in classroom parties and reduce the number of holiday and birthday celebrations at school (Behrendt, Nelson, and Bruce 2010, 1).

10. Kessler (2009), Nestle (2006), and Pollan (2008) provide some helpful ideas for how individuals and organizations can promote and enact healthy eating practices.

● REFERENCES

Aubrey, A. 2015. "Bad Day for Bacon: Processed Meats Cause Cancer, WHO Says." *NPR*, October 26. http://www.npr.org.

Behrendt, T., R. Nelson, and M. Bruce, M. 2010. "Cookie Protest: Sarah Palin Calls Pennsylvania a 'Nanny State Run Amok.'" *ABC News*, November 10. http://abcnews.go.com.

Bellavia, A., S. C. Larsson, M. Bottai, A. Wolk, and N. Orsini. 2013. "Fruit and Vegetable Consumption and All-Cause Mortality: A Dose-Response Analysis." *American Journal of Clinical Nutrition* 98 (2): 454–59. http://ajcn.nutrition.org.

Berardi, J. 2013. "Eggs: Healthy Or Not?" *The Huffington Post*, July 16. http://www.huffingtonpost.com.

"A Brief History of USDA Food Guides." 2011. *Center for Nutrition Policy and Promotion*, June. http://www.choosemyplate.gov/content/brief-history-usda-food-guides.

Centers for Disease Control and Prevention. 2013. *State Indicator Report on Fruits and Vegetables.* Atlanta, GA: Author.://www.cdc.gov/nutrition/downloads/state-indicator-report-fruits-vegetables-2013.pdf.

Centers for Disease Control and Prevention. 2015. *How to Use Fruits and Vegetables to Help Manage Your Weight.* Atlanta, GA: Author. https://www.cdc.gov/healthyweight/healthy_eating/fruits_vegetables.html.

Centers for Disease Control and Prevention. 2016. *Chronic Disease Prevention and Health Promotion.* Atlanta, GA: Author. http://www.cdc.gov/chronicdisease/overview.

Cherry-Chandler, E. 2009. "After the Reapers: Place Settings of Race, Class, and Food Insecurity. *Text and Performance Quarterly* 29 (1): 44–59.

Corapi, S. 2014. "Why It Takes More Than a Grocery Store to Eliminate a 'Food Desert.'" *PBS Newshour*, February 3. http://www.pbs.org.

Davis, C. A., P. Britten, and E. F. Myers. 2001. "Past, Present, and Future of the Food Guide Pyramid." *Journal of the American Dietetic Association* 101 (8): 881–85. http://www.adajournal. org.

Davis, C., and E. Saltos. 1999. "Dietary Recommendations and How They Have Changed over Time." In *America's Eating Habits: Changes and Consequences*, 33–50. Edited by E. Frazão. Agricultural Bulletin No. (A1B750). Washington, DC: United States Department of Agriculture.

D'Elgin, T. 2005. *What Should I Eat? A Complete Guide to the New Food Pyramid*. New York: Ballantine Books.

DiNicolantonio, J. J., J. H. O'Keefe, and S. C. Lucan. 2015. "Added Fructose: A Principal Driver of Type 2 Diabetes Mellitus and Its Consequences." *Mayo Clinic Proceedings* 90 (3): 372–81. http://www.mayoclinicproceedings.org.

Executive Summary of Formative Research. 2011. "Development of *2010 Dietary Guidelines for Americans*: Consumer Messages and New Food Icon." *United States Department of Agriculture*, June. http://www.choosemyplate.gov/health-professionals.

Fryar, C. D., M. D. Carroll, and C. L. Ogden. 2014. "Prevalence of Overweight, Obesity, and Extreme Obesity Among Adults: United States, 1960–1962 Through 2011–2012." *Centers for Disease Control and Prevention*. Atlanta, GA: Author. http://www.cdc.gov/nchs/data/hestat/obesity_adult_11_12/obesity_ adult_11_12.htm.

Gangwisch, J. E., L. Hale, L. Garcia, D. Malaspina, M. G. Opler, M. E. Payne, R. C. Rossum, and D. Lane. 2015. "High Glycemic Index Diet as a Risk Factor for Depression: Analyses from the Women's Health Initiative." *American Journal of Clinical Nutrition*. http://ajcn.nutrition. org.

Goldberg, J. P., M. A. Belury, P. Elam, S. C. Finn, D. Hayes, R. Lyle, S. St Jeor, M. Warren, and J. P. Hellwiq. 2004. "The Obesity Crisis: Don't Blame It on the Pyramid." *Journal of the American Dietetic Association* 104 (7): 1141–47.

Haack, S. A., and C. J. Byker. 2014. "Recent Population Adherence to and Knowledge of United States Federal Nutrition Guides, 1992–2013: A Systematic Review." *Nutrition Reviews* 72 (10): 613–26.

Haven, J., and P. Britten. 2006. "MyPyramid—The Complete Guide." *Nutrition Today* 41 (6): 253–59.

Hellmich, N. 2002. "Scales Tip in Favor of New Pyramid." *USA Today*, November 4.

Hellmich, N. 2005. "USDA's New Food Pyramid Is All About You." *USA Today*, April 19.

Hellmich, N. 2011. "USDA Serves Nutrition Guidelines on 'MyPlate.'" *USA Today*, June 2.

Hentges, E. J. 2006. "Foreword [Supplement to]." *Journal of Nutrition Education and Behavior* 38 (6): S77.

"Home Internet Access in U.S.: Still Room for Growth." 2009. *Nielsen Report*, March 11. http://www.marketingcharts.com.

Kamps, A. D. 2011. *What's Cooking, Uncle Sam? The Government's Effect on the American Diet.* Washington, DC: The Foundation for the National Archives.

Kennedy, E. 1998. Building on the Pyramid—Where Do We Go from Here? *Nutrition Today* 33 (5): 183–85.

Kerver, J. M., E. J. Yang, L. Bianchi, and W. O. Song. 2003. "Dietary Patterns Associated with Risk Factors for Cardiovascular Disease in Healthy US Adults." *American Journal of Clinical Nutrition* 78 (6): 1103–10.

Kessler, D. A. 2009. *The End of Overeating: Taking Control of the Insatiable American Appetite.* New York: Rodale.

Krisberg K. 2003. "Dietary Guidelines, Food Pyramid Facing Scrutiny." *The Nation's Health*, November. http://www.medscape.com.

Ledikwe, J. H., J. A. Ello-Martin, and B. J. Rolls. 2005. "Portion Sizes and the Obesity Epidemic." *Journal of Nutrition* 135 (4): 905–09.

Manella, M. 2016. "Mediterranean Diet Linked to Lower Risk of Heart Attack, Stroke." *CNN*, April 26. http://www.cnn.com.

McCoy, K. 2015. "Is Red Wine Really Good for You?" *Everyday Health*, March 12. http://www.everydayhealth.com.

Mudry, J. 2010. "Counting on Dinner: Discourses of Science and the Refiguration of Food in USDA Nutrition Guides." *Environmental Communication* 4(3): 338–54.

"MyPyramid Has a Mixed Response from Experts." 2005. *News-Medical.net*, April 20. http://www.news-medical.net.

Nestle, M. 1993. "Dietary Advice for the 1990s: The Political History of the Food Guide Pyramid." *Caduceus* 9 (3): 136–53.

Nestle, M. 2002. *Food Politics: How the Food Industry Influences Nutrition and Health* (revised edition). Berkeley: University of California Press.

Nestle, M. 2006. *What to Eat: An Aisle-by-Aisle Guide to Savvy Food Choices and Good Eating.* New York: North Point Press.

Nestle, M. 2010. *Safe Food: The Politics of Food Safety* (updated and expanded edition). Berkeley: University of California Press.

Nestle, M., and D. V. Porter. 1990. "Evolution of Federal Dietary Guidance Policy: From Food Adequacy to Chronic Disease Prevention." *Caduceus* 6 (2): 43–67.

Noland, C., and M. I. Meirelles. 2008. "Visual Representation of Health Information: A Critique of the 2005 Food Pyramid." *American Communication Journal* 10(S): 431–2. http://www.ac-journal.org.

O'Connor, A. 2015. "Coca-Cola Funds Scientists Who Shift Blame for Obesity away from Bad Diets." *New York Times*, August 9. http://www.nytimes.com.

Painter, J., J. H. Rah, and Y. K. Lee. 2002. "Comparison of International Food Guide Pictorial Representations." *Journal of the American Dietetic Association* 102 (4): 483–89.

Park, M. 2011. "Plate Icon to Guide Americans to Healthier Eating." *CNN*, June 2. http://www.cnn.com.

Perelman, A. 2011. "The Pyramid Scheme: Visual Metaphors and the USDA's Pyramid Food Guides." *Design Issues* 27 (3): 60–71.

Petre, E. A. 2012. *Iconic Images, Visual Appropriations, and Public Culture: Negotiating the Rhetorical Challenges of the USDA Food Pyramids* (Doctoral dissertation). http://opensiuc.lib.siu.edu/dissertations/492/.

Pew Research Center. 2015. *Public Trust in Government: 1958–2015.* http://www.people-press.org.

Pollan, M. 2008. *In Defense of Food: An Eater's Manifesto.* New York: Penguin Press.

"Public Response to MyPyramid." 2005. *Center for Nutrition Promotion and Policy.* http://www.cnpp.usda.gov/MyPyramidConsumerResearch.htm.

Ratzan, S. C. 2004. "Silent Threat: Non-Communicable Disease and Obesity." *Journal of Health Communication* 9 (1): 1–2.

Severson, K. 2005. "When a Food Marketer Devises Nutrition Advice." *New York Times*, April 10.

Sifferlin, A. 2015. "90% of Americans Eat Too Much Salt." *Time*, July 2. http://www.time.com.

"Start with Small Changes." 2016. *United States Department of Agriculture.* http://www.choosemyplate.gov.

Suchetka, D. 2010. "Americans Are Consuming More Calories Than Ever: Fighting Fat." *Cleveland.com*, April 5. http://www.cleveland.com.

Thomas, D. M., C. Bouchard, T. Church, C. Slentz, W. E. Kraus, L. M. Redman, C. K. Martin, A. M. Silva, M. Vossen, K. Westerterp, and … S. B. Heymsfield. 2012. "Why Do Individuals Not Lose More Weight from an Exercise Intervention at a Defined Dose? An Energy Balance Analysis." *Obesity Reviews* 13 (10): 835–47.

United States Department of Agriculture. 2011. *USDA Unveils New Food Icon.* USDA Press Release No. 0225.11. Washington, DC: Author.

United States Department of Agriculture and United States Department of Health and Human Services. 2010. *Dietary Guidelines for Americans, 2010* (7th ed.). Washington, DC: Author. http://www.dietaryguidelines.gov.

Walton, A. G. 2012. "Why We Keep Overeating and What We Can Do About It." *The Atlantic,* March 7. http://www.theatlantic.com.

Welsh, S., C. Davis, and A. Shaw. 1992a. "A Brief History of Food Guides in the United States." *Nutrition Today* 27 (6): 6–11. http://journals.lww.com/nutritiontodayonline.

Welsh, S., C. Davis, and A. Shaw. 1992b. "Development of the Food Guide Pyramid." *Nutrition Today* 27 (6): 12–23. http://journals.lww.com/nutritiontodayonline.

Willett, W. C. 2006. "Rebuilding the Food Pyramid [Special issue]." *Scientific American* 16 (4): 12–21. http://www.ScientificAmerican.com.

● IMAGE CREDITS

SECTION **SIX**

SOCIAL PROBLEMS IN FAMILIES

American families have experienced a number of significant changes over the years. Divorce, cohabitation, and single parenthood are much more likely now than they were fifty years ago. These are subjective social problems: some see them as problems while others welcome the increased options available. The purpose of this section is to examine these and other changes in American family life over time and to explore additional social problems related to the family, such as the motherhood wage penalty and issues related to domestic violence.

● CHANGES IN AMERICAN FAMILY LIFE OVER TIME

The American family has experienced a number of changes over the years. Prior to World War II, the American divorce rate was low, having children outside of marriage was a source of embarrassment and shame for women, and same-sex relationships were disparaged. Now, the divorce rate is high, it is more common than not to live together prior to getting married, and same-sex marriage is legal in all fifty states. While support for all of these phenomena has risen over time, Americans who are more traditional and conservative see them as being social problems.

Divorce

The divorce rate in the United States rose steadily from the mid-1800s, with peaks after both world wars, until an ultimate high in 1980. It has been slightly declining since. However, the current rate is still high, as couples marrying now have an approximately 40 percent chance of divorcing. Prior to the 1970s, divorce was very stigmatizing, and being divorced often became a master status for people, suggesting failure. Plenty of people were unhappy in their marriages, but they would stay together due to societal expectations of stability, especially for children. In addition, most Americans were married in churches and were more active in organized religions than people are today. People felt that it was important to honor their commitment and remain as members in good standing in their respective houses of worship. Also, most women did not have the resources to live independently of their husbands if they were to get divorced.

Marriage has changed over time, in that it used to be more of an economic partnership and less about love (Coontz 2006). Increasingly, romantic love has become the basis for marriage and therefore marriages are less stable. Americans' current perspective on marriage emphasizes self-development, where each person should develop a fulfilling, independent self within the marriage; flexible roles, where people should be willing to take on different tasks to contribute to the household; and open communication, including mutually shared emotional disclosures. We tend to expect a lot from our spouses, potentially too much, as the number of people we confide in has decreased over time. It is frankly easier for marriages to fail than in previous eras. The good news is that when couples are able to satisfy these criteria, their chances are high for a secure and fulfilling marriage. In fact, the odds of divorcing decrease the longer a couple has been married.

Cohabitation

Cohabitation was almost unthinkable in America fifty years ago. It went against the teachings of most religions and people's moral beliefs. People believed in the sanctity of marriage to a much more elevated degree than most people do today. Many people who do not believe in cohabitation do not believe in sex before marriage and maintain a traditional view of marriage. Historically, people used the language of "living in sin" to describe cohabitation. Even today, the Mormon,

Catholic, and evangelical Christian faiths have clear doctrines against people living together outside of marriage. However, fewer Americans practice organized religion than in the past and this is particularly the case for young people.

Beginning around 1970, the proportion of young adults who cohabited prior to marrying increased sharply. Now, the majority of first marriages are preceded by (at least one) cohabitation. It is becoming the norm. This is connected to the later age at first marriage, as couples put off marriage until they have some financial stability. Most cohabitations in America are short term, meaning that couples either break up or marry. Cohabitation is even more common after a first marriage than before it: whether someone remarries or not, she or he is likely to cohabit at least once after a marriage ends. And increasing numbers of people do not marry at all, either remaining single or cohabiting without marriage.

Same-Sex Marriage

Even though it has been legalized in every state, same-sex marriage is still very controversial. Many traditional and conservative people take issue with it because they argue that it goes against religious teachings. Opponents of same-sex marriage also reference procreation, saying that only a man and a woman can create children, which is an important aspect of a family. For a sizeable but shrinking segment of the country, same-sex marriage is a social problem. It indicates a decline in traditional values and behaviors and should therefore be stopped. These folks think that they should be able to refuse services to same-sex couples who are planning to marry, as it goes against their religious and moral beliefs.

A large percentage of Americans, however, openly support same-sex marriage and problematize the second-class treatment of gay people as discriminatory. Same-sex marriage is quickly becoming more accepted by Americans, as shown in an ongoing Pew Research Center study (2016). A majority, at 55 percent, expressed support for same-sex marriage in 2016, up from 35 percent just fifteen years ago. And since the oldest generation is the most opposed, it is likely that support will continue to increase over time. Unsurprisingly, adults who are not affiliated with organized religion are more supportive than religious people. However, support has increased over time even for religious groups, especially for Catholics and white mainline Protestants.

Single Parenthood

In 1960, a mere 5 percent of American children were born to unmarried parents. Today that number is 40 percent. One related trend is that the marriage rate has declined over time. In 1960, just 9 percent of adults aged twenty-five and older had never been married, whereas now it is 20 percent, an all-time high (Pew Research Center 2014). Couples are more likely to wait until they feel financially secure to marry, and for some that time does not come. But people may not be as willing to forego or delay childbearing, resulting in children born outside of marriage. Also, with divorce more of an option than it used to be, some children are born after a divorce.

Attitudes toward single parenthood in America are not as positive as those toward other changes such as cohabitation and same-sex marriage. In a recent poll, a full 69 percent of American adults maintained that the trend toward more single women having children is a bad thing for society, and "a majority (61%) still believe that a child needs both a mother and a father to grow up happily" (Pew Research Center 2016). Not surprisingly, younger people and those who are less traditional religiously or politically are more accepting of single parenthood than older and more traditional people. However, Americans generally believe that children should be raised in two-parent households, even as fewer of them are.

Social Class and American Families

All of these trends are correlated with social class in America. In her piece, "Social Class and Diverging Family Structures," Monahan Lang discusses the growing inequality between working-class and poor people on one end, and middle- and upper-middle-class people on the other end, in their family lives. In conjunction with the cumulative advantage and disadvantage discussed in Section 1, Monahan Lang shows that Americans with higher education levels, professional jobs, and higher incomes are more likely to get and stay married in today's economy. As people put off marriage until financial security and subsequently marry others who are like themselves socioeconomically, those on the higher rungs of the ladder lead more secure and fulfilling family lives than those who are more precarious economically. More privileged Americans also tend to live in affluent neighborhoods so their children can attend well-funded schools. This is another form of inequality that is growing in contemporary American society.

THE MOTHERHOOD PENALTY

Social scientists have developed a concept called the motherhood penalty that identifies that women with children face a host of challenges that women without children do not typically face. Many people perceive that women without children are more committed to employment than women with children, which ultimately negatively impacts the pay, hiring, and promotion of mothers. Interestingly, fathers do not experience this. There is not a fatherhood penalty for men. In fact, employed men with children are often celebrated for being good dads and solid family men. Among other things, this reaffirms that many aspects of parenthood are still gendered.

In "Gender Pay Equity in Advanced Countries: The Role of Parenthood and Policies," Misra and Strader identify two very interesting trends. One is that there is a convergence between men's and women's wages in most developed countries. The second is that mothers in these countries earn substantially less money, on average, than childless women. In the United States, for example, research shows that women experience, on average, a 7 percent wage penalty per child. Meanwhile, fathers are likely to earn a little more money than childless men. In addition to explaining these social trends, Misra and Strader outline two strategies aimed at reducing the gender gap in earnings: expanding maternity and paternity leave and publicly subsidizing childcare.

DOMESTIC VIOLENCE IN THE UNITED STATES

One social problem that is more objective than divorce and cohabitation is domestic violence. Although there are exceptions, the general trend is that men perpetrate injurious violence against women. In the United States, rates of domestic violence are quite high and take a variety of different forms, including physical, sexual, emotional, and economic abuse. Millions of American women endure the fear, humiliation, and intimidation that goes along with being in a relationship with a violent partner.

In her article, "Domestic Violence and the Family: Mothers Experiencing Homelessness," Hetzler provides a history of domestic violence in the United

States and shows just how common it is. In addition to establishing some of the reasons why domestic violence takes place, she establishes the connection between domestic violence and mothering. From there, Hetzler describes how many domestic violence shelters and programs have been established to help women and children whose lives are affected by domestic violence. Her piece concludes with a description of the challenges and opportunities that women and children staying at New Beginnings, a shelter for victims of such violence, experience.

References

Coontz, S. 2006. *Marriage, A History: How Love Conquered Marriage*. New York: Penguin Books.

Pew Research Center. 2014. *Record Share of Americans Have Never Married: As Values, Economics and Gender Patterns Change*. http://www.pewsocialtrends.org/2014/09/24/record-share-of-americans-have-never-married/.

Pew Research Center. 2016. *Changing Attitudes on Gay Marriage*. http://www.pewforum.org/2016/05/12/changing-attitudes-on-gay-marriage/.

CHAPTER 20

Social Class and Diverging Family Structures

By Molly Monahan Lang

I t is difficult to define a successful family life. The standard definition in the United States has been a family that is begun with a heterosexual marriage, includes children, and avoids divorce. But that normative definition has given way to many varieties of families. Over the last several decades, as the upper middle class has grown and the gap between the wealthy and the poor has increased, family lives have become more divided by social class. In the following chapter, I discuss how marriage and divorce have changed over time, as well as how marriage and divorce rates currently differ by social class. I also discuss the increase in single parenthood and its relation to social class. I then show how both economic and familial changes have resulted in growing inequalities between children growing up in different social classes. Children's lives are increasingly divided along socioeconomic lines, and unless major changes occur, this trend is likely to continue.

● MARRIAGE AND DIVORCE

Andrew Cherlin has written extensively on marriage in America (2004, 2010). He has developed a typology that discusses three main kinds of marriage over time. The institutional marriage describes marriage prior to the 1900s in America. This type of marriage is characterized by duty and conformity, meaning that every man was supposed to marry a woman and every woman was supposed to marry a man, as part of their obligation to society. The local community, the church, and the law all supported this type of marriage. Men were expected to be the heads of their households. The marriage was to be Christian-based, with God at the top. So men were to be subservient to God, and women were to be subservient to their husbands and to God. At the time, romantic love was not considered an acceptable reason for marriage (Coontz 2006). Marriage was a practical arrangement frequently planned by extended family members, which resulted in an exchange of services. These were primarily colonists and their ancestors living on homesteads. There was a lot of work to be done, and romantic love would not help it to get accomplished.

Keep in mind that during the time of the institutional marriage, divorce was fault based and difficult to achieve. There were very few acceptable grounds for divorce, including adultery and desertion. With the patriarchal structure of the time, it was rare for women to be granted divorces. More frequently, men would accuse women of a fault to be able to divorce. Even so, divorce was quite rare. There were stepfamilies, certainly, but they were more likely to be preceded by death than divorce. In fact, marriages in general were much more likely to dissolve with death than divorce. Divorce was simply unacceptable and shameful in the early decades of the United States.

As America modernized through the process of industrialization, a new form of marriage emerged. Cherlin (2004) refers to this as the companionate marriage. He places the beginnings of this type of marriage in the early 1900s, but it had its heyday in the 1950s. The companionate marriage includes a breadwinner and a homemaker. As men moved away from the homesteads, or came from other countries to find work in industry, a segmentation between home and employment occurred. And though plenty of women worked, whether employed at home or away from home, married women were expected to prioritize home and family life and limit or curtail provisioning. In this type of marriage, the husband is the authority figure, but less so than in earlier eras. Coontz (2006) refers to this as "affectionate inequality," because husbands and wives were to feel and show affection for each other, but they were not equals, socially or otherwise. While friendly with each other, men still were to have other men as friends, and women were to congregate and socialize mainly with other women. All members of couples were expected to find meaning in their family roles: men were to be fulfilled as breadwinners and disciplinarians, women were to be fulfilled as housewives and mothers. And while divorce was beginning to increase, it remained fault based until the 1970s.

Cherlin's third type of marriage, the individualized marriage, emerged after 1960. This form of marriage should be the most familiar to you. It emphasizes self-development, in that each person should be able to develop and maintain a fulfilling, independent self within the marriage. Individualized marriages are characterized by flexible roles, depending on what each person brings to the couple and the stage of life the couple is in. For example, if the woman can earn more money or gets more satisfaction from her occupation, she may be the primary breadwinner, but this could change if the man earns a degree that gets him a job outside of the area. When children are young, the husband's and wife's roles may be different than later in the marriage.[1] All of this relies on regular and open communication with mutually shared disclosures. As can be seen, couples are meant to be each other's close friends, perhaps their closest friends. As Coontz (2006) has written, this can put a lot of pressure on one relationship. Indeed, marriages in the current era can be highly satisfactory, if all of the ingredients are present, but they are also incredibly fragile.

As marriage has become more individualized, it has also become less common in America. For example, in 1960, 9 percent of people aged twenty-five and up had never been married. By 2012, that percentage had increased to 20 percent (Pew Research Center 2014). People are also marrying later in life, with the average age of first marriage at 27 years old for women and 29 for men. Consider this: in 1960, fully 68 percent of adults between the ages of 20 and 29 were married. As the companionate marriage declined and the individualized marriage became more prevalent, that percentage had decreased to 26 percent by

2008 (Pew Research Center 2010). It has become more common for Americans to delay marriage or avoid marriage altogether.

When it comes to marriage rates, there are differences by group. Education and income have become major predictors of marriage. In 1960, there was very little difference between the percentage of college graduates and the percentage of those who had not gone to college who were married (76% and 72%, respectively; Pew Research Center 2010). By 2008, not only had those percentages decreased, the gap had grown dramatically: 64 percent of college graduates were married while only 48 percent of those who had not gone to college were. Marriage has declined much more for those without a college degree than for those with one. Other more recent studies have also shown that people with college degrees are more likely than those without to be married (U.S. Bureau of Labor Statistics 2014). People with lower incomes are also less likely to be married than people with higher incomes (Pew Research Center 2010).

Why is this? The best argument is that individuals, especially women, want a marriage partner who is able to contribute financially. But men's real wages have been falling for decades, especially young men's. And in this economy, men with a high school degree or less are more likely to be unemployed than those with higher education (U.S. Bureau of Labor Statistics 2016). Women have increased their education levels and increased their earning potential over time, decreasing their reliance on marriage or men for financial well-being. It may be more costly for some women to marry than to delay marriage or forego it altogether.

As more people, especially more women, are earning college degrees, people who do marry are likely to marry someone with a similar education level to themselves. And since the college educated are more likely to marry, this means that the college educated are not only more employable but also more likely to be married to each other. This increases the inequality between themselves and those who have not finished college.

Divorce trends add to this inequality. While divorce was rare for all groups during the time of the institutional marriage, and was still considered shameful through the 1950s, it began a steep rise during the 1960s and 1970s. Interestingly, the divorce rate peaked in 1980 and has been either level or slightly declining since. Of course, America's divorce rate is still quite high, with 40 percent of couples predicted to divorce. However, divorce is now more likely for particular groups. Poor people divorce at higher rates than other social classes, for example (Amato 2010). And college-educated people are less likely to divorce than those without a college degree (Stevenson and Wolfers 2007; U.S. Bureau of Labor Statistics 2013). This may reflect, in part, the tendency for college-educated people to marry at a later age than their less-educated counterparts.

What all of this means is that college-educated people are more likely to get married and to stay married in contemporary America. Therefore, children raised by parents with a college degree are more likely to have married parents. And since the longer couples are married, the lower their chances of divorce, such children stand a good chance of avoiding the disruption of divorce.

● SINGLE PARENTHOOD

In addition to the trends described above, single parenthood has grown quite common in America. Whereas just 5 percent of babies were born to unmarried mothers in 1960, fully 40 percent of babies are today (Hamilton, Martin, Osterman, Curtin, and Mathews 2015). One reason for this is the decrease in marriages that occur between conception and birth—what have been termed "shotgun marriages" (Akerlof, Yellen, and Katz 1996). Cohabitation has also increased substantially over the years, especially for those with low levels of education (Copen, Daniels, and Mosher 2013). Unmarried births are three times as common for the poor as for the affluent (Edin and Kefalas 2011). The mothers are often in a relationship with the father of the child, and such pregnancies may be unintended or intended, or somewhere in between (England and Edin 2007).

Families deemed "fragile" due to the parents being unmarried while raising a child have become increasingly common, particularly among those with lower incomes (Carlson, McLanahan, and England 2004). Edin and Kefalas's 2011 study of low-income single mothers in Philadelphia identifies some reasons why women may have children with men who they would not (yet) marry. Though women in general are expected to want children, and most do, poor women are more likely than affluent women to see childlessness as tragic. Children are also likely to give poor women's lives meaning in a way that careers or other relationships may do for well-educated, professional women. And yet, the men to which poor women have access are likely to have low education levels, low incomes, and a high likelihood of contact with the criminal justice system (Edin and Kefalas 2011). These men are not seen as marriage material. Women may want to get married but they want to marry a man with a steady job (Pew Research Center 2014). Recognizing that this may never happen, they do not want to give up the possibility of ever having children.

One result of the decrease in shotgun marriages, the unemployment of men with low education levels, and increased cohabitation, is multiple-partner fertility, or men and women having children with more than one partner. Though multiple-partner fertility is not new, as it can occur after the death of a spouse or after a divorce, what is new is that it is occurring more frequently outside of marriage (Kuzzo 2014). While Americans are unique in terms of their high number of relationship transitions (marriages, divorces, cohabitations; Cherlin 2010), the poor have a particularly high rate of family complexity, requiring poor children to have to adapt to frequent changes in their family lives.

● A GROWING GAP IN CHILDREN'S LIVES

When discussing the rising income and wealth inequality in America, the focus is frequently on adults. However, many of the households on both ends of the socioeconomic spectrum have children in them. As the upper middle class as grown, children in these households have benefited from increased material comfort as well as the family stability that comes with their parents' higher education and employment prospects. At the same time, the gap between their experiences and children of the poor and working class has resulted in a substantial proportion of children lacking the proper resources and experiences that portend success in American society.

Owens (2016) analyzed large metropolitan areas from 1990 to 2010 in America and found increases during that time period in residential income segregation among households with children that were not apparent in households without children. It appears as though having children has resulted in affluent parents being more likely to choose to live amongst other affluent people. This is directly related to school districts: affluent parents can afford to choose which schools they wish to send their children to, and to buy housing within those districts. Well-educated parents are more likely than other parents to view the choice of school as a crucial socializing decision for their children (Pugh 2009). Therefore, for those with children, rising income inequality results in greater residential segregation as well as school segregation by income. Children's lives are increasingly divided by social class in America: children tend to live near and go to school with children who share their social class, with the advantages or disadvantages that go along with that.

Parenting also tends to differ by social class. Lareau (2003) developed a typology of parenting based on her research observing and interviewing parents and children in different social classes. She describes the parenting of the working class and poor as an "accomplishment of natural growth." With this approach there is a clear social distance between parents and children, including directives such as "Stop grabbing your sister!" or "Don't talk back to me," and less negotiation or reasoning. There is also more contact with extended family members, whether they are sharing living spaces or living nearby. Children have a lot of free time when they are not in school, hanging out in their homes or in their neighborhoods. I would argue that this describes most Americans' upbringings in the twentieth century. Only recently has income and wealth inequality grown to allow for a different approach to childrearing that Lareau calls "concerted cultivation."

In contrast to natural growth, parents using concerted cultivation have less social distance from their children. In place of directives, these parents frequently give their children reasons for why they would like them to behave differently. Such parents are also more likely to tolerate—and perhaps even encourage—negotiations from their children, whereas natural growth parents would see such behavior as "talking back" or disrespectful. Children in these families tend to be busy with structured activities, as parents are likely to believe that children's interests and potential should be nurtured and maximized. In contrast, data show a decrease over time in the percentage of lower-income children who participate in extracurricular activities (Badger 2015).

In addition to the material benefits of living in an upper-middle-class home (and frequently, neighborhood), children raised with concerted cultivation tend to gain more social, cultural, and human capital than children raised in poor or working-class homes. Social capital refers to the people you know and the people in your social networks. Children raised in upper-middle-class homes are likely to have access to professionals in a variety of fields, such as law, education, and politics. These contacts can be beneficial for access to opportunities such as schooling or jobs, but they can also help when a second chance is needed after a mistake or failure. Cultural capital refers to social skills such as eye contact and personability, vocabulary, and well-rounded knowledge of areas ranging from art to engineering (Bourdieu 1986). Having the right kind of cultural capital can be impressive when being considered for school admissions or a job. Finally, human capital means educational and other credentials that people earn in their lives. People with college-educated parents are more likely to earn a college degree themselves.

As a result of their upbringing, children raised with concerted cultivation tend to be more comfortable in settings with professional people in them. They are raised to see themselves as professionals-in-training, as potential equals to those in positions of authority. In contrast, Lareau (2003) finds that working class and poor children are socialized to practice constraint with authority figures. In the days when most parents used more of a natural growth approach to parenting, there was more of what Durkheim (1933/1997) called a "collective conscience" concerning the roles of central figures in children's lives. Parents tended to agree that teachers should be left alone to teach, supported and not interfered with, and that doctors should diagnose and treat their children as they see fit, and not be questioned. But with increasing inequality, a new approach to dealing with such figures has arisen, whereby educated/professional parents believe that good parents—especially mothers—are involved with their children's schooling and medical treatment (Hays 1998). Nowadays, assertiveness tends to result in parents getting their children individualized education plans and tailored medical attention. So those who are still practicing natural growth, either out of respect for or distrust of authority figures, are left at a disadvantage. Poor children and working-class children are not as likely to see themselves as "special" or entitled to individualized treatment, nor are they likely to have access to the resources, teachers, and medical practitioners that can help them maximize their potential, academically or otherwise.

● CONCLUSION

Discussions of growing income and wealth inequality in America tend to focus on the very rich billionaires who hold the great majority of the wealth, contrasted with the rest of us. However, I agree with Putnam (2015) when he differentiates between those with a college education and those without. After all, the upper class represents a tiny fraction of people in the United States, whereas the upper middle class is more substantial. And whereas they are not likely to see themselves as "rich" (and are certainly lacking financially when compared to the upper-class billionaires), the upper middle class are quite privileged in comparison to most Americans and indeed most people throughout the world.

At the same time, poverty in America has persisted. Indeed, 21 percent of children are living below the federal poverty line, and even more are precariously close to it (Jiang, Ekono, and Skinner 2016). And increasingly, children in upper-middle-class families and children in poor families are living apart from each other and going to different schools. While parenting strategies used to be similar in the past, they are diverging by social class over time. And while getting and staying married used to be the norm, in our deindustrialized economy this is more likely to be accomplished by college-educated professionals.

Altogether, children growing up in different social classes are leading disparate lives socioeconomically, residentially, and educationally. Professionals are more and more distanced from those with less education, and poor people are increasingly disadvantaged socially and economically in society. Housing policies to integrate neighborhoods and fair funding policies for schools could help equalize children's experiences, as could attention to the student loan crisis in higher education. Job growth for men with low levels of education is needed, as well as a greater cultural acceptance of men in feminized fields such as nursing and teaching (Reeves and Sawhill 2015). But unless these and other changes occur, we can expect such trends to continue. Until then, American children's family lives will be increasingly affected by the social class of their parentage.

● NOTES

1. While the focus here is on heterosexual marriages, with the legalization of same-sex marriage many of these concepts and trends may apply to same-sex marriages as well.

● REFERENCES

Akerlof, G. A., J. L. Yellen, and M. L. Katz. 1996. "An Analysis of Out-of-Wedlock Childbearing in the United States." *The Quarterly Journal of Economics* 111 (2): 277–317.

Amato, P. 2010. "Research on Divorce: Continuing Trends and New Developments." *Journal of Marriage and Family* 72 (3): 650–66.

Badger, E. 2015. "The Terrible Loneliness of Growing Up Poor in Robert Putnam's America." *The Washington Post*, March 6. https://www.washingtonpost.com/news/wonk/wp/2015/03/06/the-terrible-loneliness-of-growing-up-poor-in-robert-putnams-america/?tid=a_inl.

Bourdieu, P. 1986. "The Forms of Capital." In *Handbook of Theory and Research for the Sociology of Education,* 241–58. Edited by J. Richardson. New York: Greenwood Press.

Carlson, M., S. McLanahan, and P. England. 2004. "Union Formation in Fragile Families." *Demography* 31 (2): 237–61.

Cherlin, A. 2004. "The Deinstitutionalization of American Marriage." *Journal of Marriage and Family* 66 (4): 848–61.

Cherlin, A. 2010. *The Marriage-Go-Round: The State of Marriage and the Family in America Today.* New York: Vintage Books.

Coontz, S. 2006. *Marriage, a History: How Love Conquered Marriage.* New York: Penguin Books.

Copen, C. E., K. Daniels, and W. D. Mosher. 2013. *First Premarital Cohabitation in the United States: 2006–2010 National Survey of Family Growth.* Hyattsville, MD: National Center for Health Statistics.

Durkheim, E. 1933. *The Division of Labor in Society,* rev. ed. (repr. New York: The Free Press, 1997).

Edin, K., and M. Kefalas. 2011. *Promises I Can Keep: Why Poor Women Put Motherhood Before Marriage.* Berkeley: University of California Press.

England, P., and K. Edin. 2007. *Understanding Low-Income Unmarried Couples with Children.* Briefing Paper for the Council on Contemporary Families.

Hamilton, B. E., J. A. Martin, M. J. K. Osterman, S. C. Curtin, and T. J. Mathews. 2015. *Births: Final Data for 2014.* Hyattsville, MD: National Center for Health Statistics.

Hays, S. 1998. *The Cultural Contradictions of Motherhood*. New Haven, CT: Yale University Press.

Jiang, Y., M. Ekono, and C. Skinner. 2016. *Basic Facts About Low-Income Children: Children Under 18 Years, 2014*. New York: National Center for Children in Poverty.

Kuzzo, K. B. 2014. "New Partners, More Kids: Multiple-Partner Fertility in the United States." *The ANNALS of the American Academy of Political and Social Science* 654 (1): 66–86.

Lareau, A. 2003. *Unequal Childhoods: Class, Race, and Family Life*. Berkeley: University of California Press.

Owens, A. 2016. "Inequality in Children's Contexts: Income Segregation of Households with and Without Children." *American Sociological Review* 81 (3): 549–74.

Pew Research Center. 2010. *The Decline of Marriage and Rise of New Families*. http://www.pewsocialtrends.org/2010/11/18/the-decline-of-marriage-and-rise-of-new-families/.

Pew Research Center. 2014. *Record Share of Americans Have Never Married: As Values, Economics and Gender Patterns Change*. http://www.pewsocialtrends.org/2014/09/24/record-share-of-americans-have-never-married/.

Pugh, A. 2009. *Longing and Belonging: Parents, Children, and Consumer Culture*. Berkeley: University of California Press.

Putnam, R. 2015. *Our Kids: The American Dream in Crisis*. New York: Simon & Schuster.

Reeves, R. V., and I. V. Sawhill. 2015. "Men's Lib!" *The New York Times*, November 14. http://www.nytimes.com/2015/11/15/opinion/sunday/mens-lib.html?_r=0

Stevenson, B., and J. Wolfers. 2007. "Marriage and Divorce: Changes and Their Driving Forces." *Journal of Economic Perspectives* 21 (2): 27–52.

U.S. Bureau of Labor Statistics. 2013. *Marriage and Divorce: Patterns by Gender, Race, and Educational Attainment*. Washington, DC: Author. http://www.bls.gov/opub/mlr/2013/article/marriage-and-divorce-patterns-by-gender-race-and-educational-attainment.htm.

U.S. Bureau of Labor Statistics. 2014. *College Graduates More Likely Than Those with Less Education to Be Married at Age 27*. Washington, DC: Author. http://www.bls.gov/opub/ted/2014/ted_20140328.htm.

U.S. Bureau of Labor Statistics. 2016. *Labor Force Statistics from the Current Population Survey*. Washington, DC: Author. http://www.bls.gov/cps/cpsaat07.htm.

CHAPTER 21

Gender Pay Equity in Advanced Countries: The Role of Parenthood and Policies

By Joya Misra and Eiko Strader

D espite the increase in employment numbers and earnings for women globally over the past several decades, there remains a persistent and substantial gender wage gap, with women earning less than men. This gap is prevalent across a broad range of advanced, wealthy countries in Oceania, Europe, and North America. For example, as of 2010, women with full-time employment in the United States earned approximately 77 percent of what their male peers earned.[1] Although the gap has narrowed—that figure was 60 percent in 1960—U.S. gender wage parity would not occur until 2056 at that rate of change.[2] Scholars in disciplines ranging from economics, public policy, and sociology have shown that women's earnings have increased relative to men's due to rising education levels, increased employment opportunities, and the passage of anti-discrimination legislation. Yet it is also true that the gender wage gap narrowed in a relative sense, as men's wages have fallen due to deindustrialization and the decline of labor unions.[3]

Rather than declining over time as the gender gap has done, the motherhood penalty remains stable, controlling for factors such as education and experience.

This convergence in wages, however, primarily reflects the experience of childless men and women. Mothers continue to earn substantially less than other workers in most countries. While mothers earn significantly less than childless women with the same characteristics—referred to as a motherhood penalty—fathers earn somewhat more than childless men with the same characteristics—referred to as a fatherhood bonus. Research shows that rather than declining over time as the gender gap has done, the motherhood penalty remains stable, controlling for factors such as education and experience.[4]

We focus on the intersection of gender and parenthood in eleven countries. Through our analysis, we found that parenthood and specifically, actual and perceived caregiver responsibilities that are entrenched in employers' perceptions and reinforced through legislation and policies, are central factors in explaining the persisting gender wage gap. Wage gaps may reflect the market value of differing levels of human capital. A woman who is less educated or has lost marketable professional experience by taking time out of the workforce receives a lower wage. Yet even controlling for those variables, research continues to find substantial differences in wages by parenthood status and gender.[5] We first review the existing literature that has attempted to explain the persistence of motherhood penalties and fatherhood bonuses. By analyzing available earnings data from eleven advanced economies, we illustrate how parenthood contributes to the gender wage gap and how it differs across those countries. Finally, we examine some existing public policies and propose some key ones aimed at reducing the gender wage gap, specifically taking into account the notion of gendered parenthood.

● PARENTHOOD & EARNINGS

In most advanced economies, mothers earn substantially less than childless women, while fathers earn somewhat more than childless men.[6] These phenomena have been termed the motherhood penalty and fatherhood bonus, respectively.

In the United States, while researchers identify a 7 percent wage penalty per child, only one-third of this penalty can be attributed to the loss of work experience.[7] There are two major explanations that have been advanced to account for these outcomes. Some scholars theorize that gendered specialization in the household is a key driver of wage differentials.[8] Consider a household composed of a married man and woman. If each focuses on different household roles—with the man emphasizing paid employment and the woman emphasizing caregiving responsibilities—this might affect workplace productivity. The man may work harder and longer while the woman may work less due to her engagement in caregiving responsibilities outside of the work environment. Research finds that time spent on household tasks that are typed as "female," such as meal preparation and housekeeping, reduces the wages of both men and women. Women tend to engage in those tasks more on average. This suggests that those tasks may drive the gender wage gap.[9] A longitudinal study examining changes in women's wages over time found that the motherhood penalty is primarily realized when mothers interrupt their employment due to childcare responsibilities.[10] However, findings do not always support this specialization theory. For example, motherhood penalties in the United States vary by race and ethnicity, with white women paying the largest penalties. Yet this does not explain why Latinas do not see a motherhood penalty, despite more traditional divisions of labor among men and women in Latino households.[11]

Researchers also explore the effect of specialization on wage bonuses for men. Drawing upon some of the research mentioned above, one can theorize that only men who benefit from a partner who "specializes" in unpaid work would earn a wage bonus. For each additional hour an American wife works, her husband's wage gains reduce, which may support the idea that a heterosexual married man's higher wages are due to higher productivity.[12] Research also suggests that white and Latino men, whose families have more traditional breadwinner or caregiver divisions, do appear to earn larger fatherhood bonuses—4 percent and 8 percent, respectively.[13] Yet these effects do not hold for African-American men.[14] Employer perceptions, rather than differences in productivity, may play a role. The employers "may be less likely to view black fathers as committed breadwinners, and black men may experience less of a labor market bonus for fatherhood."[15]

Other research considers the role of employer discrimination. One study looks at a worker's race and gender and compares their employer's productivity descriptions with the employee's actual work records. The results demonstrate that some employers discriminate against women—particularly African-American women—stereotyping them as less committed or productive, even when their work records do not indicate any basis for such characterization.[16] Experimental research similarly suggests that employers stereotype mothers as less competent and committed. In a laboratory experiment carried out with undergraduate volunteers, the students assessed application materials for a mid-level marketing position; the materials established that candidates had the same credentials, experience, and productivity, but varied resumes by the first name of the worker, indicating race and gender, and listed that they volunteered in a community organization or for a parent-teacher organization. The researchers found that those who were believed to be mothers were less likely to get positions, and of those who were, they were offered lower salaries—7.9 percent less than perceived childless women and 8.6 percent less than fathers.[17]

The same study carried out an audit of actual employers advertising employment vacancies to see how they responded to applications. Some of the employee applications included a cover letter mentioning that the potential employee was relocating to the city, while others noted that they were specifically relocating with their families to the city. Women who mentioned families were half as likely to be interviewed than women who did not mention families, while men who mentioned families were slightly more likely to be interviewed than men who did not.[18] Therefore, employers' assumptions about mothers' productivity may help account for some of the gender wage gap.

There remain important gendered distinctions behind wage penalties and bonuses, rather than productivity differences due to specialization.

Well-designed studies based on survey data may also challenge the specialization argument. One study compares partnered and single men and women, both childless and parents, and argues that if specialization explains wage differences, both partnered women and mothers would see penalties. Instead, both partnered men and women see wage premiums, relative to single men and women, though the gain is larger for men.[19] In addition, if the specialization theory holds true, both men and women who have full-time working partners should experience penalties. Yet men's wages are higher when their partners work less than full-time, while the same is not true for partnered women. Moreover, while mothers appear to alter employment hours, job traits, and tenure in ways similar to fathers, whose wages increase, mothers experience a substantial wage penalty.[20] In conclusion, there remain important gendered distinctions behind wage penalties and bonuses, rather than productivity differences due to specialization.

Both motherhood penalties and fatherhood bonuses vary cross-nationally. Considering this may allow us to analyze the factors driving these penalties and bonuses, since these reflect different patterns in employment, caregiving, and policies aimed at addressing work-family conflict. More research considers how motherhood wage penalties differ across countries, while considerably less examines the fatherhood bonus across countries.[21] Wage premiums exist for fathers in all countries. However, these premiums are only robust in a few countries after controlling for variables such as human capital, marital status, and work hours. This bonus also links to their partners' employment status. Men with a caregiving partner are more likely to earn the premium in a number of countries.[22] Motherhood penalties are more consistent across a wide range of countries, controlling for human capital, marital status, and work hours, though they vary dramatically in degree.[23] Previous cross-national studies suggest that work-family policies, such as paid leaves and state-subsidized childcare, may help explain this variation, a point we will examine below.

● HOW PARENTHOOD PENALTIES & BONUSES RELATE TO GENDER GAPS

We explored gender gaps and parenthood effects using cross-national data collected by the Luxembourg Income Study (LIS) for Australia, Canada, Finland, France, East Germany, West Germany, Luxembourg, the Netherlands, Sweden, the United Kingdom, and the United States around the mid-2000s (Wave VI).[24] We examined the former East and former West Germany ("East Germany" and

"West Germany") separately, because there remain significant socio-political and cultural differences after reunification, due to different histories of women's employment. We also looked at wages by comparing the percentile rankings, which corrects for differences in wage structures and makes interpretation fairly simple.[25] Lastly, in order to enhance the comparability of data, we excluded those who are self-employed or in the armed forces.

Figure 21.1 shows remarkable variation in the gender gap across all eleven countries, even after controlling for major determinants of earnings such as age, age-squared, education, marital status, and part-time employment among workers between twenty-five and forty-nine years of age.[26] Women in the Netherlands suffer from the highest earnings gap, whereas women in East Germany with equivalent demographic and human capital characteristics experience the lowest gap. More specifically, these estimates indicate that Dutch women on average rank twenty-eight percentiles lower on the earnings distribution than men with the same human capital, while women in East Germany rank ten percentiles lower than men. Interestingly, East Germany and West Germany have very different gender gaps; East German women were strongly engaged in the labor force for a number of decades, and the gender gap is much smaller than that in West Germany.[27]

Figure 21.1 Gender Gap in Wage Across Eleven Countries in the mid-2000s

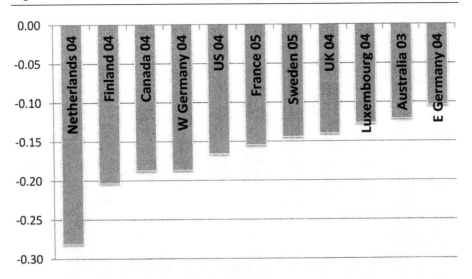

Source: Author's data analysis, Luxembourg Income Study Database (LIS).

In Figure 21.2, we took the wages of childless men as the baseline and considered how the wages of fathers, childless women, and mothers diverge from these, controlling for the same determinants as in Figure One.[28] Countries are listed in the order of gender wage gap estimates taken from Figure One, which do not account for the effect of parenthood. The gap between childless women and childless men is much smaller than that between mothers and fathers, while parenthood effects vary considerably across these cases.

In three countries—East Germany, Luxembourg, and Sweden—there is no significant fatherhood bonus. Yet in every other country, fathers do appear to earn a premium, relative to childless men. Fatherhood bonuses are particularly strong in West Germany and the Netherlands; Dutch fathers earn almost ten percentiles more than childless men with the same characteristics. This suggests that in most countries, fathers receive earnings bonuses, though the size of these bonuses varies.

A gap remains between childless men's and childless women's earnings in all but one country—East Germany. This suggests that childless women in East Germany are more likely to experience gender parity.[29] Figure Two shows that in

Figure 21.2 Wage Divergences from Childless Men's Wages Across Eleven Countries in the mid-2000s

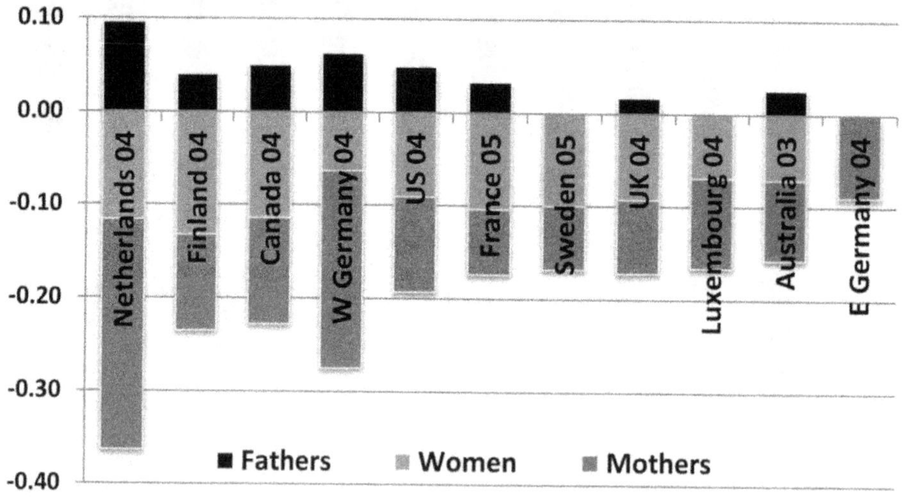

Source: Author's data analysis, Luxembourg Income Study Database (LIS).

most countries, childless women earn approximately zero percentiles (in East Germany) to thirteen percentiles (in Finland) less than childless men. Since gender gaps vary between ten percentiles in East Germany and twenty-eight percentiles in the Netherlands, as shown in Figure 21.1, it is clear that childless women face a smaller penalty than women more broadly. On the other hand, mothers pay a large penalty. Their wages are not only significantly smaller than those of childless men, they are also significantly smaller than those of childless women. Here we see that mothers earn between nine percentiles (East Germany) and thirty-six percentiles (the Netherlands) less than childless men.

Motherhood penalties, relative to childless women, are smaller than ten percentiles less in a number of countries, including Australia, East Germany, France, Luxembourg, Sweden, and the United Kingdom. We see very large motherhood penalties, or more than twenty percentiles less, in both the Netherlands and West Germany—two countries with very high levels of part-time employment. In these two countries, motherhood wage penalties may reflect the perception of employers that consider mothers as less career-focused, even for those working full-time. Canada, Finland, and the United States have moderate motherhood penalties.

On the whole, Figures 21.1 and 21.2 make several points clear. First, gender wage gaps capture only part of the story. Pay gaps differ not only between men and women, as displayed in Figure One, but also among childless men and fathers and among childless women and mothers, as displayed in Figure Two. Second, if we compare the gender gap in Figure One with the gap between childless men and women in Figure Two, it becomes clear that a great deal of the overall gender gap can be attributed to parenthood differences—the bonuses fathers see and the penalties paid by mothers. Finally, the remarkable variation in these gaps across countries suggests that there are societal-level factors that are shaping these outcomes. In the next section, we turn to considering the policies that may most effectively mediate the motherhood penalty and the fatherhood bonus.

● POLICIES AIMED AT REDUCING THE GENDER GAP

There are many policies that aim at reducing the gender gap, such as the U.S. Civil Rights Act of 1964.[30] In a meta-analysis, researchers find that equal treatment laws are associated with lower gender wage gaps cross-nationally, although protective labor legislation targeted at women, usually excluding them from particular types of dangerous or hazardous work, tends to increase gender wage gaps.[31] Hence, equal opportunity policies may lose power over time if enforcement mechanisms are not in place.[32] In the U.S., for example, the Equal Pay Act of 1963 has a number of loopholes that make it less effective at fighting gender wage discrimination.[33]

Much of the gender wage gap can also be attributed to occupational gender segregation, with women earning less in occupations traditionally staffed by women.[34] This leads to a range of policy approaches, such as comparable worth and other policies aimed at integrating occupations.[35] These policies, if designed effectively, also have the potential of making strong inroads regarding gender inequality.

In addition to these approaches, however, we believe that there are other policies that can address the gender wage gap, and particularly the gaps that reflect parenthood, including motherhood penalties and fatherhood bonuses. We argue for two major sets of policies that can effectively mediate these inequalities. The first are moderate-length, gender-neutral, paid-leave policies, which allow both parents to share care for infants and toddlers. A second policy set includes publicly-funded childcare that aims at providing employment support for the parents, as well as caring for and educating toddlers and preschoolers and providing afterschool and vacation care.

Leave Policies

Leave policies include maternity and paternity leaves—aimed at supporting mothers and fathers after the immediate birth or adoption of a child—as well as parental leaves, which are often longer and meant to enable parents to care for infants and young toddlers. These leaves may be paid or unpaid. In most countries, maternity and paternity leaves are well-paid, while parental leaves vary more in compensation. Parental leaves are often gender-neutral by design, but are generally taken by mothers, particularly if they earn less, and leaves are paid as a proportion of usual income. The most effective gender-neutral parental leave policies have relatively high compensation rates and include "use it or lose it" periods of leave that can only be taken by fathers.[36]

Maternity leave policies are integral to maintaining women's continuing labor force participation, especially when children are first born or adopted.[37] Mothers who reside in countries with short unpaid or non-mandatory leave policies often must leave the labor force to care for infants. They then face the prospect of reentering the work force with less experience.[38] Paid maternity leaves are common across wealthy countries, although the U.S. and, until recently, Australia, have been outliers.[39] In the U.S., while some workers qualify for twelve weeks of unpaid leave as provided by the Family and Medical Leave Act (FMLA), this leave is an unaffordable right for many working-class and poor families.[40]

Scholars have long argued that lost tenure from labor force withdrawal may explain a large proportion of the gender wage gap and the motherhood wage penalty.[41] Paid leave programs can ensure that women remain attached to the labor force. When California implemented a paid leave program in 2004, researchers found that it doubled the overall use of maternity leave, particularly for less advantaged groups, and increased the weekly working hours and incomes for mothers with children between one and three years of age.[42]

Parental leaves also help parents care for young children. Indeed, in many countries, these policies are aimed at and primarily taken advantage of by mothers. When parental leave policies are well-paid, families can provide care for infants and toddlers without losing ties to the labor market. However, the design of the policy matters a great deal in terms of compensation, length of the leave, and whether part of the leave is reserved for fathers. When parental leaves are unpaid or poorly paid, some families may not be able to use the leave. Very short parental leaves can also be less effective because of the difficulties in finding childcare for newborn infants. On the other hand, moderate-length paid leaves can have more positive effects, particularly when coupled with measures to increase men's caregiving. Yet when parental leaves are very long and primarily taken by women, mothers lose valuable job experience and may find little prospect for career advancement later on. The leaves may discourage employers from hiring women by placing them on a so-called "mommy track," rather than a regular career track.

Indeed, the relationship between mothers' earnings and length of leave is curvilinear.[43] Motherhood wage penalties exceed 6 percent per child in countries with less than one year or more than three years of job-protected leave, while the per child penalty is only slightly more than 1 percent in countries with moderate job-protected leave, controlling for other factors known to affect wages.[44] This suggests that while paid leaves are important to mediate the gender gap and motherhood penalty, leaves need to be designed so as to avoid long absences from the labor force.

For example, until recently, parental leave in Germany was almost three years in length.[45] While parental leaves may help women maintain links to employment, very long leaves may lead to employers placing mothers on a separate career track. As Figure 21.2 shows, the motherhood penalty is very strong in West Germany. Although the same leave policies existed in East Germany, women were less likely to take very long leaves, given the history of women's employment, as well as better availability of childcare places in East Germany, which we discuss below.

Research based in Hungary finds that employers explicitly blame long leave policies for their attempts to screen out mothers in the hiring process.[46] Employers also channel women with childbearing aspirations into lower-level positions. In addition, employers restructure positions in order to terminate workers despite job guarantees, route returning workers into positions with lower authority, and pressure exceptional workers into taking shorter leaves.[47] This research suggests why women in countries with long parental leaves may be disadvantaged.

Countries with leaves aimed at fathers may further reduce the penalties faced by mothers, as well as the bonuses provided to fathers. For example, fathers in Sweden are entitled to two weeks of fully paid paternity leave, and two months of paid parental leave that can only be taken by fathers, referred to as "use it or lose it." As a result, as shown in Figure 21.2, there is a much smaller motherhood penalty in Sweden than in other countries, while the fatherhood bonus disappears. Swedish employers tend to view both men and women as caregivers; these roles are not stigmatized in the Swedish labor market.

Publicly Subsidized Childcare

In addition to leaves, research shows that publicly subsidized childcare significantly increases the wages and employment attachment of mothers, especially for those with children ages three and younger.[48] Most wealthy countries have universal preschool in place for children between ages three and six, although these programs differ by how many hours are available.[49] Research consistently shows positive outcomes from publicly subsidized childcare and educational programs, including after school programs and programs over vacations.[50] While publicly subsidized care for infants and toddlers varies more across wealthy countries, where it exists, employment and wages are higher and risk of poverty is lower.[51]

Countries with greater access to childcare for infants and toddlers have lesser motherhood penalties. East Germany, France, and Sweden are often noted as having better publicly subsidized childcare coverage as compared to other industrialized nations, and they indeed have lesser motherhood wage penalties than those countries, such as the U.S. and West Germany.[52] In countries with minimal publicly subsidized childcare, mothers are less likely to be employed while those who are employed see larger wage penalties. The per-child wage penalty is roughly 10 percent in countries with limited public childcare and only

4 percent in countries with generous childcare coverage, after controlling for relevant wage determinants.[53]

Another policy that is often recommended to address work-family conflict and the gender gap in pay is flexible working hours, including part-time employment. Yet we do not include this policy among our recommendations because this approach tends to relegate women to lower status positions in the labor market. For example, the Netherlands is often touted for its Work and Care Act that encourages flexible work schedules. However, many have criticized this scheme for sustaining gender wage gap and motherhood wage penalty by encouraging part-time employment among women and full-time employment among men.[54] As Figure 21.2 demonstrates, even though we control for part-time employment, mothers in the Netherlands clearly suffer from significant wage penalty, while fathers benefit from nearly a ten percentile ranking increase in their earnings.

● CONCLUSION

We have discussed how the motherhood penalty and fatherhood bonus together explain a large portion of gender wage disparities across wealthy countries and have highlighted the importance of specific public policies in narrowing the gaps. Research on the gender wage gap often focuses on explaining why women as a whole earn less than men, which leads to an emphasis on broad policies designed to improve employment conditions for women. However, our analysis makes it clear that policies can encourage, discourage, or sustain various gendered employment patterns that reflect not only gender, but also gendered parenthood. Understanding this nuance is critical to gaining forward momentum in the pursuit of gender wage equality.

We argue that a multi-faceted approach to achieving gender wage equality is warranted for two main reasons. First, to provide short- and long-term support for parenthood, both leave policies and the provision of publicly subsidized childcare should be discussed. Publicly subsidized childcare alone will not meet the needs of parents with newborns, while leave policies without a concomitant investment in childcare may lead to gendered divisions of care responsibilities, which may support employer perception of "juggling" mothers and committed fathers. Paying attention to the design of the policies, with an aim to equalizing the involvement of *both* parents in caregiving and employment, will lead to better outcomes.

In addition, policies need to be designed in recognition of differences in cultural contexts and attitudes toward care for children. For example, policies are most effective when the culture supports maternal employment.[55] This finding suggests that the gender earnings gap in the U.S. might shrink with the right policies in place, since Americans tend to value maternal employment.[56] Investing in early education and childcare programs, together with paid, gender-neutral, moderate-length leaves, is likely to pay off in strong dividends regarding lower levels of gender inequality.

Understanding the different mechanisms behind gender wage gaps across these eleven countries allows us to suggest more effective policy recommendations. Countries with very large motherhood penalties should focus primarily on policy solutions aimed at addressing how gendered parenthood affects employment and earnings. This is not to suggest that policies aimed at the gender gap more broadly—such as those targeting discrimination, comparable worth, or occupational gender segregation—are not useful, as they are important mechanisms for addressing gender inequality more broadly. However, we hope this paper highlights the complexity of mechanisms behind the gender wage gap and suggest that future studies and policy analyses consider the differential impact of gendered parenthood on wages,

● ENDNOTES

1. Ariane Hegewisch, Claudia Williams, and Amber Henderson, "The Gender Wage Gap: 2010" (IWPR Fact Sheet #C350, The Institute for Women's Policy Research, Washington, DC: April 2011), 1, http://www.iwpr.org/publications/pubs/the-gender-wage-gap-2010-updated-march-2011/at_down-load/file.

2. Ibid.

3. See Annette Bernhardt, Martina Morris, and Mark S. Handcock, "Women's Gains or Men's Losses? A Closer Look at the Shrinking Gender Gap in Earnings," *American Journal of Sociology* 101, no. 2 (1995), 302–328; Francine D. Blau and Lawrence M. Kahn, "In the 1990s: Slowing Convergence," *Industrial and Labor Relations Review* 60, no. 1 (2006), 45–66; Maria Charles, "A World of Difference: International Trends in Women's Economic Status," *Annual Review*

of Sociology 37, no. 1 (11 August, 355–371; Margaret Mooney Marini and Pi-ling Fan, "The Gender Gap in Earnings at Career Entry," *American Sociological Review* 62, no. 4 (1997), 588–604; Joshua D. Pitts and Charles Kroncke, "Forum for Social Economics Educational Attainment and the Gender Wage Gap: A Comparison of Young Men and Women in 1984 and 2007," *Forum for Social Economics* (2012), 37–41.

4. Sarah Avellar and Pamela J. Smock, "Has the Price of Motherhood Declined Over Time? A Cross-Cohort Comparison of the Motherhood Wage Penalty," *Journal of Marriage and Family* 65, no. 3 (August 2003), 597–607.

5. Francine D. Blau and Lawrence M. Kahn, "Gender Differences in Pay," *Journal of Economic Perspectives* 14, no. 4 (2000), 75–99; Michelle J. Budig and Paula England, "The Wage Penalty for Motherhood," *American Sociological Review* 66, no. 2 (2001), 204–225; Alexandra Killewald and Margaret Gough, "Does Specialization Explain Marriage Penalties and Premiums?," *American Sociological Review* 78, no. 3 (26 April 2013), 477–502.

6. Michelle J. Budig and Melissa Hodges, "Differences in Disadvantage: Variation in the Motherhood Penalty Across White Women's Earnings Distribution," *American Sociological Review* 75, no. 5 (8 October 2010), 705–728; Budig and England; Deborah J. Anderson, Melissa Binder, and Kate Krause, "The Motherhood Wage Penalty Revisited: Experience, Heterogeneity, Work Effort, and Work-Schedule Flexibility," *Industrial and Labor Relations Review* 56, no. 2 (2003), 273–294; Jane Waldfogel, "The Effect of Children on Women's Wages," *American Sociological Review* 62, no. 2 (1997), 209–217; Shelley J. Correll, Stephen Benard, and In Paik, "Getting a Job: Is There a Motherhood Penalty?," *American Journal of Sociology* 112, no, 5 (2007), 1297–1339; Rebecca Glauber, "Race and Gender in Families and at Work: The Fatherhood Wage Premium," *Gender & Society* 22, no. 1 (February 2008), 8–30; Killewald and Gough; Wendy Sigle-Rushton and Jane Waldfogel, "Motherhood and Women's Earnings in Anglo-American, Continental European, and Nordic Countries," *Feminist Economics* 13, no. 2 (2007), 55–91; Rebecca Glauber, "Marriage and the Motherhood Wage Penalty Among African Americans, Hispanics, and Whites *Journal of Marriage and Family* 69, no. 4 (November 2007), 951–961.

7. Budig and England.

8. Mary C. Noonan, "The Impact of Domestic Work on Men's and Women's Wages," *Journal of Marriage and Family* 63, no. 4 (2001), 1134–1145; Shelly Lundberg and Elaina Rose, "Parenthood and the Earnings of Married Men and Women," *Labour Economics* 7, no. 6 (November 2000), 689–710; Hyunbae Chun and Injae Lee, "Why Do Married Men Earn More: Productivity or Marriage Selection?" *Economic Inquiry* 39, no. 2 (April 2001), 307–319.

9. Noonan.

10. Lundberg and Rose.

11. Glauber (2007).

12. Chun and Lee.

13. Glauber (2008), 22.

14. Ibid.

15. Ibid., 25.

16. Irene Browne and Ivy Kennelly, "Stereotypes and Realities: Images of Black Women in the Labor Market," in *Latinas and African American Women at Work,* ed. Irene Brown (New York: Russell Sage Foundation, 1999), 302–326.

17. Correll, Benard, and Paik, 1323.

18. Ibid, 1330.

19. Killewald and Gough.

20. Ibid.

21. For research focused on the motherhood penalty, see Michelle J. Budig, Joya Misra and Irene Boeckmann, "The Motherhood Penalty in Cross-National Perspective: The Importance of Work- Family Policies and Cultural Attitudes," *Social Politics: International Studies in Gender, State & Society* 19, no. 2 (17 May 2012), 163–193; Joya Misra, Michelle J. Budig and Stephanie Moller, "Reconciliation Policies and the Effects of Motherhood on Employment, Earnings and Poverty," *Journal of Comparative Policy Analysis Research and Practice* 9, no. 2 (2007), 135–155; Sigle-Rushton and Waldfogel (2007). For research that investigated the fatherhood bonus, see Irene Boeckmann and Michelle J. Budig, "Fatherhood, Intra-household Employment Dynamics, and Men's Earnings in a Cross-National Perspective" (LIS working paper series, no. 592, June 2013).

22. Boeckmann and Budig (2008).

23. Budig, Misra, and Boeckmann (2012); Misra, Budig, and Moller (2007); Joya Misra, Michelle Budig, and Irene Boeckmann, "Work-family Policies and the Effects of Children on Women's Employment Hours and Wages," *Community, Work & Family* 14, no. 2 (May 2011), 139–157.

24. *Luxembourg Income Study Database (LIS),* www.lisdatacenter.org (multiple countries; 8 July-15 August, 2013), Luxembourg: LIS.

25. Francine D. Blau and Lawrence M. Kahn, "Wage Structure and Gender Earnings Differentials: an International Comparison," *Economica* 63 (1996), S29-S62.

26. This age restriction minimizes the effect of variance in the timing of educational milestones and excludes most parents whose children no longer reside in the same household.

27. Jennifer Hunt, "The Transition in East Germany: When Is a Ten-Point Fall in the Gender Wage Gap Bad News?," *Journal of Labor Economics* 20, no. 1 (2002), 148–169; Rachel A. Rosenfeld, Heike Trappe, and Janet C. Gornick, "Gender and Work in Germany: Before and After Reunification," *Annual Review of Sociology* 30, (2004), 103–124.

28. The horizontal line at zero represents a baseline average earning level for childless men, while the black column at the top of each bar represents any significant difference in the pay of fathers (since it is above zero, it refers to a fatherhood bonus), relative to childless men with the same characteristics. The light gray column in the middle of each bar represents the

difference between the earnings of childless women and childless men (a gender penalty). The column at the bottom of each bar represents the additional wage gap mothers incur (the motherhood penalty).

29. Although this finding may also reflect some selection bias in the labor force. See Hunt.

30. Ann Orloff, "From Maternalism to 'Employment for AH': State Policies to Promote Women's Employment across the Affluent Democracies," in *The State after Statism,* ed. Jonah D. Levy (Cambridge, MA: Harvard University Press, 2006), 230–268.

31. Doris Weischelbaumer and Rudolf Winter-Ebmer, "International gender wage gaps: The effects of competition and equal treatments laws on gender wage differentials," *Economic Policy* (April 2007), 235–287.

32. Kevin Stainback and Donald Tomaskovic-Devey, *Documenting Desegregation* (New York, NY: Russell Sage Foundation, 2012).

33. Joel P. Rudin and Kimble Byrd, "U.S. Pay Equity Legislation: Sheep in Wolves' Clothing," *Employee Responsibilities and Rights Journal* 15, no. 4 (December 2003), 183–190.

34. Asaf Levanon, Paula England, and Paul Allison, "Occupational Feminization and Pay: Assessing Causal Dynamics Using 1950–2000 U.S. Census Data," *Social Forces* 88, no. 2 (December 2009), 865–891; Maria Charles and David B. Grusky, *Occupational Ghettos: The Worldwide Segregation of Women and Men* (Palo Alto: Stanford University Press, 2004); Donald Tomaskovic-Devey and Sheryl Skaggs, "Sex Segregation, Labor Process Organization, and Gender Earnings Inequality," *American Journal of Sociology* 108, no. 1 (2002), 102–128.

35. Rudin and Byrd; Joan Acker, *Doing Comparable Worth* (Philadelphia: Temple University Press, 1989); Levanon, England, and Allison; Paula England, "Uneven and Stalled," *Gender & Society* 24, no. (2010), 149–166.

36. "Maternity at Work: A Review of National Legislation" (ILO report, Geneva: 2010), http://www.ilo.org/wcmsp5/groups/public/@dgreports/@dcomm/@publ/documents/publication/wcms_124442. pdf.

37. Anne Gauthier, "Family Policies in Industrialized Countries: Is There Convergence?," *Population* 57, no. 3 (2002), 447–474; J.C. Gornick and M.K. Meyers, *Families That Work: Policies for Reconciling Parenthood and Employment* (New York: Russell Sage Foundation, 2005).

38. Becky Pettit and Jennifer L. Hook, *Gendered Tradeoffs: Family, Social Policy, and Economic Inequality in Twenty-One Countries* (New York: Russell Sage Foundation, 2009); Misra, Budig and Boeckmann, (2011); Boeckmann, Misra and Budig, "Mothers' Employment in 19 Wealthy Western Countries: How Do Cultural and Institutional Factors Shape the Motherhood Employment and Working Hours Gap?" (conference draft, New Orleans: April 2013).

39. Regarding Australia's recent adoption of paid maternity leave, see Ray Broomhill and Rhonda Sharp, "Australia's Parental Leave policy and Gender Equality: An International Comparison" (Australian Workplace Innovation and Social Research Centre, The University of Adelaide, Australia: 2012), http://www.adelaide.edu.au/wiser/pubs/

WISeR_Parental_Leave_Policy_and_Gender_Equality_an_ international_comparison_re-port.pdf.

40. Naomi Gerstel and Amy Armenia, "Giving and Taking Family Leave: Right or Privilege?," *Yale Journal of Law & Feminism* 21, no. I (2009), 161–184.

41. Waldfogel; Budig and England.

42. Mary Rossin-Slater, Christopher J. Ruhm, and Jane Waldfogel, "The Effects of California's Paid Family Leave Program on Mothers' Leave-Taking and Subsequent Labor Market Outcomes," *Journal of Policy Analysis and Management* 32, no. 2 (2013), 224–245.

43. Pettit and Hook; Michelle J. Budig, Joya Misra, and Irene Boeckmann, "The Wage Penalty for Motherhood in a Cross-National Perspective: Relationships with Work-Family Policies and Cultural Attitudes" (Population Association of America conference paper, April 2010), 21.

44. Ibid.

45. This source includes data on the lengths of leaves. Irene Boeckmann, Michelle Budig and Joya Misra, "The Work-Family Policy Indicators" (Sociology Department, University of Massachusetts-Amherst: 2010), 4, http://www.lisdatacenter.org/wp-content/uploads/resources-other-work-family-policy-indicators.pdf.

46. Christy Glass and Eva Fodor, "Public Maternalism Goes to Market: Recruitment, Hiring, and Promotion in Postsocialist Hungary," *Gender & Society* 25, no. 1 (20 January 2011), 5–26.

47. Ibid.

48. Misra, Budig, and Moller; Misra, Budig, and Boeckmann (2011); Budig, Misra, and Boeckmann, (2012); Pettit and Hook; Budig, Misra, and Boeckmann (2010).

49. Jane Lewis, *Work-Family Balance, Gender, and Policy* (Northampton, MA: Edward Elgar, 2009).

50. Gornick and Meyers; Pettit and Hook.

51. Misra, Budig, and Boeckmann (2011); Misra et al., "Family Policies, Employment and Poverty Among Partnered and Single Mothers," *Research in Social Stratification and Mobility* 30, no. 1 (March 2012), 113–128; Misra, Budig, and Moller (2007); Budig, Misra, and Boeckmann (2010); Budig, Misra, and Boeckmann (2012); Boeckmann, Misra, and Budig (2013).

52. Irene Boeckmann, Michelle Budig, and Joya Misra, "The Work-Family Policy Indicators" (Sociology Department, University of Massachusetts-Amherst: 2010), 4, http://www.lisdata-center.org/wp-content/uploads/resources-other-work-family-policy-indicators.pdf.

53. Budig, Misra, and Boeckmann (2010), 21.

54. Janneke Plantenga and Chantal Remerv, "The Provision of Childcare Services: A Comparative Review of 30 European Countries" (report, Office for Official Publications of the European Communities, Luxembourg: 2009).

55. Budig, Misra, and Boeckmann (2010).

56. Ibid., 172.

CHAPTER 22

Domestic Violence and the Family: Mothers Experiencing Homelessness

By Olivia R. Hetzler

When many people ponder the concept of family, images such as intimacy, trust, warmth, and comfort are often evoked. However, as many of us well know, these images do not apply to all families at all times. In fact, the family, for many, can be a source of fear, victimization, and violence. As this chapter demonstrates, domestic violence touches a significant number of families in our society. Domestic violence is not limited to intimate partners that cohabitate, as the term suggests; it also extends to dating teen couples and adult couples. Reported incidents of domestic violence totaled 634,610 in 2015 (Truman and Langton 2015). However, it is widely known that domestic violence, as well as other forms of gendered violence (for example, stalking and sexual assault) are often underreported, so it is likely that this number is a small reflection of the reality of this social problem. According to a survey conducted by the Centers for Disease Control and Prevention, almost one in four women (22.3%) have been the victim of severe physical violence by an intimate partner (Breiding et al. 2011). One in seven men (14%) have also experienced this same violence (Breiding et al. 2011). This social problem touches many individuals and many families. This chapter explores the relationship between domestic violence and homelessness through an ethnographic account of victims who reside at a temporary domestic violence shelter with their children. As you will see, doing family in a place that is not your own is a challenging and daunting task.

● THE HISTORY OF DOMESTIC VIOLENCE IN THE UNITED STATES

Although it is rarely disputed that domestic violence is a contemporary social issue, this has not always been the case. Like many social problems, the issue must first be considered troubling and also gain a degree of support or consensus within the social setting at a particular point in time. While embedded in our social world, the history of domestic violence has only recently begun to be addressed through governmental policies and social services. Domestic violence (DV) became a visible social problem in the late 1960s as a result of the battered women's movement and the emerging feminist movement. As Donileen Loseke (1992) explains, not only did this new social problem become defined and constructed in a new way, it also established new language, as terms such as the "battered woman" emerged. Further, a new type of social service was created to manage the battered woman through the creation of battered women's shelters, each as a way to respond to the problem of wife abuse.

Since this time, the terminology has shifted. Instead of the term "wife abuse," contemporary terms such as domestic violence (DV) and intimate partner violence are used. The original terminology stemmed from the battered women's movement, as the primary victims were wives. As such, most, if not all, of the services to address this issue were directed towards married women. For example, the first two shelters in the United States were created for wives of alcoholic husbands, meaning that women who were neither married nor experiencing abuse by alcoholic husbands could not access those services (Tierney 1982). As the movement continued, more resources emerged, moving from safe houses, which were often basements or space within movement participants' homes, to shelters to house victims of DV. During this time, efforts were made to also provide services and counseling to the women and children of DV households. Although the breadth of housing and counseling services are largely directed towards women and children, presently women, children, men, and transgender persons, either married or single, are offered a wide range of services compared to when the movement emerged.

Prior to the battered women's movement, violence within the household was regarded as a private issue and a problem to be dealt with inside the household (Tierney 1982). Now, it is no longer viewed as an interpersonal problem and the focus has shifted beyond the household (Schneider 2000). DV is now regarded as a cultural problem that supports male violence towards women. This is evident in the shifting of funds from managing the issue through sheltering, crisis lines, and counseling victims, to prevention through outreach to youth and batterer's programs in the hopes of preventing future violence (Schneider 2000). In the past forty years, there have been great strides made in the movement against domestic violence, including the establishment of a National DV Hotline; expansion to 1,637 DV shelters; the 1994 Violence Against Women Act (reauthorized in 2000, 2005, 2012, and 2013); expanded funding for services and programs; and a retooling of law enforcement approaches to DV, including units within law enforcement departments specifically oriented to DV in their communities (Reiter 2005). Reported incidents of DV illustrate that women are disproportionately victims of DV, which influences women in a multitude of ways. As such, this chapter focuses on the experience of DV among women with children who experience homelessness following exit from an abusive relationship.

● MOTHERING AND DOMESTIC VIOLENCE

As Schneider (2000) points out, motherhood adds complexity to societal perspectives concerning abused women. As a result of the cultural construction of mothering that dictates that women must put their children's interests first, when adequate protection has not been provided or is not perceived to be being adequate, women are subject to sanctions. These include formal sanctions, such as various child neglect charges, as well as informal sanctions, such as condemnation. Battered woman syndrome (BWS) constructs victims as helpless compared to motherhood narratives, which highlight women as responsible, take-charge people. These two narratives, victim and responsible adult, collide in the battered mother. Battered mothers must put their children's needs and interests before their own. Violations of this cultural construction call into question women's adequacies as mothers, which subjects them to contempt and often leads to them being labeled as being inadequate parents and caregivers (Schneider 2000). As such, DV victims have a precarious relationship to these standards of measuring mothering. On one hand, they are perceived as lacking agency and, on the other, they are perceived as possessing an infinite number of choices to protect their children. As research shows, children exposed to DV are at risk (Edelson 1999). Therefore, women who expose their children to DV are at risk of being labeled inadequate.

Radford and Hester (2006) point to the significant negative impacts children living with DV experience, which include educational and achievement deficits, developmental delays, health risks, welfare (bed wetting, nightmares), emotional problems (fear, anxiety, depression), and/or behavioral problems (acting out, becoming withdrawn). Furthermore, linkages have been noted in research between witnessing violence as a child and normalization of gendered violence as an adult, resulting in a cycle of violence within the family (National Resource Center on Domestic Violence [NRCDV] 2002). Moreover, researchers find correlations between child abuse and concluding that perpetrators of DV are more likely to also abuse their children (NRCDV 2002). Finally, parental stress of victims is correlated to child abuse perpetrated by DV victims (NRCDV 2002).

As risk factors for children are apparent, volunteer DV programs have begun to address children within the shelter. Peled and Dekel (2010) conducted focus group interviews with workers in DV shelters and revealed that workers held a "deficit perspective" when describing the residents' mothering skills. They tended to focus on problems and failures of mothers rather than acknowledging any strengths or competencies, which resulted in the characterization of mothers as being ineffective, indifferent, abusive, or loveless. Despite these critical appraisals of victims' mothering, workers also empathized with victims, which the authors label "excusable deficiency." Although they viewed the women's mothering practices as problematic, they couched this deficiency as a result of their abuse. Staff at this shelter held strong cultural constructions of motherhood as "instinctive, self-fulfilling, and enjoyable." As such, they expected women to be devoted to their children's needs at all times. This was difficult, however, for many mothers, as they were physically and emotionally drained from undertaking domestic responsibilities, arguing with abusers, managing the abusers' emotions and "walking on eggshells" (Radford and Hester 2006). Among other things, this served to limit opportunities for mother–child bonding.

Placing blame on mothers for children's exposure to DV is evident within shelter policy, as well as within other institutions such as state child welfare work and legal arenas. A mother may be charged with failure to protect, held liable for abuse and/or neglect, or face criminal responsibility for endangering the welfare of the child (Schneider 2000). As this section illustrates, maintaining a mothering identity alongside the identity of victim is difficult as women approach various service agencies. They are frequently faced with allegations of inadequate mothering, as well as possible institutional charges for exposing children to abuse. This leaves us to wonder about the possible ramifications that this may pose for women's relationships to their children when attempting to gain assistance as a victim of DV. Notions of inadequate mothering, either by choice of the victim, or by consequence of the abuse, has led to increased programs offered to victims who are mothers and are often instituted into shelter policy.

● DV, HOMELESSNESS, AND MOTHERS AT NEW BEGINNINGS

Domestic violence accounts for a significant proportion of the rising numbers of homeless women and children in the United States (Jasinski, Wesely, Mustaine, and Wright 2005; Jasinski, Wesely, Wright, and Mustaine 2010; Lowe, Slater, Welfley, and Beard 2005). In order to investigate the relationships between DV and the family, an ethnographic study of a domestic violence shelter was conducted over a period of ten months. The shelter, New Beginnings, is located in a mid-sized midwestern college town, and provides services for victims of domestic and sexual abuse. Services are primarily provided to women; although men are able to access these services, they are not permitted into the physical space of the shelter. New Beginnings has twenty-five beds in six rooms and serves women and their children. In 2010, New Beginnings provided shelter for 208 individuals, 104 children and 104 mothers. Almost half of the residents (43.9%) are with children, with an average of 2.6 children per resident. The average age of residents is thirty-four, and the average length of stay is twenty-eight days. New Beginnings also offers non-residential services for victims of domestic violence and sexual assault, at an alternate location, through individual and group counseling services. My research was conducted at New Beginnings' residential program for domestic abuse and sexual violence survivors, which offers temporary, emergency shelter to victims. While certain room arrangements may have the feel of a home, as residents have a place to return to each night, there is also the possibility of eviction for non-compliance to shelter rules, as well as a time limit on stays.

Entrance to New Beginnings residential program requires an assessment for potential victims prior to admittance. Simply stating that there has been an occurrence of abuse does not qualify potential victims for entrance to the shelter. Instead, potential residents must prove their victimhood, as well as qualify the abuse as meeting the criteria for needing emergency shelter. Shelter staff explained that this screening process is conducted in order to determine that the potential residents are telling the truth, as any gaps or inconsistencies in their story are interpreted as "red flags" for staff to continue with skepticism. Because many of the community's female homeless population have few resources, instances of them reporting DV in order to gain shelter has taken place. It is not uncommon to see the reason for denial listed on hotline forms listed as "homeless, no DV." Moreover, staff seek to determine that this individual is suitable for communal living, as shelter staff are not equipped to provide medical care or manage those with significant mental or physical concerns. Staff explain that this rigorous screening may help protect limited funds due to community perceptions that the agency is overly gracious to their residents. Upon exit, women are offered either funds for the first month's rent or deposit on housing, as well as many start-up supplies to furnish the home. Finally, since New Beginnings functions as an emergency shelter, victims must also provide an account that is consistent with needing emergency shelter, as determined by staff.

After admittance, women are assigned a room. Women without children are typically roomed with other women without children, or at least without children present with them at the time. Women with children are often roomed alone, especially when multiple children are present, or with other women with children. Efforts are made for women and their children to have their own beds. However, shelter rules state that this may be altered if there is a need for additional space. Women are then assigned their own cabinet in the kitchen for non-perishable items, and a shared refrigerator with one or more other residents. The shelter offers ninety days for shelter stays, although the time is sometimes extended if staff determine the woman's stay to be favorable. It is required that all adult residents attend weekly meetings, sign in and out each time they enter and leave the facility, adhere to a nonviolence contract, and protect the confidentiality of other residents.

For women who entered the shelter with children, they are required to also participate in the mother's and children's program. This program's goal is to link families with local services in order to gain stability and encourage good mothering, as many staff are under the assumption that the mother's parenting practices are faulty. The rules in place, such as the maintenance of constant contact with children and supervision, create some tension but are needed in order to receive funding. Ultimately, the many rules represent an enormous strain for mothers with children in the shelter. Mothers are expected to keep their children with them at all times. Mothers' experiences with this rule vary by the age of their children, as well as number of children present.

When Lindsay, for example, a twenty-seven-year-old mother of four, entered the shelter, she came with only her four-month-old infant daughter. Lindsay's older children (ages eight, six, and four) resided temporarily with her ex-husband, the father of the three children. Lindsay reasoned that their older age increased the likelihood that they would remember their stay at a DV shelter, which she hopes for them to avoid. When initially asked if it was difficult to parent in the shelter, prior to reunification with her three older children, Lindsay responded as follows:

Lindsay: With Annie (four-month-old daughter), it's easy (mothering in the shelter) because she's a baby.... I don't have to say, "No, here you can't run around," or what we used to do at home versus what we do here. Kind of like the other kids what was allowed at home isn't allowed here and that can be hard, so I don't have to worry about that so far.

However, when Lindsay's older children came to stay at the start of the school year, she reports that the addition of the older children changed her experience and often conflicted with her parenting choices, especially with the added exposure to parenting styles that diverged from her own. Lindsay reported feeling exhausted at having to maintain constant contact with her four children.

Despite some frustration with shelter rules, Lindsay's experience is quite different from that of June. As June, a twenty-four-year-old woman, describes, she felt that shelter rules and the dynamics of communal living had eroded her power in her relationship with her four-year-old daughter, Penny. June describes her strain with discipline at the shelter:

> Researcher: Do you feel like your parenting is constrained here?
>
> June: Yes. Like I said, I'm a firm believer in spanking. It's the only way that I can get through to her that I'm not messing. Sometimes when I talk to her she won't listen, she won't pay attention, she has real selective hearing sometimes. And so yeah, at first I'm hollerin' and spankin' and there's that no violence contract and I can't do that.

June references the commitment to nonviolence contract that is required of all residents, but applies particularly to mothers, as it specifies, "no spanking or yelling" at your children. This is a set of rules that applies to a communal living space, and also to the function of nonviolence particular to a DV shelter, in which exposure to violence or tension is desired to be at a minimum to protect victims.

The state welfare policy does not cite spanking and yelling as child abuse, and therefore does not compromise the mother–child relationship in that context; however, continued stay may be compromised by violation of this contract. As the rules for families with children detail, "this form of discipline (spanking and yelling) is not allowed and staff have the right to intervene if corporal punishment is observed during your time at the shelter." Further, mothers are reminded that staff are mandated reporters and may contact DFS to report violence. However, it is not mentioned that spanking in itself is not an illegal form of discipline, but again further stay at the shelter may be compromised. New Beginnings encourages nonviolent discipline in the forms of "encouraging positive behaviors" and "discouraging negative behaviors," accomplished through giving consequences and removal of privileges, as well as the use of time outs and giving choices to children.

June argues above that these forms of discipline are not effective with Penny, and states that spanking has been the only way to get Penny's attention. June explains:

> June: I guess I feel like that it (spanking) is the only way that I can get through to her. I didn't spank for a long time and I kept going to my stepmom and dad and asking, "What do I do with her?" and they were firm believers in not doing that (spanking), you just talk.... It wasn't working with Penny, talking doesn't work with her. And so, just in the discipline that's hard (at the shelter).

Since June's stay at the shelter is contingent upon a commitment to nonviolence, her choices for discipline are constrained and she feels forced to contend with these policies since she could be asked to leave otherwise. June discusses this fear after what she felt was a passive-aggressive problematizing of her parenting at a house meeting:

> June: They didn't pull me aside and quietly say it, but it was in one of the Tuesday meetings (house meeting). And they were like, "remember that everyone signed a no violence contract." It was just a general message to everyone, but I felt like it was direct to me, but maybe it was just my guilty conscience because I was doing it. But they said, "if we see you spanking your child," that they are mandated to report it.

Melanie, a thirty-four-year-old mother of two children, reports a similar reprimanding by staff when it is brought up at a house meeting that yelling at children will not be tolerated, reminding women that they may be asked to leave for this infraction. Melanie later approached staff and stated that she felt that this was directed at her, staff confirmed that it was meant for her, as well as the other women. Melanie became upset and tearful, telling staff that she did not realize she was yelling at her children and would stop.

In both June and Melanie's experiences with violating the rules related to yelling, it becomes clear that "yelling" is very ambiguous. This understanding of yelling is left ambiguous and therefore open to interpretation by staff, as are the possible repercussions. June feels, as a result of these policies and her need for shelter at the time, that her relationship with her daughter is being called into question, and that it influences her relationship with her daughter:

> June: It's (spanking) just a swat on the butt. And sometimes I holler and I can't do that anymore. So, I just let her rip and run. It's not like she is destructing stuff or hurting anybody, but like at home I wouldn't let her have crayons sprawled out all over the playroom.... But, yeah, I feel like it is constricting because I would like to be doing a lot more disciplining a whole lot more than I am now.

Further, June states that she fears how she will be able to regain control once exiting the shelter after Penny has been afforded such permissiveness during their stay. As June explains, she feels that Penny has gained control of the relationship during their stay at New Beginnings.

Shana expresses similar frustrations to those described by Lindsay and June when discussing her parenting choices. Shana is a thirty-three-year-old mother of three children (ages seven, nine, and thirteen). When asked whether her parenting feels constrained in the shelter, Shana replies:

> Shana: Very, very much so, like not that I would ever beat my children or yell at them more, but I feel like every little thing I do is, even if there's no one in the room, "well, so-and-so said," you know? It's taken the wrong way.... If my kids are doing something they're not supposed to do then I get in trouble for that. I feel like I can't win.

During Shana's stay, she had several encounters with staff regarding her parenting, and problems concerning her children, one of which resulted in a situation that has continuing impacts on her relationship with her oldest son.

This example highlights the power of staff perception over resident perceptions and voice; due to the power and authority of staff, their opinions and interpretations supersede accounts given by women and/or children.

> Shana: The night Tyler (thirteen-year-old son) ran away, (staff) were like, "You need to step up, you need to take over and take charge, and you gotta not back down." And so I didn't back down and he (Tyler) ran away. You know it's like, what do I do? … And I could have just left it alone, but then they were like, "You just let him get away with too much, you need to show him who's boss." … So we keep fighting over it so then I took it out of the room, so that's when, when I took it downstairs to bring it out of the room, that's when he ran away.

This encounter led to a spiraling chain of events, beginning from a staff report stating that as he left Tyler had become aggressive by "getting in her face." However, Tyler reports that she was lying down when he left and denies being aggressive. Due to the accusation by a staff member of aggressive behavior, Tyler is no longer allowed at the shelter as a resident or a visitor. Tyler is now out of her physical presence for care and Shana faces the additional difficulties of mothering from afar (Parrenas 2001; Barrow and Laborde 2008; Ferraro and Moe 2003).

Tyler's experience provides another powerful example of tensions that arise between Shana's relationship to her son, youth behavior, and the goals of the shelter. While Tyler's behavior is normal for his age, it is counter to the rules of the shelter that specify that all children must be in the care of their mothers at all times. These rules are designed to avoid liability issues, as well as clarify the perceived responsibilities of the staff. As one staff member puts it, "Our responsibility is to the women, not children. It is the mother's responsibility to their children." Shana struggles with self-blame, a frequent experience for mothers, for Tyler's recent experiences, explaining that if it were not for her actions, stemming back to moving her family in with her abuser, which resulted in homelessness, then he would not have had to endure the recent sequence of events. Further, Tyler is only communicating occasionally with Shana, as his feelings of where to place blame align with Shana's.

Shana: It's just hard, because I know it doesn't just affect me, it affects the (children) and it kills me that Tyler is going through all of this stuff because it's all from choices that I made, you know. Situations that I put him in ... and he won't talk to me about it.

Although Shana harbors most of the blame for Tyler's current predicament, she is also troubled by the plethora of advice that she has been given by staff, and consequently questions her own effectiveness as a mother:

Shana: They're (staff) talking to me like I've never disciplined my kids ever, you know. And in this place, what am I supposed to do? I can't, there's no video games, there's no ... there's not much to take away. They can't have friends over; they don't have any privileges ... like, what am I going to take away? ... I can't take my little kids swimming and tell Tyler, "Like, well you can't go," because he has to go everywhere with me ... so I just feel like it's very difficult.

Shana explains the issue of conflict between being a resident in the shelter and trying to parent, since the shelter has few options for youth and directs the program primarily towards the women and mothers.

Shana: I mean its rough (shelter life). And the kids, like we all have to stay in one room and they all go to bed at different times and they have different, you know?

June reports a similar exhaustion, as she describes her showering routine:

June: I'm like, "How am I supposed to do this?" That is not realistic with a four-year-old. Like she's going to sit in the bathroom with me while I take a shower. No.

The television became another source of disagreement with Shana's three children (ages thirteen, nine, and seven), when several residents complained that they were dominating the space, as well as the TV in favor of more juvenile shows. Further, New Beginnings rules state that in the presence of children the television must be free of violence, sexuality, or any other inappropriate choices for children. With children's constant presence in the living room, the women were frustrated due to their lack of options in more adult television programs.

Shana is correct in her assessment that staff problematize her parenting. Case notes of the children's program coordinator state that, "Mom's pretty clueless how to parent and discipline," following an incident in which Shana's children got into an argument that escalated into violence. Following this, it was suggested that Shana go to counseling. Additionally, the children's coordinator intervened with Tyler (the thirteen-year-old) to discuss house rules and to brainstorm ways to manage anger with his siblings. Again, when Shana's nine-year-old son was perceived as acting out for not participating in kid's hour, the children's coordinator interprets this event as Jamie wanting attention and recommends counseling for both Shana and Jamie.

In addition, Shana cites the ongoing problem with her oldest son, Tyler. As the rules can influence her stay, without the power to make the rules she lacks choice and freedom.

> Shana: There are certain rules and, um, I can be thrown out like, I was worried about that with my son. He wasn't following the rules and he had to go, or we all had to go, and it was hard. It was really hard.

In her explanation, her presence as a resident in the shelter altered her freedom of choice in managing the situation with Tyler, thus putting a strain on her ability to mother. As Shana illustrates above, mothering in the shelter is not an easy task. It is affected by a combination of shelter rules and the density of the physical place, which places many women and children in close contact, adding to stress, but also exposing children to alternate parenting styles.

For example, upon the return of Lindsay's three older children (ages four, six, and eight), Lindsay notes a strain that was not there previously when she had only her infant daughter. In one instance, Lindsay had allowed her three children to go down the hall to visit the five-year-old daughter of another resident. When she heard excessive noise coming from down the hall, she went to check on them and found that the children had dismantled the bunk beds to make slides from the mattresses. Lindsay was appalled and told her children to immediately put the beds back together. The other mother tried to assure Lindsay that it was fine and she did not mind. Lindsay explained that this was a delicate interaction, as she did not want to offend the mother, but wanted to make it clear that this is not acceptable in terms of her parenting, and politely states, "But it's not okay, I don't want my children doing this." Upon returning to the room, she had to explain to her children why this was not okay, despite the fact that another adult had given approval.

June also explains that she is much more permissive with her four-year-old daughter at the shelter due to shelter rules as well as the exposure to other children. At home, she requires her daughter to keep her toys put away, but since there are so many children in the shelter and the playroom, it is difficult to keep track of who is responsible for the mess. It also upsets the children's play when they are communally sharing toys. As such, June gives her daughter more freedom at the shelter, compared to when she is at home. Shana also includes density when describing the difficulty of mothering in the shelter, reporting that at times it can lead to conflict with other residents:

> Shana: There's thirteen kids here right now and they're very rarely ever here at once, but like if there's a mess and someone's child…. Like, I don't follow my kids around and it's hard for me…. Like a mom would say to me, "Well your child did this and your child did that." Well, how do you know it wasn't…. It's just little petty stuff.

The close proximity and density of the shelter also increases the surveillance of residents by each other. Shana reports a great deal of "tattling" by residents to staff, reporting that "it's like being in high school again." Shana expresses a great deal of frustration, as she explains: "They (staff) take it very seriously and will be like, 'Well, you did this and you did that,' and they don't say who said it, but you know …" Further, she cites the thin walls and joint bathroom as making privacy difficult, as well as leading to an increase in complaints.

Shana: People are always complaining that my kids are always loud and the walls are very thin, and the concrete (floors) doesn't help because everything echoes, but anyway, um, they complain. So, somebody (fellow resident) was like, "Well, if they (children) had a movie at night to lay down then maybe they'd be quiet." So, then I borrowed the DVD player and would take it back down that morning. Well, then somebody threw a fit about that. And, so now I can't do that, I can't borrow the DVD player. So I'm like, you guys are never happy.

In this and other instances, she indicates that the tattling can have negative impacts for her personally, in the form of direct or indirect reprimand by staff, which can influence the continuance of a resident's stay at New Beginnings. It can also create tension among the residents. The presence of children in a confined space can lead to conflict. Therefore, in order to avoid conflicts, many women alter their typical routines in order to cater to communal peace. For example, June reports having to alter their bedtime routine in order to prevent conflict with her roommate, and roommate's infant daughter.

June: At nighttime, when (roommate's daughter) is sleeping, and I know (roommate) is trying to get her to sleep, and my daughter is still wanting to read a book and I'm like, "No, we need to get to bed." So she'll start crying and I'm like, "Just hold the book while you're sleeping or something." And like, I'm giving in; I'm letting her walk all over me. And she (daughter) can cry, like sometimes kids will stop crying after five minutes, but she can go. And I'm not going to put (roommate) through that, so I give in and I kind of give her what she wants. We're all living together and I don't wanna … so yeah, I give in.

Both June and Shana discuss the shelter's rule regarding constant contact of mothers with children, citing it as unreasonable at times, as well as physically exhausting. For example, Shana received a formal reprimand from staff, as well as a passive aggressive address at a house meeting, when she left her son unattended in the room.

Shana: When I first got here, he (Tyler) was sleeping, he wouldn't get out of bed, the little kids were late for school and I was like, "Can I just leave him for 5 minutes?" Oh my goodness, I did and I was abandoning my child. It was brought up in a meeting, "You cannot abandon your children!"

Learning from that experience, Shana keeps her children with her at all times, which influences sleep schedules, but also the ability to discipline as suggested by New Beginnings, by reward or stripping privileges. Shana explains that the context does not fit the advice, since there are few privileges available to the children thus not much to take away as punishment. Further, since all children must be with her at all times, she must either give all of the children a privilege, or none of them, creating much stress in parenting, as well as a feeling of unfairness among the children. She reports a strain in her relationship with her children and ability to mother, as well as a personal toll.

Many of the mothers have little respite from the responsibilities of childcare. In addition, many women report nonexistent or strained social networks that may otherwise be relied upon for respite childcare. Several women did have family that lived nearby and provided intermittent respite care on the weekends for the children. Women with more stable networks can request overnight vouchers to visit family on holidays and weekends, although these trips are subject to approval by their caseworker. In fact, the entrance into the shelter has created a marked strain on both Shana and June's relationships with their support systems after their request for doubling up with family was refused, as well as their parent's seemingly distant relationship to their children.

Shana had requested that her parents take Tyler when he was no longer able to stay at Kid's House and was rebuffed. These women are quite distinct from one another in terms of education, skill sets, length of stay, age, and resources. However, a common thread is broken or strained relationships to family, which are often the base social networks one turns to in individual crisis. For these women, families were not support options, leading them to seek help at the shelter. Although not all women report the development of new social networks, most were involved in these networks to some degree. As respondents reveal, they face strained relationships with their families, and therefore find support from these network members to be unreliable or nonexistent. Researchers have found that DV victims face restrictions on contact with social networks as a form of power and control by their abusers (Thompson et al. 2000; Levendosky, Bogat, Theran, Trotter, von Eye, Davidson 2004). This diminishment of a victim's social networks leads to difficulties when attempting to flee the situation and rebuild independently. They often turn to a shelter as an alternative.

● DOMESTIC VIOLENCE VICTIMS AND CHOICE AS MOTHERS

In a program that explicitly defines empowerment as the cornerstone of their approach, these examples illustrate the unevenness of the approach between staff and residents. Although the program touts the value of all choices as valid choices, it appears that this only rings true when the choices are perceived as "good choices." This provides an excellent context for the difficulties of attempting to mother in institutional spaces, which both limit personal agency, but also negate, or disempower, the choices that are made in a mother's parenting decisions about their children. It is clear that the cultural constructions of what mothers should be, or do, are present within staff through their advice to mothers, and parallel the ideas of intensive mothering (Hays 1998).

If empowerment is seen as choice, mothers who are also victims of domestic violence face greater restrictions on access to empowerment than those without children, as a result of the extra surveillance and involvement of the shelter, and the staff's critique of their choices. This can be tied to unrealistic expectations of mothers, and the construction of inadequate mothering among DV victims that cites less-available parenting, elevated levels of stress, and delays in physical, social, and emotional development. Similar to the construction of the BWS, these models of inadequate parenting (or inadequate mothers) also assume an ideal type, which becomes embedded in the programs designed for victims of DV. While the argument for inadequate parenting claims that the source is the abuser labeling the mother's parenting as faulty, and the mother coming to believe these verbal assaults, it seems to ignore this similar reproduction of mother blaming that is present in DV work. The shelter becomes the site in which mothers encounter these discourses of the battered mother and this shapes their experience of mothering within the shelter as these discourses are embedded in shelter work, shaping the protocol of staff, and programs for women and children. This local site is an environment in which these discourses are practiced and is ordered by the relations of ruling present in DV discourse, mothering discourse, and constructions of the battered mother.

Loseke (1992) illustrated how DV was created as a social problem, bringing with it a constructed victim, a protocol for helping this "type of person," as well as creating a new industry of help work. The discourse of the battered woman shaped how institutions designed to help battered women were structured; at the same time, the creation of the battered woman as a person led to restrictions on the types of victims battered women could become. The present work takes the idea of the battered woman and combines it with mothering discourse on DV victims. This is done in order to show how DV discourse constructs a particular kind of mother, the battered mother, who is assumed to be deficient and is in need of rebuilding herself as well as learning how to mother. These discourses structure the shelter experience for battered mothers, making the experience of domestic violence sheltering very different for women with children compared to women without children present.

● REFERENCES

Barrow, S., and N. Laborde. 2008. "Invisible Mothers: Parenting by Homeless Women Separated from Their Children." *Gender Issues* 25 (3): 157–172.

Breiding, M. J., S.G. Smith, K.C. Basile, M.L. Walters, J. Chen, and M.T. Merrick 2011. "Prevalence and Characteristics of Sexual Violence, Stalking and Intimate Partner Violence Victimization—National Intimate Partner and Sexual Violence Survey, United States, 2011." *Morbidity and Mortality Weekly Report*, 2014L 63 SS–8: 1–18.

Edelson, J. L. 1999. "Children's Witnessing of Adult Domestic Violence." *Journal of Interpersonal Violence* 14 (8):839–870.

Ferraro, K. J., and A. M. Moe. 2003. "Mothering, Crime and Incarceration." *Journal of Contemporary Ethnography* 32 (1) 9–40.

Hays, S. 1998. *The Cultural Contradictions of Motherhood.* New Haven, CT: Yale University Press.

Jasinski, J., J. Wesely, E. Mustaine, and J. Wright. 2005. *The Experience of Violence in the Lives of Homeless Women: A Research Report*. *https://www.ncjrs.gov/pdffiles1/nij/grants/211976.pdf* National Institute of Justice. U.S. Department of Justice.

Jasinski, J., J. Wesely, J. Wright, E. Mustaine. 2010. *Hard Lives, Mean Streets: Violence in the Lives of Homeless Women*. Boston: Northeastern University Press.

Levendosky, A. A., G. A. Bogat, S. A. Theran, J. S. Trotter, A. von Eye, and W. S. Davidson. 2004. "The Social Networks of Women Experiencing Domestic Violence." *American Journal of Community Psychology* 34 (1–2): 95–109.

Loseke, D. 1992. *The Battered Woman and the Shelters: The Social Construction of Wife Abuse*. Albany: State University of New York Press.

Lowe, E. T., A. Slater, J. Welfley, and T. Beard. 2005. *Hunger and Homelessness Survey: A Status Report on Hunger and Homelessness in America's Cities*. Washington, D.C.: U.S. Conference of Mayors.

National Resource Center on Domestic Violence. 2002. *Children Exposed to Intimate Partner Violence*. http://vawnet.org/sites/default/files/materials/files/2016-09/NRC_Children-KeyIssue1.pdf

Parrenas, R. S. 2001. "Mothering from a Distance: Emotions, Gender, and Intergenerational Relations in Filipino Transnational Families." *Feminist Studies* 27 (2) 361–390.

Peled, E., and R. Dekel. 2010. "Excusable Deficiency: Staff Perceptions of Mothering at Shelters for Abused Women." *Violence Against Women* 16 (11): 1224–1241.

Radford, L., and M. Hester. 2006. *Mothering Through Domestic Violence*. London: Jessica Kingsley Publishers.

Reiter, B. 2005. "Many Victims Don't Know Law Provides Protection." *Des Moines Register*, February 27. http://www.ncdsv.org/images/ManyVictimsDOntKnowLawProvidesProtection.pdf.

Schneider, E. M. 2000. *Battered Women and Feminist Lawmaking*. New Haven, CT: Yale University Press.

Thompson, M. P., N. J. Kaslow, J. B. Kingree, A. Rashid, R. Puett, D. Jacobs, and A. Matthews 2000. "Partner Violence, Social Support, and Distress Among Inner–City African American Women." *American Journal of Community Psychology* 28 (1) 127–143.

Tierney, K. J. 1982. "The Battered Women Movement and the Creation of the Wife Beating Problem." *Social Problems*, 29(3).

Truman, J. L., and L. Langton. 2015. "Criminal Victimization, 2014." *Bureau of Justice Statistics*, September 2015.

SECTION **SEVEN**

SOCIAL PROBLEMS IN EDUCATION

M any people are concerned about the state of education in the United States. The gulf between well-funded, high-functioning schools and poorly funded, low-functioning schools is growing. Although programs like No Child Left Behind have been created to help address these issues and improve the quality of American education, the problem does not appear to be abating. This section consists of three chapters that identify important social problems that are connected to education: No Child Left Behind and similar legislation, bullying in schools, and the challenges that African American students face in a predominantly white college.

● NO CHILD LEFT BEHIND

American public schools are funded mostly through local property taxes. So, people living in a given district pay property taxes that are used to fund the public elementary, middle, and high schools in that district. School districts around the country have vastly different operating budgets because the people in those districts have homes that are worth different amounts of money and pay different rates of taxation. Residents of poorer districts tend to pay less in property taxes, resulting in less money being generated. This, in turn, affects teacher pay, the quality of educational resources, class sizes, and student morale.

American education experts have known for years that the current way of funding public schools is flawed. As a way to help struggling schools, the No Child Left Behind Act was signed into law in 2002 under President Bush. When Bush signed the law, he said he wanted to ensure that "every single child, regardless of where they live, how they're raised, the income level of their family, every child receive a first-class education in America" (White House Office of the Press Secretary 2002). A central component of this legislation is the standardized test. Tests such as the PSSA are used to measure students' abilities, particularly in language arts and math, and to monitor their yearly progress. Schools with students who—as a whole or in subgroups—repeatedly struggle to reach baselines have been targeted for interventions, such as replacing teachers. Vast inequalities in school quality and outcomes remain, however.

Darling-Hammond's chapter, entitled "Testing, No Child Left Behind, and Educational Equity" critically assesses No Child Left Behind. As Darling-Hammond articulates, there has been a clear and longstanding need to make changes to public education in America. High-stakes standardized testing, however, has led to teachers spending more time on the subjects being tested, particularly on multiple-choice questions like the ones on the tests, as opposed to more higher-order tasks that would better prepare students for high school and college. Breadth is also favored over depth, even if that is not pedagogically sound. This is all particularly true for schools with predominantly low-income and racial minority students. Unfortunately, the consequences for underperforming schools have not helped them, and the strategies deployed by schools to appear better—such as excluding the lowest-performing students—have resulted in lower quality or no education (i.e., dropping out) for the poorest schools. Darling-Hammond concludes this chapter by calling for the creation of a new Elementary and Secondary Education Act that measures need much differently than current legislation.

● BULLYING

Bullying is another significant social problem in the United States. Tens of thousands of youths all over the country experience emotional and physical repercussions from repeated aggression by others. Cyberbullying has also emerged in recent years and involves a person being harassed, intimidated, or threatened through electronic communication, such as texting or email messaging, Instagram, Facebook, or Twitter. There are a variety of psychological and social reasons why people engage in bullying against particular targets. It may be due to perceived exclusion or an inflated sense of self-importance. Interestingly, many bullies have been victims of bullying themselves. The consequences of bullying are dire, as it is linked to depression, anxiety, anger, and even suicide.

In her chapter, "Understanding Bullying: Insight from a Sociology of Bullying Perspective," Nicole Rosen defines what bullying is, showing how the definition used is consequential for understanding the scope of bullying and how it may change over time. She identifies characteristics of bullies and their targets. Next, she discusses various coping techniques and whether they encourage or dissuade further bullying, primarily using a psychological approach. She then innovatively offers a more sociological perspective on bullying, showing how bullying can be analyzed and addressed at the micro-, meso-, and macro-levels to not only raise awareness about bullying but to also reduce its likelihood of occurrence in the future.

● HIGHER EDUCATION AND RACE

In America, black and Hispanic students are less likely to enroll in college and less likely to graduate from college than whites. Race correlates with social class, and those who are born into a poor or working-class family are less likely to attend college than those from a more affluent background. Relatedly, students in these minority groups are not as likely to have the educational support networks that many white students take for granted. As such, many college students of color go to college and feel disconnected from others around them. Even though many colleges are striving to be more diverse, most are bastions of whiteness. Colleges tend to be located in predominantly white areas, and students and faculty are likely to be white. Therefore, the adjustment from life in high school to life in college varies for people of different racial and ethnic groups.

In his chapter, "A Qualitative Inquiry on the Multidimensional Racial Development Among First-Year African American College Students Attending a Predominately White Institution," Baber shows that there are specific challenges that African American students face while attending mostly white colleges. Since college attendance rates are on the rise, these challenges are important to address. Using the Multidimensional Model of Racial Identity (MMRI), Baber contends that racial salience, racial centrality, racial regard, racial ideology, and complexity of identity impact a variety of students' beliefs and values which, in turn, inform their self-identity and mediate their overall experiences. Baber also discusses the importance of cultural capital and resiliency for developing coping strategies and seeking support from others.

References

White House Office of the Press Secretary. 2002. *President Signs Landmark No Child Left Behind Education Bill.* Washington, DC: Author. https://georgewbush-whitehouse.archives.gov/news/releases/2002/01/20020108-1.html.

CHAPTER 23

Testing, No Child Left Behind, and Educational Equity

By Linda Darling-Hammond

T he United States is falling behind a growing number of nations in every aspect of educational achievement and attainment. High school graduation rates—once at the top of international rankings—have been stagnant at about 70 percent since the 1970s, while nations like Finland, Norway, Greece, Germany, Japan, and South Korea have surged ahead and now graduate more than 90 percent of their students (Organization for Economic Cooperation and Development 2008). And, whereas the U.S. was an unchallenged 1st in the world in higher education participation for many decades, it had slipped to 16th by 2008 (OECD 2008).

Although about 60 percent of U.S. high school graduates go off to college, only about half of these are well-enough prepared educationally and well-enough supported financially to graduate with a degree—far too few for the knowledge economy we now operate. In the end, about 38 percent of an age cohort in the U.S. gains a college degree, as compared to about 50 percent in European countries, and over 60 percent in South Korea (Douglass 2006; KEDI 2006).

For students of color in the United States, the pipeline leaks more profusely at every juncture. Only about 17 percent of African American young people between the ages of 25 and 29—and only 11 percent of Hispanic youth—had earned a college degree in 2005, as compared to 34 percent of white youth in the same age bracket (U.S. Census Bureau 2005). Although these young people of color will be a majority of public school students by 2025, investments in their education remain highly unequal and inadequate to meet today's demands for the kinds of learning needed in the labor market. The schools they attend are both more segregated than they were 25 years ago and less adequately resourced (Darling-Hammond 2010). International studies confirm that the U.S. educational system not only lags most other industrialized countries in academic achievement by high school, it is also allocates more unequal inputs and produces more unequal outcomes than its peer nations (OECD 2007).

The stark disparities in access to high-quality education at the elementary and secondary levels translate into unequal access to higher education for low-income and minority students. Meanwhile, recognition of the increasing importance of education to individual and societal well-being has spawned an education reform movement in the United States focused on the development of new standards for students and new assessments to test students' knowledge. All states have created these new standards, and many have put in place accountability systems that attach rewards and sanctions to students' scores on standardized tests. The hope is that these systems will close the achievement gap.

The largest federal education law, reauthorized at the start of the Bush administration in 2001 as the No Child Left Behind Act (NCLB), reinforces these test-based accountability systems. It requires all states receiving funding to test students annually and to enforce penalties for schools that do not meet specific test score targets each year, both for students as a whole and for groups defined by race/ethnicity, language, socio-economic status, and disability. This law is intended to rectify the inequalities that have plagued the American education system and that currently threaten the nation's future. Yet, as I describe in this chapter, NCLB has produced mixed results, including a variety of unintended negative consequences for the students it was intended to help.

Civil rights advocates initially welcomed NCLB's emphasis on improving education for disadvantaged students, and, indeed, the law contains some major breakthroughs. First, by flagging differences in student performance by race and class, it shines a spotlight on long-standing inequalities and has triggered attention to the needs of students neglected in many schools. Second, by insisting that all students are entitled to qualified teachers, the law has stimulated some productive recruitment efforts in states where low-income and "minority" students have experienced a revolving door of inexperienced, untrained teachers. This first-time-ever recognition of students' right to qualified teachers is historically significant.

However, as I discuss in this chapter, the press for greater accountability through testing has proved to be a double-edged sword. The creation of state standards to guide student learning has clarified goals, and in cases where standards are well-designed, has usefully upgraded expectations for knowledge and skills. Where assessments have been thoughtfully constructed and where standards-based reform has been implemented as intended—with greater investments in high-quality learning materials and teaching, education for under-served students has been helped to improve. However, where low-quality tests have driven a narrow curriculum disconnected from the higher-order skills needed in today's world, educational quality has declined, especially for low income students whose education has come increasingly to resemble test preparation, instead of the skills they desperately need to succeed in college and careers.

Furthermore, where high-stakes testing has occurred in lieu of investing, discouraged students and overwhelmed schools have produced higher dropout rates rather than higher standards, reducing the pipeline to higher education while growing the school-to-prison pipeline (Wald and Losen 2003). These unintended consequences have emerged in part because the Act layers onto a highly unequal school system a set of ultimately unmeetable test score targets that disproportionately penalize schools serving the neediest students and those with the most diverse school populations. I explore these complex dynamics below.

● THE PROSPECTS AND PITFALLS OF STANDARDS-BASED REFORM
Using Standards for Improvement

The original theory of standards–based reform anticipated that learning standards and assessments for students would be tied to investments in higher-quality and better-aligned learning materials, better-prepared teachers, and stronger supports for struggling students (O'Day and Smith 1993). This has, in fact, occurred in some states, especially in the first wave of such reforms in the early 1990s. Studies found that teachers and principals became more focused on state standards (DeBard and Kubow 2002; Woody *et al.* 2004), and that, in many places, schools paid greater attention to students who need support to improve their performance and invested in increased professional development for teachers (Ladd and Zelli 2002).

In some states, such as Connecticut, Kentucky, and Vermont, high-quality assessments have been used to help educators figure out what aspects of the curriculum need improvement and to direct resources toward those areas (Herman *et al.* 2000; see also reviews by Linn 2000; Shepard 2000). These states' performance assessments asked students to analyze texts; write persuasive essays; find, evaluate, synthesize, and use information; conduct and present the results of scientific investigations; and solve complex mathematical problems in real-world settings, showing their solution strategies and explaining their reasoning

States that developed performance assessments found that teachers assigned more writing and more complex mathematical problem solving, and that achievement on these higher-order skills improved (Darling-Hammond and Rustique-Forrester 2005). These results are consistent with the findings of a number of studies that have found achievement gains for students in classrooms offering a well-taught problem-oriented curriculum featuring performance assessments requiring research, writing, problem-solving, and defense of ideas (see, for example, Darling-Hammond *et al.* 2008; Newmann *et al.* 1995; Lee *et al.* 1995. These skills are the ones required in college and contemporary knowledge-based careers.

Challenges of Contemporary Test-Based Accountability

Despite the positive outcomes of performance assessments, many initiatives of the 1990s were scaled back or abandoned with the passage of No Child Left Behind in 2002. The law caused many states to revert to multiple-choice tests in order to comply with federal requirements for annual testing of every child at low cost and to meet the Education Department's approval process, which frequently rejected performance-based assessments. Unfortunately, when used in high-stakes contexts, these more narrow tests have been found to exert strong pressures to reduce the curriculum to subjects and modes of performance that are tested, and to encourage less focus on complex reasoning and performance. (For a review, see Darling-Hammond and Rustique-Forrester 2005).

Teachers often prepare students by spending substantial instructional time on exercises that look just like the test items, reverting to worksheets filled with multiple-choice questions and drill based on recall and recitation that they feel will prepare students for the tests. In the process, instructional strategies such as extended writing, research papers, investigations, and computer use are de-emphasized (Haney 2000; Jones and Egley 2004; Popham 1999).

Untested subjects or topics are also neglected. Most teachers report less attention to subjects that are not on the state test (Education Week 2001). In 2007, a study by the Center on Education Policy found that nearly half of all elementary schools had reduced time for science, social studies, arts, music, and physical education in response to the emphasis on reading and mathematics tests under No Child Left Behind (Center on Education Policy 2007). This has the additional effect of failing to provide the content knowledge upon which more complex reading skills develop and the foundations for disciplinary studies in high schools that could prepare students for college.

Teachers in high-stakes testing states have reported not only that they no longer teach science or social studies, but that that they do use computers, because the state test requires handwritten answers (Pedulla et al. 2003), impeding the acquisition of both writing skills and computer skills (Russell and Abrams 2004).

Teachers in high-stakes testing states are also more likely to report that they feel pressured to use test formats in their instruction and to teach in ways that contradict their ideas of sound instructional practice (Pedulla et al. 2003). One Florida teacher observed:

> Before FCAT [the state test], I was a better teacher. I was exposing my children to a wide range of science and social studies experiences. I taught using themes that really immersed the children into learning about a topic using their reading, writing, math, and technology skills. Now I'm basically afraid to NOT teach to the test. I know that the way I was teaching was building a better foundation for my kids as well as a love of learning. Now each year I can't wait until March is over so I can

spend the last two and a half months of school teaching the way I want to teach, the way I know students will be excited about.

Another Florida teacher added:

> I believe that the FCAT is pushing students and teachers to rush through curriculum much too quickly. Rather than focusing on getting students to understand a concept fully in math, we must rush through all the subjects so we are prepared to take the test in March. This creates a surface knowledge or many times very little knowledge in a lot of areas. I would rather spend a month on one concept and see my students studying in an in-depth manner.
>
> *(Southeast Center for Teaching Quality 2003, p. 15)*

Ironically, while U.S. teachers feel pressured to rush through topics, covering them superficially, higher-scoring countries in mathematics and science teach *fewer* concepts than most schools in the U.S. do each year, but teach them more deeply (Schmidt *et al.* 2005). Furthermore, studies show that increases in test scores on rote-oriented tests do not stimulate increases on assessments that look for analytic thinking and application of knowledge (Amrein and Berliner 2002; Klein *et al.* 2000). As a Texas teacher noted in a survey:

> I have seen more students who can pass the TAAS but cannot apply those skills to anything if it's not in the TAAS format. I have students who can do the test but can't look up words in a dictionary and understand the different meanings.... As for higher quality teaching, I'm not sure I would call it that. Because of the pressure for passing scores, more and more time is spent practicing the test and putting everything in TAAS format.
>
> *(Haney 2000, Part 6, p. 10)*

These adjustments of the curriculum to match the test happen most frequently and intensely in schools serving low-income and minority students (Darling-Hammond and Rustique-Forrester 2005), where meeting test score targets is a greater struggle, leaving these students with the least access to a rich and thoughtful curriculum that will prepare them for the higher education and jobs they need for lifelong success.

● TESTING RATHER THAN INVESTING

An equally large problem is that, while NCLB has dramatically increased the amount of testing in schools, it has not addressed the profound educational inequalities poor children experience. International studies repeatedly find that the U.S. has one of the most inequitable education systems in the industrialized world, with a 3-to-1 ratio between high- and low-spending schools in most states, multiplied further by inequalities across states (Darling-Hammond 2010). Most high-achieving countries not only provide high-quality universal early childhood care and health care for children, they also fund their schools centrally and equally, with additional funds to the neediest schools. Furthermore, they support a better-prepared teaching force, funding competitive salaries and high-quality teacher education, mentoring, and ongoing professional development for all teachers—at the state's expense (Darling-Hammond 2010).

By contrast, NCLB's small allocation—less than 10 percent of most schools' budgets—does not substantially improve the under-resourced schools where many students currently struggle to learn. Furthermore, the law does not require that states demonstrate progress toward equitable and adequate funding or greater opportunities to learn. Although NCLB requires "highly qualified teachers," the lack of a federal teacher supply policy makes this a hollow promise in many communities. School funding lawsuits brought in more than 40 states describe apartheid schools serving low-income students of color, with crumbling facilities, overcrowded classrooms, out-of-date textbooks, no science labs or art or music courses, and a revolving door of untrained teachers, while their suburban counterparts spend twice as much for students with fewer needs, offering expansive libraries, up-to-date labs and technology, small classes, well-qualified teachers, expert specialists, and luxurious facilities (Darling-Hammond 2010).

As Gloria Ladson-Billings (2006) has noted, the problem we face is not an "achievement gap" but an *educational debt* that has accumulated over centuries of denied access to education and employment and has been reinforced by deepening poverty and resource inequalities in schools. Ladson-Billings argues that until American society confronts the accumulated educational debt owed to these students and takes responsibility for the inferior resources they receive, children of color and of poverty will continue to be left behind.

The Testing Gauntlet: How Diverse Schools are Penalized

The biggest problem with NCLB is that it mistakes measuring schools for fixing them. NCLB's complex regulations for showing "Adequate Yearly Progress" (AYP) toward test score targets aimed at "100 percent proficiency" have created a bizarre situation. Projections indicate that more than 80 percent of the nation's public schools will be labeled "failing" by 2014—even many that already score high and those that are steadily improving from year to year (Packer 2004; Wiley et al. 2005), most of them because they missed just one of the many targets set for test participation rates and scores on multiple tests. These targets include specific expectations for scores and participation rates on reading and math tests for each of up to eight different groups defined by race/ethnicity, language background, disability status, and income, resulting in as many as 30 or more separate targets a diverse school might have to achieve.

As a result of the law's design, the chances that a school will be designated as failing increase in proportion to the number of demographic groups served by the school. Ironically, this makes well-integrated schools more likely to be identified as failing than segregated ones that achieve at the same levels. Two separate studies (Novak and Fuller 2003; Sunderman and Kim 2004) have found that schools serving poor, minority, and limited-English proficient students and schools with a greater number of subgroups for which they are held accountable are disproportionately identified as "needing improvement" under NCLB.

Worse still, there is an unwinnable Catch-22 for those serving English language learners and special needs students. In *Alice in Wonderland* fashion, the law assigns these students to special subgroups *because* they do not meet the proficiency standard, but for purposes of calculating AYP, they are removed from the subgroup as they become proficient, so it is impossible for the subgroup ever to become 100 percent proficient. Schools serving a significant share of these learners will inevitably be labeled failing, even if all of their students consistently make strong learning gains. Schools serving the nation's neediest students are asked to show the greatest gains in the shortest time, typically with the fewest resources, and under rules that, if they serve new English language learners, for example, label them as failing no matter how much they improve. From that starting point, other consequences unfold.

Consequences for the Neediest Schools and Students

There is growing evidence that the law's strategy for "improving" schools may, paradoxically, reduce access to education for the most vulnerable students. Research by Clotfelter, Ladd, and colleagues (2004) has found that labeling schools as failures makes it even harder for them to attract and keep qualified teachers. As one Florida principal queried, "Is anybody going to want to dedicate their lives to a school that has already been labeled a failure?" Second, schools that have been identified as not meeting AYP standards must use their federal funds to support choice and "supplementary services," such as privately provided after-school tutoring, thus leaving even fewer resources to spend on improving their core instructional programs. Unfortunately, many of the private supplemental service providers have proved ineffective (Sunderman 2007), and transfers to higher-quality schools have been impossible in communities where such schools are unavailable or uninterested in serving students with low achievement, poor attendance, and other problems that might bring their own average test scores down. Thus, rather than expanding educational opportunities for low-income students and students of color, the law further reduces the quality of education in the schools these students must attend.

Perhaps the most adverse unintended consequence of NCLB is that it creates incentives for schools to rid themselves of students who are not doing well, producing higher scores at the expense of vulnerable students' education. Paradoxically, NCLB's requirement for disaggregating data by grade and other defined subgroup creates incentives to eliminate those at the bottom of each subgroup. A number of studies have found that systems that sanction schools based on average student scores lead to schools retaining students in grade so that their grade-level scores will look better (even though these students ultimately do less well and drop out at higher rates), excluding low-scoring students from admissions, and encouraging such students to transfer or drop out (Darling-Hammond and Rustique-Forrester 2005).

Recent research in New York, Texas, and Massachusetts shows how schools have raised test scores while "losing" large numbers of low-scoring students. In one large Texas city, which served as the model for NCLB, scores soared while tens of thousands of students—mostly African American or Latino—disappeared from school. Educators reported how exclusionary policies were used to hold back, suspend, expel, or counsel out students in order to boost test scores (Vasquez Heilig and Darling-Hammond 2008). Overall, fewer than 40 percent of African American and Latino students graduated. Indeed, in part because of high-stakes testing, graduation rates for African American and Latino students have returned to pre-1954 levels in a growing number of states.

● WHAT IT WOULD TAKE TO REALLY LEAVE NO CHILD BEHIND

Hundreds of proposals for tweaking various provisions of NCLB have been made, but a more substantial paradigm shift that directly confronts both educational quality and equality is required if the nation is to move from an inequitable and inadequate education system focused increasingly on compliance to a system that is organized to support powerful learning for all students.

The Forum on Education and Accountability (2004), a group of over 100 education and civil rights organizations, has argued that "the law's emphasis needs to shift from applying sanctions for failing to raise test scores to holding states and localities accountable for making the systemic changes that improve student achievement." These organizations—which include the National Urban League, the NAACP, the League of United Latin American Citizens, Aspira, the Children's Defense Fund, the National Alliance of Black School Educators, and the Council for Exceptional Children, as well as the National School Boards Association, the National Education Association, and the American Association of School Administrators—offer proposals focused on teacher development, stronger curriculum, and supports for school improvement.

How might this be done? Among other things, a new paradigm for national education policy should be guided by twin commitments to *support learning* on the part of students, teachers, and schools and to *pay off the educational debt,* making it possible for all students to profit from more productive schools.

Support Student Learning and School Progress

A new Elementary and Secondary Education Act (ESEA) should evaluate schools on multiple measures, including such factors as student progress and continuation, graduation, and classroom performance on tasks beyond multiple choice tests. Gains should be assessed by how individual students improve over time, rather than school averages that can be influenced by changes in who is assessed. To eliminate the statistical gauntlet that penalizes schools serving the most diverse populations, the current punitive and confusing system of Adequate Yearly Progress should be replaced with a continuous improvement model.

Such a model would judge schools on whether students make progress on an index that includes multiple measures of learning, including assessments that evaluate higher order thinking and performance, that ensure appropriate assessment for special education students and English language learners, and that include progress through school and graduation rates. Schools that are lagging should be helped to improve, through a diagnostic review by experts who can help guide useful improvements and direct resources to where they are needed. "Opportunity-to-learn standards" should provide benchmarks for the provision of adequate materials, facilities, and teachers, and should be guaranteed for schools that are in need.

Pay off the Educational Debt

A new ESEA must finally address the deep and tenacious educational debt that holds our nation's future in hock. Federal education funding to states should be increased and tied to each state's movement toward equitable access to education resources. Furthermore, the obvious truth—that schools alone are not responsible for student achievement—should propel attention to programs that will provide adequate health care and nutrition, safe and secure housing, and healthy communities for children.

Major investments must be made in the ability of schools to hire and support well-prepared teachers and leaders. While NCLB sets an expectation for hiring qualified teachers, it does not include policy supports to make this possible. Federal leadership in developing an adequate supply of well-qualified teachers is needed, just as it has been essential in providing an adequate supply of physicians for more than 40 years through investments in medical training for those who prepare in shortage specialties and locate in underserved areas.

A focused and purposeful Marshall Plan for Teaching (see Darling-Hammond 2007) could ensure that all students are taught by well-qualified teachers within the next five years through a federal policy that (1) *recruits new teachers* using service scholarships that underwrite their preparation for high-need fields and locations and adds incentives for expert, veteran teachers to teach in high-need schools; (2) *strengthens teachers' preparation* through incentive grants to schools of education and districts to create professional development schools, like teaching hospitals, which offer top-quality urban teacher residencies to candidates who will stay in high-need districts; and (3) *improves teacher retention and effectiveness* by ensuring that novices have mentoring support during their early years—a period during which 30 percent of them drop out.

For an annual cost of $3 billion, or less than one week in Iraq, the nation could underwrite the high-quality preparation of 40,000 teachers annually—enough to fill all the vacancies currently filled by unprepared teachers each year; seed 100 top quality urban teacher education programs and improve the capacity of all programs to prepare teachers who can teach diverse learners well; ensure mentors for every new teacher hired each year; and provide incentives to bring expert teachers into high-need schools through targeted improvements in salaries and working conditions.

Students will not learn to higher levels unless they experience good teaching, a strong curriculum, and adequate resources. In fact, adopting tests and punitive sanctions, without making investments, does not create genuine accountability and increases the likelihood that the most vulnerable students will be more severely victimized by a system not organized to support their learning. A policy agenda that leverages equitable resources and invests strategically in high-quality teaching would support *real* accountability—that is, accountability to children and parents for providing the conditions in which students can acquire the skills they need to succeed in college and careers in the twenty-first century.

● REFERENCES

Amrein, A. and D. Berliner. 2002. High-Stakes Testing, Uncertainty, and Student Learning. *Educational Policy and Analysis Archives* 10(8). Retrieved [November 21, 2003] from: http://www.epaa.asu.edu/epaa/v10n18.

Center on Education Policy 2007, July. *Choices, Changes, and Challenges: Curriculum and Instruction in the NCLB Era.* Washington, DC: Author.

Clotfelter, C. T., H. F. Ladd, J. L. Vigdor, and R. A. Diaz. 2004. Do School Accountability Systems Make It More Difficult for Low Performing Schools to Attract and Retain High Quality Teachers? *Journal of Policy and Management* 23(2): 251–72.

Darling-Hammond, L. 2007. A Marshall Plan for Teaching: What It Will Really Take to Leave No Child Behind, *Education Week Commentary* 26(18) (January 10): 48, 28.

Darling-Hammond, L. 2010. *The Flat World and Education: How America's Commitment to Equity Will Determine Our Future.* NY: Teachers College Press.

Darling-Hammond, L. and E. Rustique-Forrester. 2005. The Consequences of Student Testing for Teaching and Teacher Quality. In Joan Herman and Edward Haertel (Eds.), *The Uses and Misuses of Data in Accountability Testing.* The 104th Yearbook of the National Society for the Study of Education, Part II, Malden, MA: Blackwell Publishing. Pp. 289–319.

Darling-Hammond, L., B. Barron, P. D. Pearson, A. Schoenfeld, E. K. Stage, T. D. Zimmerman, G. N. Cervetti, and J. L. Tilson. 2008. *Powerful Learning: What We Know about Teaching for Understanding.* San Francisco: Jossey-Bass.

DeBard, R., and P. K. Kubow. 2002. From Compliance to Commitment: The Need for Constituent Discourse in Implementing Testing Policy. *Education Policy* 16(3): 387–405.

Douglass, J. A. 2006. *The Waning of America's Higher Education Advantage.* Paper CSHE-9-06. Berkeley, CA: Center for Studies in Higher Education, University of California at Berkeley.

Education Week. 2001. *Quality Counts 2001: A Better Balance.* Bethesda, MD: Editorial Projects in Education (11 January).

Forum on Educational Accountability. 2004, as updated. *Joint Organizational Statement on No Child Left Behind.* http://www.edaccountability.org/Joint_Statement.html.

Haney, W. 2000. The Myth of the Texas Miracle in Education. *Educational Policy Analysis Archives* 8(41): http://epaa.asu.edu/epaa/v8n41/.

Herman, J. L., R. S. Brown, and E. L. Balcer. 2000. *Student Assessment and Student Achievement in the California Public School Systems.* Retrieved [November 18, 2004] from: cresst96.cge.ucla.edu/CRESST/Reports/TECHS19.pdf.

Jones, B. D. and R. J. Egley. 2004. Voices from the Frontlines: Teachers' Perceptions of High-Stakes Testing. *Education Policy Analysis Archives* 12(39). Retrieved [August 10, 2004] from http://epaa.asu.edu/epaa/v12n39/.

Klein, S. P., L. S. Hamilton, D. F. McCaffrey, and B. M. Stetcher. 2000. *What Do Test Scores in Texas Tell Us?* Santa Monica, CA: The RAND Corporation.

Korean Educational Development Institute (KEDI) 2006. Statistical Yearbook of Education, 2006. Seoul: KEDI.

Ladd, H. F. and A. Zelli. 2002. School-Based Accountability in North Carolina: The Responses of School Principals. *Educational Administration Quarterly* 38(4): 494–529.

Ladson-Billings, G. 2006. From the Achievement Gap to the Education Debt: Understanding Achievement in U.S. Schools. *Educational Researcher* 35(10): 3–12.

Lee, V. E., J. B. Smith, and R. G. Croninger. 1995. Another Look at High School Restructuring: More Evidence that It Improves Student Achievement and More Insight into Why. *Issues in Restructuring Schools.* Issue report no. 9 (Fall), Madison, WI: Center on the Organization and Restructuring of Schools, University of Wisconsin. Pp. 1–9.

Linn, R. L. 2000. Assessments and Accountability. *Educational Researcher* 29(2): 4–16.

Newmann, F. M., H. M. Marks, and A. Gamoran. 1995. Authentic Pedagogy: Standards that Boost Performance. *American Journal of Education* 104(4): 280–312.

Novak, J. and B. Fuller. 2003. *Penalizing Diverse Schools? Similar Test Scores but Different Students Bring Federal Sanctions* (December). Berkeley, CA: Policy Analysis for California Education.

O'Day, Jennifer A. and Marshall S. Smith. 1993. Systemic School Reform and Educational Opportunity. In Susan Fuhrman (Ed.), *Designing Coherent Education Policy: Improving the System*. San Francisco: Jossey-Bass.

Organisation for Economic Co-operation and Development 2007. Programme for International Student Assessment 2006: Science competencies for tomorrow's world. Paris: OECD. Accessed at: http://nces.ed.gov/surveys/pisa/index.asp.

Organisation for Economic Co-operation and Development 2008. *Education at a Glance: OECD Indicators, 2007*. Paris: OECD.

Packer, J. 2004, July 28. *No Child Left Behind and Adequate Yearly Progress Fundamental Flaws: A Forecast for Failure*. Paper presented at the Center for Education Policy Forum on Ideas to Improve the Accountability Provisions. Washington, DC.

Pedulla, J. J., L. M. Abrams, G. F. Madaus, M. K. Russell, M. A. Ramos, and J. Miao. 2003. *Perceived Effects of State-Mandated Testing Programs on Teaching and Learning: Findings from a National Survey of Teachers*. Boston: National Board on Testing and Public Policy, Boston College.

Popham, W. J. 1999. Why Standardized Test Scores Don't Measure Educational Quality. *Educational Leadership* 56(6): 8–15.

Russell, M. and L. Abrams. 2004. Instructional Uses of Computers for Writing: The Impact of State Testing Programs. *Teachers College Record* 106(6): 1332–57.

Schmidt, W. H., H. C. Wang, and C. McKnight. 2005. Curriculum Coherence: An Examination of US Mathematics and Science Content Standards from an International Perspective. *Journal of Curriculum Studies* 37(5): 525–59.

Shepard, L. A. 2000. The Role of Assessment in a Learning Culture. *Educational Researcher* 29(7): 4–14.

Southeast Center for Teaching Quality. 2003, December 3–5. *Teacher Leaders Network Conversation: No Child Left Behind*. Retrieved July 25, 2007, from http://www.teach-erleaders.org/old_site/Conversations/NCLB_chat_full.pdf.

Sunderman, G. 2007. *Supplemental Educational Services under NCLB: Charting Implementation*. Los Angeles: The Civil Rights Project, UCLA.

Sunderman, G. and J. Kim. 2004. *Inspiring Vision, Disappointing Results: Four Studies on Implementing the No Child Left Behind Act*. Cambridge, MA: Harvard Civil Rights Project.

U.S. Bureau of the Census. 2005. *Current Population Reports*, Series P-20; Current Population Survey, March 1990 through March 2005. Washington, DC: U.S. Department of Commerce.

Vasquez Heilig, J. and L. Darling-Hammond. 2008. Accountability Texas Style: The Progress and Learning of Urban Minority Students in a High-Stakes Testing Context. *Educational Evaluation and Policy Analysis* 30: 75–110. http://epa.sagepub.com/cgi/reprint/30/2/75.

Wald, M. and D. Losen. 2003. *Deconstructing the School to Prison Pipeline*. San Francisco: Jossey-Bass.

Wiley, E. W., W. J. Mathis, and D. R. Garcia. 2005. *The Impact of the Adequate Yearly Progress Requirement of the Federal "No Child Left Behind" Act on Schools in the Great Lakes Region*. Tempe, AZ: Educational Policy Studies Laboratory, Arizona State University.

Woody, E. L., M. Buttles, J. Kafka, S. Park, and J. Russell. 2004, February. *Voices from the Field: Educators Respond to Accountability*. Retrieved [November 19, 2004] from: pace.berkeley.edu/ERAP_Report-WEB.pdf.

CHAPTER 24

Understanding Bullying: Insight from a Sociology of Bullying Perspective

By Nicole L. Rosen

Over time, there has been increased attention paid to bullying in schools across the United States. However, despite several efforts that have attempted to understand this phenomenon through research, stop future incidences of bullying through prevention programs, or address current cases of bullying with zero-tolerance programs, school-aged children continually report being victimized by their peers (Sullivan 2011). If more educators, parents, children, and law enforcement are aware of bullying and are taking proactive steps to stop it, wouldn't we expect rates of bullying to decrease? Why, then, are reported rates increasing?

Various theories, along with other insights from educators and psychologists, can be used to answer this question. However, in order to adequately address the problem of bullying in schools, researchers, educators, and parents would be best served if they considered not only the characteristics of bullies and victims, but also the larger social structures that shape children's behavior. Adopting such a perspective would require us to move towards a "sociology of bullying." This will enable us to see how society influences the individual and to recognize bullying behavior as a symptom of other social issues in our culture.

This chapter has three major goals. The first is provide a concise overview of bullying. The second is to provide a summary of coping strategies that people develop in response to bullying. The third is to examine implications of remedying bullying by exploring the sociological implications of bullying.

● WHAT IS BULLYING?

Norwegian researcher Dan Olweus is considered to be the father of bullying research. His extensive research in Norway spearheaded universal attention on children "mobbing" or bullying their peers. As defined by Olweus (1993), bullying involves any unwanted aggression and behavior that occurs repeatedly and over time, often involving an imbalance of power. This definition is used by many researchers today, although the definition is not without its flaws. For instance, serious acts of aggression and sexual harassment are not considered bullying if the behavior only happens once (Finkelhor, Turner, and Hamby 2012). Meanwhile, some children are likely to categorize *any* negative behavior as bullying, regardless of the frequency of such accounts (Finkelhor et al. 2012). Children who taunt, tease, or threaten their peers are undeniably "mean," but some children may categorize a single incident of mockery as bullying. There is not always a clear imbalance of power, as evident in the frequency of relational aggression found in girls' friendships (see Simmons 2002). In addition to discrepancies in Olweus' definition of bullying, the term "bully" itself does not readily translate to other languages and therefore the term may have different meanings within various cultures (Smith et al. 2002).

While children may consider all sorts of "wrong" behavior as bullying, educators, researchers, parents, and law enforcement often rely on concrete definitions. For instance, children may shrug off what may be perceived with great alarm by parents and educators. Or, what might appear as a malicious threat may not be considered a crime by law enforcement. This is especially apparent in incidences of cyberbullying (see Hinduja and Patchin 2010). Indeed, reaching a common definition of bullying is still of great concern for many researchers (Finkelhor et al.

2012; Hamburger, Basile, and Vivolo 2011). Some researchers caution adults and children from using the term bully, since it may reinforce stigma against a child (Smith et al. 2002). Researchers also acknowledge that many children who bully their peers are victims themselves (referred to as victim/bully), often victimized by their parent(s), sibling(s), or other children (Olweus 1993). Therefore, while a child may be a bully in one setting, she or he may be a victim in other situations. In an attempt to reach common ground, the terms peer mistreatment, peer aggression, and peer victimization are often used in place of bullying (see Finkelhor et al. 2012). While often defaulting to Olweus's definition, these terms avoid reinforcing stigma and are more inclusive of inappropriate behavior that may not perfectly fit within Olweus's definition (i.e., pertaining to frequency and power imbalance).

The Scope of Bullying

Given the limitations of Olweus's (1993) definition, researchers, educators, and parents must consider how studies that report the prevalence of bullying might be skewed. Various studies may have relied on different definitions of bullying, and therefore the reported rates and prevalence of incidences may be higher or lower than actual incidences. Despite this, general trends on the frequency and types of bullying are documented throughout various studies. Nationally, 28 percent of students in sixth through twelfth grade reported being bullied in the last school year (stopbullying.gov 2014). Within high school alone (9th through 12th grade), 20 percent of students reported being bullied. Roughly 30 percent of students admitted to bullying others and approximately 70 percent reported seeing bulling behavior at their schools (stopbullying.gov 2014). While it may appear that bullying is a grave concern and a growing epidemic, some studies suggest otherwise.

According to the U.S. Department of Education's National Center for Education Statistics (NCES 2015), there has been a gradual decline in reported incidences of bullying since 2005 amongst students aged twelve to eighteen. For instance, 29–33 percent of girls ages twelve to eighteen reported being bullied in previous years, yet in 2013, approximately 24 percent of girls reported the same behavior (NCES 2015). While the declining rates are similar for girls and boys, girls still reported slightly higher rates of bullying compared to boys (NCES 2015). Despite reports that bullying in schools may be declining, many agree that the behavior still demands attention.

When compared to their peers, bullies are often characterized as being more impulsive and assertive, whereas victims are often identified as being more timid and lacking a strong support system with peers (see Sullivan 2011). Victims are targeted for an array of reasons, including their gender presentation, sexual orientation, race or ethnicity, appearance, or mental or physical disabilities (Sullivan 2011). Girls and boys are similarly at risk of being victims of bullying. However, a distinction is that boys often target girls and boys, whereas girls often target other girls (Ringrose and Renold 2010). This may reflect gender differences pertaining to socialization (Simmons 2002).

Generally, boys report higher rates of partaking in direct forms of bullying such as physical aggression, including kicking, hitting, choking, or pulling hair (Sullivan 2011). Girls often experience indirect bullying, sometimes referred to as relational aggression (Espelage, Mebane, and Swearer 2004; Fried and Fried 1996; Osterman et al. 1998; Crick and Grotpeter 1995; Sullivan 2011). Relational aggression includes nonverbal psychological bullying, which involves deliberately ignoring, isolating, or excluding someone (Espelage et al. 2004; Crick and Grotpeter 1995; Sullivan 2011). Males are perceived as being more aggressive than females (Espelage et al. 2004), and therefore are considered the main culprits and victims of bullying (Crick and Grotpeter 1995). This may be attributed to the visibility of bullying amongst boys. Physical forms of aggression are easily identified, therefore adults can more readily respond when they see boys hitting or kicking one another (Simmons 2002). Meanwhile, girls who use relational forms of aggression are much more subtle and often go undetected by adults (Simmons 2002). There is growing evidence that suggests that girls are victimized at higher rates than boys (NCES 2015; Simmons 2002).

● COPING TECHNIQUES

There is widespread agreement that in order to eradicate bullying, bullies themselves must be stopped. As such, many interventions and anti-bullying campaigns focus primarily or exclusively on bullies (see Sullivan 2011 for a comprehensive review). However, we must remember that oftentimes bullies are victims themselves (Olweus 1993). In order to stop the cycle of victimization, we must consider that victims play an important role in dissuading or encouraging future incidences of bullying. Some studies suggest that victims of bullying may actually instigate future incidences of bullying, depending on how they respond to being bullied (Cowie and Berdondini 2002; Olweus 1993). Therefore, it is important to investigate different coping techniques and examine how these strategies may deter or encourage future cases of bullying. While this may be critiqued as a "blame the victim" approach, others argue that fostering resiliency amongst school-aged children may help instill healthy coping techniques that will benefit them in other areas of their lives. In other words, focusing on the victims is not an attempt to shift the blame of bullying behavior, but instead to help children cultivate adaptive coping strategies for any adversary they may experience.

Coping requires attention and action to solve a problem using effective solutions (see Lazarus and Folkman 1984; Yuksel-Sahin 2015). Given that children do not have mature cognitive and social development, their coping techniques differ from those of adults (Fields and Prinz 1997). For instance, children have less power and status than adults and they lack experience with stressors, which influences how they perceive and cope with various stressors in their lives (Fields and Prinz 1997). As a result, the significance of stressors may be magnified for children who lack experience and effective coping strategies (Fields and Prinz 1997).

Psychologists and social psychologists have especially contributed to research on child-coping strategies (for examples see Fields and Prinz 1997; Kochenderfer-Ladd and Skinner 2002; Mahady, Wilton, Craig and Pepler 2002). There are a number of different conceptual and theoretical models of coping strategies that are applied to children and adolescents (for complete descriptions see Fields and Prinz 1997; see also Causey and Dubow 1992). The approach/avoidance model has been used in previous studies pertaining specifically to bullying behavior. Simply defined, approach strategies are often characterized as adaptive, since they involve actively responding to the stressor, whereas avoidance strategies involve avoiding the stressor and are often deemed maladaptive (Fields and Prinz 1997). Students may experience stressors from academic demands, peer relations, family turmoil, or other related experiences.

Approach Strategies

Approach strategies, often called problem-focused coping, are often used by proactive or aggressive victims and include attempts by the victim to face their stressors directly, either by seeking social support or figuring out a plan of action and following through (Fields and Prinz 1997; Kochenderfer-Ladd and Skinner 2002; Roth and Cohen 1986). Such strategies either call upon the inclusion of others (seeking social support) or being independent and solving the problem on their own, which may have gendered differences (see Kochenderfer-Ladd and Skinner 2002).

Peer support has been documented as a successful means to cope with bullying (see Cowie and Sharp 1996; Cowie and Olafsson 2000). Peers can serve as support to actively combat bullying in three ways: utilizing conflict resolution, counseling-based approaches, or befriending the target (Cowie and Sharp 1996; see also Cowie and Olafsson 2000). In general, these types of peer support involve offering skills to the victim to enable them to resolve the situation, occur relatively soon after the incident, and encourage the avoidance of placing blame and instead enable open communication between parties (Cowie and Sharp 1996; see also Cowie and Olafsson 2000). Interventions that encourage the involvement of peers to address bullying "recognize that pupils themselves have the potential to assume a helpful role in tackling bullying behaviour" (Cowie and Sharp 1996, 80; see also Cowie and Olafsson 2000). Such an approach not only helps the victim, but may also benefit the helpers, since prior to being sought out, the helpers might have merely been bystanders (see Cowie and Olafsson 2000). Therefore, the helpers' sense of usefulness is increased, knowing that they are able to assist their peers (Cowie and Olafsson 2000).

Avoidance Strategies

Whereas approach strategies reflect children taking direct action to alter their stressors, avoidance strategies reflect children's attempts to "manage their cognitive or emotional reactions" (Kochenderfer-Ladd and Skinner 2002, 268; see also Fields and Prinz 1997). Avoidance strategies, also referred to as emotional reactions, are often used by passive victims and include passive coping attempts. For instance, children might avoid or ignore the stressor (a behavioral strategy) or they may attempt to negate threat (a cognitive strategy; Fields and Prinz 1997;

Kochenderfer-Ladd and Skinner 2002; Roth and Cohen 1986). Emotional strategies that are classified as avoidance techniques are those in which the child avoids or distances themselves emotionally from the stressor (Roth and Cohen 1986).

Children who lack skills on how to manage their emotions may act out in maladaptive ways, such as yelling, shouting, or attacking their stressor (Mahady Wilton, Craig, and Pepler 2000). While such behavior requires the victim to respond directly to their stressor (either verbally or physically), within the literature, such responses are not considered approach strategies (Mahady Wilton et al. 2000). Since the victim lacks the skills to control his or her emotions in a positive way, counter aggressive responses are considered emotional reacting strategies (Mahady Wilton et al. 2000) or externalizing approaches (Causey and Dubow 1992). Counter aggressive responses to stressors are overwhelmingly maladaptive.

Based on their research in elementary schools in Canada, Mahady Wilton and colleagues (2000), for example, found that when aggressive victims respond to their bullies with counter-attacks, they often lose the fight. On the other hand, children were thirteen times more likely to de-escalate and resolve a bullying interaction if they used a problem-solving approach instead of an aggressive coping response (Mahady Wilton et al. 2000). Bullies seek dominance over their victims. Therefore, children who respond to their bullies with anger or contempt may likely ignite further retaliation from the bully, thereby placing the victim at greater risk of future attacks (Mahady Wilton et al. 2000).

● THE SOCIOLOGICAL IMPLICATIONS OF BULLYING

To reduce incidences of bullying, we should consider moving towards a sociology of bullying. This will require us to see how society influences the individual. To accomplish this, we may begin by drawing our attention to the three levels of analysis often used by sociologists: the micro-, meso-, and macro-levels.

Implications at the Micro-Level

The micro-level is the smallest level of analysis, focusing on interactions in small groups, such as within families, churches, neighborhoods, and schools. Grade school marks an important transition for children and adolescents. While family is often recognized as the primary agent of socialization, peers may actually have a greater influence during adolescence (Aseltine 1995). Schools are therefore another prominent agent of socialization during this period, since adolescents spend much of their time in schools. The manifest functions of schools are obvious, however schools also provide students with an array of unintended lessons. In addition to learning standard lessons in writing, math, and science, students indirectly learn responsibility, obedience to authority, and conformity to gender norms (Thorne 1997). Unfortunately, for girls who are routinely called "fat" and boys who are teased for being "gay," school is less about education and more about negotiating a fearful terrain, in which their peers routinely bully them. Girls and boys who are frequently punched, slapped, or pushed in the hallways learn to view school as a battlefield, not an inclusive or safe environment that cultivates respect and academic success.

Teachers, staff, and administrators at schools should capitalize on their influential role and promote prosocial behavior. As explained in the Elton Report, "The message to heads and teachers is clear. It is they have the power, through their own efforts, to improve standards of work and behaviour and the life chances of their pupils" (Elton 1989, 89). Adults working in schools have the ability to deter future incidences of bullying by promoting a positive school climate, which does not tolerate bullying behavior. The school climate refers to "the quality and character of school life," including the expectations, norms, and values that influence how people in school feel (Graves and Mirsky 2007). Research suggests that when compared to other schools, schools with a positive climate have higher student performance rates and lower rates of truancy, aggression, and violence (Berkowitz 2014; Graves and Mirsky 2007;). Similarly, students' perceived support from teachers, specifically regarding bullying, is an important aspect of deterring future incidences of aggression (Berkowitz 2014; Cowie and Olafsson 2000). Depending on the relationships with adults at school, students may refrain from defending victims if the students lack confidence in teachers (Sullivan 2011). Therefore, school personnel must consider how they are not only role models for students, but also how their attitudes and values shape the school climate.

School-wide approaches to deterring bullying should also consider promoting campaigns as "pro-belonging" instead of "anti-bullying" (Davis 2015). Focusing on a "pro-belonging" mentality may more accurately capture the overarching goals of educators who aim to foster prosocial behavior amongst their students. Shifting our perspective to focus on positive behavior may contribute to a different mindset, one that makes positive behavior the focus within schools, not wrong-doing behavior. This coincides with research on active bystanders and bullies. In exploring the effects of peer-helping interventions, Cowie and Sharp (1996) found that implementing peer-helping interventions in one school not only pacified immediate stressors, but that the school climate also improved (see also Cowie and Olafsson 2000). However, many decisions that school administrators and teachers make are limited based on the influence of meso-level institutions.

Implications at the Meso-Level

The meso-level is considered the middle ground of analysis. This level of analysis focuses on groups that are larger than day-to-day interactions and smaller than national influences. The meso-level includes municipal institutions (i.e., a school board), state or regional organizations (i.e., a political party), and entire communities.

Focusing on the education system may offer fruitful insight into considering how bullying might be stopped beyond interactions at the micro-level. The education system includes public schools from kindergarten to twelfth grade and is responsible for funding, policies, regulations, resources (i.e., supplies and technology), compensation, contracts, and administrative offices (state and district). These decisions are the responsibility of the state and local government, not individual schools (micro-level) or the nation (macro-level).

In an attempt to be "tough on crime," Congress pased the Gun-Free Schools Act 1994 (Kang-Brown, Trone, Fratello, and Daftary-Kapur 2013). For states to qualify for federal educational funding, schools districts were required to expel any student for a year if they brought a weapon to school (Kang-Brown et al. 2013). This contributed to the widespread use of zero-tolerance programs. Zero-tolerance programs are characterized by their "one strike" rule; any form of misconduct is grounds for expulsion or suspension (Graves and Mirsky 2007; Kang-Brown et al. 2013). Between 1996 and 1997, 79 percent of American schools (compelled by school districts) adopted a zero-tolerance policy (Kang-Brown et al. 2013).

Despite their widespread implementation, zero-tolerance policies have been found to be counter-productive and researchers urge schools to instead adapt values that reflect restorative justice (Graves and Mirsky 2007). Rather than suspending or expelling students who misbehave, school climates are positively influenced if wrongdoings are addressed with respect, all parties are involved (i.e., the student, school, parents, community, and law enforcement), and the culprit is integrated back into the community (Graves and Mirsky 2007; Heydenberk, Heydenberk and Tzenova 2006). At the state level, the education system may consider appointing restorative justice policies for all schools to follow. Within this framework, the meso-level (education system) has the ability to directly influence the micro-level (individual schools). Policies implemented from the education system could enable educators to "punish in private and praise in public" (Davis 2015). Also, since many bullies are also victims, the cycle of victimization for bully/victims could be deterred if they were reintegrated back into their school community and avoid being stigmatized and labeled as bad.

Implications at the Macro-Level

As the largest level of analysis, macro-level sociologists study society as a whole, entire nations, and the global community. At first glance, it may appear that bullying can be readily remedied by focusing attention on the micro- and meso-levels. However, policies and bills passed at the national level have the capability of influencing greater society. Efforts made at the micro- and meso-levels are essentially attempting to change American culture so that diversity, inclusiveness, and respect are strengthened in schools. Changes at the macro-level have the ability to trickle down to the meso- and micro-levels.

For instance, government grants may help organizations and institutions at the meso-level who are working to remedy bullying in their schools. One salient way that some organizations are attempting to promote prosocial skills amongst their students is the implementation of mentoring programs (such as Big Brothers Big Sisters). Previous studies have found that students who participate in mentoring programs have gained positive attributes in the youths' academic, behavior, and social-emotional outcomes (DuBois, Portillo, Rhodes, Silverthorn, and Valentine 2011; Larose, Savoie, DeWir, Lipman, and DuBois

2015; Rhodes 2005). Relationships formed between mentors and mentees have strengthened the mentees' self-worth, academic achievement, and social skills (Karcher, Davidson, Rhodes, and Herrera 2010) and decreased rates of substance abuse (Rhodes, Reddy, and Grossman 2005). Given the long-term benefits of mentor programs (see DuBois et al. 2011), schools would benefit if the government offered more opportunities to receive substantial grants to help fund these efforts. If funded by multi-million dollar grants, school districts would be able to implement mentor programs in their schools.

As stated previously, researchers do not readily agree on one definition of bullying and, as a result, reported rates and frequencies of bullying are not consistent (Finkelhor et al. 2012). Examining how the term bullying is used to describe various behaviors warrants further investigation. This would require researchers and educators to discern if there is a difference between how bullying, peer aggression, peer mistreatment, and peer victimization are categorized. Additionally, examining how the terms bully and victim reflect a fixed mindset might move researchers and educators away from *labeling* and redirect their efforts to focus on the *behavior*. Reaching a consensus on defining inappropriate behavior is especially imperative, given the rise of cyberbullying, sexting, and revenge porn, which warrant legal intervention (see Hinduja and Patchin 2010).

Adopting a sociology of bullying approach will enable educators, parents, students, and schools to consider the multiple factors that influence and enable bullying behavior. Similarly, through this lens, we may consider various steps to decrease incidences of bullying and advance prosocial behavior. At the micro-level, promoting healthy school climates may be one salient way that children learn to appreciate diversity, gain self-confidence and self-efficacy, and thereby minimize the tolerance for bullying and strengthen their coping techniques. At the meso-level, the education system can consider how restorative justice might be implemented in school districts, thereby fostering respect and reintegration for children involved in bullying. Lastly, large-scale change is possible if the government offers grants to help fund mentoring programs in schools, and a uniform definition of bullying is established.

● REFERENCES

Aseltine, R. H. 1995. "A Reconsideration of Parental and Peer Influences on Adolescents Deviance." *Journal of Health and Social Behavior* 36 (2): 103–21.

Berkowitz, R. 2014. "Student and Teacher Responses to Violence in School: The Divergent Views of Bullies, Victims, and Bully–Victims." *School Psychology International* 35 (5): 485–503.

Causey, D. L., and E. F. Dubow. 1992. "Development of a Self-Report Coping Measure for Elementary School Children." *Journal of Clinical Child Psychology* 21 (1): 47–59.

Cowie, H., and L. Berdondini. 2002. "The Expression of Emotion in Response to Bullying." *Emotional and Behavioural Difficulties* 7 (4): 207–14.

Cowie, H., and R. Olafsson. 2000. "The Role of Peer Support in Helping the Victims of Bullying in a School with High Levels of Aggression." *School Psychology International* 21 (1): 79–95.

Cowie, H., and S. Sharp. 1996. *Peer Counseling in School: A Time to Listen*. London: David Fulton.

Crick, N. R., and J. K. Grotpeter. 1995. "Relational Aggression, Gender, and Social-Psychological Adjustment." *Child Development* 66 (3): 710–22.

Davis, S. 2015. "Increasing Kind and Supportive Actions by Peers, Using Social Norms Approaches." Presented at *Moving Forward: Creating a Community Response to Cyberbullying Conference*, Penn State Erie, The Behrend College, May 15, 2015, Erie, PA.

DuBois, D. L., N. Portillo, J. E. Rhodes, N. Silverthorn, and J. C. Valentine. 2011. "How Effective Are Mentoring Programs for Youth? A Systematic Assessment of the Evidence." *Psychology Sciences in the Public Interest* 12 (2): 57–91.

Elton, L. 1989. *The Elton Report: Discipline in Schools*. Report of the Committee of Enquiry, Department of Education and Science and the Welsh Office. http://www.educationengland. org.uk/documents/elton/elton1989.html.

Espelage, D. L., S. E. Mebane, and S. M. Swearer. 2004. "Gender Differences in Bullying: Moving Beyond Mean Level Differences." In *Bullying in American Schools: A Social–Ecological Perspective on Prevention and Intervention*, 15–35. Edited by D. L. Espelage and S. M. Swearer. Mahwah, NJ: Lawrence Erlbaum Associates, Publishers.

Fields, L., and R. J. Prinz. 1997. "Coping and Adjustment During Childhood And Adolescence." *Clinical Psychology Review* 17 (8): 937–76.

Finkelhor, D., H. A. Turner, and S. Hamby. 2012. "Let's Prevent Peer Victimization, Not Just Bullying." *Child Abuse & Neglect* 36: 271–74.

Fried, S., and P. Fried. 1996. *Bullies & Victims: Helping Your Child Survive the Schoolyard Battlefield*. New York: M. Evans and Company, Inc.

Graves, D., and L. Mirsky. 2007. "American Psychological Association Report Challenges School Zero Tolerance Policies and Recommends Restorative Justice." *International Institute for Restorative Justice*, September 5. http://www.iirp.edu/article_detail.php?article_id=NTU3.

Hamburger, M., E., K. C. Basile, and A. M. Vivolo. 2011. *Measuring Bullying Victimization, Perpetration, and Bystander Experiences: A Compendium of Assessment Experiences*. Atlanta, GA: Centers for Disease Control and Prevention, National Center for Injury Prevention and Control.

Heydenberk, R. A., W. R. Heydenberk, and V. Tzenova. 2006. "Conflict Resolution and Bullying Prevention: Skills for School Success." *Conflict Resolution Quarterly* 24 (1): 55–69.

Hinduja, S., and J. W. Patchin. 2010. "Bullying, Cyberbullying, and Suicide." *Archives of Suicide Research* 14 (3): 206–21.

Kang–Brown, J., J. Trone, J. Fratello, and T. Daftary–Kapur, T. 2013. "A Generation Later: What We've Learned About Zero Tolerance in Schools." *Institute of Justice, Center on Youth Justice*. Issue Brief: December.

Karcher, M. J., A. J. Davidson, J. E. Rhodes, and C. Herrera. 2010. "Pygmalion in the Program: The Role of Teenage Peer Mentors' Attitudes in Shaping Their Mentees' Outcomes. *Applied Developmental Science* 14 (4): 212–27.

Kochenderfer–Ladd, B., and K. Skinner. 2002. "Children's Coping Strategies: Moderators of the Effects of Peer Victimization?" *Developmental Psychology* 38 (2): 267–78.

Larose, S., J. Savoie, J. J. DeWit, E. L. Lipman, and D. L. DuBois. 2015. "The Role of Relational, Recreational, and Tutoring Activities in the Perceptions of Received Support and Quality of Mentoring Relationship During a Community-Based Mentoring Relationship." *Journal of Community Psychology* 43 (5): 527–544.

Lazarus, R. S., and S. Folkman. 1984. *Stress, Appraisal and Coping*. New York: Springer.

Mahady Wilton, M. M., W. M. Craig, and D. J. Pepler. 2000. "Emotional Regulation and Display in Classroom Victims of Bullying: Characteristic Expressions of Affect, Coping Styles and Relevant Contextual Factors." *Social Development* 9 (2): 226–45.

NCES. 2015. "New Data Show a Decline in School-Based Bullying." U.S. Department of Education's National Center for Education Statistics. http://www.ed.gov/news/press-releases/new-data-show-decline-school-based-bullying.

Olweus, D. 1993. *Bullying at School: What We Know and What We Can Do*. Oxford: Blackwell.

Osterman, K., K. Bjorkqvist, K. M. J. Lagerspetz, A. Kaukiainen, S. F. Landau, A. Fraczek, and G. V. Caprara. 1998. "Cross-Cultural Evidence of Female Indirect Aggression." *Aggressive Behavior* 24 (1): 1–8.

Rhodes, J. E. 2005. "A Model of Youth Mentoring." In *Handbook of Youth Mentoring*, 30–43. Edited by D. L. DuBois and M. J. Karcher. Thousand Oaks, CA: Sage.

Rhodes, J. E., R. Reddy, and J. Grossman. 2005. "The Protective Influence on Mentoring on Adolescents' Substance Abuse: Direct and Indirect Pathways." *Applied Developmental Science* 9 (1): 31–47.

Ringrose, J., and E. Renold. 2010. "Normative Cruelties and Gender Deviants: The Performative Effects of Bully Discourses for Girls and Boys in School." *British Educational Research Journal* 36 (4), 575–96.

Roth, S., and L. C. Cohen. 1986. "Approach, Avoidance, and Coping with Stress." *American Psychologist* 41 (7): 813–19.

Simmons, R. 2002. *Odd Girl Out: The Hidden Culture of Aggression in Girls*. New York: Harcourt, Inc.

Smith, P. K., H. Cowie, R. F. Olafsson, A. Liefooge, A. Aimeida, and H. Araki. 2002. "Definitions of Bullying: A Comparison of Terms Used, and Age and Gender Differences, in a Fourteen-Country International Comparison." *Child Development* 73 (4): 1119–33.

Stopbullying.gov. 2014. "Facts About Bullying." U.S. Department of Health and Human Services. http://www.stopbullying.gov/news/media/facts/#listing.

Sullivan, K. 2011. *The Anti-Bullying Handbook* (2nd edition). Thousand Oaks, CA: Sage.

Thorne, B. 1997. *Gender Play: Girls and Boys in School*. New Brunswick, NJ: Rutgers University Press.

Yuksel–Sahin, F. 2015. "An Examination of Bullying Tendencies and Bullying Coping Behaviors Among Adolescents." *Social and Behavioral Sciences* 191: 214–21.

CHAPTER 25

A Qualitative Inquiry on the Multidimensional Racial Development Among First-Year African American College Students Attending a Predominately White Institution

By Lorenzo DuBois Baber

Postsecondary degree attainment has generated significant scholarly attention in recent years, particularly for traditionally underrepresented students (Bowen, Chingos, and McPherson 2009; Rosenbaum, Deil-Amen, and Person 2006; Sacks 2008). While recent evidence suggests that persistence and completion rates at four-year colleges and universities are on the rise, a closer examination of the data reveals continued disparities based racial/ethnic demographics. In particular, persistence and degree completion rates for African American students continue to lag behind White students. Among a cohort of students who began at a four-year postsecondary institution in the 2003, 21 percent of African Americans dropped out of postsecondary education three years later, compared to just 11 percent of White students. A wider gap exists in graduation rates. Among a cohort of students who began at a four-year postsecondary institution in 2001, 42 percent of African American students completed a degree within six years, compared to 60 percent of White students (Aud et al. 2010).

To address these observed educational inequities, considerable attention has been paid to the experiences of African American college students, particularly those who attend predominately White institutions (PWIs). Since *McLaurin v. Oklahoma State Regents* decision in 1950 and the Civil Rights Act of 1964 established *de jure* access to all institutions of higher education regardless of race, African American students have increasingly enrolled at PWIs. By 2001, approximately 87 percent of all African American students in postsecondary education were enrolled in a non-historically Black college or university (U.S. Department of Education 2004).

Despite increasing enrollment rates for African American students at PWIs, establishing relationships and maintaining engagement on campus continues to present unique difficulties (Allen 1992; Cabrera et al. 1999; Fries-Britt and Turner 2002; Guiffrida 2005; Hurtado et al. 1998). When compared to their White peers, African American students at PWIs are more likely to develop perceptions of a racially hostile climate on campus. Based on direct experiences and observations, these feelings often lead to a sense of alienation, inhibiting an establishment connection and commitment to the institution. The feeling of isolation among African American students attending PWIs is of particular concern during the first year of college. Most first-time college students face academic and social challenges as they transition to the institution (Elkins, Braxton, and James 2000; Pascarella and Terenzini 2005; Upcraft, Gardner, and Barefoot 2004). For African Americans attending PWIs, this difficult transition may become overwhelming, contributing to the persistence and degree completion disparities based on racial/ethnic categories.

As first-year experiences have demonstrated a strong connection to persistence and degree attainment, it is critical to examine issues related to transitional experiences of African American students attending PWIs. The purpose of this study is to examine the first-year college experiences of African American students. Specifically, through a qualitative inquiry, this study explores ways in which racial identity development shape first-year experiences of African American students at a predominately White, four-year postsecondary institution. By investigating the complex process of identity development and contextual transition among African American students, the hope is that this study sheds additional light on the consistent issue of persistence and attainment among a traditionally marginalized group.

Wijeyesinghe and Jackson (2001) noted that studies on racial identity development are like taking a "snapshot of a moving picture" (p. 2). Concepts of race and racial identity are constantly evolving for individuals and societies in response to significant sociocultural events. Similarly, research on student transition and persistence are shaped by myriad of factors, including individual actions and institutional characteristics. While limited in scope, this study aims to make a contribution to the larger landscape of research on racial identity development and transition to college through an in-depth inquiry.

● THEORETICAL FRAMEWORK

Studies on student persistence often rely on traditional theoretical frameworks of student departure which stress the assimilation and acculturation of students into the dominant culture of the institution (Berger and Braxton 1998; Gumport 2007; Rendon, Jalomo, and Nora 2000; Tanaka 2002; Tierney 1992). This perspective of student persistence often fails to question the contribution educational institutions have in reproducing racial hierarchies which tend to favor those familiar with or from the dominant culture. In contrast, student persistence theories rooted in interpretive frameworks emphasize the subjectivity of educational environments, influenced by a society increasingly stratified by race/ethnicity. As students from traditionally marginalized groups enter institutions, they confront a community that is not value-neutral, but a place that maintains certain preferences and tendencies which exclude those with dissimilar cultural experiences. For African Americans, relationships with mainstream social institutions have rarely been objective, but subjectively influenced by cultural norms grounded in racism and discrimination. As a result, African Americans have suffered from a fragmented process of identity development. Du Bois (1901) described this 'double consciousness' as a manifestation of the power of White stereotypes on African American life, exclusive practices of racism which separate African Americans from the mainstream society, and the internal conflict between selfconceptions grounded in African ancestry and American birth.

This study uses an interpretive perspective, specifically the Multidimensional Model, of Racial Identity (MMRI, Rowley et al. 1998; Sellers et al. 1997; Sellers et al. 1998) to investigate the influence of racial identity development on the educational experiences of African American students at a PWI. MMRI reflects a synthesis of multiple theoretical frameworks that attempt to understand the significance of African American identity in individual self-conceptualization and the meaning attributed to association with the African American collectivity.

MMRI proposes four dimensions of identity development among African Americans—(a) racial salience, (b) racial centrality, (c) racial regard, and (d) racial ideology. *Racial salience* "refers to the extent to which one's race is a relevant part of one's self-concept at a particular moment or in a particular situation (Sellers et al. 1998, p. 24). As racial salience is rooted in a specific event or situation, it is highly sensitive to context and the degree to which the individual 'feels' their African American self. *Racial centrality* refers to "the extent to which a person normatively defines himself or herself with regard to race (p. 25). Whereas racial salience is situation-centered, racial centrality is a stable self-perception across multiple situations. Implicit in the centrality of racial identity is its close proximity to an individual's core definition of self, challenged by other forms of identity including gender, sexual orientation, socioeconomic position, and others. The third dimension, *racial regard,* "refers to a person affective and evaluative judgment of her or his race in terms of positive-negative valence" (p. 26). It is heavily influenced by an individual's assessment of how his or her ethnic group is viewed by the broader society. Racial regard has both a private and public aspects—an internal, psychological closeness toward the African American collectivity (private), as well as external displays of African American pride (public). *Racial ideology* refers to "the person's philosophy about the ways in which African Americans should live and interact" (p. 27). MMRI suggests that, with respect to political/economic development, cultural/social activities, intergroup relations, and perceptions of the dominant group, individuals may develop an ideology along four philosophical paradigms—(a) a nationalist philosophy (emphasis on isolated self-direction for African Americans), (b) an oppressed minority philosophy (emphasis on similarities with other oppressed groups), (c) an assimilation philosophy (emphasis on similarities with dominant group), and (d) a humanist philosophy (emphasis on commonality among all humans).

The connection between racial/ethnic identity and psychosocial health has long been established through theoretical stage models (Cross, Parham, and Helms 1991; Helms 1994; Phinney 1989). These models often provide details of students moving from low levels of racial/ethnic identity to world-view perspectives on race/ethnicity. Despite this significant and valuable contribution to literature on development and African American college students, the identity development process provides perceptions and experiences within particular institutional contexts that are often left understudied. MMRI provides evidence that racial identity development is not a homogenous process across the African American collectivity. Rather, there is an intra-group variation in racial identity development based on interaction with the environment. Among African American college students attending PWIs, this interaction between racial/ethnic identity development and a racially subjective environment produce various behaviors that may contribute to persistence decisions.

● METHODS

A phenomenological approach was selected for this study as it allows for an in-depth description of the essence of lived experiences for individuals within a particular phenomenon (Creswell 1998; Sadala and Adorno 2001). Phenomenology focuses on individual perspectives and a building up of knowledge through a process of development. The task for the researcher is to analyze individual experiences, through a theoretical framework, in order to perceive how the particular phenomenon is given meaning. The phenomenon of this study was institutional experiences of first-year African American college students at a PWI. Previous research provides support for examining this phenomenon through the lens of MMRI. Strategies for selection of participants, data collection, and data analysis reflect the focus on the essence of the postsecondary transitional experience for African American students.

Participants

In working with the Office of Student Affairs, purposeful sampling chose fifteen self-identified African American students who were entering their first year at a mid-size, predominately White research institution in the mid-Atlantic region (referred to as Mid-Atlantic University). Pseudonyms were assigned to each student and to the institution in order to ensure participant anonymity. All of the students self-identified as African Americans and every participant was born and primarily socialized in the United States. The sample included nine females and six males. Six students participated in a scholarship program (given the pseudonym Drew Program for this study) aimed at increasing participation of students of color in science, technology, engineering, and mathematics (STEM) fields. Self-reported first semester grade-point averages ranged from 1.50 to 4.00 (see Table 25.1).

Table 25.1 Characteristics of Participants

NAME (PSEUDONYM)	GENDER	INTENDED MAJOR	FIRST SEMESTER GPA
Anthony	Male	Mechanical Engineering	3.80
Malik	Male	Biochemistry	4.00
Fana	Female	Pre-Med	Not provided
Bridgette	Female	Cultural Anthropology	4.00
Will	Male	Pre-Physical Therapy	3.00
Tara	Female	Biochemistry	3.80
Christopher	Male	Economics	1.70
Ron	Male	Mechanical Engineering	1.50
Gina	Female	Biology	Not provided

Eric	Male	Political Science	1.50
Jada	Female	Biochemistry	4.00
Imani	Female	Political Science	2.80
Stephanie	Female	Africana Studies	4.00
Kristina	Female	Biochemistry	4.00
Natalya	Female	Chemical Engineering	3.50

Data Collection

Each student participated in one-hour, semi-structured interviews at three times during the academic year—October, December, and March. The research questions focused on the continuing academic and social experiences at Mid-Atlantic. Interviews took place in secured study rooms located within the residence hall of the student or an alternate neutral location chosen by the student. With permission of the participant, all interviews were audio recorded using a digital recorder. Additionally, this author provided each student with a journal for recording his or her reflections between interviews. Journals were allowed to be unstructured, although students were given general instruction to record and reflect on experiences that had been important in shaping their first-year. Journal entries were collected in between interviews and recordings were often referenced during our discussions. Each student was compensated for their time, receiving a $45 stipend for participating in the nine-month study.

Data Analysis and Trustworthiness

In an effort to provide a reliable description of the lived experiences, phenomenological data analysis uses a methodology of reduction and analysis of specific statements (Creswell 1998; Sadala and Adorno 2001). Reduction brackets the description of experiences by individuals and, through critical reflection and reflexivity by the researcher, interprets participants' experiences into significant statements for analysis. Phenomenological analysis positions these statements within larger theoretical frameworks to broaden the understanding of the phenomenon of interest. For this study, the author reviewed the interview transcripts and journal entries, bracketing the perspectives they offered line by line. Then phrases were highlighted that corresponded with the research question under consideration. Using relationships with colleagues familiar with the study, my interpretations of individual perspectives were discussed after each round of interviews. This author also kept a journal to record personal reflections on how my experiences may influence interpretations. Participants were asked to review transcripts and revise as necessary. Participants were also given the opportunity to read the findings as they emerged and offer feedback. The initial analysis revealed twelve themes, six of which are presented in this article.

Reflexivity

As the instrument through which data are interpreted and analyzed, qualitative investigators are encouraged to confront subjectivity though reflexivity—articulation and clarification of assumptions, experiences, and theoretical orientation that influences study. As Patton (2002) argued "Reflexivity reminds the qualitative inquirer to be attentive to and conscious of the origins of one's own perspective" (p. 65). Throughout the study, I engaged in a process of selfreflection, exploring forms of bias developed through personal and professional identities. Foremost, as an African American, I recognized congruency between my early experiences in education and those experiences of the participants. Part of the subjectivity that I bring into the project is my sense of racial identity which may not match the meaning of participants. Therefore, after each interview, I provided each student with my summary of our conversation to ensure analysis accurately reflected his or her journey. The depth of our conversations suggests that my racial background may have also presented an advantage in this study, as participants may have felt more comfortable sharing their experiences with someone who is African American.

Limitations

There are a few cautions that should accompany the results of this investigation. As this uses a qualitative research methodology, generalization about all African American college student experiences is not intended. Additionally, studies of college student experiences cannot account for every factor that may influence educational experiences. Other environmental experiences not identified for this study may influence educational experiences of African American students. Such factors include socioeconomic background, certainty of major choice, and distance from home. As data were collected, information was highlighted about alternative explanations for variation in educational experiences as they were uncovered. Despite these limitations, distinct patterns that emerged from the students in this study regarding the role of racial identity development have implications for future research and policy development.

● FINDINGS

Five major themes which emerged from this study were (a) established racial identity; (b) reconsidering identity through heterogeneous community experience; (c) conflict between ideologies; (d) resiliency against hostility; and (e) uncovering complexity of identity. These themes convey the essence of described transitional experiences among first-year African American students at one institution through a MMRI framework.

Established Racial Identity

The first theme, *established racial identity,* represents how students entered post-secondary education with established dispositions of African American culture. These dispositions were rooted in memorable experiences (both positive and negative) within previous contexts. These experiences appeared to trigger an evaluative process where racial centrality and racial salience were influenced by connections (or misconnection) between internalized self-concepts and cultural markers attributed to the African American collectivity.

A notable example is when participants who attended majority-White high schools, were asked about experiences related to their African American identity and recalled taunts from both African American and White peers. These external judgments mocked participant's perceived disassociation with traits—in particular speech patterns or personal style—not aligned with 'typical' perceptions of the African American collectivity. For example, Anthony recalls being branded as an 'Oreo' several times during high school by both White and African American peers. As this researcher inquired about his response to the name-calling, he stated "I usually would shut down when somebody would confront me about that. I wouldn't really know how to respond to them, especially when it comes from White people." Bridgette experienced similar taunts, although her response was more matter-of-fact:

> See, you're supposed to impress your teacher and get good grades and speak correctly, but, then when you're in the hallways, if you use correct grammar ... it's like, oh you're White ... which never really bothered me ... it didn't affect me, but it affected my friends and they were kind of sad all the time and it just ... I just didn't understand.

A counterbalance to peer critiques appeared to be alternative sources that provided a broader perspective of racial identity than what participants heard from peers. These sources of support were often family members, notably older siblings or relatives closer to the age of the students. These conversations expanded definitions of African American culture and appeared to influence private and public regard among students.

Interestingly, students also discussed the influence of structural observations within high schools on conceptions of racial identity. Specifically, students discussed social isolation from other African American peers as they were often one of few, if not the only, person of color in their advanced or honors courses—even in racially diverse high schools. Will recalled that every year he would have the same reaction when entering his advanced classes, "I was just sad ... just make me think, you know ... c'mon why aren't there more Blacks in this class?" Tara further explained the conundrum she and other participants in this study faced:

> Since ninth grade I'd take honors classes ... we'd have fewer and fewer Black students and other races. The majority of them were White. And I was like, not the only ... but there were either one or two Black students and the rest were White. So I did not have many Black friends outside my (advanced) classes ... then when we made friends with the people in class ... all of a sudden we were trying to be White.

As students entered postsecondary education, it appeared that established racial identity was rooted in a response to the observations of educational structure that assigned advanced classes as spaces for White students or 'assimilated' African American students who were 'acting White.' Therefore, one may consider what is perceived as low racial centrality and regard among student is not an internalized preference for reducing one's racial identity, but a coping mechanism for struggling through contextually influenced labeling. Furthermore, contradictions to a monolithic perspective of African American culture came from sources of identity support outside the educational institution, particularly family members.

Shifting Salience and Centrality through Heterogeneous Community Experience

The second theme, *shifting salience and centrality through heterogeneous community experience,* describes peer and structural influence on racial identity development at Mid-Atlantic University. For participants in this study, shifts in racial centrality and racial regard appeared to be stimulated by connecting to a diverse mass of African American students at Mid-Atlantic. This diversity created multiple subcultures—both formal and informal—where students could find a place of support. For many students, the campus provided extended exposure to the heterogeneity of African American culture for the first time.

Kristina once felt that she did not fit in with African Americans growing up and, therefore, socialized primarily with White peers. She recalls the reactions from those peers,

> Like, a lot of my friends from (high) school, when they look on my Facebook, they're like, 'Oh my gosh! All of your friends are Black and that's not who you are!' And I'm like, 'It's who I am now.'

Gina has found a vibrant, diverse African American subculture on campus. Similar to Anthony and Kristina, she had predominately White friends in high school.

Well, it's like all my friends are African American and it's like the first time ever in my whole life because all my friends in high school, I was like the only African American girl so it's like an adjustment to have all your friends be African American.

When asked about the adjustments she has made as a result of having predominately African American friends for the first time, Gina replied

It's just more of a comfortability (sic) because they have similar views, you can talk about the things they relate to and you don't have to try and … nobody has to hold themselves back from speaking to you because they feel like they're going to offend you or anything.

The informal network, particularly in the residence hall communities, appeared to offer extended opportunities to find, as Natalya describes "like-minded African Americans." Natalya expresses connecting with a group of women in her residence hall, not necessarily members of a formal organization. "We all just kind of click and support each other. It's like a community within a community. I think we get along because we are the same in certain ways and different in others." When questioned about how the dynamics of the group differ from her high school experience, she replied

In high school, I never really had it like this, it was kind of either be in this group and act a certain way or be in that group. Like here, I don't have to make that choice. If I want to be a certain me, I hang with one group and then I have the other group too.

Approximately fourteen percent (200 out of 1400) of the first-time, traditional freshman entering in fall 2007 at Mid-Atlantic were African American. While not a high percentage, this appeared to be enough of a critical mass at the institution to develop diverse sub-cultures for students to explore and find connections. Among students, this critical mass appeared to influence movement toward a normative definition and positive racial regard related to African American collectivity. Both the formalized opportunities and informal connections seemed important to students as they transitioned to a new community.

Conflicts between Ideologies

The third theme, *conflicts between ideologies,* was particularly evident during interviews conducted after the semester break. Participants provided information about the tension they felt at home as they expressed a racial ideology that diverged from previous influences. For example, Stephanie was going to join the campus chapter of the National Association for the Advancement of Colored People (NAACP) during the fall semester. She recounted a particular reaction from her father when she wore one of her NAACP t-shirts at home,

> I always liked the shirts that they had, like Black power. Then I came home and my dad saw the shirt that I was wearing. He is much more conservative than I am and I think he thinks I might be becoming a radical or something.

When queried about her dad's perception of the NAACP, Stephanie responded, "He told me all about the NAACP and how they're not the same as they used to be in the Civil Rights Era and they didn't really want me to be in that." In the spring semester, Stephanie stated that she decided not to join the organization, "Yeah, and I decided not to (join) because of the things that they believe now are different. I like the NAACP back when Martin Luther King was involved. What they were about now, I'm not too sure about."

The tension between Will and his family arose from his reluctance to attend church over the break. During the first interview, Will identified his predominately White church community as a source of strength for his family, one of the reasons they relocated to the community from which he graduated high school. However, during a follow-up discussion at the end of the first semester, he discussed the growing disconnection with his church community. As he stated:

> I want more diversity now, because my family goes to a mostly White church, and it's not very diverse. I can't relate with them sometimes. I

began to realize that I don't even like these people that much, so I want to kind of find a new church where it's like people more like me.

For Anthony, a perceived shift in 'style' was a source of tension with his mother. Coming from a majority White community, Anthony had developed a strong network of African American friends for the first time. Connection to this new peer group began to influence a change in dress. He recalls his mother's reaction,

my mom has actually said some funny things … because I started buying a lot of my own stuff … that I look more like a hoodlum or whatever when I come home. I just told her that that was my style has always been this way. I just never really had access to get it myself or whatever.

The students in this study appeared to be shifting between various racial ideologies during their first year at Mid-Atlantic. Often the contrast becomes apparent on their return to their home community and family, particularly if the home community was connected with White-dominant community institutions. The dynamic often complicates the transition for students—the resources that contributed to successful transition to college, through connections with the critical mass of African American students, were now the same resources that stimulated conflict with the perspectives of family and previous community institutions. In the process of apprising competing values within certain community contexts (African American community at Mid-Atlantic University, White-dominant home community and family), participants appeared to struggle within the range of racial ideology spectrum.

Racial Regard Resiliency

The fourth theme, *racial regard resiliency,* represents a student resistance against perceptions or experiences with one-dimensional judgments of racial identity. Rather than internalize stereotypes and accept labels, students described ways in which they confronted challenges to their identity. Imani, who initially had described herself as a 'White girl with a really good tan,' discussed a particularly unsettling experience where she and an African American peer were questioned about their ethnic 'authenticity' based on their musical taste, "We were talking and my friend was listening to my iPod and she said, 'John Mayer! I love John Mayer!' and this White guy at the table said … his exact words were, 'You guys need a Black intervention!'" Knowing that Imani experienced 'acting White' taunts from her African American peers in high school, I inquired how she handled the situation.

> When he said it, we were the only two Black people there and it was this whole group of White people. And all of the White people were really, really uncomfortable … I wasn't going to cause a scene … But, when (Imani's peer) was yelling at him, she was saying everything I thought. She was like, 'How dare you tell me about being Black? You don't even know! You don't know anything about me! Because I like John Mayer, I'm not Black?' And he was like, 'I was just joking!' But that's not funny. It's not appropriate.

No longer accepting a Eurocentric identity, Imani seemed to gain a level of racial salience that would not allow others to define her based on what type of music they think she should be listening to. As this researcher started to move to another question, Imani quickly added a closing thought about the incident: "What does he think being Black is? Does he think that we're supposed to … does he think that we should just listen to Tupac?' Well, I *have* Tupac on my iPod *too!* So there (laughing)."

Hostility was not limited to social settings, as Malik offers an illustration from a calculus class during the spring semester:

> Our professor said that the TA came and asked her, 'Are there a lot of (minority scholarship) students in the Calculus II class?' (The professor) told (the TA) there were, and she asked him why he asked … (The TA) was like, 'There are a lot of …' (The professor) kind of finished it for him, 'There's a lot of people of color in there?' He said, 'Yeah, that's all I'm going to say.' We kind of laughed about it.

After laughing and pausing for a bit, Malik continued seriously, "Yeah, it definitely put something in me. When I came back, I told some of the other (minority scholarship) students and they were like, 'Damn.' So I was like, O.K. let's do this." Anthony concluded with a similar refrain in recalling an experience in the classroom,

> I was called up to the board and (in an instant) one of the things running through my mind was 'Are the White people in this class thinking that I won't be able to get this problem?' I want to show … to prove to people that I can do as much as they can.

The peer support, missing in previous educational contexts, appeared to both strengthen perseverance and reduce vulnerability to assumptions connected with racial identity. While this developing resiliency was a source of strength, perceptions of hostility remained, particularly in the classroom. Jada, who self-reported high grades during her first semester, describes "… they don't know what I got last semester, so I feel like I have to prove myself again."

In reviewing discussions with participants over the course of the year, students cited more examples of hostility in academic settings than in social settings, although the social incidents appeared to have much deeper meaning for students as they tended to dominate journal entries. In particular, the reflection found in journal entries appeared to represent the fragile state of resiliency during the first year of college. While resiliency was vulnerable to self-doubt, it was often stimulated by connections to sources of support, most notably peer support. Over time, heightened resiliency allowed students to find comfortable levels of racial salience and centrality.

Complexity of Identity

The fifth theme, *complexity of identity*, began to develop among students during the later stages of the first year. Students began to discuss how their racial identity interacted with other forms of identity—gender, socioeconomic background, sexual orientation—to stimulate complex reflection. The emerging influence of experiences based on socioeconomic position appeared most consistent among students at the end of this study. In the initial interviews, only Natalya presented a portrait of her family circumstances that reflected limited socioeconomic resources. At the end of the last interview, Natalya, whose father had lost his job and her family was evicted from their home, asked if she could revisit earlier questions about her identity development:

> Actually, I think socioeconomic supersedes a lot of the other stuff. Just because money … I'm reading this book and it's like, why aren't we raised to go to school and own a business? It also depends on how you look at money. People see money as their way to … if people really want to do something, then [that] is going to be a part of their lives a lot. Whereas someone who really doesn't look at money that way, they'll see different aspects of their life differently. That kind of supersedes the ethnicity thing. That is what's on TV nowadays, money.

Other participants also reflected on complex perspective of their identity during the latter stages of the study. Other participants from lower socioeconomic backgrounds revealed an emerging socioeconomic identity during the latter stages of the study. For example, Imani described her family's socioeconomic fluctuation as "definitely upper-middle class, then definitely dropped, like middle class, lower middle class, now upper-middle class again, I guess." In a later interview, in discussing how experiences during her first year at Mid-Atlantic had heightened her awareness of her mother's financial struggle, she stated "I think I'm definitely more aware of money. I'm constantly thinking about, just … I definitely don't want to be poor again. I saw how stressed out my mom was. Who wants to be poor?"

Bridgette, who described herself as from an upper middle-class family, displayed an awareness of the intersection between racial identity and socioeconomic background in the initial interview. She stated "Middle-class Blacks tend to look down on lower-class Blacks. I know I probably do, which I don't want to do, but I probably do." Toward the end of the semester, she revealed an alternate perspective:

It's awful … if you're born, if you're born poor you're gonna be poor, cause you can't get an education in this country if you're poor, a good one. Umm, it's hard to escape this Black inferiority mentality and if it's been beat in your head for so long and if you've been at the bottom for so long it's hard to come up so I think this dialogue academically about Blacks that aren't doing well has not been translated into cultural or social activism. People keep talking about it but they don't do anything. I guess when I get out I want to do something about it, I'm not sure what yet, but I'd like to do something.

Perhaps because participants did not want to add a dimension of difference to their identity as they entered a new community, initial conversations about other forms of identity were limited. However, as illustrated by Natalya and Bridgette, socioeconomic status (SES) may play a pivotal role in shaping racial salience and centrality. Additionally, as Bridgette demonstrated, students began to reinterpret their racial ideology, constructing a deeper understanding of how socioeconomic position provided advantages or disadvantages. The movement toward this awareness appeared both stimulating and unsettling.

● DISCUSSION

For the fifteen first-year students interviewed for this study, the transitional experiences were influenced by both internal reconceptualization of racial identity and access to external sources of support. Although described separately, these themes—established identity; shifting salience and centrality; conflicting ideologies; resilient regard; and identity complexity—represent a connected process. The participant descriptions provide both congruency and contrast to previous studies which examined the role of racial identity development on educational experiences of African American students.

Previous studies on college students suggested that construction of racial identity begins with a sense of self and develops continuously through experience that provides fresh opportunities for revelation (Cross 1995; Cross, Parham, and Helms 1991). Identity is not static, but changes with individual accumulation of experiences and shifts in various social contexts (Phinney 1992). The Multidimensional Model of Racial Identity (MMRI) outlines shifts in four different dimensions, (a) racial salience, (b) racial centrality, (c) racial regard, and (d) racial ideology. The experiences of these students support the static nature of identity, influenced by the internalization of experiences in external sociocultural environments. The use of MMRI as a theoretical lens offers the opportunity to move beyond examining identity development as a process of 'stages.' In following students over the course of a year, it became clear that identity development is a cyclical process where students shift within and among dimensions simultaneously, influenced by several communities—past and present communities, Eurocentric and ethnocentric communities, and home and campus communities. At a predominately White institution, African American students may find themselves primarily as an 'outsider,' but in the case of the institution for this study, they also found opportunities to be an 'insider.' During initial experiences in a new community, students were focused on positioning themselves in formal and informal communities where they are on the inside—stimulated by the pain of previous outsider experiences and the opportunities provided by a heterogeneous African American community.

The appreciation of a heterogeneous African American community supports previous studies examining the value of a critical mass of African American students enrolled at a PWI (Etzkowitz et al. 1994; Fries-Britt and Turner 2002). When there is only a small presence of a traditionally underrepresented group within the larger population, the minority population can be easily marginalized. In contrast, a large presence produces sub-communities offer valuable support to a minority population. It appeared that the institution examined for this study had a large enough presence among the African American students that formal and informal subcommunities emerged and were visible to participants in this study. However, even with the heterogeneous presence on campus, there appeared to be aspects of identity that students sought to de-emphasize. In particular, students with varied socioeconomic backgrounds appeared to consciously reduce this less visible dimension of difference to protect their insider position within sub-communities. The highly static nature of SES among the students in this study was also visible as they discussed experiencing multiple socioeconomic contexts through intergenerational upward or downward mobility. These shifting contexts also influenced their access to and comfort with various sources of identity support.

The experiences of students in this study suggest that diverse sources of support are key mechanisms for shifting dimensions of racial identity development. These sources of support may be viewed as a type of 'cultural capital' (Bourdieu and Passeron 1998; Lamont and Lareau 1998). Unlike traditional application of cultural capital theory in previous studies on college students, often rooted in access to Eurocentric values, this study supports the influence of both traditional and non-traditional states of cultural capital. Dominant cultural capital corresponds with Bourdieu's conceptualization of powerful high status attributes, while non-dominant cultural capital describes resources used by individuals to gain "authentic" cultural status within their respective communities (Carter 2003). Different, though interconnected, these two forms of capital represent varied cultural currencies, the benefits of which vary depending on the social space in which they are used. Student experiences represent the variability of cultural capital and how it shapes the many dimensions of racial identity development. Furthermore, there is evidence that the interaction between external sources of cultural capital and the internal process of racial identity development influenced campus climate perceptions and behaviors of the African American students in this study.

Perhaps the most valuable outcome of this interaction is the development of resiliency. Resiliency theory suggests that those with stable healthy personas develop coping skills that enable them to succeed in the face of perceived or actual threats (Gandara 1995; James, Jurich, and Estes 2001). Resiliency is influenced by individual attributes such as positive self-efficacy, structural support, and involvement in programs that provide a sense of support. Students in this study provided various examples of resiliency in multiple contexts during their transition. Their experiences also revealed the fragility of resilience, particularly during the first year. Specifically in the academic context, even when students experienced success in the classroom, they discussed the need to continuously prove themselves to their White peers and instructors. This suggests that while student success in culturally exclusive spaces was related to their position to dominant sources of cultural capital, they also relied heavily on non-dominant sources for additional support against perceptions or experiences with racism or stereotyping. Resiliency and its connection to formal and informal support from peers may not be unique to African American students; however, the degree to which African American students attending a PWI must continuously draw on this attribute to persistence seems particularly relevant given the connection between racial identity development and perceptions of a hostile campus environment.

Finally, as students in this study shifted between various dimensions of racial identity, they began to uncover the complexity of identity. In particular, they began a process of discovering how their multiple identities—including race and socioeconomic status—influence their experiences. This study supports previous research on the importance of examining African Americans as a heterogeneous group (Chavous et al. 2004; Harper and Nichols 2008). The experiences of students suggest that African American students from the high-SES backgrounds benefit from a position of privilege, when compared to African American students for lower-SES backgrounds; however, it appears that African American students from high-SES background have additional sources of stress that their White peers may not have. Additionally, for students in this study, identity was further complicated by conflicts with home communities and family. The same resources that appear to foster successful transition college may conflict with previous sources of support. In the process of appraising competing values within certain contexts, participants initially seemed to struggle as they processed the developing complexity of their position. It was apparent at the end of this study that this process would continue to linger beyond the first-year, particularly when students returned home for an extended period between the spring and fall semesters.

● IMPLICATIONS AND CONCLUSION

What after all, am I? Am I an American or am I a Negro? Can I be Both? Or is my duty to cease to be a Negro as soon as possible and be an American? Here it seems to me is the reading of the riddle that puzzles so many of us.

W. E. B Du Bois, *The Conversation of Races* (1897)

The voices presented in this study illustrate the progress that society has made since the Du Bois statement, as well as the challenges still to be faced as we move through the 21st century. These challenges extend not just across racial categories, but within them as well. Monolithic, stereotypical perspectives of identity serve to simplify a complex society, and inevitably limit human progress. The contributions of the participants provided a greater understanding of varied first-year experiences, confirming results from previous studies while challenging other conclusions. Most importantly, the experiences of these students suggest several implications for future consideration.

Researchers in higher education should continue to investigate how socio-economic background influences persistence within the postsecondary system. The evidence of an increasing socioeconomic divide is strong and consistent across all racial classifications (Bowen, Chingos, and McPherson 2009; Sacks 2008). One of the implications from this study is the need to address the complexity of socioeconomic background. The dynamic nature of socioeconomic status limits the ability to directly examine the influence of class background on participant experiences. Students discussed growing up in various community settings, suggesting socioeconomic experiences grounded intergenerational mobility rather than an inherited position. Therefore quantitative measurements of socioeconomic background are limited, particularly when examining students from traditionally excluded populations.

From a policy perspective, the observation that socioeconomic status is not a stationary variable among African American families, challenges suggestions that affirmative action policies that are based on socioeconomic background may adequately replace race-based affirmative action policies with little consequence for African American postsecondary enrollment. The rapid intergenerational mobility of African American families tends to place them at statistically higher socioeconomic positions based on snapshot socioeconomic measurements—education, occupation, and income. However, as Patillo-McCoy (2003) argued, the lack of wealth accumulated among African American middle-class and upper-middle class families renders socioeconomic comparisons across ethnic groups unfair. In this study, only one student could be considered having upper-middle class background based on family background. Additionally, while they may have accumulated levels of cultural capital to decrease lingering impact, students from statistically middle-class or upper-middle class families were not shielded from racism or being stereotyped on campus. This finding further supports the danger in arbitrarily replacing race with socioeconomic status in forming institutional policies.

Finally, the use of developmental frameworks which emphasize the diverse dimensions of racial identity development is critical to expanding understanding of African American student experiences. Identity development is not context-neutral. In fact, it may be quite the opposite. The experiences of students in this study demonstrate that racial salience, racial regard, racial centrality, and racial ideology are interwoven with multiple contexts. Emphasizing the role of context in identity development allows scholars to challenge the myth of campus neutrality in higher education (Kaufmann and Feldman 2004; Wolff 1969). The gatekeeping function of higher education is supported by the evidence of non-merit-based factors that influence access and persistence, including connection to dominant forms of cultural capital. With this access comes certification that maintains social position. The degree, to which this certification extends to African American from high-SES backgrounds, and the consequences for their racial identity development, should be examined.

● REFERENCES

Allen, W. R. (1992). *College in Black and White: African American students in predominantly White and historically Black public universities.* Albany: State University of New York Press.

Aud, S., Hussar, W., Planty, M., Snyder, T., Bianco, K., Fox, M., Frohlich, L,, Kemp, J., and Drake, L. (2010). *The condition of education 2010* (NCES 2010–028). Washington, DC: National Center for Education Statistics, Institute of Education Sciences, U.S. Department of Education.

Berger, J. B., and Braxton, J. M. (1998). Revising Tinto's interactionalist theory of student departure through theory elaboration. *Research in Higher Education, 39,* 106–116.

Bourdieu, P., and Passeron, J. C. (1998). *Reproduction in education, society, and culture.* London: Sage.

Bowen, W. G., Chingos, M. M., and McPherson, M. S. (2009). *Crossing the finish line: Completing college at America's public universities.* Princeton: Princeton University Press.

Carter, P. (2003). Black cultural capital, status, positioning, and schooling conflicts for low-income African American youth. *Social Problems, 50,* 136–155.

Chavous, T. M., Harris, A., Rivas, D., Helaire, L., and Green, L. (2004). Racial stereotypes and gender in context: African Americans at predominately Black and predominantly White colleges. *Sex Roles, 51,* 1–12.

Creswell, J. W. (1998). *Qualitative inquiry and research design: Choosing among five traditions.* Thousand Oaks, CA: Sage.

Cross, W. (1995). The psychology of Nigrescence: Revisiting the Cross model. In J. Pontero, J. Casas., L. Suzuki, and C. Alexander (Eds.), *Handbook of multicultural counseling* (pp. 93–122). Thousand Oaks, CA: Sage.

Cross, W. E., Parham, T, and Helms, J. (1991). The stages of Black identity development: Nigrescence models. In R. Jones (Ed.), *Black psychology* (pp. 319–338). Berkeley: Cobb and Henry.

Du Bois., W. E. B. (1897). *The conversation of races: The American Negro Academy Occasional Papers, No. 2.* Washington, DC: The Academy.

Du Bois, W. E. B. (1903). *The souls of Black folk.* New York: Bantam.

Elkins, S. A., Braxton, J. M., and James, G. W. (2000). Tinto's separation stage and its influence on first-semester college student persistence. *Research in Higher Education, 41,* 252–266.

Etzkowitz, H., Kemelgor, C., Neuschatz, M., Uzzi, B., and Alonzo, J. (1994). The paradox of critical mass for women in science. *Science New Series, 266,* 51 -54.

Fries-Britt, S., and Turner, B. (2002). Uneven stories: Successful Black collegians at a Black and a White campus. *The Review of Higher Education, 25,* 315–330.

Gandara, P. (1995). *Over the ivy walls: The educational mobility oflow-income Chicanos.* New York: State University of New York Press.

Guiffrida, D. A. (2005). To break away or strengthen ties to home: A complex question for African American students attending a predominantly White institution. *Equity and Excellence in Education, 38,* 49–60.

Gumport, P. J. (Ed.). (2007). *Sociology of higher education: Contributions and their contexts.* Baltimore, MD: Johns Hopkins University Press.

Harper, S., and Nichols, A. (2008). Are they not all the same? Racial heterogeneity among Black male undergraduates. *Journal of College Student Development, 49,* 247–269.

Helms, J. E. (1994). The conceptualization of racial identity and other "racial" constructs. In E. J. Trickett, R. J. Watts, and D. Briman (Eds.). *Human diversity: Perspectives on people in context* (pp. 285–311). San Francisco: Jossey-Bass.

Hurtado, S., Milem, J. F., Clayton-Pedersen, A. R., and Allen, W. R. (1998). Enhancing campus climates for racial/ethnic diversity through educational policy and practice. *Review of Higher Education, 21,* 279–302.

James, D. W., Jurich, S., and Estes, S. (2001). *Raising minority academic achievement: A compendium of education programs and practices.* Washington, DC: American Youth Policy Forum.

Kaufmann, P., and Feldman, K. A. (2004). Forming identities in college: A sociological approach. *Research in Higher Education, 45,* 463–496.

Lamont M., and Lareau, A. (1988). Cultural capital: Allusions, gaps and glissandos in recent theoretical developments. *Sociological Theory, 6,* 153–168.

McLaurin v. Oklahoma State Regents for Higher Education, 339 U.S. 637 (1950).

Pascarella, E. T., and Terenzini, P. T. (2005). *How college affects students: A third decade of research.* San Francisco: Jossey-Bass.

Patton, M. Q. (2002). *Qualitative research and evaluation methods.* Thousand Oaks, CA: Sage.

Phinney, J. S. (1989). Stages of ethnic identity development in minority group adolescents. *Journal of Early Adolescence, 9,* 34–49.

Phinney, J. S. (1992). The multigroup ethnic identity measure: A new scale for use with diverse groups. *Journal of Adolescent Research, 7,* 156–176.

Rendon, L. I., Jalomo, R. E., and Nora, A. (2000). Theoretical considerations in the study of minority student retention in higher education. In J. M. Braxton (Ed.) *Reworking the student departure puzzle* (pp. 127–156). Nashville, TN: Vanderbilt University Press.

Rosenbaum, J. E., Deil-Amen, R., and Person, A. E. (2006). *After admission: From college access to college success.* New York: Russell Sage Foundation.

Rowley, S. J., Sellers, R. M., Chavous, T. M., and Smith, M. A. (1998). The relationship between racial identity and self-esteem in African American college and high school students. *Journal of Personality and Social Psychology, 74,* 715–724.

Sacks, P. (2008). *Tearing down the gates.* Berkeley, CA: University of California Press.

Sadala, M, and Adorno, R. (2001). Phenomenology as a method to investigate the experiences lived: A perspective from Husserl and Merleau-Ponty's thought. *Journal of Advanced Nursing, 37,* 282–293.

Sellers, R. M., Rowley, S. A. J., Chavous, T. M., Shelton, J. N., and Smith, M. A. (1997). Multidimensional inventory of Black identity: A preliminary investigation of reliability and construct validity. *Journal of Personality and Social Psychology, 73,* 805–815.

Sellers, R. M., Smith, M. A., Shelton, J. N., Rowley, S. A. J., and Chavous, T. M. (1998). Multidimensional model of racial identity: A reconceptualization of African American racial identity. *Personality and Social Psychology Review, 2,* 18–39.

Tanaka, G. (2002). Higher education's self-reflexive turn: Toward an intercultural theory of student development. *The Journal of Higher Education, 73,* 263–296.

Tierney, W. G. (1992). An anthropological analysis of student participation in college. *The Journal of Higher Education, 63,* 603–618.

Upcraft, M. L., Gardner, J. N., and Barefoot, B. O. (Eds.). (2005). *Challenging and supporting the first-year student: A handbook for improving the first year of college.* San Francisco: Jossey–Bass.

U.S. Department of Education. (2004). *Historically Black colleges and universities, 1976 to* (NCES Publication No. 2004–062). Washington, DC: U.S. Department of Education, National Center for Education Statistics.

Wijeyesinghe, C. L., and Jackson, B. W. (2001). *New perspectives on racial identity development: A theoretical and practical anthology.* New York: New York University Press.

Wolff, R. P. (1969). *The ideal of the university.* Boston: Beacon Press.

SECTION EIGHT

ENVIRONMENTAL SOCIAL PROBLEMS

This last section considers a range of environmental social problems that exist in the United States. The state of the environment affects our lives on a daily basis. Our air and water quality are directly related to our health and well-being. And changes in the atmosphere impact all living things. Some people are also more likely than others to be negatively impacted by environmental problems. In this section, social problems relating to pollution, environmental health, environmental racism, and consumption are considered.

● POLLUTION AND ENVIRONMENTAL HEALTH

Pollution is a grave social problem that affects all of us. Air pollution, water pollution, ozone depletion, and carbon dioxide emissions each represent a significant social problem. Pollution from transportation and factories has resulted in smog, which has compromised the air quality of densely populated American cities such as Los Angeles and New York City. Air pollution is also responsible for acid rain, where the pH of the precipitation is reduced, resulting in highly acidic water in lakes and rivers. This kills wildlife and impacts the reproduction of fish and other animals.

Water pollution is another very serious social problem. Agriculture, golf courses, industry, and fracking are chief causes of this phenomenon. Farms and golf courses use fertilizers and pesticides that leach into the soil, are absorbed into the water table, and end up in bodies of water that we use for drinking water. Fertilizer and pesticide exposure are linked to cancer, birth defects, and reproductive issues. In spite of the Clean Water Act that was passed in 1972, levels of mercury, lead, and other toxic compounds are still very high in the Great Lakes and other bodies of water throughout the country. Exposure to these chemicals has also resulted in a number of environmental health hazards contributing to organ failure and neurological damage. People who live near fracking operations have experienced problems related to fracking fluid and natural gas contaminating their drinking water.

Ozone depletion is another significant environmental problem. Chlorofluorocarbons (CFCs) were common agents used in air conditioning, aerosols, and the making of Styrofoam through the mid-1990s. The use of CFCs resulted in the thinning of the ozone layer in the atmosphere, leaving us more exposed to ultraviolet A and B radiation. Skin cancers, the great majority of which are caused by ultraviolet radiation, constitute the most common form of cancer. In southern countries like Australia and Chile that are near an actual hole in the ozone layer, rates of cancer and other illnesses are even higher. Although rates of illness are high, there is cause for optimism. Almost two hundred countries have signed the Montreal Protocol, which is an important piece of international legislation that phased out CFC usage around the world.

Perhaps the most prominent environmental issue of our time is global warming. Nine of the ten hottest years on record have been in the 2000s and this warming trend has impacted weather patterns, Antarctic glaciers, wildlife, and agriculture around the world. Global warming is caused by increased carbon dioxide emissions from cars, power plants, homes, and factories into the atmosphere. These emissions result in an expanded layer of carbon dioxide in the atmosphere that allows the heat from the sun to pass through it on the way to earth, but not pass through it as easily upon being reflected back from the earth's surface. This results in even more heat being directed towards the earth. Some people call this the "greenhouse effect" because carbon dioxide has the same thermal properties as glass. We have all gone to our cars on a hot summer day when the inside of the car is even hotter than the outside. That is because the heat is able to get through the glass much easier than it can escape. That is what is happening in our atmosphere.

Chapter 26 is called "Impacts of Climate Change on People and Communities of Rural America." In this piece, Wright Morton and Rudel document how temperature increases have affected precipitation patterns, water runoff, pollination cycles, and other aspects of nature that are essential to the American rural way of life. Upon establishing the general concerns that many people have with climate change, they examine the impacts of climate change in three rural places. The first case is the wildfires in the western mountain states, where warmer temperatures have resulted in less snow pack and drier conditions. The second case is the rash of flooding along the Mississippi and Ohio rivers caused by heavy snowmelt and rainfall. The third case describes how changing weather patterns have affected the hunting and fishing patterns of indigenous people living in coastal Alaska.

● ENVIRONMENTAL RACISM

Environmental racism can be defined as the disproportionate exposure to pollution of minorities. Sociologists and other academics have established a social pattern involving many American manufacturing firms and waste management facilities. Many factories and other polluting facilities are located in minority neighborhoods, meaning that the noise, air, and water pollution that they generate are more likely to affect minorities. This practice also occurs internationally when companies located in the developed world operate factories in the developing world to take advantage of lower wages and fewer environmental restrictions. In response to environmental racism, the concept of environmental justice has emerged. The environmental justice social movement seeks to end the practice of environmental racism and promote more social and environmentally friendly behaviors around the world.

In their chapter, "Native Americans and Social and Environmental Justice: Implications for Criminology," Lynch and Stretesky establish that Native Americans have very high rates of exposure to environmental hazards. The authors assert that Native Americans experience environmental injustice because they are excluded from environmental decision making and are disproportionately exposed to various forms of pollution. Using five case studies, Lynch and Stretesky document the extent to which exposure to polychlorinated biphenyls (PCBs) and other chemicals found in industrial pollution in New York, Quebec, and Ontario; uranium exposure among miners in the American southwest; and the sinking of the Exxon Valdez in Alaska have negatively impacted the lives of native peoples throughout North America.

● CONSUMPTION

Many people have described Western lifestyles as representative of a "throwaway" or "disposable" culture. When people use this language, they emphasize how many resources we use and how big our proverbial ecological footprint is. Our lifestyles have become very resource-intensive. When we buy new things, we do not typically consider all of the resources used to manufacture them. For example, consider the plastic, paper, and metals used to create and package iPhones. Add to that the transportation-related pollution associated with bringing such products from China and you can see the clear connection between consumption and the environment.

In his piece, "The United States of Consumption (and Debt)," Lang explores rates of American consumption and debt over time. It is not just that we consume more products than our parents and grandparents; we also maintain higher rates of personal debt than previous generations of Americans. Of course these two phenomena are related. And research shows that people with substantial debt have more physical and mental health problems, a reduced quality of life, higher rates of divorce, and higher rates of bankruptcy than people without such high levels of debt.

CHAPTER 26

Impacts of Climate Change on People and Communities of Rural America[1]

By Lois Wright Morton and Tom Rudel

Three great patterns dominate the earth and are of tremendous importance to man—the pattern of climate, the pattern of vegetation, and the pattern of soils. When the three patterns are laid one upon the other, their boundaries coincide to a remarkable degree because climate is the fundamental dynamic force shaping the other two ... the fourth pattern laid upon the three is that of human culture, or civilization. (USDA Climate and Man Yearbook 1941, 98)

The year 2011 saw fourteen extreme weather events in the United States costing more than $1 billion each and with carnage that represented a devastating "new normal" in a global context of increasingly extreme weather events (Coumou and Rahmstorf 2012; Hansen, Sato, and Ruedy 2012). Rural people have always assessed changing weather conditions—evaluating the shape and color of the clouds as predictors of an early snowfall, sniffing the moisture in the air to predict rain and make planting and harvest decisions, and scanning green-tinted skies in the calm before a tornado touches down. Despite the unpredictability of where lightning will strike, how long a drought will last, and when the first frost will occur and the last snows will melt, rural peoples have used past weather patterns to guide their daily behavior.

In an era of climate change, weather events seem even more fraught with uncertainty. The Intergovernmental Panel on Climate Change (IPCC) assessments for North America document increases in annual mean air temperature since 1955, with the greatest warming occurring in Alaska, substantial warming in the continental interior, and modest warming in the southeast (IPCC 2001; 2007; Field et al. 2007). Spring and winter temperatures have changed the most, with daily minimum (nighttime) temperatures warming more than daily maximums (daytime). Earlier spring warming has lengthened growing seasons, with an average increase of two days per decade since 1950. Annual precipitation has increased particularly in northern regions, but has decreased in the southwestern United States. Although effects vary among regions of the United States, all production systems dependent upon precipitation and reliable water sources are affected to some degree by changes in climate (Walthall et al. 2012). In Box 26.1 we summarize many of the key North American findings on how temperature

---

Box 26.1: Key North American and US findings on climate change effects adapted from the 3rd and 4th Assessment Report on Climate (Field et al. 2007) and USDA Climate Change and Agriculture in the United States: Effects and Adaptation (Walthall et al. 2012).

Resources and Ecosystems

- In western snowmelt-dominated watersheds, shifts in seasonal runoff, with more in winter.

- Increased regional and seasonal variability in availability and management of water resources, including rain-fed and irrigated agriculture.

- Changes in pressures associated with weeds, diseases, and insect pests, and with the timing and coincidence of pollinator lifecycles.

- Changes in the abundance and spatial distribution of species important to commercial and recreational fisheries.

- Increased production costs and productivity loses associated with animal products (e.g., meat, eggs, and milk) with prolonged exposure to extreme temperatures.

- Benefits from warming for food production but with strong regional differences.

- Increases in the productivity of forests.

- More pervasive disturbances in forest ecosystems, with longer fire seasons and wider areas subjected to high fire danger.

- Likely losses of cold-water ecosystems, high alpine areas, and coastal and inland wetlands.

Human Settlements

- Less extreme winter cold in northern communities, and more extreme heat.

- Heightened risk of storm surges (e.g., Hurricanes Katrina and Sandy), water scarcities, and floods.

- Increased frequency and severity of heat waves leading to more illness and death, particularly among the young, elderly, and frail. Respiratory disorders may be exacerbated by warming-induced deterioration in air quality.

- Expanded ranges of vector-borne and tick-borne diseases.

- Increased weather-related losses since the 1970s, with rising insured losses reflecting growing affluence and movement into vulnerable areas.

- Coverage, since the 1980s, by disaster relief and insurance programs of a large fraction of flood and crop losses, possibly encouraging more human activity in at-risk areas.

- Reduced availability of disaster insurance from insurers.

and precipitation changes have affected ecosystems and rural human settlements to date.

While climate has always shaped both natural and human communities (USDA Climate and Man Yearbook 1941), its influence now seems much more uncertain with records and models of temperature, precipitation, and atmospheric conditions indicating increased variability and more frequent extreme events (Hatfield et al. 2011). The vulnerabilities and risks associated with these uncertainties present new challenges that people of rural places must recognize and plan for in order to adapt, survive, and thrive.

People do not always see these challenges in the same way. Despite Intergovernmental Panel on Climate Change (IPCC) reports over the last twenty years that document climate change, a great deal of disbelief and uncertainty persists among the general US population (Donner 2011; McCright and Dunlap 2011; Weber and Stern 2011). The natural variability of local weather conditions from day to day and year to year is a significant barrier to public recognition of human impacts on the global climate. Climate changes occur over the course of decades and centuries, sometimes in incremental ways, so it is easy for this long-term signal to get lost in the midst of weekly and seasonal fluctuations in weather (Gleick 2012).

The challenges of understanding and responding to climate change have been amplified by controversies over the legitimacy of climate change science. While more than 90 percent of publishing climate scientists agree that climate change is occurring and caused primarily by human activities, in 2011 only 15 percent of the American public believed there is a high degree of scientific agreement (Leiserowitz et al. 2011). The agricultural community illustrates this skepticism, and at its 2010 national conference the Farm Bureau established, as its official position, that "there is no generally agreed upon scientific assessment of the exact impact or extent of carbon emissions from human activities, their impact on past decades of warming or how they will affect future climate changes" (Winter 2010). At its 2012 conference, it reiterated its position that climate change is not human induced (Clayton 2012). Fossil fuel producers, worried about the threat to their livelihoods by efforts to reduce fossil fuel use, have sought through misinformation campaigns to discredit the consensus view of climate change among scientists (McCright and Dunlap 2011). Until recently, the press amplified the voices of climate change denialists through its desire to present all sides of the controversy, without regard to the very large differences in the rigor of science underlying different positions (Boykoff 2011).

A social-ecological framework of press-like processes of incremental change and pulse-like processes of sudden, event-driven changes provides a useful way to understand the interactions among climates, rural peoples, their natural resource bases, and their livelihoods. Case studies of wildfires in the western mountain states, flooding in the Midwest, and warming in Inuit coastal communities in Alaska exemplify the ways climate change has begun to impact rural peoples. The differences in impacts and perceptions of risk have created different discourses. Programs of planned adaptation vary from isolated individuals and households living in poor rural communities to highly capitalized communities of interest like agribusiness and forestry. The former people are especially vulnerable to climactic disturbances as natural resource dependent populations with few resources.

● PRESS-PULSE DYNAMICS IN COUPLED HUMAN AND NATURAL SYSTEMS

The human-dominated landscapes of North America represent a coupled human and natural system (CHANS) that changes through a mix of press and pulse processes. *Press processes* alter the structure of a system in small increments, while *pulse events* transform social and ecosystem functions suddenly through "shocks" (Collins et al. 2011). Population growth, agricultural and forestry expansion, yield increases, and coastland erosion represent typical press processes that are less visible than pulse processes, which occur suddenly and make structural changes highly visible. Pulse events transform rural places, livelihoods, and quality of life in short intervals of time. For Americans, pulse events are more salient than press events. They foresee deaths and injuries due to pulse events such as floods, hurricanes, winter storms, and wildfires, but are less concerned about press threats to water resources, plants and animals, public infrastructure (roads, schools, sewer systems), and crop productivity (Leiserowitz et al. 2011).

Press-pulse dynamics entail a recursive dimension in which humans adapt to the perturbation. These responses include actions to sustain flows of goods and services and to bolster the resilience of communities (Jackson et al. 2010). Adaptation often begins with efforts to resist and attempts to manage change, such as building new or strengthening existing levees and seawalls to protect towns, businesses, and farmland against hurricanes, sea level rise, and flooding. Adaptation strategies focused on resilience try to increase the capacity of the rural community to be more flexible and cope without changing the baseline structure—e.g., shifting the types of agricultural crops grown or diversifying the community's economic or social infrastructure to be prepared for warmer, wetter, or drier conditions, but not changing the basic nature of land uses or rural livelihoods. Transformative adaptive responses might include moving settlements out of coastal regions facing rising sea levels (see Gramling and Laska in this volume), returning floodplains and bottomlands to seasonal wetlands rather than levee protected agricultural uses (Morton and Olson 2013), or creating public policies that incentivize agrobiodiversity and the creation of different livelihoods congruent with changing conditions.

Weather refers to day-to-day temperature and precipitation, whereas *climate* refers to the average temperature, precipitation, and atmospheric conditions over longer periods of time. These short- and long-term patterns influence how rural people chose livelihoods and create desirable places to live. Changes in these patterns can represent threats to economic, physical, and social well-being, particularly when temperature and precipitation vary considerably from human expectations and preparedness. When changes in the frequency, intensity, and variation of temperature, precipitation, and atmospheric conditions (pulses) occur, they inevitably intersect with the steady presses of human activity and land use changes. Given the intense use of the natural resource base—row crop cultivation, cattle grazing, mining, fishing, and building on floodplains—these systems have little redundancy built into them so unanticipated events like drought can quickly compromise their capacities.

Pulse events such as floods, droughts, and tornados are highly visible, dramatic events that grab media headlines and pose immediate threats to human livelihoods. During the southwestern United States drought of late 2011 and early 2012, newspapers headlined, "Texas Rice Farmers Lose Their Water" and reported that the $394 million Texas rice industry would suffer a shortage of water for irrigation if the Lower Colorado River (Texas) Authority cut off water to farmers for the first time in seventy-eight years (Koppel 2012). A climate pulse occurred in March 2012 in the interior United States when meteorological conditions spawned a series of unusually powerful tornados from the Gulf of Mexico to the Great Lakes. This event left behind fourteen dead in Indiana and twelve dead in Kentucky, leveled small towns, transformed rural homes into piles of debris, flattened a fire station, and ripped roofs off of schools and prisons, leaving survivors without power and emotionally stunned (Associated Press 2012). Rural communities and outlying homes without good warning systems are particularly vulnerable. Further, strong winds, hail, and heavy rains increase water runoff and loss of nutrients and soil in agricultural regions, with effects on annual and future yields when they occur during the growing season. Totaling up the various types of extreme weather events from the first half of 2011, the National Oceanographic and Aeronautics Administration (NOAA) declared that the year had already become one of the most extreme weather years in history (Morello 2011).

Water problems originate through press processes. The IPCC documents decreased stream discharge in the Colorado River Basin since 1950, and warming trends that have reduced the amount of winter snow in the mountain headwaters of the Colorado River and the timing of snowmelt (one to four weeks earlier in 2002 than in 1948). As the fraction of annual precipitation falling as rain rather than snow increases (an increase of 74 percent in the US western mountain states from 1949 to 2004), landslides and flooding occur more often. When more rapid rain-based runoff replaces slow release from snow melt, there is an increased need for greater reservoir capacity to capture and hold water for the dry season, which in turn complicates the availability of water for agricultural production, population and economic growth, and mining industries.

Climate disasters in one rural region may create opportunities for another rural region (Lal, Alavalapati, and Mercer 2011). The increase in the growing season, warmer temperatures, higher levels of CO_2, and more precipitation have increased agricultural productivity in the upper Midwest and Pacific Northwest, leading to record yields of corn, wheat, and soybeans. At the same time, other agricultural regions, like northern China, have experienced crop failures due to droughts and flooding. While price volatility in commodity markets is not unexpected, economists find that the volatility of the last few years seems attributable to an unusual mix of market inelasticities associated with public policies, scarcity of global land supply, and grain supply shortfalls caused by adverse weather events in major agricultural regions of the world (Diffenbaugh et al. 2012).

Persistent drought, high temperatures, and loss of forage have caused declines in cattle herds in the southwestern United States, giving a competitive advantage to northeastern US cattle and dairy producers who have experienced more precipitation, lower heat intensities, and abundant forage. Some analysts suggest that more intense heat in southern regions may shift crops northward, with pork and chicken production moving from the Southeast to the Northeast, and fruit tree production shifting from crops such as apples and pears, which require cold dormancy, to peaches, nuts, and vegetables. This might be beneficial to northeastern rural communities engaged in agriculture and forest related activities. The Southwest and Southeast may continue to experience water scarcity and increased energy costs as temperatures rise and precipitation patterns shift. Similar dynamics of regional losses and gains appear to be affecting non-farm, amenity-rich rural areas in the United States. The loss of southern ski areas in New England has arguably benefited ski areas in northernmost New England and the Colorado Rockies (Hamilton, Brown, and Keim 2007).

● CLIMATE IMPACTS ON THREE RURAL PLACES

Although climate scientists agree that the world is getting warmer, they are not certain about how global patterns impact local and regional conditions. Some parts of rural America are experiencing drought and heat stress; other parts are too wet from unprecedented flooding; and still others have had their town infrastructure as well as homes and lives destroyed by tornados, hurricanes, and melting permafrost. The following three case studies illustrate the range of variation in climactic impacts across different rural regions.

Wildfires in the Western Mountain States

The western United States has experienced a significant increase in wildfires during the summer months. Geographical analyses of the fires' locations have tied the increase in fires to smaller snowpacks at the higher elevations in the Rocky Mountains. More fires have begun at high elevations because with the smaller snowpack, these places have, in a press-like process, become drier and more prone to fire than they were during years with longer, colder, more snow-abundant winters (Westerling et al. 2006). Prolonged drought conditions have also accompanied the warming trends, and together they have contributed to substantial increases in the numbers of fires. The annual area burned has increased from less than 500,000 hectares prior to 1985 to more than 1,200,000 hectares after 2005 (Riley 2009). The number of large fires, pulse-like events, has also increased over the same two decade period at a rate of about seven fires a year. The increasing size of the fires stems in part from the drier conditions in which ignition events like lightning strikes occur.

The growing size of the fires stresses the firefighters who struggle to contain them. The firefighters, usually young men from rural backgrounds, work in small teams of five to fifteen people with responsibility for limited areas of forest. When large fires break out, forest service dispatchers bring in teams of firefighters from elsewhere in an attempt to bring the blazes under control before they destroy homes and endanger lives. In 2002, hundreds of firefighters from around the Southwest fought to subdue the Rodeo Chediski fire for several weeks. They brought it under control only after it burned almost 200,000 hectares of forest and destroyed 400 homes. The Wallow fire of 2011 burned for more than a month and consumed even more forest than the Chediski fire. Fires along the front range of the Rockies in Colorado during June and July 2012 destroyed comparable amounts of forests and hundreds of homes. The growth in the size of fires and the organizational demands of throwing together teams of unacquainted firefighters to fight large fires has exposed increased numbers of firefighters to dangerous situations (Desmond 2007). Even experienced teams are exposed to danger. In August 2013, nineteen members of one specially trained team of firefighters were killed in Arizona.

Cairo, Illinois, Levees, and the New Madrid Floodway

River flooding along the Mississippi and Ohio rivers is a pulse process that impacts adjacent agricultural lands and port infrastructure; exacerbates poverty, unemployment, and declining rural populations of the river towns; and heightens the racial tensions embedded in their social-political histories (Gellman and Roll 2011). Cairo, Illinois, situated at the confluence of the Ohio and Mississippi rivers, marks the divide between the Upper and Lower Mississippi River and is surrounded by an extensive system of levees and floodwalls. Formerly a vibrant river city and transportation hub with a population of 15,203 in 1920, Cairo in 2011 has a declining (2,900 inhabitants), aging (18 percent are sixty-five and older living alone), and impoverished (more than one-third of residents living below the poverty line) population.

The Mississippi and Ohio river bottomlands were historically riparian forests, transition ecosystems between the river and uplands that experienced the seasonal pulse of flooding with little damage to human settlements or activities (Morton and Olson 2013). These rivers also represented physical, social, economic, and symbolic divides between slave and free states, the opposing sides in the Civil War, and opposed positions about minority civil rights. Over 2.5 million acres of agricultural bottomlands in Missouri and Arkansas are protected by hundreds of miles of levees on the western border of the Lower Mississippi River south of Cairo.

Heavy snowmelt and rainfall ten times greater than average across the eastern half of the Mississippi watershed (~200,000 mi^2) in spring and summer of 2011 produced a flood to rival the destructive 1927 and 1937 floods and strained the capacity of the entire levee system (Camillo 2012; Olson and Morton 2013). On 2 May 2011, the USACE deliberately breached the Birds Point fuse plug levee in the New Madrid Floodway to protect the town of Cairo and other downstream cities from levee failures and loss of human life by diverting floodwaters into the agricultural lands of the Floodway. This decision reignited racially charged and class-based tensions between agricultural landowners and urban populations.

The 2011 Floodway decision altered agricultural lands as the force of the water rushed through the breaches and created hundreds of acres of deep gully fields and crater lakes, displaced tons of soil, and damaged irrigation equipment, farms, and homes.

Stream flows in the eastern United States have increased 25 percent in the last sixty years (Field et al. 2007) with increasing flows in winter and spring. While opening the Floodway reduced the water pressure on the Cairo levee system and enabled it to withstand the record flood, more than a year later depressions and sink holes in roads and on private properties remain; weakened levees and the floodwall require significant re-engineering and repair in preparation for future flood events; and the social and economic life of the rural town is struggling to recover. As a single 100- or 500-year event, the floods of 2011 might be considered a once-in-a-century or five-century event, except many of these rural communities have experienced one-hundred-year floods in both 2007 and 2008, suggesting a pattern of frequency and unpredictability not experienced before.

The Inuit in Alaskan Coastal Communities

Climate change exposes some North American populations to particularly large stresses. For example, the indigenous peoples of North America exhibit a special vulnerability to climate change. In disproportionate numbers, they reside in rural areas and engage in natural resource dependent occupations like fishing, trapping, or hunting, so markets with sources of supply all over the world do not buffer the impacts of climate change for American Indians as they do for urban residents. Further, a large proportion of them live in poverty, so they have fewer personal resources to draw upon in trying to cope with climate change. Some American Indians, like the Inuit, are particularly vulnerable to the effects of climate change given that the magnitude of change increases in the high latitudes where they live. Parts of Alaska have experienced an increase of four degrees Fahrenheit in average temperatures over the past thirty years.

The climate-related misfortunes visited upon the Inuit have come in various forms. Severe storms and melting permafrost have damaged the infrastructure in Inuit communities. Houses, roads, boardwalks, and even entire villages have begun to sink into the melting permafrost on which they were built. Ocean storms have eaten away at coastal shorelines and destroyed houses, docks, and fish-drying racks in coastal villages. Marine-based livelihoods have changed dramatically. Hunting and fishing regimens have been disrupted by thinning ice that has made it too dangerous to venture forth on the winter ice floes (Alaska Native Science Commission 2010) to fish or hunt for seals. Invasive species like spruce beetles have begun to decimate forests at higher rates. More generally, climate change has jeopardized the rural poor by destroying natural resources, like seal populations and fisheries, vital to Inuit livelihoods.

Climate change has had social as well as physical effects on American Indian communities. As one Inuit observer puts it, "the seasons are getting very fast and are all mixed up … These seasons are in too much of a hurry now." Another remarks, "Our elders tell us that our earth is getting old and needs to be replaced" (Alaska Native Science Commission 2010). These changes, occurring more or less simultaneously, have sharpened problems of food security in Inuit households as they have disrupted seasonal routines for obtaining foodstuffs (Ford and Beaumier 2011). Attachment to place among the Inuit has also declined with disruptions in subsistence routines and changes in landscapes brought about by melting permafrost (Willox et al. 2012). More generally, climate change has disabled the habitus surrounding Inuit activities, and, in so doing, has ushered in a period of rapid social change (Bourdieu 1977). These misfortunes test the resilience of Inuit communities. Because the Inuit do not have as much social and economic capital to draw upon as other populations, they have become more dependent on outside aid, with its complications, for their survival.

● THE MANY FACES OF CLIMATE CHANGE: VARYING PERCEPTIONS OF VULNERABILITY AND RISK

The varying forms that climate change takes in different locales coupled with the different scales at which people experience and visualize climate means that groups of people in different places perceive the threats very differently. The discourses surrounding climate change reflect these regional disparities in impacts. Discussions have focused on specific local experiences and emergency responses as well as planning to minimize future damages. Farmers in the upper Mid-west have invested in measures to cope with unusually large spring floods while ranchers in the southern Great Plains have explored ways to cope with historically unprecedented drought conditions, and residents of the western mountain states have expressed concern about the large increase in the number and scale of forest fires during the summer months. At a national scale, officials and academics have begun thinking in more concerted ways about extreme weather events and efficacious ways of addressing them.

Much of the discussion concerns the vulnerability of people to the adverse effects of climate change. A community's vulnerability varies with the magnitude of events, types of events, rates of change, community exposure, sensitivity to events, and adaptive capacity (Lal, Alavalapati, and Mercer 2011; Howden et al. 2007). In this highly variable context, climate scientists face major challenges when they try to communicate with non-specialist audiences about the risks and uncertainties associated with climate change (Pidgeon and Fischhoff 2011). The concept of risk means different things to different people. Expert judgments of risk stem from technical estimates while lay judgments of risk are sensitive to everyday perceptions of catastrophic potential, controllability, and threat to the future (Slovic 2009).

New discursive currents have entered agricultural communities. Many officials in larger agricultural NGOs now acknowledge the reality of climate change and assert the need to plan for it. The 25x'25 Alliance, a national organization of voluntary agricultural and forestry organizations with a goal to provide 25 percent of the nation's energy by 2025, has created a Climate Change Sub-committee to develop adaptation strategies to achieve its goal (Yoder 2012). Foresters may perceive the opportunity to sequester carbon and proactively engage in mitigation discussions and actions. Row crop agronomists have been more reticent to acknowledge climate change and are particularly resistant to mitigation efforts. The continuing absence of a consensus point of view is reflected in the results from a 2011 Iowa Farm and Rural Life Poll, in which neither the scientific consensus about the anthropogenic origins of climate change nor the denialist position received support from a majority of Iowa farmers (Arbuckle, Morton, and Hobbs 2013). Prescriptions for dealing with the problem vary accordingly. Many farmers do not want government action, believing that businesses and individuals are best suited to solve the problem. Those who believe climate change is happening, but is naturally caused, may not take adaptive actions for a variety of reasons including a fatalism that it is beyond their control (Pidgeon and Fischhoff 2011; Donner 2011).

Rural residents and scientists often offer dramatically different perspectives on climate change. Rural residents base their views on memories of past weather and are preoccupied with current weather (such as flooding, drought, shifts in seasonality). Scientists track large-scale global patterns and model scenarios of climate change decades into the future. The diversity of viewpoints has frustrated not just lay people but also scientists (Pidgeon and Fischhoff 2011). The challenge is how to communicate about complex scientific findings in a context of shifting and volatile discourses, and about current climate conditions in ways that prepare and protect rural peoples, their livelihoods, and their quality of life.

● RESILIENCE AND ADAPTATION IN RURAL AMERICA

The unprecedented numbers of extreme weather events in recent years have raised questions about the resilience of rural communities in the face of these disturbances. Communities of interest as well as communities of place have begun to respond to climate change in ways that should enable them to survive disturbances. In other instances where communities may not have the internal resources to cope with the changes, outside interventions have become more important to their survival.

Agribusinesses, farmers, land grant university experiment stations, and the United States Department of Agriculture (USDA) have all initiated lines of research intended to respond to anticipated and actual changes in temperature, precipitation, and atmospheric CO_2 concentration (Hatfield et al. 2011). In 2011, the USDA Agriculture and Food Research Initiative (2011) invested more than $113 million in research and extension programming related to climate change, agriculture, and forestry with foci on reducing greenhouse gas emissions (GHG), increasing carbon sequestration in agricultural and forest production systems, and preparing the nation's agriculture and forests to adapt to changing climates.

The range of adaptive strategies pursued by agricultural communities includes marketing as well as field management practices (see Box 26.2). For example, some farmers and foresters are particularly interested in carbon trading as it relates to climate mitigation and the sequestration of carbon to reduce atmospheric

Box 26.2: Producers of corn, rice, soybeans, and wheat (which provide 75 percent of calories consumed by the world's population; the United States provides about 23 percent of calories) are likely to experience the following disruptive changes related to weather and make adaptations:

1. A longer growing season means producers can plant earlier and can use longer season hybrids.

2. Wetter springs leave a smaller window of time to plant and increase the need for larger machinery.

3. More summer precipitation in the north central United States will support higher plant densities for higher yields and change management practices.

4. Wetter springs and summers are likely to lead to closer spacing of subsurface tile drainage and tiling of sloped surfaces.

5. Increased precipitation variability (flooding and drought) may alter management practices and increase the need for conservation structures and different crop varieties and breeds.

6. Increased changes in seasonal temperatures are likely to increase demand for new crop varieties and breeds, improved IPM practices, and pest-suppression technologies.

7. Higher humidity and more pathogens will lead to more problems with fall dry-down, a need for wider bean heads for faster harvest, and a shorter harvest period during daytime (e.g., because of dew period).

8. Drier autumns could result in delayed harvests to take advantage of natural dry downs condition and reduce fuel costs.

CO_2. This has led to increased interest in developing global carbon budgets and has accelerated evaluations of forest and land management impacts on vegetation and soil carbon dynamics and storage (Pan et al. 2011).

Other rural communities, in particular those that have few resources like the Inuit or that face large scale floods and fires, cannot possibly cope with these disturbances by themselves because they do not have the scale of services necessary to bring the floods and fires under control. Similarly, larger fires have led to more property damage, made restoration efforts increasingly expensive, and placed a large fiscal burden on governments. These events increase the magnitude of government transfer payments to rural regions and communities, both to counter the destructive climatic events and to restore productive activities in the burnt-over districts. In the words of one report, the "economic damage from severe weather has increased dramatically, due largely to increased value of the infrastructure at risk. Annual costs to North America have now reached tens of billions of dollars in damaged property and economic productivity" (Field et al. 2007, 619).

In this context, extreme weather events have elicited historically unprecedented relief efforts. In some instances, professions and NGOs have organized to deal with these contingencies—e.g., among fire fighters and relief groups. Higher-level authorities have also intervened. State level mobilizations and federal assistance programs (such as the Federal Emergency Management Agency and the USDA Risk Management Agency) have grown in scale. Disaster capitalist firms, some of them unscrupulous, have also sprung up (Klein 2007). Incremental social changes associated with migration and agricultural commodity price fluctuations now occur in a context increasingly marked by abrupt and disruptive changes following disasters that test the adaptive capacities of governing institutions at all scales. While outside interventions are crucial to efforts to restore basic services and sometimes the social fabric, such interventions inevitably exact a toll on the local autonomy of rural communities.

● CONCLUSIONS

Rural America is a repository of American wealth. It covers 80 percent of the land area and contains a significant portion of the nation's natural resource assets. For this reason rural places and peoples will shoulder the brunt of the direct impacts from climate change. Because the productivity of natural resources varies with changes in precipitation, heat, humidity, and seasonality, climate change has begun to disrupt well-established routines for utilizing natural resources. This dynamic makes rural communities more vulnerable than their urban counterparts to climate-change-related disruptions. Rural populations are vulnerable because they depend on natural resources for their livelihoods and because they have fewer social and economic resources to employ in recovering from weather related disasters.

A variety of local, state, and national initiatives, such as the United States Global Change Research Program (2012), promise to assist rural America in addressing the impacts of climate change. It is important that rural citizens not only be engaged with their local leadership in identifying issues and pro-actively seeking adaptive strategies, but also that public and private resources and partnerships outside rural communities be available. The ad hoc and fragmented field of responder organizations limits both timely and effective responses. Sunk costs and the expense of small-scale reconstruction make it difficult to repair and restore services; extractive industries with their boom-bust cycles preoccupy rural workers, and the growing prevalence of absentee ownership cripples the capacity of local governments to mobilize and respond to climate change (Majumdar and Bailey 2011). Only a comprehensive re-sponse, engaging all sectors and scales of society, would seem sufficient to meet these challenges.

How can rural sociologists contribute to this effort? First, adaptation to climate change will require multidisciplinary teams of researchers to formulate and then evaluate adaptations that appropriately and effectively address farmers' agricultural production practices, inland and coastal land use and water manage-ment, and rural communities' weather emergency action plans. Rural sociologists, trained to speak the languages of other scientific disciplines, could play pivotal roles in these team efforts. Second, the mitigation of GHG poses particularly acute challenges for rural residents because they have lower incomes than other Americans, so strategies that entail the purchase of expensive clean energy devices seem less affordable for rural populations. With their detailed knowledge of rural cultures and social structures, rural social scientists could make major contri-butions to these mitigation efforts. Third, climate change threatens Americans with far-reaching social transformations, and sociologists with their knowledge about these processes seem well positioned to aid communities in turning these moments of change into opportunities. Lastly, sociologists can facilitate public dialogue and help bridge the knowledge divide between the accepted science of changing climate conditions and the realities of adapting to and even affecting the course of climate change.

● ENDNOTES

1. This research was supported in part by the USDA-NIFA, Award No. 2011–68002–30190 "Cropping Systems Coordinated Agricultural Project (CAP): Climate Change, Mitigation, and Adaptation in Corn-Based Cropping Systems" and Iowa State University College of Agriculture and Life Sciences.

● REFERENCES

Alaska Native Science Commission. 2010. "Impact of Climate Change on Alaska Native Communities." Accessed 15 February 2012. http://www.nativescience.org/pubs/afn%20 2005%20impact%20of%20climate%20change%20on%20alaska%20native%20 communities. pdf.

Arbuckle, J.G., L.W. Morton, and J. Hobbs. 2013. "Farmer Beliefs and Concerns about Climate Change and Attitudes toward Adaptation and Mitigation: Evidence from Iowa." *Climatic Change* 118 (3–4): 551–63. http://dx.doi.org/10.1007/s10584-013-0700-0.

Associated Press. 2012. "Gulf to Great Lakes, Storms Leave Carnage." *Des Moines Register*, 3 March, front page.

Bourdieu, P. 1977. *Outline of a Theory of Practice*. Cambridge, UK: Cambridge University Press. http://dx.doi.org/10.1017/CBO9780511812507.

Boykoff, M. 2011. *Who Speaks for the Climate? Making Sense of Media Reporting about Climate Change*. Cambridge, UK: Cambridge University Press. http://dx.doi.org/10.1017/ CBO9780511978586.

Camillo, C.A. 2012. *Divine Providence: The 2011 Flood in the Mississippi River and Tributaries Project*. Vicksburg, MS: Mississippi River Commission.

Clayton, C. 2012. "Getting to the Heartland of the Climate Debate." *Progressive Farmer*, 17 February.

Collins, S.L., S.R. Carpenter, S.M. Swinton, D.E. Orenstein, D.L. Childers, T.L. Gragson, N.B. Grimm, J.M. Grove, S.L. Harlan, J.P. Kaye, et al. 2011. "An Integrated Conceptual Framework for Long-Term Social-Ecological Research." *Frontiers in Ecology and the Environment* 9 (6): 351–7. http://dx.doi.org/10.1890/100068.

Coumou, D., and S. Rahmstorf. 2012. "A Decade of Weather Extremes." *Nature Climate Change* 2: 491–6.

Desmond, M. 2007. *On the Fireline: Living and Dying with Wildland Firefighters.* Chicago, IL: University of Chicago Press. http://dx.doi.org/10.7208/chicago/9780226144078.001.0001.

Diffenbaugh, N.S., T.W. Hertel, M. Scherer, and M. Verma. 1 July 2012. "Response of Corn Markets to Climate Volatility under Alternative Energy Futures." *Nature Climate Change* 2: 514–18. Medline:23243468.

Donner, S.D. 2011. "Making the Climate a Part of the Human World." *Bulletin of the American Meteorological Society* 92 (10): 1297–302. http://dx.doi.org/10.1175/2011BAMS3219.1.

Field, C.B., L.D. Mortsch, M. Braklacich, D.L. Forbes, P. Kovacs, J.A. Patz, S.W. Running, and M.J. Scott. 2007. "Climate Change 2007: Impacts, Adaptation and Vulnerability." In *Contribution of Working Group II to the Fourth Assessment Report of the Intergovernmental*

Panel on Climate Change, ed. M.L. Parry, O.F. Canziani, J.P. Palutikof, P.J. van der Linden, and C.E. Hanson, 617–52. Cambridge, UK: Cambridge University Press.

Ford, James D., and M. Beaumier. 2011. "Feeding the Family during Times of Stress: Experience and Determinants of Food Insecurity in an Inuit Ccommunity." *Geographical Journal* 177 (1): 44–61. http://dx.doi.org/10.1111/j.1475-4959.2010.00374.x. Medline:21560272.

Gellman, E.S., and J. Roll. 2011. *The Gospel of the Working Class.* Urbana-Champaign: University of Illinois Press.

Gleick, P. 2012. "Climate Change, Disbelief, and the Collision between Human and Geologic Time." *Forbes*, 16 January. http://www.forbes.com/sites/petergleick/2012/01/16/climate-change-disbelief-and-the-collision-between-human-and-geologic-time/.

Hamilton, L.C., B.C. Brown, and B.D. Keim. 2007. "Ski Areas, Weather and Climate: Time Series Models for New England Case Studies." *International Journal of Climatology* 27 (15): 2113–24. http://dx.doi.org/10.1002/joc.1502.

Hansen, J., M. Sato, and R. Ruedy. 2012. "Perception of Climate Change." Proceedings of the National Academy of Sciences, early edition. http://www.pnas.org/content/109/37/E2415.

Hatfield, J.L., K.J. Boote, B.A. Kimball, L.H. Zisha, R.C. Izaurralde, D. Ort, A.M. Thomson, and D. Wolfe. 2011. "Climate Impacts on Agriculture: Implications for Crop Production." *Agronomy Journal* 103 (2): 351–70.

Howden, S.M., J.F. Soussana, F.N. Tubiello, N. Chhetri, M. Dunlop, and H. Meinke. 11 December 2007. "Adapting Agriculture to Climate Change." *Proceedings of the National Academy of Sciences of the United States of America* 104 (50): 19691–6. http://dx.doi.org/10.1073/pnas.0701890104. Medline:18077402.

IPCC. 2001. *Climate Change 2001: Synthesis Report. A Contribution of Working Groups I, II, and III to the Third Assessment Report of the Intergovernmental panel on Climate Change.* Cambridge, UK: Cambridge University Press.

IPCC. 2007. *Climate Change 2007: Synthesis Report. Contribution of Working Groups I, II, and III to the Fourth Assessment Report of the Intergovernmental Panel on Climate Change.* Cambridge, UK: Cambridge University Press.

Jackson, L., M. van Noordwijk, J. Bengtsson, W. Foster, L. Lipper, M. Pulleman, M. Said, J. Snaddon, and R. Vodouhe. 2010. "Biodiversity and Agricultural Sustainability: From Assessment to Adaptive Management." *Current Opinion in Environmental Sustainability* 2 (1–2): 80–87. http://dx.doi.org/10.1016/j.cosust.2010.02.007.

Klein, N. 2007. *The Shock Doctrine: The Rise of Disaster Capitalism.* New York: Henry Holt.

Koppel, N. 2012. "Texas Rice Farmers Lose their Water." *Wall Street Journal*, 3–4 March, A3.

Lal, P., J.R. Alavalapati, and E.D. Mercer. 2011. "Socio-economic Impacts of Climate Change on Rural United States." *Mitigation and Adaptation Strategies for Global Change* 16 (7): 819–44. http://dx.doi.org/10.1007/s11027-011-9295-9.

Leiserowitz, A., E. Maibach, C. Roser-Renouf, and N. Smith. 2011. "Global Warming's Six Americas." May. Yale University and George Mason University. New Haven, CT: Yale Project on Climate Change and Communication.

Majumdar, M., and C. Bailey. 2011. "Relationship between Absentee Landownership and Quality of Life in Alabama." Paper presented at the annual meeting of the Rural Sociological Society, Boise, ID, July 2011.

McCright, A.M., and R.E. Dunlap. 2011. "The Politicization of Climate Change and Polarization in the American Public's Views of Global Warming 2001–2010." *Sociological Quarterly* 52 (2): 155–94. http://dx.doi.org/10.1111/j.1533-8525.2011.01198.x.

Morello, L. 2011. "NOAA Makes it Official: 2011 among Most Extreme Weather Years in History." *Scientific American*, June 17. http://www.scientificamerican.com/article.cfm?id=noaa-makes-2011-most-extreme-weather-year.

Morton, L.W., and K.R. Olson. 2013. "Birds Point-New Madrid Floodway: Redesign, Reconstruction, and Restoration." *Journal of Soil and Water Conservation* 68 (2): 35A–40A. http://dx.doi.org/10.2489/jswc.68.2.35A.

Olson, K.R., and L.W. Morton. 2013. "Soil and Crop Damages as a Result of Levee Breaches on Ohio and Mississippi Rivers." *Journal of Earth Science and Engineering* 3 (3): 1–20.

Pan, Y., R.A. Birdsey, J. Fang, R. Houghton, P.E. Kauppi, W.A. Kurz, O.L. Phillips, A. Shvidenko, S.L. Lewis, J.G. Canadell, et al. 19 August 2011. "A Large and Persistent Carbon Sink in the World's Forests." *Science* 333 (6,045): 988–93. http://dx.doi.org/10.1126/science.1201609. Medline:21764754

Pidgeon, N., and B. Fischhoff. 2011. "The Role of Social and Decision Sciences in Communicating Uncertain Climate Risks." *Nature Climate Change* 1 (1): 35–41. http://dx.doi.org/10.1038/nclimate1080.

Riley, K. 2009. "Measuring Trends in Wildfire Severity and Magnitude." Presentation at the 4th International Fire Ecology Conference, Savannah, GA.

Slovic, P. 2009. *The Perception of Risk*. Sterling, VA: Earthscan Publications Ltd.

United States Global Change Research Program. 2012. Accessed 13 March 2012. http://www.globalchange.gov/.

United States Global Change Research Program. 2012. *Our Changing Planet*. Annual Report to Congress. Washington, DC.

USDA Agriculture and Food Research Initiative. 2011. "NIFA Announces Grant to Study the Effects of Climate Change on Agricultural and Forest Production." 18 February. http://www.nifa.usda.gov/newsroom/news/2011news/02181_climate_change_cap.html.

USDA Climate and Man Yearbook. 1941. "House document No. 27, 77th Congress, 1st Session." United States Department of Agriculture, Washington, DC, US Government Printing Office.

Walthall, C., J. Hatfield, P. Backlund, L. Lengnick, E. Marshall, M. Walsh, S. Adkins, M. Aillery, E.A. Ainsworth, C. Ammann, et al. 2012. *Climate Change and Agriculture in the United States: Effects and Adaptation*. USDA Technical Bulletin 1935, Washington, DC.

Weber, E.U., and P.C. Stern. May–June 2011. "Public Understanding of Climate Change in the United States." *American Psychologist* 66 (4): 315–28. http://dx.doi.org/10.1037/a0023253. Medline:21553956.

Westerling, A.L., H.G. Hidalgo, D.R. Cayan, and T.W. Swetnam. 18 August 2006. "Warming and Earlier Spring Increase Western U.S. Forest Wildfire Activity." *Science* 313 (5,789): 940–43. http://dx.doi.org/10.1126/science.1128834. Medline:16825536.

Willox, A. Cunsolo, S.L. Harper, J.D. Ford, K. Landman, K. Houle, and V.L. Edge, and the Rigolet Inuit Community Government. August 2012. "'From This Place and of This Place:' Climate

Change, Sense of Place, and Health in Nunatsiavut, Canada." *Social Science & Medicine* 75 (3): 538–47. http://dx.doi.org/10.1016/j.socscimed.2012.03.043. Medline:22595069.

Winter, A. 2010. "Farm Bureau Fires Back against Climate Bill's 'Power Grab.'" *New York Times*, January 11. http://www.nytimes.com/cwire/2010/01/11/11climatewire-farm-bureau-fires-back-against-climate-bills-93758.html.

Yoder, F. January 2012. "Agriculture and Forestry in a Changing Climate: The Road Ahead." A product of the 25x'25 Adaptation Initiative.

CHAPTER 27

Native Americans and Social and Environmental Justice: Implications for Criminology

By Michael J. Lynch and Paul B. Stretesky

● INTRODUCTION

Despite attending to social and economic justice issues, criminologists have said little about environmental justice (Zilney, McGurrin, and Zahran, especially among underrepresented populations such as Native Americans (for an exception, see Seis, 1996).[1] This review examines the social, economic, and environmental injustices Native Americans face by drawing on health and medical literature.[2]

Environmental injustice occurs when minority groups and/or the poor are excluded from environmental decision-making (including methods of production), or are disproportionately exposed to environmental hazards (Stretesky and Hogan, 1998). Environmental injustice against Native Americans occurs, in part, because of social and economic injustice. Brooks (1998) argues that contemporary injustice against Native Americans is an extension of the historical process of genocide, and should be understood within that framework.[3] The health care and medical literature provides considerable support for Brooks' contention. This review focuses on five examples of environmental injustice against Native Americans, using as empirical documentation the Akwesasne Nation, Church Rock (New Mexico), the Four Comers Region of the United States, the upper West or Plains area, and Prince William Sound (Alaska). To put that injustice in context, we begin with a review of some general information on Native American populations and then summarize general indicators of social and economic well-being.

Native American Lands and Population

Native populations exist throughout the United States, living both inside and outside reservations, and are extensively surveyed by *The Harvard Project on American Indian Development* (Taylor and Kalt, 2005). The 2000 Census indicates there were 310 reservations and 40 Indian statistical areas (ISA) in the continental United States, which were home to 511,000 American Indians, or 21.3 percent of the estimated 2.4 million self-identified American Indian/Native Americans (*Ibid.:* 2). An additional 97,000 Native Americans live in Alaska, 3,000 in Hawaii, and 229,000 in Indian Statistical Areas (ISAs). The population of Native Americans living outside reservations and ISAs is significantly larger (1.6 million) than the Native populations living on reservations and ISAs (0.8 million). The majority of America Indians living on reservations and ISAs (66 percent) live on non-gaming reservation, which are typically the most economically and socially disadvantaged (*Ibid.*).

Social and economic inequality is widespread among Native Americans. That inequality helps to explain the degree and extent of environmental injustice experienced in Native American communities. The environmental justice literature is replete with findings indicating an association between income and measures of environmental injustice, a relationship that could be expected to extend to Native Americans given their deprived economic standing. Below we review several relevant indicators of social and economic inequality among Native Americans in comparison to other racial groups as described in Taylor and Kalt's national study.

Poverty and Income Unemployment. Per capita income for Native Americans is approximately one-half the U.S. mean. American Indians living on reservations fare far worse than those who live outside the reservations on this measure. American Indians who live on reservations have a per capita income level that is 33 percent of the U.S. average, compared to 45 percent for those living on gaming reservations and 35 percent for those who live on non-gaming reservations (*Ibid.*: 8).

Per capita income for American Indians on reservations is inflated by the inclusion of ISA populations, since those who live on ISAs earn, on average, more than other Native Americans. If ISA residents are excluded, the per capita income of American Indians on non-gaming ($7,365) and gaming ($8,466) reservations compares poorly to mean per capita income for all races ($21,587) (*Ibid.*: 11). These data imply that legalized gaming has not contributed significantly to Native Americans' income or to economic equity, and may be detrimental with respect to related social problems such as alcohol use and crime.

As a group, the Navajo, who comprise the largest proportion of American Indians living on reservations, suffer from significant poverty. Excluding them from the computation tells a dramatic story with respect to American Indian per capita income. Once Navajo are excluded, the per capita income of American Indians on gaming reservations *rises* by 19.7 percent, or $1,451 (*Ibid.*: 12–13).

Poverty rates for Native Americans are substantial: 37 percent on no gaming reservations and 27 percent on gaming reservations, significantly higher than the nine percent national average for all U.S. families (*Ibid.*: 20). These findings extend to child poverty indicators as well (*Ibid.*: 21–23).

American Indian poverty and per capita and family income differences have a significant relationship to unemployment across racial groups. In 2000, American Indians living on non-gaming (22 percent) and gaming reservations (15 percent) experienced significantly higher official unemployment than the U.S. mean unemployment rate for that year (6 percent) (*Ibid.*: 27–30). Labor force participation rates for Native Americans are also lower (47 percent no gaming, 59 percent gaming) when compared to other races (69 percent).

Education. Educational achievement and access provide another measure of social inequality. American Indians are overrepresented among those with less than a ninth-grade educational attainment level (*Ibid.*: 44). On non-gaming reservations, 19 percent have less than a ninth-grade education in contrast to eight percent for those living on gaming reservations, with the latter figure being equivalent to the U.S. average (*Ibid.:* 44). There are significant educational differences in relation to holding college degrees: these are held by 11 percent of American Indians living on non-gaming reservation, 16 percent of those living on gaming reservations, and 31 percent of the U.S. population (*Ibid.:* 40–41). Educational difference, then, partially explains economic differences across racial groups.

Housing Conditions. Inequality can also be measured by quality of life indicators. One such indicator is crowded housing, defined as the number of occupants per room, with more than one occupant per room defined as crowded (Taylor and Kalt, 2005). Twenty-four percent of American Indians living on non-gaming reservations reside in crowded housing compared to 10 percent on gaming reservations, and six percent of the general population (*Ibid.:* 34–35).

Lack of indoor plumbing and lack of a complete kitchen are other quality of life indicators. Twenty-four percent of housing units in no gaming reservations lack indoor plumbing compared to three percent on gaming reservations and onepercent of all U.S. housing (*Ibid.:* 36–37). Among American Indians living on non-gaming reservations, 26 percent of housing units lack a complete kitchen, compared to three percent for those on gaming reservation and one percent for other races (*Ibid.:* 38–39).

Health and Health Care. Access to health care and adequate health conditions are important indicators of social and economic justice. Native populations fare quite poorly on these measures compared to other races. Recent research indicates that there are significantly higher rates of sexually transmitted diseases among American Indians teens aged 15 to 19 in Arizona (Winscott, Taylor, and Kenney, 2010). This finding extends to other sexually transmitted diseases (e.g., HIV; see Duran et al., 2010) and Native populations.

Especially significant problems for Native populations are a high incidence of cancer and lack of access to cancer treatment, screening, and prevention services (Guadagnolo, Cina, et al., 2009). There is also evidence of disparities in cancer mortality between Native and other populations (Lanier et al., 2008). Due to poor delivery of cancer services, Native Americans are usually diagnosed with cancers at more advanced stages of the disease. This outcome relates to lack of access to medical services, Native American cultural values, and lower levels of cancer screening knowledge (Guadagnolo, Peteriet et al., 2009). Similar conclusions apply to a variety of forms of cancer among Native Americans, including colorectal (Perdue et al., 2008; Schumacher et al., 2008), gallbladder (Lemrow et al., 2008), primary liver (Jim et al., 2008), cervical (Becker et al., 2008), gastric (Wiggins et al., 2008), and kidney cancer (Wilson et al., 2008)—though there is significant regional variation among these rates (Wiggins et al., 2008).

Numerous studies have raised concerns about the incidence of specific forms of cancer among particular groups of Native Americans. For example, elevated rates of lung cancer remain a concern among American Indian miners exposed to uranium in Colorado. These rates have not declined substantially since the 1980s, even though mining employment for Native Americans has decreased (Schubauer, Daniels, and Pinkerton, 2009). Radiation exposure has also been associated with higher rates of pancreatic cancer among American Indians when compared to whites (Reddy and Bhutani, 2009). Breast cancer incidence, survival, and mortality have been increasing among Native populations. Compared to other minority groups, Native women have the lowest levels of mammogram screening. This pattern may reflect cultural or economic differences, since women of lower socioeconomic standing are more likely to present with late-stage cancer (Baquet and Commiskey, 2000); or it may be due to limited access to medical care and treatment on reservations and in rural areas (Eberth, Huber, and Rene, 2010).

Cardiovascular disease is also a significant problem among Native Americans. A recent study of a sample of American Indians and Native Alaskans indicated that over a 10-year period, while risk factors for cardiovascular disease (i.e., diabetes, obesity, and hypertension) remained constant, cardiovascular disease increased by as much as 26 percent (Jerrigan et al., 2010). This result invalidates the traditional medical assumption that such diseases are related to individual behavioral choices and risk factors. Since the distribution of the disease correlates remained constant over time, other causes for the increase must be suspected. Research suggests that certain chemical pollutants may be the culprits, and that structural factors may be correlated with heart disease among Native populations. For example, Weaver (2010) related cancer outcomes to the prevalence of toxins in the environment, rather than to the "usual" medical suspects—diet, smoking, and alcohol intake. Because Native populations rely more heavily on hunting and fishing for subsistence than other groups do, Weaver has argued that the food chain to which Natives have access is widely contaminated by toxins found in and around the reservations. The connection between environmental toxins and disease and other negative outcomes in Native communities is reviewed more extensively below.

Therefore, a number of strategies are needed to tackle these problems, especially policies that focus on elevating the economic status of Native populations. Unfortunately, medical researchers tend to propose more limited approaches, such as targeted clinical interventions designed to enhance access of American Indians to cancer screening protocols by increasing the delivery of services to this population (Guadagnolo, Cina, et al., 2009).

In sum, each measure reviewed above—per capita income, individual, family, and childhood poverty, unemployment, labor force participation, housing quality, and health care and disease—indicates that Native Americans fare much more poorly than other races. As a group, they face a variety of forms of social and economic inequality and injustice. There is significant regional variation in life conditions and these average differences may not represent the condition of all Native Americans. However, it is evident that Native Americans as a group are much more likely than other racial groups to live in conditions that can be described as unequal and unjust.

Environmental Justice

Native populations are exposed to a wide variety of environmental hazards and suffer extensive environmental injustice both in terms of production (e.g., dangerous mining operations) and of distribution (e.g., disposal of military weapons and waste). It is important to consider the occurrence of environmental hazards in Native American territories, since they affect the quality of life of Native populations and contribute to social and economic inequality, and in particular to health inequities and high disease rates.

Proximity to Toxic Hazards. In a study of the relationship between proximity to hazardous waste sites and occurrence of birth defects among 28,401 individuals born in California from 1983 to 1988, Orr and others (2002) found the strongest association between toxic exposure and congenital defects among Native American populations. Other research indicates that proximity to soil lead and lead dust pollution from mining waste poses a more significant health concern for American Indians than for other populations (Malcoe, 2002; see also Anderton, 1997, on Superfund sites; Bullard et al., 2007, on commercial toxic waste facilities). Gowda and Easterling (2000) discovered that environmental injustice also occurred in the planning stages of hazardous waste sites, which targeted Native American lands without any input from the population. Hooks and Smith (2004) examined the distribution of military nuclear waste and unexploded military ordinance, finding that Native American populations were more likely to be exposed to the dangerous conditions these sites present. In particular, Hooks and Smith argued that American Indians had been unequally exposed to the military waste produced by the Cold War, which was disposed of on reservations—resembling how low-income urban areas suffer from the legacy of toxic waste industries left behind in them (Kreig, 1995).

Toxic Hazards and Natural Resource Extraction. Another significant environmental justice issue for Native populations concerns the effects of natural resource extraction on lands inhabited by or in close proximity to Native communities. The extraction of natural resources has numerous environmental, social, and economic justice implications for Native communities, especially because the lands granted to Native Americans under reservation treaties were later discovered to store significant resources desired by corporations and the federal government. American Indian reservations, for example, hold large quantities of copper, oil, coal, and uranium (Churchill and LaDuke, 1992). To facilitate access to these resources, the federal government employed various mechanisms that disadvantaged Native Americans, including rescinding or modifying the treaties to retake control of the land, reorganizing American Indian forms of governance, and entering into coercive contract arrangements, a practice that has also been followed by the corporate mining sector (*Ibid.*; Forbes, 1979; LaDuke, 1979).

The following sections examine these health and environmental issues in five Native American communities: the Akwesasne Nation; Church Rock, New Mexico; the Four Comers Region; the upper West, or Plains area; and Prince William Sound, Alaska.

Environmental Justice and the Akwesasne Nation. Numerous studies of the consequences of environmental pollution have been undertaken on Akwesasne Nation territory, facilitated by the collaboration between researchers and the Akwesasne Task Force on the Environment. The Akwesasne Mohawks, who consist of approximately 12,000 members, inhabit upper-eastern New York and the lower portions of the Canadian provinces of Quebec and Ontario along the St. Lawrence, St. Regis, and Raquette rivers. Industrial pollution in this region is significant.

Pollution studies have uncovered various risks for the Akwesasne peoples, the local waterways, and the wildlife that are integral to Akwesasne traditional subsistence lifestyles. Industrial pollution contributes to high levels of exposure to polychlorinated biphenyls (PCBs), hexachlorobenzene (HCB), and p,p'-dichlorophenyldichloroethylene (p,p'-DDE) (Manning, 2005). De Solla and others (2000) found elevated levels of PCBs and organochlorine pesticide in wild snapping turtle eggs, which are part of the Akwesasne diet. Exposure studies among the Akwesasne have confirmed PCB levels well above the national average (Haase et al., 2009) and discussed their impact on Akwesasne women and infants (Fitzgerald et al., 1998, 2004; Hwang, Fitzgerald, and Bush, 1996).

The prevalence of organic pollutants in the Akwesasne region is important for several reasons. PCBs are classified as probable carcinogens by the U.S. Environmental Protection Agency and as reasonably likely carcinogens by the National Toxicological Program. Studies indicate a link between PCB exposure and cancers of the liver, gallbladder, gastrointestinal tract, brain, and possibly breast and skin (Johnson et al., 1999). Children of women exposed to PCBs during pregnancy experience significant neurological and motor skill deficiencies, low IQ, poor short-term memory, lower birth weight, and reduced head size (Jacobson and Jacobson, 1996; Johnson et al., 1999). PCBs also disrupt the normal functioning of the hormonal system, including the thyroid (Chevrier et al., 2008) and immune system (Schell et al., 2003), and are suspected of influencing coronary heart disease (Goncharov et al., 2009, 2008; Hay and Tarrel, 1997; Sergeev and Carpenter, 2005). Organochlorine pesticide exposure, also widespread in this region, is associated with additional health consequences, including pancreatic cancer, non-Hodgkins lymphoma, breast cancer, preterm births, neurological defects, and memory, attention, and verbal skills deficits in children (Chevrier et al., 2008; Cohn et al., 2007; Garabrant et al., 1992; Jurewicz and Hanke, 2008; Korrick and Sagiv, 2008; Longnecker et al., 2001; Rathore et al., 2002).

Other studies also indicate the direct effects of persistent organic pollutants on the Akwesasne (DeCaprio et al., 2005; Kinney et al., 1997).[4] Two important studies by Newman and others (2009, 2006) documented a measurable decline in cognitive functioning, including long-term memory, comprehension, and knowledge, which "provides evidence of subtle negative effects of PCB exposure" (Newman et al., 2009: 439–445). Other studies confirm the hormonal effects of PCBs among the Akwesasne, including early menarches (Denham et al., 2005), low serum testosterone levels among Akwesasne men (Goncharov et al., 2009), and the occurrence of diabetes (Codru et al., 2007) and thyroid disease (Sukdolova et al., 2000; but see also Schell et al., 2004).

A series of studies examined the relationship between fish eating and PCB exposure among the Akwesasne (Fitzgerald et al., 1996). These findings indicated elevated levels of PCBs among occupationally exposed men (Fitzgerald et al., 2004, 2001, 1998, 1995). and in relation to fish eating for men (Fitzgerald et al., 1999, 1996) and women (Fitzgerald et al. 1998, 1995). Similar relationships have been found for pregnant women and breast-feeding mothers, which is especially troubling since PCB contamination can be passed from mother to child during pregnancy and breast feeding (Fitzgerald et al., 2004, 2001, 1998, 1995).

The Church Rock Nuclear Spill. On July 16, 1979, the largest yet most neglected nuclear accident in U.S. history (1,100 tons and 95 million gallons of nuclear waste) occurred on the Navajo reservation at the United Nuclear Corporation facility in Church Rock, New Mexico (Brugge, deLemos, and Bui, 2007). The spill was caused by a defect in the earthen dam system used to contain nuclear mine mill wastes that was known to United Nuclear's executives and to federal and state investigators (*Ibid.*: 1598).

Church Rock is a small Navajo community with a population of 1,633 in 1980 (U.S. census). Approximately 12 percent of that population was employed in uranium mining. Given the low income of the community and its dependence on the Puerco River as a water source, the extensive groundwater contamination produced by the incident had numerous consequences for the Navajo community. Even before the spill, the Church Rock population had experienced significant health problems from uranium exposure (Brugge, deLemos, and Bui, 2007).

Following the spill, United Nuclear claimed financial hardship, petitioned the federal government to resume operations, and was granted that request. It continued to use the damaged retention and burrow pits. Ongoing use of these unlined retention areas produced extensive groundwater contamination, and by 1983 Church Rock was added to the U.S. EPA's National Priorities list as a Superfund site. In 1982, United Nuclear suspended work at the facility, which never reopened, leading to immediate, long-term unemployment for members of the Church Rock community. The consequences of the Church Rock spill have never been adequately addressed.

Recent studies by deLemos et al. (2009) detail some concerns associated with the spill. For example, rates of kidney disease—a condition caused by uranium exposure—among the Navajo are three times higher than the age-adjusted rate for the U.S. population. Several related conditions may be responsible. For example, between 50 and 80 percent of Navajo living in the area obtained water from unregulated sources, indicating that they were potentially accessing water sources contaminated by the spill and by the general uranium mining operation. DeLemos and colleagues also note that some Navajo residences are located within a few hundred feet of uranium mining waste, and that there is contamination in the Navajo's food chain and livestock.

Church Rock is the best known of the uranium mining accidents that affected this region. According to Quartaroli (2002), the U.S. Nuclear Regulatory Commission acknowledges at least 10 additional incidents in this region between 1959 and 1977. In addition, a 1984 flash flood caused four tons of high-grade uranium ore to wash into the Colorado River and Kanab Creek. In Moab, Utah, the 130-acre mine tailing site left by Atlas Mining leaks 57,000 gallons of radioactive contamination into the Colorado River each day. And Ship Rock, New Mexico, is the site of a 72-acre, 1.7-ton pile of mine tailings (see below).

The health consequences of exposure to uranium, while not well studied among Native populations in this area, are well known. Uranium exposure among Native Americans has been linked to elevated rates of lung cancer among the occupationally exposed (Brugge and Goble, 2002) and to a variety of diseases among American Indians in nuclear test areas (Dawson and Madsen, 1995; Eichstaedt, 1994; Frohmberg et al., 2000; Shields et al., 1992; U.S. Environmental Protection Agency, 2006).

Uranium Mining in the Four Corners Region. The uranium exposure risk for Native Americans goes beyond nuclear accidents. In the Four Corners region (southwest Colorado, northwestern New Mexico, northeastern Arizona, and southeastern Utah), the site of the largest uranium mining endeavors initiated toward the end of World War I, uranium exposure is linked to mining waste remains. Mining here accelerated from the 1940s through the 1960s, facilitated by new mining methods, government incentives for uranium prospecting and deposit discoveries, and guaranteed minimum ore prices (Quartaroli, 2002). Only in the 1960s did health officials and researchers begin to recognize these problems.

The Navajo probably understood little about uranium mining and its effects, because as Brugge and Goble (2002: 1411) note, they lived in relative isolation, and many spoke Native languages that did not contain a word for radiation. In the early 1960s, the first cases of lung cancer among Navajo uranium miners surfaced (Brugge and Goble, 2002:1415; see also Brugge, Benally, and Yazzie-Lewis, 2006).

At these sites, mining processes produced "yellow cake," or enriched uranium that results from discarding low-grade ore and mining extracts. This creates extensive mine waste or mine tailings, since it takes one ton of uranium ore to produce 2.24 ounces of yellow cake (LaDuke, 1979). Kerr McGee's Ship Rock mining operation left behind 71 acres of highly radioactive mine tailings just 60 feet from the San Juan River *(Ibid.)*. The legality of the uranium mining and waste disposal process in the Four Comers area has been questioned. In 1977, for example, the Department of the Interior waived 13 protective regulations to grant Exxon a mining lease on 625 square miles of the Navajo reservation *(Ibid.)*.

Several studies speak to the issue of toxic exposure among American Indians who worked in the uranium extraction industry (Dawson, 1992; Dawson and Madsen, 1995; Gilliland et al., 2000; Roscoe et al., 1995). Dawson interviewed 55 Navajo uranium workers in Arizona and New Mexico. Several workers claimed to have been uninformed about the dangers of uranium mining radiation exposure. In hindsight, they said, the lack or withholding of relevant safety information lead them to feel betrayed by the government and unable to make rational decisions about employment opportunities or their health. Roscoe and other's (1995) postmortality examination of 757 Navajo uranium miners from the Colorado Plateau offers evidence of the extent of this problem. They found elevated rates of lung cancer, tuberculosis, pneumoconiosis, and other respiratory diseases. Nearly 25 years after their last occupational exposure, Navajo miners continued to face excessive mortality risks from these diseases.

In their study of uranium exposure effects, Raymond–Whish and others (2007) found that uranium disrupts endocrine systems. They related these results to the health of American Indians in the Four Corners region. Of particular concern are the estimated 1300 abandoned uranium mines there (Raymond–Whish et al., 2007: 1711), which pollute the air, water, soil, and food chain (Brugge and Goble, 2002). As Raymond–Whish and others (2007) point out, the Oak Ridge National Laboratories estimated that 10,000 gallons of uranium-laced water leaks into the Colorado River every day. Forty percent of tested water sources contain uranium in excess of EPA standards, some with concentration 38 times higher than standards allow, while at least one-half of the Navajo obtain drinking water from unregulated, non-municipal water systems.

Shields and others' examination of birth defects (1992), stillbirths, and other adverse pregnancy outcomes among 13,329 Navajos born in the Ship Rock area between 1964 and 1981 revealed the presence of 320 different congenital defects. Other research has revealed the adverse psychological effects of radioactive exposure (Markstrom and Charley, 2003).

Uranium Mining in Upper-Western Native Lands. Uranium mining has had notable impacts on American Indians and reservations in South and North Dakota, Wyoming, and Montana. Few studies have examined the effects of uranium mining on Native Americans in these locations, despite the extensive criticism of mining and federal and corporate policies affecting Native Americans there (Churchill, 1999). In recent years, Native populations have collected and posted data on the extent of the uranium problem *(www.eaglerocktradingpost. com/uranium.htmtm)*. In Cave Hill, South Dakota, the Grand River is affected by mine runoff from 89 abandoned mines. At one mine, the radioactivity level is 120,000 times above the regional background levels. Mine runoff also affects the Cheyenne River Indian Reservation, the Morreau River, and several Pine Ridge Indian Reservations. Dragnet studies on the Cheyenne River confirm the effects of radiation on local wildlife, and have lead to the erection of radioactivity warning signs along the river near Hermosa, South Dakota *(www.de/endblackhills. org)*. According to the South Dakota Cancer Report (2003), counties on the Pine Ridge have a "significantly higher rate of cancer, diabetes, and infant mortality than the SD state average for the time period of 2001–2005," when cancers declined for white residents and increased for Native Americans.[5] American

Indians believe President Nixon's secret 1972 Executive Order declaring this four-state region a "National Sacrifice Area" is responsible for the problems *(www. eaglerocktradingpost.com/uranium.htm)*.

Exxon Valdez Oil Spill and Native Americans. Fossil fuel extraction, processing, and transportation significantly affects Native American communities in many locations, contaminating Native American water sources and exposing local populations to various chemicals (Grahame and Sisk, 2002). Ironically, although significant coal reserves are located on Native American lands, many Native Americans lack access to electricity *(Ibid.)*. The *Valdez* represented the largest shipping oil spill in U.S. history (258,000 barrels of oil or 10.8 million gallons). This March 1989 accident affected 1,200 miles of coastline and 15 Native Alaskan communities in Prince William Sound, Alaska (Davis, 2010). A number of studies have examined the effect of the oil spill on Native Alaskan communities and diverse ethnic groups (Palinkas et al., 2004, 1993, 1992; Palinkas, Peterson, and Downs, 1993; U.S. Department of the Interior, 1990). Sufficient evidence exists to examine its environmental justice impact on Native Alaskan communities. Of particular importance is that the spill produced a decline in subsistence-based economic activities such as fishing, as well as adverse effects on mental health and drug and alcohol use among Native Alaskans (Dyer, Gill, and Picou, 1992; Picou and Gill, 1996; Picou et al., 1992). Dyer (1993) noted that the patterns of stress produced by the oil spill have long-term consequences for Native communities because of loss of tradition, a decline in subsistence activities, and eroded traditional social support mechanisms and networks. Supporting this conclusion, Palinkas and others (2004) found elevated indicators of post-traumatic stress disorder among both Alaskan Natives and whites.

At the time of the oil spill, a study of social life in the Alaskan villages in the Prince William Sound area had been underway since 1986. Following the spill, the researchers expanded the study to examine its effects on local communities. This study revealed that residents perceived a significant decline in the availability and quality of natural resources, and that these perceptions were related to proximity to the spill and to the extent to which communities relied on local natural resources for subsistence and employment. Of particular concern was the effect of the spill on employment in the fishing industry. Fall and Field's study among 2,200 Alaskan Natives in 10 of 15 affected communities found that fishing catches declined by as much as 77 percent after the spill (Fall and Field, 1996; see also Fall et al., 2001). Native Alaskan's reliance on local fish consumption declined due to fears related to the effect of the oil spill on local fish populations. A three-year task force study that examined tissue samples from fish, marine mammals, and invertebrates concluded that fish but not invertebrates were safe to consume. Following its release, Native Alaskan reliance on subsistence fishing increased despite continued fears. Such fears appear to be well founded. More than a decade after the incident, evidence of the spill remained on beach surfaces where weathered, hardened oil could be found, and below beach surfaces, where liquid oil deposits are waiting to be unearthed by erosion *(wwwxifsc.noaa.gov/ Quarterly/jas2001/feature_JasOl htm)*.

Discussion and Implications for Criminologists

American Indians are exposed to a variety of social, economic, and environmental injustices. They are among the poorest populations in the United States, suffer from hypersegregation, live in inadequate housing, lack access to educational and life resources other groups take for granted, have a higher incidence of a number of diseases, lack access to adequate medical screening and treatment, and have experienced a long historical process that reduced Native landholdings to a fraction of their "original" size. Taken together, these conditions of life have a strong impact on the average life course of Native Americans. Moreover, these conditions are evidence of a structural injustice against Native populations, amounting to a long- lasting social and economic war that can be described as a long-term act of genocide.

Why have criminologists failed to address those concerns and issues? Part of the answer lies in the effect of mainstream cultural practices on criminological discourse. Disciplines are not immune from the effects of larger structural practices and patterns, unless adherents in those disciplines make a concerted effort to address, undermine, and correct those influences. In the case of Native Americans, that has not occurred within criminology.[6] Beyond external structural influences, factors internal to the discipline of criminology also promote the neglect of Native population concerns and problems.

Despite long-entrenched criticisms from radical criminologists of its orientation, criminology has been less concerned with correcting and addressing injustice than with explaining the causes of crime. Its frame of reference has been individual characteristics and defects and its policies have sought to improve the efficiency of criminal justice responses, so as to reduce crime. Beginning in the early 1970s, Herman and Julia Schwendinger, among others, set out an alternative radical definition of crime that also included injustice. The forms of injustice they describe as crimes are evident in the cases reviewed above. Yet, even among radical/critical criminologists, the injustice experienced by Native Americans has received little attention.

In general terms, criminology's disciplinary preference for individual-level explanations of crime precludes efforts to understand how structural forces such as history, economy, and social and political factors affect both crime and justice. To be sure, several minority groups experience social, economic, and environmental injustice. Minority communities that experience environmental injustice are also likely to be located at the lower end of the economic spectrum, to live in substandard housing, to show elevated rates of poverty and unemployment, and to have reduced access to medical treatment—or in the traditional language of sociology and criminology, to experience deficits in social, economic, and cultural capital. With respect to American Indians, forced cultural exclusion and assimilation, hypersegregation, and genocide intersect to create a unique contextual situation.

In Native communities subject to environmental injustice, the origins of exposure to toxic hazards relate to the wealth of natural resources found beneath their lands. Native cultural values treat these lands and resources much differently than predominant capitalist values do (Seis, 1996), and the cultural reverence for nature in Native communities clashes with the exploitive, monetary values of capitalism. With the aid of the U.S. government, capital has treated Native lands in the same way it that treats Third World areas—as ripe for resource exploitation. Once capital's foothold is established, the exploitation and exportation of resources accelerate, leaving little behind, including capital. Instead, capital leaves behind a depleted resource base and widespread environmental problems that exceed the economic ability of Native communities to remediate them. This outcome illustrates a form of super-exploitation, wherein capital uses the labor power of Native populations and consumes the raw materials found in Native lands without just compensation. Native communities, which are rich in raw materials but deficient in capital, become excellent targets for the methods of capital, are stripped of their wealth, and of any economic power they potentially possess.

No simple solution exists for this historically grounded situation, which is backed by the power of the state and capital. As researchers have noted (Churchill, 1999; Churchill and LaDuke, 1992; LaDuke, 1979), an important dimension of the problem relates to the form of political governance the federal government has imposed on Native American reservations. It requires Americans Indians to adopt nontraditional forms of political rule and to establish a model that benefits the interests of the federal government and the corporations. This new form of governance effectively created a patronage system similar to the general U.S. political model. The more diffuse model of governance found in American Indian communities is reduced and superceded by a power structure that facilitates ties to the federal government and corporate interests. Thus, the first step in restoring justice in Native American communities would be to promote relations of governance that benefit collective Native interests over external interests.

Policies also needed to address social and environmental injustice in Native communities could include: reservation-specific environmental laws and regulations that promote safe environmental practices and offer more stringent regulations; fees paid by corporations to operate oversight mechanisms; enhanced penalties for violating environmental laws on Native lands; legal provisions that adjust corporate fees paid to Native landholders in accordance with commodity market prices; resource extraction contracts that incorporate the provision of enhanced medical and social services on reservations; and wage contracts tied to mean wages in the extraction industry rather than to depressed wage scales in Native communities.

One article is not sufficient to analyze the widespread forms of injustice affecting Native Americans. From a disciplinary point of view, criminologists need to make greater efforts to address Native American injustice in its variety of forms and manifestations.

Notes

1. It is tempting to argue that this neglect reflects the fact that because Native populations comprise only one percent of the U.S. population, they are less worthy of attention. Yet, the criminological literature is filled with studies of much smaller populations, such as homicide

offenders and prison inmates. Thus, population size alone does not explain the criminological neglect of Native Americans.

2. We use the term "Native Americans" to refer to the aggregation of the primary race groups that inhabited the territories now recognized as the United States. These groups are American Indians, Native Alaskans, and Native Hawaiians.

3. There is often an obvious collusive agreement between the private sector and the state that facilitates these forms of injustice, suggesting that these activities could also be examined as state-corporate crimes (Lynch, Bums, and Stretesky, 2010). However, it is not our intention here to examine Native American social, economic, and environmental injustice as a state-corporate crime. We leave this topic to future research explorations.

4. For example, research has shown the effects from PCBs, p,p'-dichlorophenyldichloroethylene (p,p'-DDE), and HCB on young Akwesasne Mohawk adults and breast-feed infants (Schell et al., 2009).

5. See *http://censored-news.blogspot.com/2007/08/uranium-mining-oglala-lakota-people-and. htmi*for water assessment information, see *http://pubs.usgs.gov/wri/wri994063*.

6. Structural conditions and impediments are often overlooked, and a key indicator of this tendency is the relative exclusion of Native American issues from media coverage. When the media deal with Native American issues, they often focus on unusual incidents or stereotypes—for example, those related to casinos—rather than on the social and economic inequalities affecting Native American communities.

References

Anderton, 1997 D. "Environmental Equity in Superfund: Demographics of the Discovery and Prioritization of Abandoned Toxic Sites." *Evaluation Review* 21: 3–26.

Baquet, C.R., and P. Commiskey 2000 "Socioeconomic Factors and Breast Carcinoma in Multicultural Women." *Cancer* 88, 5: 1256–1264.

Becker, T.M., D.K. Espey, H.W. Lawson, M. Saraiya, M.A. Jim, and A.G. Waxman 2008 "Regional Differences in Cervical Cancer Incidence Among American Indian and Alaskan Natives, 1990–2004." *Cancer* 113, 5: 1234–1243.

Brooks, D. 1998 "Environmental Genocide: Native Americans and Toxic Waste." *The American Journal of Economics and Sociology* 57: 105–113.

Brugge, D., T. Benally, and E. Yazzie-Lewis 2006 *The Navajo People and Uranium Mining.* Albuquerque, NM: University of New Mexico Press.

Brugge, D., J.L. de Lemos, and C. Bui 2007 "The Sequoyah Corporation Fuels Release and the Church Rock Spill: Unpublicized Nuclear Releases in American Indian Communities." *American Journal of Public Health* 97, 9: 1595–1600.

Brugge, D. and R. Goble 2002 "The History of Uranium Mining and the Navajo People." *American Journal of Public Health* 92, 9: 1410–1419.

Bullard, R.D., P. Mohai, R. Saha, and B. Wright 2007 *Toxic Wastes and Race at Twenty: 1987–2007. Grassroots Struggles to Dismantle Environmental Racism in the United States.* Cleveland, OH: United Church of Christ, Justice and Witness Ministries. At *http://www.ejnetarg/ej/twart. pdf.*

Chevrier, J., B. Eskenazi, N. Holland, A. Bradman, and D.B. Barr 2008 "Effects of Exposure to Polychlorinated Biphenyls and Organochlorine Pesticides on Thyroid Function During Pregnancy." *American Journal of Epidemiology* 168, 3: 298–310.

Churchill, W. 1999 "The Radioactive Colonization of Native North America." *American Indian Culture and Research Journal* 23, 4: 23–69.

Churchill, W. and W. LaDuke 1992 "Native North America: The Political Economy of Radioactive Colonialism." M.A. Jaimes (ed.), *State of Native America: Genocide, Colonization and Resistance.* Cambridge, MA: South End Press: 241–266.

Codru, N., M. Schymura, S. Negoita, R. Rej, and D. 2007 Carpenter "Diabetes in Relation to Serum Levels of Polychlorinated Biphenyls and Chlorinated Pesticides in Adult Native Americans." *Environmental Health Perspectives* 115, 10: 1442–1447.

Cohn, B., M. Wolff, P. Cirillo, and R. Sholtz 2007 "DDT and Breast Cancer in Young Women." *Environmental Health Perspectives* 115: 1410–1414.

Davis, N. 2010 "The Exxon Valdez Oil Spill, Alaska." J.K. Mitchell (ed.), *The Long Road to Recovery: Community Responses to Industrial Disaster.* New York: United Nations University Press: 231–272.

Dawson, S.E. 1992 "Navajo Uranium Workers and the Effects of Occupational Illnesses: A Case Study." *Human Organization* 51, 4: 389–397.

Dawson, S.E. and G. Madsen 1995 "American Indian Uranium Mill Workers: A Study of the Perceived Effects of Occupational Exposure." *Journal of Health & Social Policy* 7: 19–31.

DeCaprio, A., G. Johnson, A. Tarbell, D. Carpenter, J. Chiarenzelli, G. Morse, A. Santiago-Rivera, and M J. Schymura 2005 "Polychlorinated Biphenyl (PCB) Exposure Assessment by Multivariate Statistical Analysis of Serum Congener Profiles in an Adult Native American Population." *Environmental Research* 98: 284–302.

de Lemos, J.L., D. Brugge, M. Cajero, M. Downs, J.L. Durant, C.M. George, S. Henio-Adeky, et al. 2009 "Development of Risk Maps to Minimize Uranium Exposures in the Navajo Churchrock Mining District." *Environmental Health* 8: 29–44.

de Solla, S., C. Bishop, H. Lickers, and K. Jock. 2000 "Organochlorine Pesticides, PCBs, Dibenzodioxin, and Furan Concentrations in Common Snapping Turtle Eggs (Chelydra Serpentina Serpentina) in Akwesasne, Mohawk Territory, Ontario, Canada." *Archives of Environmental Contamination and Toxicology* 40: 410–417.

Denham, M,, L. Schell, G. Deane, M. Gallo, J. Ravenscroft, and A. DeCaprio 2005 "Relationship of Lead, Mercury, Mirex, DDE, HCB, and PCBs to Age at Menarche among Akwesasne Mohawk Girls." *Pediatrics* 115: 125–134. At *http://pediatricsmappublications.org/content/115/2/el27.fullhtml*.

Duran, I J., C.R. Pearson, Y. Jiang, K. Foley, and M. Harrison 2010 "Risk Factors for HIV Disease Progression in a Rural Southwestern American Indian Population." *Public Health Reports* 125, 4: 43–50.

Dyer, C. 1993 "Traditional Loss as Secondary Disaster: Long-Term Cultural Impacts of the Exxon Valdez Oil Spill." *Sociological Spectrum* 13: 65–88.

Dyer, C., D.A. Gill, and S. Picou 1992 "Social Disruption and the Valdez Oil Spill: Alaskan Natives in a Natural Resource Community." *Sociological Spectrum* 12: 105–126.

Eberth, J.M., J.C. Huber, and A. Rene 2010 "Breast Cancer Screening Practices and Correlates among American Indian and Alaskan Native Women, 2003." *Women's Health Issues* 20, 2: 139–145.

Eichstaedt, P. 1994 *If You Poison Us: Uranium and Native Americans.* Santa Fe, NM: Red Crane Books.

Fall, J.A. and LJ. Field 1996 "Subsistence Uses of Fish and Wildlife Before and After the Exxon Valdez Oil Spill." *American Fisheries Symposium* 18: 819–836.

Fall, J., R. Miraglia, W. Simeone, C. Utermohle, and R. Wolfe 2001 *Long Term Consequences of the Exxon Valdez Oil Spill for Costal Communities of South-central Alaska.* Technical Paper #264. Division of Subsistence, Alaskan Department of Fish and Game: Juneau, Alaska. At *http://www-subsistence.adfg.state.ak.us/TechPap/tp264.pdf*.

Fitzgerald, E., S. Hwang, M. Gomez, B. Bush, B. Yang, and A. Tarbell 2007 "Environmental and Occupational Exposures and Serum PCB Concentrations and Patterns among Mohawk Men at Akwesasne." *Journal of Exposure Analysis and Environmental Epidemiology* 17: 269–278.

Fitzgerald, E., S. Hwang, G. Lambert, M. Gomez, and A. Tarbell 2005 "PCB Exposure and in Vivo CYP1A2 Activity Among Native Americans." *Environmental Health Perspectives* 113: 272–277.

Fitzgerald, E., S. Hwang, K. Langguth, M. Cayo, B. Yang, B. Bush, P. Worswick, and T. Lauzon 2004 "Fish Consumption and Other Environmental Exposures and Their Associations with Serum PCB Concentrations among Mohawk Women at Akwesasne." *Environmental Research* 94: 160–170.

Fitzgerald, E., S. Hwang, K. Langguth, M. Cayo, B. Yang, B. Bush, P. Worswick, and T. Lauzon 2001 "The Association Between Local Fish Consumption and DDE, Mirex, and HCB Concentrations in the Breast Milk of Mohawk Women at Akwesasne." *Journal of Exposure Analysis and Environmental Epidemiology* 11: 381–388.

Fitzgerald, E., S. Hwang, M. Gomez, B. Bush, B. Yang, and A. Tarbell 1999 "Local Fish Consumption and Serum PCB Concentrations among Mohawk Men at Akwesasne." *Environmental Research* 80: 97–103.

Fitzgerald, E., S. Hwang, B. Bush, K. Cook, and P. Worswick 1998 "Fish Consumption and Breast Milk PCB Concentrations Among Mohawk Women at Akwesasne." *American Journal of Epidemiology* 148: 164–172.

Fitzgerald, E., K. Brix, D. Deres, S. Hwang, B. Bush, G. Lambert, and A. Tarbell 1996 "Polychlorinated Biphenyl (PCB) and Dichlorodiphenyl Dichloroethylene (DDE) Exposure Among Native American Men from Contaminated Great Lakes Fish and Wildlife." *Toxicology and Industrial Health* 12: 361–368.

Fitzgerald, E., S. Hwang, K. Brix, B. Bush, and P. Worswick 1995 "Fish PCB Concentrations and Consumption Patterns among Mohawk Women at Akwesasne." *Journal of Exposure Analysis and Environmental Epidemiology* 5: 1–19.

Forbes, J.D. 1979 *The Papago-Apache Treaty of 1853: Property Rights and Religious Liberties of the 'O'odham, Maricopa, and Other Native Peoples.* Davis, CA: University of California, Davis.

Frohmberg, E., R. Goble, V. Sanchez, and D. Quigley 2000 "The Assessment of Radiation Exposures in Native American Communities from Nuclear Weapons Testing in Nevada." *Risk Analysis* 20: 101–111.

Garabrant, D., J. Held, B. Langholz, J. Peters, and T. Mack 1992 "DDT and Related Compounds and Risk of Pancreatic Cancer." *Journal of the National Cancer Institute* 84: 764–771.

Gilliland, F., W. Hunt, M. Pardilla, and C. Key 2000 "Uranium Mining and Lung Cancer among Navajo Men in New Mexico and Arizona, 1969–1993." *Journal of Occupational & Environmental Medicine* 42: 278–283.

Goncharov, A., R. Haase, A. Santiago-Rivera, G. Morse, R. McCaffrey, R. Rej, and D. Carpenter 2008 "High Serum PCBs Are Associated with Elevation of Serum Lipids and Cardiovascular Disease in a Native American Population." *Environmental Research* 106: 226–239.

Goncharov, A., R. Rej, S. Negoita, M. Schymura, A. Santiago-Rivera, G. Morse, the Akwesasne Task Force on the Environment, and D. Carpenter 2009 "Lower Serum Testosterone Associated with Elevated Polychlorinated Biphenyl Concentrations in Native American Men." *Environmental Health Perspectives* 117: 1454–1460.

Gowda, R. and D. Easterling 2000 "Voluntary Siting and Equity: The MRS Facility Experience in Native America." *Risk Analysis* 20: 917–930.

Grahame, J. and T. Sisk (eds.) 2002 *Canyons, Cultures and Environmental Change: An Introduction to the Land-Use History of the Colorado Plateau*. At *http://www.cpluhna.nau.edu*.

Guadagnolo, B.A., K. Cina, P. Helbig, K. Molloy, M. Renier, E.F. Cook, and D.G. Peteriet 2009 "Assessing Cancer Stage and Screening Disparities Among Native American Cancer Patients." *Public Health Reports* 124, 1: 79–89.

Guadagnolo, B.A., D.G. Peteriet, P. Helbig, D. Koop, P. Kussman, E. Fox-Dunn, and A. Patniak 2009 "Involving American Indians and Medically Underserved Rural Populations in Cancer Clinical Trials." *Clinical Trials* 6: 610–617.

Haase, R., R. McCaffrey, A. Santiago-Rivera, G. Morse, and A. Tarbell 2009 "Evidence of an Age-Related Threshold Effect of Polychlorinated Biphenyls (PCBs) on Neuropsychological Functioning in a Native American Population." *Environmental Research* 109: 73–85.

Hay, A. and J. Tarrel 1997 "Mortality of Power Workers Exposed to Phenoxy Herbicides and Polychlorinated Biphenyls in Waste Transformer Oil." *Annals of the New York Academy of Science* 837: 138–156.

Hooks, G. and C. Smith 2004 "The Treadmill of Destruction: National Sacrifice Areas and Native Americans." *American Sociological Review* 69: 558–575.

Hwang, S., E. Fitzgerald, and B. Bush 1996 "Exposure to PCB's from Hazardous Waste among Mohawk Women and Infants at Akwesasne." *Technology Journal of the Franklin Institute* 333A: 17–23.

Jacobson, J. and S. Jacobson 1996 "Intellectual Impairment in Children Exposed to Polychlorinated Biphenyls in Utero." *New England Journal of Medicine* 335: 783–789.

Jerrigan, V.B., B. Duran, D. Ahn, and M. Winkleby 2010 "Changing Patterns in Health Behaviors and Risk Factors Related to Cardiovascular Disease Among American Indians and Native Alaskans." *American Journal of Public Health* 100, 4: 577–583.

Jim, M.A., D.G. Perdue, L.C. Richardson, D.K. Espey, J.T. Redd, H J. Martin, J J. Kelly, J.A. Henderson, and F. Ahmed 2008 "Primary Liver Cancer Incidence Among American Indians and Alaskan Natives, US, 1999–2004." *Cancer* 113, 5: 1244–55.

Johnson, B,, H. Hicks, W. Cibulas, O. Faroon, A. Ashizawa, and C. De Rosa 1999 "Public Health Implications of Exposure to Polychlorinated Biphenyls (PCBs)." Agency for Toxic Substances and Disease Registry. At *wwwxitsdrcdc.gov/DTI pcb007html*.

Jurewicz, J. and W. Hanke 2008 "Prenatal and Childhood Exposure to Pesticides and Neurobehavioral Development: Review of Epidemiological Studies." *International Journal of Occupational Medical and Environmental Health* 21: 121–132.

Kinney, A., E. Fitzgerald, S. Hwang, B. Bush, and A. Tarbell 1997 "Human Exposure to PCBs: Modeling and Assessment of Environmental Concentrations on the Akwesasne Reservation." *Drug Chemistry and Toxicology* 20:313–328.

Korrick, S. and S. Sagiv 2008 "Polychlorinated Biphenyls, Organochlorine Pesticides and Neurodevelopment." *Current Opinion in Pediatrics* 20: 198–204.

Kreig, E. 1995 "A Socio-Historical Interpretation of Toxic Waste Sites." *American Journal of Economics and Sociology* 54: 1–14.

La Duke, W. 1979 "Uranium Mines on Native Land: The New Indian Wars." *The Harvard Crimson* (May 2). At *http.i/pubs.usgs.gov/wri/wri994063/*.

Lanier, A.P., G.E. Day, J J. Kelly, and E. Provost 2008 "Disparities in Cancer Mortality Among Alaskan Native People, 1994–2003." *Alaska Medical Journal* 49, 4: 120–125.

Lemrow, S.M., D.G. Perdue, L.C. Richardson, M.A. Jim, H.T. French, J. Swan, B.K. Edwards, C. Wiggins, L. Dickie, and D.K. Espy 2008 "Gallbladder Cancer Incidence Among American Indians and Native Alaskans, 1999–2004." *Cancer* 113, 5: 1266–1273.

Longnecker, M., M. Klebanoff, H. Zhou, and J. Brock 2001 "Association Between Maternal Serum Concentration of the DDT Metabolite DDE and Preterm and Small-for-Gestational-age Babies at Birth." *The Lancet* 358:110–114.

Lynch, M.J. and R. Michalowski 2006 *Primer in Radical Criminology.* New York: Criminal Justice Press.

Lynch, M J., R.G. Bums, and P.B. Stretesky "Global Warming as a State-Corporate Crime: The Politicalization of Global Warming During the Bush Administration." *Crime, Law and Social Change* 54, 3: 213.

Malcoe, L., R. Lynch, M. Kegler, and V. Skaggs 2002 "Lead Sources, Behaviors, and Socioeconomic Factors in Relation to Blood Lead of Native American and White Children: A Community-Based Assessment of a Former Mining Area." *Environmental Health Perspectives* 110, 2: 221–231.

Manning, J. 2005 "PCBs (Polychlorinated Biphenyls) in New York's Hudson River." At *http://EnvironmentalChemistry.comlyogilenvironmental/2005l0hudsonriverpcbs.html*.

Markstrom, C. and P. Charley 2003 "Psychological Effects of Human Caused Environmental Disasters: Examination of the Navajo and Uranium." *American Indian and Alaska Native Mental Health Research* 11: 19–45.

Newman, J., A.G.Aucompaugh, L.M. Schell, M. Denham, A.P. DeCaprio, M.V. Gallod, J. Ravenscroft, et al. 2006 "PCBs and Cognitive Functioning of Mohawk Adolescents." *Neurotoxicology and Teratology* 28, 4: 439–445.

Newman, J., M. Gallo, L. Schell, A. DeCaprio, M. Denham, G. Deane, and the Akwesasne Task Force on the Environment 2009 "Analysis of PCB Congeners Related to Cognitive Functioning in Adolescents." *Neurotoxicology* 30: 686–696.

Orr, M., F. Bove, W. Kaye, and M. Stone 2002 "Elevated Birth Defects in Racial or Ethnic Minority Children of Women Living Near Hazardous Waste Sites." *International Journal of Hygiene and Environmental Health* 205, 1–2: 19–27.

Palinkas, L., M.A. Downs, J.S. Patterson, and J. Russell 1993 "Social, Cultural and Psychological Consequences of the Exxon Valdez Oil Spill." *Human Organization* 52, 1: 1–13.

Palinkas, L., J. Peterson, J. Russell, and M. Downs 2004 "Ethnic Differences in Symptoms of Post-Traumatic Stress after the Exxon Valdez Oil Spill." *Prehospital and Disaster Medicine* 19: 102–112.

Palinkas, L., J. Peterson, and M. Downs 1993 "Community Patterns of Psychiatric after the Exxon Valdez Oil Spill." *American Journal of Psychiatry* 150: 1517–1523.

Palinkas, L,, J. Russell, M. Downs, and J. Peterson 1992 "Ethnic Differences in Stress, Coping and Depressive Symptoms after the Exxon Valdez Oil Spill." *The Journal of Nervous and Mental Disease* 180: 287–295.

Perdue, D.G., C. Perkins, J. Jackson-Thompson, S.S. Coughlin, F. Ahmed, D.S. Haverkamp, and M.A. Jim 2008 "Regional Difference in Colorectal Cancer Incidence, State and Subsite Among American Indians and Alaskan Natives, 1999–2004." *Cancer* 113, 5: 1179–1180.

Picou, S. and D. Gill 1996 "The Exxon Valdez Oil Spill and Chronic Psychological Stress." *American Fisheries Society Symposium* 18: 879–893.

Picou, S., D. Gill, C. Dyer, and E. Curry 1992 "Disruption and Stress in an Alaskan Fishing Community: Initial and Continuing Impacts of the Exxon Valdez Oil Spill." *Industrial Crisis Quarterly* 6: 235–257.

Quartaroli, M.L. 2002 "Leetso, the Yellow Monster: Uranium Mining on the Colorado Plateau." J. Grahame and T. Sisk (eds.), *Canyons, Cultures and Environmental Change.* At *www.cpluhna.nau. edu/.*

Rathore, M., P. Bhatnagar, D. Mathur, and G. Saxena 2002 "Burden of Organochlorine Pesticides in Blood and Its Effect on Thyroid Hormones in Women." *The Science of the Total Environment* 295: 207–215.

Raymond-Whish, S., L. Mayer, T. O'Neal, A. Martinez, M. Sellers, P. Christian, S. Marion et al. 2007 "Drinking Water with Uranium below the U.S. EPA Water Standard Causes Estrogen Receptor-Dependent Responses in Female Mice." *Environmental Health Perspectives* 115: 1711–1716.

Reddy, N.K. and M.S. Bhutani 2009 "Racial Disparities in Pancreatic and Radon Exposure." *Pancreas* 38, 4: 391–395.

Roscoe, R., J. Deddens, A. Salvan, and T. Schnorr 1995 "Mortality among Navajo Uranium Miners." *American Journal of Public Health* 85: 535–540.

Schell, L., M. Gallo, J. Ravenscroft, and A. DeCaprio 2009 "Persistent Organic Pollutants and Anti-Thyroid Peroxidase Levels in Akwesasne Mohawk Young Adults." *Environmental Research* 109: 86–92.

Schell, L., M. Gallo, A. DeCaprio, L. Hubicki, M. Denham, J. Ravenscroft, and The Akwesasne Task Force on the Environment 2004 "Thyroid Function in Relation to Burden of Polychlorinated Biphenyls (PCB's), p,p'-DDE, HCB, Mirex, and Lead among Akwesasne Mohawk Youth: A Preliminary Study." *Environmental Toxicology and Pharmacology* 18: 91–99.

Schell, L., L. Hubicki, A. DeCaprio, M. Gallo, J. Ravenscroft, A. Tarbell, A. Jacobs, D. David, P. Worswick, and The Akwesasne Task Force on the Environment 2003 "Organochlorines, Lead, and Mercury in Akwesasne Mohawk Youth." *Environmental Health Perspective* 111: 954–961.

Schubauer-Berigan, M.K., R.D. Daniels, and L.E. Pinkerton 2009 "Radon Exposure Mortality among White and American Indian Uranium Miners: An Update of the Colorado Plateau Cohort." *American Journal of Epidemiology* 169, 6: 718–730.

Schumacher, M.C., M.L. Stanley, A.P. Lanier, K.N. Ma, S. Edwards, E.D. Ferrucci, and L. Tom-Orme 2008 "Prevalence and Predictors of Cancer Screening Among American Indians and Native Alaskan People: The EARTH Study." *Cancer Causes and Control* 19, 7: 725–737.

Seis, M. 1996 "A Native American Criminology of Environmental Crime." S.M. Edwards, T.M. Edwards, and C. Fields (eds.), *Environmental Crime and Criminology.* New York: Garland.

Sergeev, A.V. and D.O. Carpenter 2005 "Hospitalization Rates for Coronary Heart Disease in Relation to Residence Near Areas Contaminated with Persistent Organic Pollutants and Other Pollutants." *Environmental Health Perspectives* 113, 6: 756–761.

Shields, L., W. Wiese, B. Skipper, B. Charley, and L. Banally 1992 "Navajo Birth Outcomes in the Shiprock Uranium Mining Area." *Health Physics* 63: 542–551.

Stretesky, P.B. and MJ. Hogan 1998 "Environmental Justice: An Analysis of Superfund Sites in Florida." *Social Problems* 45: 268–287.

Sukdoıová, V., S. Negoita, L. Hubicki, A. DeCaprio, and D. Carpenter 2000 "The Assessment of Risk to Acquired Hypothyroidism from Exposure to PCBs: A Study among Akwesasne Mohawk Women." *Central European Journal of Public Health* 8: 167–168.

Taylor, J.B. and J.P. Kalt 2005 *American Indians on Reservations: A Databook of Socioeconomic Change Between the 1990 and 2000 Census.* The Harvard Project on American Indian Development, John F. Kennedy School of Government. Boston, MA: Harvard University.

United States Department of the Interior 1990 "Impact of Potential Oil Spills in the Arctic Ocean on Alaska Natives." *Federal Register* 55, 27: 43144.

United States Environmental Protection Agency 2006 "Abandoned Uranium Mines (AUM) on the Navajo Nation: Eastern AUM Screening Assessment Report. (U.S. EPA Region 9.)" San Francisco: U.S. EPA.

Weaver, H.N. 2010 "Native Americans and Cancer Risks: Moving Toward Multifaceted Solutions." *Social Work in Public Health* 25, 3: 272–285.

Wiggins, C.L., D.K. Espey, P.A. Wingo, J.S. Kaur, J.T. Wilson, J. Swan, B.A. Miller, M.A. Jim, J.J. Kelly, and A.P. Lanier 2008 "Cancer Among American Indians and Native Alaskans in the United States, 1999–2004." *Cancer* 113, 5: 1142–1152.

Wiggins, CL., D.G. Perdue, JA. Henderson, M.G. Bruce, A.P. Lanier, J.J. Kelly, B.F. Seats, and D.K. Espey 2008 "Gastric Cancers Among American Indians and Native Alaskans in the United States, 1999–2004." *Cancer* 113, 5: 1225–1233.

Wilson, R.T., L.C. Richardson, JJ. Kelley, J. Kaur, M.A. Jim, and A.P. Lanier 2008 "Cancers of the Urinary Tract Among American Indians and Native Alaskans in the United States, 1999–2004." *Cancer* 113, 5: 1213–1224.

Winscott, M., M. Taylor, and K. Kenney 2010 "Sexually Transmitted Diseases Among American Indians in Arizona: An Important Public Health Disparity." *Public Health Reports* 125, 4: 51–60.

Zilney, L.A., D. McGurrin, and S. Zaharan 2006 "Environmental Justice and the Role of Criminology: An Analytic Review of 33 Years of Research." *Criminal Justice Review* 31, 1: 47–62.

CHAPTER 28

The United States of Consumption (and Debt)

By Brandon Lang

Consumption and debt are a package deal in the United States. Today, Americans not only consume more than people in past generations, but we finance many of our purchases with borrowed money. We have bigger homes, nicer cars, more expansive wardrobes, and fancier gadgets than our parents and grandparents did and these are, for the most part, financed with credit. Many of us want the nicest things and we tend to want them right away, even if we cannot afford them.

There are some clear benefits to credit cards and credit, in general. They can help us out in a pinch and enable us to make sizeable purchases without having to carry large sums of cash. Plus, using a credit card establishes a person's credit history, which is likely to improve his or her credit score, lower his or her interest rates, and increase the amount of money that she or he can borrow. There are also many concerns with credit, mostly because many of us are not responsible users of credit and credit cards. Many of us have access to so much credit that we are tempted to buy things that we cannot afford, spend beyond our means, and rack up huge amounts of debt.

The purposes of this chapter are twofold. The first is to examine consumption patterns over time and compare people's consumer spending habits with those of people living in past eras. The second is to examine the consequences of debt. Personal debt is a social problem that is linked with anxiety and other health concerns, bankruptcy, divorce, and even suicide.

● BACKGROUND

Many of our parents and grandparents took the idea of living within their means very seriously. They lived in homes that they could afford, purchased things outright and only when they could afford them, and saved as much money as they could. The idea of saving money for a rainy day was a mantra that people born through the 1930s believed. Many people born after World War II, however, do not share that perspective. Recent statistics show that Americans' savings are going down while our levels of debt are increasing. By 2010, Americans were borrowing almost twice as much, consuming over 50 percent more, and saving almost 50 percent less than people did in 1970 (Cohen 2014). Cohen reports that Americans saved between 9 and 10 percent of their post-tax incomes in 1970, compared to 2.4 percent of their post-tax incomes in 2007. Similarly, total household debt levels were between 45 and 50 percent of the nation's Gross Domestic Product (GDP) in the 1970s and almost 99 percent of the GDP in 2007 (Cohen 2014).

The typical American's lifestyle was more modest in past decades than it is today. Many of our parents and grandparents lived in modest homes that were much smaller than many of us would consider living in today. In fact, the average home size went from 1,100 square feet in 1950 to 2,340 square feet in 2002, meaning that the average home size has more than doubled over that time (Wilson and Boehland 2005). With the average household family size actually decreasing between 1950 and now, the average household member has three times more space than people did in 1950 (Wilson and Boehland 2005).

In addition to being smaller than many of the homes that people live in today, the homes that people lived in through the 1950s and 1960s had fewer amenities than are found in many contemporary homes. Unlike today, most people did not have dishwashers or central air conditioning, for example. On average, people's homes had fewer rooms, in general, and fewer bathrooms and bedrooms, in particular. It was very common through the 1970s for families to have just one car, for siblings to share bedrooms, and for houses to have only one bathroom. The U.S. Census Bureau (2016) also reports that more than half (53.2%) of all homes were paid for in 1950, while that rate is now 29.3 percent (Lazo 2013). This helps to explain why the amount of people's average household debt relative to their tangible household assets doubled from 0.24 in 1954 to 0.48 in 2005 (Campbell and Hercowitz 2006).

It is not just that many people's homes are bigger than before. Today, most Americans are spending a higher percentage of their incomes on health care, recreation, and education than they did in times past. In terms of health care, Fuchs (2012) reports that per capita health care costs have increased by a factor of eight since 1950. In 1950, health care costs represented 4.6 percent of the GDP, and had risen to over 17 percent by 2009 (Fuchs 2012). Costs have gone up due to the development of more advanced medical equipment and procedures, higher malpractice insurance premiums for medical professionals, and expensive pharmaceutical products. Research conducted by the Kaiser Family Foundation (2011) reports that per capita health care costs are higher in the United States than in any other developed country in the world. In short, Americans spend more on health care than people living in other countries, which leaves us even less money to cover other expenses. Moreover, uninsured and underinsured people who do need medical treatment represent a large proportion of people who claim bankruptcy. In their study, Himmelstein, Thorne, Warren, and Woolhandler (2009) found that medical problems contributed to 46.2 percent of bankruptcies.

Over time, the amount of money that Americans spend on recreation has increased. According to the U.S. Census Bureau (2016), Americans' total recreation expenditures increased almost threefold to $897 billion between 1990 and 2008. We do not necessarily go to more sporting events, concerts, or movies than people did in the 1950s. Rather, the cost relative to our incomes has increased. One interesting trend is that food expenditures have gone down while people are buying a greater proportion of their food in restaurants. In 1950, Americans spent 17.8 percent of their food expenditures away from home, compared to 38 percent in 1997 (U.S. Census Bureau 1999).

Lastly, education costs have also increased over time. Watson (2013) reports that college tuition has increased by 1,120 percent since the early 1980s. We have recently hit the point where Americans collectively owe $1 trillion in student loans, an amount that exceeds the total car loans and credit card debt combined (Watson 2013). In addition, interest rates for student loans are also often higher than they are for home loans, meaning that people are paying much bigger percentages of their income to pay off these loans than ever before. Suze Orman, a popular television-based financial advisor, differentiates between good and bad debt. College loans have historically represented good debt because they expand people's range of professional options. Unfortunately, with the state of today's economy, not all college graduates will get jobs in their fields of study and make the money that is needed to pay off their loans. As with other forms of debt, having to write a significant check every month to pay off these loans is stressful for many people.

Since the 1950s, two additional trends have emerged. The first is that men have gradually increased their weekly working hours. The second is that more women have entered the paid workforce. In their study, Campbell and Hercowitz (2006) have found a direct relationship between people's debt and the number of hours that they work per week. It appears as though many people are working as many hours as they can to pay off debt and generate more income to purchase even more consumer goods.

Juliet Schor, a sociologist at Boston University, has studied and written about these trends in her books *The Overworked American* (1992) and *The Overspent American* (1999). She is also credited with developing the concept of the work/spend treadmill. The work/spend treadmill explains that people work long hours in order to generate the income that they need to sustain their lifestyles. Because they work so hard and forego time off, they are likely to purchase consumer goods and services that serve as a reward for their hard work. Maybe they go out for an expensive dinner or get an expensive haircut. Even after many extra hours of work, a lot of people are still not able to cover all of their expenses. This prompts them to work more which, in turn, prompts them to reward their hard work with consumer expenditures. Thus, a cycle is established where they work hard, spend a lot of money, and need to work even harder to cover those costs. As discussed below, the mental strain is but one of the many consequences of living beyond one's means and working more hours to try and pay down debt.

● CURRENT TRENDS

The amount of debt that is owed by the typical American is much higher than it has ever been. Many Americans not only have mortgages, student loans, and credit card debt, they are also paying off furniture, car, computer, wedding, and even vacation loans. The U.S. Census Bureau (2016) reports that the average American has $117,000 in home debt, $10,000 in vehicle debt, $3,530 in credit card debt, and $17,000 in other loans. In terms of credit cards, the average card-holder has 3.7 cards and pays an average of 12.2 percent interest per year (Ray and Ghahremani 2009). There were 20.2 billion credit card transactions in 2009, with a total purchase volume of $1.76 trillion (Soll, Keeney, and Larrick 2013). Clearly, debt has become a way of life for most Americans, who appear to be very comfortable borrowing vast sums of money against future earnings to meet their needs and wants.

● WHY DO AMERICANS HAVE SO MUCH DEBT?

There are several reasons why the typical American has so much debt. The first relates to how easy it is for most people to obtain credit. The second is based on very high amounts of interest that Americans pay every month. The third reason is the aggressive marketing campaigns used by corporations to sell us consumer goods. The fourth reason is the hyper-consumerism that we often exhibit.

1. Easy Access to Credit

It is very easy for most people to access credit in the United States. When we go to the mall, we see numerous offers to open a store card and get 10 or 15 percent off that day's purchase. When we go to sporting events, fans are offered free beach towels, footballs, or baseball caps if they apply for a card. Car dealerships all over the country have "sign and drive" promotions where qualified people can buy a car without paying any money down. Most of us receive unsolicited offers from credit card companies in the mail wooing us with one offer or another to open a card. In short, we are inundated with opportunities to open lines of credit and purchase consumer goods that we will likely pay off over time.

When stores and banks offer sign-up promotions, they do so not for altruistic reasons. Rather, these incentives are motivated by profit. All of these companies know that if they give people a discount the first time that they use a card, they will probably spend beyond their means and purchase more goods than they are able to pay off. Yes, consumers may get 10 or 15 percent off their purchase, but they will end up paying 20 percent or more in interest on the unpaid amount, thereby offsetting any discount. The same holds true for airline miles and other cash back offers. Often times, there is a lot of proverbial fine print that keeps any deal from being as good as it may seem.

The early 2000s was, arguably, the easiest period in recent history to obtain credit. Banks came out with thirty-year mortgages, people could buy homes with $0 down and new types of short-lived loans emerged. One loan type that became popular during this period was the interest-only loan. With an interest-only loan, people would pay only the interest on the loan for first ten years and pay the entirety of the principal over the remaining years on the loan. The problem with this is that people's payments would skyrocket after ten years to the point of putting many in a position where they could not make their monthly payments. Another loan type was the sub-prime loan. Similar to the interest-only loan, people would pay a reduced amount of interest during the first part of the loan only to have higher payments after that period ended. Like interest-only loans, sub-prime loans had very high default rates. Both of these loan types were discontinued by banks after 2008.

2. High Amounts of Interest

When credit cards first took hold in the late 1970s and early 1980s, they were meant to be paid off at the end of every billing cycle. Unlike today, most credit card holders did not carry over monthly balances to the next month. According to the US Census Bureau (2016), more than half of Americans do not pay off their entire credit card bills, but instead carry over monthly balances. Today, most credit cards require a 2 percent minimum payment every year. This may spell relief for people between jobs or in need of short-term financial assistance, but it also carries with it many concerns. Ultimately, this means that a person can take up to fifty years to pay off his or her credit card. At 20 or 22 percent interest per year, this becomes a very expensive proposition.

Credit card companies make a lot of their money through compound interest, or interest accruing on interest. If someone owes $100 on a credit card with an interest rate of 20 percent that goes unpaid for a year, she or he will owe $120. After a second year of going unpaid, another 20 percent interest will be levied on the $120, making the new balance $144. After fifty years of nonpayment, that original value of $100 would grow to over $2 million.

There are numerous Americans who either have paid such little money down or have such high interest rates or long amortization periods that they owe more money on their cars, homes, boats, or pieces of furniture than they are actually worth. This has come to be known as being "upside down" on a loan. Oftentimes when people with brand new cars, for example, are in car accidents, the amount of money owed on the vehicle exceeds its replacement value by the insurance companies. In fact, most insurance companies offer something called gap insurance for an additional fee. Gap insurance covers the difference between the value of a car that has been totaled and the amount of money that is owed on it. This same concept also applies to people who bought homes in the early 2000s and paid elevated amounts due to the growth of the housing bubble. When the bubble collapsed ten years later, people all over the country owed more on their homes than they were worth, meaning that if they were in the market to sell, they would take a (sometimes significant) loss.

3. Aggressive Marketing

All of us are exposed to hundreds, if not thousands, of commercial messages every day that appear on computers, televisions, billboards, buses, and so on. There is also product placement in the movies we watch and commercial messages in the music that we listen to. Companies pay billions of dollars to marketing firms to help them build a brand identity and target certain demographics of consumers. A concern that many have with this practice is that marketing strategies are often so effective that they convince people to buy things that they probably do not need.

The purpose of advertising and marketing is to convince people that they cannot live without a certain product. The newly developed term "content marketing" takes this to the next level. Brands that engage in content marketing like Red Bull and Whole Foods are selling an idea as much as physical goods. Through direct marketing in the form of blogs, videos, texts, emails, and newsletters, companies like Whole Foods work very hard to convince people that shopping at their store is a healthy lifestyle choice. In other words, their goal is to sell people on the idea that shopping at that particular store is going to make them a healthier and happier person.

4. Consumerism

Another main reason for high levels of debt is materialism. Many people want the latest clothing styles, phone models, cars, or home appliances. Newness is an American value, replacing the restraint of previous generations. People also want the latest consumer goods in order to fit in with others. Having an old phone, car, or computer can be stigmatizing. As it turns out, this plays right into the hands of the companies that make the goods that we use every day. It simply means that we regularly replace perfectly good consumer goods with newer versions.

Marcus Barber coined the term "enoughness" in 2008 to describe a state where people feel that their material needs are satisfied (Morgan and Hines 2013). Enoughness involves a simpler lifestyle where people feel that what they currently have meets their needs. They do not feel the need to constantly upgrade. Whatever phone, car, or clothes that they have may not be the latest styles or have all of the features that more recent versions have, but they still work well. In short, enoughness is similar to voluntary simplicity, the idea that people consciously choose to consume less. Unfortunately, this is a very tough sell in the contemporary United States.

One book that helps to make sense of this phenomenon, especially as it applies to children, is *Longing and Belonging: Parents, Children and Consumer Culture* by Allison Pugh. In this book, Pugh writes about scrip, an experience or consumer good that gives children legitimacy in the eyes of their peers. One of Pugh's (2009, 55) main points is that youth use scrip as a means of gaining entry into the "ongoing conversation" of their peers. This may be based on an experience like going to Disneyland, or playing a certain sport, watching a certain television show, or having a certain model of phone. Regardless of the type of scrip, Pugh (2009) explains that it serves to confer status and reinforce in-group/out-group boundaries. Pugh also writes about the competing value systems that kids create to establish a hierarchy of belonging. It is not just about having Game Boys or American Girl dolls. The number of games and accessories that a child has impacts their role in this ongoing conversation. All told, Pugh contends that scrip helps to alleviate social anxiety in kids, in part, because it includes them in the ongoing conversation and transmits the message to others that they are "cared for."

Pugh's (2009) concept of scrip can also be applied to older children and adults. Adults routinely share inside jokes about certain television shows they have watched or concerts they have attended. Adults use scrip to convey to others that they belong in the conversation as well. Maybe this involves having a certain phone or a valued type of engagement ring. Perhaps it involves going to the right vacation spot or being friends with certain people. In the same way that people name-drop to make themselves feel important and convey to others that they are successful, scrip allows people to "product-drop" and "experience-drop." When people talk about the latest iPhone features, you can be part of the conversation because you have the latest model of iPhone. When people talk about going to the Bahamas, again, you can be part of the conversation because you have been there.

● WHY SHOULD WE BE CONCERNED ABOUT DEBT?

Social scientists have conducted dozens of studies that identify the negative consequences of debt. This section will discuss five areas of interest. The first of these is ill health, both physical and mental. A second consequence is lower quality of life or a lack of fulfillment and satisfaction with life. A third consequence of debt is divorce. Many studies also establish the link between debt and bankruptcy.

Lastly, many scholars have established a correlation between indebtedness and criminal behavior.

1. Ill Health

Dozens of social scientific studies have been undertaken that clearly establish the mental and physical strain that is associated with being in debt. In fact, the term "debt stress" has been created to show the negative impacts of debt upon people's health, happiness, and family relationships (Dunn and Mirzaie 2012). In their article "The High Price of Debt: Household Financial Debt and its Impact on Mental and Physical Health", Sweet, Nandi, Adam, and McDade (2013) document that debt has been shown to negatively impact people's blood pressure, quality of sleep, eating habits, and job performance, while being positively associated with substance abuse, depression, and suicide. There is no question that being in debt, especially severe debt, becomes a source of preoccupation for many people who are regularly thinking about making payments and staying a step ahead of their creditors.

As mentioned above, stress is linked to numerous mental health issues. In their study of 7,461 English respondents, Meltzer, Bebbington, Brugha, Farrell, and Jenkins (2013) observed that those in debt were three times more likely to have a common mental disorder (anxiety, depression, eating disorder, panic) than those who were not in debt. They also found that approximately 50 percent of respondents in debt had a common mental disorder (CMD) and conclude that debt is "a major risk factor" for CMD (Meltzer et al. 2013). In their study of 1,463 mostly older respondents in south Florida, Drentea and Reynolds (2012) found that indebtedness is associated with depression, anxiety, and anger. In their study of 250 people undergoing foreclosure in the Philadelphia region, Pollock and Lynch (2009) found that 36.7 percent of them met the screening criteria for major depression. These findings are consistent with those found in dozens of other studies (see Bridges and Disney 2010; Dossey 2007; Dudley 2000; Selenko and Batinic 2011).

Stress can trigger a number of physical ailments, as well. People who are stressed are tired, immune compromised, and therefore susceptible to disease. In their study of 276 respondents living in twenty-nine different OECD-member countries, Clayton, Liñares-Zegarra and Wilson (2015) found that long-term household debt reduces life expectancy and increases premature mortality. They conclude that higher household debt is linked to poorer general health. In their study of German respondents over a ten-year period from 1999 to 2009, Keese and Schmitz (2014) found that debt was strongly correlated with personal health dissatisfaction, mental health problems, and obesity. In an older study of British respondents, Nettleton and Burrows (1998) found that levels of personal debt impacted the number of health problems that respondents reported and the changes in the number of health problems that they experienced over time. As with mental health problems, researchers have found clear evidence that debt impacts people's physical health.

2. Reduced Quality of Life

In addition to mental and physical health, studies have shown that there is an inverse relationship between debt and quality of life. Quality of life taps into how happy, fulfilled, and satisfied people are. People with high quality of life scores tend to have good friends, a genuine sense of community with others, and an overall sense of contentment. Interestingly, wealth and quality of life are not correlated; people report high and low quality of life scores across all income brackets (Putnam 2000).

The relationship between debt and quality of life has not been studied as extensively as the one between debt and health. Nevertheless, several studies report very interesting findings. For example, in their study of 355 students at the University of Canterbury in England, Zhang and Kemp (2009) found that as respondents' debt increased, their happiness decreased. Similarly, Nepomuceno and Laroche (2015) found that debt negatively impacted people's overall happiness. Based on a recent Gallup poll of college graduates between 1990 and 2014, Belkin (2014) reports that graduates with no outstanding college loans were more financially secure, physically healthy, and had a better sense of purpose than graduates with $50,000 or more in college loans. According to Belkin (2014), debt has ripple effects that affect people for years. People who borrow money to go to college may take well-paying jobs that they do not like just for the extra pay, and work more hours to try to get ahead. Belkin (2014) also documents studies showing that people with college loans experience delays in home ownership and marriage, which is probably connected to lower satisfaction with community and social relationships.

3. Divorce

The divorce rate is already very high in the United States. One group that has higher risk factors for marital conflict and divorce are people who are in debt. Using longitudinal data from the National Survey of Families and Households, Dew (2011) found that consumer debt is a predictor of divorce. In another study, Dew (2008) found that newlywed couples who assumed consumer debt were less happy in their marriage than newlywed couples who did not assume such debt. Similar results have been found in studies conducted by Grafova (2007), Moen (2011), and Papp, Cummings, and Goeke-Morey (2009). Other findings show that materialism (Dean, Carroll, and Yang 2007), over spending by one spouse (Britt, Grable, Goff, and White 2008) and conflicting views over debt (Rick, Small, and Finkel 2011) are also associated with higher rates of divorce.

It makes sense that debt is a contributing factor to divorce. Being in debt is stressful and frustrating for people. It leads to arguments and often leaves people feeling resentful. If a family is in debt because one person made a misguided spending decision or brought a lot of debt into the relationship, chances are, the other person will resent it. Owing money can also be distracting for people and keep them from spending quality time with their spouse. Being in debt may also prompt people to work more hours, thereby spending less time with their spouse. It is also likely that members of a couple will have different strategies for dealing with household debt. If one member wants to aggressively pay back debt, she or he will probably be annoyed with a spouse who is less concerned about the problem, or less willing to cut back in certain areas.

4. Bankruptcy

Many people have such high rates of seemingly insurmountable debt that they file for bankruptcy. In the United States, there are different kinds of bankruptcy, and Chapter 7 is the most common. Bankruptcy is for individuals and business who have fallen far behind in their payments to their creditors and owe them much more money than they are able to repay. For people in this situation, bankruptcy serves as a form of protection that allows them to have bank loans, credit card loans, pay day loans, medical bills, and other debts discharged. Interestingly, bankruptcy does not discharge student loans, criminal fines, alimony, or child support. Bankruptcy is also only meant to be used as a last resort when alternative payment plans and debt consolidation have not worked.

In 2014, there were 936,795 bankruptcy filings in the United States (debt.org 2016). One of the biggest reasons that people declare bankruptcy is because of insurmountable medical bills. Although there are many different figures relating to this, Austin (2014) estimates that around 25 percent of all bankruptcy cases are brought on by unpaid medical bills. People who are uninsured or underinsured and receive medical treatment for car accidents, heart attacks, and virtually any other severe illness are still responsible for paying their bills, which are often in the tens of thousands of dollars. Many medical procedures are so expensive that it follows that Americans may not be able to pay for them in cash and would have to sell their homes, cars, and other assets to even come close to doing so. In cases where people have liquidated their assets and still cannot pay off their medical bills or other debt, bankruptcy becomes a viable option.

5. Crime

A final consequence of debt is crime. In their review of thirty-six different studies that examine the relationship between debt and crime among youth, Hoeve et al. (2014) report that there is a strong association between debt and criminal activity. Using a sample consisting of more than sixty thousand young adults, they report that about half of the respondents had some debt, more than a third had credit card debt, and 40 percent had student loans. They also found that female respondents and minority respondents had, on average, higher levels of debt than male and white respondents, respectively (Hoeve et al. 2014). Their results show that the association between financial problems and delinquency increases with age and that there is a relatively strong relationship between debt and recidivism. In other words, juvenile offenders with criminal histories were more likely to have debt than those without criminal records. Lastly, they found that there is a relationship between persistent offending over the life course and future financial problems for both males and females.

In their article, Hoeve et al. (2014) establish that young people today have more expenses than historically was the case due to higher education costs and cell phone expenses. As such, several studies contend that paying down debt is a contributing factor to crime among youth. The authors use Merton's strain theory to explain this. According to strain theory, crime occurs when people's needs and desires do not correspond with their opportunities. As such, people are more likely to engage in property crime, drug dealing, and other criminal acts to generate the money that they need. With regards to debt, the thought here is that people engage in theft, fraud, gambling, or racketeering to generate money to service their personal debt. The authors also establish that this might be enhanced by a lack of self-control among the offenders.

● CONCLUSION

Consumption and debt are rampant in the United States. While using a loan or a credit card to buy a nice car, watch, or gift for somebody may provide people with a great feeling in the short-term, the long-term consequences of both consumption and debt tend to be negative. Debt is associated with higher rates of mental and physical illness, lower life expectances, and lower quality of life. The stress of being in debt is contributing to high rates of anxiety, depression, substance abuse, and even suicide all over the country. Indebtedness is also a contributing factor to divorce, bankruptcy, and crime. All told, it has become more and more apparent that the costs of credit are much higher than any of the benefits.

The good news is that the negative effects of debt are wholly reversible. All of us can redefine what enoughness means for us and do many things to get off of the work/spend treadmill. People all over the country are doing this in a variety of different ways. People are trimming costs by using refillable water bottles instead of disposable ones, for instance. People are waiting to buy a home until they can afford it. Relatedly, there is the growing phenomenon of the tiny house. People all over the country are buying flatbed trailers and building one to two hundred square foot living spaces on them. Although everything is compact and the space is limited, most can pay for them outright and not worry about monthly rent or mortgage payments. Plus, the confined space puts people in a situation where they can keep only what is really important and meaningful for them. This means that they are likely going to have fewer possessions, in general.

In fact, many tiny house owners are flipping the quality/quantity script and choosing to go from having a high quantity of medium-quality goods to having a much smaller quantity of higher-quality goods that are more durable and longer lasting. Of course, all of us are not going to join the tiny house movement, but we can surely learn from what they are doing. We do not have to literally and figuratively buy into the notion that the newer and the more stuff that we have, the better off we are.

● REFERENCES

Austin, D. 2014. "Medical Debt as a Cause of Consumer Bankruptcy." *Maine Law Review* 67: 1.

Belkin, D. (2014). "College Loans Are a Burden Long After Graduation, Poll Finds." *Wall Street Journal* August 7.

Bridges, S., and R. Disney. 2010. Debt and Depression. *Journal of Health Economics* 29 (3): 388–403.

Britt, S., J. E. Grable, B. S. N. Goff, and M. White. 2008. "The Influence of Perceived Spending Behaviors on Relationship Satisfaction." *Journal of Financial Counseling and Planning* 19 (1): 31.

Campbell, J. R., and Z. Hercowitz. 2006, November. "The Macroeconomic Transition to High Household Debt." In *Financial Innovations and the Real Economy,* conference sponsored by the Center for the Study of Innovation and Productivity, Federal Reserve Bank of San Francisco, San Francisco, CA, 16–17.

Clayton, M., J. Liñares–Zegarra, and J. O. Wilson. 2015. "Does Debt Affect Health? Cross Country Evidence on the Debt-Health Nexus." *Social Science & Medicine* 130 (April): 51–58.

Cohen, J. N. 2014. "The Myth of America's 'Culture of Consumerism': Policy May Help Drive American Household's Fraying Finances." *Journal of Consumer Culture,* 16(2), 531–554.

Dean, L. R., J. S. Carroll, and C. Yang. 2007. "Materialism, Perceived Financial Problems, and Marital Satisfaction." *Family and Consumer Sciences Research Journal* 35 (3): 260–81.

Debt.org. 2016. "Bankruptcy Statistics." https://www.debt.org/bankruptcy/statistics.

Dew, J. 2008. "Debt Change and Marital Satisfaction Change in Recently Married Couples." *Family Relations* 57 (1): 60–71.

Dew, J. 2011. "The Association Between Consumer Debt and the Likelihood of Divorce." *Journal of Family and Economic Issues* 32 (4): 554–65.

Dossey, L. 2007. "Debt and Health." *Explore: The Journal of Science and Healing* 3 (2): 83–90.

Drentea, P., and J. R. Reynolds. 2012. "Neither a Borrower Nor a Lender Be: The Relative Importance of Debt and SES for Mental Health Among Older Adults." *Journal of Aging and Health* 24 (4): 673–95.

Dudley, K. M. (2000). *Debt and Dispossession: Farm Loss in America's Heartland.* Chicago, IL: University of Chicago Press.

Dunn, L. F., and I. A. Mirzaie. 2012. Determinants of Consumer Debt Stress: Differences by Debt Type and Gender. Unpublished manuscript, Department of Economics, Ohio State University, Columbus, Ohio.

Fuchs, V. R. 2012. "Major Trends in the US Health Economy Since 1950." *New England Journal of Medicine* 366 (11): 973–77.

Grafova, I. B. 2007. "Your Money or Your Life: Managing Health, Managing Money." *Journal of Family and Economic Issues* 28 (2): 285–303.

Himmelstein, D. U., D. Thorne, E. Warren, and S. Woolhandler. 2009. "Medical Bankruptcy in the United States, 2007: Results of a National Study." *The American Journal of Medicine* 122 (8): 741–46.

Hoeve, M., G. J. J. Stams, M. van der Zouwen, M. Vergeer, K. Jurrius, and J. J. Asscher. 2014. "A Systematic Review of Financial Debt in Adolescents and Young Adults: Prevalence, Correlates and Associations with Crime." *PloS one* 9 (8): e104909.

Kaiser Family Foundation. 2011. "Snapshots: Health Care Spending in the United States and Selected OECD Countries." http://kff.org/health-costs/issue-brief/snapshots-health-care-spending-in-the-united-states-selected-oecd-countries/

Keese, M., and H. Schmitz. 2014. "Broke, Ill, and Obese: Is There an Effect of Household Debt on Health?" *Review of Income and Wealth* 60 (3): 525–41.

Lazo, A. 2013. "Nearly One-Third of Homeowners Have No Mortgage." *The Los Angeles Times*, January 10.

Meltzer, H., P. Bebbington, T. Brugha, M. Farrell, and R. Jenkins. 2013. "The Relationship Between Personal Debt and Specific Common Mental Disorders." *The European Journal of Public Health* 23 (1): 108–13.

Moen, D. A. 2011. Newlywed to Established Marriage: A Longitudinal Study of Early Risk and Protective Factors that Influence Marital Satisfaction. Unpublished manuscript.

Morgan, X. and Hines, A. (2013). Shifting Values: Hope and Concern for "Waking Up". On the Horizon, 21 (3), 187–196.

Nepomuceno, M.V., and M. Laroche. 2015. "The Impact of Materialism and Anti-Consumption Lifestyles on Personal Debt and Account Balances." *Journal of Business Research* 68 (3): 654–64.

Nettleton, S., and R. Burrows. 1998. "Mortgage Debt, Insecure Home Ownership and Health: An Exploratory Analysis." *Sociology of Health & Illness* 20 (5): 731–53.

Papp, L. M., E. M. Cummings, and M. C. Goeke-Morey. 2009. "For Richer, for Poorer: Money as a Topic of Marital Conflict in the Home." *Family Relations* 58 (1): 91–103.

Pollack, C. E., and Lynch, J. (2009). Health Status of People Undergoing Foreclosure in the Philadelphia Region." *American Journal of Public Health* 99 (10): 1833–1839.

Pugh, A. J. 2009. *Longing and Belonging: Parents, Children, and Consumer Culture* (1st edition). Berkeley: University of California Press.

Putnam, R. D. 2000. *Bowling Alone: The Collapse and Revival of American Community*. Simon & Schuster.

Ray, D. P., and Y. Ghahremani. 2009. "Credit Card Statistics, Industry Facts, Debt Statistics." http://www.nasdaq.com/article/credit-card-statistics-industry-facts-debt-statistics-cm21786

Rick, S. I., D. A. Small, and E. J. Finkel. 2011. "Fatal (Fiscal) Attraction: Spendthrifts and Tightwads in Marriage." *Journal of Marketing Research* 48 (2): 228–37.

Schor, J. B. (1999). *The Overspent American: Why We Want What We Don't Need*. New York City: Perenial.

Schor, J. (1991). *The Overworked American: The Unexpected Decline of Leisure*. New York City: Basic.

Selenko, E., and B. Batinic. 2011. "Beyond Debt. A Moderator Analysis of the Relationship Between Perceived Financial Strain and Mental Health." *Social Science & Medicine* 73 (12): 1725–32.

Soll, J. B., R. L. Keeney, and R. P. Larrick. 2013. "Consumer Misunderstanding of Credit Card Use, Payments, and Debt: Causes and Solutions." *Journal of Public Policy & Marketing* 32 (1): 66–81.

Sweet, E., A. Nandi, E. K. Adam, and T. W. McDade. 2013. "The High Price of Debt: Household Financial Debt and Its Impact on Mental and Physical Health." *Social Science & Medicine* 91 (August): 94–100.

U. S. Census Bureau. 1999. *Statistical Abstract of the United States*. U. S. Census Bureau.

U. S. Census Bureau. 2016. *Statistical Abstract of the United States*. U. S. Census Bureau.

Watson, B. 2013. "The High Cost of Higher Education Explained in One Simple Graphic." https://www.aol.com/on/college-costs-tuition-rising-student-debt-infographic//.

Wilson, A., and J. Boehland. 2005. "Small Is Beautiful: US House Size, Resource Use, and the Environment." *Journal of Industrial Ecology* 9 (1–2): 277–87.

Zhang, J., and S. Kemp. 2009. "The Relationships Between Student Debt and Motivation, Happiness, and Academic Achievement." *New Zealand Journal of Psychology* 38 (2): 24–29.

Conclusion

As a result of reading and discussing the chapters in this book, we hope that you have learned important concepts and facts that you can take with you after this course ends. We could not include every social problem in the contemporary United States, but we wanted you to have a solid overview of the main areas sociologists who specialize in social problems study. We have particularly emphasized social problems at the college level, in order to make it easier for you to connect them to your everyday lives. For example, as discussed in Chapter 3, first-generation college students often struggle to complete their degrees for a variety of reasons. If you yourself are first-generation, we hope that reading this research helps you in your college journey. On the other hand, if your parents graduated from college and/or you grew up at least middle class, this research will hopefully make you more aware of the constraints experienced by first-generation or low-income college students, and encourage you to find common ground across social class boundaries.

The reading on sexual assault, Chapter 16, identifies that college-aged women are more likely than other women to be sexually assaulted. It also discusses how "suitable targets" and "motivated offenders" are likely in the college atmosphere, especially due to the probability of alcohol intoxication. Relatedly, in our introduction to the section, we discuss consent as a crucial concept to consider with sexual assault. We hope that you reflect on consent and what it means to you, and discuss this with your friends. We also encourage you to investigate bystander intervention so that you can be part of the solution rather than a passive witness to potential sexual assault.

Mental health is another social problem that is particularly significant on college campuses. Chapter 18 concerns depression and its correlates, and identifies that certain groups of students, such as LGBT students, may be more susceptible to depression than others. The authors identify the factors that may mitigate the relationship between depression and academic performance, such as sleep and relationship difficulties. Importantly, this reading should help sensitize you to depression among yourselves or your friends in order to seek help if necessary. Most depression is treatable, and depression may be situational or temporary.

A study of the experiences of first-year African American college students in predominantly white institutions, Chapter 25, also offers pertinent information. The author's findings show an ongoing interactional focus on race that African American students are likely to endure. Blackness comes up frequently as an issue and this attention to race is something that white students are not likely to encounter. The author also identifies the importance for these students of finding others who are similar to themselves in salient ways, something that is important for students of all racial-ethnic categories. In addition, the reading discusses the challenges that students have with reconciling who they are at "home" with who they are becoming in college. This is a phenomenon that many college students can relate to, even if the particularities differ.

In Chapter 24, on bullying, the focus is, rightly so, on adolescents. However, the author discusses the school climate as being an important factor to consider with bullying. When there is a positive school climate—when the norms and values of a school contribute to students, faculty, and staff feeling good—there is less truancy and aggression. These ideas can be applied to the college environment as well. For example, Chapter 11 focuses on discrimination against transgender people and their response to it. Transgender people are increasingly visible on college campuses and are likely to experience harassment and aggression as a result of their gender minority status. It is our hope that your school has a positive climate and that you participate in maintaining that. And if you see bullying, including cyberbullying, occurring at your school, again we encourage you to be an active rather than passive bystander, to intervene.

The final reading in the book relates to consumption and debt. College students are all too aware of the increase in student loan debt that people are carrying. And while this debt may be worth it for some, it is too high to benefit others. (This appears to be particularly true for students in for-profit schools or those who do not complete their degrees.) In addition, college students often feel pressures to have the "right" products, which may be expensive. And credit card companies like to target college students because they suspect that college students will want to spend money they do not have, and will carry a balance over from month to month (which gives the company more interest, as is discussed in the chapter). It is important for you to be informed of the negative consequences of debt, so that you can try to avoid them if possible.

Many of the readings in this book can be used as springboards for you to remain informed about the issues of the day. If you are informed, you can form opinions and hopefully vote in favor of candidates or legislation with which you agree. For example, one popular piece of the Affordable Care Act (discussed in Chapter 17) is the increase in the age of children that parents can keep on their insurance policies. Prior to 2010, the age limit was typically nineteen, or twenty-three for full-time college students. Now it is twenty-six. This is something that a lot of you are likely to support. Student loans, discussed in Chapter 28, are also an important issue in contemporary America. It is in your best interest to study how student loan debt has increased over time, and what can be done to ease the burden for the millions of people who attend college each year.

These are just some of the takeaways we foresee from this book. In general, we hope that these readings encourage you to be an active participant in your social world, to be informed and contributory, so that the negative effects of these and other social problems may be lessened over time.

About the Authors

Brandon Lang is an associate professor of sociology at Bloomsburg University in Central Pennsylvania, where he teaches a variety of sociology courses including contemporary social problems, the sociology of music, environmental sociology, and the sociology of gender. His PhD is from North Carolina State University, and he also graduated from Goddard College in Vermont (MA), and Trent University in Ontario (BA Hons). He is married to his collaborator, Molly Monahan Lang, and they have three young children together.

Molly Monahan Lang is a part-time faculty member in the Department of Applied Sociology and Social Work at Mercyhurst University and a lecturer of sociology at Penn State Erie, The Behrend College, both in Erie, Pennsylvania. Her interests include families, gender, social stratification, and medical sociology (especially as it pertains to death and dying). She earned her PhD and MS in sociology with a doctoral minor in gender studies from North Carolina State University, and her BA in sociology from the Pennsylvania State University.

Mallary Allen, PhD, is an assistant professor of sociology at Concordia College in Moorhead, Minnesota. Her research interests include gender, families, and social movements, and she has studied the pro-choice movement in the United States extensively.

Ali Awadi, PhD, is currently employed at Cleary University as a part-time graduate studies professor, and at Henry Ford College as an administrator and adjunct professor in leadership, US foreign policy, management, and business administration. His research interests focus on how public policy affects the sociological and psychological behavior of society. With over twenty-six years of experience in in the business and social science sectors, Dr. Awadi has worked as a rule of law adviser in Iraq, where he has assisted in the training of U.S. Army military police, Iraqi police, and Iraqi judicial members in the Wasit Province.

Lorenzo D. Baber, PhD, is an associate professor in the School of Education at Iowa State University. He also serves on the editorial and advisory board for *The Journal of Negro Education*.

Dr. Gina Castle Bell is an Assistant Professor at Saint John's University. She studies race related social justice issues in the U.S., and Black and White intercultural communication in particular.

Richard Craig, PhD, is an assistant professor of communication at George Mason University. His research centers on mass media political economy, addressing the production, distribution, and consumption of media content.

Linda Darling-Hammond, EdD, is an emeritus professor of education at Stanford University. She has authored or edited more than a dozen books and three hundred articles on education policy and practice. She also served as the faculty director of the Stanford Center for Opportunity Policy in Education.

Kathryn Edin, PhD, is the Bloomberg Distinguished Professor of sociology at Johns Hopkins University. She is a trustee of the Russell Sage Foundation and on the Department of Health and Human Services advisory committee for the poverty research centers at Michigan, Wisconsin, and Stanford. Professor Edin is also a founding member of the MacArthur Foundation–funded Network on Housing and Families with Young Children and a past member of the MacArthur Network on the Family and the Economy. In 2014, she became a member of the National Academy of Sciences and the American Academy of Political and Social Sciences.

Patricia Fabiano, PhD, teaches in the Woodring College of Education at Western Washington University.

Jamie Flexon, PhD, is an associate professor of criminal justice at Florida International University. Her research interests involve juvenile delinquency primarily among minority youth, criminal justice issues related to punishment (i.e., capital punishment), and policy evaluation.

Sarah Halpern-Meekin, PhD, is an associate professor of human development and family studies at the University of Wisconsin–Madison. Her current research includes examining how premarital experiences are associated with later relationship outcomes; how government-funded relationship education programs are experienced by their participants; and how changes to the welfare state, like the rise of the Earned Income Tax Credit, affect low-income families.

Olivia Hetzler, PhD, is an assistant professor of sociology at Lincoln University in Jefferson City, Missouri. She studies mothering, gendered violence, and homelessness.

Mark C. Hopson, PhD, is an associate professor of communication at George Mason University, where he is co-director of the doctoral program. His research interests include critical intercultural communication and diversity, rhetorical studies, and the communication of violence prevention.

Veronyka James, PhD, is an assistant professor of criminology at Virginia Union University. Her research interests are sexual assault victimization and reporting, stigma management, policing (particularly police misconduct), and "senseless" violence (e.g., serial killers and mass shooters).

Rosalind Kichler, MA, is a PhD student at the University of Nebraska-Lincoln. Her research interests include gender, sexuality, culture, feminist theory, and qualitative methodology. She also studies the ways in which gender and sexuality minority people (LGBTQIA+) construct and negotiate their identities and communities within a rapidly changing cultural context.

Carrie R. Leana, PhD, is the George H. Love Professor of Organizations and Management at the University of Pittsburgh, where she holds appointments in the Katz Graduate School of Business, the School of Medicine, the Graduate School of Public and International Affairs, and the Learning Research and Development

Center. She is director of the University of Pittsburgh's Center for Health and Care Work, serves on the board of directors of the Aging Institute, and on the national advisory board of the School of Public Health. She is also on the advisory board of the European Union Center and the Center for West European Studies. Professor Leana's research and training are in the area of organizational behavior.

Eric G. Lesneskie, PhD, is an assistant professor in the Department of Sociology, Social Work, and Criminal Justice at Bloomsburg University. His research interests include communities and crime, adolescent residential and school mobility, and offender risk.

Billie J. Lindsey, EdD, is an associate professor emeritus of community health at Western Washington University.

Michael J. Lynch, PhD, is a professor of criminology at the University of South Florida. He is the series co-editor of *Green Criminology*, the founding editor of *Social Pathology: A Journal of Reviews*, and head of the editorial collective of *The Critical Criminologist*.

Michael Maly, PhD, is an associate professor of sociology and the director of the Policy Research Collaborative at Roosevelt University.

Sanjay S. Mehta, PhD, is a professor of marketing at Sam Houston State University. He studies such issues as franchising, electronic commerce, and the problems with online trading.

Joya Misra, PhD, is professor of sociology and public policy at the University of Massachusetts. Her teaching and research focus primarily on inequality. She is also the editor of *Gender & Society*.

Vikas Mittal, PhD, is the J. Hugh Liedtke Professor of Marketing at the Jones Graduate School of Business at Rice University. Dr. Mittal has published extensively in leading marketing journals such as *Journal of Marketing*, *Journal of Marketing Research*, *Journal of Consumer Research*, and *Marketing Science*.

John J. Newbold, PhD, is an associate professor of marketing at Sam Houston State University.

Matthew A. O'Rourke, MBA, is the director of search engine optimization at Blue Moon Digital, Inc., in Denver, Colorado.

C. J. Pascoe, PhD, is an associate professor of sociology at the University of Oregon, where she teaches courses on sexuality, masculinity, social psychology, and gender. Her current research focuses on masculinity, youth, homophobia, sexuality, and new media.

Elizabeth A. Petre, PhD, is an assistant professor in the Department of Communication Studies at Bloomsburg University of Pennsylvania. Her research focuses on rhetorical approaches to organizational communication in various contexts. Elizabeth teaches courses in public speaking, leadership and team building, communication for business professionals, and gender issues in communication.

James T. Petre, PhD, is an assistant professor in the Department of Communication Studies at Bloomsburg University of Pennsylvania. His primary research focus is rhetorical theory and criticism, particularly related to politics and economics. He teaches a variety of different classes including persuasion, rhetorical criticism, political campaign communication, public speaking, and business and professional communication.

Nicholas W. Robinson, MA, is a graduate student in communication studies at Texas Tech University.

Nicole L. Rosen, PhD, is a project director and research associate at the Susan Hirt Hagen Center for Community Outreach, Research, and Evaluation (CORE) at Penn State University, Behrend. She is also the mentor coordinator for the Mentor Project at Behrend, associated with the Prevention of Aggression Resource Center (PARC) at Penn State Behrend. As a qualitative researcher, Nicole's research interests include gender inequality, poverty, peer mistreatment, social change, and culture. She is published in ASA Trails: Teaching Resources and Innovations Library for Sociology.

Thomas Rudel, PhD, is a professor of human ecology at Rutgers University. He conducts research on land use change and has researched the driving forces behind tropical deforestation both through case studies in the Ecuadorian Amazon and through quantitative analyses at the global scale.

Abigail C. Saguy, PhD, is professor of sociology and gender studies at UCLA. She is the author of *What's Wrong with Fat?* (2013, Oxford University Press) and *What Is Sexual Harassment? From Capitol Hill to the Sorbonne* (2003, University of California Press). Her teaching and research interests include gender, culture, the body, politics, law, and public health.

Meena Sharma, PhD, is a professor in sociology at Henry Ford College, where she teaches many courses including introductory sociology, marriage and the family and sociology of deviant behavior. Dr. Sharma's research interests are in the area of race and ethnicity, family, immigration, and mental health. Specifically, her research focuses on the relationship between country of origin, conflict experiences between the generations in immigrant families, and the mental health results of family members, to Canada and the United States.

Nicole A. Shoenberger, PhD, is an assistant professor of sociology at Penn State University, Behrend. She is also the assistant director of the Susan Hirt Hagen Community Outreach Research and Evaluation Center (CORE) and a faculty affiliate of the Prevention of Aggression Resource Center. Her main areas of research focus on positive deviance, social inequality within the criminal justice system, peer mistreatment, and stigmatized deviant groups such as new religious movements. She has recently published in *Deviant Behavior, Trails*, and the *Journal of Religion and Society.*

Chris Stark is the research associate for Western Washington University's Office of Survey Research. He holds degrees in political science and psychology, and has a professional background in institutional research.